Theatre in Europe: a documentary history

This is the first volume to be published in the series *Theatre in Europe: a documentary history*. The authors have compiled a documentary account of the theatre in Britain during the Restoration and Georgian period, which covers some 120 years of theatrical activity. It was an exciting period that saw the first arrival of the scenic stage in the public theatres of London, bringing with it a whole new approach to staging and performance. The development outlined in the volume shows the progression of the theatre from a tightly controlled, court-based institution in the Restoration to an ebullient, bustling, commercial undertaking with wide popular appeal in the late Georgian period.

The collection of primary source material (both verbal and visual) documents changes in government control and censorship, company management, actors and acting styles, stage presentation, playhouse design and audience response. A number of documents are eye-witness accounts of major actors in specific roles; others give detailed descriptions of playhouse interiors, stage settings and lighting devices. Acting theory and the development of theatre criticism are also fully illustrated. The compilers include the source location for each document as well as a complementary list of alternative sources (where appropriate) and indications of secondary sources offering previously printed transcripts.

Theatre in Europe: a documentary history

General editors:

Glynne Wickham
John Northam
John Gould
W.D. Howarth

This series will present a comprehensive collection of primary source materials for teachers and students and will serve as a major reference work for studies in theatrical and dramatic literature. The volumes will focus individually on specific periods and geographical areas, encompassing English and European theatrical history. Each volume will present primary source documents in English, or in English translation, relating to actors and acting, dramatic theory and criticism, theatre architecture, stage censorship, settings, costumes, and audiences. These sources include such documents as statutes, proclamations, inscriptions, contracts and playbills. Additional documentation from contemporary sources is provided through correspondence, reports, and eyewitness accounts. The volumes will also provide not only the exact source and location of the original documents, but also complementary lists of similar documents. Each volume contains an Introduction, narrative linking passages, notes on the documents, a substantial bibliography and an index offering detailed access to the primary material.

Theatre in Europe: a documentary history

Restoration and Georgian England, 1660–1788

Compiled and introduced by
DAVID THOMAS
Professor of Theatre Studies and Dramatic Arts
University of Warwick

and

ARNOLD HARE
Formerly Reader in Theatre History
University of Bristol

Edited by
DAVID THOMAS

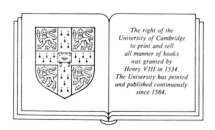

The right of the
University of Cambridge
to print and sell
all manner of books
was granted by
Henry VIII in 1534.
The University has printed
and published continuously
since 1584.

CAMBRIDGE UNIVERSITY PRESS
Cambridge
New York   Port Chester   Melbourne   Sydney

Published by the Press Syndicate of the University of Cambridge
The Pitt Building, Trumpington Street, Cambridge CB2 IRP
40 West 20th Street, New York, NY 10011, USA
10 Stamford Road, Oakleigh, Melbourne 3166, Australia

First published 1989

Printed in Great Britain by the University Press, Cambridge

British Library cataloguing in publication data
Restoration and Georgian England 1660–1788.
–Theatre in Europe: a documentary
history).
1. England. Theatre, 1632–1642
1. Thomas, David   II. Hare, Arnold
III. Series
792'.0942

Library of Congress cataloguing in publication data

Restoration and Georgian England. 1660–1788 / compiled by David Thomas
    and Arnold Hare ; edited by David Thomas.
       p.   cm. – (Theatre in Europe)
    Bibliography.
    ISBN 0 521 23380 1
    1. Theater – England – History – 17th century – Sources.   2. Theater –
England – History – 18th century – Sources.   I. Thomas, David, 1942–.
    II. Hare, Arnold, 1921–.   III. Series.
PN2592.R66   1989
792'.094 – dc19   88–21148   CIP

ISBN 0 521 23380 1

Contents

List of documents

General editors' preface

In appointing appropriately qualified editors for each of the sixteen volumes of this documentary history it has been our aim to provide a comprehensive collection of primary source materials for teachers and students on which their own critical appraisal of theatrical history and dramatic literature may safely be grounded.

Each volume presents primary source documents in English, or in English translation, relating to actors and acting, dramatic theory and criticism, theatre architecture, stage censorship, settings, costumes and audiences. Editors have, in general, confined their selection to documentary material in the strict sense (statutes, proclamations, inscriptions, contracts, working-drawings, playbills, prints, account books, etc.), but exceptions have been made in instances where prologues, epilogues, excerpts from play texts and private correspondence provide additional contemporary documentation based on author's authority or that of eye witnesses to particular performances and significant theatrical events.

Unfamiliar documents have been preferred to familiar ones, short ones to long ones; and among long ones recourse has been taken to excerpting for inclusion all passages which either oblige quotation by right of their own intrinsic importance or lead directly to a clearer understanding of other documents. In every instance, however, we have aimed to provide readers not only with the exact source and location of the original document, but with complementary lists of similar documents and of secondary sources offering previously printed transcripts.

Each volume is equipped with an introductory essay, and in some cases introductory sections to each chapter, designed to provide readers with the appropriate social background – religious, political, economic and aesthetic – as context for the documents selected; it also contains briefer linking commentaries on particular groups of documents and concludes with an extensive bibliography.

Within this general presentational framework, individual volumes will vary considerably in their format – greater emphasis having to be placed, for example, on documents of control in one volume than in another, or with dramatic theory and criticism figuring less prominently in some volumes than in others – if each volume is to be an accurate reflection of the widely divergent interests and concerns of different European countries at different stages of their historical development, and the equally sharp differences in the nature and quality of the surviving documents volume by volume.

The editors would like to thank Michael Black and Sarah Stanton at Cambridge University Press for their unwavering interest, encouragement and practical support in bringing this enterprise forward from thoughts and wishes expressed at a Conference in 1979 to publication of the first volume to reach maturity a decade later.

Glynne Wickham (Chairman)
Bristol University, 1988

Editor's preface

In approaching the task of collecting and editing material for this volume, the two authors divided their responsibilities on a chronological basis. Arnold Hare was responsible for selecting and commenting on material for the period 1737–88; David Thomas was responsible for selecting and commenting on material for the earlier period, 1660–1737. As editor, David Thomas was also responsible for the overall structure and shape of the volume and its constituent sections.

Our collaboration on this volume has been a most happy task, one which we both have viewed as an extension of a friendship that stretches back over some twenty years. In addition to subjecting our material to each other's critical gaze, we have at times benefited from the painstaking advice and suggestions of a number of colleagues working in this same area. We are particularly grateful for the help and advice of Judith Milhous, Rob Hume, Graham Barlow, Kathleen Barker and the detailed help and encouragement of the General Editors Glynne Wickham, Bill Howarth, John Northam and John Gould.

We also owe a debt of gratitude to the staff of the British Library; the Print Room of the British Museum; the Public Records Office; the University Library Bristol; Dr Jim Fowler of the Theatre Museum; Ann Brooke Barnett, Keeper of the University of Bristol Theatre Collection; the Keeper of the Duke of Devonshire's Collection at Chatsworth; the Curator of the Mander and Mitchenson Theatre Museum; Gordon Kelsey, photographer in the Faculty of Arts Photographic Unit, University of Bristol. Finally, we are especially grateful for the patience and encouragement shown us by Sarah Stanton of Cambridge University Press who has helped us in every conceivable way during the lengthy period of planning and preparing this volume.

TECHNICALITIES

In preparing the text for this volume, the orthography of the original documents has been consistently modernised. Not only is this the agreed policy for all the volumes in this series, it makes particular sense in respect of the Restoration and

Georgian period where spelling, abbreviations and use of capital letters are frequently idiosyncratic and seem to have been very much left to individual whim and taste. The gain in clarity more than compensates for any loss of authenticity.

In addition, we have decided to retain capital letters for all play titles, but to avoid the use of capital letters (except in the case of names and titles) in respect of other source material, articles and studies. Our punctuation has been deliberately light. In those Georgian documents that have lengthy sentences held together with a profusion of semicolons, we have consistently shortened the sentences by replacing semicolons with full stops whenever this seemed feasible.

Sources are given in full the first time they are listed; thereafter we have used abbreviated references where practicable. Studies are referred to by the author's surname, followed by the date of publication of the study in brackets.

BIBLIOGRAPHY

The bibliography has been divided into five sections:
1 Works of reference
2 Manuscript sources
3 Published sources
4 Studies
5 Articles

Reference is made in square brackets to source material used in a numbered document. Pictorial sources are not listed in the bibliography, but are given in full whenever a pictorial source is used as a numbered document.

ABBREVIATIONS

The following abbreviations have been used throughout the volume:

Add.Ch: Additional Charter
Add.MS: Additional Manuscript
BD: *A biographical dictionary of actors, actresses, musicians, dancers, managers and other stage personnel in London, 1660–1800* (Carbondale and Edwardsville: Southern Illinois University Press, 1973–)
BL: British Library
BM: British Museum
Eg.Ch: Egerton Charter
LS: *The London stage* (Carbondale and Edwardsville: Southern Illinois University Press, 1960–5)
PMLA: *Publications of the Modern Language Association of America*
PRO: Public Records Office
STR: Society for Theatre Research
TN: *Theatre Notebook*
TS: *Theatre Survey*

PUBLISHED SOURCES

In respect of published source material referred to in this volume, the authors, in most cases, have not identified a specific library where a given published source may be consulted. Apart from the inevitable overlap of holdings in the crown copyright libraries, the public reference libraries of major cities, and many university libraries, the vast majority of published source material may be found in the British Library. In those few instances where the British Library does not possess a copy of a book used as a primary source, the authors have drawn attention to a major library or collection where the item in question may be found.

NEWSPAPERS AND PERIODICALS

A comprehensive list of newpapers and periodicals published before 1800 may be found in *BUCOP* or *British Union Catalogue of Periodicals (seventeenth century to the present)*. This does not, however, indicate which titles contain significant theatrical material. The following list of newspapers and journals, while not aiming to be comprehensive, gives some indication of titles that do contain notices relevant to the theatre of the period. If the newspaper or periodical was published throughout the period covered by this volume, only the starting date of publication is given. In most cases, the newspapers may be consulted on microfilm in the British Library or in the public reference library of the place of publication. The periodicals may be consulted at the British Library.

London newspapers

Daily Courant, 1702–35
London Daily Post and General Advertiser, 1726 (later *Public Advertiser*, 1752–94)
London Evening Post, 1727
London Advertiser and Literary Gazette, 1751–3
The World, 1753–74
Dodsley's London Chronicle, 1757
St James's Chronicle, 1761
Morning Chronicle and London Advertiser, 1769
Morning Post and Daily Advertising Pamphlet, 1772

Provincial newspapers

Bath Journal, 1744
Bath Chronicle, 1760
Bristol Journal (Felix Farley's), 1743
Bristol Journal (Bonner and Middleton's), 1774
Bristol Gazette and Public Advertiser, 1767
Birmingham Gazette (Aris's), 1741

Chester Weekly Journal, 1721–33
Chester Chronicle, 1775
Derby Mercury (Drewry's), 1753
Faulkner's Dublin Journal, 1725
The Public Register, or Freeman's Journal (Dublin), 1763
The Hibernian Journal (Dublin), 1718
Edinburgh Chronicle, 1759–60
Edinburgh Evening Courant, 1718
Glasgow Herald and Evening Intelligencer, 1783
Hampshire Chronicle, 1772
Kentish Gazette, 1768
Leicester and Nottingham Journal, 1753
Liverpool Advertiser, 1756
Gore's General Advertiser, 1765
Manchester Mercury (Harrap's), 1752
Newcastle Courant, 1711
Newcastle Chronicle, 1764
Norfolk Chronicle or Norwich Gazette, 1761
Norwich Mercury, 1721
Norwich Gazette, 1711
Nottingham Journal (Cresswell and Burbage's), 1732
Salisbury and Winchester Journal, 1729
Sheffield Advertiser, 1761
Stamford Mercury, 1712
York Chronicle, 1772

Periodicals

Read's Weekly Journal, 1725–61
London Magazine, or Gentleman's Monthly Intelligencer, 1732
Gentleman's Magazine, 1736
Common Sense, or the Englishman's Journal, 1737–43
The Universal Museum and Complete Magazine, 1762–72
Town and Country Magazine, 1769
The Theatrical Monitor, 1767–8
European Magazine, 1782
The Tatler, 1709–11
The Spectator, 1711–12, 1714
The Theatre, 1720

COLLECTIONS OF PLAYBILLS

Major collections of playbills in Great Britain may be found in the British Library (Burney Collection and many volumes of London and provincial bills); the

Enthoven Collection in the Theatre Museum; the Garrick Club; the National Library of Scotland; York Minster Library (Hailstone Collection 1766–1812); the public libraries of Bath, Birmingham, Bristol, Edinburgh, Liverpool, Manchester; Trinity College Library, Dublin. In the USA, major collections may be found at the Folger Shakespeare Library, Washington; Harvard Theatre Collection; Huntington Library, San Marino, California.

PICTORIAL SOURCES

In identifying specific sources for visual items used as numbered documents, the authors have attempted to concentrate, where possible, on easily accessible and well catalogued collections of theatrical material in London and Bristol: notably the British Museum in London and the University Theatre Collection in Bristol. This does not, however, imply that the collection in question holds the only available illustration of a particular item. In London alone, for instance, there is considerable overlap between the holdings of the British Museum, the Theatre Museum and the Mander and Mitchenson Theatre Collection, to name but three. Furthermore, in the case of most eighteenth-century theatre prints and frontispieces, copies are extant in the hands of private collectors (including the two authors of this volume), in addition to the public collections. Formal acknowledgements are therefore given below where a library, museum or theatre collection has provided, specifically for this volume, a photographic illustration of an item from its holdings or possesses the copyright of an original portrait, design sketch, plan or drawing. Acknowledgements for items in private hands have been given where, after consultation, this has been requested.

ACKNOWLEDGEMENTS

The institutions listed below have kindly given permission to reproduce visual material from their collections, as indicated by the document numbers. The authors would particularly like to express their thanks for the generosity of the Warden and Fellows of All Souls College, Oxford; the Art Institute of Chicago; the University Library, Bristol; the Trustees of the British Museum; the British Library; the Chatsworth Settlement Trustees; the Folger Library; the Trustees of Sir John Soane's Museum; J.A. Mitchley Esq; the National Theatre; the Provost and Fellows of Worcester College, Oxford; all of whom have greatly assisted this academic publishing venture by giving permission to reproduce the visual material listed below without charge.

The Warden and Fellows of All Souls College, Oxford: [56, 60]
Art Institute, Chicago: [64]
University of Bristol Theatre Collection: [69, 222, 225, 226, 233, 237, 238, 246, 247, 248a, 285, 316]

University Library, Bristol: [67, 71, 101, 108, 174, 334]
By permission of the British Library: [46, 47, 58, 80, 82, 86, 94, 158, 242, 254]
The Trustees of the British Museum: [93, 98, 125, 129, 229, 258, 260, 261, 275, 280b, 283, 317, 322, 331, 332, 337, 357]
The Devonshire Collection, Chatsworth. Reproduced by kind permission of the Chatsworth Settlement Trustees: [75]
Edinburgh City Libraries: [250]
Folger Shakespeare Library, Washington DC: [73]
The Iveagh Bequest, Kenwood: [339b]
By courtesy of the Trustees of Sir John Soane's Museum: [234]
The Mander and Mitchenson Theatre Collection: [318, 337]
J.A. Mitchley, Private Collection: [252]
The Museum of London: [362]
The National Museums and Galleries on Merseyside (Walker Art Gallery): [326]
The National Theatre: [328]
The Theatre Museum, London: [85, 89, 244a, 267, 289b]
The Provost and Fellows of Worcester College, Oxford: [45, 50]

Introduction

This documentary history of the theatre in Britain during the Restoration and Georgian period covers some 120 years of theatrical activity. It was an exciting period that saw the first arrival of the scenic stage in the public theatres of London, bringing with it a whole new approach to staging and performance. It was also a period that saw a distinct shift from the Restoration, when the theatre was an extension of court life, to the late Georgian period when theatre-going had become an essential part of fashionable middle-class social life. However, the development we shall be tracing in this volume begins in the aftermath of a national disaster, the Civil War of the 1640s.

The Civil War marks a watershed in the development of the theatre in Britain. Even before the outbreak of hostilities in the 1640s, academics, lawyers, merchants and craftsmen of puritan persuasion were united in their hostility towards the theatre, which was seen as an organ for Royalist values and perceptions. The 1642 Act of Parliament, which closed the theatres and prohibited the performing of all plays, was the inevitable culmination of a long process of covert and overt opposition to the theatre on the part of the puritan middle classes. The Civil War had a devastating effect on the burgeoning theatre traditions of London and the provinces. At a stroke it removed the popular base for theatre in Britain, bringing to an abrupt end the tradition of outdoor theatre performances in London in large unroofed playhouses and curtailing professional theatre activity in the provinces, which had enjoyed varying degrees of civic support.

The Restoration of Charles II in the summer of 1660 brought with it an entirely new style of theatre. After his years of exile in Paris, Charles was intent on ensuring that the theatre could be kept under tight control while outwardly reflecting appropriate visual and verbal images of a French-inspired courtly culture. In Restoration England, one no longer finds the large open-air playhouses of Elizabethan England: in their place came converted indoor tennis court theatres, modelled on those of Paris. Changeable scenery, inspired by French and Italian practice, was introduced to appeal to the sophisticated tastes of an elite audience, marking yet another break with the traditions of the pre-Civil-War theatre. Finally, as in Paris, actresses now appeared, by Royal command, on the stages of London's public playhouses. Together, these various individual changes amounted to a complete revolution in theatrical activity.

There were of course many links with the past. Not only in terms of the repertoire of plays written during the early part of the century and before, but also in the continuity of acting traditions handed on by those players who had somehow eked out a professional living after the cessation of hostilities in the 1650s. Despite this, the revolutionary nature of the changes effected in the Restoration theatre cannot be too strongly emphasised.

The continuing opposition towards the theatre on the part of academics, lawyers and merchants, until well into the eighteenth century, ensured that the theatre was destined to make only slow progress in regaining the ground it lost during the Civil War as a popular institution of national significance. To begin with it deliberately reflected the values and aspirations of Charles and his courtiers (even on those occasions when it subjected these values to a mildly satirical treatment). Genuine political satire or comment was out of the question.

By the turn of the century, there was a discernible shift in respect of theatre organisation, management and repertoire policy. The court was no longer so intimately associated with the theatre. Hence it was easier for management to concentrate on the task of maximising profit rather than pleasing courtly patrons. The move towards a more distinctly commercial style of management was accelerated by the fact that broader and less educated sections of the population were being attracted to performances. Even in the provinces there was evidence of renewed theatrical activity. It was now that the first signs of *rapprochement* were made between the middle classes and the theatre they had previously eschewed. The first theatre criticisms appeared in print in the 1700s, reflecting the puritan values of the middle classes; these same values informed the first sentimental comedies written at the beginning of the eighteenth century, demonstrating the possibility of a puritan approach to playwriting. There was still residual hostility towards the theatre in middle-class circles, but it was no longer a uniform or even a majority view.

By the late 1720s, London's theatres were reflecting in their repertoire the often heated political debates of the period. The rumbustious political farces and ballad operas of the day (some of which were performed in the slowly increasing number of small, unlicensed playhouses in the capital) delighted a wide cross-section of the theatre-going public, but caused increasing concern to Walpole's administration. This was the immediate prelude to the Licensing Act of 1737, which was to arrest and stunt the growth of theatrical activity in London and the provinces for many decades. This was bad enough, but arguably the most serious effect of the Act was to dissuade, because of its draconian censorship provisions, most committed or gifted writers from expressing their ideas in dramatic form.

Eventually, the growing popularity of theatre amongst middle-class patrons proved an effective counterweight to parliamentary legislation. In London the managers of the two patent houses at Drury Lane and Covent Garden fought effectively to retain their privileged monopoly position, although some legislative chinks were opened up by the end of the century, making it possible for competitors to play for gain in the quiet of the summer season. It was, however, in the provinces that an astonishing development of theatrical activity took place. From the 1760s onwards, a spate of individual letters patent were granted to a whole series of theatres in major provincial centres. This in its turn reflected the thriving popular base that the theatre had by then acquired in provincial England.

By the 1780s, most, but not all, of the ground lost as a result of the Civil War in the 1640s had been regained in London: in the provinces real advances had been made. The theatre was once again a thriving national institution. It boasted some of the finest actors in Europe. It enjoyed a rich and varied repertoire, even if exciting new authors were few and far between. The architectural solutions pioneered by Davenant and Wren in the Restoration proved to be viable blueprints for the provincial theatre buildings erected as from the 1750s. Finally, many of the problems associated with financing and touring scenic productions were solved by the creation of effective touring networks and the judicious use of stock scenery.

Throughout the eighteenth century, theatre-goers proved remarkably effective in their attempts to prevent increases in ticket prices. Even the threat of an increase was enough to provoke a riot. As a result, managers found themselves having to increase the capacity of their houses in order to ensure a proper financial return on their operations. This meant the gradual loss of the forestage, which was such a striking feature of the Restoration playhouse, and the building of gallery seating in the roof space. Eventually, it would entail a whole new design philosophy, ushering in the large roofed playhouses of the early nineteenth century.

Something of the overall effect of the development sketched here may be gleaned from a comparison of the two following maps. The first, a detailed section from Rocque's map of London, 1746 (BM), shows the two patent houses at Drury Lane and Covent Garden licensed specifically for theatrical performances in mid-eighteenth-century London (the King's Theatre in the Haymarket was licensed for operatic performances).

A detailed section from Rocque's Map of London, 1746 (BM)

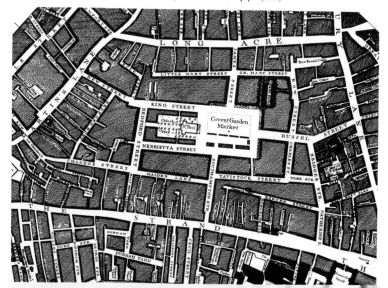

The second lists a representative selection (approximately a third) of the those provincial centres that acquired a theatre by the 1790s. While the development of the theatre in London had been deliberately suppressed so that it remained virtually unchanged in scope from the Restoration period, the position in the remainder of England was radically different. All over the country, there was a thriving network of theatrical activity growing at an almost exponential rate.

Distribution of theatres in the British Isles outside London, *c.* 1790

ENGLAND[1]

(1) Penzance	(24) Wells	(47) Lowestoft	(72) *Manchester*
(2) *Plymouth*	(25) Taunton	(48) *Norwich*	(73) *Liverpool*
(3) *Exeter*	(26) Bideford	(49) Peterborough	(74) Blackburn
(4) Dorchester	(27) Bristol	(50) Northampton	(75) Bradford
(5) Weymouth	(28) *Bath*	(51) Warwick	(76) Harrogate
(6) Lymington	(29) *Newbury*	(52) *Birmingham*	(77) York
(7) *Southampton*	(30) *Reading*	(53) Kidderminster	(78) Scarborough
(8) *Portsmouth*	(31) *Windsor*	(54) Shrewsbury	(79) Ripon
(9) *Chichester*	(32) *Richmond*	(55) Stafford	(80) Lancaster
(10) Newport	(Surrey)	(56) Lichfield	(81) Northallerton
(IOW)	(33) *Edmonton*	(57) Leicester	(82) Whitby
(11) *Brighton*	(34) Chelmsford	(58) Stamford	(83) Richmond
(12) *Lewes*	(35) Aylesbury	(59) Boston	(Yorks.)
(13) Eastbourne	(36) Oxford	(60) *Grantham*	(84) Kendal
(14) Hastings	(37) Cheltenham	(61) Nottingham	(85) Darlington
(15) Dover	(38) Gloucester	(62) Derby	(86) Durham
(16) *Margate*	(39) Hereford	(63) Chester	(87) Keswick
(17) Canterbury	(40) Worcester	(64) Buxton	(88) Carlisle
(18) *Maidstone*	(41) Banbury	(65) Sheffield	(89) *Newcastle upon*
(19) *Tunbridge*	(42) Bedford	(66) Doncaster	*Tyne*
Wells	(43) Cambridge	(67) Gainsborough	(90) Sunderland
(20) Guildford	(44) Bury	(68) Lincoln	(91) Alnwick
(21) *Winchester*	St Edmunds	(69) Grimsby	(92) Berwick on
(22) *Andover*	(45) Colchester	(70) Hull	Tweed
(23) Salisbury	(46) Ipswich	(71) Leeds	

WALES

(93) Cardiff	(95) Brecon	(97) Carmarthen	(99) Presteigne
(94) Monmouth	(96) Swansea	(98) Aberystwyth	(100) Montgomery

SCOTLAND

(101) Dumfries	(104) Edinburgh	(107) Dundee	(110) Inverness
(102) Ayr	(105) Stirling	(108) Inverary	
(103) Glasgow	(106) Perth	(109) Aberdeen	

IRELAND

(111) Cork	(114) Kilkenny	(116) Galway	(118) Belfast
(112) Waterford	(115) Dublin	(117) Newry	(119) Londonderry
(113) Limerick			

[1] Italic entries indicate playhouses illustrated in James Winston: *The theatric tourist* (London: T. Woodfall, 1805).

Doubtless the artificial limits imposed on the London theatres contributed to the swift growth of theatrical activity in the provinces. There was simply not enough scope in London for talented actors and actor managers. Nevertheless, this was a remarkable demonstration of the way the theatre, by the 1790s, had won back a dedicated and loyal theatre-going public. Once again it had become an artistic medium for all the people, and not simply a propaganda organ for a ruling house. Indeed, such was the strength and vigour of the touring tradition established in the provinces that many of its practitioners were moved to carry their skills to the West Indies and America in search of new audiences amongst British settlers. Although this aspect of theatrical activity falls outside the scope of the present study, it will re-appear in a later volume of the series.

The development outlined here shows the progression of the theatre from a tightly controlled, court-based institution in the Restoration to an ebullient, bustling, commercial undertaking with wide popular appeal in the late Georgian period. It is by and large a joyful story. It has its villains and traitors but also its fair share of heroes, some adored by a glittering public in London, others long forgotten and largely unsung in the outer reaches of the provinces. We have greatly enjoyed the process of trawling through the period to identify major developments in terms of government control, company contracts, playhouse design, scenic presentation, acting styles and achievements, audience responses and theatre criticism. The account presented here is far from complete. Indeed we have agonised at length over material we have had to omit through lack of space. Our final choice of material was often determined by the need to use documents that facilitated valuable cross-references or which illustrated more than one specific point. The debt we owe to previous studies is considerable and is freely acknowledged in our footnotes and source references. Finally, we hope that our readers will share our sense of enjoyment, as they explore with us the theatre of this period, and will savour some of the human gems that we have unearthed during our investigations.

1660–1737

I   Documents of Control

INTRODUCTION

Between the Restoration of Charles II in 1660 and the implementation of the Licensing Act in 1737, the theatre in London developed from a Royalist institution, with patent companies established by Royal warrant and controlled directly by the Lord Chamberlain, to a discernibly commercial enterprise, regulated by Act of Parliament. (Although the licensing functions were left in the hands of the Lord Chamberlain, he was effectively answerable to the politicians in his role of censor and licensing agent.)

At the Restoration, groups of enterprising actors had hoped to revive the pattern of theatrical activity that had obtained in London in the 1630s, with rival groups of actors competing for the attention and custom of a wide and disparate audience. These same hopes were clearly nurtured by Sir Henry Herbert, the Master of the Revels, who had previously been responsible for licensing plays and all acting troupes, which in turn had furnished him with a reliable source of known fee income.

These various expectations were dashed by Charles II who decided, shortly after his Restoration, to establish only two patent companies of actors under Royal patronage. These were to be managed by two courtiers, Thomas Killigrew and Sir William Davenant, and all other companies were to be banned. Cutting across established practice in the theatre, Charles provoked a troubled period of wrangles and legal disputes involving the actors, the new managers and Sir Henry Herbert. What eventually emerged from this was a basic theatre structure, shaped around two patent houses, that was to last to the end of the eighteenth century.

As sworn servants of the King the actors normally enjoyed the protection of the Lord Chamberlain, notably when they were pressed for civil offences such as debt. They were also relatively free from day-to-day interventions in the running of their affairs. Major interventions by the Lord Chamberlain occurred during periods of poor management when company disputes threatened the stability or even viability of one of the companies. And this seems to have happened on a regular twenty-year cycle: in the mid 1670s, the mid 1690s, around 1709 and in the 1730s.

Generally, the tone of the documents of control reprinted here reflects the changing temper of the age. Even Royal patents or licences, seemingly couched in the traditional terminology of Royalist absolutism, are nevertheless worded with more than just a passing reference to the major concerns of the age. And so one finds, for instance, in a licence granted by Queen Anne a concern for banishing immorality and profanity from the stage that clearly reflects the issues raised by contemporary morality debates.

Sir Richard's Steele's brush with authority in the early 1720s, when he was for a period relieved of his licence for refusing to acknowledge the controlling power of the Lord Chamberlain and his political allies, is symptomatic of the conflicts that were to come to a head in the 1730s. By then the theatres had enjoyed several decades with little or no direct intervention by government. The result of such *laissez-faire* policies was that theatre companies threatened to proliferate beyond the immediate control of the Lord Chamberlain, and plays were performed that questioned the policies and behaviour of those in power and subjected them to hard-hitting personal satire. At that point it was inevitable that a formal redefinition of the government's power to license plays and theatres would occur, which is precisely what happened in the Licensing Act of 1737.

THE FIRST MONTHS AFTER THE RESTORATION

At the Restoration of King Charles II in May 1660, several enterprising groups of actors formed themselves into theatrical companies. Michael Mohun gathered together a group of experienced players at the Red Bull, most of whom had been active in pre-Commonwealth days. These were: William Wintershall, Robert Shatterall, William Cartwright, Walter Clun, Charles Hart and Nicholas Burt.[1] John Rhodes the bookseller brought together another company at the Cockpit in Drury Lane. His actors were younger men, some of whom were destined to play a crucial role in Restoration theatre: Thomas Betterton, Thomas Sheppey, Thomas Lovell, Thomas Lillieston, Cave Underhill, Robert Turner, James Dixon, Robert Nokes as well as others who regularly acted women's parts, including Edward Kynaston and James Nokes.[2] A third theatre at Salisbury Court was owned by William Beeston who was intent on setting up yet another troupe. To this end, he obtained a licence from Sir Henry Herbert, the Master of the Revels, probably in June 1660 [*see* 1].[3] There is evidence to suggest that he had found a visiting company as tenants later that summer, almost certainly a troupe led by George Jolly.[4] In his dealings with Beeston and the actors at the Red Bull, Sir Henry Herbert was intent on re-asserting the legal and financial control over the theatre he had exercised prior to the Commonwealth period [*see* 2].

[1] See Downes (Summers ed.), pp. 1–2; and Nicoll, vol. 1 (1952), p. 288.
[2] See Downes (Summers ed.), pp. 17–18; and Nicoll, vol. 1 (1952), p. 289.
[3] This date is suggested by Malone (1790), p. 239.
[4] See Nicoll, vol. 1 (1952), p. 292.

1   A licence for Salisbury Court Playhouse, June 1660

BL Add.MS 19,256, f. 100. Reproduced in Malone (1790), p. 239; Adams (1917), p. 81

Whereas the allowance of plays, the ordering of players and playmakers, and the permission for erecting of playhouses has, time out of mind [. . .] belonged to the Master of his Majesty's Office of the Revels. And whereas Mr William Beeston has desired authority and licence from me to continue the house called Salisbury Court Playhouse in a playhouse, which was formerly built and erected into a playhouse by the permission and licence of the Master of the Revels.

These are therefore by virtue of a grant under the Great Seal of England, and of the constant practice thereof, to continue and constitute the said house called Salisbury Court Playhouse into a playhouse, and to authorise and license the said Mr Beeston to set, let or use it for a playhouse, wherein comedies, tragedies, or tragi-comedies, pastorals and interludes may be acted, provided that no persons be admitted to act in the said playhouse but such as shall be allowed by the Master of his Majesty's Office of the Revels. [. . .]

2 The Red Bull players submit to Herbert's authority, 14 August 1660

PRO CP 40/2751, Mem. 317. Reproduced in Hotson (1928), p. 202[1]

We whose names are here underwritten do hereby promise and covenant to pay or cause to be paid to Sir Henry Herbert, Knight, Master of his Majesty's Office of the Revels, or to his deputy or agent, the sum of ten pounds on Saturday next after the date hereof. And what plays soever we shall act for the future, to pay or cause to be paid to the said Sir Henry Herbert, his deputy or agent, for every new play 40s and for every revived play 20s, as fees anciently belonging to the Master of the Revels. And we do hereby furthermore promise and covenant to pay or cause to be paid four pounds to the said Master of the Revels, his deputy or agent, on every Saturday successively next after the date hereof. In witness whereof we have hereunto set our hands and seals the fourteenth day of August, 1660. These covenants are to be made good during the time of acting under the said Master of the Revels. Michael Mohun, Robert Shatterall, William Cartwright, William Wintershall, Walter Clun, Charles Hart and Nicholas Burt.

[1] Another version of this document, signed only by Nicholas Burt may be found in BL Add.MS 19,256, f. 64. It is reproduced in Adams (1917), pp. 84–5.

SIR HENRY HERBERT PETITIONS THE KING

Sir Henry Herbert's hopes of re-asserting his authority over the stage suffered a severe blow in July 1660 when Charles II acceded to requests made to him by two courtiers, namely Thomas Killigrew and Sir William Davenant, to be granted permission to establish theatre companies under the direct authority of the King. All other theatre companies were to be suppressed. Charles's instructions to the Attorney General, dated 9 July 1660,[1] stung Sir Henry Herbert into submitting an immediate protest against the threatened diminution of his powers [see 3]. Even Palmer, the Attorney General, when asked to look into the matter, clearly viewed the proposed grant of a theatrical monopoly under the Great Seal with some misgivings. He was well aware of the legal complications it would cause in view of the earlier powers vested in the Office of the Master of Revels. His memorandum to Charles on the issue is, however, cautious and circumspect [see 4].

[1] PRO SP 29/5, no. 158. Reproduced in Hotson (1928), p. 400.

3 Sir Henry Herbert's petition to King Charles II, 4 August 1660

BL Add.MS 19,256, f. 48. Reproduced in Malone (1790), pp. 241–3; Adams (1917), pp. 86–7

To the King's most excellent Majesty. The humble petition of Sir Henry Herbert, Knight, Master of your Majesty's Office of the Revels shows: that whereas your petitioner by virtue of several grants under the Great Seal of England has executed the said Office as Master of the Revels for about 40 years, in the times of King James and of King Charles, both of blessed memory, with exception only to the time of the late horrid rebellion.

And whereas the ordering of plays, players and playmakers, and the permission for erecting of playhouses are peculiar branches of the said Office, and in the constant practice thereof by your petitioner's predecessors in the said Office and himself [. . .]. And that no person or persons have erected any playhouses or raised any company of players, without licence from your petitioner's said predecessors or from your petitioner, but Sir William Davenant, Knight, who obtained leave of Oliver and Richard Cromwell to vent his operas in a time when your petitioner owned not their authority.[1]

And whereas your Majesty has lately signified your pleasure by warrant to Sir Geoffrey Palmer, Knight and Baronet, your Majesty's Attorney General, for the drawing of a grant for your Majesty's signature to pass the Great Seal, thereby to enable and empower Mr Thomas Killigrew and the said Sir William Davenant to erect two new playhouses in London, Westminster, or the suburbs thereof, and to make choice of two companies of players, to be under their sole regulation, and that no other players shall be authorised to play in London, Westminster, or the suburbs thereof but such as the said Mr Killigrew and Sir William Davenant shall allow of.

And whereas your petitioner has been represented to your Majesty as a person consenting to the said powers expressed in the said warrant, your petitioner utterly denies the least consent or foreknowledge thereof, but looks upon it as an unjust surprise, and destructive to the powers granted under the Great Seal to your petitioner, and to the constant practice of the said Office, and exercised in the said Office ever since players were first admitted by authority to act plays and cannot legally be done as your petitioner is advised. And it may be of very ill consequence, as your petitioner is advised, by a new grant to take away and cut off a branch of the ancient powers granted to the said Office under the Great Seal.

Your petitioner therefore humbly prays that your Majesty would be justly as graciously pleased to revoke the said warrant from your Majesty's said Attorney General or to refer the premises to the consideration of your Majesty's said Attorney General to certify to your Majesty of the truth of them and his judgement on the whole matters in question betwixt the said Mr Killigrew, Sir William Davenant and your petitioner, in relation to the legality and consequence of their demands and your petitioner's rights.[2]

---

[1] Davenant had in fact been granted a patent to set up a theatre company by Charles I in 1639 [see G.E. Bentley: *The Jacobean and Caroline stage*, vol. 6 (Oxford: The Clarendon Press, 1968), pp. 305–9]. Herbert does his best to discredit Davenant by drawing attention to his theatrical activity in the time of the Commonwealth. Davenant had indeed come close to compromising himself through his determination to mount operatic performances in Cromwellian London. But Charles obviously attached more importance to honouring a patent granted by his father than to distancing himself from a once loyal courtier who had shown a remarkable ability to ingratiate himself with Cromwell and his ministers.

[2] Charles duly referred the matter to his Attorney General, Sir Geoffrey Palmer, who reported on 14 September 1660 that he had seen the parties to the dispute separately, but that Davenant and Killigrew had failed to attend a meeting he had arranged at which Sir Henry Herbert would also be present. He went on to add: 'I have forborne to proceed further; having received an intimation by letter from Sir William Davenant that I was freed from further hearing this matter' [BL Add.MS 19,256, f. 48].

4   Sir Geoffrey Palmer's note to Charles II on the proposed grant
PRO SP 29/10, no. 108. Reproduced in Hotson (1928), p. 200

May it please your Majesty, the humble representation which I made to your Highness concerning the provided grant to Mr Killigrew and Sir William Davenant was only that the matter was more proper for a toleration than a grant under the Great Seal of England, and did not interpose any other obstacle; nor do find cause to object against the two warrants they have now produced.

CHARLES II GRANTS A WARRANT TO KILLIGREW AND DAVENANT

Sir Henry Herbert's tenacity in clinging to his ancient privileges was matched by the dedicated single-mindedness with which Killigrew and Davenant set about establishing their new empires. Davenant at least had some claim to theatrical distinction. He had worked as a dramatist for the King's Men from 1626 to 1640. He had also worked with Inigo Jones on court masques during the 1630s and had obtained a theatre patent from Charles I in 1639. In addition, he had attempted to introduce new theatrical ideas into England (including changeable scenery)[1] during the difficult years of the Commonwealth in the late 1650s. Killigrew had a strong love of the theatre and had written several plays, but he was above all a man eager for financial perquisites after the long years of exile he had shared as one of Charles's closest companions.

Despite Herbert's shrill protests and the tactfully phrased objections of the Attorney General, Charles took the first steps towards giving Killigrew and Davenant the theatrical empires they wanted in August 1660. The stated excuse was entirely spurious, namely the King's desire to suppress any plays containing 'much matter of profanation and scurrility'. Astute politician that he was, Charles knew that this moral aim would appeal to strong puritan sentiments in the City of London while providing a convenient screen for his real purpose, which was to reward his loyal courtier friend Tom Killigrew and to honour the patent granted to Davenant by Charles I. As so often in the history of the theatre, the excuse of moral outrage was used as a means of concealing more pragmatic aims. It is worth noting, however, that Charles's commitment to Killigrew and Davenant proved to be less than whole-hearted. By December 1660 he had granted a theatrical licence to George Jolly who was to be a troublesome competitor to Killigrew and Davenant.[2]

[1] See pp. 84–91 below.
[2] See p. 18 below.

5   Warrant granted by Charles II to Killigrew and Davenant, 21 August 1660
BL Add.MS 19,256, f. 47. Reproduced in Malone (1790), pp. 244–6; Adams (1917), pp. 87–8; Fitzgerald, vol. 1 (1882), pp. 23–4

Charles the Second, by the grace of God, of England, Scotland, and Ireland, King, Defender of the Faith, etc., to all whom these presents shall come, greeting. Whereas we are given to understand that certain persons in and about our City of London, or the suburbs thereof, do frequently assemble for the performing and acting of plays and interludes for rewards, to which diverse of our subjects do for their entertainment resort: which said plays, as we are informed, do contain much matter of profanation and scurrility, so that such kind of entertainments which if well managed might serve as moral instructions in human life, as the same are now used, do for the most part tend to the debauching of the manners of such as are present at them, and are very scandalous and offensive to all pious and well-disposed persons. We, taking the premises into our princely consideration, yet not holding it necessary totally to suppress the use of theatres, because we are assured that if the evils and scandal in the plays that now are or have been acted were taken away, the same might serve as innocent and harmless divertissement for many of our subjects; and having experience of the art and skill of our trusty and well-beloved Thomas Killigrew, Esq., one of the Grooms of our Bedchamber, and of Sir William Davenant, Knight, for the purposes hereafter mentioned, do hereby give and grant unto the said Thomas Killigrew and Sir William Davenant full power and authority to erect two companies of players, consisting respectively of such persons as they shall choose and appoint, and to purchase, build, and erect or hire at their charge, as they shall think fit, two houses or theatres with all convenient rooms and other necessaries thereunto appertaining, for the representation of tragedies, comedies, plays, operas, and all other entertainments of that nature in convenient places: and likewise to settle and establish such payments to be paid by those that shall resort to see the said representations performed as either have been accustomely given and taken in the like kind, or as shall be reasonable in regard of the great expenses of scenes, music, and such new decorations as have not been formerly used:[1] with further power to make such allowances out of that which they shall so receive to the actors and other persons employed in the said representations in both houses respectively as they shall think fit; the said companies to be under the government and authority of them, the said Thomas Killigrew and Sir William Davenant. And in regard to the extraordinary licentiousness that has lately used in things of this nature, our pleasure is, that there shall be no more places of representation nor companies of actors of plays, or operas, and recitations, music or representations by dancing and scenes and any other entertainments on the stage, in our Cities of London and Westminster, or in the liberties of them than the two to be now erected by virtue of this authority. Nevertheless, we do hereby by our authority royal strictly enjoin the said Thomas Killigrew and Sir William Davenant that they do not at any time hereafter cause to be acted or represented any play, interlude, or opera, containing any matter of profanation, scurrility, or obscenity; and we do further hereby authorise and command the said Thomas Killigrew and Sir William Davenant to peruse all plays that have been formerly written, and to expunge all profanities and scurrility from the same before they be represented or acted. And this our grant and authority made to the said Thomas Killigrew and Sir William Davenant shall be effectual and remains in full force and virtue, notwithstanding any former order or direction by us given, for the suppression of playhouses and plays and any other entertainments of the stage.

---

[1] It is worth noting the reference to scenery here, which implies that both patent holders intended at this point to erect scenic theatres. Davenant's earlier patent granted in 1639 is worded quite

differently: 'And that it shall and may be lawful to and for the said William Davenant, his heirs, executors, administrators and assigns to take and receive of such our subjects as shall resort to see or hear any such plays, scenes and entertainments whatsoever, such sum or sums of money as is, are, or hereafter from time to time shall be accustomed to be given or taken in other playhouses and places for the like plays, scenes, presentments and entertainments' [Thomas Rymer: *Foedera* (London: Tonson, 1735), p. 378]. The wording used in the August 1660 warrant is repeated in all later patents granted during the Restoration and throughout the eighteenth century.

THE ACTORS PETITION THE KING

Killigrew and Davenant swiftly consolidated their position and acquired sites for their new theatre buildings.[1] Killigrew took over the group of older and more experienced actors from the Red Bull; Davenant acquired the younger actors from the Phoenix. Both groups of actors united on a temporary basis in one company at the Phoenix during the autumn of 1660, while the new theatre buildings were being made ready. Because Killigrew's company included most of the older actors, they enjoyed exclusive performance rights to pre-Restoration plays. Davenant was obliged to petition the King in December 1660 for the right to perform at least some old plays; a small concession was granted him in a warrant from the Lord Chamberlain dated 12 December 1660.[2] He was given exclusive performance rights to eleven plays, nine of which were by Shakespeare. He was further given exclusive rights to perform his own pre-Restoration plays. And for the space of two months he was allowed to perform six plays that had previously been the property of Rhodes's company.[3] Meanwhile, Sir Henry Herbert continued to assert his rights by harrassing the actors at the Phoenix and requiring them to submit to his authority.[4] In some desperation, the actors petitioned the King on 13 October 1660.

[1] See pp. 58–60 below.
[2] PRO LC 5/137, pp. 343–4. Reproduced in Nicoll, vol. 1 (1952), pp. 352–3.
[3] For further details, see Milhous (1979), pp. 15–17 and John Freehafer: 'The formation of the London Patent companies in 1660' *TN* 20 (1965–6), 26–7.
[4] Warrants issued by Sir Henry Herbert on 10 and 13 October 1660, are reproduced in Adams (1917), pp. 93–4.

6   The petition of the Cockpit [Phoenix] players, 13 October 1660

BL Add.MS 19,256, f. 71. Reproduced in Malone (1790), pp. 248–9; Adams (1917), pp. 94–6

To the King's most excellent Majesty. The humble petition of Michael Mohun, Robert Shatterall, Charles Hart, Nicholas Burt, William Cartwright, Walter Clun, and William Wintershall humbly shows that your Majesty's humble petitioners, having been suppressed by a warrant from your Majesty, Sir Henry Herbert informed us it was Mr Killigrew had caused it, and if we would give him so much a week, he would protect them against Mr Killigrew and all powers. The complaint against us was: scandalous plays, raising the price, and acknowledging no authority;[1] all which ended in so much per week to him; for which we had leave to play and promise of his protection: the which your Majesty knows he was not able to perform, since Mr Killigrew, having your Majesty's former grant, suppressed us, until we had by covenant obliged ourselves to act with women, a new theatre, and habits according to our scenes.[2] And according to your Majesty's approbation, from the companies we made election of one company; and so far Sir Henry Herbert has been from protecting us, that he has been a continual disturbance unto us, who were [united] by your Majesty's command under Mr Killigrew, as Master of your Majesty's Comedians; and we have annexed unto our petition the date of the warrant by which we were suppressed, and for a protection against that warrant he forced from us so much a week. [. . .].

The premises considered, your petitioners humbly beseech your Majesty to be graciously pleased to signify your royal pleasure to the Lord Chamberlain, that your petitioners may not be molested in their calling. [. . .]

[1] See Adams (1917), pp. 93–4.
[2] This suggests some opposition amongst the actors to all three, namely working with women, working in a new theatre and working with painted scenery and costumes to match.

HERBERT AND THE PATENT HOLDERS COME TO AN AGREEMENT

Killigrew's company, known initially as the King's Men, started playing at Gibbon's Tennis Court in Vere Street, Clare Market, on 5 November 1660. Davenant's company, known initially as the Duke's Men, began performances at Salisbury Court on the same date.[1] As sworn Royal servants, the actors enjoyed the status of 'grooms of the chamber in ordinary without fee'[2] and were entitled to wear Royal liveries.[3] Despite the royal favour and protection they enjoyed, Herbert continued to harrass the patent holders and their actors. He brought a successful lawsuit against Mohun and other actors in Killigrew's troupe in December 1661.[4] In February 1662 he served a writ against Killigrew and Davenant but he lost the case.[5] Undeterred, he brought another lawsuit against Davenant in June 1662, and this time he won. In some desperation, Davenant sent a petition to Charles asking him to clarify the position.[6] Charles referred the matter to the Lord Chancellor and the Lord Chamberlain. Meanwhile, in May 1662 Herbert had already served yet another writ, this time against Betterton, who was acting in Davenant's company.[7] By June 1662 Killigrew had reached a compromise with Herbert and legal articles were drawn up. He agreed to pay Herbert the traditional fees for licensing plays as well as generous compensation for all the trouble he had caused. For his part Herbert effectively relinquished his claim to license playhouses and players and agreed not to molest Killigrew any further. There is no record of Davenant's agreement with Herbert, but it may be assumed that a similar compromise was reached or imposed by the Lord Chancellor and the Lord Chamberlain who summoned Herbert and Davenant to appear before them in July 1662.[8]

[1] Although there are no records of performances until January 1661, evidence suggesting performances as from 5 November 1660 may be found in Herbert's lawsuit against Betterton of 1662, where Herbert claims compensation for unpaid licensing fees for ten new plays and 100 revived plays between 5 November 1660 and 6 May 1662. See Adams (1917), pp. 109–10 and Hotson (1928), pp. 208 and 239, n. 27.
[2] See PRO LC 5/137, pp. 332–3.
[3] Livery warrants may be found in PRO LC 5/119; PRO LC 5/137, pp. 31, 43, 173; and PRO LC 5/138, pp. 55, 65, 71, 271–2.
[4] Fitzgerald, vol. 1 (1882), p. 58.
[5] *Ibid.* and Hotson (1928), p. 211.
[6] The petition is printed in full in Hotson (1928), pp. 211–12. The original may be found in BL Add.MS 19,256, f. 74.
[7] BL Add.MS 19,256, ff. 67–8. See Hotson (1928), p. 212.
[8] BL Add.MS 19,256, f. 74.

7   **Articles of agreement between Herbert and Killigrew, 4 June 1662**

BL Add.MS 19,256, f. 66. Reproduced in Malone (1790), pp. 262–4; Adams (1917), pp. 113–15

[. . .] Imprimis, it is agreed that a firm amity be concluded for life between the said Sir Henry Herbert and the said Thomas Killigrew.

Item, the said Thomas Killigrew, Esquire, does for himself covenant, promise, grant and agree to pay or cause to be paid unto Sir Henry Herbert or to his assigns, on or before the fourth day of August next, all moneys due to the said Sir Henry Herbert from the King's and Queen's Company of Players, called Michael Mohun, William Wintershall, Robert Shatterall, William Cartwright, Nicholas Burt, Walter Clun, Charles Hart, and the rest of that company, for the new plays at forty shillings a play and for the old revived plays at twenty shillings a play [that] they the said players have acted since the eleventh of August in the year of our Lord 1660.

Item, the said Thomas Killigrew, Esquire, does for himself covenant, promise, grant and agree, to pay or cause to be paid unto the said Sir Henry Herbert or to his assigns, on or before the fourth day of August next, such moneys as are due to him for damages and costs obtained at law against Michael Mohun, William Wintershall, Robert Shatterall, William Cartwright, Nicholas Burt, Walter Clun and Charles Hart, upon an action of the case brought by the said Sir Henry Herbert in the court of Common Pleas against the said Michael Mohun (etc.), whereupon a verdict has been obtained as aforesaid against them. [. . .]

Item, the said Thomas Killigrew, Esquire, does for himself covenant, promise, grant and agree, that the said Michael Mohun and the rest of the King's and Queen's Company of Players shall, on or before the said fourth day of August next, pay or cause to be paid unto the said Sir Henry Herbert or his assigns, the sum of fifty pounds, as a noble present from them for his great damages sustained from them and by their means.

Item, that the said Thomas Killigrew, Esquire, does covenant, promise, gr[ant, and] agree to be aiding and assisting unto the said Sir Henry Herbert [in the] due execution of the Office of the Revels, and neither directly nor indirectly to aid or assist Sir William Davenant, Knight, or a[ny of] his pretended company of players, or any other company of play[ers] to be raised by him or any other company of players whatsoever. [. . .]¹

And the said Sir Henry Herbert does for himself covenant, promise, grant and agree not to molest the said Thomas Killigrew, Esquire, or his heirs in any suit at law or otherwise to the prejudice of the grant made unto him by His Majesty or to disturb the receiving of the profits arising by contract from the King's and Queen's Company of Players to him, but to aid and assist the said Thomas Killigrew in the d[ue] execution of the legal powers granted unto him by His Majesty f[or the] ordering of the said Company of Players, and in the levying and receiving of the moneys due to him the said Thomas Killigrew, Esquire, or which shall be due to him from the said Company of Players by any contract made or to be made between them concerning the same, and neither directly nor indirectly to hinder the payment of the said moneys to be made weekly or otherwise by the said Company of Players to the said Thomas Killigrew, Esquire, or to his assigns, but to be aiding and assisting to the said Thomas Killigrew, Esquire and his assigns therein, if there be cause for it, and that the said Thomas Killigrew desire it of the said Sir Henry Herbert. [. . .]

¹ At this juncture, Herbert had not reached any agreement with Davenant and was intent on driving a wedge between the two patentees.

CHARLES II GRANTS INDIVIDUAL PATENTS FOR KILLIGREW AND DAVENANT

After the opening of their converted tennis court theatres, Killigrew and Davenant managed to persuade Charles and his officials to grant them individual patents to replace their initial warrants. These effectively consolidated their position, confirming the long-term nature of the royal grant under the Great Seal. The excuse for giving them a theatrical monopoly was the same as before, but there were also important new provisions concerning women players. These the patentees presumably suggested to Charles, as they were arguments they had used in silencing the actors at the Cockpit [Phoenix].¹

¹ See the petition of the Cockpit [Phoenix] players, pp. 13–14 above.

8   Killigrew's patent, 25 April 1662
Original in the possession of The Theatre Museum. Copy at PRO c/66/3013. Reproduced in Fitzgerald, vol. 1 (1882), pp. 77–80

[. . .] Know ye that we of our especial grace, certain knowledge and mere motion [. . .] do give and grant to the said Thomas Killigrew, his heirs and assigns, full power, licence and authority, that he, they, and every of them, [. . .] shall and may lawfully, quietly and peaceably frame, erect, new build and set up in any place within our cities of London and Westminster, or the suburbs thereof, where he or they shall find best accommodation for that purpose, to be assigned and allotted out by the surveyor of our works, one theatre or playhouse, with necessary tiring and retiring rooms and other places convenient, of such extent and dimension as the said Thomas Killigrew, his heirs or assigns shall think fitting, wherein tragedies, comedies, plays, operas, music, scenes and all other entertainment of the stage whatsoever may be shown and presented. And we do hereby for us, our heirs and successors, grant unto the said Thomas Killigrew, his heirs and assigns, full power, licence and authority, from time to time to gather together, entertain, govern, privilege and keep such and so many players and persons to exercise and act tragedies, comedies, plays, operas, and other performances of the stage within the house to be built as aforesaid, or within any other house where he or they can be best fitted for that purpose, within our cities of London and Westminster or the suburbs thereof. Which said company shall be the servant of us and our dear consort, and shall consist of such number as the said Thomas Killigrew, his heirs or assigns, shall from time to time think meet; and such persons to permit and continue at and during the pleasure of the said Thomas Killigrew, his heirs or assigns from time to time to act plays and entertainment of the stage of all sort peaceably and quietly without the impeachment or impediment of any person or persons whatsoever, for the honest recreation of such as shall desire to see the same: and that it shall and may be lawful to and for the said Thomas Killigrew, his heirs and assigns, to take and receive of such our subjects as shall resort to see or hear any such plays, scenes and entertainment whatsoever, such sums of money as either have accustomably been given or taken in the like kind or as shall be thought reasonable by him or them in regard of the great expenses of scenes, music and such new decorations as have not been formerly used; and further, for us, our heirs and successors, we do hereby give and grant unto the said Thomas Killigrew, his heirs and assigns, full power to make such allowances out of that which he shall so receive by the acting of plays and entertainment of the stage aforesaid to the actors and other persons employed in acting, representing or in any qualities whatsoever about the said theatre, as he or they shall think fit; and that the said company shall be under the sole government and authority of the said Thomas Killigrew, his heirs and assigns, and all scandalous and mutinous persons from time to time by him and them to be ejected and disabled from playing in the said theatre. And for that we are informed that diverse companies of players have taken upon them to act plays publicly in our said cities of London and Westminster, or the suburbs thereof, without any authority for that purpose, we do hereby declare our dislike of the same, and will and grant that only the said company to be erected and set up by the said Thomas Killigrew, his heirs and assigns by virtue of this present, and one other company to be erected and set up by Sir William Davenant, Knight, his heirs or assigns and none other, shall from henceforth act or represent comedies, tragedies, plays or entertainment of the stage within our said cities of London and Westminster and the suburbs thereof, which said company to be erected by the said William Davenant, his heirs or assigns, shall be subject to his or their government and authority, and shall be styled the Duke of York's Company. And better to preserve amity and correspondence betwixt the said companies, and that the one may not encroach upon the other by any indirect means, we will and ordain that no actor or other person employed about either the said theatres ejected by the said Thomas Killigrew and Sir William Davenant or either of them, or deserting his company, shall be received by the governor of the said other company to be employed in acting or in any manner relating to the stage without the consent or approbation of the governor of the company whereof the person so ejected or deserting was a member, signified under his hand and seal. And we do by this present declare all other company and companies before mentioned to be silenced and suppressed, and for as much as many plays formerly acted do contain several profane, obscene and scurrilous passages, and the women's parts therein have been acted by men in the habit of women, at which some have taken offence,[1] for the preventing of these abuses for the future, we do hereby strictly command and enjoin that from henceforth no new play shall be acted by either of the said companies containing any passages offensive to piety and good manners, nor any old or revived play containing any such offensive passages as aforesaid, until the same shall be corrected and purged by the said master or governors of the said respective companies from all such offensive and scandalous passages as aforesaid. And we do likewise permit and give leave that all the women's parts to be acted in either of the said two companies for the time to come may be performed by women so long as their recreations, which by reason of the abuses aforesaid were scandalous and offensive, may by such reformation be esteemed not only harmless delight, but useful and instructive representations of human life, to such of our good subjects as shall resort to the same. [. . .]

¹ The excuse of wishing to avoid giving offence was used to cloak the real motives for introducing women on stage, namely the patentees' desire to offer contemporary audiences an additional, commercially profitable attraction.

GEORGE JOLLY AND THE PATENTEES

Despite the new patents Killigrew and Davenant had obtained from Charles II, they still had one theatrical competitor in London, namely George Jolly. On 24 December 1660 the King had given him a licence to perform plays in London, notwithstanding his former grant to Killigrew and Davenant.¹ This was presumably because Jolly had agreed to surrender his lease of Salisbury Court Playhouse in November 1660 to make way for Davenant's company. There is evidence that Jolly's troupe played in different London theatres throughout 1661 and 1662.² By December 1662 he formally agreed to lease his warrant to the patentees, having obtained Herbert's permission to play in the provinces.³ In his absence, Killigrew and Davenant informed the King that Jolly had in fact sold them his warrant and asked that they might use it to set up a third theatre in London, a Nursery for young actors. Charles accordingly revoked the warrant in July 1663 and gave the patentees permission to set up a Nursery.⁴

Jolly was naturally incensed at the double-dealing of the patentees and continued to play in defiance of their monopoly. A series of stern warnings was delivered to him, culminating in his arrest in January 1668.⁵ After this event, Jolly agreed to the compromise suggestion of the patentees that he should manage their new Nursery in Hatton Garden.

¹ PRO SP 29/44, no. 37. Reproduced in Hotson (1928), pp. 177–8.
² See Nicoll, vol. 1 (1952), pp. 309–10.
³ The agreement is printed in Hotson (1928), pp. 179–82.
⁴ PRO SP 44/15, pp. 117–19. Draft in PRO SP 29/77, no. 38.
⁵ PRO LC 5/186, p. 184. Reproduced in Nicoll, vol. 1 (1952), p. 313.

9   Charles II orders George Jolly to surrender his licence, March 1667

PRO SP 29/195, no. 109, p. 173. Reproduced in Hotson (1928), p. 186

Whereas we are informed that by virtue of a patent by us granted unto you, you are now presuming to set up a playhouse notwithstanding that you have been several times commanded the contrary. We have thought fit hereby to require you forthwith to deliver your said patent into the hands of one of our Principal Secretaries of State, there to remain until our further pleasure in this behalf, whereof you may not fail as you will answer to the contrary.

THE KING INTERVENES IN THE RUNNING OF KILLIGREW'S COMPANY

The basic pattern of theatre work in London was now firmly established and was to remain unchanged until the two companies united in 1682. Both companies were instructed to cease acting during the Plague between June 1665 and December 1666,[1] which involved considerable loss of revenue. Both companies also committed themselves to heavy expenditure in the early 1670s through the building of new theatres. The Duke's Company opened their new theatre at Dorset Garden in November 1671 and the King's Company opened their new Theatre Royal in Drury Lane in March 1674, after a fire had destroyed their earlier theatre in Bridges Street in January 1672.[2]

Killigrew proved to be a feckless and incompetent manager, and his troupe was restive under his control. They attempted on several occasions in the early 1660s to petition the King, but without success.[3] Further disputes took place in 1674 and 1676.[4] On the latter occasion, the actors actually refused to perform and had to be instructed by the Lord Chamberlain, on behalf of the King, to resume their duties [see 10]. Killigrew was appointed Master of the Revels in April 1673. Four years later, in 1677, he became embroiled in a bitter lawsuit with his own son, Charles. The conflict was resolved in February 1677 when he handed over to his son his patent and subsequently the Office of the Revels. Charles Killigrew proved no better than his father as a theatre manager, and even the King was moved to express his dissatisfaction with the management of the theatre in July 1677 [see 11]. By 1682, profits had sunk so low that the Theatre Royal had to close, leaving the two companies to amalgamate.[5] A year after this merger, on 19 March 1683, old Thomas Killigrew died.

The Duke's Company were better managed, even after Sir William Davenant's death in 1668. His widow held financial control until their son Charles was old enough to play a nominally more active role in the affairs of the theatre in 1673. Meanwhile, the practical management of the theatre was given over to Thomas Betterton and Henry Harris. Betterton in particular proved to be an able and astute manager, and it was largely due to his efforts that the Duke's Company were still in relatively good shape when the two companies united in 1682.[6]

---

[1] PRO LC 5/138, p. 417. The order is reproduced in Nicoll, vol. I, p. 299.
[2] See p. 69 below.
[3] See Hotson (1928), pp. 244–5 and Nicoll, vol. I (1952), p. 299.
[4] See Nicoll, vol. I (1952), pp. 323–5.
[5] See pp. 39–40 below.
[6] For information on the profits of the Company, see Judith Milhous: 'The Duke's Company's profits, 1675–77' *TN* 32 (1978), 76–88.

---

10   The Lord Chamberlain orders the actors at the Theatre Royal to resume acting, 14 February 1676

PRO LC 7/1, p. 5. Reproduced in Nicoll, vol. I (1952), p. 325

His Majesty, understanding that his Company of Comedians have left off acting upon private differences and disagreements between themselves, is very much displeased thereat and has commanded me to require and order the said Company forthwith to act and play as formerly. And that none of the same Company presume to leave off acting.

II   Letter from the Lord Chamberlain to the Attorney General, expressing the King's dissatisfaction with the management of the Theatre Royal, 30 July 1677
PRO LC 5/142, p. 98. Reproduced in Nicoll, vol. I (1952), p. 326

His Majesty being dissatisfied with the government of the players, His Servants at the Royal Theatre, upon their humble petition which I here send you, is pleased to gratify them in their proposition of governing themselves but withall, that Mr Killigrew's right to his shares and profits may be preserved and that he may have also security given him to indemnify him from those articles and debts, which he alleges he is liable unto, as you will see in his answers to their petition which I here also send you. His Majesty desires it may be despatched by you with all conveniency that the Company may begin to play to support themselves because they suffer every day they lie still.

DISSENSION IN THE UNITED COMPANIES

The United Companies survived the uncertainties created by the death of Charles II in 1685 and the ill-fated reign of James II from 1685–8. There were minor troubles and disputes during this period,[1] but nothing compared to the turmoil experienced after December 1693 when Christopher Rich, a lawyer, and Sir Thomas Skipwith, an 'adventurer'[2] acquired control over the Company through a series of stealthy financial moves.[3] Rich's main aim appears to have been to extract the maximum profit from the enterprise without regard to the feelings or the skill of his actors. When he began cutting actors' salaries and redistributing acting roles from senior to junior members, he provoked the leading members of the troupe into open revolt. In December 1694, this group of actors, led by Betterton, submitted a petition to the Lord Chamberlain, outlining their grievances. It proved impossible to reconcile the parties, and in March 1695 Betterton and his colleagues were granted a licence to set up a new and separate company of actors.[4] They moved into their newly converted theatre in Lincoln's Inn Fields in April 1695.

[1]   See Nicoll, vol. I (1952), p. 332.
[2]   'Adventurers' were investors who had acquired whole or part shares in a theatre. They were not normally directly involved in the running of the theatre.
[3]   See Nicoll, vol. I (1952), p. 333 and Hotson (1928), pp. 284–8.
[4]   PRO LC 7/3, f. 7.

I2   Petition of the players, December 1694
PRO LC 7/3, ff. 2–3. Reproduced in Nicoll, vol. I (1952), p. 368 and Milhous (1979), pp. 225–9

The humble petition of their Majesties' Servants and Comedians shows that your petitioners whose names are here subscribed being no longer able to suffer and support themselves under the unjust oppressions and violations of almost all the by-laws, customs and usages that have been established among us from the beginning and which remained unviolated till after Dr Davenant sold his patent and shares to his brother Alexander under whom and by whom several titles have been claimed by diverse persons, and sometimes a trust in him only pretended whereby many have been defrauded, with other pretences and combinations whereby several persons have been let in who seek after their own interest to recover their debts. [. . .]

Our humble petition to your Lordship is that, out of your goodness and compassion, you would be pleased to appoint a day of hearing our just complaints and, if we make out what we allege, to deliver us from our oppressions which are so intolerable and heavy that, unless relieved, we are not able to act any longer.

Thomas Betterton, Cave Underhill, Edward Kynaston, Jos. Williams, Thomas Doggett, George Bright, Samuel Sandford. Elizabeth Barry, Anne Bracegirdle, Susanna Verbruggen, Elizabeth Bowman, Mary Betterton, Ellen Leigh, John Bowman.

¹ The detailed grievances are set out in PRO LC 7/3, ff. 3–4; the lengthy reply of the patentees in PRO LC 7/3, ff. 8–20. Extracts are printed on p. 42 below.

THE STAGE FACES DEMANDS FOR REFORM

The mutual hostility of the two playhouses led to several injunctions from the Lord Chamberlain instructing the two companies not to employ actors from each other without the agreement of the respective managers and the permission of the Lord Chamberlain.¹ From the late 1690s onwards there were also concerted attempts by successive Lord Chamberlains to re-establish a credible form of licensing in respect of the plays performed by the two companies² [see 13]. This was partly prompted by the desire to placate the increasingly vociferous puritan opponents of the stage (some of whom attempted unsuccessfully to prosecute actors for uttering obscene and profane expressions on stage);³ but it was also intended as a means of regaining political control over an important public medium. This consideration ensured that there was continued pressure on the stage throughout the early decades of the eighteenth century, culminating in the Licensing Act of 1737⁴ [see 14].

In December 1704, Congreve and Vanbrugh were given a licence by Queen Anne, permitting them to open a new playhouse in the Haymarket, designed by Vanbrugh. (In the same month, John Downes informs us, 'Mr Betterton assigned his licence and his whole company over to Captain Vanbrugh to act under his [licence] at the theatre in the Haymarket'.)⁵ The wording of the licence for Vanbrugh and Congreve clearly reflects the new moralising tone of the age.

¹ PRO LC 5/152, p. 15; PRO LC 7/1, pp. 40 and 42; PRO LC 7/3, f. 21. The latter two are reproduced in Nicoll, vol. I (1952), pp. 338–9.
² PRO LC 7/1, p. 43; PRO LC 5/152, p. 162; PRO LC 5/153, p. 433. Reproduced in Krutch (1929), pp. 180–4.
³ See PRO LC 7/3, ff. 159 and 166. See also Krutch (1929), pp. 168–76.
⁴ See pp. 205–10 below.
⁵ Downes (Summers ed.), pp. 47–8. Judith Milhous queries whether Vanbrugh initially intended to invite Betterton to join forces with him at the Haymarket. See Milhous (1979), pp. 169–70.

13   Order to the managers of the Haymarket and Drury Lane governing the registering of actors and plays, 24 December 1709
PRO LC 5/154, ff. 256–7

[. . .] That from and after the first day of January next no new representations be brought upon the stage which are not necessary to the better performance of comedy or opera, such as ladder dancing, antique postures, etc.,[1] without my leave and approbation first had. That you forthwith prepare and transmit to me an exact list of all such comedies which you propose to act the next year that were licensed before her Majesty's accession to the Crown in order to their being more carefully revised and new licensed by the Master of the Revels. And that from and after Lady Day next you shall not suffer or permit any such play to be acted till it has received new licence. And you are hereby strictly required not to allow anything to be acted upon the stage that has been struck out by the Master of the Revels nor any new prologues or epilogues to be spoken without his licence upon pain of being silenced for such neglect.

[1] Rich had taken the lead in introducing various forms of mime and acrobatics into his repertoire in order to attract a larger audience to his theatre.

14   Queen Anne's licence for Congreve and Vanbrugh, 14 December 1704

PRO LC 5/154, p. 35/f. 22. Reproduced in Krutch (1929), p. 186 and in Nicoll, vol. 2 (1952), p. 275

Whereas we have thought fit for the reforming the abuses and immorality of the stage that a new company of comedians should be established for our service under stricter government and regulations than have been formerly. We therefore reposing especial trust and confidence in our trusty and well-beloved John Vanbrugh and William Congreve, Esquire, for the due execution and performance of this our will and pleasure, do give and grant unto them the said John Vanbrugh and William Congreve full power and authority to form, constitute and establish for us, a company of comedians with full and free licence to act and represent in any convenient place, during our pleasure, all comedies, tragedies, plays, interludes, operas, and to perform all other theatrical and musical entertainments whatsoever and to settle such rules and orders for the good government of the said company, as the Chamberlain of our Household shall from time to time direct and approve of.

By her Majesty's command. Kent.

INTERVENTIONS BY THE LORD CHAMBERLAIN 1705–15

The opening of the Queen's Theatre in the Haymarket in 1705 ushered in a decade of instability for London's theatres. There were many complex management changes, sudden shifts of allegiance involving the actors of the two houses, frequent interventions by the Lord Chamberlain and even open mutiny by the actors.[1]

In broad terms the decade was marked by Vanbrugh's ill-fated attempts to introduce Italian opera into London and Rich's ill-judged attempts to extort as much money as possible from his actors. In December 1707, Vanbrugh persuaded the Lord Chamberlain to give him a monopoly of opera production at the Haymarket [see 15]. Although he had a genuine interest in Italian opera, he was in large part driven to seek a monopoly of opera production because the theatre he had designed proved acoustically unsuited to acting. The opera monopoly was a costly error. By the spring of 1708 he had lost so much money that he was obliged to lease his licence and stock to his manager Owen Swiney. (Congreve had already lost enough money to make him quit by December 1705.) Rich, for his part, was defeated by his own deviousness at Drury Lane. In the season 1708-9, his unremitting attempts to withhold benefit money owing to his actors led them to complain bitterly to the Lord Chamberlain. Kent, the Lord Chamberlain, responded by silencing the whole company in June 1709, effectively putting Rich out of business [see 16]. The actors petitioned him to be allowed to resume acting,[2] and, on 8 July 1709, he allowed them to do so, giving them permission to act four days a week in the Haymarket on the grounds that they were not involved in Rich's contempt.[3] A lengthy document of complaint was drawn up by the 'adventurers', questioning the legality of the Lord Chamberlain's arbitrary intervention. But the 'adventurers' decided not to press the matter at law, even though they clearly had a strong case [see 17].

In the stormy period that followed these events, a Tory MP called William Collier outmanoeuvred his fellow 'adventurers' by successfully applying for a licence to run Drury Lane in November 1709; he asserted his right by forcibly occupying the theatre. However, the actors were restive under his manager, Aaron Hill, and staged a full-scale riot in June 1710 [see 18]. What emerged from this chaos was a triumvirate of actors to manage Drury Lane under Collier's licence (initially Wilks, Cibber and Doggett and then Wilks, Cibber and Booth). Following the death of Queen Anne in August 1714, the three actor-managers invited Richard Steele to become their licensee in place of William Collier.

Meanwhile, at the Haymarket Owen Swiney went bankrupt in the season 1712-13 and fled to the continent, leaving his debts (and his actors) unpaid. Thereafter the Haymarket housed a succession of opera companies all of which eventually foundered because of the high cost involved in mounting operas. (It was not until 1719 when a Royal Academy of Music was established at the Haymarket, with Handel's operas as the cornerstone of its repertoire and with generous financial support from the King and wealthy subscribers, that Italian opera enjoyed a stable production base in London.)[4]

After the death of Queen Anne, the irrepressible Rich managed to persuade George I to renew his patent (the original amalgamated patent of Killigrew and Davenant) for a newly built theatre in Lincoln's Inn Fields. He died shortly before his theatre opened, but his son, John Rich, became the main patentee in November 1714. At that point, the theatres in London had reverted to what was effectively the structure first established in the Restoration.

[1] The complete picture of these turbulent years has only recently been unravelled by Judith Milhous and Robert D. Hume in *Vice Chamberlain Coke's theatrical papers, 1706-1715* (Carbondale and Edwardsville: Southern Illinois University Press, 1982), pp. xvii-xxix.
[2] BL Add.MS 20,726, f. 20.
[3] PRO LC 5/154, p. 446/f. 232.
[4] The proposals accepted by George I in April 1719 for establishing a Royal Academy of Music are set out in PRO LC 7/3, f. 52. For further details and MS information, see Judith Milhous and Robert D. Hume: 'New light on Handel and The Royal Academy of Music in 1720' in *Theatre Journal* 35, no. 2 (1983), 149-67.

15   Vanbrugh is given a monopoly of opera at the Haymarket, 31 December 1707

PRO LC 5/154, ff. 299-300. Copy in BL Add.MS 20,726, ff. 36-7. Reproduced in Milhous and Hume (1982), pp. 49-50

Whereas by reason of the division of her Majesty's Comedians into two distinct houses or companies the players have not been able to gain a reasonable subsistence for their encouragement in either company, nor can plays always be acted to the best advantage. And whereas the charge of maintaining a company of comedians with performers of opera in the same house is now become too great to be supported. Therefore to remedy those inconveniences and for the better regulation and support of the theatres I do hereby order and require:

That all operas and other musical presentations be performed for the future only at her Majesty's Theatre in the Haymarket under the direction of the manager or managers thereof, with full power and authority to receive, admit and employ any performers in music, dancing, etc. whom he or they shall judge fit for their service. And I do hereby strictly charge and forbid the said manager or managers from and after the 10th day of January next to represent any comedies, tragedies or other entertainments of the stage that are not set to music or to erect any other theatre for that purpose upon pain of being silenced for breach of this my order.

I do likewise hereby give leave to the manager or managers of the theatres in Drury Lane and Dorset Garden, etc.[1] full power and authority to receive and admit into their company any players or actors of tragedy or comedy they shall think fit to entertain, notwithstanding any articles or engagements they may be under in any other playhouse at the same time, strictly charging and requiring the said managers not to perform any musical entertainment upon their stage or to receive into their service any dancers or performers in music, other than such instrumental music as are not employed in the operas and are necessary for such entertainments, upon the like pain of being silenced for breach of this order. [. . .] To the Managers of the Theatre in Drury Lane and Dorset Garden. Kent.

[1] Dorset Garden still belonged to the company controlled by Rich. It was finally demolished in 1709.

16   Rich is silenced by the Lord Chamberlain, 6 June 1709
PRO LC 5/154, p. 437/f. 227. Reproduced in Nicoll, vol. 2 (1952), p. 282

Whereas by an order dated the 30th day of April last upon the petition of several players, I did then direct and require you to pay to the respective comedians who had benefit plays last winter the full receipt of such plays, deducting only from each the sum of £40 for the charges of the house, pursuant to the articles made with you at the theatre in the Haymarket and which were promised to be made good upon their removal to the theatre in Covent Garden.[1]

And whereas I am informed that in contempt of the said order you still refuse to pay and detain from the said comedians the profits of the said benefit plays, I do therefore for the said contempt hereby silence you from further acting and require you not to perform any plays or other theatrical entertainments till further order. And all her Majesty's sworn Comedians are hereby forbid to act any plays at the theatre in Covent Garden or elsewhere without my leave, as they shall answer the contrary at their peril and, etc. To the Manager or Managers of her Majesty's Company of Comedians, for their patentees. Kent.

[1] The theatre in Covent Garden is another way of describing the Theatre Royal, Drury Lane.

17   The adventurers question the legality of the Lord Chamberlain's intervention, October 1709

BL Add.MS 20,726, ff. 22–3. Reproduced in Judith Milhous and Robert D. Hume: 'The silencing of Drury Lane in 1709', *Theatre Journal* 32 (1980), 439–40

That the Right Noble the Marquess of Kent, Lord Chamberlain of your Majesty's Household, has been pleased to make several orders and given directions to his secretary to make several significations of his pleasure, and orders to the patentees and their managers and the players and performers belonging to them, and in particular:

1st. Several orders in November and December 1705 relating to the establishing another playhouse and restraining your petitioners' power to treat and agree with such actors and others, as they should think necessary for their business.

2ndly. Several orders and significations in December and January 1708 for restraining your petitioners from acting any operas and from employing such persons as they should conceive fit for singing and dancing, under the penalty of silencing.

3rdly. An order of the 30th April 1709 ordering your petitioners' treasurer to pay moneys to their actors, without any agreement or consent of your petitioners and another of the 6th of June last, silencing your petitioners and their actors for not so doing.

Which orders, letters and significations are not only extraordinary in their own nature and contradictory one to another, but were made without ever calling your petitioners before his Lordship, or ever hearing them in relation to the matters thereof; and, as we are advised, are contrary and in prejudice to the powers, privileges, authorities, rights and interests granted by your Royal Majesty's predecessors by the said respective Letters Patent and tend to the subversion of the same and to the destruction of your petitioners' estates, rights, properties and interests, and of those claiming under the said patents.

18   Collier is ordered to suspend actors after the 1710 riot, 14 June 1710

PRO LC 5/155, f. 11. Reproduced in Nicoll, vol. 2 (1952), p. 292

Whereas complaint has been made to me that five of the actors belonging to her Majesty's Company of Comedians under your management, viz. George Powell, Barton Booth, Jonathan Bickerstaffe, Theophilus Keen and Francis Lee, did not only refuse to obey the orders of Mr Hill who is appointed by you to take care of the said company, but that they did also lately in a riotous manner break open the doors of the playhouse, beating and abusing the said Mr Hill and with their swords drawn threatening his life and have also committed several other insolencies and disorders.

These are therefore to charge and require you immediately to dismiss and remove the said Powell from the service of her Majesty's Company, he having been formerly guilty of the like offences,[1] and that you suspend Barton Booth,

Theophilus Keen, Jonathan Bickerstaffe and Francis Lee from further acting, without my leave first had and obtained. Kent.

[1] Powell had been silenced on previous occasions for unruly behaviour. Furthermore, Rich was silenced briefly in March 1707 for allowing Powell to appear on stage while he was suspended. See PRO LC 5/154, p. 224/f. 122.

RICHARD STEELE ATTEMPTS TO RESIST THE CONTROL OF THE LORD CHAMBERLAIN

Richard Steele was granted a patent for the Theatre Royal in January 1715: it followed much the same pattern as the earlier patents given to Killigrew and Davenant, except that, unlike theirs, his was limited to his lifetime and three years thereafter. Steele claimed that the wording of his patent (identical to that of the earlier patents), clearly gave the patentee full powers to peruse and correct all old and new plays prior to performance, which meant that there was no need to refer plays to the Master of Revels for perusal and licensing [*see* 19]. Accordingly he refused to submit plays for licensing and paid no licensing fees to the Office of the Revels.

However, when Thomas Pelham-Holles, first Duke of Newcastle, was appointed Lord Chamberlain in 1717, he resolved to re-establish the ancient authority of his staff over the theatres. In the autumn of 1717 he invited Steele and the three actor-managers to surrender their 'licence' and exchange it for a less powerful one. Steele declined. In October 1718, Holles took legal advice on the validity of Steele's position.[1] A year later, in December 1719, he demanded the dismissal of Cibber, one of the managers.[2] Again Steele refused. In order to avoid any legal battles, Holles persuaded the King to revoke Steele's 'licence' (not the full patent) on 23 January 1720 [*see* 20]. He then silenced the theatre on 25 January 1720.

The three actor-managers agreed to accept the Lord Chamberlain's authority and were granted a licence to resume acting on 27 January 1720. Steele was furious at his exclusion. Adding insult to injury, the Duke of Newcastle refused to deal with him directly. In response Steele wrote an irate and threatening note to the Duke's private secretary on 27 May 1720 [*see* 21]. Subsequently, he petitioned the King as he had threatened, but without success.[3] Denied any legal redress, he responded by founding a periodical called *The Theatre*, in order to attack Holles whom he had once regarded as a close friend and patron. He was not re-instated as patentee until May 1721, when changes in the government forced the Lord Chamberlain to relent.

Steele had obtained his patent in 1715 as a political reward for the considerable journalistic services he had rendered the Whigs during the reign of Queen Anne. In 1720 he lost his licence for Drury Lane, not only because he opposed the authority of the Lord Chamberlain, but also because he had offended the Whig Establishment by speaking and voting against the Peerage Bill in the House of Commons. Significantly, he regained his full patent in 1721 a matter of months after his long-standing friend and ally Walpole was made Chancellor of the Exchequer[4] [*see* 22].

[1] See PRO LC 5/157, pp. 142–4/ff. 81–2. See also Loftis (1952), pp. 125–6.
[2] See PRO LC 5/157, p. 265/f.137.
[3] 'Petition to the King's Majesty in Council against being deposed as governor of Drury Lane' (BL Add.MS 32,685, f. 40).
[4] The full details of the quarrel are given in Loftis (1952), pp. 121–80.

19   Steele's patent, 19 January 1715
PRO c/66/3501. Reproduced in Fitzgerald, vol. 1 (1882), pp. 401–4

[. . .] Know ye that we, of our special grace, certain knowledge and mere motion, and in consideration of the good and faithful services which the said Richard Steele has done us, and does intend to do for the future, have given and granted, and by these presents for us, our heirs and successors, do give and grant unto him, the said Richard Steele, his executors, administrators and assigns, for and during the term of his natural life, and for and during in full end and term of three years to be computed next and immediately after the decease of him, the said Richard Steele, full power, licence and authority to gather together, form, entertain, govern, privilege and keep a company of comedians for our service, to exercise and act tragedies, plays, operas and other performances of the stage. [. . .]

And for the better attainment of our royal purposes in this behalf, we have thought fit hereby to declare that henceforth no representations be admitted on the stage by virtue, or under colour, of these our Letters Patent, whereby the Christian religion in general or the Church of England may in any manner suffer reproach, strictly inhibiting every degree of abuse or misrepresentation of sacred characters, tending to expose religion itself and bring it into contempt; and that no such character be otherwise introduced or placed in other light than such as may enhance the just esteem of those who truly answer the end of their sacred function. We further enjoin the strictest regard to such representations as any way concern civil policy or the constitution of our government, that these may contribute to the support of our sacred authority and the preservation of order and good government. And it being our royal desire that, for the future, our theatre may be instrumental to the promotion of virtue and instructive to human life, we do hereby command and enjoin that no new play, or any old or revived play, be acted under the authority hereby granted containing any passages or expressions offensive to piety and good manners, until the same be corrected and purged by the said governor from all such offensive and scandalous passages and expressions. [. . .]

20   The King's warrant for revoking the licence granted to Steele and the other managers at Drury Lane, 23 January 1720

PRO LC 5/157, p. 279/f. 144

Whereas by our royal licence bearing the date the 18th day of October 1714, we did give and grant unto Richard Steele Esq., now Sir Richard Steele, Knight, Mr Robert Wilks, Mr Colley Cibber, Mr Thomas Doggett and Mr Barton Booth, full power, licence and authority to form, constitute and establish for us a company of comedians with free licence to act and represent comedies, tragedies and other theatrical performances, subject to such rules and orders for the good government therein as they shall receive from time to time from the Chamberlain of our Household, such licence to continue during our pleasure and no longer.

And having received information of great misbehaviours committed by our Company of Comedians now acting at the theatre in Drury Lane for want of a regular management of our said company and from the neglect of a due subordination and submission to the authority of our Chamberlain and other officers of our Household.

Therefore for reforming and regulating the comedians in our service and for establishing the just and ancient authority of the officers of our Household and more especially of our Chamberlain, we have thought fit to revoke the above mentioned licence given by us to the said Richard Steele, Robert Wilks, Colley Cibber, Thomas Doggett and Barton Booth. By His Majesty's Command. Holles, Newcastle.

21   Steele's letter of protest to the Duke of Newcastle's private secretary, 27 May 1720
BL Add.MS 32,685, ff. 31–2

As you delivered a verbal message to forbid the writing to the Duke of Newcastle himself, you will pardon me that I give you this trouble, which is to desire you would obtain for me His Grace's direct answer whether he will recall the order of silence which he sent to Drury Lane upon a pretence of the King's revocation of all authorities granted by His Majesty for acting plays.

I told you when you brought the message that I should be always ready when the Duke should please to alter his mind to receive His Grace's commands, but if my Lord insists to keep me out from my right, I must plainly tell you, that is, His Grace by you, that the right of petitioning the King in Council, the Parliament sitting or the judges in Westminster Hall shall be utterly taken from me before I will suffer my very good Lord to send my children a starving.

22   Holles terminates Steele's suspension, 2 May 1721
PRO LC 5/157, pp. 415–16/ff. 212–13. Reproduced in Loftis (1952), p. 158

Whereas application has been made to me in behalf of Sir Richard Steele, on occasion of the regulation under which his Majesty's Company of Comedians has been lately placed exclusive of the said Sir Richard Steele and his pretensions. I do hereby order and direct you to account with the said Sir Richard Steele for all past and future share arising from the profits of the theatre as he would have been entitled to by any agreement between you and him, if the said regulations had never been made, and to pay him hereafter from time to time his said share till further orders from me, or determination of that point be made by due course of law. For which this shall be your sufficient warrant.
Holles, Newcastle.

THEATRICAL CONTROVERSY IN THE EARLY 1730s

Holles's instructions to the managers to 'account with' Sir Richard Steele led to prolonged financial wrangles and a fiercely contested lawsuit that Steele eventually lost.[1] After Steele's death in 1729, the Theatre Royal was controlled by the three actor-managers until they themselves were granted a patent for twenty-one years in April 1732.[2] Later that year Wilks died and Booth died in 1733. The theatre now faced a renewed period of instability. In July 1732, John Highmore, a wealthy man of leisure, purchased Booth's share and took over the running of the theatre as a speculative venture. By the end of his first season, his incompetence as a manager prompted the actors, led by Colley Cibber's son Theophilus, into open rebellion and they began working as a rival company.

John Rich, who had moved from Lincoln's Inn Fields into a splendid new theatre in Covent Garden in December 1732, joined forces with Highmore in attempting unsuccessfully to prosecute the rebellious actors as vagrants.[3] By February 1734, Highmore had lost so much money that he made way for another dilettante manager, Charles Fleetwood.

The stage mutiny, as it came to be known, prompted two contemporary artists into publishing a satirical view of the event. John Laguerre, Rich's principal scene painter, published his caricature of the mutiny in July 1733. With obvious relish, he satirised all parties to the dispute. Theophilus Cibber is shown as Ancient Pistol, leading his band of actors under the banner of 'liberty and property'. Highmore points at a scroll he is holding on which it states that it cost £8000. Behind Highmore the widow of Wilks in her weeds shouts, 'we'll starve 'em out'. Colley Cibber sits downstage left, with money bags in his lap, pointing ironically at Highmore [*see* **23**].

A few months later, Hogarth utilised Laguerre's original in his view of Southwark Fair (delivered to his subscribers in January 1734). The acting booth of Theophilus Cibber is shown collapsing onto the unsuspecting world as he and his actors attempt a pretentious performance of the *Fall of Bajazet*. The Laguerre drawing hangs as a sign above the booth[4] [*see* **24**].

[1] See Loftis (1952), pp. 57–61. See also R.J. Smith: *A collection of material towards a history of the English stage*, vol. 21 (BL, 1825–40), f. 89.

[2] PRO LC 5/160, p. 175.

[3] See Fitzgerald, vol. 2 (1882), p. 84 and R.J. Smith, vol. 21 (BL, 1825–40), f. 129.

[4] See Paulson (1971), vol. 1, pp. 319–24.

23   John Laguerre: *The Stage Mutiny*, 1733
The Burney Collection of Theatrical Portraits, vol. 2, no. 160, p. 86 (Print Room, BM).
Reproduced in Paulson, vol. 1 (1971), p. 323

24   Hogarth: *Southwark Fair*, January 1734

The Burney Collection of Theatrical Portraits, vol. 2, no. 162, p. 88 (Print Room, BM). Reproduced in Paulson, vol. 1 (1971), p. 319

2 *Contractual and company documents*

INTRODUCTION

Although Davenant and Killigrew were given the opportunity of establishing a theatrical monopoly at the Restoration, they nevertheless took as the model for their companies the structural pattern evolved in the very different world of London theatres during the 1630s. Leading actors were made shareholders in the company and their income was thus dependent upon the profits derived from collective endeavour. In contrast, actresses, young actors, musicians, craftsmen, scenemen and servants – all these enjoyed a less exalted status and were paid on a salaried basis.

The number of shares to be divided amongst the two companies was carefully calculated, so as to ensure that the patent holders, Killigrew and Davenant, kept the largest proportion for themselves. Apart from allowing them to draw an appropriate managerial fee, this practice was intended to cover the costs of stock scenery and costume as well as the salaries of the actresses. Obviously, it was open to abuse, and in the case of Killigrew it was soon used as a means of borrowing money to service a substantial burden of debt.

After a promising start, in which profit was healthy and morale was high, the building programmes of the two companies and Killigrew's abysmal record as a manager soon led to acute financial embarrassment. A number of documents reprinted here illustrate the internal tensions facing the companies and their playwrights, as their fortunes waned, prior to the union of the companies, in the late 1670s and early 1680s. Others illustrate interventions by the Lord Chamberlain in response to petitions from aggrieved actors and groups of players.

By the 1690s a blatantly commercial style of management had replaced the old order, provoking a short-lived actors' revolt at Lincoln's Inn Fields: a final attempt to set up a commonwealth of actors, all equal sharers and partners in an artistic enterprise. It proved unworkable. But the ruthless managerial style of the lawyer Christopher Rich was in its turn just as unsuccessful. What emerged from the chaotic first decade of the eighteenth century was the actor-manager structure that became the hallmark of the eighteenth-century theatre.

By the mid 1710s, the two patent theatres were run by actor-managers who employed their fellow actors on salary rather than share and supplemented the basic salary offered their employees with benefit nights. The managers also entered into a cartel agreement to prevent actors moving from one company to another without the express permission of the two managements: this gave them not only a powerful weapon to enforce company discipline but also ensured that salary levels were not subject to undue competitive pressure. In general, the financial structure adopted by the patent companies in the 1700s remained in force for the remainder of the century. (It was not until much later in the century, however, that widespread provision for sickness and accident benefit was made, as had been clearly anticipated in the actors' company formed at Lincoln's Inn Fields in 1695.)

The overall picture to emerge from these company documents is of a transition in London's theatre world from Restoration theatre practice, built on Jacobean and Caroline example, with its emphasis on sharers and a commonwealth of interests, to the more obviously commercial theatre of the eighteenth century, reflecting the growing mercantile interests of the country, with its clear distinction between actor-managers and salaried staff.

DAVENANT'S ARTICLES OF AGREEMENT WITH HIS COMPANY OF ACTORS

On 5 November 1660, Davenant began performances with his company of players at Salisbury Court.[1] That same day he signed articles of agreement with the leading actors in the company and his scene painter, Henry Harris (later an actor), in order to provide a firm contractual basis for their work at Salisbury Court and in the new playhouse being made ready at Lisle's Tennis Court in Lincoln's Inn Fields.

A number of important features are built into this agreement. Davenant is to have ultimate authority over the company, although the actors are given specific areas of delegated managerial control. The profits, after deducting the house charges and the cost of male hirelings, are to be divided up into fifteen shares. These shares are then to be split between the patent holder and the company on a two to one basis: ten shares to Davenant and five to the company. The imbalance in the shareholding is partly explained by a number of expenses Davenant agreed to cover – the cost of scenery, costumes and the salaries of the actresses – but also by the fact that Davenant intended to sell off a proportion of his shares, in order to establish a building fund for the new theatre. Within a year, he had sold seven of his ten shares, in half and whole share lots at between £600 and £800 for each whole share, to provide the necessary capital for his new theatre at Lincoln's Inn Fields.[2] (Killigrew, in contrast, set up a separate building fund, with building sharers, in January 1662 when he undertook to build a new theatre in Bridges Street.)[3]

The distinction between company sharers, on the one hand, and hirelings and salaried actors, on the other, was to remain a basic feature of theatre contracts throughout the Restoration period. It also became common practice for patent holders to sell off or mortgage their company and building shares to 'adventurers' in order to fund capital expenditure or merely service their debts. By 1673, for instance, Killigrew had sold off or mortgaged all his building shares, as well as his company shares and his patent, in order to settle a variety of pressing debts.[4] In 1716, Richard Steele was equally profligate, mortgaging his patent and company shares for £4000 as a means of satisfying his creditors.[5]

---

[1] See p. 14 above.
[2] The details of these transactions are set out in Hotson (1928), pp. 219–22.
[3] The detailed arrangements are described in Hotson (1928), pp. 243–5. The agreement between Killigrew and the building sharers of 1662 is reproduced in Fitzgerald, vol. 1 (1882), p. 82.
[4] See Hotson (1928), p. 258.
[5] The detailed transactions are set down in Loftis (1952), pp. 91–8. The Lord Chamberlain's concern over these negotiations is expressed in PRO LC 5/157, pp. 142–4/ff. 81–2.

25   Articles of agreement between Davenant and the company of players at the Cockpit [Phoenix] in Drury Lane, 5 November 1660

BL Add.Charter 9295. Also in BL Add.MS 19,256, ff. 53–60. Reproduced in Malone (1790), pp. 250–5 and in Adams (1917), pp. 96–100[1]

[. . .] Imprimis, the said Sir William Davenant does for himself, his executors, administrators and assignees, covenant, promise, grant and agree, to and with the said Thomas Betterton, Thomas Sheppey, Robert Nokes, James Nokes, Thomas Lovell, John Mosely, Cave Underhill, Robert Turner and Thomas Lillieston, that he the said Sir William Davenant by virtue of the authority to him derived for that purpose does hereby constitute, ordain and erect them [. . .] and their associates to be a company, publicly to act all manner of tragedies, comedies and plays whatsoever in any theatre or playhouse erected in London or Westminster or the suburbs thereof, and to take the usual rates for the same, to the uses hereafter expressed, until the said Sir William Davenant shall provide a new theatre with scenes.

Item, it is agreed by and between all the said parties to these presents that the said company (until the said theatre be provided by the said Sir William Davenant) be authorized by him to act tragedies, comedies and plays in the playhouse called Salisbury Court Playhouse or any other house, upon the conditions only hereafter following, viz.:

That the general receipts of money of the said playhouse shall (after the house rent, hirelings and all other customary and necessary expenses in that kind be defrayed) be divided into fourteen proportions or shares, whereof Sir William Davenant shall have four full proportions or shares to his own use, and the rest to the use of the said company.

That during the time of playing in the said playhouse (until the aforesaid theatre be provided by the said Sir William Davenant), the said Sir William Davenant shall depute the said Thomas Betterton, James Nokes and Thomas Sheppey, or any one of them particularly, for him and on his behalf, to receive his proportion of those shares, and to survey the accounts conducing thereunto and to pay the said proportion every night to him the said Sir William Davenant or his assignees, which they do hereby covenant to pay accordingly.

That the said Thomas Betterton, Thomas Sheppey and the rest of the said company shall admit such a consort of musicians into the said playhouse for their necessary use, as the said Sir William shall nominate and provide, during their playing in the said playhouse, not exceeding the rate of 30s the day, to be defrayed out of the general expenses of the theatre before the said fourteen shares be divided.

That the said Thomas Betterton, Thomas Sheppey and the rest of the said company so authorized to play in the Playhouse in Salisbury Court or elsewhere, as aforesaid, shall at one week's warning given by the said Sir William Davenant, his heirs or assignees, dissolve and conclude their playing at the house and place aforesaid, or at any other house where they shall play, and shall remove and join with the said Henry Harris and with other men and women provided or to be provided by the said Sir William Davenant, to perform such tragedies, comedies, plays and representations in that theatre to be publicly provided by him the said Sir William as aforesaid.

Item, it is agreed by and between all the said parties to these presents in manner and form following, viz.:

That when the said company, together with the said Henry Harris, are joined with the men and women to be provided by the said Sir William Davenant to act and perform in the said theatre to be provided by the said Sir William Davenant, that then the general receipts of the said theatre (the general expense first being deducted) shall be divided into fifteen shares or proportions, whereof two shares or proportions shall be paid to the said Sir William Davenant, his executors, administrators or assignees, towards the house rent, buildings, scaffolding and making of frames for scenes, and one other share or proportion shall likewise be paid to the said Sir William, his executors, administrators and assignees, for provision of habits, properties and scenes, for a supplement of the said theatre.

That the other twelve shares (after all expenses of men hirelings and other customary expenses deducted) shall be divided into seven and five shares or proportions, whereof the said Sir William Davenant, his executors, administrators or assignees shall have seven shares or proportions to maintain all the women that are to perform or represent women's parts in the aforesaid tragedies, comedies, plays or representations; and in consideration of erecting and establishing them to be a company, and his the said Sir William's pains and expenses to that purpose for many years. And the other five of the said shares or proportions is to be divided amongst the rest of the persons (parties) to these presents, whereof the said Henry Harris is to have an equal share with the greatest proportions in the said five shares or proportions.

That the general receipts of the said theatre (from and after such time as the said company have performed their playing in Salisbury Court or in any other playhouse, according to and no longer than the time allowed by him the said William as aforesaid) shall be by ballatine or tickets sold for all doors and boxes.

That Sir William Davenant, his executors, administrators or assignees shall at the general charge of the whole receipts provide three persons to receive money for the said tickets in a room adjoining to the said theatre; and that the actors in the said theatre, now parties to these presents, who are concerned in the said five shares or proportions, shall daily or weekly appoint two or three of themselves, or the men hirelings deputed by them, to sit with the aforesaid three persons appointed by the said Sir William, that they may survey or give an account of the money received for the said tickets. That the said seven shares shall be paid nightly by the said three persons by the said Sir William deputed, or by any of them, to him the said Sir William, his executors, administrators or assignees.

That the said Sir William Davenant shall appoint half the number of the doorkeepers necessary for the receipt of the said tickets for doors and boxes, the wardrobe keeper, barber and all other necessary persons as he, the said Sir William, shall think fit, and their salary to be defrayed at the public charge.

That when any sharer amongst the actors of the aforesaid five shares and parties to these presents shall die, that then the said Sir William Davenant, his executors, administrators or assignees, shall have the denomination and appointment of the successor and successors. And likewise that the wages of the men hirelings shall be appointed and established by the said Sir William Davenant, his executors, administrators or assignees.

That the said Sir William Davenant, his executors, administrators or assignees, shall not be obliged out of the shares or proportions allowed to him for the supplying of clothes, habits and scenes, to provide either hats, feathers, gloves, ribbons, sword belts, bands, stockings or shoes for any of the men actors aforesaid, unless it be to properties.[2]

That a private box be provided and established for the use of Thomas Killigrew, Esquire, one of the Grooms of his Majesty's Bedchamber, sufficient to contain six persons, into which the said Mr Killigrew and such as he shall appoint, shall have liberty to enter without any salary or pay for their entrance into such a place of the said theatre as the said Sir William Davenant, his heirs, executors, administrators or assignees shall appoint.

That the said Thomas Betterton, Thomas Sheppey, Robert Nokes, James Nokes, Thomas Lovell, John Mosely, Cave Underhill, Robert Turner and Thomas Lillieston, do hereby for themselves covenant, promise, grant and agree, to and with the said Sir William Davenant, his executors, administrators and assignees, by these presents, that they and every of them shall become bound to the said Sir William Davenant in a bond of £5000 conditioned for the performance of these presents. And that every successor to any part of the said five shares or proportions shall enter into the like bond before he or they shall be admitted to have any part or proportion of the said shares or proportions. [. . .][3]

Item, it is mutually agreed by and between all the parties to these presents, that the said Sir William Davenant alone shall be master and superior and shall from time to time have the sole government of the said Thomas Betterton, Thomas Sheppey, Robert Nokes, James Nokes, Thomas Lovell, John Mosely, Cave Underhill, Robert Turner and Thomas Lillieston and also of the said Henry Harris and their associates, in relation to the plays [playhouse] by these presents agreed to be erected.

---

[1] Summaries of this document may be found in Hotson (1928), p. 207; Nicoll, vol. 1 (1952), p. 300; Fitzgerald, vol. 1 (1882), pp. 85–6; and Milhous (1979), pp. 9–10.

[2] Actors continued to have the responsibility for providing these items throughout the eighteenth century.

[3] The sum of £5000 is the total bond. In addition to the nine actors named in the document, Henry Harris was also required to enter into the same bond, which means that the bond amounted to £500 per person.

KILLIGREW SIGNS AN AGREEMENT WITH BUILDING SHARERS IN 1673

In order to fund the building of his new Theatre Royal in Drury Lane in 1673, Killigrew established a group of building investors or sharers who raised between them the required capital sum for the new building in thirty-six investment shares. Killigrew owned nine of these shares; leading actors two each; and the various named individuals in the documents below owned the remainder.[1]

The agreement between Killigrew and the builders provides for a daily rent to be paid of £3 10s for every day the building is used for performance, assuming the final cost of the building is £2400. If the final cost is greater, a proportionally larger rent will be paid. As Hotson points out, the eventual rent paid was £5 14s per acting day, which means that the actual cost of the Theatre Royal came to approximately £3908.[2] Each building share was therefore worth some £109. (The building shares for the first Theatre Royal in Bridges Street were worth £66 13s 4d when the agreement was signed in January 1662. By November 1663, these shares were selling at a price of £215 each.)[3]

The practice of paying rent to the building sharers only when the theatre was used for performance was an important financial safeguard for theatre companies who were frequently silenced at short notice by the Lord Chamberlain for a wide variety of reasons (ranging from the plague to the misbehaviour of individual actors) and whose acting season was in any case normally limited to thirty-three weeks in the year. The same practice of paying rent only on acting days persisted throughout the eighteenth century.

[1] See Hotson (1928), p. 279, n. 29.
[2] Ibid., pp. 254–5.
[3] Ibid., p. 249.

26   Contract between Killigrew and builders, 17 December 1673

BL Add.MS 20,726, ff. 8–9. Copy in BL Add.MS 12,201, f. 132. Further copy at PRO c7/298/35. Reproduced in Fitzgerald, vol. 1 (1882), p. 138

Articles inter Thomas Killigrew, John Dryden, Robert Lewright, Charles Hart, Michael Mohun, Nicholas Burt, John Lacy, Robert Shatterall, William Cartwright, William Wintershall and Edward Kynaston of the one part, and Edmond Ashton, Thomas Shippey, John Wolf, John Tombes, Joseph Nickens and Thomas Jonson, builders, on the other part; reciting that the former theatre called the Theatre Royal had been lately demolished by fire; therefore the said Thomas Killigrew, Dryden, etc., covenant with Ashton, Shippey and the rest of the builders that Killigrew, Dryden, etc., should with all convenient speed after the said theatre should be rebuilt and finished make use of the same to act and represent comedies, tragedies, etc., and should not at any time afterwards make use of any other house or place in or about London, and that the charges in rebuilding the said former theatre did amount to £2400. And the said Hart and the rest of the company should [pay] or cause to be paid unto and amongst the builders and owners the sum of £3 10s per diem for every day the said house was so used and employed. The said Thomas Killigrew, Dryden, etc., do covenant as before that they and such other persons as should then after be admitted and taken into the said company should pay or cause to be paid to and amongst the said builders, their executors, etc. their respective interests and shares of £3 10s per diem for every day the said theatre should be so used and employed, and for such further sums of money as had or should be laid out in rebuilding, finishing and adorning the same over and above the £2400. And Killigrew, Dryden, etc., and their successors should for every day the said theatre should be used pay and divide amongst the builders a further sum of money, rent, or payment over and above the said £2400, as £3 10s *per diem* did bear £2400.

KILLIGREW IN DISPUTE WITH HIS ACTORS

Not long after the opening of the new Theatre Royal, Drury Lane, in March 1674, the company of actors became embroiled in a series of disputes with their manager Killigrew.[1] The actors felt disinclined to obey the directives of a manager who had sold or mortgaged his entire interest in the theatre and whose main concern, it seemed, was to extract from the enterprise what remaining profit he could. Killigrew complained to the Lord Chamberlain in January 1675 that money due to him was being withheld by the actors, which led to a new formal agreement being signed between them.[2] In December 1675, an attempt was made to re-impose some form of company discipline, with the articles signed below. There was, however, continued disorder in the company, and by February 1676 certain actors refused to act and had to be ordered to resume their duties by the Lord Chamberlain.[3]

[1] See Nicoll, vol. 1 (1952), pp. 323–4.
[2] PRO LC 5/138, pp. 376 and 411. Reproduced in Nicoll, vol. 1 (1952), pp. 323–4.
[3] See p. 19 above.

27   Articles of agreement for the better regulating their Majesties' Servants, the comedians of the Theatre Royal, 9 December 1675

PRO LC 5/141, p. 307. Reproduced in Nicoll, vol. 1 (1952), pp. 324–5

1. That no man or woman shall dispose of their parts without the consent of the Company. Subpoena, 20 shillings.

2. That neither man or woman shall refuse any part the Company shall think fit for. Subpoena, a week's wages.

3. That no hired man or woman neglect rehearsal upon forfeiture as formerly.

4. Whereas by experience we find our clothes tarnished and imperilled by frequent wearing them out of the playhouse, it is thought fit no woman presume to go out of the house with the playhouse clothes or properties upon penalty of their week's pay.

5. That neither man or woman make use of either scenes or clothes without the general consent of the whole Company.

6. Upon complaint of people of quality of Mrs Meggs's several maids[1] offending them in the pit besides offending the stage with their noise and treading upon their clothes and other affronts, we desire she may be obliged to strictly observe her covenants.

7. That no hired man or woman quit the Company without three months' warning and that given to Mr Thomas Killigrew under their hands.

8.   That no man or woman be entertained in the Company without the general knowledge and consent of the Company for the future and that they play three months without salary by way of approbation, according to ancient articles.

9.   That neither feathers nor clothes nor ribbons nor anything relating to the stage be taken up without the consent of the Company, upon penalty of paying for them themselves.

10.   To prevent the disorders of the sharing table by an inundation of people that press upon them in their business, Henry Hayles is appointed to stand at the door and there to admit them as they are called and by one to deliver up their charge and so dismiss them.[2]

11.   To avoid the future inconveniency of strangers' frequent egress and regress when a play is done in the house, it is thought fit that some one or two be appointed to stand at the tiring house door till the house is discharged, the persons appointed are David Middleton and Brittain.

12.   That no persons unconcerned in the business of the play be admitted to stand between the scenes.[3]

13.   Henry Hayles is ordered to take up all forfeits.

Killigrew, Lacy, Kynaston, Shatterall, Hart, Wintershall, Mohun, Cartwright and Burt.

[1] Mary Meggs, otherwise know as 'Orange Moll', had been granted a licence by Killigrew, on payment of £100 in February 1663, 'to sell oranges, lemons, fruit, sweetmeats and all manner of confectioners' wares and commodities' [see Hotson (1928), pp. 291–2]. She was in charge of the orange wenches of whom the actors here complain.

[2] The sharing table was the place where the proceeds of each evening were paid in before the various proportions owing to each company and building sharer were calculated.

[3] This appears to have been a recurring problem for the theatre companies. At frequent intervals from the Restoration onwards, the Lord Chamberlain published injunctions forbidding members of the audience to 'stand between the scenes'. See pp. 179–80 below.

THE ACTORS COMPLAIN OF DRYDEN'S CONDUCT

In the spring of 1668, the playwright John Dryden had been made a sharer in Killigrew's company (with one and a quarter shares) on the understanding that he would write three new plays for the King's Company every season.[1] This was a unique privilege for a playwright in the Restoration period. (Killigrew's agreement with the builders in 1673, quoted above, includes John Dryden's name as one of the company sharers.) Although Dryden never fulfilled his obligations (he wrote only nine plays for the company between 1668 and 1678), the other sharers tolerated his breach of the agreement until such time as the rapidly declining fortunes of the Theatre Royal in the late 1670s moved Dryden to offer his new plays to the rival house. In some dismay, his fellow sharers at the Theatre Royal drew up a formal complaint over Dryden's conduct in February 1678. There is some doubt, however, as to whether it was actually submitted to the Lord Chamberlain.[2] Dryden was clearly unmoved by the complaint of his fellow sharers and from then on gave his new plays to the Duke's Theatre in Dorset Garden.

[1] See Osborn (1940), p. 186.
[2] *Ibid.*, p 191.

28   Complaint at Dryden's conduct, February 1678

Reproduced in Osborn (1940), pp. 188–9; Nicoll, vol. 1 (1952), p. 329; Fitzgerald, vol. 1 (1882), p. 150

Whereas, upon Mr Dryden binding himself to write three plays a year, he the said Mr Dryden was admitted and continued as a sharer in the King's Playhouse for diverse years and received for his share and a quarter, three or four hundred pounds, communibus annis;[1] but though he received the moneys, we received not the plays, not one in a year. After which, the House being burnt, the Company in building another, contracted great debts, so that the shares fell much short of what they were formerly. Thereupon Mr Dryden complaining to the Company of his want of profit, the Company was so kind to him, that they not only did not press him for the plays which he so engaged to write for them (and for which he was paid beforehand), but they did also at his earnest request, give him a third day for his last new play, called 'All for Love'.[2] (He promising before most part of the Company that they should have the refusal of all his plays thenceforward)[3] and at the receipt of the money of the said third day, he acknowledged it as a gift and a particular kindness of the Company. Yet notwithstanding this kind proceeding, Mr Dryden has now jointly with Mr Lee (who was in pension with us to the last day of our playing and shall continue), written a play called 'Oedipus' and given it to the Duke's Company, contrary to his said agreement, his promise and all gratitude, to the great prejudice and almost undoing of the company, they being the only poets remaining to us. [. . .] Charles Killigrew, Charles Hart, Nicholas Burt, Cardell Goodman, Michael Mohun.

[1] Hotson views this as a highly inflated view of the value of one and a quarter shares. See Hotson (1928), p. 245.

[2] This was the accepted method of paying authors who were not contractually bound to a particular company: namely, the proceeds of the third night a play ran, less the house charges. If the play ran less than three nights, no payment was made. Dryden was granted his third night in addition to his share. ('Attached' authors received a stipend, normally £50 per annum, for offering their work to a particular company. Dryden was unique as a 'sharer' in the Restoration period, whereas in the pre-Civil-War era a number of authors had enjoyed this privilege.)

[3] The comment in brackets is crossed out in the original document, which is reproduced in Osborn (1940) between pp. 186–7.

ARTICLES OF UNION AND MOHUN'S PETITION

Internal dissension and increasing financial problems eventually brought about the closure of the Theatre Royal in 1682. On 4 May 1682, Charles Killigrew signed Articles of Union with Charles Davenant, under which the two patents were to be amalgamated, the stock of plays made over to the Duke's Theatre and the company of players at the Theatre Royal dispersed [see 29]. Killigrew's action, taken without consultation, was fiercely contested by some of the company sharers and a lawsuit followed.[1] However, more than half the building sharers were prepared to accept Killigrew's proposals for leasing the Theatre Royal to Davenant by June 1682;[2] by the beginning of the autumn season 1682, the Union was fully effected.

Some of the younger actors from the Theatre Royal joined the Duke's Company, while a number of older actors retired. At least one, Michael Mohun, who had played a substantial part in re-establishing theatrical activity in London at the Restoration, was shabbily treated and petitioned the King for redress [*see* 30]. Charles II acceded to his petition and instructed the Managers of the United Company to offer Mohun the same conditions as offered to Hart and Kynaston [*see* 31 **a and b**].

¹ See Hotson (1928), pp. 271–2.
² *Ibid.*, p. 273.

29   Charles Killigrew's and Charles Davenant's Articles of Union, 4 May 1682

BL Add.MS 20,726, ff. 10–13. Copy in BL Add.MS 12,201, ff. 136–38. Reproduced in Fitzgerald, vol. 1 (1882), pp. 154–5

[. . .] And whereas upon mature deliberation and weighty considerations had and taken by the said parties that it would be much more convenient and beneficial for all parties concerned that all authorities and privileges in and by the said Letters Patent should be united, therefore the said Charles Killigrew does thereby covenant and agree with Charles Davenant that all the powers and authorities put in the first Letters Patent should be joined and united with the powers in the second Letters Patent and from thenceforth the same should be as one and so for ever continued. And it is mutually covenanted and agreed by and between all the parties to these presents that all plays as should then after be acted by virtue of the said Patents or either of them should be acted by the company then employed at the theatre in Dorset Garden called the Duke's Playhouse in such manner as by the said Charles Killigrew and Charles Davenant and their heirs should be directed and appointed and not otherwise. [. . .] And Charles Killigrew covenants with Davenant that he will procure the present company of players now belonging to and which have usually acted at the said Theatre Royal within six days next after the date of the said Indenture to be wholly dispersed and dissolved, and should within the same time deliver up unto the said Charles Davenant, his heirs or assignees, for the joint use and benefit of him and them and of the said Charles Killigrew, his heirs and assignees, all the plays particularly mentioned in a schedule to the Indenture annexed, to the intent all or any the said plays should be only acted as the said Charles Killigrew and Charles Davenant, their respective heirs and assignees, should direct or appoint. And the peaceable possession of the said Theatre Royal, with the appurtenances except the scenes and scene rooms, should be delivered up to the said Charles Davenant, his heirs and assignees, to and for the sole use of the said united Letters Patent and that the same should be thereafter from time to time held and employed for the acting of plays and entertainments of the stage when it shall be thought expedient. [. . .]

30   Mohun's petition to Charles II

PRO LC 5/191, p. 102. Reproduced in Nicoll, vol. 1 (1952), pp. 365–6

[. . .] That it being your Majesty's pleasure to reduce the two companies into one, your petitioner is deprived of his share and a quarter in the scenes, clothes and plays (that cost about £4000) by Mr Charles Killigrew who has rented them to Mr

Davenant for a share (as your petitioner is informed) and tells him if your petitioner has any right thereto, he must get it by law. And instead of a share and a quarter, which your petitioner had formerly in your Majesty's company for acting, he is now only proffered 20s a day when they have occasion to use him, so that they having not studied our plays nor your petitioner [acting] therein, he cannot conceive the same will amount to above £20 per annum. Wherefore your petitioner most humbly prays that your Majesty will be graciously pleased to order the present Company to allow him the same conditions as Mr Hart and Mr Kynaston have (whose shares were all equal before) whereby he may be enabled to support himself and five children.

31   The Lord Chamberlain instructs the Managers of the United Company to make a just settlement with Mohun

(A) NOVEMBER 1682 PRO LC 5/191, p. 103

It is His Majesty's pleasure and command that the persons concerned in managing the comedians and profits of the plays at the Royal Theatre and His Royal Highness's Theatre (being now united into one company) do give and allow unto Mr Michael Mohun the same conditions which they allow unto Mr Hart and Mr Kynaston (their share having been equal formerly). 23 November 1682. Arlington.

(B) DECEMBER 1682 PRO LC 5/191, p. 105. Reproduced in Nicoll, vol. I (1952), p. 366

Upon the former petition of Mr Michael Mohun, it was again thus ordered:
It is His Majesty's pleasure that their Majesties' Comedians do give an allowance to Mr Michael Mohun, the same allowance for his weekly pension and for his acting as is allowed and given unto Mr Charles Hart; the same to commence for the three and twentieth day of November last; and to be employed presently and to have his own parts to act. 5 December 1682. Arlington.

THE BENEFIT SYSTEM IS ESTABLISHED

According to Colley Cibber, the practice of granting actors (and other company members) an annual benefit, i.e. a performance where they would be given the proceeds of the evening, less the house charges, began as a concession to the actress Elizabeth Barry, 'in King James's time'.[1] Pepys, in his diary, however, mentions the fact that he was invited to a collective benefit performance for the actresses in the King's company on 28 September 1668: 'Up betimes and Knepp's maid comes to me to tell me that the women's day at the playhouse is today and that therefore I must be there to increase their profit'.

In the early 1690s, the concession to Elizabeth Barry was subject to formal agreement between Mrs Barry and the managers of the United Company. Later, Thomas Davenant, on behalf of the managers, gave her an assurance that the profit from her benefit would be made up to £70, even if the house takings did not cover the sum. When Rich took control of the United Company in December 1693, he refused to honour this agreement [*see* 32]. He also refused the request of Anne Bracegirdle for a benefit night on which she offered to meet the 'constant charge' of the house, i.e. the fixed overheads as opposed to the 'incident charge' associated with a specific production.[2] Both points emerge from the actors' complaint to the Lord Chamberlain in December 1694 and from Rich's subsequent reply [*see* 33].

[1] Cibber (Lowe ed.), vol. 1 (1966), p. 161.
[2] In PRO LC 7/3, f. 155, the two charges are defined as follows:
   The Constant Charge. 19 men actors, 14 women actors, house rent, 2 office keepers, 1 check on the office, 12 box and door keepers, 2 wardrobe keepers, 4 fire men, 4 carpenters, 20 music[ians], 1 candle keeper, book holder, house keeper, 2 barbers, 2 porters, 3 necessary women.
   The Incident Charge. Clothes, scenes, candles (wax and tallow), printer, 4 bill carriers, properties, trumpets, drummer, attendants, washer-women, man taylors, painter, dancers and singers (constant or incident as the occasion shall require), coals.

32   Petition of the players, December 1694
PRO LC 7/3, ff. 2–4[1]

[. . .] 7. Mrs Barry made an agreement with Dr Davenant, Mr Killigrew, Mr Smith and Mr Betterton for 50 s per week and the profit of a play every year. Upon a second agreement with Mr Thomas Davenant,[2] it added, if the day's charges being deducted there wanted of £70, they were to make it up. What was above £70, she was to have. This agreement has been performed to her many years. But now the present claimers refuse to make the £70 good to her if the day's receipt fall short of it, and besides would take a third part of the profit of Mrs Barry's play from her to give to Mrs Bracegirdle.

[. . .] 12. Mrs Bracegirdle reasonably proposes to pay the constant charge of an old play. And what more shall be agreed to by her playing, whatever the play will bring in. The sum got above by the assistance of her friends is all she desires for herself. [. . .][3]

33   The reply of the patentees, 10 December 1694
PRO LC 7/3, f. 14[4]

[. . .] 7. May it please your Lordship that Mr Betterton himself took notice that Mrs Barry made so great advantage of a play given her one day in the year that the same, with her salary, was more than his £5 per week. And we, observing that although the receipts of late had been less than usual, yet the constant and incident charges are higher and consequently needful to be retrenched. And Mrs Barry, having declared that Mr Thomas Davenant had released her of her bargain and that she would not be obliged to play unless she came to a new agreement with us, it was proposed that she would continue at her usual salary of 50 s per week and remit one third of the profits of the day's play to Mrs Bracegirdle, which we believed would, by the addition of Mrs Bracegirdle's friends, so increase the receipts as that Mrs Barry would not be a great loser. [. . .]

[. . .] 12. As to Mrs Bracegirdle's proposition of having parts of the clear profits of an old play. May it please your Lordship, we did, before she asked anything, propose the third of the profits of a play in the answer to the 7th Article concerning Mrs Barry's memorandum. Therefore we have the greater reason to take her joining in Betterton's mutiny most unkindly and humbly hope your Lordship will think it reasonable her presentations be left to our consideration since we were the first movers of advancing her. [. . .]

[1] A summary of the grievances is given in Nicoll, vol. 1 (1952), pp. 368–70 and a complete transcription in Milhous (1979), pp. 225–9.

[2] Nicoll mistakenly records the later agreement as being with Thomas Betterton. Nicoll, vol. 1 (1952), p. 369.

[3] The wording is not entirely clear, but the meaning is. Mrs Bracegirdle wants whatever sum the play will bring her, by her playing to her friends, after deducting the fixed or constant charges of the house.

[4] The first of these two extracts is reproduced in full in Nicoll, vol. 1 (1952), p. 375. The second is summarised in Nicoll, vol. 1 (1952), p. 378. The whole of the 'Reply' is reproduced in Milhous (1979), pp. 230–46.

THE BENEFIT SYSTEM DEVELOPS

After the dissolution of the United Company in 1695, the benefit system spread quickly through the two rival companies. Doggett's contract with the Skipwith–Rich management, signed when Doggett defected from Lincoln's Inn Fields, is a typical example [see 34]. (The contract also indicates some of the complexities involved in the system of taking salary or share.)

In 1708 Rich began to withhold large proportions of benefit money due to individual actors. After petitions from various actors, the Lord Chamberlain ordered him in April 1709 to pay his actors, 'their full benefit pursuant to their articles'.[1] His continued refusal to do so led to his being silenced by the Lord Chamberlain two months later.[2] Only too aware of the heated passions and jealousies aroused by the benefit system, the Lord Chamberlain attempted to stamp it out in his draft 'Regulations for the Directors of the Playhouse' of 1710 [see 35]. Future interventions were prompted by specific complaints from aggrieved actors or actresses, as in the case of Mrs Oldfield and Mrs Porter in 1720 [see 36].

[1] PRO lc 5/154, p. 417/f. 218.

[2] See [16]. For a full account of Rich's silencing, see Robert D. Hume: 'The silencing of Drury Lane in 1709' Theatre Journal 32 (1980), 427–47.

34   Articles of agreement between Thomas Doggett and Sir Thomas Skipwith, 3 April 1696
PRO lc 7/3, f. 73

[. . .] 3. Item. In consideration of the premises, the said Sir Thomas Skipwith, for himself, his heirs, executors and administrators, does covenant and grant to and with the said Thomas Doggett [that he] [. . .] shall and may from and after the said tenth day of October next have and receive out of the receipts of the said theatre or theatres the sum of four pounds per week salary (accounting six acting days to the week, excepting only when the young people act for themselves) or else share up to the [same] height as shall be paid to Mr George Powell or Mr John Verbruggen or any other of the company for acting, and at such time and times and in such manner as they respectively shall be paid; that is to say, when in salary, once every week, and when in share, at the time of every dividend, all which payments to be set down in the incident charge. And the said Thomas Doggett is on the tenth day of October next, and on the tenth day of October in each of the two next following years, to declare whether he will for the year then next ensuing stand to an actor's share whatever it shall happen to be or at four pounds per week salary as aforesaid.

4. Item. That in further consideration of the premises that he, the said Thomas Doggett, shall and may receive and have full receipts and profits of any one old play, which he shall choose to be acted by this company on any Wednesday or Friday in the Lent time after Christmas next, so as he act a part therein himself and do pay out of such receipts all the charges of such day, both constant and incident. [. . .]

35   Regulations for the Directors of the Playhouse, undated rough memorandum

PRO LC 7/3, f. 5. Reproduced in Nicoll, vol. 1 (1952), p. 280

[. . .] That there be no poet's night, but that the board agree for performing plays at certain rates both as well as for the printing as the acting, which are after to be licensed by the Master of the Revels, with the prologues, epilogues and songs and which are to be printed by the direction of the board.

That no benefit plays be allowed, nor tickets given to any person.[1]

[1] 'Ticket nights' were another form of benefit, when an actor or employee might be given a number of tickets to be sold for his or her profit. See Troubridge (1967), pp. 26–7.

36   Orders to the Theatre in Drury Lane in respect of Mrs Oldfield's and Mrs Porter's benefit night, 2 February 1720

PRO LC 5/157, p. 284/f. 147

Whereas I have thought fit for the better regulation and government of His Majesty's Theatre in Drury Lane to require you the manager or managers of the said company acting under His Majesty's licence, to take care that no benefit nights be allowed for the future to any actor before Mrs Oldfield's and Mrs Porter's benefit night. And that the prices of the house be never raised without my leave first had.[1] Holles, Newcastle.

[1] Steele's attempts to increase ticket prices prior to 1720 had provoked various complaints.

A NEW STYLE OF MANAGEMENT AT LINCOLN'S INN FIELDS

The troupe of dissident actors who left Drury Lane in 1695 attempted, in the theatre at Lincoln's Inn Fields, to establish themselves on a new financial and organisational basis. Instead of setting up a group of building sharers to fund the re-conversion of Lisle's Tennis Court into a theatre, much of the capital expenditure involved was met through a subscription raised by 'several persons of quality'.[1] The actors then constituted themselves as a company of equal sharers in which no-one was given overall control. The document printed below, signed by eight leading actors, sets out the details. The implicit aim of this democratic management structure was to achieve a harmonious pattern of work through shared responsibility. Differences of opinion and temperament eventually put an end to such hopes. By November 1700, the Lord Chamberlain, having been informed that there were, 'frequent disorders amongst the players', appointed Betterton to be in charge, although he was given only limited powers to impose fines and handle relatively small sums of money.

[1] See Hotson (1928), p. 294 and Cibber (Lowe ed.), vol. I, p. 194.
[2] PRO LC 5/153, p. 23. For a full discussion of Betterton's new role after the Lord Chamberlain's intervention, see Milhous (1979), p. 116.

37   Sharers' agreement at Lincoln's Inn Fields, 25 March 1695
PRO LC 7/3, f. 22[1]

[. . .] It is [. . .] resolved and agreed by the consent of the whole company that the shares do never exceed the number of ten.

It is further resolved and agreed that every whole sharer dying or quitting the company fairly shall after the expiration of five years from the establishment of the said company have the sum of one hundred pounds paid him or his executor after his decease or quitting the company by the rest of the sharers as his or their interest for the share in the clothes, scenes, properties, etc. That is to say the sum of twenty pounds to a whole sharer for the first year, twenty pounds more for the second year and so on to one hundred pounds at the five years' end. And so to all other parts of shares in proportion to a whole share.

But in consideration of the great expenses the first three years being more than reasonably can be supposed for the like term to come, it is agreed that any whole sharer dying at or after the expiration of three years shall have the sum of one hundred pounds paid his executor as well and fully as if the whole term of five years was expired so in proportion to every under sharer. That is to say, this payment is to be made upon no other account but the death of the party.

If any sharer be made incapable of his business in the company by sickness or any other accident, every whole sharer so disabled shall have forty shillings per week allowed him every week the company shall act. And every person under the degree of a whole sharer shall have an allowance in proportion to his part of a share he then enjoyed when he was so disabled.

If any sharer shall hereafter be received into any proportion of share, he shall be obliged to sign the said articles and be conformable to all orders and agreements made by the company before his admission.

If any sharer shall be adjudged incapable of acting, he shall be obliged[2] to quit his share and take the salary provided in that case above mentioned. Before a twelvemonth be expired, in which space of a twelvemonth, if he recover so to perform his business as formerly, he shall then enjoy his share as formerly.

If any hired servant whose salary exceeds twenty shillings the week be made incapable of his business by sickness or any other accident on the stage, he shall have such a weekly allowance proportionable to his salary as the majority of the sharers shall settle upon him.

If any actor in share or salary shall quit this company and afterwards shall be acting or otherwise assist any other company, he shall be incapable of receiving any benefit of these articles. And also every actor quitting the said company shall be obliged to give sufficient security for his performing the conditions of this article before he shall receive his proportion of clothes.

It is further agreed by the consent of the whole company that, as the number of sharers are not to exceed ten, so no person shall have any proportion above one share in consideration of acting.

Betterton, Verbruggen, Bowman, Underhill, Bright, Mrs Barry, Mrs Bracegirdle, Mrs Leigh.

[1] Nicoll prints the version of this agreement given in PRO LC 7/1, p. 44. There are some differences of wording. See Nicoll, vol. 1 (1952), pp. 361–3.
[2] In PRO LC 7/1 the secretary of the Lord Chamberlain has made a transcription error and states, 'he shall not be obliged'. Nicoll retains this error in vol. 1 (1952), p. 362.

A NEW STYLE OF MANAGEMENT AT DRURY LANE

A more successful innovation in management structure came when a triumvirate of actors – Wilks, Cibber and Doggett – was appointed in 1710 to take charge of Drury Lane. Although Doggett was displaced by Booth in 1713 (involving acrimonious legal disputes that dragged on for several years),[1] the basic pattern of three actor-managers, jointly responsible for the running of the theatre, proved a viable and stable system of company management. The original agreement between the managers, approved by the Lord Chamberlain presumably in 1710 (the actual document is undated), clearly sets out their individual rights and collective responsibilities.

When Steele was appointed as patentee in 1715, it was hoped by the managers that he would attend some of their meetings, write plays for the house and generally use his position and contacts at Court and in Parliament to promote the interests of the company.[2] Until his exclusion by the Lord Chamberlain in 1720, Steele took his duties seriously, but his contribution did not affect the basic managerial structure adopted by the triumvirate of actor-managers.

[1] See Fitzgerald, vol. 1 (1882), pp. 352–60.
[2] See Loftis (1952), pp. 36–7.

38   Undated rules and regulations for the management of Drury Lane[1]

PRO LC 7/3, f. 149. Reproduced in Nicoll, vol. 2 (1952), pp. 280–1

We, the managers of Her Majesty's Company of Comedians, acting under Her Majesty's royal licence at the Theatre in Drury Lane, do hereby agree for the better regulation and management of the said Company, and for the prevention of any disputes that may arise among us, the said managers in the execution or conduct of our respective rights or power granted by the said royal licence, do agree and jointly subscribe ourselves to the true and punctual observation of the following rules and orders, viz.:

1.   That once a week at least, or oftener (if any two of them require it), there shall be a meeting of all the managers at the office to consult and order all matters relating to the Company.

2.   That all orders shall be entered in a book kept for that use by the Treasurer and shall not be revoked or contradicted, without the consent of all the three managers.

3.   That all orders be signed by all the three managers and that nothing be an order that has not all their three hands to confirm it, excepting any little necessaries that may be wanting, not exceeding the value of twenty shillings, which any one of the said managers may from time to time direct to be bought or provided. And if any one of the said managers shall refuse or neglect to be present at the said weekly meetings, then the other managers there present shall have full power to order and direct all matters whatsoever relating to the Company, as if such absent manager had been present.

4.   That no new play be received that is not approved by all the managers, nor any play revised or the parts of it cast, without the approbation of all three under their hands.

5.   That no actor, officer, or servant be discharged, taken down, or raised, without the consents and hands of all three.

6.   That all tradesmen's bills be signed by all three and paid every week, if there be money enough received; and no money shall be shared till all debts and disbursements be discharged.

7.   That the Treasurer shall not pay or refuse to pay any money contrary to these orders, upon penalty of being discharged.

All which rules and orders we oblige ourselves to observe and be subject to, and upon any difference or dispute arising from them, to appeal to the Lord Chamberlain.

---

[1] In their catalogue of PRO LC 7 in *TN* 1981, Milhous and Hume suggest a possible date of 1712. Earlier attempts at dating suggested a date of 1710. See Judith Milhous and Robert D. Hume: 'An annotated guide to the theatrical documents in the PRO LC 7/1, 7/2 and 7/3', *TN* 35 (1981), 85.

CONTRACTUAL RESTRICTIONS IN THE 1670s

As from the Restoration, sharers and salaried actors alike needed the written consent of the company manager, if they wished to leave their acting company. This stipulation was part of the original patents granted to Killigrew and Davenant.[1] Actors were therefore legally at the mercy of their managers, which did not prevent them, however, from playing off one manager against the other. Fully aware of this, the Lord Chamberlain reminded all parties of King Charles II's stipulation in 1674 when there was growing discontent in Killigrew's company; this was presumably to prevent widespread defection from the Theatre Royal.

---

[1] See p. 17 above.

39   No players to leave the house they belong to without leave, 16 May 1674

PRO LC 7/1, p. 3. Reproduced in Nicoll, vol. 1 (1952), p. 360

It is His Majesty's pleasure, according to a clause in His Majesty's Letters Patent for erecting the two companies for the two theatres, that no person whatsoever that are hired or anyways entertained by any bargain or agreement or have acted or practised either in His Majesty's theatre or His Royal Highness's theatre shall depart from either the said theatres without giving three months warning. And that neither of the said theatres do entertain, hire or desire to act or practise any person that has been so entertained in any ways as aforesaid at the other theatre, unless the person do first show a certificate under the hands and seals of such as are appointed by that company to give the same, that he or she is discharged from their theatre. And this order is to take effect from the day of the date hereof. Arlington.

CONTRACTUAL RESTRICTIONS AT THE TURN OF THE CENTURY

After the dissolution of the United Company in 1695, the fierce and bitter rivalry of the two companies led to frequent attempts by one or other company to seduce away actors from their rivals and to equally frequent reminders from the Lord Chamberlain that any actor changing companies needed his permission and the written consent of the company he was leaving. His reminders were normally prompted by the aggrieved complaints of one or other manager or company spokesman.

40   Mr Rich complains to the Lord Chamberlain of Her Majesty's household, December 1705

PRO LC 7/3, f. 92[1]

That Mr Vanbrugh and Mr Congreve (in violation of the standing orders and rules of the Lord Chamberlain's Office concerning the playhouses) and contrary to the laws of the land, have seduced away and entertained Mrs Mary Hooke, alias Harcourt, to act in the Playhouse in the Haymarket, although they were acquainted and well know that in October 1702 she entered into articles with Mr Rich for five years with security for performance. That she lately returned from Dublin on purposed to serve out her articles with Mr Rich. But Mr Vanbrugh and Mr Congreve, bidding her a much higher salary than she expected or (as Mr Rich believes) they intend to pay her, she has deserted Mr Rich's service.

He now humbly prays his Lordship that she may be restrained from acting in the company in the Haymarket until she has served out her articles with him.

[1] Nicoll gives a summary of this complaint in vol. 2 (1952), p. 289.

CONTRACTUAL AGREEMENTS IN THE 1720S

In the more stable, though no less competitive theatre climate of the 1720s, the two patent holders, John Rich and Richard Steele, signed an agreement in which they formally promised not to engage actors from each other's company. Any transfers or discharges that did take place needed the written consent of both managements, with provision for a modest fine of £20 for any breach of the agreement. This cartel agreement clearly suited the managers, but it was to become a growing source of discontent amongst the actors of the period.

41   An agreement between Richard Steele and John Rich, 12 April 1722

BL Add.Charter 9308. Copy in BL Add.MS 12,201, ff. 13–24. Reproduced in Judith Milhous and R.D. Hume: 'The London theatre cartel of the 1720s: British Library additional charters 9306 and 9308' *Theatre Survey* 26 (May 1985), 21–35

Now these presents witness that for the considerations aforesaid and for the considerations hereafter mentioned and for diverse other good causes and considerations, the said Sir Richard Steele, Robert Wilks, Colley Cibber and Barton Booth [. . .] do severally covenant, promise and agree to and with the said John Rich and Christopher Mosyer Rich, by these presents, that if the said Sir Richard Steele, Robert Wilks, Colley Cibber and Barton Booth or any of them do or shall at any time or times from the day of the date of these presents to the tenth day of June next inclusive or from the first day of September to the tenth day of June inclusive in any year during so long time as they or any of them shall be master or masters, manager or managers of the said Theatre Royal in or near Drury Lane, or any other theatre or theatres within the limits of the weekly bills of mortality, permit or suffer all or any of the said person or persons whose names are mentioned in the said schedule or inventory (no. 1) hereunto annexed[1] publicly to act or perform any part or parts in any tragedy, comedy, farce or other theatrical performance whatsoever within or upon the stage of or belonging to the said Theatre Royal in or near Drury Lane or any other theatre or theatres as is aforesaid (unless the same be from time to time by and with the previous mutual consent in writing of all the said parties to these presents or such of them as shall continue to be masters or managers aforesaid) that then and in such case and as often as it shall so happen without such consent as aforesaid, they the said Sir Richard Steele, Robert Wilks, Colley Cibber and Barton Booth or such of them as shall then be master or masters, manager or managers as aforesaid, shall and will well and truly pay or cause to be paid unto the said John Rich and Christopher Mosyer Rich or either of them that shall then be master or masters, manager or managers as aforesaid, his or their assignees, the full sum of twenty pounds of lawful money of Great Britain, if they or either of them shall be then master or masters, manager or managers as aforesaid. [. . .][2]

Item the said Sir Richard Steele, Robert Wilks, Colley Cibber and Barton Booth, do severally covenant, promise and agree to and with the said John Rich and Christopher Mosyer Rich by these presents that if they, the said Sir Richard Steele, Robert Wilks, Colley Cibber and Barton Booth or any of them do or shall at any time or times hereafter so long as they or any of them shall be master or masters, manager or managers as aforesaid, admit or receive any other person or persons than what are named in the said schedule or inventory (no. 2) hereunto annexed to be an actor or actress, or actors or actresses under their or any of their management or direction, that then and within one calendar month next after every or any such admission or reception, they the said Sir Richard Steele, Robert Wilks, Colley Cibber and Barton Booth or such of them as shall then be master or masters, manager or managers as aforesaid, shall and will by writing under their or any of their hands directed to the said John Rich and Christopher Mosyer Rich or either of them that shall be then master or masters, manager or managers as aforesaid signify and declare such admission or reception and the name or names of the person or persons so from time to time admitted or received. [. . .]

¹ The full list of actors and actresses annexed to the agreement is printed in Milhous and Hume (1982), p. 24.
² The same provisions are repeated at this point for the Lincoln's Inn Fields managers in respect of the Drury Lane company.

COMPANY FINANCES

Prior to the eighteenth century, there are no documents extant that give a complete picture of theatre company finances. The first such document preserved in the Public Records Office relates to a proposal made in 1703 for a new united company.¹ Although the proposal was never implemented, the document nevertheless gives a very clear picture of the scope and complexity of a London theatre company at the very beginning of the century. A number of salient points emerge from a close reading of the document.

Hitherto actors had been employed on salary or share. In this proposal, no-one is to be employed on a share basis. All actors are to receive a salary, with some actors earning a lower basic salary than others, to be supplemented by a 'guinea' each time they act. Within a decade, the triumvirate at Drury Lane was to implement a differential salary structure for their company, with no-one, apart from the managers, receiving a share of the profits.

Two sets of salary figures are quoted. Judith Milhous argues convincingly that the lower figure is likely to represent the salary earned at the time by each actor, whereas the higher figures represent what the proposers of the union hoped each actor would earn in a united company.²

The proposed salaries range from a mere £30 for the lowest paid actor to £150 for Betterton at the top of the scale; he is also to receive an additional £50 for training young actors.

The annual receipts of the company are calculated to come to £9000, based on an acting year of 280 days; which means that the daily cost of running the theatre or daily 'charge' was just over £32. (By the 1780s, the daily charge for running Covent Garden had almost trebled to £83.)³ It is suggested that the stock debt of the company, i.e. money already owing in respect of scenery and costume, be covered by a levy of two shillings in the pound on all salaries, whereas the directors should advance £200 each for the purchase of new scenery and costumes, these sums to be repaid at the end of the year out of receipts.

The latter suggestion does not recur in any later company documents; managers soon learnt to be more circumspect in the way they manipulated the stock debt [see 214]. This may well have been the main reason why this particular proposal was doomed to failure from the outset.

¹ Allardyce Nicoll, following his transcription of the document in vol. 2 (1952), suggests a date of 1707 for the document (p. 278). Judith Milhous presents convincing circumstantial evidence for a 1703 dating. See Judith Milhous: 'The date and import of the financial plan for a united theatre company in PRO LC 7/3' in *Maske und Kothurn* 21 (1975), 81–8.

[2] *Ibid.*, p. 88.
[3] See *LS*, pt iv.

42   A detailed financial proposal for a united company in 1703

PRO LC 7/3, f. 161. Reproduced in Nicoll, vol. 2 (1952), pp. 276–8[1]

AN ESTABLISHMENT FOR THE COMPANY

Men		pr an.	Women		
	Betterton	150	Barry	150	120
	more to teach	50	Bracegirdle	150	120
120	Verbruggen	150	Rogers	60	60
120	Powell	150	Bowman	70	60
120	Wilks	150	Lee	60	50
80	Cibber	100	Oldfield	80	70
80	Booth	100	Porter	40	35
70	Bowman	80	Willis	40	35
60	Mills	60	Prince	40	35
40	Bailey	50	Mountford	30	30
50	Griffin	50	Betterton Housekeeper		
			& to teach to act	80	80
		1090			
				800	695

Besides a guinea a time when he acts:

60	Underhill	80	Dancers	
100	Dogget	100	Master to compose & teach	
100	Johnson	100	L'Abbé	60
70	Pinkethman	80	De Ruell	40
50	Bullock	60	Charrier	30
40	Norris	50	Mrs Elford	40
40	Bright	40	Mrs Mayers	40
40	Pack	40	Devonshire girl	20
30	Leigh	40	Miss Evans	20
30	Trout	30		
				250
1400[2]		620		

To be allowed besides – every time they dance which, with the charge of additional dancers, amounts to   250

Men	1090
	620
Women	800
Pensions & young actors	190
(deleted)	2600
Tot:	2700

Tot: 500

	Singers		Music	
Master to teach		Master to oversee the music	
Leveridge	40	Mr Eccles	40
Hughes	20	Twenty musicians allowing near	20
Cook	20	shillings per week to each for 40 weeks	
Mrs Hudson	30	comes to	760
Lindsey	20		
Mills	20		800
	150	House rent	600
To be allowed each when they sing		Candles, wax, tallow	
which, with the charge of additional		and oil	600
singers, amounts to	200	3 Managers	600
			1800
Tot:	350		

Under Officers

2 Treasurers of Office Keepers at	
75 each	150
12 Doorkeepers at 20 each	240
Wardrobe Keeper & servant	60
4 Tiremen at 20 each	80
4 Tirewomen at 25 each	100
4 Scenemen that are carpenters	
at 25 each	100
2 men to look after the candles at	
15 each	30
Prompter & his clerk	60
2 Barbers	40
4 Bill-carriers 10 each	40
3 Necessary women at 10 each	30
	930

Totals

Players	2700
Dancers	500
Singers	320
Under Officers	930
Rent, candles, managers	1800
Music	800
Remaining for incidentals, as scenes, clothes, printing, new plays, coals and composition of music etc.	1950
Tot: charge	9000

Note that gloves, ribbons, periwigs, shoes etc. that may be worn abroad are not to be provided out of the public stock but out of their respective salaries.

A CALCULATION OF THE RECEIPTS

Supposing that for the six winter months or 180 days the house receive £50 *per diem*, one day with another, and that all the receipts of 100 days more which they act in the year be thrown in to make up the sum, the receipts of the house will then amount to £9000,[3] which will be sufficient to bear the charge of the intended establishment.

Two shillings in the pound to be stopped out of salaries or £600 till the receipts can discharge the debt of clothes and scenes, after which to be repaid. The directors with salaries to advance £200 each towards buying clothes and scenes to be repaid them at the end of the year out of the receipts.

¹ Another document is printed in PRO LC 7/3, f. 163, identical to the one printed here, except that the singers are put down as costing £350 and the incidentals at £1920.

² The correct total is £1300. The proposer or scribe has made a transcription error in recording the total as £1400. Nicoll made a further transcription error when reproducing the document and recorded this total as £1460 (p. 277).

³ In the original document the proposer or scribe had made a transcription error and put down £90000!

3   Playhouses

INTRODUCTION

The Restoration period was characterised by a zest for experiment in terms of theatre design. Both Killigrew and Davenant were keen to provide roofed public playhouses for their patrons, with provision for changeable scenery. Both signalled their desire for innovation by converting indoor tennis courts into theatre structures (following the example of the Théâtre du Marais in Paris) rather than use the remaining 'private' playhouses from the pre-Commonwealth era at Salisbury Court and Drury Lane. In the event, Killigrew settled for a compromise opening a non-scenic stage at the Clare Market, probably similar in style to the Phoenix at Drury Lane but with improved seating capacity; while Davenant waited patiently until his scenic stage was ready at Lincoln's Inn Fields.

The design features incorporated into Davenant's tennis court theatre – pit and tiered boxes with seats for all patrons; apron stage with stage doors on either side; rear scenic stage with painted wings and shutters – established a basic framework or idiom within which later architects could work. The design concept of Lincoln's Inn Fields was both functional and cost-effective and was to recur in countless variations throughout the eighteenth century.

The main challenges to this architectural idiom came, on the one hand, from neo-classic purists and, on the other, from Baroque extremists. During the 1620s and 1630s, Inigo Jones had been working towards a neo-classic purism of line in his theatre designs that suited the High Renaissance ideals of Charles I. It was this tradition that was probably continued in the design of Killigrew's second theatre at Bridges Street, but it proved to be less flexible and functional than Davenant's theatre and had to be altered soon after its opening.

The solution of Baroque ornateness was attempted at the Dorset Garden theatre, following Davenant's death. Although it was equipped with up-to-date continental stage machinery and was well suited to mounting lavish productions, Dorset Garden never seemed to enjoy genuine popular esteem. Within a decade of its opening, it was more or less neglected by the United Company and by 1709 had become so delapidated that it was pulled down.

In his design for the Theatre Royal, Drury Lane, Wren clearly relied heavily on the pragmatic idiom that had been tried and tested at Lincoln's Inn Fields. In so doing, he achieved a fine working compromise between the traditional English preference for simplicity and understatement and the continental pull towards the two extremes of neo-classic purism, on the one hand, and Baroque extravagance, on the other.

Vanbrugh's opera house, known as the Queen's Theatre in the Haymarket, marked a deliberate attempt to weave together and celebrate these two opposing strands of continental thought. In terms of design concept, his theatre was a deliberate attempt to recreate the purism of Palladio; while the embellishment was unashamedly Baroque. Magnificent as it was, the theatre proved to be a costly failure. Function had been sacrificed to form. While an audience might be willing to admire the purity of line in the design or the imaginative vigour of the décor, they also wanted to be able to hear and see the performance for which they had bought expensive tickets.

The remaining theatres built by Christopher and John Rich in the early decades of the eighteenth century relied heavily on the successful design concept of Wren's Drury Lane, while at times drawing on some of Vanbrugh's more interesting ideas in terms of embellishment and line.

THE FIRST RESTORATION PLAYHOUSES

At the Restoration, the existing playhouses in London all had a number of disadvantages in the eyes of Killigrew and Davenant. The Red Bull, although large, was unroofed [see **43**][1] and it had always had a reputation for attracting poor-quality actors and rowdy audiences.[2] Pepys, who visited the theatre in March 1661, confirms that such was still the case after the Restoration [see **44**]. The Phoenix or the Cockpit (as it was also called) in Drury Lane and the Salisbury Court Playhouse were too small for the audience capacity Killigrew and Davenant envisaged. Both playhouses would also have been unsuited to the scenic innovations that Davenant and Killigrew[3] wished to introduce, although Davenant had used the Phoenix for two of his productions in the late 1650s using rudimentary changeable scenery.[4]

There is no certainty as to the design and interior disposition of these two theatres. A detailed section and ground-plan by Inigo Jones for a roofed private playhouse has been variously ascribed by scholars as a possible design for the Salisbury Court playhouse, on the one hand, and the Phoenix, on the other (see **45**). Glynne Wickham has argued that the likely dimensions of Jones's ground-plan and elevation are best suited to the Salisbury Court site,[5] while John Orrell has argued that Jones's design may be seen as providing the likely basis for the Phoenix, Drury Lane.[6] John Orrell's argument presupposes that the Phoenix was a new theatre building erected upon the site of the original cockpit, whereas Glynne Wickham assumes that the shape and dimensions of the original cockpit were retained in the Phoenix. (He goes on to argue that the evidence of the *Roxana* and *Messalina* vignettes, published in respectively 1632 and 1640, seems to confirm that a private theatre of cockpit dimensions was in use in London during the 1630s. The angled thrust stage shown in both woodcuts can easily be accommodated within the octagonal shape of a cockpit theatre.)[7]

The issue is further complicated by an illustration from Kirkman's *The Wits*, published in 1673, showing a tapestry-hung, rectangular thrust stage from the Civil-War period [see **46**]. (The dating is suggested by the martial scenes depicted on the gallery panels.) This illustration seems to indicate that something like a roofed private playhouse with cockpit dimensions was still operational in London in the 1640s. But if James Wright was correct in asserting in 1699 that the private playhouses of Caroline London were all 'alike for form and bigness', there is no certainty as to which of the private playhouses (if any) was depicted here.[8]

---

[1] There is controversy over the question as to whether or not the Red Bull had been roofed by the Restoration. Hotson (1928) argues convincingly against this notion (p. 87).

[2] See Adams (n.d.), p. 303 and *Historia Histrionica*, reproduced in Cibber (Lowe ed.) (1966), pp. xxiv–xxvii.

[3] The fact that Killigrew as well as Davenant intended to introduce scenic settings is clear from the wording of the warrant granted them on 21 August 1660. See pp. 11–13 above.

[4] *The Cruelty of the Spaniards in Peru* (1658) and *The History of Sir Francis Drake* (1659).

[5] See Wickham (1972), pp. 144–7.

[6] See Orrell (1985), pp. 39–77.

[7] See Wickham (1972), pp. 83–9.

[8] Several scholars have claimed this to be an illustration of the stage at the Red Bull. Apart from the fact that an unroofed public playhouse would not have chandeliers and footlights, as confirmed in [43], it is also clear that the theatre shown here is of more intimate dimensions, even allowing for artistic licence, than one might expect of the Red Bull. The most recently published volume to repeat this claim is *LS*, pt i, pp. 64–5. Hotson (1928) was the first scholar to argue convincingly that the Kirkman drawing was not an illustration of the Red Bull playhouse. Edward Langhans (in 'The Vere Street and Lincoln's Inn Fields Theatres in pictures' *Educational Theatre Journal* 20 (1968), 178) speculates on whether the illustration might be from Killigrew's Vere Street Theatre. This seems less likely, as the performance of drolls after the Restoration was confined to fairs, taverns and mountebank's booths, as Kirkman himself points out on the title page of *The Wits*.

43   James Wright describes the playhouses of the 1630s

Historia Histrionica: An historical account of the English stage, showing the ancient use, improvement and perfection of dramatic representations in this nation, in a dialogue of plays and players (London: William Haws, 1699). Reprinted in *A select collection of old plays*, vol. 9 (London, 1744). Also in Cibber (Lowe ed.), vol. 1 (1966), pp. xix–li

The Blackfriars, Cockpit and Salisbury Court were called private houses[1] and were very small to what we see now. The Cockpit was standing since the Restoration, and Rhodes's Company acted there for some time. [. . .] they were all three built almost exactly alike, for form and bigness.[2] Here they had pits for the gentry and acted by candle-light. The Globe, Fortune and Bull were large houses and lay partly open to the weather, and there they always acted by day light. [. . .]

44   Pepys visits the Red Bull

Samuel Pepys: *The diary of Samuel Pepys*, edited by Robert Latham and William Matthews, vol. 2 (London: G. Bell & Sons, 1970), p. 58.
23 MARCH 1661

Dined at home. And then out to the Red Bull (where I have not been since plays came up again); but coming too soon I went out again and walked all up and down the Charterhouse yard and Aldersgate Street.[3] At last came back again and went in, where I was led by a seaman that knew me, but is here as a servant, to the tiring-room where strange the confusion and disorder that there is among them in fitting themselves, especially here, where the clothes are very poor, and the actors but common fellows. At last into the pit, where I think there was not above ten more than myself, and not 100 in the whole house. And the play, which is called *All's Lost by Lust* [William Rowley], poorly done; and with so much disorder, among others, that in the music room the boy that was to sing a song, not singing it right, his master fell about his ears and beat him so, that it put the whole house in an uproar.

[1] The origin of the term 'private playhouse' is difficult to locate with precision, but it stretches back to the first commercial performances organised by the boy actors' companies at Blackfriars Hall in the 1570s. In order to avoid licensing problems, these performances were restricted to a select, possibly

invited and hence 'private' audience. Thereafter the smaller, roofed playhouses of Elizabethan and Jacobean England were all termed 'private playhouses' as opposed to the large unroofed 'public playhouses'. See Adams (n.d.), pp. 22–3.

² Blackfriars was built in a hall 46 ft broad and 66 ft long, Salisbury Court (including outbuilding) was built on a site 42 ft broad and 140 ft long. See Adams (n.d.), p. 350 and Hotson (1928), p. 106.

³ The Red Bull was situated at the upper end of St John's Street, Clerkenwell.

45   Inigo Jones's designs for a roofed private playhouse

Worcester College, Oxford. Reproduced in Wickham (1972), plates xxiv and xxv; Leacroft (1973), p. 71 and Orrell (1985), pp. 40–1

(A) PLAN

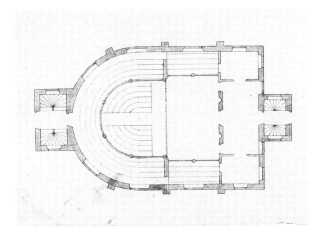

(B) SECTION THROUGH AUDITORIUM   (C) SECTION THROUGH STAGE

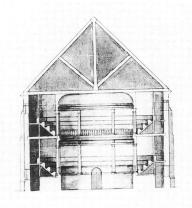
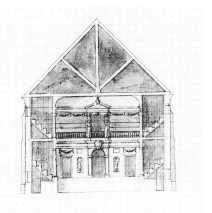

46   Francis Kirkman: *The Wits* Frontispiece

Francis Kirkman: *The Wits or sport upon sport, being a curious collection of several drolls and farces, presented and shown for the merriment and delight of wise men and the ignorant, as they have been sundry times acted in public and private: in London at Bartholomew Fair, in the country at other fairs, in halls and taverns, on several mountebanks' stages at Charing Cross, Lincoln's Inn Fields and other places by several strolling players, fools and fidlers and the mountebanks' zanies* (London: published by the author, 1673).

Reproduced in *LS*, pt i, p. 64; Mander and Mitchenson: *A picture history of the British Theatre* (London: Hulton Press, 1957), p. 19 and Wickham (1972), plate xxiii

THE TENNIS COURT THEATRES

The tennis court theatres, opened by Killigrew at Gibbons's Tennis Court in Vere Street, Clare Market on 8 November 1660 and by Davenant at Lisle's Tennis Court in Lincoln's Inn Fields on 28 June 1661, were both compromise structures [*see* **47**]. Killigrew had clearly intended to make provision for changeable scenery [*see* **5**], but there is no evidence that in the event he did so. One can only speculate as to the reasons. He may have been impatient to open his playhouse swiftly and to avoid the inevitable delays involved in building a scenic stage. He may also have met considerable resistance from the older actors in his troupe who were schooled in pre-Civil-War production methods. Even without the advantage of scenery, Pepys was enthusiastic about the new playhouse on his first visit [see 48].

Davenant's conversion took a lot longer to complete but it had provision for scenes and machines. The building itself was probably some 106 ft long and 42 ft broad, with additional space for workshops and scenery stores.[1] Although no illustrations exist of the interior, modern studies of the stage directions of plays performed at Lincoln's Inn Fields (along with the brief descriptions of contemporary patrons) indicate a theatre in which the auditorium was divided into a pit and a series of side boxes, probably two tiers with a possible further gallery above.[2] The stage area was divided into two sections: a down-stage acting area in the auditorium, approached through one or two pairs of stage or proscenium doors with balconies above them[3] and an up-stage scenic area, separated from the acting area by a proscenium arch. Although the rectangular shape of the tennis court imposed many of these features, the use of an acting area in the auditorium, approached through fixed stage doors, was a logical extension and refinement of the Elizabethan stage, reflecting the continuation of an acting tradition (and the importance for the Restoration of a body of plays) handed on from the Elizabethan and Jacobean theatre. In the Elizabethan theatre, the stage doors and balconies above them were placed in the centre of the stage.[4] In Davenant's theatre, they were moved to the side, in order to permit an uninterrupted view of the scenic stage.[5] This pattern, evolved at Lincoln's Inn Fields, established the basic shape and structure of most subsequent theatres built in Britain in the Restoration period and eighteenth century and in North America during the colonial era.[6]

[1] Hotson's estimate of the size of the building is considerably smaller, namely 75 ft by 30 ft [see Hotson (1928), p. 123]. Apart from the fact that a building as small as this would have offered no advantage over the private playhouses already in existence, there is evidence to support the larger figures. (See Graham Barlow's unpublished doctoral dissertation: *From tennis court to opera house* (University of Glasgow, Ph.D, 1983), pp. 75–7. See also Graham Barlow: 'Gibbons's tennis court: Hollar v. Wilkinson' *Theatre Research International* 8, no. 2 (1983), 130–46.)

[2] See E.A. Langhans: 'Notes on the reconstruction of the Lincoln's Inn Fields Theatre' *TN* 10 (1955–6), 112–14. See also Barlow's dissertation (1983), pp. 89–90.

[3] Barlow argues at length in his dissertation in favour of one pair of stage doors and a pair of stage boxes (pp. 95–105).

[4] Leacroft (1973) argues the case for obliquely placed doors on the sides as well as the back of the second Globe Theatre built in 1614. See pp. 44–50 for his conjectural reconstruction.

[5] See Leacroft (1973), pp. 80–1 and Richard Southern: 'Theatre and scenery' in *The Revels History of Drama in English*, vol. 5 (London: Methuen, 1976), p. 92.

[6] The development of playhouses in colonial America will be covered in a later volume of the series.

47   Hollar's engraving of West-Central London, *c.* 1657

Map room, BL. Reproduced in Hotson (1928), p. 129
Gibbons's Tennis Court is the long thin building in the centre left section, Lisle's Tennis
Court is the building jutting into the fields on the far right.

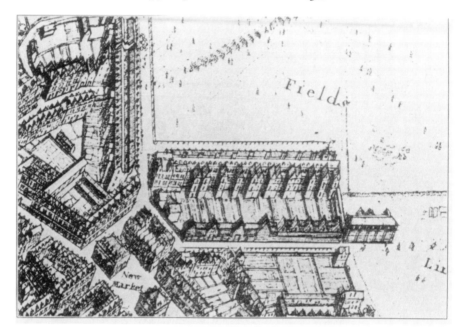

48   Pepys visits Gibbons's Tennis Court

Pepys (Latham and Matthews eds.), vol. 1 (1970), p. 297
20 NOVEMBER 1660

[. . .] To the new playhouse near Lincoln's-Inn-Fields (which was formerly
Gibbons's Tennis Court) [. . .]. And indeed it is the finest playhouse, I believe, that
ever was in England.

49   Pepys visits Lincoln's Inn Fields

Pepys (Latham and Matthews eds.), vol. 2 (1970), pp. 130–1
2 JULY 1661

[. . .] Took coach and went to Sir William Davenant's opera; this being the fourth
day that it has begun, and the first that I have seen it. Today was acted the second
part of *The Siege of Rhodes*. We stayed a very great while for the King and the Queen
of Bohemia. And by the breaking of a board over our heads, we had a great deal of
dust fell into the ladies' necks and the men's hair, which made good sport. The
King being come, the scene opened; which indeed is very fine and magnificent; and
well acted, all but the Eunuch, who was so much out that he was hissed off the
stage.[1]

¹ The part of the eunuch was played by John Downes who later became the prompter for Davenant's company. He blames his poor performance on the sight of the King who, according to Downes, was making his first visit to a public theatre. 'The sight of the august presence spoiled me for an actor too.' Downes (Summers ed.), p. 34.

THE COCKPIT-IN-COURT

Alongside the public theatres that were prepared for performance in the first few months after the Restoration, the court theatre at Whitehall, known as the Cockpit-in-Court, was extensively refurbished during the first two years of the Restoration period.¹

A ground-plan of the Cockpit-in-Court and elevation of the stage, showing a Palladian *frons scenae*, closely matches the description of building works carried out at the Cockpit between 1629 and 1632, which may be found in the accounts of the Office of Works.² Scholars such as G.E. Bentley and Glynne Wickham have argued that the close match of visual and verbal evidence establishes beyond doubt that the ground-plan and elevation show the actual theatre built by Inigo Jones between 1629 and 1632.³ Glynne Wickham has also argued that these designs should be seen as a masterly compromise between Jones's enthusiasm for Palladian design principles, as exemplified by the Teatro Olimpico at Vicenza, and the demands of the leading actors of the day for an intimate, non-scenic stage at court [*see* **50**].⁴

Claims have been made by other scholars that the ground-plan and elevation of the Cockpit are the work of John Webb (Jones's most distinguished pupil who survived into the Restoration period) and show a provisional scheme for rebuilding the theatre in 1660 on the basis of Jones's original designs.⁵ In view of the close matching of verbal and visual evidence noted above, it seems far more likely that the drawings are indeed those for the original conversion, although the draftsman's hand may well be that of John Webb (who was already working for Jones at the time) and there may be some slight residual doubt as to whether the Cockpit by 1630 already had the square walls shown in the ground-plan.⁶

As part of the 1660 refurbishment, the upper tiring room (located immediately behind the stage area) had to be altered to accommodate the actresses who were now beginning to appear in command performances at court. The warrant from the Lord Chamberlain, dated 10 December 1662, sets out in fascinating detail what was required to achieve the necessary alterations [*see* **51**].

¹ A detailed account of this work may be found in Boswell (1932), pp. 10–21, with relevant warrants and accounts reproduced in an appendix on pp. 235–41.
² These accounts are reproduced in full in R.F. Hill (ed.): 'Dramatic records in the declared accounts of the Office of Works, 1560–1640' in *Collections*, vol. 10 (Malone Society, 1977), pp. 40–3. They are also quoted extensively in Bentley, vol. 6 (1968), pp. 271–3.
³ See Bentley, vol. 6 (1968), pp. 267–84 and Wickham (1972), pp. 119–122.
⁴ Glynne Wickham: 'The Cockpit reconstructed' *New Theatre Magazine* 7, no. 2 (1967), 26–35.
⁵ See Leacroft (1973), pp. 73–5.
⁶ William Keith: 'John Webb and the Court theatre of Charles II' *The Architectural Review* 57, no. 2 (1925), 49–55.

50   Stage elevation and ground-plan of the Cockpit-in-Court, 1630/1660

Library of Worcester College Oxford. Reproduced in E.K. Chambers, *The Elizabethan Stage*, vol. 6 (1923), frontispiece; Wickham (1972), plates xix–xxi; Orrell (1985), pp. 98–9

(A) THE STAGE. PLAN AND ELEVATION

(B) GROUND-PLAN

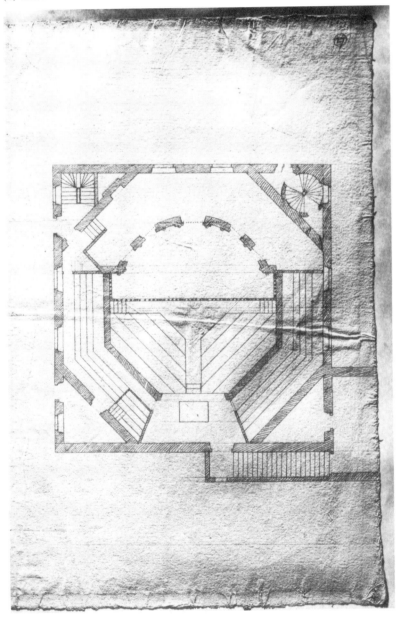

51   A warrant for the upper tiring room at the Cockpit-in-Court, 10 December 1662

PRO LC 5/119. Reproduced in Boswell (1932), p. 18

These are to signify unto your Lordship his Majesty's pleasure that you forthwith provide and deliver or cause to be provided and delivered to John Carew, Yeoman of the Revels in Ordinary to His Majesty for His Majesty's service in the Cockpit Playhouse in St James's Park, the parcels and particulars following, viz.: for the upper tiring room in the Cockpit, the walls being unfit for the rich clothes, one hundred and ten yards of green baize at three shillings four pence the yard; one looking glass of twenty seven inches for the women comedians dressing themselves; twenty chairs and stools; three tables; two stands; six candlesticks; two pieces of hangings and great curtain rods to make partitions between the men and women; two pair of hand-irons; two pair of tongs; two fire shovels and bellows; one lantern and one iron pan; one property bed with a red taffeta coverlet and taffeta curtains and quilt; and one couch. And this shall be your Lordship's warrant. Given under my hand this 10th day of December 1662, in the 14th year of the reign of our Sovereign Lord the King.

To the Right Honourable Edward, Earl of Sandwich, Master of His Majesty's Great Wardrobe or to his Deputy there.

Manchester.

THE THEATRE ROYAL, BRIDGES STREET
The lease

Two days after he had visited Davenant's new scenic theatre on 2 July 1661, Pepys saw a play at Killigrew's theatre and commented: 'But strange to see this house that used to be so thronged, now empty since the Opera began: and so will continue for a while, I believe'. The comment proved to be prophetically accurate. Killigrew responded swiftly and began planning a new scenic theatre, only too aware that Davenant had gained a significant advantage over him. Already by December 1661 he had arranged to lease a suitable site from the Earl of Bedford.

52   The lease for the site at Bridges Street, 20 December 1661

BL Add.MS 20,726, f. 15. Also in BL Add.MS 12,201, ff. 116–17. Reproduced in Fitzgerald, vol. 1 (1882), pp. 81–2

[. . .] The said Earl of Bedford, in consideration of the rent, etc. and in consideration that Sir Robert Howard, Thomas Killigrew and the rest, except Hewitt and Clayton,[1] should before Christmas 1662 expend and lay out £1500 in building a playhouse upon the piece or parcel of ground situated in [the] parishes of St Martin's-in-the-Fields and St Paul's, Covent Garden, known by the name of the Riding Yard, containing in length from east to west 112 ft, and in breadth from north to south at the east end 59 ft and at the west end 58 ft, did at the nomination and appointment of Sir Robert Howard, Killigrew, etc. demise to Hewitt and Clayton the said piece of ground for the term of 41 years from Christmas next at the rent of £50 in trust for Howard, Killigrew, etc. And Howard, Killigrew and all the rest, except Hewitt and Clayton, covenant to pay the £50 rent.

[1] Hewitt and Clayton were appointed trustees.

THE THEATRE ROYAL, BRIDGES STREET
The design concept

The Theatre Royal, Bridges Street, as it came to be known, was opened on 7 May 1663, by which time its projected building costs of £1500 had risen to £2400.[1] As in the case of the tennis court theatres, there are no contemporary illustrations of either the exterior or the interior.

From contemporary descriptions, it is clear that the building had a sizeable cupola, which was probably unglazed. Apart from the architectural problems involved in designing supports for a heavy glazed cupola,[2] any combination of daylight and candlelight in a roofed playhouse produces a most unsatisfactory lighting state.[3] It seems most likely that the cupola was a decorative feature above the rounded auditorium.[4] All we know for certain is that it let in the rain. Pepys commented on 1 May 1668: 'a disorder in the pit by its raining in from the cupola at top, it being a very foul day, and cold'.

There are a number of fleeting descriptions of the interior in the memoirs of various visitors to London. A consistent feature to emerge from these sources is the semi-circular shape of the auditorium [see 53 and 55]. Although the stage shape is not described in any contemporary source, it seems likely that it will have echoed the semi-circular line of the auditorium (following the Italian neo-classic practice of Palladio and Serlio). This would have entailed a curved *frons scenae* (as in the Cockpit-in-Court), with symmetrically placed proscenium doors and with the addition of a large central opening to reveal the scenic stage. A design sketch in the Wren collection at All Souls Oxford gives some idea of what the lay-out may have been [see 56].[5] Similar ideas had been explored by Inigo Jones in the 1630s when High Renaissance ideas were in fashion at court.[6] The intervening Civil-War period had done much to discredit such neo-classic purism.

In 1663, Pepys, as a typical representative of the Restoration, was less impressed by the symmetry of the design than by the purely practical disadvantages imposed by the purist rigour of the theatre's lay-out [see 57]. His misgivings were obviously shared by others. In 1665–6, during the enforced closure of the theatre because of the plague, Killigrew attempted, in a major rebuilding programme, to remedy some of the design flaws built into the theatre [see 78a]. In most subsequent Restoration theatres (with the notable exception of Vanbrugh's Haymarket Theatre),[7] the circular or elliptical form derived from Palladio and Serlio was abandoned in favour of the pragmatic compromise between Elizabethan stage practice and the demands of the scenic stage evolved by Davenant at Lincoln's Inn Fields.

[1] See Hotson (1928), p. 249.
[2] See Donald Mullin: 'The Theatre Royal, Bridges Street. An architectural puzzle' *TN* 25 (1970–1), 14–19.
[3] This fact I established empirically in experiments with painted scenery and candlelight carried out in the studio theatre of the Department of Drama in Bristol in 1971.
[4] Donald Mullin, in an earlier paper than the one quoted in note 2, suggested that the cupola, following Vitruvian example, may have been a semi-circular opening above the pit (*Educational Theatre Journal*, 19 (1967), 24–5). In view of the expensive green cloth on the pit benches and the fine leather work decorating the boxes, this seems most unlikely [see 53].
[5] Edward Langhans suggests this may have been a design sketch for The Theatre Royal. See 'Pictorial material on the Bridges Street and Drury Lane Theatre' in *TS* 7 (1966), 80–100. Leacroft (1973)

disputes this view (pp. 84–5) and argues that the sketch is more likely to be a projected adaptation of the Tudor Hall at Whitehall.
⁶ See Campbell (1923), plate v, between pp. 204 and 205.
⁷ *See* [64–7].

53   A visit to the theatre by Monsieur de Monconys, 22 May 1663
Journal des voyages de Monsier de Monconys, vol. 2 (Lyons: Horace Boissat, 1666), p. 25. Reproduced in Campbell (1923), p. 235

The theatre is the neatest and tidiest I have ever seen, completely covered in green baize, including the boxes that are also covered with strips of gold-tooled leather. All the benches of the pit, where people of rank also sit, are shaped in a semi-circle, each row higher than the next. The scene changes and the machines are most ingeniously thought out and executed.

54   Samuel Sorbière describes the theatre, 1663
Samuel Sorbière: *Relation d'un voyage en Angleterre* (Paris: Thomas Jolly, 1664), p. 166
Samuel Sorbière: *A voyage to England, containing many things relating to the state of learning, religion and other curiosities of that Kingdom* (London: J. Woodward, 1709), p. 69

The playhouse is much more diverting and commodious [than Hyde Park or St James's Park]; the best places are in the pit, where men and women promiscuously sit, everybody with their company. The stage is very handsome, being covered with green cloth;¹ the scenic area is quite open, with many scene changes and perspective views. [. . .]

55   Prince Cosmo III of Tuscany visits the theatre in 1669
Lorenzo Magalotti: *Travels of Cosmo the Third, Grand Duke of Tuscany, through England* (London: J. Mawman, 1821), pp. 190–1

After dinner he recommenced his visits to the ladies, going towards evening to the King's Theatre to hear the comedy in His Majesty's box. This theatre is nearly of a circular form, surrounded, in the inside, by boxes separated from each other and divided into several rows of seats, for the greater accommodation of the ladies and gentlemen who, in conformity with the freedom of the country, sit together indiscriminately; a large space being left on the ground-floor for the rest of the audience. The scenery is very light, capable of a great many changes, and embellished with beautiful landscapes. [. . .]²

¹ The following clause differs from the 1709 translation, which merely states that: 'the scenes often change, and you are regaled with new perspectives'.
² John Orrell suggests that Magalotti incorrectly ascribed this visit to the Theatre Royal. Citing the evidence of another follower of Cosimo, Filippo Corsini, along with records of payments for command performances to the Duke's Company, he argues persuasively that Magalotti's description in fact applies to the Duke's Theatre in Lincoln's Inn Fields. The circumstantial evidence is convincing; what is less convincing is the architectural feasibility of accommodating a commercially viable semi-circular auditorium shape within the likely overall dimensions of Lisle's Tennis Court in Lincoln's Inn Fields. In order to meet this point, Barlow in his thesis (pp. 89–90) suggests a possible U-shaped design for the auditorium at Lincoln's Inn Fields. This would allow a commercially viable seating configuration, but would hardly justify the theatre being described as 'nearly of a circular form'. See John Orrell: 'Filippo Corsini and the Restoration theatre' *TN* 34 (1980), 4–9.

56   Unidentified theatre design by Sir Christopher Wren

Library of All Souls College, Oxford. Reproduced in Campbell (1923), plate vii, between pp. 242 and 243.

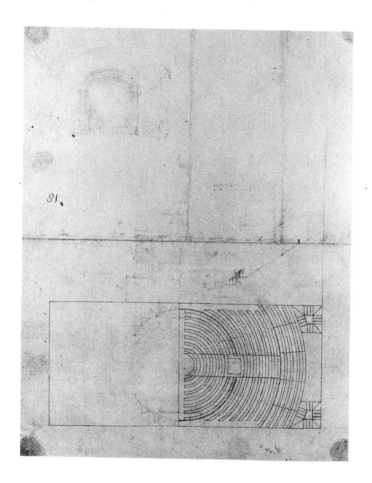

57   Pepys describes his first visit to the Theatre Royal

Pepys (Latham and Matthews eds.), vol. 5, p. 128
8 MAY 1663

[. . .] Took my wife [. . .] to the Theatre Royal, being the second day of its being opened. The house is made with extraordinary good contrivance, and yet has some faults, as the narrowness of the passages in and out of the pit, and the distance from the stage to the boxes, which I am confident cannot hear; but for all other things it is well, only, above all, the music being below, and most of it sounding under the very stage, there is no hearing of the basses at all, nor very well of the trebles, which sure must be mended. [. . .]

THE DUKE'S THEATRE, DORSET GARDEN

Location and exterior view

After the death of Sir William Davenant in 1668, his widow and the leading actors in the company made plans for a new and larger playhouse to replace their tennis court conversion at Lincoln's Inn Fields. Initially, they considered a site immediately behind Salisbury House in the Strand, but eventually chose another part of the grounds giving onto the Thames at Dorset Stairs. The Duke's Theatre, Dorset Garden opened on 9 November 1671.[1] The building was some 140 ft long by 57 ft wide.[2]

Illustrations of the exterior show a main entrance set back in a pleasing colonnade; the upper stories supported by the colonnade being divided into two apartments. One of these apartments was occupied by Richard Middlemore, a sharer in the theatre, and the other by Betterton who was appointed keeper of the theatre, in addition to his duties as company manager.[3]

[1] There is no firm evidence to support the generally held view that the theatre was designed by Sir Christopher Wren. Diana de Marly puts the case for seeing Robert Hooke as the architect in a convincingly argued paper: 'The architect of Dorset Garden Theatre' *TN* 29 (1975), 119–24.
[2] See Robert D. Hume: 'The Dorset Garden Theatre: a review of facts and problems' *TN* 33 (1979), 8.
[3] See Hotson (1928), pp. 233–4.

58   The exterior of Dorset Garden Theatre, 1673

Frontispiece engraved by W. Dolle for the 1673 edition of Elkanah Settle's play *The Empress of Morocco*, published by William Cademan, London

The stage and auditorium

Settle's play *The Empress of Morocco* was performed at Dorset Garden in 1673. The published edition of the play includes a set of engravings by W. Dolle illustrating scenes from the Dorset Garden production. These show a richly embellished stage area, divided, as at Lincoln's Inn Fields, into two distinct sections: a forestage acting area located downstage of the proscenium arch and an upstage scenic area. In front of the ornate proscenium opening, a pair of proscenium doors with balconies above them give onto the stage.[1] Behind the proscenium, with its drape curtain, there is a large upstage scenic area, clearly capable of handling a number of complex scene changes and 'discoveries', as is shown by the set of illustrations from Settle's play.[2] At the top of the proscenium opening, a sizeable music room, with its own windows and curtains, juts out over the acting area [see 80].

Although there is no illustration of the auditorium, a brief description from Brunet, yet another foreign visitor to London, confirms that the seating was arranged in amphitheatre form [see 59]. By comparison with the Theatre Royal, Bridges Street, Dorset Garden marked a decisive shift away from a rigorously sustained neo-classic design concept. In its place, the architect lavished a profusion of Baroque detail and ornamentation on the interior. The basic shape, however, was a functional compromise between the practical advantages of the tennis court thrust and scenic stage, and the Palladian preference of Inigo Jones and John Webb for semi-circular forms in the auditorium.

[1] Only one pair of doors is shown in the illustrations. Scholars are divided in their opinion as to whether there were more. See Leacroft (1973), p. 86. See also John R. Spring: 'Platforms and picture stages: a conjectural reconstruction of the Duke of York's Theatre, Dorset Garden, 1669–1709' *TN* 31 (1977), 6–19 and 'Dorset Garden Theatre: playhouse or opera house' *TN* 34 (1980), 60–9. See also Robert D. Hume: 'The Dorset Garden Theatre: a review of facts and problems' *TN* 33 (1979), 4–17.
[2] See pp. 95–9 below.

59   François Brunet describes the interior of the Duke's Theatre, 1676

François Brunet: *Voyage en Angleterre* (unpublished manuscript, 1676), BL Add.MS 35,177, ff. 79–80. Reproduced in Summers (1934), p. 63

The auditorium is infinitely more beautiful and well-kept than those in the playhouses of our French actors. The audience is seated in the pit, arranged in the form of an amphitheatre, and there is no noise. There are only seven boxes, holding twenty persons each. There are the same number of boxes up above and, higher still, there is the gallery.

Wren's longitudinal section

Killigrew's Theatre Royal in Bridges Street was burned down in January 1672 in a disastrous fire that engulfed a number of surrounding buildings. The company moved to Lisle's Tennis Court at Lincoln's Inn Fields, recently vacated by the Duke's Company, while Wren was commissioned to design them a new playhouse on the same site between Bridges Street and Drury Lane. Additional land was leased to provide a new scene room and workshop. Wren's new Theatre Royal, Drury Lane, opened on 26 March 1674. It was some 112 ft long by 58 ft broad; the newly added scene room extended the length of the site to a total of 140 ft.[1]

There is no contemporary illustration of the interior, but a drawing in Wren's papers marked simply 'Playhouse' is generally thought to be a longitudinal section through The Theatre Royal at Drury Lane. On the basis of this design sketch, scholars and architects have built scale models and drawn three-dimensional views of the interior.[2] However, Wren's drawing is torn into four pieces, which may indicate some doubt or dissatisfaction on the architect's part. And there is no final certainly that the design sketch does indeed show the interior of Drury Lane.

60   Wren's longitudinal section of a playhouse
Library of All Souls, Oxford. Reproduced in Leacroft (1973), p. 90[3]

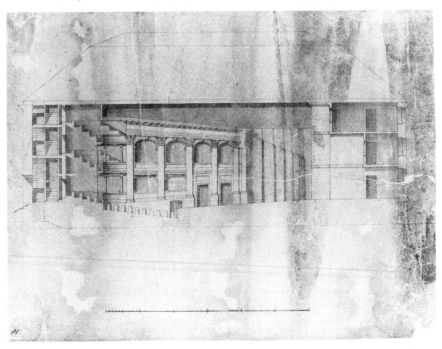

[1] See Hotson (1928), p. 256.
[2] See, for instance, Leacroft (1973), p. 95 and Southern (1952), p. 176 (see chapter 4).
[3] Richard Southern's model, based on this section drawing, is housed in the Theatre Collection of the University of Bristol. A picture of the model is reproduced in Southern: *Changeable scenery* (London: Faber & Faber, 1952) between pp. 176 and 177.

THE THEATRE ROYAL, DRURY LANE
The design concept

Colley Cibber, writing of the alterations made to the theatre by Rich in 1696, implies that there were originally only two sets of stage pilasters at the proscenium opening, to which Rich may have added an additional set when he made his alterations [*see* **61**]. Leacroft interprets Cibber's phrase as meaning that the Corinthian columns in the auditorium had been removed some time before Rich's alterations in 1696.[1] There is no evidence to prove that any such rebuilding and alteration work took place before 1696.

Barlow interprets Cibber's words as meaning that there were originally one pair of stage doors and a pair of stage boxes that were moved upstage during the alterations.[2] However, this interpretation would appear to be contradicted by the evidence of a frontispiece published in 1721 showing Joe Haines on the fore-stage of Drury Lane in 1697 (the year after Rich's alterations). The space formerly occupied by the two stage doors has now been turned into two stage boxes, with balconies still above them. The stage has been shortened and straightened, as Cibber describes, so that it now terminates where the stage boxes meet the side boxes. In contrast to Wren's section, however, the stage boxes and side boxes follow an unbroken line round the auditorium [see 158].

Even allowing for the usual artistic licence that is taken in eighteenth-century theatrical prints, the visual detail here seems to indicate that Drury Lane did indeed have two pairs of narrow stage boxes (in place of the original two pairs of doors) following the 1696 alterations and that the stage no longer projected as far into the auditorium as it had done during the Restoration period.

Juxtaposing this evidence with the known design features of later theatres modelled on Wren's original, notably the Theatre Royal at Bristol (1764–6), would seem to indicate that Wren, instead of building the theatre as shown in his section drawing, in fact adapted his design so as to confine the massive Corinthian columns to the proscenium area.

In the Theatre Royal at Bristol, where large pairs of pilasters were confined to the area of the proscenium and orchestra pit,[3] even the slender supporting columns of the side boxes (now called the side dress circle) still pose a distinct sight-line hazard for audiences. If Wren's playhouse had been built as shown in his section drawing, the width of the Corinthian columns would have meant that high-ranking members of the audience in the side boxes would have seen little of the action on the thrust stage and nothing of the splendours of the scenic stage. This is a design fault that any experienced theatre manager would surely have queried. It also seems quite inconceivable that Killigrew and his leading actors would have approved a second flawed theatre design after all the problems they had experienced with the first Theatre Royal.

Assuming the remaining features of the theatre were much as shown in Wren's drawing, which seems to be confirmed by Cibber's and Misson's descriptions [see 62], as well as the Joe Haines illustration, this new theatre clearly marked an even more satisfying solution than the ornate Duke's Theatre in Dorset Garden to the problem of achieving a working compromise between native English traditions in the theatre and neo-classic design concepts spreading to England from the Continent. The modified thrust stage, retained from the Elizabethan theatre, allowed every inflection of the actors' voices to be heard and every gesture seen; the scenic stage provided ample depth for visual spectacle when required; while the gently curving shape of the pit benches and front boxes reflected the neo-classic desire for symmetry and curved harmony of line.[4]

In his design concept for the Theatre Royal, Drury Lane, Wren successfully married together the best features of English theatre traditions with Continental neo-classic theory and practice. Elegant in its simplicity, functionally attractive to both actors and audiences, it provided an effective blueprint for theatre architects in England throughout the eighteenth century.

[1] See Leacroft (1973), p. 91.
[2] See Barlow (1983), p. 102.
[3] Illustrated in Leacroft (1973), p. 113.
[4] There is still controversy over the exact shape of the auditorium. Leacroft (1973) argues that it was fan-shaped (pp. 93–5). Mullin and Koenig, in TN 21 (1966–7), 180–7, argue that the side walls were parallel and only the pit seating and rear walls followed an oval line. Langhans argues for a smooth U-shaped line to the boxes in TN 18 (1963–4), 91–100. Sheppard, in *Survey of London*, vol. 35 (London: Athlone Press, 1970), p. 44, supports Leacroft.

61   Colley Cibber's description of the Theatre Royal, Drury Lane, prior to 1696

An apology for the life of Mr Colley Cibber, written by himself, edited by R.W. Lowe (New York: AMS Press, 1966), vol. 2, pp. 84–6

It must be observed then that the area or platform of the old stage projected about four foot forwarder, in a semi-oval figure, parallel to the benches of the pit; and that the former lower doors of entrance for the actors were brought down between the two foremost (and then only) pilasters; in the place of which doors now the two stage boxes are fixed. That where the doors of entrance now are, there formerly stood two additional side-wings, in front to a full set of scenes, which had then almost a double effect in their loftiness and magnificence.

By this original form, the usual station of the actors, in almost every scene, was advanced at least ten foot nearer to the audience than they now can be; because, not only from the stage's being shortened in front, but likewise from the additional interposition of those stage boxes, the actors (in respect to the spectators that fill them) are kept so much more backward from the main audience than they used to be. But when the actors were in possession of that forwarder space to advance upon, the voice was then more in the centre of the house so that the most distant ear had scarce the least doubt or difficulty in hearing what fell from the weakest utterance: all objects were thus drawn nearer to the sense; every painted scene was stronger; every grand scene and dance more extended; every rich or fine-coloured habit had a more lively lustre; nor was the minutest motion of a feature (properly changing with the passion or humour it suited) ever lost, as they frequently must be in the obscurity of too great a distance. And how valuable an advantage the facility of hearing distinctly is to every well-acted scene, every common spectator is a judge. [. . .]

62   Henri Misson describes the Theatre Royal, Drury Lane, 1698

Henri Misson: *Memoirs and observations in his travels over England,* translated by John Ozell (London: D. Browne, 1719), pp. 219–20

There are two theatres at London (a third is lately opened), one large and handsome, where they sometimes act operas and sometimes plays; the other something smaller, which is only for plays. The pit is an amphitheatre,[1] filled with benches without backboards and adorned and covered with green cloth. Men of quality, particularly the younger sort, some ladies of reputation and virtue, and abundance of damsels that hunt for prey, sit all together in this place, higgledy-piggledy, chatter, toy, play, hear, hear not. Farther up, against the wall, under the first gallery and just opposite to the stage, rises another amphitheatre, which is taken up by persons of the best quality, among whom are generally very few men. The galleries, whereof there are only two rows, are filled with none but ordinary people, particularly the upper one.

[1] The use of the word amphitheatre in French does not necessarily imply a semi-circular shape. In the French theatre of the period it was used to describe either a standing pit or a space of tiered seating behind the front boxes.

THE QUEEN'S THEATRE, HAYMARKET
Vanbrugh's original design

In designing his theatre in the Haymarket in 1703, Vanbrugh's primary aim was to establish a centre for opera productions in London, and appropriately his theatre was normally referred to as the opera house. At some stage in his planning (and the precise stage is far from clear),[1] he approached Betterton and offered to accommodate the Lincoln's Inn Fields troupe in his new theatre, on the understanding that Betterton would relinquish control of the troupe in favour of Vanbrugh. He raised the building capital by a subscription of twenty-nine persons of quality who each paid a share of 100 gns.[2] Many of his friends in the Kit-Cat Club contributed, although Defoe hinted that some sharers were reluctant to part with their money.[3]

As Vanbrugh began work on the design in 1703 (the interior was to be substantial in size, 124 ft long by 55 ft wide),[4] he boasted to his friend Tonson that the interior was, 'very different from any other house in being' [see 63]. Although there is no undisputed visual illustration of the interior as he first designed it, it does seem likely that a number of design sketches by Thornhill, showing a great arched proscenium, do in fact refer to the Queen's Theatre in its first years of existence[5] [see 64]. Colley Cibber's description makes it clear that Vanbrugh's conscious departure from the design concept evolved by Wren at Drury Lane was an unfortunate error of judgement [see 65]. Functional simplicity was sacrificed to an unwieldy combination of Palladian rigour and Baroque excess. A lofty decorative ceiling with ornately gilded cornices; a lavishly embellished, elliptical proscenium arch; a wastefully proportioned amphitheatre for the pit and boxes; huge Corinthian pilasters not only flanking proscenium doors and balconies, but even extending into the stage area itself;[6] all contributed to make this a design of self-indulgent extravagance, unsuited to fulfilling the basic functional objective of a theatre, namely to allow an audience to see and hear a company of actors presenting a play.

[1] See Milhous (1979), pp. 169–70.
[2] Barlow (1983) reproduces examples of the covenants made by individual subscribers. See pp. 270–1.
[3] See Downes (Summers ed.), p. 41.
[4] See Leacroft (1973), p. 99; *Survey of London*, vol. 29, p. 227 and Barlow (1983), p. 308.
[5] In his book *Changeable scenery* (1952), Richard Southern argues that an unidentified water-colour of a stage scene from the Burney Collection in the British Library may in fact be an illustration of the proscenium arch and scenic stage in the original Queen's Theatre. (See the frontispiece and pp. 182–7.) Barlow (1983) opposes this ascription and argues with convincing documentation that a number of Thornhill sketches provide a more accurate picture of the proscenium of the Queen's Theatre. See pp. 335–53.
[6] See Barlow (1983), pp. 346–8.

63   Vanbrugh's letter to Jacob Tonson, 13 July 1703
The works of Sir John Vanbrugh, edited by Geoffrey Webb, vol. 4 (London: Nonesuch Press, 1927), p. 9

[. . .] The ground is the second stable yard going up the Haymarket. I gave £2000 for it, but have laid such a scheme of matters that I shall be reimbursed every penny of it by the spare ground; but this is a secret lest they should lay hold on it to lower the rent. I have drawn a design for the whole disposition of the inside, very different from any other house in being. But I have the good fortune to have it absolutely approved by all that have seen it. [. . .] The book you mention which I wanted, you'll oblige me to get. 'Tis Palladio in French, with the plans of most of the houses he built. There is one without the plans, but 'tis that with them I would have. [. . .]

64   Sir James Thornhill: First Great Flat Scene. Scenic Curtain, showing Atlas, Neptune, etc.

Pen and wash, Leonora Hall Gurley Memorial Collection, 1922. 1617. Art Institute of Chicago

65   Colley Cibber describes Vanbrugh's playhouse
Cibber (Lowe ed.), vol. I, pp. 321–2

As to their other dependence,[1] the house, they had not yet discovered that almost every proper quality and convenience of a good theatre had been sacrificed or neglected to show the spectator a vast triumphal piece of architecture! And that the best play, for the reasons I am going to offer, could not but be under great disadvantages, and be less capable of delighting the auditor here than it could have been in the plain theatre they came from. For what could their vast columns, their gilded cornices, their immoderate high roofs avail, when scarce one word in ten could be distinctly heard in it? Nor had it then the form it now stands in, which necessity, two or three years after, reduced it to. At the first opening it, the flat ceiling that is now over the orchestra, was then a semi-oval arch that sprung fifteen feet higher from above the cornice; the ceiling over the pit, too, was still more raised, being one level line from the highest back part of the upper gallery to the front of the stage. The front boxes were a continued semi-circle to the bare walls of the house on each side: this extraordinary and superfluous space occasioned such an undulation from the voice of every actor that generally what they said sounded like the gabbling of so many people in the lofty aisles in a cathedral. The tone of a trumpet or the swell of an eunuch's holding note, 'tis true, might be sweetened by it, but the articulate sounds of a speaking voice were drowned by the hollow reverberations of one word upon another. To this inconvenience, why may we not add that of its situation; for at that time, it had not the advantage of almost a large city, which has since been built in its neighbourhood. Those costly spaces of Hanover, Grosvenor and Cavendish Squares, with the many and great adjacent streets about them, were then all but so many green fields of pasture, from whence they could draw little or no sustenance, unless it were that of a milk diet. The City, the Inns of Court and the middle part of the town, which were the most constant support of a theatre and chiefly to be relied on, were now too far out of the reach of an easy walk, and coach hire is often too hard a tax upon the pit and gallery. [. . .]

[1] The reference is to Betterton's troupe.

THE QUEEN'S THEATRE, HAYMARKET
Alterations in 1708

Although Vanbrugh expended considerable energy in his attempts to make a success of this theatre, he found himself at every turn hampered by the design flaws of his building. Audiences found it impossible to hear spoken dialogue clearly and were therefore loath to pay good seat prices even when Vanbrugh offered them attractive new comedies from his own pen. (*The Confederacy* and *The Mistake*, both adaptations from Continental sources, were written for the autumn and winter of 1705 but failed to draw large houses.) In December 1707, Vanbrugh abandoned any hope of combining opera and drama in his new theatre and persuaded the Lord Chamberlain to give him a monopoly of opera production in London.[1] Although his theatre was better suited to opera, the Palladian purism of the auditorium shape limited the house capacity, despite its size. This was a serious shortcoming in view of the high costs (in terms of scenery, costume and singers' fees) involved in mounting Italian opera. Vanbrugh soon discovered that his hopes of achieving a working profit were vain. When he finally relinquished control of the theatre to his manager, Owen Swiney, in the spring of 1708, he had accumulated substantial debts that were to remain with him for many years to come [see 66].

As soon as Owen Swiney took over control of the theatre from Vanbrugh, he embarked on a substantial programme of rebuilding, probably between May and December 1708 when the theatre remained closed. His aim was to make good the worst of the theatre's defects. (Vanbrugh may well have supervised these alterations.) The ceiling was lowered, the proscenium design may have been altered[2] and the seating capacity improved. There is no certainty as to the exact extent of the alterations made in 1708, but a ground-plan and section published by Dumont in 1774 give some idea of the changes made [see 67].

[1] See pp. 22–4 above.
[2] Pictorial evidence from the early 1730s suggests that the proscenium may not have been radically altered in the 1708 rebuilding. See p. 000 below.

66   Vanbrugh writes to Jacob Tonson, 1719
The works of Sir John Vanbrugh, vol. 4, edited by Geoffrey Webb (London: The Nonesuch Press, 1927), p. 123

But to tell you the truth; I have no money to dispose of. I have been many years at hard labour, to work through the cruel difficulties that Haymarket undertaking involved me in; notwithstanding the aid of a large subscription. Nor are those difficulties quite at an end yet.

67   The King's Theatre in 1774: plan and section by Dumont
G.P.M. Dumont: *Parallèle des plans des plus belles salles de spectacles d'Italie et de France* (Paris: [s.n.], 1774). [University Library, Bristol][1]
(see facing page)

THE NEW THEATRE IN LINCOLN'S INN FIELDS AND COVENT GARDEN THEATRE

After his silencing in 1709, Christopher Rich acquired the lease of the theatre in Lincoln's Inn Fields, using an actor called Penkethman as his front man. He made plans for demolishing the old building and erecting a new theatre on the site but had to wait patiently until a change of monarch and government offered concrete hope of rehabilitation. In 1714, in the first year of his reign, George I agreed to revoke the silencing order imposed upon Rich. At once Rich drew up agreements for building his new theatre at Lincoln's Inn Fields and for establishing the financial structure of the company. An indenture dated 3 September 1714, concerned with the latter, provides a straightforward factual description of the site [see 68].

Unhappily, Christopher Rich died before the opening of his new theatre in November 1714, but his two sons John Rich and Christopher Mosyer Rich took control of the company and the patent. John Rich was the dominant figure, although at first he proved to be a less than competent manager. In the early years of his regime, the company came close to bankruptcy. But as from 1722 he was increasingly successful. He could be as devious and wily as his father, but his meticulous grasp of detail eventually helped to make him an able theatre manager. He was himself a talented dancer who appeared as Harlequin in the

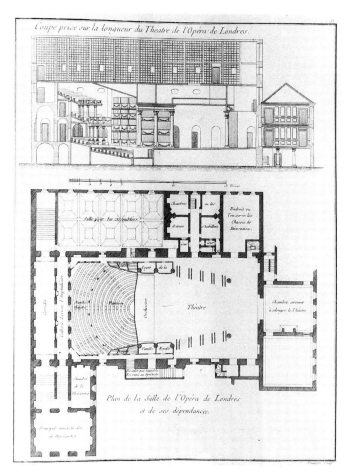

67   The King's Theatre in 1774

<hr />

[1] Dumont's printer has reversed the engraving. A correct version may be found in *Survey of London*, vol. 29, plate xxvi.

pantomimes and after-pieces for which his theatre became well known during the 1720s. His most famous theatrical success came with the mounting of Gay's *Beggar's Opera*, which ran for an unprecedented sixty-two performances in 1728.

During his long stay at Lincoln's Inn Fields, he frequently refurbished the theatre, adding structural and decorative features that delighted his contemporaries: superb 'looking glasses on both sides of the stage' in 1720; splendid ceiling paintings in 1722; 'gilding, painting, scenes and columns of pier glass, raised for the better illuminating the stage and other parts of the house' in 1725.[1]

The best illustration of the interior may be seen in Hogarth's burlesque of *The Beggar's Opera*, which clearly shows the attractive finish to the side and stage boxes and equally clearly shows one of the distinctive features of the stage area: the satyr statues flanking the proscenium opening [*see* **69**]. The theatre was generously proportioned within an overall site that was 130 ft long and 47 ft 6 inches wide at its Western end and 71 ft 6 inches wide at its Eastern end. The likely interior dimensions were: auditorium 43 ft wide and 64 ft long; forestage 15 ft deep and 27 ft wide; scenic stage, 28 ft deep from proscenium to Eastern wall and at least 45 ft wide.[2]

It was almost certainly the success of *The Beggar's Opera* that prompted Rich to consider moving to a new and better equipped theatre in 1730. In January 1731 he invited subscriptions from wealthy backers, and in March 1731 took out a lease with the Duke of Bedford for a 'parcel of ground contiguous to Bow Street and Covent Garden',[3] the site being 120 ft in length from east to west and 100 ft in width from north to south. Rich engaged the architect Edward Shepherd to design his new building and drew up formal articles with him in June 1731. Shepherd was to receive £5600 out of a capital sum of £15000, to be raised from the sale of fifty shares at £300 each. The residue of £9400 was to be retained by Rich. Recent research has established that Rich did indeed achieve his subscription target of £15000, making a handsome profit for himself in the process.[4]

After the building was completed, Rich became embroiled in a lawsuit with Shepherd. The substance of his claim was that Shepherd had failed to meet the agreed specification in terms of both structural and decorative detail. (And Rich always paid close attention to detail.) The legal depositions in this case provide a valuable source of descriptive evidence in respect of the interior [*see* **70**].

[1] The above quotations are taken from *LS*, pt ii, vol. 1, p. xxxiii.
[2] See Barlow (1983), pp. 210, 227 and 235.
[3] *LS*, pt iii, vol. 1, p. xxviii. See also *Survey of London*, vol. 35, p. 71 and *LS*, pt iii, vol. 1, p. xxviii.
[4] *Survey of London*, vol. 35, pp. 73–4. Previously, scholars have argued that Rich failed to achieve the target of £15000. See, for instance, *LS*, pt iii, vol. 1, pp. xxviii–xxx.

68   Indenture between Christopher Rich and Rupert Clarke, dated 3 September 1713
BL Add.Charter 9303

[. . .] All that great and lately new erected messuage tenement theatre or playhouse upon the ground and room of all that great messuage or playhouse and building which before such new erection was commonly called Lisle's Tennis Court or the Theatre or Playhouse in Little Lincoln's Inn Fields, and the same is intended hereafter to be called the New Theatre or British Theatre, together with all erections and buildings thereupon and on the north side thereof and upon any part or parcel thereof, all which premises are situate lying and being at or near Little Lincoln's Inn Fields.

69   The interior of Lincoln's Inn Fields theatre in Hogarth's caricature of *The Beggar's Opera*, 1728
University of Bristol Theatre Collection. Further copy in The Burney Collection of theatrical portraits, vol. 4, no. 43, p. 21 (Print Room, BM). Reproduced in *The Revels history of drama in English*, vol. 5 (1976), plate 18

(see facing page)

69   The interior of Lincoln's Inn Fields theatre in 1728

70   Rich's bill of complaint against Shepherd, 1732
PRO c11/2662/1. Reproduced in *Survey of London*, vol. 35 (1970), p. 86

[. . .] That the stage, the front and side boxes, galleries and benches should be finished in as good a manner in all respects as those at the Theatre in Lincoln's Inn Fields (except the lining of the boxes and seat coverings, history painting, gilding, all glasses which were not to be done by the said Edward Shepherd but by your orator).[1] That the vaults under the intended great lobby and the boxes and passages leading thereto should be joisted and boarded. That the outside passages where no rooms were intended to be built over should be roofed and tiled with glazed pantiles or plain tiles, according to the said annexed plan or otherwise finished as requested by your orator, and should be paved with purbeck stone from end to end of the east and west sides of the said intended theatre. That the lodgements above the stage for the flyings should be framed with good yellow joists to be seven inches by nine inches and the common joists, seven inches by three inches, covered with yellow deals without sap on each side of the stage fifteen foot wide. That the boxes over the stage door and the boxes over the two side boxes adjoining to the King's and Prince's Boxes[2] should be ornamented with entablature (as delineated in the said plan). That there should be in and about the said theatre as many staircases as designed by the said plan which should be finished in a good, proper and substantial manner. The music room, treasurer's, box keeper's and other offices and all other conveniencies necessarily appertaining to a theatre (and as that at Lincoln's Inn Fields) should be done and finished with good and substantial yellow boarded floors without sap. And that a carpenter's workshop, a painting room, such wardrobes and other conveniencies (as should be required by your orator) should be made in the roof of the said intended theatre. [. . .] that there be as many benches in each box as at Drury Lane Theatre, the benches should be altered so that each person sitting might have as proper a view of the stage as the place would admit, which they would not have as they were then placed. [. . .]

¹ Namely, Rich.
² Although a Royal front box was provided, this was the first occasion on which Royal side boxes were located, in the French manner, on either side of the forestage.

COVENT GARDEN THEATRE
The design concept

The theatre was built in a shell 112 ft long by 56 ft broad. It was announced in *The Daily Advertiser* of 2 March 1731 as being, 'after the model of the Opera House in the Haymarket'.¹ The fan-shaped lay-out of the auditorium does indeed show some resemblance to the semi-circular design of the auditorium in Vanbrugh's theatre as rebuilt in 1708. In addition, the treatment of the stage pilasters is strikingly similar to Vanbrugh's design. But the dimensions of the theatre are closer to those of Wren's Drury Lane than the Haymarket, and the essentially functional approach of Shepherd (for instance, his ingenious extension of the upper tiers of the top two galleries over the ground-floor foyers and the pragmatic line of the pit benches, cut in straight lengths rather than in purist curves) marked an imaginative refinement of Wren's elegantly simple design concept rather than an echo of Vanbrugh's Baroque excess and extravagance. The theatre opened on 7 December 1732 with a performance of *The Way of the World*. Despite Rich's complaint over Shepherd's workmanship, the auditorium was widely praised for its elegant shape and excellent acoustic.

¹ Quoted from *Survey of London*, vol. 35 (1970), p. 86.

71   Covent Garden in 1774: plan and section by Dumont

G.P.M. Dumont: *Parallèle de plans des plus belles salles de spectacles d'Italie et de France* (Paris: [s.n.], 1774). [University Library, Bristol]¹

(see facing page)

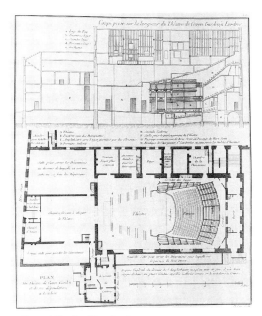

71   Covent Garden Theatre in 1774

¹ As in the case of the Haymarket Opera House engraving, Dumont has printed this engraving in reverse in his book. A corrected illustration may be seen in *Survey of London*, vol. 35 (1970), plate 40.

THE THEATRE IN AYLIFFE STREET, GOODMAN'S FIELDS

In October 1729, Thomas Odell opened a small theatre in Ayliffe Street, Goodman's Fields, in a converted throwster's shop.¹ Despite opposition from the Justices of the Peace, and an unsuccessful attempt by the Lord Chamberlain to silence the playhouse in April 1730,² the theatre continued to prosper.

In September 1731, Odell relinquished control of the theatre to Henry Giffard who proved to be an able manager and entrepreneur. By the end of the year, Giffard had published plans to erect a new theatre in the same area. He obtained a sixty-one-year lease from Sir William Leman and succeeded in persuading twenty-three subscribers to advance £100 each by May 1732, in order to establish a building fund of £2300.³ Edward Shepherd, who was at the time designing the new playhouse at Covent Garden, was engaged as architect. By the early summer of 1732, building work had started; in July 1732, the building was roofed; and by October 1732 the theatre was completed. It opened on 2 October 1732 with a performance of 1 *Henry IV*.⁴

The theatre was of modest dimensions, 88 ft long by 47 ft wide, with pit, boxes and one gallery. It was an intimate structure for which Shepherd almost certainly utilised a variation of the fan-shaped auditorium he was designing for Covent Garden.⁵ No contemporary illustration survives of the theatre (and it ceased functioning as a theatre after Garrick had made his London début there in October 1741). However, the late eighteenth-century scene designer, William Capon, visited the shell of the building in 1786 and 1802 (it finally burnt down in 1802) and, after his last visit, drew a hypothetical reconstruction of the ground plan, based on his detailed observations of the structural features he observed.⁶

1 See S. Rosenfeld: 'Theatres in Goodman's Fields' *TN* 1 (1946), 48–50.
2 See pp. 203–4 below. According to a newspaper report of 1729, Odell obtained letters patent for his new theatre. But there is no record of this in the Lord Chamberlain's warrant books. See *LS*, pt iii, vol. 1, p. xxi.
3 See *LS*, pt iii, vol. 1, p. xxiii.
4 *Ibid.*
5 See Leacroft (1973), pp. 110–11.
6 See R. Eddison: 'Capon and Goodman's Fields' *TN* 14 (1959–60), 127–32.

72   From Capon's notes on the theatre in Goodman's Fields, 1802

Reproduced in R. Eddison: 'Capon and Goodman's Fields' *TN* 14 (1960), 132

[. . .] On the ceiling were painted the portraits of Shakespeare, Betterton, Dryden, on the left; Congreve, on the right, done by W. Oram. [. . .] The whole length of the building from east to west was 88 ft exactly outside the walls, 47 ft wide inside the walls, and $2\frac{1}{2}$ bricks thick the front walls on the south next Alie Street. The width of the pit 30 ft only. Depth to the orchestra 15 ft and seven seats only. The colour of the inside [of] the boxes, a light flesh colour or pink. [. . .]

73   Capon's hypothetical reconstruction of the theatre in Goodman's Fields, 1802

Folger Library. Reproduced in Leacroft (1973), p. 111; *LS*, pt iii, vol. 2, between pp. 224 and 225.

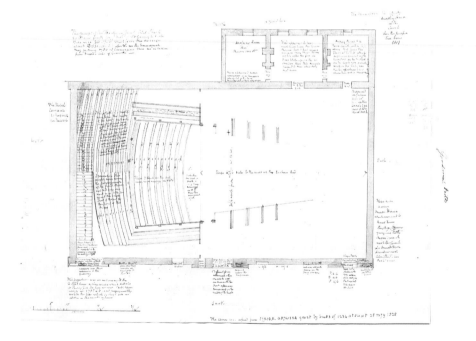

4 Stage presentation

INTRODUCTION

In much the same way that Davenant established the basic idiom of Restoration theatre architecture in his converted tennis court at Lincoln's Inn Fields, he also established the basic framework and structure of the scenic stage that was to become such a prominent feature in the Restoration theatre. His collaborator and designer in this venture was initially John Webb who had been one of Inigo Jones's most gifted pupils in the 1630s. Together Davenant and Webb, in their production of *The Siege of Rhodes* at Rutland House in 1656, established the scenic conventions that were to become the norm in terms of Restoration and eighteenth-century theatre practice. The whole set was built around the principle of perspective painting, with a vanishing point upstage centre. Pairs of receding wings were designed to follow the geometry of the vanishing point, and shutters were inserted between them (corresponding to the perspective) to indicate changes of location. The shutters met in the centre of the stage and were drawn on and off in grooves laid across the stage floor. With the help of *trompe l'oeil* painting, an illusion of space was given even though the stage space available was relatively cramped.

The Restoration stage was a compromise between the non-scenic thrust stage of pre-Commonwealth theatre and the fully scenic stage of Venetian opera houses and the salle à machines in Paris. It was a compromise that was determined in large measure by the need to reconcile the demands of the scenic stage with the acting traditions and repertoire handed on from the Elizabethan and Jacobean theatre. Much of the action in both tragedies and comedies could be played on the apron stage, with the wings and shutters of the scenic stage offering no more than a pleasing visual background against which the actors stood out in relief. However, for discovery scenes, scenes of state and scenes in public parks and piazzas, the long vista opened up by the scenic stage offered the possibility of an attractive visual framework within which the action could be played out. In both tragedies and comedies, the ease with which the setting could be changed, simply by opening or closing a shutter, ensured the smooth progression of the action. And shutters could be opened and closed as actors moved upstage or downstage, making the scenery an integral part of the action.

During the Restoration period, comedies were generally the most popular form of entertainment in the theatre. The evidence of some of the visual material shown below indicates that the blocking conventions used by Restoration actors were surprisingly natural and even naturalistic, to the point where actors were clearly prepared to turn their backs to the audience. In complete contrast, the operatic versions of Shakespearean and other tragedies used the full gamut of spectacular staging conventions available at the time: traps, flying machines, special lighting effects, swift scene changes of wings and borders as well as shutters.

By the early eighteenth century, a less sophisticated audience was attracted into the theatre by different kinds of spectacle: grotesque dancing, tightrope walking, pantomime. All of these entertainments were offered as afterpieces to the main programme; especially in the case of pantomime, the afterpiece was often more popular than the play performed as the major part of the evening's entertainment.

An elegant and attractive tradition of visual staging was established with the introduction of Italian opera onto the London stage after 1705. It proved a popular form of entertainment with wealthy and genteel audiences who enjoyed the combination of musical virtuosity and visual splendour.

Restoration comedy continued to be a popular attraction, side by side with the new sentimental comedies of Cibber and Steele; and the staging conventions for both remained largely unchanged from the Restoration. Even a ballad opera, such as *The Beggar's Opera*, used the relatively simple staging conventions of Restoration comedy, including the natural blocking.

Apart from isolated attempts at unusual staging effects, such as Lediard's 'transparent theatre' shown to London audiences in the 1730s, the scenic practices and conventions of London theatres in the 1730s differed very little from those established by Davenant in his theatres just before and at the very beginning of the Restoration period.

SIR WILLIAM DAVENANT'S OPERAS IN THE 1650S

Throughout the 1650s, a troupe of actors led by Andrew Cane mounted performances at the Red Bull, defying parliamentary ordinances and risking fines and imprisonment. They survived by living from hand to mouth and by bribing the Captain of the Guard; even so, they were subjected to frequent raids by the soldiers. Because of the threat of such raids, a new form of compressed entertainment was evolved at the Red Bull; programmes were made up of so-called 'drolls', or short comic scenes culled from a variety of sources. These collections of drolls were extremely popular with audiences who were otherwise starved of live entertainment.[1]

However, a programme of farcical drolls could not in the long run satisfy the more refined tastes of the many upper-class Royalists who had returned to London after the end of the Civil War. Already by the 1640s, there are records of private performances in houses in Kensington and Knightsbridge,[2] but it was not until Sir William Davenant began his theatrical activities in 1656 that this particular need was met.

As Charles I's poet laureate, Davenant had supplied the text for some of Inigo Jones's sumptuous court masques in the late 1630s. He was therefore intimately acquainted with the kind of elegant visual entertainments that appealed to aristocratic taste at the time. He had hoped to introduce opera and visual spectacle to London audiences when Charles I granted him a patent to build a new theatre in London in 1639, but the outbreak of the Bishops' Wars in 1640 put an end to his plans.[3]

After a flamboyant career during the Civil War as Queen Henrietta Maria's personal messenger, followed by a lengthy spell in the Tower as a result of his capture at sea in 1651, Davenant, in July 1654, managed to obtain a full pardon for his Royalist activities from Oliver Cromwell. (He had a peculiar gift for flattering those in power and talking himself both into and out of the most impossible situations.)

In May 1656, Davenant used the influence of a few friends in high places, notably

Bulstrode Whitelocke who was Lord Commissioner of the Treasury, and obtained permission to mount a series of musical and visual representations in the house he was renting at the time, Rutland House in fashionable Charterhouse Yard. What he offered London audiences was a first taste of visual spectacle in the theatre, along with a moral debate on the pros and cons of theatrical performance, all encompassed within a musical framework. It was called *The First Day's Entertainment at Rutland House* and was intended to be a curtain-raiser for the opera that was to follow in a short space of time.[4] The success of this theatrical debate encouraged him to press on with preparations for his first opera production *The Siege of Rhodes*, which was presented probably in September 1656.

As his scenic designer, Davenant engaged John Webb who was related by marriage to Inigo Jones and had also been one of Jones's star pupils. Despite the cramped space available in Rutland House, for which Davenant was most apologetic in the printed text [*see* **74**], John Webb's settings gave London audiences a first glimpse of the staging techniques Inigo Jones had pioneered in the court masques of the 1630s. A false proscenium established the framework for a perspective setting using pairs of straight rather than angled wings[5] and with shutters in grooves (along with cut-out relieves) providing an elegant but simple method of showing different locations and settings. The only visual innovation was the addition of painted crowds and armies on the shutters, which may possibly have been a technique Davenant had seen in Paris during his period of exile there [*see* **75**].[6]

As in Italy, where opera productions were the means of introducing the world of courtly masques and scenic splendour onto the public stage (as from 1637), so it was in London. On a much more humble scale, necessitated by the privations of the times, Davenant introduced his contemporaries to the delights of the scenic stage through the medium of opera [*see* **76**].

Following his success with *The Siege of Rhodes* at Rutland House, Davenant transferred the production to the rebuilt Phoenix (or Cockpit) in Drury Lane in 1658.[7] He also mounted two further productions at the Phoenix, *The Cruelty of the Spaniards in Peru* (July 1658) and *The History of Sir Francis Drake* (winter, 1658–9).[8] In both he used the same basic approach to staging as in *The Siege of Rhodes*. However, a number of visual devices were introduced into the staging of *The History of Sir Francis Drake* to entertain the audience. A ship was seen to lower its sail, while a rowing boat was seen moving towards the shore [p. 3]; there was also a sensational tableau scene showing 'a beautiful lady tied to a tree, adorned with the ornaments of a bride, with her hair dishevelled' [p. 27]. Such devices may have been intended to compensate for the re-appearance of some of the same scenery as in *The Cruelty of the Spaniards in Peru* but they were to recur in later Restoration productions.[9]

---

[1] See Francis Kirkman's preface to *The Wits*.
[2] See Hotson (1928), pp. 23–4.
[3] See Nethercot (1938), pp. 169–70.
[4] The official report of a government observer at *The First Day's Entertainment* suggests that Davenant had overestimated his potential audience's willingness to pay high ticket prices. The report is reproduced by Hotson (1928), p. 150.
[5] Jones and Webb had used the angled wings of the Serlian stage in their design for *Florimène*, a French pastoral mounted at the great hall in Whitehall in December 1635. See Nicoll (1938), pp. 79–80 and 112–13, and Orrell (1985), pp. 128–48.
[6] See Hotson (1928), p. 154.
[7] See Orrell (1985), pp. 68–71.
[8] Following the destruction of the interior in 1649, William Beeston had rebuilt and refurbished the theatre in 1651 in the vain hope of establishing a theatre company there: all Davenant had to do was install scenery and some machinery for visual effects.
[9] See pp. 96 and 99 below.

74   Davenant's address to the Reader in *The Siege of Rhodes,* September 1656

Sir William Davenant: *The Siege of Rhodes. Made a representation by the art of prospective in scenes and the story sung in recitative music. At the back part of Rutland House in the upper end of Aldersgate Street, London* (London: Henry Herringman, 1656)

To the Reader. It has been often wished that our scenes (we having obliged ourselves to the variety of five changes, according to the ancient dramatic distinctions made for time) had not been confined to eleven foot in height and about fifteen in depth, including the places of passage reserved for the music. This is so narrow an allowance for the fleet of *Solyman* the Magnificent, his army, the island of *Rhodes* and the varieties attending the siege of that city that I fear you will think we invite you to such a contracted trifle as that of the Caesars carved upon a nut. [. . .]

We conceive, it will not be unacceptable to you if we recompense the narrowness of the room by containing in it so much as could be conveniently accomplished by art and industry: which will not be doubted in the scenes by those who can judge that kind of illustration and know the excellency of Mr John Webb who designed and ordered it. [. . .]

75   Illustrations and stage directions from *The Siege of Rhodes,* Rutland House, September 1656

Illustrations from the Chatsworth Settlement. Reproduced in Southern (1952), between pp. 160 and 161. Quotations from the 1656 edition of *The Siege of Rhodes*

(A) FRONTISPIECE AND WINGS

The ornament which encompassed the scene consisted of several columns of gross rustic work, which bore up a large frieze. In the middle of the frieze was a compartment wherein was written RHODES. The compartment was supported by diverse habiliments of war, intermixed with the military ensigns of those several nations who were famous for defence of that island: which were the French, Germans and Spaniards, the Italians, Avergnois and English. The renown of the English valour made the Grand Master Villerius to select their station to be most frequently commanded by himself. The principal enrichment of the frieze was a crimson drapery, whereon several trophies of arms were fixed. Those on the right hand representing such as are chiefly in use amongst the Western nations, together with the proper cognisance of the Order of Rhodian Knights. And on the left, such as are most esteemed in the Eastern countries. And on an antique shield, the Crescent of the Ottomans [pp. 1–2].

(B) THE FIRST SHUTTER: THE PROSPECT OF THE CITY OF RHODES

The scene before the first entry.

The curtain being drawn up, a lightsome sky appeared, discovering a maritime coast, full of craggy rocks and high cliffs, with several verdures naturally growing upon such situations. And, afar off, the true prospect of the city of Rhodes when it was in prosperous estate: with so much view of the gardens and hills about it, as the narrowness of the room could allow the scene. In that part of the horizon

terminated by the sea was represented the Turkish fleet making towards a
promontory some few miles distant from the town. The entry is prepared by
instrumental music [pp. 2–3].

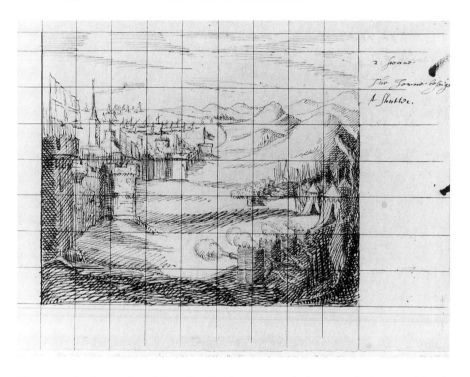

The scene is changed and the city Rhodes appears beleaguered at sea and land.
The entry is again prepared by instrumental music. The second entry [p. 7].

(D) FIRST RELIEVE: SOLYMAN'S THRONE

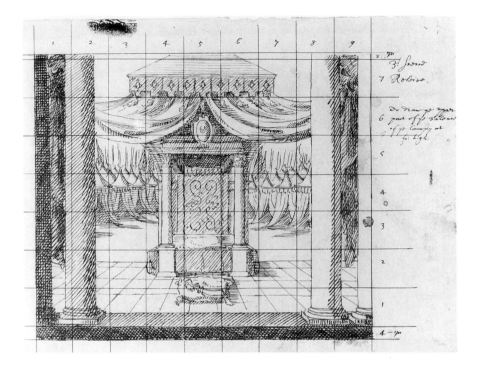

The further part of the Scene is opened and a Royal Pavilion appears displayed, representing Solyman's imperial throne. And about it are discerned the quarters of his bassas and inferior officers. The entry is prepared by instrumental music. The third entry [p. 14].

(E) SECOND RELIEVE: MOUNT PHILERMUS

The scene is varied to the prospect of Mount Philermus. Artificers appearing at work about that castle which was there, with wonderful expedition, erected by Solyman. His great army is discovered in the plain below, drawn up in battalia; as if it were prepared for a general assault. The entry is again prepared by instrumental music. The fourth entry [p. 22].

(F) THIRD SHUTTER: THE GENERAL ASSAULT

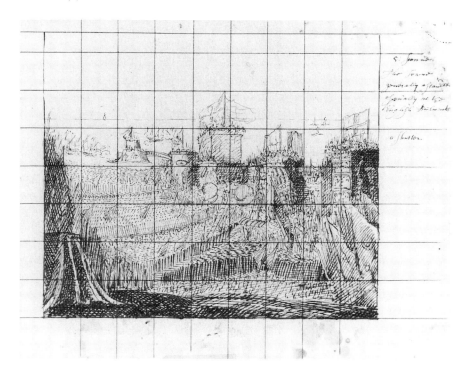

The scene is changed into a representation of a general assault given to the town; the greatest fury of the army being discerned at the English station. The entry is again prepared by instrumental music. The fifth entry [p. 29].

76   John Evelyn sees one of Davenant's operas in 1659
John Evelyn: *The diary of John Evelyn*. Edited by E.S. de Beer (Oxford: Clarendon Press, 1955), vol. 3, p. 229
5 MAY 1659

I went to visit my brother and next day to see a new opera, after the Italian way, in recitative music and scenes, much inferior to the Italian composure and magnificence; but what was prodigious that in a time of such public consternation such a vanity should be kept up or permitted. I being engaged with company could not decently resist the going to see it, though my heart smote me for it.

After the Restoration of Charles II in 1660, there are tantalisingly few descriptions of contemporary theatre practice. There was no formal theatre criticism as such, and there were no official reports on productions written by government observers (as happened in Davenant's case during the interregnum). All that remains are fleeting references to specific theatre visits in the few letters and diaries that are preserved from the period, notably the diaries of Pepys and Evelyn [see 77 and 78], and equally fleeting references to theatrical events in contemporary newsletters such as *The London Gazette*,[1] as well as the Newdigate Newsletters.[2]

The only essay written specifically about the contemporary theatre and its origins was Richard Flecknoe's *Short discourse of the English stage* (1664). Flecknoe was a much travelled Catholic (possibly a priest), who had returned to London in the early 1650s. In his first play, *Love's Dominion* published in 1654, he had made a remarkable plea for the restoration of the stage as a useful moral institution.[3] His talents as a dramatist were limited (Dryden in particular had a very low opinion of him). But his essay on the English stage is an enterprising thumb-nail sketch of English dramatic and theatrical history, providing some useful if basic information. Its reliability as a documentary source is, however, diminished in its closing paragraphs where a number of contradictory statements are made on the issue of stage spectacle in the theatre prior to the Restoration [see 79].[4]

[1] The first daily newspaper in London, *The Daily Courant*, was not started until 1702. Prior to that, various newsletters had been published throughout the seventeenth century, providing their readers with much abridged versions of political and religious news. There were also occasional reports of unusual or sensational events. Items of news from the London theatres were reported only when they fell into the latter category. See Charles H. Gray: *Theatrical Criticism in London to 1795* (New York: Columbia University Press, 1931), pp. 28–9.

[2] See John Harold Wilson: 'Theatre notes from the Newdigate Newsletters' *TN* 15 (1960–1), 79–84 and 'A theatre in York House' *TN* 16 (1961–2), 59. See also Philip Hines Jr: 'Theatre items from the Newdigate Newsletters' *TN* 39 (1985), 76–83.

[3] See Summers (1936), p. 207.

[4] See Kenneth Richards: 'Changeable scenery for plays on the Caroline stage' *TN* 23 (1968–9), 6–20.

77   John Evelyn comments on the scenery in *The Indian Queen*

Evelyn (de Beer ed.), vol. 3, pp. 368–9
5 FEBRUARY 1664

I saw acted *The Indian Queen*, a tragedy well written, but so beautified with rich scenes as the like had never been seen here or haply (except rarely anywhere else) on a mercenary theatre.

78   Pepys comments on the effects of stage lighting and theatre music, 1666–8

Pepys (Latham and Matthews eds.), vol. 7, pp. 76–7

(A) 19 MARCH 1666

After dinner we walked to the King's playhouse, all in dirt, they being altering of the stage to make it wider. But God knows when they will begin to act again. But my business here was to see the inside of the stage and all the tiring rooms and machines; and indeed, it was a sight worthy seeing. But to see their clothes and the various sorts, and what a mixture of things there was – here a wooden leg, there a ruff, here a hobby-horse, there a crown – would make a man split himself to see with laughing. And particularly Lacy's wardrobe and Shattrell's. But then again, to think how fine they show on the stage by candle light and how poor things they are to look now too near hand is not pleasant at all. The machines are fine and the paintings very pretty.

(B) 12 MAY 1669 (vol. 4, pp. 552–3)

[. . .] After dinner my wife and I to the Duke of York's playhouse and there, in the side balcony over against the music, did hear but not see a new play the first day acted, *The Roman Virgin*, an old play and but ordinary I thought;[1] but the trouble of my eyes with the light of the candles did almost kill me.

(C) 27 FEBRUARY 1668 (vol. 9, pp. 93–4)

[. . .] With my wife and Deb to the King's House, to see *The Virgin Martyr*, the first time it has been acted a great while; and it is mighty pleasant; not that the play is worth much but it is finely acted by Becke Marshall. But that which did please me beyond anything in the whole world was the wind music when the angel comes down, which is so sweet that it ravished me and indeed, in a word, did wrap up my soul so that it made me really sick, just as I have formerly been when in love with my wife; that neither then, nor all the evening going home, and at home, I was able to think of anything but remained all night transported. [. . .]

[1] Pepys is referring in this conflated statement to the fact that Betterton's new play *The Roman Virgin* was in fact an adaptation of Webster's *Appius and Virginia*. Any possible confusion here was of Pepys's own making, as Betterton did not publish *The Roman Virgin* as one of his plays, nor did he ever claim that it was anything other than an adaptation.

79   Flecknoe's comments on the scenic stage of the Restoration, 1664

Richard Flecknoe: *A short discourse of the English stage* (London: R. Wood, 1664)

Now for the difference betwixt our theatres and those of former times. They were but plain and simple, with no other scenes nor decorations of the stage but only old tapestry, and the stage strewed with rushes (with their habits accordingly), whereas ours now for cost and ornament are arrived to the height of magnificence. But that which makes our stage the better makes our plays the worse perhaps, they striving now to make them more for sight than hearing. Whence that solid joy of the interior is lost and that great benefit which men formerly received from plays from which they seldom or never went away, but far better and wiser than they came. [. . .]

For scenes and machines, they are no new invention, our masques and some of our plays in former times (though not so ordinary) having had as good or rather better than any we have now.[1]

They are excellent helps of imagination, most grateful deceptions of the sight and graceful and becoming ornaments of the stage, transporting you easily without lassitude from one place to another; or rather by a kind of delightful magic, whilst you sit still, does bring the place to you. Of this curious art the Italians (this latter age) are the greatest masters, the French good proficients, and we in England only scholars and learners yet, having proceeded no further than to bear-baiting and not arrived to the stupendous wonders of your great engineers, especially not knowing yet how to place our lights for the advantage and illumination of the scenes. [. . .]

[1] Flecknoe's reference to the use of scenes and machines before the Restoration may of course be exclusively concerned with productions at court, where pastorals as well as masques were performed on scenic stages. This may be the implication of his comment in brackets that such productions were 'not so ordinary'.

SETTLE'S *EMPRESS OF MOROCCO*

While there are few descriptive accounts of Restoration theatre practice, there is if anything even less visual material extant or so far discovered. There are no original scene designs and very few published engravings showing contemporary theatre settings. Only one play was published during the period containing a set of illustrations from the current production: namely, the 1673 edition of Settle's play *The Empress of Morocco*, presented at Dorset Garden in the same year. However, this unique set of five illustrations does give a fascinating insight into some aspects of Restoration staging methods. (The main omission is in the area of lighting.)

If one looks at the complete set of illustrations, it seems clear that both wings and borders were changed at significant points in the action, which means that this was obviously a spectacular and expensive production; what is also shown is the way the scenic area was used by the actors during 'discoveries' and in scenes requiring large numbers of characters on stage.

80   Stage settings for Settle's *The Empress of Morocco* at Dorset Garden, 1673

Elkanah Settle: *The Empress of Morocco. A tragedy with sculptures. As it is acted at the Duke's Theatre* (London: William Cademan, 1673)

(A) ACT ONE

The opening dungeon scene in Act 1 shows three pairs of wings, three sets of arched borders, a back shutter and what may have been a practical lantern suspended over the scenic area. Muly Labas and Morena are clearly revealed acting within the scenic stage at this juncture.

First act, scene the first. Scene opens, Muly Labas appears bound in chains, attended by guards. Enter Morena bound [pp. 1–2].

(B) ACT TWO

The setting for Act 2, scene i shows one pair of wings behind which there is presumably a practical sea-scape made up of revolving water-rows. Several sailing ships are depicted, some of which were probably capable of lowering their sails, and there is a rowing boat moving towards the shore. Both of these scenic devices had first been shown to London audiences by Sir William Davenant in *The History of Sir Francis Drake* (1658–9) at The Phoenix [Cockpit] in Drury Lane.[1]

Act the second, scene the first. The scene opened is represented the prospect of a large river with a glorious fleet of ships, supposed to be the navy of Muly Hamet. After the sound of trumpets and the discharging of guns, enter King, Young Queen, Hametalhaz and attendants [p. 8].

(C) ACT TWO

The third illustration has no details of the wings and back shutters; however, the stage directions imply that the whole length of the scenic stage is used for 'a state', a scene that has to accommodate a large throng of actors, dancers and musicians. A large practical palm tree is brought onto the stage as a centre piece, fulfilling a function similar to a relieve.

The scene opened. A state is presented, the King, Queen and Mariamne seated, Muly Hamet, Abdelcador and attendants. A Moorish dance is presented by Moors in several habits, who bring in an artificial palm tree about which they dance to several antique instruments of music. In the intervals of the dance, this song is sung by a Moorish priest and two Moorish women; the chorus of it being performed by all the Moors [. . .] [p. 13].

(D) ACT FOUR

The masque scene from Act 4 seems to be a deliberate visual reference to the kind of masquing house used in the early 1600s, notably in Ben Jonson's *Masque of Queens*.[2] Furies rise from below the stage and are flown from above. There are no wings shown, but we are given a glimpse of what may be the main drapes behind the proscenium arch or possibly the hint of a traverse curtain as used by Inigo Jones in these early masques.[3] Once again, the scenic area is crowded with characters for this spectacular scene.

Act four, scene three. The Masque. The scene opened is presented a hell, in which Pluto, Proserpine and other women spirits appear seated, attended by furies. The stage being filled on each side with Crimalhaz, Hamet, Queen Mother and all the court in masquerade. After soft music, enter Orpheus [p. 46].

(E) ACT FIVE

The final scene illustrated is from the end of Act 5. The villain Crimalhaz is discovered impaled on a wall set with spikes. This too seems to be an example of a scenic device first introduced by Davenant in his production of *The History of Sir Francis Drake*: the 'discovery' of a spectacular visual tableau.[4] The figures impaled in the background beyond two sets of wings and borders were probably papier mâché or cardboard figures slung over a relieve scene.

Act five, final scene. Here the scene opens and Crimalhaz appears cast down on the gaunches, being hung on a wall set with spikes of iron. Enter again Abdelcador:

> See the reward of treason; death's the thing
> Distinguishes the usurper from the King [p. 70].

Other scenes from the play were not illustrated. These included palace interiors and exteriors and were presumably stock shutters that allowed the far upstage scenic area to be prepared for the next flamboyant visual spectacle or 'discovery'.

[1] See Nethercot (1938), p. 33 who first drew attention to these devices, set out in the stage directions of the opera.
[2] For a full account of this masque, see Southern (1962), pp. 188–93.
[3] See Southern (1962), p. 193.
[4] See Campbell (1923), p. 228 and Nethercot (1938), p. 333.

Throughout the Restoration period, the most spectacular effects on stage were reserved for operatic productions. These were expensive to mount but their popularity with contemporary audiences offered the prospect of rich rewards. The new theatres at Dorset Garden and Drury Lane (particularly the former) were well equipped with scenes and machines to show their audiences what could be achieved in terms of visual spectacle.

Generally, Davenant and Betterton led the way with their spectacular productions: Davenant at Lincoln's Inn Fields in the 1660s and Betterton at Dorset Garden in the 1670s. (Killigrew's troupe tended to follow their lead.) Betterton obviously shared Davenant's passion for the scenic stage and acquired from him an invaluable technical expertise. Throughout his career as a company manager, Betterton mounted a series of lavish and lovingly conceived operatic productions that delighted his contemporaries.[1] John Downes, Betterton's prompter, makes a number of brief but appreciative comments on the success of these productions in his *Roscius Anglicanus* of 1708 [see **81**].

[1] On average this meant one production per season, apart from the decade 1678–88 when political upheavals diminished theatre audiences to the point where the financial risk was too great. For the complete list, see Milhous (1979), pp. 44–5.

81   John Downes comments on the success of different operas during the 1670s

John Downes: *Roscius Anglicanus or an historical review of the stage*, edited by Montague Summers (London: The Fortune Press, n.d.)

(A) THE TRAGEDY OF *MACBETH*, 1673 [p. 33]

The tragedy of *Macbeth*, altered by Sir William Davenant; being dressed in all its finery, as new clothes, new scenes, machines, as flyings for the witches; with all the singing and dancing in it. The first composed by Mr Locke, the other by Mr Channell and Mr Joseph Priest. It being excellently performed, being in the nature of an opera, it recompensed double the expense; it proves still a lasting play.

(B) *THE TEMPEST*, 1674 [pp. 34–5][1]

The year after in 1673.[2] *The Tempest, or the Enchanted Island* made into an opera by Mr Shadwell, having all new in it, as scenes, machines. Particularly one scene painted with myriads of ariel spirits, and another flying away with a table furnished with fruits, sweetmeats and all sorts of viands just when Duke Trinculo and his companions were going to dinner. All things performed in it so admirably well that not any succeeding opera got more money.

(C) *PSYCHE*, 1675 [pp. 35–6]

In February 1672.[3] The long expected opera of *Psyche* came forth in all her ornaments: new scenes, new machines, new clothes, new French dances. This opera was splendidly set out, especially in scenes. The charge of which amounted to above £800. It had a continuance of performance about eight days together. It proved very beneficial to the company. Yet *The Tempest* got them more money.

(D) *CIRCE*, 1677 [pp. 36–7]

Circe, an opera written by Dr Davenant. [...] All the music was set by Mr Banister, and being well performed, it answered the expectation of the company.

(E) *ALBION AND ALBANIUS*, 1685 [p. 40]

In anno 1685. The opera of *Albion and Albanius* was performed, written by Mr Dryden and composed by Monsieur Grabut. This being performed on a very unlucky day, being the day the Duke of Monmouth landed in the West. The nation being in a great consternation, it was performed but six times, which not answering half the charge they were at, involved the company very much in debt.

[1] For a detailed account of this production, see Powell (1984), pp. 62–83.
[2] Downes is referring to the next season, i.e. 1673–4.
[3] This is an error of memory or transcription. *Psyche* opened in February 1675.

Drury Lane

In the increasingly competitive atmosphere of the 1670s, Killigrew's troupe attempted to emulate Betterton's success with operatic productions in their newly opened playhouse in Drury Lane. In March 1674, they mounted a production of a French opera called *Ariadne: or, the Marriage of Bacchus* originally composed by Pierre Perrin, but set to music for this production by M. Grabut, Master of His Majesty's Music. There is no record of how the production was received,[1] nor of who sang in it. (Though it seems likely that some of the French singers who were to act in *Calisto* in the following season may have already been in London.)[2] However, the published libretto of the opera contains some fascinating stage directions for a number of spectacular scenes in which full use is made of traps, flying machines and water-rows [see **82b** and **c**]. Echoes of court masques from the 1630s may be detected in the regal pomp and splendour of the final scene. The published libretto contains, in addition, an illustration showing the stage setting for the prologue to the opera, as it was presented at Drury Lane in 1674. This is the only surviving illustration of an opera production during the Restoration period.

The illustration suggests that a false proscenium had been constructed at the front of the forestage,[3] behind which are shown six sets of flats in perspective, depicting a palace setting. As Allan Jackson has demonstrated, the palace setting seems based on Michelangelo's Campidoglio, Palace of the Conservator in Rome.[4] Upstage of the wings, a series of water-rows permit a machine fronted by a large scallop shell to rise from the waves and convey onto the stage a number of river goddesses. Above them a set of cupids are seen in the Heavens, flown in by a suitable cloud machine. Despite the Italian flavour of the palace setting depicted on the wings, the back shutter shows a view of contemporary London [see **82a**]. Throughout the period, scene painters made skilful reference to earlier and contemporary styles of architecture and painting, and views of contemporary London were always greatly favoured.[5]

[1] In his account of the production, Jocelyn Powell suggests that *Ariadne* was not a success [p. 48]. There is, however, no firm evidence to support such a view.
[2] See *LS*, pt. 1, p. 215.
[3] This was a standard practice for spectacular operatic productions, as is clear from the printed stage directions to Dryden's *Albion and Albanius*. See pp. 104–5 below.
[4] See Allan S. Jackson: 'Restoration scenery, 1656–80' *Restoration and eighteenth-century theatre research* 3, no. 2 (November 1964), 28–9.
[5] *Ibid.* pp. 29–33.

82   The setting for the Prologue and two spectacular scenes from the opera *Ariadne* at Drury Lane in 1674

Ariadne; or, the Marriage of Bacchus. An opera or a vocal representation, first composed by Monsieur P.P. Now put into music by Monsier Grabut, Master of His Majesty's Music. And acted by the Royal Academy of Music at the Theatre Royal in Covent Garden (London: Tho. Newcombe, 1674)

(A) THE FRONTISPIECE

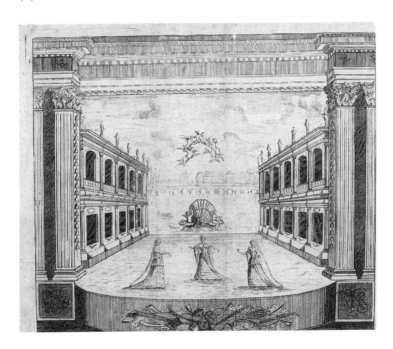

(B) THE PROLOGUE

First opening of the theatre by a symphony, showing a prospect of [the] Thames opposite to London, on the waves of which is seen floating a great shell, as it were of mother of pearl, bearing three nymphs representing three rivers: Thames, Tiber and Seine. Which nymphs sing the prologue thus. The first representing the Thames, inviting the other two to approach, sings this the Prologue:

THAMES.   Approach, approach fair sisters, cross the main,

    To come and taste my sweets, ye Tiber and Seine. [. . .]

These three nymphs having near done singing, a fourth appears born as the former, representing the river Po.

(C) FIRST AND SECOND MASQUE ENTRY [pp. 21–2]

First Masque Entry

The Bacchants, abhorring the falsity of Theseus, run Fury-like, their burning torches in their hands, to burn him in his ship as they see him sail on the sea; but the waves and billows do force them back to the shore. During the conflict, Thetis the goddess of the sea, who is of kin to Bacchus and sees their bold attempt, surges up out of the water and strives to oppose their rage. The Bacchants, persisting in their design, the sea gods enter.

Second Masque Entry

A huge sea monster swimming near the shore where the Bacchants are still striving against the waves enters combat with them. The Bacchants leave their torches and with darts wound the monster, whereupon he vomits out of his jaws several sea gods and plunges into the sea. These fall a wrestling with the Bacchants and do form a regular fight, after which they grasp each other fast in their arms and precipitate themselves all into the sea.

(D) ACT 5, SCENE VII [pp. 49–52]

All the actors are seen in this last scene. Oboes and symphonists of Venus playing. Shepherds, shepherdesses and clowns.

A glittering palace comes down from Heaven, on the middle of which is seen a royal throne; over the throne hangs a crown made of seven precious stones, the crown suspended by four little cupids flying. Venus with the three Graces sits on the throne with bands of symphonists about her. During the symphony, the palace and throne descend slowly upon the theatre, where being fixed, Venus and the Graces come down from the throne and, taking the new married pair, lead them by the hand and place them on the same, Bacchus in the middle, Ariadne on his right, Venus on his left hand and the Graces at their feet. Symphonists playing. [. . .]

The seven gems which composed her crown are inflamed of a sudden and changed into so many bright stars, known in Heaven by the name of Ariadne's Hair. [. . .]

The clowns dance to the sound of voices and instruments all the while the palace is drawing up.

Albion and Albanius at Dorset Garden

The popularity of contemporary visual references in opera productions is shown yet again in the setting for Dryden's opera *Albion and Albanius*, presented at Dorset Garden in 1685. Despite his earlier disparaging comments on opera in his prologue for the opening of Drury Lane (which he called 'a plain built house' by comparison with Dorset Garden where 'scenes, machines and empty operas reign'), Dryden was tempted to write this masque-like opera at a time when the royalist position was once again under threat. Unfortunately for him and the United Companies, Monmouth's rebellion put a stop to the opera's run after only six performances [see 81]. The detailed stage directions, prepared by Betterton from his prompt copy, not only show just how much contemporary reference was made in the different settings, but also give a vivid impression of the spectacular effects created on stage [see 83].

83   The Frontispiece and some of the settings for Dryden's opera *Albion and Albanius,* as described by Betterton, 1685

John Dryden: *Albion and Albanius: an opera.* Performed at the Queen's Theatre in Dorset Garden (London: Tonson, 1685)

(A) THE PREFACE

[. . .] The descriptions of the scenes and other decorations of the stage I had from Mr Betterton who has spared neither for industry nor cost to make this entertainment perfect, nor for invention of the ornaments to beautify it.

(B) THE FRONTISPIECE

The curtain rises and a new frontispiece is seen, joined to the great pilasters, which are on each side of the stage. On the flat of each basis is a shield, adorned with gold; in the middle of the shield, on one side, are two hearts, a small scroll of gold over them and an imperial crown over the scroll. On the other hand, in the shield, are two quivers full of arrows saltire, etc. Upon each basis stands a figure bigger than the life: one represents peace, with a palm in one and an olive branch in the other hand; the other plenty, holding a cornucopia and resting on a pillar. Behind these figures are large columns of the Corinthian order, adorned with fruit and flowers. Over one of the figures on the trees is the King's cypher; over the other, the Queen's. [. . .]

(C) DECORATIONS OF THE STAGE IN THE FIRST ACT [p. 1]

The curtain rises and there appears on either side of the stage, next to the frontispiece, a statue on horseback, of gold on pedestals of marble enriched with gold and bearing the imperial arms of England. One of these statues is taken from that of the late King at Charing Cross; the other from that figure of his present Majesty (done by that noble artist Mr Gibbons) at Windsor.

The scene is a street of palaces, which lead to the front of the Royal Exchange. The great arch is open and the view is continued through the open part of the Exchange to the arch on the other side and thence to as much of the street beyond as could possibly be taken.[1]

(D) ACT 2, SCENE I [p. 10]

The scene is a poetical hell. The change is total; the upper part of the house as well as the side scenes. There is the figure of Prometheus, chained to a rock, the vulture gnawing his liver. Sisyphus rolling the stone, the Belides, etc. Beyond, abundance of figures in various torments. Then a great arch of fire. Behind this three pyramids of flames in perpetual agitation. Beyond this, glowing fire which terminates the prospect.

(E) ACT 3, SCENE I [pp. 25 and 27]

The cave of Proteus rises out of the sea; it consists of several arches of rock work, adorned with mother of pearl, coral and abundance of shells of various kinds. Through the arches is seen the sea and parts of Dover pier. In the middle of the cave is Proteus asleep on a rock adorned with shells, etc. like the cave. [. . .]

A machine rises out of the sea. It opens and discovers Venus and Albanius sitting in a great scallop shell, richly adorned. Venus is attended by the Loves and Graces, Albanius by heroes. The shell is drawn by dolphins. It moves forward, while a symphony of flutes-doux, etc. is playing, till it lands them on the stage and then it closes and sinks.

[1] The mixture of an imaginary or Italianate palace setting shown on the wings and a back shutter (in this case with a relieve), showing a London scene, is the same as in the production of *Ariadne*.

OPERA AND STAGE SPECTACLE AT THE TURN OF THE CENTURY

Following the actors' rebellion of 1695 and the establishment of a new acting company at Lincoln's Inn Fields, there was intense and ruthless competition between Drury Lane and Lincoln's Inn Fields. In order to attract larger audiences into their rival theatres, including relatively unsophisticated members of the public, the two companies began to introduce a variety of additional entertainments into their repertoires: initially dancers and singers (often engaged at great expense), but later acrobats, animal shows and separate afterpieces. The two houses also offered an increasing amount of music and musical drama in their repertoires, including commemorative masques such as the one performed at Lincoln's Inn Fields to celebrate King William's triumph at the battle of Namur in the autumn of 1695.[1]

Inevitably, the intense competition between the two houses also involved an increasing use of stage spectacle and scenic effects, with Rich determined to outshine his rivals at Lincoln's Inn Fields, particularly Betterton who was the acknowledged master of spectacular and operatic theatre. The process began with a sumptuous production of Settle's opera *The World in the Moon* at Dorset Garden in June 1697 (Rich still controlled Dorset Garden at the time, though his company normally played at Drury Lane). Despite lavish new scenic effects, the summer première proved to be a great disadvantage. Much to the relief of the company at Lincoln's Inn Fields, Rich failed on this occasion to capture the enthusiasm of London's audiences.

After further operatic competition between the two companies in the late 1690s,[2] Rich once again decided to mount another spectacular production of an opera by Settle in May 1701. *The Virgin Prophetess*, performed this time at Drury Lane, marked a high point in terms of visual extravagance, unequalled by any later eighteenth-century production on the London stage.[3] Unfortunately, there are no illustrations or design sketches extant for this production, but the very detailed stage directions give some indication of the visual splendours achieved, with multiple settings giving the illusion of enormous height and depth to the stage.

[1] See Milhous (1979), p. 94.
[2] *Ibid.*, pp. 139–40.
[3] See Rosenfeld (1973), p. 58.

84   The setting for Cupid's Palace in Settle's opera *The Virgin Prophetess*

Elkanah Settle: *The Virgin Prophetess: or the fate of Troy. An opera performed at the Theatre Royal by His Majesty's Servants* (London: A. Roper, 1701), pp. 21–2

The scene opens and discovers Paris and Helen seated upon thrones between the scenes, etc. In the middle of the scenes and under the second grand arch, a painted curtain hangs down to the ground, reaching upwards only thirteen foot and the like in width, the whole prospect of the roof of the scenes being seen about eleven foot over it. Before this curtain, upon two rich couches, lie two painted cupids as big as the life.

Here a symphony plays and immediately the two cupids start from their couches and, flying up, take hold of the upper corners of the curtain and draw it up: two more cupids of the same bulk, absconded before behind the couches, rising with the curtain at the two lower corners.

Here is discovered a small set of scenes, being twelve foot high and the like breadth, consisting of three pairs of wings and a flat scene: the objects being a palace of cupid with blue pillars, with silver bases and capitals, hung round with wreaths of flowers, the inner prospect terminating in bowers, fountains, etc.

The symphony still continuing, out of this set are drawn forth on each side, two more sets of scenes exactly in unison with the inner set, the first set being no ways diminished and the whole three perspectives now reaching to twenty-five foot width. Here the curtain advances yet higher and discovers a fourth set of scenes over the middle set, in which Cupid sits in glory; while from the sides of this set spring two scenes which cover the two outmost palaces. This machine now filling the whole house and reaching twenty-four foot high, making so many vistas of palace work.

Arsinoe

The production of *The Virgin Prophetess* proved less of a success than Rich would have liked. It was not until 1705 that he mounted his next operatic production, goaded into doing so by the prospect of Vanbrugh opening his new Haymarket theatre with a series of operas. Before the Haymarket was ready to open its doors to the public, Rich offered London audiences his most successful operatic work to date: *Arsinoe, Queen of Cyprus*, with music by Thomas Clayton and the libretto translated by Peter Motteux. The opera opened on 16 January 1705 and was an enormous public success. Although sung in English, Clayton admitted in his preface to the published libretto that his aim was 'to introduce the Italian manner of music on the English stage, which has not been before attempted'.[1]

The stage settings for *Arsinoe* were designed by Sir James Thornhill, and four of his design sketches for the production have fortunately been preserved. Although these represent an early stage in the design process, they nevertheless give some idea of the variety and scope of operatic scenery at the turn of the century.

The production was clearly an expensive one. All four settings use quite different wing flats, although the arched borders for the two interior settings appear to be the same, and the two exterior settings use standard cloud borders. The wings for the 'garden by moonlight' and 'a room of state' do not use symmetrically matched designs, but offer visual variations on the central theme of each setting. The garden wings have statues and trees stage right, counterbalanced by foliage-clad pillars with decorative fountain basins stage left. The room of state has a series of alcoves painted at contrasting angles on the wings of either side of the stage.

The back shutters for all four settings are very detailed, offering a pleasing variety of pastoral exterior settings and one ornate Baroque interior [see **85b**]. The general aim, especially in the pastoral views, is to give the illusion of a lengthy perspective, culminating in a series of distant views: formal gardens, with an ornamental pond and a river [see **85c**]; formal gardens with ships on a great river and mountains in the background [see **85d**]; a splendid mansion with a large fountain in the foreground and a mountain landscape in the distance [see **85a**]. In two of the settings [see **85a** and **b**], Arsinoe is shown reclining on a couch that is set either mid-stage or upstage. This seems to indicate the use of the scenic stage for a significant part of the action.

¹ Thomas Clayton: *Arsinoe, Queen of Cyprus*. An opera after the Italian manner. As it is performed at the Theatre Royal in Drury Lane by Her Majesty's Servants (London: Tonson, 1705), The Preface.

85   Sir James Thornhill's design sketches for Clayton's setting of *Arsinoe*, 1705

Theatre Museum, London. Reproduced in *The Revels history of drama in English*, vol. 5 (1976), plates 10–13

(A) ACT I, SCENE I
Arsinoe sleeping. A garden by moonlight.

(B) ACT I, SCENE III
A room of state with statues and busts. Arsinoe on a couch.[1]

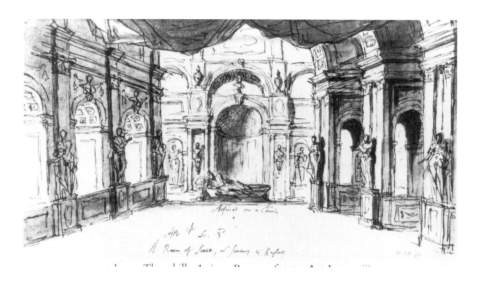

(C) ACT 2, SCENE I
A great hall looking out on a garden.

(D) ACT 2, SCENE III
Arsinoe in a fine garden, with ships, haven, etc.[2]

[1] The stage directions in the printed libretto state: Act 1, scene x. The Queen's apartment. Arsinoe alone upon a couch [p. 10].
[2] The stage directions in the printed libretto state: Act 2, scene viii: Arsinoe alone. A garden. She sits down and reposes her arm [p 23].

RESTORATION COMEDY AND THE SCENIC STAGE

One of the frustrations confronting theatre historians of the Restoration period is the dearth of pictorial material showing the staging of Restoration comedy. There are various portraits of Restoration actors in costume, and there are many illustrations in editions of the plays published in the early decades of the eighteenth century that show the characters involved in key scenes. In neither case is any significant stress placed on stage setting.

One point is, however, clearly demonstrated in these various frontispiece illustrations. The frequency with which characters are shown standing with their backs to the viewer indicates a willingness, on behalf of contemporary audiences, to accept what today might be regarded as almost naturalistic blocking. Actors and actresses are shown facing resolutely upstage as they stand or kneel [see **86a** and **86b**]. The same point is confirmed in Hogarth's painting of *The Beggar's Opera* where Lucy Lockit is depicted kneeling with her back to the audience [see **98**].

86   Natural blocking in plays by Etherege and Centlivre

(B) SUSANNA CENTLIVRE: *The Busy Body*
(London: Bernard Lintot, 1732), frontispiece

(A) SIR GEORGE ETHEREGE: *THE MAN
OF MODE, OR, SIR FOPLING FLUTTER*
(London: Tonson, 1735), frontispiece.
Reproduced in Summers (1935), p. 416

The stage directions in Restoration comedies tend to be far shorter and far less informative than those required by elaborate operas and semi-operas. However, a number of points may be inferred from the admittedly brief but nonetheless precise directions printed in certain plays.

It is quite clear that the practical stage doors were of great use to actors for indoor settings that required doors to be locked or knocked forcefully. Equally, they were found useful in exterior settings where an element of sexual pursuit was involved [*see* **87**].

Much of the action obviously took place on the forestage, in front of shutters showing stock interiors.[1] However, at some point in the action of most comedies, groups of characters are 'discovered' in the scenic area when the downstage shutters are drawn apart. The action continues without a break, and the characters either remain in the scenic area or, as happens more frequently when there are only one or two characters on stage, they move forward onto the thrust stage. On some occasions, when the dialogue suggests that the characters move downstage into another room, the directions specify that a shutter closes behind them [*see* **88**].

---

[1] In his book, *The ornament of action* (1979), Peter Holland argues that the main scenic distinction between Restoration comedy and tragedy may be seen in the way comedy was played predominantly on the forestage and tragedy in the scenic stage: 'Restoration tragedy was based on theatrical illusion, the separation from the audience that was practicable by acting principally behind the proscenium: Restoration comedy emphasised its close connection with its audience – and hence its claim, through its *vraisemblance* in acting and locale, to comment on the audience's morals – by placing the action principally on the forestage' [p. 29]. Although the stage directions of Restoration tragedies clearly imply a more frequent use of the scenic stage than in comedy, the evidence of asides and later illustrations indicates that tragic actors made frequent use of the forestage.

87   The use of stage doors in Restoration comedy

Sir George Etherege: *She would if she could* (London: Henry Herringman, 1668), pp. 16–17

Act 2, scene i. The Mulberry Garden.

(*Enter Ariana and Gatty with vizards and pass nimbly over the stage. [...] Freeman and Courtall go after the women. Enter women again and cross the stage. [...] The women go out and go about behind the scenes to the other door. Enter Courtall and Freeman. [...] Enter the women and after them Courtall at the lower door and Freeman at the upper on the contrary side.*)

88   The use of shutters in Restoration comedy

Sir John Vanbrugh: *The Confederacy* (London: Tonson, 1705), pp. 64–5

Act 5, scene ii.

(*Scene opens. Araminta, Corinna, Gripe and Moneytrap at a tea table, very gay and laughing. Clarissa comes into them.*) [...] (*Enter Mr Clip.*) [...]

GRIPE. Well, Mr Clip, no news yet of my wife's necklace?

CLIP. If you please to let me speak with you in the next room, I have something to say to you.

GRIP. Ay, with all my heart. Shut the door after us.

(*They come forward and the scene shuts behind them.*)

Well, any news?

The only illustration that conveys something of the flavour of a Restoration comedy setting, albeit on the cramped stage of the Little Theatre in the Haymarket, is an engraving from 1737 showing a performance of Fielding's satiric comedy *Pasquin*. In this illustration the forestage is much shortened by comparison with normal Restoration practice, but the drawing clearly shows the use of a stock downstage shutter with a neutral interior setting. It also shows the hooped stage lights suspended above the acting area. Above all, it indicates the intimacy of contact between stage and auditorium that was a key feature of the Restoration and early eighteenth-century stage [*see* **89**].

89   The Little Theatre in the Haymarket, 1737

Henry Fielding: *Pasquin. A dramatic satire on the times, being the rehearsal of two plays, a comedy called the election and a tragedy called the life and death of common sense. As it is acted at the theatre in the Haymarket*. Tenth edition (London: Ed. Cook, 1737), frontispiece. [Theatre Museum] Reproduced in Fiske (1973), facing p. 49

J. Smith Inv.t et Sculp.t

ITALIAN OPERA IN LONDON

The failure of English composers and librettists to build effectively on the tradition of Purcell's semi-operas from the 1690s left the way open in the 1700s to the Italian style of operatic writing. Following the success of Clayton's *Arsinoe* in 1705, which was effectively an Italian opera sung in English, there was a gradual increase every season in the numbers of Italian or Italianate operas offered to London audiences: to begin with sung in English, then partly in English and partly in Italian, finally completely in Italian with published translations for audiences to follow during the performance.

Thomyris at Drury Lane in 1706–7 was the first opera to use an Italian castrato. *Pyrrhus and Demetrius* at the Queen's Theatre in 1708–9 was the first bilingual opera and included in its cast the famous Italian castrato Nicolini. Various illustrations have survived of this production in rehearsal (and rehearsals were often conducted in public).[1]

Following this successful production, *Idaspe* in October 1709 was the first opera to be sung wholly in Italian at the Queen's Theatre [*see* **90a**]. From this point the popularity of Italian opera was beyond dispute. When Handel arrived in London in 1711, he found receptive audiences for the series of Italian operas he wrote, beginning in February 1711 with *Rinaldo*.

The sets for Italian opera were sometimes less spectacular than those used for earlier English masques and semi-operas. Often what was required was a palace setting, reminiscent of the 'palais à volonté' of the French neo-classic stage. Hogarth's caricature of a 1723 production of *Rinaldo* gives some idea of a typical generalised palace setting of the period [*see* **91**]. The settings for such Italian operas were clearly pleasing to the eye and of comparable standard to those of the Paris and Italian theatres, as confirmed by foreign visitors to London in 1710 and 1726 [*see* **90a** and **90b**].

[1] For the complete set of illustrations see Eric Walter White: 'The rehearsal of an opera' *TN* 14 (1959–60), 79–90 and plates 1–6

90   Foreign visitors comment on Italian opera in London

(A) HERR VON UFFENBACH COMMENTS ON OPERA AT THE QUEEN'S THEATRE IN 1710

London in 1710. From the travels of Z.C. von Uffenbach, translated and edited by W.H. Quarrell and M. Mare (London: Faber & Faber, 1934), pp. 17–18. The original text may be found in Z.C. von Uffenbach: *Merkwürdige Reisen durch Niedersachsen, Holland und Engelland*, vol. 2 (Ulm and Memmingen: Johann Friedrich Gaum, 1753), pp. 440–2

In the evening we went to the opera *Hidaspis*, which was being given for the last time, because it was summer, when the Lords for the most part reside in the country. The opera house is in the Haymarket, which is a large square. It is not at all large but is certainly very massive and handsomely built. The opera was very lovely in all respects, in composition, music and representation. I am sure that, as far as the first two items are concerned, nothing could be better, even in Italy. The singers were few in number but all were excellent, especially the principal and the Director Nicolai who has already been much admired in Venice but has greatly advanced himself here, because he earns prodigiously large sums of money. The best of the females is Margarite de l'Epine who has also done very well for herself. The orchestra too is so well composed that it could not be better. They are all foreigners, mostly Germans and then French, for the English are not much better musicians than the Dutch, and they are fairly bad. The conductor is Pepusch from Brandenburg, who is known everywhere for his amazingly elegant compositions. The scenery and properties had all been made expressly for the opera and were very fine, though not as costly as those in Italy; but the costumes were of the finest and the performances were in all things most natural and uncommonly elegant. In especial the representation of the lion with which Hidaspes has to fight was incomparably fine. The fellow who played him was not only wrapped in a lion-skin, but moreover nothing could be seen of his feet, which usually betray the fact that a man is hidden within. We were filled with surprise at the way in which the fellow could spring about so nimbly on the ground on all fours as well as on his hind legs. The singers expressed so well the emotions they must represent that I have never seen the like, above all Nicolini, who excels all actors in the world in this respect.

(B) M. DE MURALT COMMENTS ON LONDON OPERA IN 1726
Béat Louis de Muralt: *Letters describing the character and customs of the English and French nations*, second edition (London: T. Edlin, 1726), p. 32

The English have their operas too, but they don't make any great noise about them, nor will I say much on the subject. The music seems to me to be but indifferent, the machines are near as good as those at Paris, the decorations are fine, but above all that made of satin is extraordinary magnificent. They don't dance as well as the French, but on the other hand, they dance less frequently and perhaps more to the purpose. The same thing may be said of their singing; they sing only the airs and rehearse[1] the rest. There's something uncommon and agreeable in these airs and in my opinion is more suitable to the taste of melancholy people than others.

[1] The translation here is a little misleading: 'perform the rest in recitative' would be more accurate. This is clear from the original French version which reads, 'ils ne chantent que les airs, et récitent le reste'.

91   Hogarth caricature of Handel's *Rinaldo*, 1723
Burney Collection of Theatrical Portraits, vol. 3, no. 188, p. 92 (Print Room, BM).
Reproduced in Southern (1952), plate 32

THE FIRST PANTOMIMES

Following the growing popularity of Italian opera during the 1710s, the only alternative genre open to English composers, musicians and dancers, at least until the late 1720s, was a form of entertainment known as pantomime. Pantomimes were normally short afterpieces that followed the main play of the evening. Colley Cibber gives a brief account of their inception in his *Apology*.

92   Colley Cibber describes the inception of pantomime in 1717
Cibber (Lowe ed.), vol. 2, pp. 179–80

I have upon several occasions already observed that when one company is too hard for another, the lower in reputation has always been forced to exhibit some new-fangled foppery to draw the multitude after them. Of these expedients, singing and dancing had formerly been the most effectual. But at the time I am speaking of, our English music had been so discountenanced since the taste of Italian operas prevailed that it was to no purpose to pretend to it. Dancing therefore was now the only weight in the opposite scale, and as the new theatre sometimes found their account in it, it could not be safe for us wholly to neglect it.

To give even dancing therefore some improvement, and to make it something more than motion without meaning, the fable of *Mars and Venus* was formed into a connected presentation of dances in character, wherein the passions were so happily expressed and the whole story so intelligibly told by a mute narration of gesture only, that even thinking spectators allowed it both a pleasing and a rational entertainment. Though, at the same time, from our distrust of its reception, we durst not venture to decorate it with any extraordinary expense of scenes or habits; but upon the success of this attempt it was rightly concluded that, if a visible expense in both were added to something of the same nature, it could not fail of drawing the town proportionably after it. From this original hint then (but every way unequal to it) sprung forth that succession of monstrous medlies that have so long infested the stage and which arose upon one another alternately, at both houses, outvying in expense, like contending bribes on both sides at an election, to secure a majority of the multitude.

PANTOMIMES AT LINCOLN'S INN FIELD AND DRURY LANE

Weaver's *Loves of Mars and Venus*, performed at Drury Lane on 2 March 1717, was probably the first pantomime afterpiece mounted in London, although John Rich at Lincoln's Inn Fields rapidly established his pre-eminence in the genre.[1] Rich was a gifted dancer who appeared under the stage name of Lun, apparently the name of a famous Parisian dancer who always represented Harlequin.[2] He appeared as the *commedia dell'arte* figure Harlequin in a series of pantomimes throughout the 1720s that were enormously popular with London audiences.

The fables of these various pantomimes were taken from mythology or legend (the Faustus legend was frequently used); grotesque scenes were much in demand, as were scenes set in Hell or Hades. The story was normally recounted in arias that were sung at intervals in the action, and the mime was accompanied by appropriate music. The stage settings were spectacular and made frequent use of complex scene changes and flying machines. (There are records of occasional accidents involving the stage machinery, which caused serious injury and even death.)[3]

In 1723, both Drury Lane and Lincoln's Inn Fields offered Faustus pantomimes to their audiences. *Harlequin Dr Faustus* opened at Drury Lane on 26 November 1723 and John Rich's version, *The Necromancer or Harlequin Dr Faustus* opened at Lincoln's Inn Fields a month later on 20 December 1723. A contemporary drawing shows Rich as Faustus, wearing Harlequin's motley costume under Faustus's academic robes.[4] The stage setting is only lightly sketched in, but it shows three sets of formal neo-classic wings and a back shutter, with a practical table and chair mid-stage [*see* 93].

A later illustration from the satiric poem *Harlequin Horace* (1735) shows John Rich as Lun, helping Punch to kick Apollo, while the works of Shakespeare, Rowe and Jonson lie discarded on the stage floor. The setting is an attractive townscape, with cloud borders and a back shutter showing trees and clouds [*see* 94].

Apart from the comic appeal of the various *commedia dell'arte* figures in these pieces, the pantomimes of the 1720s offered London audiences a pleasing aesthetic combination of virtuoso dancing, attractive music and visual spectacle. (It might be argued that the pantomime of this period, in a popular down-to-earth form, continued the aesthetic traditions of the seventeenth-century masque.) Rich's pantomimes in particular were justly popular with English and foreign theatre-goers, as emerges from the travelogue of M. de Saussure. His account of a visit to Lincoln's Inn Fields in 1728 gives a vivid impression of the spectacular devices used at the time [*see* **95**].

[1] See Fiske (1973), p. 70.
[2] *Ibid.* and Tate Wilkinson: *Memoirs*, vol. 4 (1791), p. 153.
[3] See Fitzgerald, vol. 1 (1882), pp. 428–9.
[4] This print has been wrongly attributed in the past to the Drury Lane production. The sculptured figure of a satyr stage right, which was a feature of Lincoln's Inn Fields, makes it clear that the production in fact refers to the Lincoln's Inn Fields version of *Dr Faustus*. See Hogarth's caricature of *The Beggar's Opera* [*see* **69**] for another view of the Lincoln's Inn Fields stage.

93   **Stage setting for *The Necromancer or Harlequin Dr Faustus* at Lincoln's Inn Fields in 1723**
Anon. English 1972.U.517 (Print room, BM)

94   Harlequin helping Punch to kick Apollo, 1735

James Miller: *Harlequin Horace; or the art of modern poetry*, third edition (London: Lawton Gilliver, 1735), frontispiece. Reproduced in *The Revels history of drama in English*, vol. 5 (1976), plate 15

95   M. de Saussure describes a visit to Lincoln's Inn Fields in 1728

César de Saussure: *A foreign view of England in the reigns of George I and George II*, translated and edited by Mme van Muyden (London: John Murray, 1902), pp. 273–6

The theatre at Lincoln's Inn Fields is famous for its pantomimes, which follow the comedy. These entertainments are composed of two parts, serious and comical.

The first is taken from a mythological fable; gods, goddesses and heroes sing their parts; the decorations are very fine and the machinery extraordinarily so. The second part, in which the actors are Harlequin, Columbine, Scaramouche and Pierrot is acted and not spoken, but the gestures and the machinery allow you to follow the intrigue easily, and it is generally very comical.

Mr Rich, the director of this theatre, spends a great deal of money on plays of this sort; two well-known ones are the *Rape of Europa* and *Orpheus in the Lower Regions*. In the former play a part of the theatre represents hell, in which are seated gods and goddesses. It rises gradually into the clouds; at the same instant, out of the earth rises another stage. The scene represents a farmhouse, in front of which is a dunghill with an egg, the size of an ostrich's on it. This egg, owing to the heat of the sun, grows gradually larger and larger; when it is of a very large size, it cracks open and a little Harlequin comes out of it. He is of the size of a child of three or four years old, and little by little attains a natural height.

It is said Mr Rich spent more than £4000 sterling on Orpheus. The serpent that kills Eurydice is of enormous size, and is covered all over with gold and green scales and with red spots; his eyes shine like fire, and he wriggles about the theatre with head upraised, making an awful but very natural hissing noise. The first night this pantomime was given, the King was there, and I had the good fortune to be present. One of the two grenadiers of the guard, who are posted at either side of the stage with their backs turned to the actors, noticed the serpent only when he was at his feet, and this reptile was so natural that the man dropped his musket, and drawing his sword made as though he would cut the monster in two. I do not know whether the soldier was really alarmed or whether he was acting, but if so it was admirably done and the spectators laughed again and again. This piece is full of wonderful springs and clockwork machinery. When Orpheus learns that his beloved is dead, he retires into the depth of the stage and plays on his lyre. Presently out of the rocks appear little bushes; they gradually grow up into trees, so that the stage resembles a forest. On these trees flowers blossom, then fall off and are replaced by different fruits, which you see grow and ripen. Wild beasts, lions, bears, tigers creep out of the forest, attracted by Orpheus and his lyre. It is altogether the most surprising and charming spectacle you can imagine.

Mr Rich plays the part of harlequin with great agility and address, and he is said to be the best actor of this part in Europe. In pantomimes most good dancers are French men and women from Paris. Ladies attend these plays in great numbers and are always beautifully dressed.

PANTOMIME CRITICISED

Pantomime was, however, not without its critics. Many of the better educated members of London's audiences felt that it threatened the artistic integrity of the theatre by undermining the popular appeal of genuine comic and tragic writing. This is precisely the point made in an anonymous burlesque drawing entitled *The Stage's Glory*, published probably in 1730 or 1731 (the date is suggested by references in the drawing to productions of *The Beggar's Opera*, *Tom Thumb* and *Hurlothrumbo*, all of which had taken place between 1728 and

1730) [*see* **96**]. The drawing emphasises the rich commercial rewards to be gained from pantomimes that pander to popular taste, while works of literary merit lie neglected.[1]

A more prosaic critique can be found in an anonymous satiric work (probably published in 1739) entitled *Letters from a Moor at London*. Here Rich's pantomimes are criticised from the kind of common-sense, no-nonsense standpoint that was typical of London's literary circles at the time [*see* **97**].[2]

[1] Another point of interest to emerge from this drawing is the similarity between the ornamental arch shown in its centre and the same arch featured in Thornhill's design sketches for the Queen's Theatre [*see* **64**]. This would not only seem to confirm Barlow's argument that the arch shown in Thornhill's sketches is indeed the unusually shaped proscenium arch of the Queen's Theatre (pp. 313–28), it might also indicate that the basic shape of the proscenium was not altered during the 1708 rebuilding programme.

[2] Aaron Hill argued vigorously though politely against the contemporary passion for pantomimes in *The Prompter* (see, for instance nòs. 128 and 129 published on 30 January 1736 and 3 February 1736). James Miller, the author of the anonymously published work *Harlequin Horace* (first published in 1731), was rather less gentle in his critique of Rich. In the Preface, dedicated ironically to Rich, he accused him of pandering to the lowest tastes of contemporary audiences by offering them knavery, profanity, obscenity and buffoonery in place of art.

96   The Stage's Glory. An anonymous caricature of pantomime productions, probably 1731

Burney Collection of Theatrical Portraits, vol. 7, no. 189, p. 93 (Print Room, BM)

(see facing page)

97   A satiric account of pantomimes at Covent Garden in the 1730s

Letters from a Moor at London (London: F. Noble, [?] 1739), p. 109

Covent Garden Square is a noble piazza; in this square is a very fine church, as likewise a playhouse, much resorted to by the English people. But their dramatic pieces are now much neglected, and the most ridiculous nonsense introduced, as Harlequin turned into an old woman selling pears; Harlequin coming out of an egg; Harlequin running away with men's wives. But the most diverting scene is to see a number of English cuckolds applauding Harlequin when he runs away with a man's wife. Harlequin is such a hero among the English that nothing can be done without him. He skips, dances, runs about, but says nothing; all's done by dumb signs and motions. This Harlequin wears a fool's coat, a deformed face, a wooden sword, and has such a number of wooden actions that all these theatrical performances are fit for nothing but to divert wooden heads.

THE BEGGAR'S OPERA, 1728

On 29 January 1728 John Gay's *Beggar's Opera* opened at Lincoln's Inn Fields. Although its cast members were relatively inexperienced, it was destined to run for sixty-two performances, making it the most profitable theatrical success of the century. The thrust of the piece was satiric. In his ballad opera, Gay, who was a romantic Tory, directed his satire skilfully at the Whig Prime Minister Walpole and the values he represented; he also extended his satire to include the aesthetic taste of the age, with its preference for Italian opera. The improbable plots, the complex arias, and even the rivalry between Faustina and

96   The Stage's Glory. An anonymous caricature of pantomime productions, probably 1731

Cuzzoni, the leading sopranos of the day, are all effectively mocked in Gay's low-life ballad opera.

Two illustrations by Hogarth make it quite clear that the opera used conventional scenic devices and therefore required little by way of additional expense. The first illustration is a formal colour portrait of the actors (and certain members of the audience) in a scene from the beginning of Act 3, 'When my hero in court appears'. The actors are placed just downstage of the proscenium; the grouping is distinctly cramped, as additional, free-standing stage boxes have been built for high-ranking members of the audience immediately in front of the usual structural stage boxes. The upstage prison set is depicted on what looks like two pairs of wings and a back shutter. The wings, as in *Arsinoe*, are not symmetrically matched in terms of design. The statue of a satyr stage left, a distinctive feature of the stage at Lincoln's Inn Fields, is clearly shown [see **98**].

A second illustration by Hogarth shows a caricatured version of the production, with leading actors wearing animal masks on a thrust stage. Lockit is a bull, Macheath an ass, Polly a pig and Lucy a cat. (Hogarth's view of the ballad opera is quite good-natured: the real satire in the piece is directed at the contemporary rage for Italian opera. On the right of his drawing he shows a diva surrounded by rich admirers offering her presents. Meanwhile 'harmony' takes flight.)[1] Of more interest to theatre historians is the detailed picture he gives of the auditorium and stage set. The embellishments of stage and side boxes are clearly shown, as are the ornamental urns at the proscenium, supported on each side of the stage by statues of satyrs. The scenic stage depicts a number of London houses on the wings, with a practical gallows stage left. The back shutter depicts trees and clouds [see **69**]. The visual approach taken in the set is not unlike that shown in the pantomime scene of Harlequin helping Punch to kick Apollo.[2]

[1] For further details, see Moore (1948), p. 87.
[2] See [94].

98   Hogarth's portrait of actors and audience in *The Beggar's Opera*, 1728

Engraving by blake after Hogarth. Burney Collection of Theatrical Portraits. vol. c218. f. 10. no. R. 10–83 (Print Room. BM). Original portrait in Tate Gallery

(see facing page)

98   Hogarth's portrait of actors and audience in *The Begger's Opera*

'ENGLISH OPERA' IN THE EARLY 1730S

In the season 1732–3, an enterprising attempt was made by a group of young composers and musicians, notably Thomas Arne and John Frederick Lampe, to combat the all-pervasive popularity of Italian opera by mounting a series of newly composed or revised English operas. For this venture, they hired the Little Theatre in the Haymarket and Lincoln's Inn Fields, following Rich's move to Covent Garden. Only two of the eight operas they performed met with any success.[1] However, a remarkable fold-out illustration has survived in the published libretto for one of these operas showing the stage setting designed by Thomas Lediard for Lampe's opera *Britannia*, as performed at the Little Theatre on 16 November 1732 [*see* **99a**]. The design was based on what Lediard himself in his introduction called the 'transparent theatre', a system that used transparent wings, borders and relieves that could be lit from behind to produce a pleasing multi-coloured effect. The scene depicted in the frontispiece shows Public Virtue stage left as a nymph, Honour stage right as a Roman hero, with an equestrian statue of George I upstage. Fame hovers overhead and at the foot of the statue sits Britannia on a throne, next to Europe, Africa and America. The figures at the back are Victory and Valour. These and other details are carefully set out by Lediard in his prefatory 'Description of the Transparent Theatre' in the published libretto of *Britannia* [*see* **99b**]. The 'Description' contains an unusual amount of explanatory information, including details of two splendid machines that descend at key points in the action. (Both machines are illustrated in the frontispiece.)

The set represents an ingenious attempt to achieve a sense of Baroque *trompe l'oeil* in the cramped surroundings of the Little Theatre, but the production with its naive, masque-like allegories did not succeed in firing the enthusiasm of London's theatre goers, who were by now used to a more satirical response to figures of authority.

[1] For details of the repertoire, see Fiske (1973), p. 133.

99   Lediard's stage setting for Lampe's *Britannia* at The Little Theatre in the Haymarket, 1732

Britannia. An English opera. As it is performed at the New Theatre in the Haymarket. With the representation and description of a transparent theatre, illuminated and adorned with a great number of emblems, mottoes, devices and inscriptions, and embellished with machines in a manner entirely new. By Mr Lediard, Late secretary to His Majesty's envoy extraordinary in Hamburg and many years director of the opera house in that city. The music composed after the Italian manner by Mr Lampe (London: J. Watts, 1732)

(A) THE FRONTISPIECE

(B) A DESCRIPTION OF THE TRANSPARENT THEATRE
[pp. 5–10]

This theatre is [. . .] intended to represent the Temple of Honour, illuminated and adorned by the deity with transparent pyramids, emblems, mottoes, inscriptions, devices etc. to celebrate a festival to the glory of BRITANNIA and her AUGUST MONARCH.

The entrance into the Temple of Honour out of the Temple of Virtue is through a triumphal arch, resting upon transparent pillars of the Corinthian order, wreathed with foliage and flowers and adorned with gilt capitals, etc. Before these pillars sit upon two elevated thrones:

On the right hand	On the left hand
PUBLIC VIRTUE	HONOUR
Represented as a beautiful nymph, having in her right hand a spear, and in her left a garland of laurel, with a sun on her bosom.	Represented as a hero in Roman habit, [. . .] crowned with laurel, a chain of gold about his neck [. . .].

Within this triumphal arch is, on each side of the temple, a row of transparent pillars, like those of the arch, of the Corinthian order, wreathed with foliage and flowers and adorned with gilt capitals, supporting three more arches, adorned with foliage, festoons and other ornaments.

Amidst the ornaments of these and the front arch are [. . .] emblems with their mottoes in honour of the British nation of which the English lion is set as the typical resemblance. [. . .]

Between these pillars stand on both sides twelve transparent pyramids, supported on pedestals, each by two gilt lions. The pyramids are adorned with foliage, festoons, etc. and, at the foot of each upon the pedestal, is a bust of one of the Roman Emperors, famous for some virtue or laudable quality which might entitle him to a place in the Temple of Honour. [. . .]

Behind these arches are discovered three piazzas of transparent pillars in the same order and adorned in the same manner as the former.

Under the arch of the middle piazza is a stately equestrian statue of HIS SACRED MAJESTY, gilt in the habit of a Roman Emperor, on a pedestal of white marble, trampling envy and tyranny under his horse's feet. [. . .]

Over His Majesty's statue hovers fame, holding with one hand a crown of laurel over his head and with the other a trumpet, on the fane of which is the inscription: *Intaminatis fulget honoribus*/He shines with unsullied honours.

At the four corners of the pedestal are four figures representing Europe, Asia, Africa and America, signifying that HIS MAJESTY has dominions in all these four parts of the world.

And on a throne at the foot of the pedestal is seated BRITANNIA. On each side of the equestrian statue sit:

VICTORY

Represented by a maiden in the habit of an Amazon, holding a branch of palm in her right hand.

VALOUR

Represented as a young hero in a Roman habit.

In the sixth scene of the third act descends a machine in the middle of the stage, in which are seated together:

PEACE

MARS

This machine is adorned

(On the side of Peace) with branches of olives, laurel and palm, among which lie at her feet a lion sporting with a lamb, over her head a rainbow with the inscription:

(On the side of Mars) with all sorts of arms and trophies, with the inscription:

Pax meta belli

Peace is the scope of war

In fulcrum pacis

For the support of peace.

In the middle between them is a bust of His Sacred Majesty, with the inscription: *Aureum condit seculum*/He restores the Golden Age.

In the last scene descends, at the end of the stage, a large machine of clouds, which takes in the whole breadth of it, on which is seated Jupiter in the middle of the assembled Gods.

5 Actors and acting

Contemporary accounts of the work of the great Restoration actors emphasise that the older generation of actors, men such as Hart, Mohun and Shatterall, continued the virile acting traditions of the Caroline period which they had learnt in their apprenticeship as boy actors. Even the young actors of Davenant's company, notably Thomas Betterton, were schooled by Davenant in the pre-Commonwealth acting tradition that Davenant had likewise observed and experienced at first hand during the 1630s.

In the Restoration actors were expected to be versatile and to present their audience with a range of both comic and tragic roles; only outstanding comic actors such as Lacy were allowed the luxury of working exclusively in one particular genre. A tragic actor such as Betterton often found himself giving accounts of various comic roles.

The most important innovation as far as acting was concerned was the introduction of professional actresses on the stage. In the rarefied court masques of the 1630s, noblewomen and the Queen herself had played important roles in works intended to underline the stability and supremacy of the Royal house. In the Restoration, the self-confident, even assertive work of the first actresses on the public stage in England was not simply a sign of Cavalier pleasure-seeking; it was also in part a product of women's greater self-confidence in society following the Civil-War period when they had been called on to fight, plead at law and argue as vigorously as their menfolk. The actresses of the Restoration were both tough and talented and they had an immediate impact on contemporary authors, audiences and theatre managers. Significantly, the first person to be granted the honour of a benefit performance was an actress, Elizabeth Barry.

A distinctive tragic style was established in the later Restoration period by Elizabeth Barry and Thomas Betterton. It was based on powerful emotional involvement, and audiences valued highly the emotional intensity of their acting. In contrast, gifted comic actresses at the turn of the century, such as Anne Bracegirdle and Anne Oldfield, relied upon their ability to project their intelligence, wit and erotic charm in their performances.

After the death of Betterton in 1710, tragic acting styles became more mannered and externalised. Wilks and Quin were the most mannered, but even Booth who attempted to model his work on Betterton was not free from obvious mannerism in his work. Until the appearance of Macklin and, above all, Garrick in the 1740s, the emotional depth of Betterton and Barry seemed a distant memory.

At periods when the theatre flourished, strict rehearsal discipline was maintained, with the leading actors in the company or the actor-managers taking a responsible and serious interest in rehearsing their fellow actors and training youngsters. Authors were often involved in the rehearsals for new plays they had written, but not always with unqualified success. The prompter played an important part in holding together company and rehearsal discipline. One of the major concerns of older actors throughout the period was to hand on to young actors a sense of an acting tradition stretching back over several generations.

The early eighteenth century saw the publication of the first manuals in England on acting theory. Between them, Charles Gildon and Aaron Hill share this honour. They disagreed on the importance of classical rhetoric in the training of actors, and on the importance of external aids to the art of rehearsing (such as the use of a mirror or the study of fine art), but both shared the view that emotional involvement and imaginative effort were crucial to great acting. In particular, Aaron Hill stressed these qualities in his essays written in the mid-1730s and so doing, he clearly prefigured the return to a more intense, emotional acting style that Garrick was shortly to bring onto the London stage.

RESTORATION ACTORS AND THE PRE-COMMONWEALTH TRADITION

At the Restoration, a number of distinguished actors, who had served their apprenticeships as boy actors in the private playhouses of the Caroline era, resumed their interrupted careers. Some, such as Charles Hart and Nicholas Burt, had attempted to eke out a living as actors during the late 1640s and 1650s, performing illegally at the Phoenix [Cockpit] in Drury Lane, the Red Bull and in private houses.[1] Michael Mohun, on the other hand, followed Charles II into exile in Flanders and, having served there as a major in the army, is known to have performed as an actor in Antwerp.[2] At the Restoration he returned to London to lead the group of players at the Red Bull [see **101**]. These men formed the essential nucleus of Killigrew's company at Gibbons's tennis court in Vere Street [see **100**].

The glowing testimony of various contemporaries is sufficient to confirm their commanding stature as individual actors, and it also underlines the strength and vigour of the acting traditions these actors brought with them from the Caroline theatre of the 1630s. Hart and Mohun in particular elicited warm praise from their contemporaries for their acting in the plays of Jonson, Shakespeare and Beaumont and Fletcher. John Lacy was regarded as the outstanding comic actor of his generation [see **102**].[3] A measure of the regard he enjoyed may be seen in the fact that Charles II in 1662 commissioned a triple painting of him in three of his favourite roles. Langbaine records that these were: 'Teague in *The Committee*, Mr Scruple in *The Cheats* and M. Galliard in *The Variety*'[4] [see **103**]. Despite this unique favour shown him by Charles, Lacy deeply offended his patron when he played in Edward Howard's *The Change of Crowns* in 1667 and wittily embellished a part in which he was expected to criticise the King and court for their corruption. Lacy was briefly imprisoned, the King's Company silenced, and a furious row broke out between actor and author [see **104**].

Neither the 'distracted times' of the Civil War, nor the oppressive rigour of Cromwellian rule had succeeded in destroying the fine acting traditions established in the early decades of the seventeenth century. Critics looking back from the vantage point of the turn of the century seem to regard the acting of Mohun, Hart and Lacy with an affection bordering on reverence [see **105**]. Even allowing for a certain amount of romanticised nostalgia in these accounts, they are an impressive testimony to the standing and reputation enjoyed by these early Restoration actors.

[1] See *Historia Histrionica*, in Cibber (Lowe ed.), vol. 1, pp. xxix–xxx. See also *BD*, vol. 2, pp. 432–4 for an account of Nicholas Burt's life and work and vol. 7, pp. 147–53 for Charles Hart.
[2] See Nicoll, vol. 1 (1952), p. 288, n. 2. See also *BD*, vol. 10, pp. 271–6.
[3] See *BD*, vol. 9, pp. 98–104.
[4] See Langbaine (1691), p. 317. In his *Brief lives*, Aubrey asserts that the characters depicted were, 'Teague, Lord Vaux, the Puritan' (Clark ed.), vol. 2, p. 28. Both attributions are disputed by Charles

W. Cooper, on grounds of dating, in his article 'The triple portrait of John Lacy' *PMLA* 47 (1932), 759–65. He argues that the three figures are: Wareston, a Scotch laird, in *The Rump*, M. Galliard in *The Variety* and Ananias, the anabaptist deacon in Jonson's *Alchemist*.

100   The theatrical apprenticeship of the older actors at the Restoration

Historia Histrionica, in Cibber (Lowe ed.), vol. 1, pp. xxiv–xxv

Hart and Clun were bred up boys at the Blackfriars and acted women's parts. Hart was Robinson's boy or apprentice; he acted the Duchess in the tragedy of *The Cardinal*, which was the first part that gave him reputation. Cartwright and Wintershall belonged to the private house in Salisbury Court. Burt was a boy first under Shank at the Blackfriars, then under Beeston at the Cockpit; Mohun and Shatterall were in the same condition with him at the last place. There Burt used to play the principal women's parts, in particular Clariana in *Love's Cruelty*; and at the same time Mohun acted Bellamente, which part he retained after the Restoration.[1] [. . .]

[1] The play is Shirley's *Love's Cruelty* and the part is clearly a man's role, which means that Mohun had graduated from boys' roles before the outbreak of Civil War.

101   Portrait of Mohun, May 1663

University Library, Bristol. Further copy in Burney Collection of Theatrical Portraits, vol. 6, no. 55, p. 68 (Print Room, BM)

102   Contemporary descriptions of the older actors at the Restoration

(A) JOHN DOWNES
Downes (Summers ed.), pp. 16–17

I must not omit to mention the parts in several plays of some of the actors, wherein they excelled in the performance of them. First, Mr Hart in the part of Arbaces in *King and no King*; Amintor in *The Maid's Tragedy*; Othello; Rollo; Brutus in *Julius Caesar*; Alexander, towards the latter end of his acting. If he acted in any one of these but once in a fortnight, the house was filled as at a new play. Especially Alexander, he acting that with such grandeur and agreeable majesty that one of the court was pleased to honour him with this commendation: that Hart might teach any king on earth how to comport himself. He was no less inferior in comedy; as Mosca in *The Fox*; Don John in *The Chances*; Wildblood in *The Mock Astrologer*; with sundry other parts. In all the comedies and tragedies [in which] he was concerned he performed with the exactness and perfection that not any of his successors have equalled him.

Major Mohun, was eminent for Volpone; Face in *The Alchemist*; Melantius in *The Maid's Tragedy*; Mardonius in *King and no King*; Cassius in *Julius Caesar*; Clytus in *Alexander*; Mithridates, etc. An eminent poet[1] seeing him act this last vented suddenly this saying: 'Oh Mohun, Mohun! Thou little man of mettle, if I should write a hundred plays, I'd write a part for thy mouth'. In short, in all his parts he was most accurate and correct.

Mr Wintershall was good in tragedy as well as in comedy, especially in Cokes in *Bartholomew-Fair*; that the famous comedian Nokes came in that part far short of him.

Then Mr Burt, Shatterall, Cartwright and several other good actors, but to particularize their commendations would be too tedious. [. . .]

---

[1] Said to be Nathaniel Lee. See Downes (Summers ed.), p. 149.

(B) THOMAS RYMER
Thomas Rymer: *The tragedies of the last age considered and examined by the practice of the ancients and by the common sense of all ages* (London, 1678). Reproduced in J.E. Spingarn (ed.): *Critical essays of the seventeenth century*, vol. 2 (Oxford: Clarendon Press, 1908), pp. 184 and 205

They say, for instance, *A King and no King* pleases. I say the comical part pleases.

I say that Mr Hart pleases. Most of the business falls to his share and what he delivers every one takes upon content; their eyes are prepossessed and charmed by his action before aught of the poets can approach their ears. And to the most wretched of characters he gives a lustre and a brillant which dazzles the sight, that the deformities in the poetry cannot be perceived. [. . .]

We may remember (however we find this scene of Melanthius and Amintor in the book) that at the theatre we have a good scene acted. There is work cut out and both an Aesopus and Roscius are on the stage together. Whatever defect may be in Amintor and Melanthius, Mr Hart and Mr Mohun are wanting in nothing. To these we owe for what is pleasing in the scene; and to this scene we may impute the success of *The Maid's Tragedy*.

(C) SAMUEL PEPYS
Pepys (Latham and Matthews eds.)

20 NOVEMBER 1660 (vol. 1, p. 297)

Mr Sheply and I to the new playhouse near Lincoln's Inn Fields (which was formerly Gibbons's tennis court), where the play of *Beggar's Bush* [Fletcher and Massinger] was newly begun. And so we went in and saw it. It was well acted (and here I saw the first time one Mohun who is said to be the best actor in the world, lately come over with the King).

22 NOVEMBER 1660 (vol. 1, p. 300)

I to the new playhouse and saw part of *The Traitor* [James Shirley], a very good tragedy, where Mohun did act the traitor very well.

12 JUNE 1663 (vol. 4, p. 181)

At noon to the Exchange, and so home to dinner and abroad with my wife by water to the Royal Theatre and there saw *The Committee* [Sir Robert Howard], a merry but indifferent play, only Lacy's part, an Irish footman, is beyond imagination.

13 AUGUST 1667 (vol. 8, p. 384)

Sir W. Penn and I to the King's House and there saw *The Committee*, which I went to with some prejudice, not liking it before, but I do now find it a very good play and a great deal of good invention in it; but Lacy's part is so well performed that it would set off anything.

(D) JOHN EVELYN
Evelyn (de Beer ed.), vol. 3, p. 345

27 NOVEMBER 1662

At night saw acted *The Committee*, a ridiculous play of Sir Robert Howard's, where the mimic Lacy acted the Irish footman to admiration: a very Satyrus or Roscius.

103   John Lacy painted for Charles II, 1662

Triple portrait painted by Michael Wright, Hampton Court. Reproduced in Powell (1984), plate 37

104   Lacy in disgrace with Charles II

Pepys (Latham and Matthews eds.)

16 APRIL 1667 (vol. 8, pp. 168–9)

Knepp tells me the King was so angry at the liberty taken by Lacy's part to abuse him to his face that he commanded they should act no more till Mohun went and got leave for them to act again, but not this play [*The Change of Crowns*]. The King mighty angry, and it was bitter indeed, but very true and witty.

20 APRIL 1667 (vol. 8, pp. 172–3)

At noon dined and went with my wife to the King's House, but there found the bill torn down and no play acted; and so, being in the humour to see one, went to the

Duke of York's House [. . .] Here met with Rolt who tells me the reason of no play today at the King's house. That Lacy had been committed to the porter's lodge for acting his part in the late new play [*The Change of Crowns*] and that being thence released he came to the King's house, there met with Ned Howard, the poet of the play, who congratulated his release. Upon which Lacy cursed him as that it was the fault of his nonsensical play that was the cause of his ill usage. Mr Howard did give him some reply, to which Lacy [answered] him that he was more a fool than a poet. Upon which Howard did give him a blow on the face with his glove; on which Lacy, having a cane in his hand, did give him a blow over the pate. Here Rolt and others that discoursed of it in the pit this afternoon did wonder that Howard did not run him through, he being too mean a fellow to fight him. But Howard did not do anything but complain to the King of it; so the whole house is silenced and the gentry seem to rejoice much at it, the house being become too insolent.

105   Late seventeenth-century views on Restoration actors

(A) JAMES WRIGHT
Historia Histrionica, Cibber (Lowe ed.), vol. I, pp. xxiii–iv

LOVEWIT We have indeed poets of a different genius, so are the plays. But in my opinion, they are all of 'em (some few excepted) as much inferior to those of former times as the actors now in being (generally speaking) are, compared to Hart, Mohun, Burt, Lacy, Clun and Shatterall, for I can reach no farther backward.

TRUMAN I can and dare assure you, if my fancy and memory are not partial (for men of my age are apt to be over indulgent to the thoughts of their youthful days) I say the actors that I have seen before the wars – Lowin, Taylor, Pollard and some others – were almost as far beyond Hart and his company as those were beyond these now in being.

LOVEWIT I am willing to believe it but cannot readily because I have been told that those whom I mentioned were bred up under the others of your acquaintance and followed their manner of action, which is now lost. So far that when the question has been asked why these players do not revive *The Silent Woman* and some other of Jonson's plays (once of highest esteem), they have answered truly: because there are none now living who can rightly humour those parts, for all who related to the Blackfriars, where they were acted in perfection, are now dead and almost forgotten.

(B) GERARD LANGBAINE ON LACY
Gerard Langbaine: *An account of the English dramatic poets* (Oxford: George West and Henry Clements, 1691), p. 317

A comedian whose abilities in action were sufficiently known to all that frequented the King's Theatre, where he was for many years an actor, and performed all parts that he undertook to a miracle, insomuch that I am apt to believe that, as this age never had, so the next never will have his equal – at least not his superior. He was so well approved of by King Charles the Second, an undeniable judge in dramatic arts, that he caused his picture to be drawn in three several figures in the same table, viz. that of Teague in *The Committee*, Mr Scruple in *The Cheats* and M. Galliard in *The Variety*, which piece is still in being in Windsor Castle.

THE NEW GENERATION OF ACTORS AT THE RESTORATION

The company of young and untried actors under Davenant's leadership at Lincoln's Inn Fields had to face several years of stiff competition from the experienced actors in Killigrew's troupe. Initially, their main counter-attraction was the scenic spectacle that the energetic and inventive Davenant presented for the first time to London's audiences. Cibber suggests in his *Apology* that Davenant introduced scenic spectacle in his theatre with the specific aim of counterbalancing the superior acting strength of the King's Company [*see* 106]. This perfectly plausible view (indicative of Cibber's own shrewd commercial sense) takes no account of Davenant's personal fascination with scenic spectacle nor of the fact that the older actors in the King's Company enjoyed the exclusive performance rights to most pre-Restoration plays. To attract an audience at all, Davenant had to offer his patrons something unusual.[1] It also takes no account of the fact that Killigrew clearly intended to introduce scenery into his theatre and may only have refrained from doing so because of opposition within the company.

Davenant was well aware that he needed talented actors as well as his scenic stage. At some point in the autumn or winter of 1660/1 he successfully managed to persuade Betterton to leave Killigrew's troupe, even though the Lord Chamberlain issued a note on 12 December 1660 forbidding the moving of actors from one company to another.[2] He also engaged the talented painter and actor Henry Harris, offering him a generous contract (but not sufficiently generous in Harris's eyes).[3] Betterton and Harris, though very different in temperament and not always on the best of terms,[4] were to prove an attractive and popular combination on stage. Following Davenant's death in 1668, they were to become the joint managers of the company, confirming Davenant's sound judgement in his initial choice of leading actors.

When Betterton joined Davenant's troupe at the age of twenty-two, having trained originally to be a bookseller, his talent was such that he was at once given a variety of major roles, performing them with a skill and assurance that delighted contemporary audiences [*see* 107]. He was a sober and cautious individual who lived a life dedicated to his profession. In December 1662, he married one of the actresses in Davenant's troupe, Mary Saunderson, having lived with her for a brief period beforehand. Together they established a happy and stable household as well as an outstanding acting partnership. In an age of scandal and satire, the Bettertons were universally admired and respected.[5]

Henry Harris could not have been more different. He was a quick-witted man about town, a lively drinking companion, a knowledgeable connoisseur of paintings, whom Pepys much admired. He was at times arrogant and overbearing but on stage, his performances often equalled those of Betterton.[6] A portrait has survived of him playing the role of Cardinal Wolsey in *Henry VIII* [*see* 108]. Betterton played the King in the same production and Downes describes the acting of both players in these roles in glowing terms [*see* 109]. Downes also makes it clear that Betterton's work was based on an acting tradition handed on by successive players from the Shakespearean period itself [*see* 107 and 109].

[1] See Milhous (1979), pp. 16–19.
[2] PRO LC 5/137, p. 343. See John Freehafer: 'The formation of the London patent companies in 1660' *TN* 20 (1965–6), 26. See also *BD*, vol. 2, p. 75.
[3] In July 1663 Harris temporarily left the company after unsuccessfully demanding a higher fee than Betterton. He returned in December of the same year. (See Pepys, 22 July and 10 December 1663.)
[4] See Lowe (1891), p. 117.
[5] See *BD*, vol. 2, pp. 73–101.
[6] See *BD*, vol. 7, pp. 123–32.

106   Colley Cibber comments on the competition between the acting companies at the Restoration
Cibber (Lowe ed.), vol. 1, pp. 93–4

These two excellent companies were both prosperous for some few years till their variety of plays began to be exhausted. Then of course the better actors (which the King's seem to have been allowed) could not fail of drawing the greater audiences. Sir William Davenant therefore, master of the Duke's Company, to make head against their success, was forced to add spectacle and music to action; and to introduce a new species of plays, since called dramatic operas, of which kind were *The Tempest, Psyche, Circe,* and others, all set off with the most expensive decorations of scenes and habits, with the best voices and dancers.

This sensual supply of sight and sound coming in to the assistance of the weaker party, it was no wonder they should grow too hard for sense and simple nature, when it is considered how many more people there are that can see and hear than think and judge. So wanton a change of the public taste therefore began to fall as heavy upon the King's Company as their greater excellence in action had before fallen upon their competitors. Of which encroachment upon wit several good prologues in those days frequently complained.

107   Descriptions of Betterton as a Shakespearean actor

(A) JOHN DOWNES
Downes (Summers ed.), p. 21

Hamlet being performed by Mr Betterton, Sir William (having seen Mr Taylor of the Blackfriars Company act it, who being instructed by the author Mr Shakespeare) taught Mr Betterton in every particle of it; which by his exact performance of it gained him esteem and reputation, superlative to all other plays. [. . .] No succeeding tragedy for several years got more reputation or money to the company than this.

(B) SAMUEL PEPYS
Pepys (Latham and Matthews eds.)

24 AUGUST 1661 (vol. 2, p. 161)

And then I straight to the Opera and there saw *Hamlet Prince of Denmark*, done with scenes very well. But above all, Betterton did the prince's part beyond imagination.

28 MAY 1663 (vol. 4, p. 162)

And so to the Duke's House and there saw *Hamlet* done, giving us fresh reason never to think enough of Betterton.

(C) COLLEY CIBBER
Cibber (Lowe ed.), vol. 1, pp. 100–2

You have seen a Hamlet perhaps, who, on the first appearance of his father's spirit, has thrown himself into all the straining vociferation requisite to express rage and fury, and the house has thundered with applause; though the misguided actor was all the while (as Shakespeare terms it) tearing a passion into rags – I am the more bold to offer you this particular instance, because the late Mr Addison, while I sat by him to see this scene acted, made the same observation, asking me with some surprise if I thought Hamlet should be in so violent a passion with the ghost, which, though it might have astonished, it had not provoked him?[1] For you may observe that in this beautiful speech the passion never rises beyond an almost breathless astonishment or an impatience, limited by filial reverence, to enquire into the suspected wrongs that may have raised him from his peaceful tomb and a desire to know what a spirit so seemingly distressed might wish or enjoin a sorrowful son to execute towards his future quiet in the grave. This was the light into which Betterton threw this scene; which he opened with a pause of mute amazement! Then rising slowly to a solemn, trembling voice, he made the ghost equally terrible to the spectator as to himself! And in the descriptive part of the natural emotions which the ghastly vision gave him, the boldness of his expostulation was still governed by decency, manly, but not braving; his voice never rising into that seeming outrage or wild defiance of what he naturally revered. But alas! To preserve this medium, between mouthing and meaning too little, to keep the attention more pleasingly awake by a tempered spirit than by mere vehemence of voice, is of all the master strokes of an actor the most difficult to reach. In this none yet have equalled Betterton.

[1] The reference is almost certainly to Wilks playing Hamlet.

108   John Greenhill's portrait of Henry Harris as Cardinal Wolsey, 1663

Bristol UL. Further copy in Burney Collection of Theatrical Portraits, vol. 4, no. 140, p. 85 (Print Room, BM). Original at Magdalen College, Oxford

109   Downes describes Betterton and Harris in *Henry VIII*, 1663

Downes (Summers ed.), p. 24

King Henry VIII. This play, by order of Sir William Davenant, was all new clothed in proper habits: the King's was new, all the lords, the cardinals, the bishops, the doctors, proctors, lawyers, tipstaves, new scenes. The part of the King was so right and justly done by Mr Betterton, he being instructed in it by Sir William, who had it from old Mr Lowin that had his instructions from Mr Shakespeare himself, that I dare and will aver, none can or will come near him in this age in the performance of that part. Mr Harris's performance of Cardinal Wolsey was little inferior to that, he doing it with such just state, port and mien that I dare affirm, none hitherto has equalled. [. . .] Every part by the great care of Sir William being exactly performed, it being all new clothed and new scenes, it continued acting 15 days together with general applause.

THE FIRST ACTRESSES ON THE RESTORATION STAGE

In the Restoration theatre, there was a clear link with the acting traditions of the pre-Commonwealth theatre (as shown in the previous section); there was also a complete break with Jacobean and Caroline acting conventions following the appearance of professional actresses on stage. Within a matter of months after the Restoration (the exact date is disputed),[1] actresses displaced the boy actors who had earlier played women's roles. This was a major innovation and its importance cannot be overstated. It not only reflected an enormous shift in public opinion (a mere thirty years earlier, the presence of women in a visiting French troupe of actors had provoked a public outcry),[2] it also meant that for the first time ever, English playwrights could write women's roles for women, giving them the same weight and complexity in the overall fabric of their plays as the male characters. Colley Cibber emphasises the importance of this in his *Apology* [see **110a**].

It seems highly probable that Davenant had taken the initiative in persuading Charles II to insert his directive into the 1662 patents that, 'all the women's parts to be acted in either of the said two companies for the time to come may be performed by women'.[3] Davenant had already written parts for women members of the court of Charles I, including Queen Henrietta Maria, who acted in the court masques of the 1630s. He had seen professional actresses in the public and court theatres of Paris after the Civil War. And in his opera *The Siege of Rhodes*, performed in 1656 at Rutland House, he had already cast a woman singer, Mrs Coleman, in the leading female role of Ianthe. With these experiences behind him, it would obviously have seemed to him a natural and logical step to introduce women onto the public stage in London. One may also presume that both he and Killigrew were well aware that such a move would prove commercially advantageous.

The first actresses of the Restoration period came largely from the middle classes; they belonged to the 'genteel poor'. Had they not tried their luck on stage, the most they might have hoped for was a dull life of domestic service.[4] Family pressures prevented girls of higher social rank joining the profession,[5] while a lack of basic educational skills would exclude most daughters of the lower classes (above all the need to read, study and memorise a large number of roles). Some of the girls were clearly intent on finding rich keepers (as were some of the young male actors);[6] many faded away into a life of poverty, prostitution and disease; but a small and highly talented minority (including Mary Betterton and the Marshall sisters, Anne and Rebecca) gradually emerged as the artistic equals of the male actors [see **110b** and **c**]. (The equality of talent was not reflected in their salaries.)[7]

Some of the strengths and the weaknesses of these first actresses may be glimpsed in the fleeting comments of their contemporaries. Most were warm and appreciative, particularly when actresses played popular breeches parts; some were laconic and others openly disapproving [see **111**]. In addition, the erotic excitement and attraction of mingling with quick-witted actresses in the tiring rooms, in the auditorium and in the town clearly emerges from diary entries, prologues and portraits [see **112**].

---

[1] See Wilson (1958), pp. 4–8.
[2] See Lanier (1930), pp. 23–6. See also Bentley (1941–68), vol. 6, pp. 225–6.
[3] See p. 18 above.
[4] See Wilson (1958), pp. 9–10.
[5] Colley Cibber gives an illustration in his *Apology* of how a lady with a title, abandoned by her family because of some misdemeanour, was nevertheless prevented by her family from making a living on stage: 'For here you find her honest endeavour to get bread from the stage was looked upon as an addition of new scandal to her former dishonour!' (Lowe ed.), vol. 1, p. 75.
[6] For a full account of a young male actor who sought and found a rich female 'keeper', see Wilson (1964), pp. 85–96.
[7] It emerges, for instance, from the reply of the patentees in 1695 that leading male actors were then receiving between £3 and £5 per week, while 30s a week was considered adequate for a popular actress such as Mrs Cory. 50s a week was considered a generous salary for Mrs Verbruggen. See PRO LC 7/3, f. 6 and Nicoll, vol. 1 (1952), pp. 378–9.

110   The impact of the first actresses on stage

(A) COLLEY CIBBER
Cibber (Lowe ed.), vol. 1, pp. 90–1

The other advantage I was speaking of is that before the Restoration no actresses had ever been seen upon the English stage. The characters of women on former theatres were performed by boys or young men of the most effeminate aspect. And what grace or master-strokes of action can we conceive such ungain hoydens to have been capable of? This defect was so well considered by Shakespeare that in few of his plays he has any greater dependence upon the ladies than in the innocence and simplicity of a Desdemona, an Ophelia, or in the short specimen of a fond and virtuous Portia. The additional objects then of real, beautiful women could not but draw a proportion of new admirers to the theatre. We may imagine too that these actresses were not ill chosen, when it is well known that more than one of them had charms sufficient at their leisure hours to calm and mollify the cares of empire.[1]

(B) SAMUEL PEPYS
Pepys (Latham and Matthews eds.)

30 SEPTEMBER 1662 (vol. 3, p. 209)

After dinner we took coach and to the Duke's playhouse, where we saw *The Duchess of Malfy* well performed, but Betterton and Ianthe to admiration.[2]

1 FEBRUARY 1664 (vol. 5, pp. 33–4)

Took my wife out immediately to the King's Theatre, [...] and there saw *The Indian Queen* [Sir Robert Howard and Dryden] acted; which indeed is a most pleasant show and beyond my expectation. The play good but spoiled with the rhyme, which breaks the sense. But above my expectation most, the eldest Marshall [Anne Marshall] did do her part most excellently well as I ever heard woman in my life; but her voice not so sweet as Ianthe's [Mary Betterton]. But, however, we came home mightily contented.

27 FEBRUARY 1668 (vol. 9, pp. 93–4)

With my wife and Deb to the King's House, to see *The Virgin Martyr* [Massinger and Dekker], the first time it has been acted a great while; and it is mighty pleasant; not that the play is worth much, but it is finely acted by Becke Marshall.

1 The reference is to Nell Gwyn and Moll Davis who became mistresses of Charles II.
2 Ianthe was the leading female role in *The Siege of Rhodes* in which Mary Saunderson, later Betterton, became famous. Pepys always called her by the name of this character rather than her own name.

111   Contemporary comments on Restoration actresses

(A) SAMUEL PEPYS
Pepys (Latham and Matthews eds.)

12 FEBRUARY 1661 (vol. 3, p. 35)

[. . .] By coach to the theatre and there saw *The Scornful Lady* [Beaumont and Fletcher] now done by a woman, which makes the play appear much better than ever it did to me.[1]

2 MARCH 1667 (vol. 8, p. 91)

After dinner, with my wife to the King's house to see *The Maiden Queen*, a new play of Dryden's, mightily commended for the regularity of it and the strain and wit; and the truth is, there is a comical part done by Nell, [Nell Gwyn] which is Florimell, that I never can hope ever to see the like done again by man or women. The King and Duke of York were at the play. But so great performance of a comical part was never, I believe, in the world before as Nell does this, both as a mad girl then most and best of all when she comes in like a young gallant and has the motions and carriage of a spark the most that ever I saw any man have. It makes me, I confess, admire her [. . .]

22 AUGUST 1667 (vol. 8, p. 395)

To the King's playhouse and there saw *The Indian Emperor*, where I find Nell come again, which I am glad of;[2] but was most infinitely displeased with her being put to act the emperor's daughter; which is a great and serious part, which she do most basely. [. . .]

28 DECEMBER 1667 (vol. 8, p. 594)

With my wife and girl to the King's House and there saw *The Mad Couple* [James Howard], which is but an ordinary play. But only Nell's and Hart's mad parts are most excellently done, but especially hers; which makes it a miracle to me to think how ill she does any serious part, as the other day just like a fool or changeling, and, in a mad part, does beyond all imitation almost.

(B) JOHN DOWNES
Downes (Summers ed.), p. 35

Mrs Davenport, Mrs Davis, Mrs Jennings, etc. The three last by force of love were erept the stage.[3]

(C) JOHN EVELYN
Evelyn (de Beer ed.)

9 JANUARY 1662 (vol. 3, p. 309)

I saw acted the second part of *The Siege of Rhodes*. In this acted the fair and famous comedian called Roxolana for that part she acted; and I think it was the last, (she being) then taken to be the Earl of Oxford's Miss (as at this time they began to call lewd women). It was in recitative music.

18 OCTOBER 1666 (vol. 3, pp. 465–6)

This night was acted my Lord Broghill's[4] tragedy called *Mustapha* before their majesties at court, at which I was present, very seldom at any time going to the public theatres for many reasons now as they were abused to an atheistical liberty; foul and indecent women now (and never till now) permitted to appear and act which, inflaming several young noblemen and gallants, became their whores and to some their wives: witness, the Earl of Oxford, Sir Robert Howard, Prince Rupert, the Earl of Dorset and another greater person than any of these,[5] who fell into their snares to the reproach of their noble families and ruin of both body and soul.

[1] Downes lists Anne Marshall as the actress playing the title role. See Downes (Summers ed.), p. 6.
[2] In July 1667 Nell Gwyn had briefly left the theatre to live with Charles Sackville, Lord Buckhurst, as his mistress. Pepys describes the short-lived arrangement in his diary entry of 13 July 1667.
[3] Hester Davenport was inveigled into a false marriage by Aubrey de Vere, Earl of Oxford, in January 1662. See *BD*, vol. 4, pp. 194–5. Mary or 'Moll' Davis left the stage in 1668 to become one of Charles II's mistresses. See *BD*, vol. 4, pp. 222–30. Mrs Jennings had been one of the original actresses in Davenant's acting troupe; little is known of her private life. See *BD*, vol. 8, p. 154.
[4] The Earl of Orrery.
[5] The Earl of Oxford's mistress and 'wife' was Hester Davenport. Sir Robert Howard's mistress and then wife was Mary Uphill. Evelyn confuses her with the actress Susannah Uphill. Prince Rupert's mistress was Peg Hughes. The mistress of Charles Sackville, Lord Buckhurst, Earl of Dorset was Nell Gwyn who of course later became the mistress of 'another greater person', the King himself.

112   Actresses off stage

(A) SAMUEL PEPYS
Pepys (Latham and Matthews eds.)

5 OCTOBER 1667 (vol. 8, pp. 463–4)

To the Duke of York's playhouse, but the house so full, it being a new play *The Coffee House* [Sir Thomas St Serfe], that we could not get in, and so to the King's house. And there, going in, met with Knepp and she took us up into the tiring rooms and to the women's shift where Nell was dressing herself and was all unready and is very pretty, prettier than I thought. And so walked all up and down the house above and then below into the scene room and there sat down and she gave us fruit; and here I read the questions to Knepp while she answered me through her part of *Flora's Figary* [*Flora's Vagaries* by Richard Rhodes] which was acted today. But Lord! to see how they were both painted would make a man mad and did make me loath them; and what base company of men comes among them and how lewdly they talk! and how poor the men are in clothes and yet what a show they make on the stage by candle light is very observable. But to see how Nell cursed for having so few people in the pit was pretty, the other house carrying away all the people at the new play, and is said nowadays to have generally most company, as being better players.

7 APRIL 1668 (vol. 9, p. 155)

I by coach to the King's playhouse and there saw *The English Monsieur* [James Howard], sitting for privacy sake in an upper box: [. . .] After the play done, I down to Knepp and did stay her undressing herself; and there saw the several players, men and women, go by; and pretty to see how strange they are all, one to another, after the play is done. Here I saw a wonderful pretty maid of her own that came to undress her and one so pretty that she says she intends not to keep her for fear of her being undone in her service, by coming to the playhouse.

(B) WILLIAM WYCHERLEY
The prologue to *The Country Wife*, 1676

We set no guards upon our tiring room,
But when with flying colours there you come,
We patiently, you see, give up to you
Our poets, virgins, nay, our matrons too.

(C) PORTRAIT OF NELL GWYN HOLDING A NOSEGAY
Burney Collection of Theatrical Portraits, vol. 4, p. 59, no. 101 (Print Room, BM)

Following the retirement of the leading actors of the pre-Commonwealth era in the early 1680s (notably Hart and Mohun), and with the uniting of the two acting companies in 1682, Betterton's pre-eminence as the leading actor of the age was beyond dispute. He now had all the major acting roles available to him that had previously been the property of Killigrew's actors and proceeded to test himself in a variety of plays taken over from the King's Company.[1] Hitherto his wife had acted with him as one of the leading tragic heroines of the Duke's Company, but in the late 1670s, Elizabeth Barry joined the Duke's Company and soon proved to be an actress whose talent was comparable to that of Betterton [see 113].[2] Together they established a distinctive style of acting that dominated the late Restoration stage.

It is clear from Anthony Aston's description [see 114] and Kneller's portrait [see 115] that Betterton was not particularly attractive. Nor was Elizabeth Barry a great beauty [see 114 and 116]. Their strength as performers came not from any obvious physical charm (as, for instance, in the case of Kynaston or Nell Gwyn), but from the power of their personalities focused with emotional intensity on the roles they played. In the case of Elizabeth Barry, this may well have followed from her initial training as an actress by the Earl of Rochester. It was he who first encouraged her to make up for defects of voice and ear by concentrating instead on communicating an emotional depth of understanding [see 117].[3]

Aston's description of Betterton's stance – 'his left hand frequently lodged in his breast between his coat and waistcoat, while with his right he prepared his speech' – conveys a vivid impression of Augustan deportment, restraint and decorum. His acting style depended upon economy of movement and gesture. Cibber's description of his acting, on the other hand [see 118], leaves us in no doubt that Betterton could use his powerful voice and swiftly changing facial expressions to elicit an attentive silence from the rowdiest members of a typical Restoration audience. (Something of the elegance and charisma of Betterton's personality is conveyed in Kneller's portrait.)

Both Betterton and Barry prepared their parts assiduously, taking due note of any previous interpretations or, in the case of newly written works, consulting the authors carefully on points of detail.[4] The real basis of their preparation, however, was emotional identification with the parts they were studying. This is stressed by a variety of writers, as is the classical source in Horace for such an approach to art [see 119 and 120]. For Betterton and Barry, emotional identification with their different roles was the bedrock of their acting, which enabled them to offer their audiences an emotional complexity and intensity in their portrayal of differing characters [see 121 and 122]. Their finished performance was, however, always carefully modulated and controlled. Theirs was an art of acting in which an inner intensity was carefully balanced by an exterior poise and decorum. Their finely judged performances were seen as a norm against which one could measure the quality and diversity of the work of later actors.

---

[1] Downes gives a list of these plays, which included: *The Scornful Lady, The Plain Dealer, The Mock Astrologer, Bartholomew Fair, Othello, Rollo.* See Downes (Summers ed.), pp. 39–40.

[2] See *BD*, vol. 1, pp. 313–25.

[3] Some scholars are inclined to query the veracity of Curll's account. He is seldom a reliable witness and is generally more interested in sensation and gossip than fact. This particular story does, however, have the ring of truth about it, so that the authors of the *BD* are inclined to believe that it is at least partly correct. See *BD*, vol. 1, p. 313.

[4] See Gildon (1710), p. 16.

113   Downes describes Elizabeth Barry's rise to fame
Downes (Summers ed.), pp. 37–8

The Orphan, or the Unhappy Marriage, wrote by Mr Otway. Castalio acted by Mr Betterton [. . .] Monimia, Mrs Barry [. . .] All the parts being admirably done, especially the part of Monimia. This, and Belvidera in *Venice Preserved, or a Plot Discovered*, together with Isabella in *The Fatal Marriage*, these three parts gained her the name of famous Mrs Barry, both at court and city. For whenever she acted any of those three parts, she forced tears from the eyes of her auditory, especially those who have any sense of pity for the distressed.

114   Anthony Aston describes Thomas Betterton and Elizabeth Barry
Anthony Aston: *A brief supplement to Colley Cibber Esq, his lives of the famous actors and actresses* (London, 1747). Reproduced in Cibber (Lowe ed.), vol. 2, pp. 299–303

Mr Betterton (although a superlative good actor) laboured under an ill figure, being clumsily made, having a great head, a short thick neck, stooped in the shoulders and had fat short arms which he rarely lifted higher than his stomach. His left hand frequently lodged in his breast between his coat and waistcoat, while with his right he prepared his speech. His actions were few, but just. He had little eyes and a broad face, a little pock-fretten, a corpulent body and thick legs with large feet. He was better to meet than to follow, for his aspect was serious, venerable and majestic, in his latter time a little paralytic. His voice was low and grumbling, yet he could tune it by an artful climax which enforced universal attention, even from the fops and orange girls. He was incapable of dancing, even in a country dance, as was Mrs Barry, but their good qualities were more than equal to their deficiences. [. . .] Mr Betterton was the most extensive actor from Alexander to Sir John Falstaff, but in that last character he wanted the waggery of Estcourt, the drollery of Harper, the sallaciousness of Jack Evans. [. . .] Powell attempted several of Betterton's parts, as Alexander, Jaffier, etc. but lost his credit, as in Alexander he maintained not the dignity of a king but out-heroded Herod, and in his poisoned mad scene out-raved all probability; while Betterton kept his passion under and showed it most (as flame smokes most when stifled). Betterton, from the time he was dressed to the end of the play kept his mind in the same temperament and adaptness as the present character required. [. . .]

I must say of him as Hamlet does of his father: 'He was a man (take him for all in all) I cannot look upon his like again.'

His favourite Mrs Barry claims the next in estimation. They were both never better pleased than in playing together. Mrs Barry outshone Mrs Bracegirdle in the character of Zara in *The Mourning Bride*, although Mr Congreve designed Almeria for that favour. And yet this fine creature was not handsome, her mouth opening most on the right side, which she strove to draw the other way and at times composing her face, as if sitting to have her picture drawn. Mrs Barry was middle-sized and had darkish hair, light eyes, dark eye-brows and was indifferently plump. Her face somewhat preceded her action, as the latter did her words, her face ever expressing the passions. Not like the actresses of late times who are afraid of putting their faces out of the form of non-meaning, lest they should crack the cerum, white-wash or other cosmetic, trowelled on. Mrs Barry had a manner of drawing out her words which became her, but not Mrs Braidshaw and Mrs Porter. To hear her speak the following speech in *The Orphan* was a charm:

> I'm ne'er so well pleased as when I hear thee speak,
> And listen to the music of thy voice. [. . .]

Neither she, nor any of the actors of those times had any tone in their speaking (too much lately in use). In tragedy she was solemn and august, in comedy alert, easy and genteel, pleasant in her face and action, filling the stage with variety of gesture. She was woman to Lady Shelton of Norfolk (my Godmother) when Lord Rochester took her on the stage; where for some time, they could make nothing of her. She could neither sing nor dance, no, not in a country dance.

115   Kneller's portrait of Betterton

[Betterton, Thomas]: *The history of the English stage from the Restoration to the present time* (London: E. Curll, 1741), frontispiece. A further copy of the engraving in Burney Collection of Theatrical Portraits, vol. 1, no. 236, p. 101 (Print Room, BM)

116   Kneller's portrait of Elizabeth Barry

Burney Collection of Theatrical Portraits, vol. 1, no. 154, p. 66.2 (Print Room, BM)

117   Edmund Curll describes Elizabeth Barry's training by the Earl of Rochester

[Thomas Betterton]: *The history of the English stage from the Restoration to the present time* (London: E. Curll, 1741), pp. 15–16

The first parts Lord Rochester chose to teach Mrs Barry were the Little Gipsy in the comedy of *The Rover* by Mrs Behn and Isabell, the Hungarian Queen, in the tragedy of *Mustapha* by the Earl of Orrery: which (besides the private instructions he gave her) he made her rehearse near 30 times on the stage and about 12 in the dress she was to act in. He took such extraordinary pains with her, as not to omit the least look or motion, nay, I have been assured from those who were present that her page was taught to manage her train in such a manner so as to give each movement a peculiar grace.

[. . .] it was certain that Mrs Barry was mistress of a very good understanding, yet she having little or no ear for music, which caused her to be thought dull when she was taught by the actors because she could not readily catch the manner of their sounding words, but ran into a tone, the fault of most young players, this defect my Lord perceiving, he made her enter into the nature of each sentiment, perfectly changing herself, as it were, into the person, not merely by the proper stress or sounding of the voice but feeling really and being in the humour, the person she represented was supposed to be in.

118   Cibber describes Betterton's skill in obtaining an attentive silence from his audiences
Cibber (Lowe ed.), vol. 1, pp. 109–10

Betterton had so just a sense of what was true or false applause that I have heard him say he never thought any kind of it equal to an attentive silence. That there were many ways of deceiving an audience into a loud one, but to keep them hushed and quiet was an applause which only truth and merit could arrive at. Of which art there never was an equal master to himself. From these various excellencies, he had so full a possession of the esteem and regard of his auditors that upon his entrance into every scene he seemed to seize upon the eyes and ears of the giddy and inadvertent! To have talked or looked another way would then have been thought insensibility or ignorance. In all his soliloquies of moment, the strong intelligence of his attitude and aspect drew you into such an impatient gaze and eager expectation that you almost imbibed the sentiment with your eye before the ear could reach it.

119   Cibber comments on emotional identification in Betterton's acting
Cibber (Lowe ed.), vol. 1, pp. 102–3

The actor doubtless is as strongly tied down to the rules of Horace as the Writer.

Si vis me flere, dolendum est
Primum ipsi tibi –[1]

He that feels not himself the passion he would raise will talk to a sleeping audience. But this never was the fault of Betterton. And it has often amazed me to see those who soon came after him throw out in some parts of a character a just and graceful spirit which Betterton himself could not but have applauded; and yet in the equally shining passages of the same character have heavily dragged the sentiment along like a dead weight, with a long-toned voice and absent eye, as if they had fairly forgot what they were about.[2]

[1] Horace: *On the art of poetry*, line 102: 'If you want to move me to tears, you must first feel grief yourself.'
[2] Lowe claims that the reference here is to Barton Booth.

120   Gildon comments on emotional identification in the acting of Elizabeth Barry
Charles Gildon: *The life of Mr Thomas Betterton the late eminent tragedian* (London: Robert Gosling, 1710), pp. 39–40

Among those players who seem always to be in earnest, I must not omit the principal, the incomparable Mrs Barry. Her action is always just and produced naturally by the sentiments of the part which she acts, and she everywhere observes those rules prescribed to the poets by Horace and which equally reach the actors:

> We weep and laugh as we see others do,
> He only makes me sad, who shows the way,
> And first is sad himself [. . .]
> Lord Roscommon's translation.

She indeed always enters into her part and is the person she represents. Thus I have heard her say that she never said, 'Ah! poor Castalio!' in *The Orphan* without weeping. And I have frequently observed her change her countenance several times as the discourse of others on the stage have affected her in the part she acted. This is being thoroughly concerned, this is to know her part, this is to express the passions in the countenance and gesture.

121   Cibber describes the convincing variety of effect achieved by Betterton in his different roles
Cibber (Lowe ed.), vol. 1, pp. 103–8

A farther excellence in Betterton was that he could vary his spirit to the different characters he acted. Those wild impatient starts, that fierce and flashing fire which he threw into Hotspur, never came from the unruffled temper of his Brutus (for I have more than once seen a Brutus as warm as Hotspur). When the Betterton Brutus was provoked in his dispute with Cassius, his spirit flew only to his eye; his steady look alone supplied that terror which he disdained an intemperance in his voice should rise to. Thus, with a settled dignity of contempt, like an unheeding rock, he repelled upon himself the foam of Cassius. [. . .]

There cannot be a stronger proof of the charms of harmonious elocution than the many even unnatural scenes and flights of the false sublime it has lifted into applause. In what raptures have I seen an audience at the furious fustian and turgid rants in Nat Lee's *Alexander the Great*! For though I can allow this play a few great beauties, yet it is not without its extravagant blemishes. Every play of the same author has more or less of them. [. . .] When these flowing numbers came from the mouth of a Betterton, the multitude no more desired sense to them than our musical connoisseurs think it essential in the celebrate airs of an Italian opera. Does not this prove that there is very near as much enchantment in the well-governed voice of an actor as in the sweet pipe of an eunuch? [. . .]

[. . .] but to show you too that though Betterton never wanted fire and force when his character demanded it; yet, where it was not demanded, he never prostituted his power to the low ambition of a false applause. And further that when, from a too advanced age he resigned that toilsome part of Alexander, the play for many years after never was able to impose upon the public. And I look upon his so particularly supporting the false fire and extravagancies of that character to be a more surprising proof of his skill than his being eminent in those of Shakespeare. Because there, truth and nature coming to his assistance, he had not the same difficulties to combat and consequently we must be less amazed at his success where we are more able to account for it.

122   Cibber describes the variety of effect achieved by Elizabeth Barry

Cibber (Lowe ed.), vol. 1, pp. 160–1

Mrs Barry, in characters of greatness, had a presence of elevated dignity, her mien and motion superb and gracefully majestic; her voice full, clear and strong, so that no violence of passion could be too much for her. And when distress or tenderness possessed her, she subsided into the most affecting melody and softness. In the art of exciting pity she had a power beyond all the actresses I have yet seen or what your imagination can conceive. Of the former of these two great excellencies she gave the most delightful proofs in almost all the heroic plays of Dryden and Lee; and of the latter in the softer passions of Otway's Monimia and Belvidera. In scenes of anger, defiance or resentment, while she was impetuous and terrible, she poured out the sentiment with an enchanting harmony. And it was this particular excellence for which Dryden made her the above-recited compliment upon her acting Cassandra in his *Cleomenes*.[1] But here I am apt to think his partiality for that character may have tempted his judgement to let it pass for her masterpiece, when he could not but know there were several other characters in which her action might have given her a fairer pretence to the praise he has bestowed on her for Cassandra. For in no part of that is there the least ground for compassion as in Monimia, nor equal cause for admiration as in the nobler love of Cleopatra, or the tempestuous jealousy of Roxana.[2] 'Twas in these lights I thought Mrs Barry shone with a much brighter excellence than in Cassandra.

[1]   Cibber quotes Dryden's preface to *Cleomenes* where he states: 'Mrs Barry, always excellent, has in this tragedy excelled herself and gained a reputation beyond any woman I have ever seen on the theatre' (p. 158).
[2]   In *The Rival Queens*.

ANNE BRACEGIRDLE AND THE RESTORATION COMEDY OF WIT

According to Edmund Curll, Anne Bracegirdle made her acting début as a child actress in the 1680 production of *The Orphan*.[1] She began to make her mark as a mature performer in the early 1690s. Carefully trained and instructed by the Bettertons during her adolescence, she was clearly destined for a distinguished career.[2]

Where Betterton was an outstanding tragic actor who regularly turned in fine comic performances, Anne proved to be a gifted comic actress who was also well suited to roles calling for tragic pathos. She was a gifted singer as Downes notes with enthusiasm [see 123].

It was above all as a quick-witted comic actress that she excelled. She inspired Congreve to write two of his most complex female roles for her, Angelica in *Love for Love* and Millamant in *The Way of the World*; both roles were clearly modelled on her elusive and fiercely independent personality. In his description of her acting, Cibber comments on the close affinity of art and life in her case [see 124]. The strength of her acting lay, not in the intense emotional identification practised by Betterton and Barry, but in the carefully controlled projection of her own intelligence, wit and erotic charm. These were pre-eminently the qualities required of an outstanding actress in the sophisticated social comedies of the Restoration period.

An engraved portrait by James Stow and Antony Aston's description of her both contain telling features. In the portrait we are shown an idealised image of beauty. The oval face, the high forehead, arched brows and small mouth with its upper lip in the shape of cupid's bow were all qualities the age particularly valued. The playfully smiling face and erotically charged elegance of the décolleté complete the visual effect [see **125**]. Aston's description of the powerfully pleasing image she left with her audiences even after her exit, conveys something of the charisma that made her the leading comic actress of her day [see **126**].[4]

¹ See [Thomas Betterton]: *The history of the English stage from the Restoration to the present time*, vol. 1 (London: Edmund Curll, 1741), p. 26.

² See *BD*, vol. 2, pp. 269–81.

³ Lucyle Hook claims that her fame as a singer led to her portrait appearing in the frontispiece of a collection of songs in 1695. See 'Portraits of Elizabeth Barry and Anne Bracegirdle' *TN* 15 (1960–1), 133.

⁴ Her charisma was sufficiently powerful to drive some of her male admirers to acts of violence and even murder. One of these, Captain Richard Hill, was so besotted with her and so incensed at her refusal of his attentions that he attempted unsuccessfully to abduct her and then proceeded to murder the actor William Mountfort whom he suspected of having an affair with her. See *BD*, vol. 2, pp. 273–6.

123   Downes describes the effect of Anne Bracegirdle's singing
Downes (Summers ed.), p. 45

Justice Busy, a comedy written by Mr Crowne; 'twas well acted, yet proved not a living play. However, Mrs Bracegirdle, by a potent and magnetic charm in performing a song in it, caused the stones of the streets to fly in the men's faces.

124   Cibber describes the close affinity of art and life in the career of Anne Bracegirdle
Cibber (Lowe ed.), vol. 1, pp. 172–3

[. . .] she had no greater claim to beauty than what the most desirable brunette might pretend to. But her youth and lively aspect threw out such a glow of health and cheerfulness that on the stage few spectators that were not past it could behold her without desire. It was even a fashion among the gay and young to have a taste or tendre for Mrs Bracegirdle. She inspired the best authors to write for her, and two of them,[1] when they gave her a lover in a play, seemed palpably to plead their own passions and make their private court to her in fictitious characters. In all the chief parts she acted, the desirable was so predominant that no judge could be cold enough to consider from what other particular excellence she became delightful. To speak critically of an actress that was extremely good were as hazardous as to be positive in one's opinion of the best opera singer. People often judge by comparison where there is no similitude in the performance. So that, in this case, we have only taste to appeal to and of taste there can be no disputing. I shall therefore only say of Mrs Bracegirdle that the most eminent authors always chose her for their favourite character and shall leave that uncontestable proof of her merit to its own value. Yet let me say, there were two very different characters in which she acquitted herself with uncommon applause. If anything could excuse that desperate extravagance of love, that almost frantic passion of Lee's Alexander the Great, it must have been when Mrs Bracegirdle was his Statira. As when she acted Millamant, all the faults, follies and affectations of that agreeable tyrant were venially melted down into so many charms and attractions of a conscious beauty. In other characters, where singing was a necessary part of them, her voice and action gave a pleasure which good sense in those days was not ashamed to give praise to.

[1] Congreve and Rowe.

125   Engraved portrait of Anne Bracegirdle by J. Stow

[Silvester and Edward Harding]: *The biographical mirrour, comprising a series of ancient and modern English portraits of eminent and distinguished persons, from original pictures and drawings*, vol. 3 (London: Silvester and Edward Harding, 1795–1802), plate 4

126   Anthony Aston describes Anne Bracegirdle's powerful charm and charisma

Aston: *Brief supplement* in Cibber (Lowe ed.), vol. 2, p. 305

She was of a lovely height, with dark brown hair and eye-brows, black sparkling eyes and a fresh blushy complexion. And whenever she exerted herself had an involuntary flushing in her breast, neck and face, having continually a cheerful aspect and a fine set of even white teeth. Never making an exit but that she left the audience in an imitation of her pleasant countenance. Genteel comedy was her chief essay and that too when in men's clothes, in which she far surmounted all the actresses of that and this age. Yet she had a defect scarce perceptible, viz, her right shoulder a little protended which, when in men's clothes, was covered by a long or campaign peruke. She was finely shaped and had very handsome legs and feet; and her gait or walk was free, manlike and modest, when in breeches.

COLLEY CIBBER AS A LATE RESTORATION FOP

Colley Cibber was one of the most successful and yet likeable opportunists of the early eighteenth-century stage.[1] He had a peculiar genius for being in the right place at the right time, and he exploited his various acting and managerial talents with a skill bordering on virtuosity. Having begun his acting career in 1692 on a less than auspicious note [see **127**], he wisely remained with Rich at Drury Lane when Betterton and the other leading actors seceded in 1694. Their departure opened up acting opportunities to Cibber that might otherwise not so easily have come his way.

As an actor, Cibber himself realised that he lacked the powerful and resonant voice required for tragedy,[2] which did not prevent him, however, from making a number of unwise attempts at tragic acting. For these he was roundly satirised by Aaron Hill in *The Prompter* [see **128**]. It was as a comic actor that Cibber excelled, and particularly when playing the type-cast role of the fop. In 1696 he wrote for himself the first of his famous fop roles, Sir Novelty Fashion, in his play *Love's Last Shift* (an opportunistic exploitation of the new sentimental temper of the age). Later that same year, Vanbrugh completed his triumph by writing an ironic sequel to *Love's Last Shift*, called *The Relapse*, and asked Cibber to play the part of Lord Foppington.

The role of Foppington allowed him to turn all his deficiencies as an actor to their best advantage. His weak and occasionally cracked voice, his 'hatchet face', his affected pronunciation and pert gait: all these contributed to making his acting of Foppington an amusing *tour de force* of satiric precision.[3] Grisoni's portrait shows the attention to visual detail that Cibber lavished on his portrayal of this late Restoration fop [see **129**].

[1] For an assessment of his strengths and weaknesses, see *BD* vol. 3, pp. 213–40.
[2] Cibber comments ruefully on his weak voice in his *Apology*. See Cibber (Lowe ed.), vol. 1, p. 221.
[3] See *The Laureat*, p. 103. See also Lois Potter: 'Colley Cibber: the fop as hero' in J.C. Hilson, M.M.B. Jones and J.R. Watson (eds.): *Augustan worlds* (Leicester University Press, 1978), pp. 153–64.

127   Thomas Davies describes Cibber's inauspicious start as an actor

Thomas Davies: *Dramatic miscellanies*, vol. 3 (London: Thomas Davies, 1784), pp. 417–18

Cibber and Verbruggen were two dissipated young fellows who determined, in opposition to the advice of friends, to become great actors. Much about the same time, they were constant attendants upon Downes, the prompter of Drury Lane, in expectation of employment. What the first part was in which Verbruggen distinguished himself cannot now be known. But Mr Richard Cross, late prompter of Drury Lane theatre, gave me the following history of Colley Cibber's first establishment as a hired actor. He was known only for some years by the name of Master Colley. After waiting impatiently a long time for the prompter's notice, by good fortune he obtained the honour of carrying a message on the stage in some play to Betterton. Whatever was the cause, Master Colley was so terrified that the scene was disconcerted by him. Betterton asked, in some anger, who the young fellow was that had committed the blunder. Downes replied, 'Master Colley'. – 'Master Colley! then forfeit him.' – 'Why, sir' said the prompter, 'he has no salary.' – 'No!' said the old man, 'why then put him down ten shillings a week and forfeit him 5 shillings.'[1]

[1] When actors commenced their apprenticeship, they were normally expected to work for a trial period without pay.

128   Aaron Hill comments satirically on Colley Cibber as a tragic actor

The Prompter, no. 3, Tuesday, 19 November 1734 (Appleton and Burnim edition), pp. 6–8

Mr Cibber must be allowed to have a great deal of merit, in his way, but it will be necessary to distinguish what way that is. And the answer is not difficult. Nature herself limits parts to a player by the voice, the figure and conception. In every one of these three she meant Mr Cibber for a comedian. It is not possible to look at him without acknowledging this remarkable talent and confessing he was born to be laughed at.

So strong is this characteristical impression upon everything which he does or says that it is not in his own power to divest himself of the distinction. A man must be prejudiced beyond pardon who is not charmed with his exquisite propriety of affectation, whether he squeaks, bows, ogles, dresses, laughs, or any other way exerts the coxcomb, in Sir Courtly and Lord Foppington. But when we observe in the rugged Syphax[1] too the same debilitated perversion of gesture – when the dreadfully collected calmness of cruelty, the apprehensive tyrannic sagacity which should be visible in Richard the Third, is so unequally represented by the same unseasonable grimaces, the same low, mincing curtails of magnanimity – when instead of forecast and disturbed reflection we see a succession of comic shruggings, and in place of menaces and majestic transports the distorted heavings of an unjoined caterpillar – what less can be concluded by the most partial of his rational friends but that personal foibles and absurd ideas are desirable blessings to a comic actor, and that we often mistake for the excellence of a player's judgement what is, in truth, but the imperfection of his nature.

[1] Syphax was a character in Addison's play *Cato*.

129   Grisoni's portrait of Cibber as Lord Foppington

Engraving by J. Simon after Grisoni. Burney Collection of Theatrical Portraits, vol. 2 no. 154, p. 81 (Print Room, BM). Original portrait in The Garrick Club

(see next page)

ACTING STYLES IN THE EARLY EIGHTEENTH CENTURY
Wilks and Booth

By the turn of the century, a more externalised form of acting began to find its way onto the stage. Robert Wilks and George Powell substituted, in their rants, volume and vehemence for Betterton's emotional intensity; whereas Barton Booth, who modelled himself on Betterton, lacked his mentor's emotive power and all too readily fell back on a tragic monotone. Booth had made his début on the London stage as early as 1700, but it was not

129   Grisoni's
        portrait of
        Cibber as
        Lord Foppington

until April 1713 that he finally achieved fame and success in the title role of Addison's Augustan tragedy *Cato*. On this occasion, his measured delivery and controlled stage decorum was admirably suited to the role Addison had written. (His success in the production was such that it helped him to achieve his long nurtured ambition of joining the triumvirate of managers at Drury Lane.)[1] In his *Apology*, Cibber wrote a fascinating comparison between Wilks and Booth, both of whom he knew intimately as his colleagues in the Drury Lane triumvirate. In a judiciously balanced evaluation, he gives a convincing assessment of their respective merits and weaknesses [*see* 130].

Benjamin Victor's account of Booth's acting is rather more enthusiastic than Cibber's; it also suggests that Booth devoted a good deal of thoughtful preparation to his major roles, paying particular attention to pauses and phrasing. Victor provides a fascinating illustration of the way Booth broke up a lengthy speech in *Othello* with pauses and changes of pace and tone to convey the emotional progression in the speech [*see* 131]. In this his most famous role, Booth clearly proved himself to be an able and worthy pupil of Betterton his mentor.

[1] See L.B. Campbell: 'The rise of a theory of stage presentation in England during the eighteenth century' in *PMLA* 32 (June 1917), 163–200. See also Alan S. Downer: 'Nature to advantage dressed: eighteenth-century acting' in *PMLA* 58 (December 1943), 1002–37. Reprinted in John Loftis (ed.): *Restoration drama: modern essays in criticism* (New York and London: Oxford University Press, 1966), pp. 328–71.

130   Colley Cibber compares the acting of Wilks and Booth
Cibber (Lowe ed.), vol. 2, pp. 241–4

Wilks, from his first setting out, certainly formed his manner of acting upon the model of Mountfort, as Booth did his on that of Betterton. But [. . .] I cannot say either of them came up to their original. Wilks had not that easy regulated behaviour or the harmonious elocution of the one, nor Booth that conscious aspect of intelligence nor requisite variation of voice that made every line the other spoke seem his own natural self-delivered sentiment. Yet there is still room for great commendation of both the first mentioned, which will not be so much diminished in my having said they were only excelled by such predecessors, as it will be raised in venturing to affirm it will be a longer time before any successors will come near them. [. . .]

Booth and he were actors so directly opposite in their manner that if either of them could have borrowed a little of the other's faults, they would both have been improved by it. If Wilks had sometimes too violent a vivacity, Booth as often contented himself with too grave a dignity. The latter seemed too much to heave up his words, as the other to dart them to the ear with too quick and sharp a vehemence. Thus Wilks would too frequently break into the time and measure of the harmony by too many spirited accents in one line, and Booth, by too solemn a regard to harmony, would as often lose the necessary spirit of it. So that (as I have observed) could we have sometimes raised the one and sunk the other, they had both been nearer to the mark. Yet this could not be always objected to them: they had their intervals of unexceptionable excellence that more than balanced their errors. The masterpiece of Booth was Othello. There he was most in character and seemed not more to animate or please himself in it than his spectators. 'Tis true he owed his last and highest advancement to his acting Cato; but it was the novelty and critical appearance of that character that chiefly swelled the torrent of his applause. [. . .]

In sorrow, tenderness or resignation, Wilks plainly had the advantage and seemed more pathetically to feel, look and express his calamity. But in the more turbulent transports of the heart, Booth again bore the palm and left all competitors behind him. A fact perhaps will set this difference in a clearer light. I have formerly seen Wilks act Othello and Booth the Earl of Essex,[1] in which they both miscarried. Neither the exclamatory rage or jealousy of the one or the plaintive distresses of the other were happily executed or became either of them; though in the contrary characters they were both excellent.

[1] In Banks's *Unhappy favourite.*

131   Benjamin Victor describes Booth's acting of Othello

Benjamin Victor: *The history of the theatres of London and Dublin from the year 1730 to the present time*, vol. 2 (London: Thomas Davies, 1761), pp. 10–13

In the first capital scene, Iago works Othello into jealousy and takes his leave [. . .] I look upon this soliloquy to be the touchstone for every new actor. When Iago has left him, after a long pause, the eye kept looking after him, Booth spoke the following remark in a low tone of voice:

This fellow's of exceeding honesty

And knows all qualities, with a learned spirit,
of human dealings.
　　　(*Then a pause, the look starting into anger.*)
　　　　　If I do find her haggard,
Though that her jesses were my dear heart-strings,
I'd whistle her off and let her down the wind
To prey on fortune!
　　　(*A long pause, as to ruminate.*)
　　　　　Haply, for I am black,
And have not those soft parts of conversation
That chamberers have – Or, for I am declined
Into the vale of years – yet that's not much –
　　　(*After a pause, the following start of violent passion.*)
She's gone! I am abused! and my relief
Must be to loath her! O curse of marriage!
That we can call those delicate creatures ours,
And not their appetites!
　　　(*What follows in a quicker, contemptuous tone.*)
　　　　　I'd rather be a toad
And live upon the vapour of a dungeon,
Than keep a corner in the thing I love
For other's uses!
　　　(*A look of amazement, seeing Desdemona coming.*)
　　　　　Look where she comes!
　　　(*A short pause, the countenance and voice softened.*)
If she be false, O then heaven mocks itself!
I'll not believe it.

In this soliloquy the transitions are frequent and require such judicious pauses, such alteration of tones and attitudes, such corresponding looks, that no actor since Booth has been quite complete in it.

In the distressful passages, at the heartbreaking anguish of his jealousy, I have seen all the men susceptible of the tender passions in tears.

Anne Oldfield

Amongst the actresses who joined the stage at the turn of the century, the generally acknowledged successor to Elizabeth Barry and Anne Bracegirdle was Anne Oldfield. By 1707 she had proved so popular with contemporary audiences that she was given preferential treatment in the allocation of benefit performances. One of her biographers asserts that this was the primary cause for the sudden retirement of Elizabeth Barry and Anne Bracegirdle from the stage in 1708 [see **132**]. A number of handsome contemporary etchings show her with a book of poems in her hands, facing the viewer with an intelligent, ironic smile, much as one might expect from a Millamant in Act 4 of *The Way of the World* [see **133**]. (And this became one of her most popular roles.) Anne Oldfield herself claimed to prefer acting in comic parts, and her skill as a comic actress is emphasised by Cibber in his Preface to his play *The Provoked Husband* [see **134**]. She nevertheless excelled in a number of tragic roles. Contemporary descriptions of her as a tragic actress indicate that she achieved in her work a balance of emotional intensity and technical control that was reminiscent of the acting tradition established by Betterton and Barry [*see* **135**].

132   The rivalry between Anne Oldfield, Elizabeth Barry and Anne Bracegirdle

E. Curll [pseud William Egerton]: *Faithful memoirs of the life, amours and performances of the justly celebrated and most eminent actress of her time, Mrs Anne Oldfield* (London: [*s.n.*] 1731), p. 20

Some differences arising between Rich and his company, they joined in with the company at the Haymarket, acting under the licence of Vanbrugh and Congreve, where Mrs Barry and Mrs Bracegirdle, both famous in their way, had been for some time. But Mrs Oldfield's voice, figure and manner of playing soon made her shine out, even here the brightest star. Upon the preference being given to her in the benefit plays and other disputes fomented among the managers, Mrs Barry and Mrs Bracegirdle entirely quitted the business and left Mrs Oldfield sole empress of the stage.[1]

[1]   Curll is not the most reliable of witnesses. Anne Oldfield, although a fine actress, was a ruthless operator, which may have played some part in persuading the other two actresses to retire. This is indicated by a document entitled 'The memorial of Jane Rogers, humbly submitted to the town' (Harvard Theatre Collection), reproduced by Judith Milhous and Robert D. Hume in their article: 'Theatrical politics at Drury Lane: new light on Letitia Cross, Jane Rogers, and Anne Oldfield' in *Bulletin of research in the humanities* (1982), 412–29: 'As Mrs Bracegirdle, a woman of equal merit to any that ever appeared on the stage, left her employment upon Mr Swiney's ill treatment of her to oblige Mrs Oldfield, I have reason to fear that I who have much less merit than Mrs Bracegirdle, shall find it very hard to oppose Mrs Oldfield's malice and great interest with the present managers.'

133   Portrait of Anne Oldfield

Burney Collection of Theatrical Portraits, vol. 6, no. 222, p. 97 (Print Room, BM)

134   Colley Cibber describes Anne Oldfield's skill as a comic actress in *The Provoked Husband*, 1727
Colley Cibber: 'To the reader', Preface to *The Provoked Husband* (London, 1728)

But there is no doing right to Mrs Oldfield, without putting people in mind of what others, of great merit, have wanted to come near her. 'Tis not enough to say, she here outdid her usual excellence. I must therefore justly leave her to the constant admiration of those spectators who have the pleasure of living while she is an actress. But as this is not the only time she has been the life of what I have given the public, so perhaps my saying a little more of so memorable an actress may give this play a chance to be read, when the people of this age shall be ancestors. – May it therefore give emulation to our successors of the stage to know that, to the ending of the year 1727, a contemporary comedian relates that Mrs Oldfield was then in her highest excellence of action, happy in all the rarely found requisites that meet in one person to complete them for the stage. She was in stature just rising to that height, where the graceful can only begin to shew itself; of a lively aspect and a command in her mien that, like the principal figure in the finest paintings, first seizes and longest delights the eye of the spectators. Her voice was sweet, strong, piercing and melodious: her pronunciation voluble, distinct and musical; and her emphasis always placed where the spirit of the sense, in her periods, only demanded it. If she delighted more in the higher comic than in the tragic strain, 'twas because the last is too often written in a lofty disregard of nature. But in the characters of modern practised life, she found occasions to add the particular air and manner which distinguished the different humours she presented. Whereas in tragedy, the manner of speaking varies as little as the blank verse it is written in.[1] She had one peculiar happiness from nature, she looked and maintained the agreeable at a time when other fine women only raise admirers by their understanding. The spectator was always as much informed by her eyes as her elocution; for the look is the only proof that an actor rightly conceives what he utters, there being scarce an instance where the eyes do their part that the elocution is known to be faulty. The qualities she had acquired were the genteel and the elegant. The one in her air, and the other in her dress, never had her equal on the stage; and the ornaments she herself provided (particularly in this play) seemed in all respects the paraphernalia of a woman of quality. And of that sort were the characters she chiefly excelled in. But her natural good sense and lively turn of conversation made her way so easy to ladies of the highest rank, that it is a less wonder if on the stage she sometimes *was* what might have become the finest woman in real life to have supported.

[1] Cibber's revealing comment here perhaps explains why he himself never mastered the art of tragic acting.

135   The prompter William Chetwood describes the acting of Anne Oldfield
William Rufus Chetwood: *A general history of the stage* (London: W. Owen, 1749), pp. 201–2

I remember, in her full round of glory in comedy, she used to slight tragedy. She would often say, 'I hate to have a page dragging my tail about. Why do they not give Porter[1] these parts? She can put on a better tragedy face than I can.' When *Mithridates* was revived, it was with much difficulty she was prevailed upon to take part; but she performed it to the utmost length of perfection and after that she seemed much better reconciled to tragedy. What a majestical dignity in Cleopatra and indeed in every part that required it: such a finished figure on the stage was never yet seen. In *Calista, the Fair Penitent*, she was inimitable in the third act with Horatio when she tears the letter, with:

> To atoms! thus!
> Thus let me tear the vile detested falsehood,
> The wicked lying evidence of shame!

Her excellent clear voice of passion, her piercing flaming eye, with manner and action suiting, used to make me shrink with awe and seemed to put her monitor Horatio into a mouse hole. I almost gave him up for a troublesome puppy. And though Mr Booth played the part of Lothario, I could hardly lug him up to the importance of triumphing over such a finished piece of perfection that seemed to be too much dignified to lose her virtue. [. . .]

[1] Mary Porter was a rival tragic actress in the Drury Lane company.

James Quin

With the death of Wilks, Booth and Anne Oldfield by the early 1730s, the undisputed master of tragic acting during the 1730s was James Quin, who had begun his career in 1718. He was firmly committed to an artificial tragic style that depended entirely on technique at the expense of feeling. His use of a dignified but carefully measured monotone provoked both admiration and opposition [*see* 136a and b]. The contrast between his restrained acting style and the natural liveliness of Garrick in the early 1740s seemed quite startling to many contemporaries. The dramatist Richard Cumberland recalls the effect of seeing both men on stage together in 1746 [*see* 137].

136   Contrasting views of Quin's acting

(A) QUIN AS MACBETH
Davies, vol. 2 (1784), p. 133

Quin's figure and countenance in this character spoke much in his favour; but he was deficient in animated utterance and wanted flexibility of tone. He could neither assume the strong agitation of mind before the murder of the king, nor the remorse and anguish in consequence of it: much less could he put on that mixture of despair, rage and frenzy that mark the last scenes in Macbeth. During the whole representation he scarce ever deviated from a dull, heavy monotony.

(B) QUIN AS PIERRE IN *VENICE PRESERVED*
John Hill: *The actor: a treatise on the art of playing* (London: R. Griffiths, 1750), pp. 50–2 and p. 99

Whoever has heard these and the rest of the keen and disdainful reproaches which Pierre justly throws on his friend, uttered from the mouth of Mr Quin, will agree with us that the whole compass of the English stage affords nothing greater; and yet these, in this judicious performer, are but the sequel of a whole part, and that a long one, kept up throughout with due dignity and spirit. [. . .] No man ever arrived at an equal perfection in speaking the sublime with Mr Quin.

137   Quin and Garrick in *The Fair Penitent*

Richard Cumberland: *Memoirs* (London: Lackington, Allen & Co., 1806), pp. 59–60

Quin presented himself upon the rising of the curtain in a green velvet coat embroidered down the seams, an enormous full bottomed periwig, rolled stockings and high-heeled, square-toed shoes. With very little variation of cadence, and in a deep full tone, accompanied by a sawing kind of action, which had more of the senate than of the stage in it, he rolled out his heroics with an air of dignified indifference that seemed to disdain the plaudits that were bestowed upon him. [. . .] I first beheld little Garrick, then young and light and alive in every muscle and in every feature, come bounding on the stage, and pointing at the wittol Altamont and the heavy-paced Horatio – heavens, what a transition! – it seemed as if a whole century had been stept over in the transition of a single scene. Old things were done away, and a new order at once brought forward, bright and luminous and clearly destined to dispel the barbarisms and bigotry of a tasteless age, too long attached to the prejudices of custom and superstitiously devoted to the illusions of imposing declamation. This heaven-born actor was then struggling to emancipate his audience from the slavery they were resigned to, and though at times he succeeded in throwing in some gleams of new-born light upon them, yet in general they seemed to love darkness better than light and, in the dialogue of altercation between Horatio and Lothario, bestowed far the greater show of hands upon the master of the old school than upon the founder of the new. [. . .]

REHEARSALS AND REHEARSAL METHODS

Very little is known in detail about rehearsals in the Restoration theatre, but a number of conclusions can be drawn from circumstantial evidence and from fleeting comments by contemporary sources. The swiftly changing repertoire indicates that only a minimum number of rehearsals could be expected for a new production and even fewer for revivals. Performances took place at 3 p.m. in the 1660s and at 5 p.m. by 1700:[1] rehearsals were scheduled for the mornings and, in certain cases where there were additional dances to choreograph, in the early evening immediately following the day's performance. Pepys was invited to attend one such early evening rehearsal in 1667.

---

[1] The later performance time in the 1700s is a clear indication that the theatres were by then keen on attracting patrons who needed to earn their living.

138   Pepys is invited to stay for a dance rehearsal after a performance at the King's house

Pepys (Latham and Matthews eds.), vol. 8, pp. 27–8

23 JANUARY 1667

Here in a box above we spied Mrs Pierce, and, going out, they called us and so we stayed for them. And Knepp took us all in and brought us to Nelly, a most pretty woman, who acted the great part of Celia today very fine and did it pretty well: I kissed her and so did my wife, and a mighty pretty soul she is. [. . .] Knepp made us stay in a box and see the dancing preparatory to tomorrow for *The Goblins*, a play of Suckling's not acted these twenty-five years; which was pretty. And so away thence, pleased with this sight also and especially kissing of Nell. [. . .]

The read-through and learning of parts

New plays were given a first read-through by their authors, some of whom were accomplished readers but others, including Dryden and Congreve, were apparently ill at ease with this particular task [*see* 139]. Meanwhile the prompter had prepared written parts for the actors with cue lines, exits and entrances marked on them, and the actors were expected to take these away and memorise their lines. The few ensuing rehearsals were devoted to blocking and 'instruction'. The disadvantage of this procedure, as Aaron Hill pointed out in May 1735, was that actors often had little notion of the overall context into which their part fitted [*see* 140]. The result was that first-night performances sometimes had the feel of a dress rehearsal, as Pepys bitterly complained in March 1662 [*see* 141].

139   Cibber contrasts Nat Lee and Dryden reading their own plays to the actors

Cibber (Lowe ed.), vol. 1, pp. 113–14

As we have sometimes great composers of music who cannot sing, we have as frequently great writers that cannot read. And though without the nicest ear no man can be master of poetical numbers, yet the best ear in the world will not always enable him to pronounce them. Of this truth Dryden, our first great master of verse and harmony, was a strong instance. When he brought his play of *Amphytrion* to the stage, I heard him give it his first reading to the actors in which, though it is true he delivered the plain sense of every period, yet the whole was in so cold, so flat and unaffecting a manner that I am afraid of not being believed when I affirm it.

On the contrary, Lee, far his inferior in poetry, was so pathetic a reader of his own scenes that I have been informed by an actor who was present that while Lee was reading to Major Mohun at a rehearsal, Mohun in the warmth of his admiration threw down his part and said, 'Unless I were able to play it as well as you read it, to what purpose should I undertake it?' And yet this very author whose elocution raised such admiration in so capital an actor, when he attempted to be an actor himself, soon quitted the stage in an honest despair of ever making profitable figures there.

140   Aaron Hill comments on the disadvantages of actors learning their roles in isolation

The Prompter, no. 51, Tuesday 6 May 1735 (Appleton and Burnim eds.), p. 60

The want of order and propriety in rehearsals is very often the occasion of confusion when the play comes to be acted. If an actor does not know precisely the minute circumstances that relate to his role, as to entrances, exits, the part of the stage he is to fill up and the action he is to be in when he has nothing to say, he may be very perfect in the sense and meaning of the author and yet commit most egregious blunders in the representation. This is what actors generally trust to their memory, instead of performing at rehearsals, on which account it seldom happens that a play is well acted the first night which, as I observed before, ought to be the most exact of all.

One thing more which the actor (though highly necessary for him to know) very often neglects is the making himself master of the whole subject of the play. They content themselves with knowing with whom they are principally to be engaged and think no further, by which means a delicate circumstance is often unfeelingly blundered over or perhaps omitted.

141   Pepys comments on the imperfections of a first-night performance

Pepys (Latham and Matthews eds.), vol. 3, p. 39

I MARCH 1662

My wife and I to the Opera and there saw *Romeo and Juliet*, the first time it was ever acted. But it is the play of itself the worst that ever I heard in my life and the worst acted that ever I saw these people do, and I am resolved to go no more to see the first time of acting, for they were all of them out more or less.

The conduct of rehearsals

For new plays, certain rehearsals might be led by the author. This procedure is satirised in Buckingham's play *The Rehearsal* which shows the author Mr Bayes (a caricature of Dryden) sowing confusion and chaos as he attempts to direct his actors [*see* 142]. Swift gives us a more laconic account of Addison rehearsing his new play *Cato* at Drury Lane in 1713 [*see* 143]. In productions of pre-Restoration plays, the leading actors or actor-managers 'instructed' the players. Both Davenant and Betterton attached great value to 'instruction', and for both of them their specific aim in instructing the actors was to try and preserve the acting tradition handed on from actor to actor since the days of Shakespeare. Downes's references to this practice have already been quoted.[1] Thomas Davies, in his *Dramatic miscellanies*, mentions another occasion when Betterton was trying to recall a particular inflection used by Hart in the part of Alexander in *The Rival Queens* and rewarded one of the actors who managed to repeat the line in question just as Hart had performed it [*see* 144].

[1] See [107a].

142 The Duke of Buckingham draws a satirical portrait of an author rehearsing a new production of his work

George Villiers, second Duke of Buckingham: *The Rehearsal* (London, 1673), Act 2, scene v

1ST SOLDIER	Stand. Who goes there?
2ND SOLDIER	A friend.
1ST SOLDIER	What friend?
2ND SOLDIER	A friend to the house.
1ST SOLDIER	Fall on.
	(*They all kill one another. Music strikes.*)
BAYES	(*To the music*) Hold, hold! (*It ceases.*) – Now here's an odd surprise; all these dead men you shall see rise up presently at a certain note that I have made in Effaut flat, and fall adancing. Do you hear, dead men? Remember your note in Effaut flat – (*to the music*) Play on. Now, now, now! (*The music plays his note and the dead men rise but cannot get in order.*) Oh Lord! Oh Lord! Out, out, out! Did ever men spoil a good thing so? No figures, no ear, no time, nothing! Udzookers, you dance worse than the angels in *Harry the Eight* or the fat spirits in *The Tempest*, egad.
1ST SOLDIER	Why Sir 'tis impossible to do anything in time to this tune.
BAYES	Oh Lord! Oh Lord! impossible! Why, gentlemen, if there be any faith in a person that's a Christian, I sat up two whole nights in composing this air and adapting it for the business. For if you observe, there are two several designs in this tune; it begins swift and ends slow. You talk of time and time; you shall see me do it. Look you now; here I am dead (*Lies down flat on his face.*) Now make my note Effaut flat. Strike up, music. Now! (*As he rises up hastily, he falls down again.*) Ah, gadzookers, I have broke my nose.
JOHNSON	By my troth, Mr Bayes, this is a very unfortunate note of yours in Effaut.
BAYES	A plague of this damned stage, with your nails and your tenter-hooks, that a gentleman can't come to teach you to act but he must break his nose and his face and the devil and all. Pray, Sir, can you help me to a wet piece of brown paper?

143 Swift describes a rehearsal of Addison's play *Cato* in 1713

Jonathan Swift: *Journal to Stella*, edited by Harold Williams, vol. 2, p. 654

LETTER LXII 6 APRIL 1713

I was this morning at 10 at the rehearsal of Mr Addison's play called *Cato*, which is to be acted on Friday. There were not above half a score of us to see it. We stood on the stage, and it was foolish enough to see the actors prompted every moment and the poet directing them; and the drab [Mrs Oldfield][1] that acts Cato's daughter out in the midst of a passionate part and then calling out, 'What's next?' The Bishop of Cloghor [St George Ashe] was there too; but he stood privately in a gallery.

[1] Swift was offended at the sight of a very pregnant Anne Oldfield playing the role of a virtuous virgin. She was not married to the man whose child she was carrying, and her pregnancy ended the first run of the play.

144   Betterton at a rehearsal of *The Rival Queens* by Nat Lee
Davies, vol. 3 (1784), pp. 271–2

Betterton, after the re-union of the companies, acted Alexander with as much eclat as any of his other characters. This accomplished and yet modest player, when rehearsing this character, was at a loss to recover a particular emphasis of Hart, which gave a force to some interesting situation of the part; he applied for information to the players who stood near him. At last one of the lowest of the company repeated the line exactly in Hart's key. Betterton thanked him heartily and put a piece of money in his hand as a reward for so acceptable a service.

Rehearsal discipline

In periods when company discipline broke down, insufficient attention was paid to personal and company rehearsals. This was clearly the case in the actors' company in Lincoln's Inn Fields in the late 1690s. Betterton is reported by Gildon to have complained bitterly of lax rehearsal discipline in the early 1700s by comparison with the theatre in Davenant's day [*see* **144**]. However, in periods when the theatre flourished, as under the triumvirate of Wilks, Cibber, and Booth, a vigorous rehearsal policy was maintained, with proper guidance and instruction for younger actors, which undoubtedly contributed to the successful running of the acting company [*see* **146**].

145   Betterton complains of lax rehearsal discipline in the theatre at the turn of the century
Gildon (1710), p. 15

When I was a young player under Sir William Davenant, we were under a much better discipline. We were obliged to make our study our business, which our young men do not think it their duty now to do. For they now scarce ever mind a word of their parts but only at rehearsals and come thither too often scarce recovered from their last night's debauch.

146   Benjamin Victor praises the rehearsal methods of the triumvirate
Victor, vol. 2 (1761), pp. 4–5

But the first instance of their judgement appeared in their regular and masterly manner of governing their rehearsals, over which one of the three managers presided weekly. If a new play was coming on, the first three readings fell to the share of the author. If a revived play, it fell to the share of that manager who was the principal performer in it. The readings over, there followed a limited number of rehearsals with their parts in their hands; after which, a distant morning was appointed for every person in the play to appear perfect, because the rehearsals only then begin to be of use to the actor. When he is quite perfect in the words and cues, he can then be instructed and practise his proper entrances, emphasis, attitudes and exits. Thus the rehearsals went on, under the eye of a person who had ability to instruct and power to encourage and advance those of industry and merit, and to forfeit and discharge the negligent and worthless. They soon found by experience that regularity was the first step to success, and not only the merits of the great actors appeared by that in their full lustre, but even those of the lowest class acquired a decency that saved them from contempt.

The role of the prompter

In the modern theatre the roles of company manager, stage manager and prompter are normally kept quite separate. In the Restoration theatre the prompter fulfilled all three roles and was a figure of some importance. He was responsible for rehearsal discipline, (which included the levying of fines and forfeits for misdemeanours) as well as for ensuring the smooth running of all productions. He wrote out the actors' parts, and he could nurture the careers of younger players by recommending them for walk-on roles. In rehearsals and performances he not only prompted but also ensured the smooth running of the show by marshalling and commanding his army of scene shifters, stage hands and green-room messengers with his bell and whistle. (The whistle was blown at scene changes and the bell was rung at act endings and as a cue for the musicians.)[1] Aaron Hill in *The Prompter* gives a full description of the prompter's role in the very first number of the periodical [*see* **147**].

[1] See Langhans (1981), p. xxvii.

147   Aaron Hill describes the role of the prompter

The Prompter, no. 1, Tuesday, 12 November 1734 (Appleton and Burnim eds.), pp. 2–3

He stands in a corner, unseen and unobserved by the audience, but diligently attended to by everyone who plays a part. Yet though he finds them all very observant of him, he presumes nothing upon his own capacity; he has a book before him, from which he delivers his advice and instructions. [. . .]

He takes particular care not only to supply those that are *out* in their parts with hints and directions proper to set them right but also, by way of caution, drops words to those who are perfect, with an intention to keep them from going wrong. I have often observed the most expert and courageous generals tremble through fear of missing his instructions and the wisest of monarchs lend him an attentive ear. [. . .]

I have already taken notice of the scouts and messengers which attend him. By dispatching one of these he can, at a minute's warning, bring the greatest characters of antiquity or the pleasantest of the present times upon the stage, for the improvement or diversion of the audience. [. . .]

Among his *Instrumenta regni*, his implements of government, I have taken particular notice of a little bell which hangs over his arm. By the tinkling of this bell, if a lady in tragedy be in the spleen for the absence of her lover or a hero in the dumps for the loss of a battle, he can conjure up soft music to soothe their distress. Nay, if a wedding happens in a comedy, he can summon up the fiddlers to dispel care by a country dance. [. . .]

Another tool of his authority is a whistle which hangs about his neck. This is an instrument of great use and significance. I won't say but the sound of a boat-swain's whistle may be sometimes more terrible, but I am sure it cannot be more punctually obeyed. Dr Faustus's celebrated wand has not a more arbitrary and extensive power than this musical machine. At the least blast of it I have seen houses move as it were upon wings, cities turned into forests and dreary deserts converted into superb palaces. I have seen an audience removed in a moment from Britain to Japan and the frozen mountains of Zembla resembling the sunny vales of Arabia Felix. I have seen Heaven and Earth pass away and chaos ensue, and from thence a new creation arise, fair and blooming as the poet's fancy, and all by the powerful magic influence of this wonder-working whistle. [. . .]

ACTING THEORY IN THE EARLY EIGHTEENTH CENTURY
Charles Gildon

The earliest attempt at elaborating a theory of acting in England was made by a hack writer and journalist, Charles Gildon, in his book entitled *The life of Mr Thomas Betterton the late eminent tragedian*, published in 1710. The title is misleading, as only the first few pages are concerned with Betterton's life and work. The remainder is a manual for actors, a set of precepts and advice expressed by an imaginary 'Betterton', but in fact put together by Gildon himself.[1] His freely acknowledged sources were classical works on oratory, notably Quintilian, as well as more modern French works.[2] Much of the advice seems far removed from anything resembling actual stage practice. The detailed descriptions of permitted gestures and facial expressions are clearly those of the classically trained orator, not the actor [see **148a**]. Equally the advice to budding actors to practise in front of a mirror and to study works of art to find telling gestures and expressions seems of little relevance to the everyday practicalities of acting [see **148b**]. But on occasions, Gildon seems to be making a concerted effort to build up a theory of acting that combines many of the qualities he saw in Betterton's acting: viz. emotional identification combined with measured decorum [see **148c**].

[1] Gildon disarmingly admits the point on p. 3: 'Plato and Xenophon introduce Socrates in their discourses to give the greater authority to what they say. I shall therefore make the same use of Mr Betterton, on a subject in which he may reasonably be thought a competent judge.'
[2] See Duerr (1962), pp. 206–7.

148   Charles Gildon's advice to actors in England's first acting manual, 1710
Gildon (1710)

(A) THE RULES OF ORATORY APPLIED TO ACTING
[pp. 71–7]

You must lift up or cast down your eyes, according as the nature of the things you speak of. Thus, if of heaven, your eyes naturally are lifted up; if of earth or hell or any thing terrestrial, they are as naturally cast down. Your eyes must also be directed according to the passions, as to deject them on things of disgrace and which you are ashamed of, and raise them on things of honour which you can glory in with confidence and reputation. In swearing or taking a solemn oath or attestation of anything to the verity of what you say, you turn your eyes, and in the same action lift up your hand, to the thing you swear by or attest.

Your eyebrows must neither be immoveable nor always in motion; nor must they both be raised on everything that is spoken with eagerness and consent, and much less must one be raised and the other cast down. But generally they must remain in the same posture and equality which they have by nature, allowing them their due motion, when the passions require it. That is, to contract themselves and frown in sorrow; to smooth and dilate themselves in joy; to hang down in humility, etc.

The mouth must never be writhed, nor the lips bit or licked, which are all ungenteel and unmannerly actions, and yet what some are frequently guilty of. Yet in some efforts or starts of passion, the lips have their share of action, but this more on the stage than in any other public speaking, either in the pulpit or at the bar. [. . .]

Though to shrug up the shoulder be no gesture allowed in oratory, yet on the stage the character of the person and the subject of his discourse may render it proper enough. Though I confess, it seems more adapted to comedy than tragedy, where all should be great and solemn, and with which the gravest of orators' actions will agree. [. . .]

We come now to the hands, which as they are the chief instruments of action, varying themselves as many ways as they are capable of expressing things, so is it a difficult matter to give such rules as are without exception. [. . .]

It is impossible to have any great emotion or gesture of the body, without the action of the hands to answer the figures of discourse which are made use of in all poetical as well as rhetorical diction [. . .].

In the lifting up the hands, to preserve the grace, you ought not to raise them above the eyes. To stretch them farther might disorder and distort the body; nor must it be very little lower because that position gives a beauty to the figure. Besides, this posture, being general on some surprise, admiration, abhorrence, etc. which proceeds from the object that affects the eye, nature by a sort of mechanic motion throws the hands out as guards to the eyes on such an occasion.

You must never let either of your hands hang down, as if lame or dead, for that is very disagreeable to the eye and argues no passion in the imagination. In short, your hands must always be in view of your eyes and so corresponding with the motions of the head, eyes and body that the spectator may see their concurrence, every one in its own way to signify the same thing, which will make a more agreeable, and by consequence, a deeper impression on their senses and their understanding. [. . .]

(B) GILDON ADVISES ACTORS TO PRACTISE IN FRONT OF A MIRROR AND TO
STUDY WORKS OF ART
[pp. 55 and 62–3]

As to all the other parts of action indeed a glass may prove very advantageous,
since in it you have a faithful representation not only of the face in all its variations
of the countenance, but of the whole body, likewise in all its postures and motions
and the agreeableness and harmony of one to the other, and the parts with the
whole and the whole with the parts. So that you may thus easily discover any *habit*
or *gesture* that wants grace and agreeableness and any action which may add
them to your person and in them that force and influence to [what] you utter.

For want of such a glass there is but a more difficult thing to be applied to, and
that is some friend who is a perfect master in all the beauties of *gesture* and *motion*
and can correct your errors, as you perform before him, and point out those *graces*
which would render your action completely charming. [. . .]

The studying history painting would be very useful [. . .] because the knowledge
of the figure and lineaments of the represented (and in history pieces almost all
who are represented are to be found) will teach the actor to vary and change his
figure, which would make him not always the same, as I have said, in all parts, but
his very countenance so changed that they would not only have other thoughts
themselves but raise others in the audience.

(C) GILDON EMPHASISES THE IMPORTANCE OF EMOTIONAL INVOLVEMENT IN
ACTING
[pp. 68 and 113]

If the grief of another touches you with a real compassion, tears will flow from
your eyes, whether you will or not. And this art of weeping, as I have read, was
studied with great application by the ancient players. And they made so extraordinary progress in it, and worked the counterfeit so near a reality, that their faces
used to be all over blurred with tears when they came off the stage.

They used several means of bringing this passionate tenderness to perfection;
yet this they found the most effectual. They kept their own private afflictions in
their mind and bent it perpetually on real objects and not on the fable or fictitious
passion of the play which they acted. [. . .]

When you are therefore to speak, you ought first with care to consider the
nature of the thing of which you are to speak and fix a very deep impression of it in
your own mind before you can be thoroughly touched with it yourself, or able by
an agreeable sympathy to convey the same passion to another. The string of a
musical instrument sounds according to the force and impulse of the master. If the
touch be gentle and soft, the sound is so too; if strong, the sound is vivid and strong.
It is the same in speaking as in music, if violent passion produce your speech, that
will produce a violent pronunciation; but if it arise only from a tranquil and gentle

thought, the force and accent of the delivery will be gentle and calm. So that the speaker ought first to fix the tone and accent of his voice to every passion that affects him, be it of joy or sorrow, that he may by a sympathetic force convey it to others.

Aaron Hill

Some twenty years passed before the next attempt was made to set out a considered theory of acting. The writer concerned was Aaron Hill, who had endured a most unhappy season as the hapless theatre manager at Drury Lane during the actors' riot of 1710. Hill was still a very young man at the time: a mere twenty-four years of age. (After this disaster he moved on to the opera at the Haymarket and had a far more successful season as Owen Swiney's manager; indeed one of his greatest claims to fame as a man of the theatre is that he had the honour of first introducing Handel to London's opera audiences with a production of *Rinaldo* in 1711.)[1]

For most of the 1720s he was engaged in lucrative commercial enterprises. In the 1730s, however, he once again turned his attention to the theatre. He made an unsuccessful bid for the Drury Lane patent in 1733 (Highmore sold the patent to Fleetwood) and thereafter published (jointly with William Popple)[2] a twice-weekly journal called *The Prompter* between November 1734 and July 1736.

Hill was a talkative eccentric, often dismissed as a 'colossal bore' by his contemporaries,[3] but he could write perceptively on the theatre. In *The Prompter* he addressed himself to a wide range of theatrical issues, including repertoire policy; the taste for opera and panto-mime; the moral role of the theatre; scenery and costume; rehearsal practice; and the training of actors. In considering the training of actors, Hill made a plea for the establishing of a formal acting academy (the actors' nursery of the Restoration had not survived into the eighteenth century): he also set out his ideas on the theory of acting that should underpin such training. In *The Prompter* his ideas were scattered amongst disparate papers, notably nos. 64, 66, 113 and 118; later he expanded his thinking on the subject into an 'Essay on the art of acting' published posthumously in 1753 in his collected works. As in the case of Charles Gildon, he placed considerable stress on the importance of emotional involvement, but went a lot further in attempting to develop a method of refining and honing the actor's ability to feel and express changing emotional states. He also specifically rejected Gildon's advice to actors to observe the strict rules of oratorical gesture [*see* **149a**], and Gildon's suggestions that actors should practise in front of mirrors or study gestures and facial expressions in works of art [*see* **149c**]. Hill's own suggestions are in their turn more schematic than practical. But his stress on the need for genuine commitment and feeling in acting (a commitment that should physically exhaust the actor) and his awareness of the primary importance of the imagination as the lynch pin of all acting endeavour [*see* **149b**] clearly prefigure the changes in acting style that Macklin and Garrick were soon to introduce.

[1] See *BD*, vol. 7, pp. 296–7. This was a claim to fame that almost certainly embarrassed him by the 1730s, when he had developed a passionate dislike of the 'irrational' operatic entertainments that London audiences had come to admire.
[2] His collaborator, William Popple, was like Hill a failed dramatist and an ardent admirer of the theatre.
[3] See William W. Appleton and Kalman A. Burnim: Preface to *The Prompter* (New York: Benjamin Blom, 1966), p. vii.

149   Aaron Hill outlines a theory of acting in *The Prompter*

The Prompter (Appleton and Burnim eds.)

(A) AARON HILL REJECTS THE USE OF ORATORICAL DEVICES IN ACTING
No. 64, 20 June 1735 [pp. 82–3]

One prime cause of all this theatrical burlesque in the players, upon high life and its passions, is a custom that prevails with the managers to form their judgement of an actor without regard to any other of his qualities than merely the tone or extent of his voice, never dreaming (in the midst of a crowd of examples) that the finest natural voice may be useless and insignificant to its possessor unless accompanied by a power to discover passions and express them; whereas a voice of much less depth and capacity, supposing it clear and articulate, being helped by those passionate changes which are the beauties and essentials of tragedy, shall outcharm any natural sweetness of tone and reach not the ear only, but the heart, with its meaningly musical harmony.

As they err in their notions of voice, they are equally mistaken when they discourse of or consider the action, for instead of examining nature, they look into Quintilian, not reflecting that the lessons he teaches his orator were directed to the bar, not the stage, and in consequence of that error falling into mistakes and absurdities which are so much the more ridiculous by that pretence of authority whereon they would ground their establishment. One example will serve to make good my assertion. Quintilian lays it down as a rule that the orator, enforcing his eloquence by action, is 'never to raise his hands above the height of his eyes'. Now who does not see and acknowledge the necessity of this caution in a pleader because, addressing himself to the superior power of his judges, he ought to govern his gesture by a conscious regard to his inferiority and dependence. In such a situation, no doubt, the hands raised higher than the head would form too bold and presuming an attitude. But what is all this to the player who is sometimes to act a monarch who has no superior and in whom actions of menace or sudden transports of indignation carry neither indecorum nor impropriety? Or, how shall he express with proper gesture any passionate appeals to heaven, any strong postures of starting and astonishment, without throwing up his arms to a height beyond the rule of Quintilian?

Thus narrow, or thus blind, are almost all our stage maxims. [. . .]

(B) AARON HILL STRESSES THE IMPORTANCE OF EMOTIONAL INVOLVEMENT
AND IMAGINATION IN ACTING
No. 66, 27 June 1735 [pp. 83–5]

An actor is the professor of an art that represents, to the eyes and ears of an audience, the whole diversity of passions whereby human life is distinguished throughout all its conditions, whether of good or bad fortune. Now he whose trade it is to represent human passion cannot be qualified for that trade without a knowledge of those passions and a power to put on, at will, the marks and colours which distinguish them. The distinction is two-fold – to the eye, by the look and movement – and to the ear, by the tones of the voice, not only from its elevation and depression, but in a certain significant impregnation of that sound with an animated sensation of purpose.

There are but six dramatic passions which are capable of being strongly expressed by the look and which, intermingling their differences on the visage, give us all the soul-moving variety of pain, pleasure or suspension which the heart can be strikingly touched by. These six passions are joy, sorrow, fear, scorn, anger and amazement. There are many other auxiliary passions which cannot, in their own simple character, be impressed upon the countenance yet may be well enough represented by a mixture of two or more of the six capital dramatics. Such are jealousy, revenge, love, pity. The reader might presently convince himself of the truth of this remark and discover, by an easy trial, that jealousy, to express it on the features, requires a combination of three passions – fear, scorn and anger. Revenge mixes only the two last. Love cannot be looked but with a joy that is tempered by fear. And pity, to express it on the face, must qualify that fear by a mixture of sorrow.

It is so far from a difficulty to enliven and make eloquent the look by a successive assumption of all these pictures of the passions that there is nothing at once more wonderful and ridiculous than that men should appear on the stage without knowing them to be necessary or, that knowing them to be so, they should not habituate themselves to the practice.

The whole that is needful in order to impress any passion on the look is first, to conceive it by a strong and intent imagination. Let a man, for instance, recollect some idea of sorrow, his eye will, in a moment, catch the dimness of melancholy, his muscles will relax into languor and his whole frame of body sympathetically unbend itself into a remiss and inanimate lassitude. In such a passive position of features and nerves, let him attempt to speak haughtily and he will find it impossible. Let the sense of the words be the rashest and most violent anger, yet the tone of his voice shall sound nothing but tenderness. The modification of his muscles has affected the organs of speech, and before he can express sounds of anger in his voice he must, by conceiving some idea of anger, inflame his eye into earnestness and new-knit and brace up his fibres into an impatience, adapted to violence – and then not only the voice will correspond with the visage but the step, air and movement, all, recovering from the languid and carrying marks of the impetuous and the terrible, flash a moving propriety from the actor to the audience that, communicating immediately the sensation it expresses, chains and rivets our attention to the passions we are moved by.

Thus the happiest qualification which a player should desire to be master of is a plastic imagination. This alone is a Faustus for the theatres and conjures up all changes in a moment. In one part of a tragic speech the conscious distress of an actor's condition stamping humility and dejection on his fancy, straight his look receives the impression and communicates affliction to his air and his utterance.

Anon, in the same speech, perhaps the poet has thrown in a ray or two of hope. At this the actor's eye should suddenly take fire and invigorate with the glow of liveliness both the action and the accent till, a third and fourth variety appearing, he stops short, upon pensive pauses and makes transitions (as the meanings vary) into jealousy, scorn, fury, penitence, revenge or tenderness – all kindled at the eye by the ductility of a flexile fancy and appropriating voice and gesture to the very instant of the changing passion.

I question whether threshing is a more laborious exercise than acting, in the manner above described. We see in our real passions what effects their struggle at the heart produces in the body. Our first intense reflection on any sudden and vexatious accident induces a cold sweat upon the forehead. But if the thoughts become inflamed and agitate resentment into violence, what a weariness and waste of spirits succeeds the short-lived madness! Yet the player, blindly ignorant or arrogantly obstinate, presumes to imitate these whirlwinds of the soul with all the calmness of stupidity. Let the scene-man sweat; it is beneath the actor's dignity! A puffed, round mouth, an empty vagrant eye, a solemn silliness of strut, a swing-swang slowness in the motion of the arm, and a dry, dull, drawling voice that carries opium in its detestable monotony – these are the graces of the modern stage! These are the fruits of the two royal patents!

It may be objected that nature qualifies few men with a capacity to know and to copy her. Suppose it so. Those few, then, were formed for actors.

(C) AARON HILL ADVISES ACTORS AGAINST PRACTICE IN FRONT OF A
MIRROR OR THE STUDY OF PAINTINGS AND STRESSES THE IMPORTANCE OF
IMAGINATION
No. 118, 26 December 1735 [p. 140]

So that, you see, The Art of Acting is no more than a connected deduction of these plain and natural consequences:
1st – The imagination assumes the idea.
2ndly – Its marks and characteristical impressions appear first in the face, because nearest to the seat of the imagination.
3rdly – Thence, impelled by the will, a commissioned detachment of the animal spirits descending into the dependent organisation of the muscles, and swelling and adapting them in its progress, bends and stimulates their elastic powers into a position apt to execute the purpose (or to express the warmth of) the idea.
4thly – Thus the look, air, voice and action proper to a passion, preconceived in the imagination, become a mere and mechanical necessity, without perplexity, study or difficulty. [. . .]

For want of some such reduction of the art (of expressing the passions dramatically) into an easy and practical theory, to what an infinite variety of difficulties have not actors been exposed by wide and distant pursuits of a skill that lies close within their natural compass [. . .].

Some have formed tedious and laborious schemes of adjusting their gesture at looking-glasses, but for want of conceiving the above . . . disclosed dependence of the action on the idea, their imaginary graces forsook 'em and, in the very instant of their wanting them, were vanished quite out of their memory. Others, by experience of this insufficiency, have concluded all study of deportment to be useless, so abandoned themselves to a wild expectation that proper actions would spontaneously arise and present themselves in the moment of utterance. But here too they were mistaken because, adhering to no cause, they could depend upon no consequence.

A third class of actors, calling in the painters to their assistance, have expected to succeed by observation of certain lineal and expressive distinctions of the passions as they vary on the visage. But should a player endeavour to form his countenance by the too minute and individual particularities which have been enumerated by the master of the pencil for the instruction of their scholars, they would attain but the art of making mouths and distorting their faces into a scholastic and technical confusion between the ridiculous and the horrible. [. . .]

Idea, then, is the great First Mover, and an actor, by that single principle, secures a consequent and necessary perfection in look, voice and action.

6 Audiences, repertoire, morality debates, criticism

INTRODUCTION

Between the Restoration and the 1730s a decisive shift takes place in the composition and attitudes of audiences, which has far-reaching consequences for theatre managers, actors and playwrights. At the Restoration, the theatre is predominantly a court-based institution. The actors are liveried servants of the Royal household (although their salaries or profits are derived from a commercial undertaking); the audiences are drawn from an educated and elite section of society; the repertoire is designed to appeal to their tastes. The only conduct in the theatre that is censured or punished is an attack on the King and his retinue; desultory attempts are made from time to time to regulate audience behaviour, but to little effect. There are frequent intrigues involving actresses and actors and their would-be keepers from the gentry or nobility. Conversely, a gradual increase in the numbers of citizens and prentices attending the theatres meets with the disapproval of an avid theatre-goer like Pepys who belongs to the civil-service establishment. Gossip and hearsay fulfil the function of theatre criticism.

By the early 1700s, this pattern has changed quite discernibly. The theatre is now a largely commercial undertaking, quite separate from the court, even though the Lord Chamberlain remains in direct control of theatre affairs. The audiences are increasingly drawn from a less sophisticated section of society, and corresponding changes in the repertoire have to be made. The verbal subtleties and innuendoes of Restoration drama need to be made palatable by the addition of entr'acte and afterpiece entertainment that is less intellectually challenging: songs, dances and pantomimes all now begin to find their way on to the repertoire and play an increasingly important role in the commercial popularity of a given theatre.

By the 1720s, there is a marked split in the interests of theatre audiences. The nobility and gentry find themselves increasingly attracted by the musical and visual splendours of Italian opera; the less sophisticated members of London's theatre-going public are drawn to the pantomimes of John Rich; while the main attraction of straight theatre is a series of plays with clear political import.

Arguably the most significant development, however, is the growth of a puritan base for theatre criticism around the turn of the century. The morality debates sparked off by the Jeremy Collier controversy in the late 1690s mark a watershed in the history of the theatre in England. The polemic tracts published in the wake of the controversy, the essays published by Steele and Addison in 1708–9, all mark the inception of formal theatre criticism and indicate a fundamental shift in audience expectation from the subtle satirical approach of Jacobean and Restoration theatre to the moralising, sentimental approach of the eighteenth century. These early examples of moralising, puritan theatre criticism (only opposed by a few Tory satirists) set the tone and pattern of most theatre criticism in England for the remainder of the eighteenth century and beyond.

AUDIENCE BEHAVIOUR, COMPOSITION AND PRICES OF ADMISSION

Samuel Pepys's diary is the major source of information on audience responses during the Restoration. His scattered references to theatre-going experiences during the nine years in which he wrote his diary (1660–9) provide a lively account of subjects as diverse as the behaviour of individual members of the audience [*see* 150]; the changing composition of audiences [*see* 151]; prices of admission [*see* 152]; and the orange wenches [*see* 153].

A number of salient points emerge from his account. The most important is the fact that the theatre of the Restoration was an unashamedly social institution, a place to be seen and heard, not simply a place to sit and listen [*see* 150b]. The Restoration audience was lively and boisterous but also warm and appreciative. On the other hand, any play or actor falling short of the audience's expectations would be met by a barrage of comment and repartee. There were also frequent distractions: quarrels amongst young bloods [*see* 153c and d], noisy orange wenches plying their trade [*see* 153] and the intrigues of the wealthy and the beautiful.

The Restoration audience was acutely aware of rank and hierarchy. Pepys was a typical member of the civil-service establishment who knew his worth and his place. And he was greatly put out when his social inferiors – prentices and citizens at Christmas or New Year [*see* 151a and b] or clerks from his own office [*see* 151c] – sat in a better place than he did. The prices charged for admission were 12 *d* for the top gallery; 18 *d* for the middle gallery; 2 *s* 6 *d* for the pit; and 4 *s* for the boxes [*see* 151b and 152b]. It was not until 1667 that Pepys sat for the first time in a box. Premières often saw the prices doubled, which sent the frugal Pepys up into the top gallery [*see* 152a]. On the other hand, Pepys and his contemporaries availed themselves of the tacitly accepted (although officially prohibited) [*see* 154a] privilege of seeing the final act of a play without payment [*see* 152c and d]. The prices charged reflect an established sense of social hierarchy.

The overall impression to emerge from Pepys's account is of an audience that was often fractious and noisy, deeply aware of social rank, but generally warm-hearted and well informed.

150   Pepys comments on the behaviour of individual members of the audience
Pepys (Latham and Matthews eds.)

18 FEBRUARY 1667 (vol. 8, pp. 71–2)

To the King's House to *The Maid's Tragedy*; but vexed all the while with two talking ladies and Sir Charles Sedley, yet pleased to hear their discourse, he being a stranger. And one of the ladies would and did sit with her mask on, all the play and, being exceedingly witty as ever I heard woman, did talk most pleasantly with him; but was, I believe, a virtuous woman and of quality. He would fain know who she was, but she would not tell; yet did give him many pleasant hints of her knowledge of him, by that means setting his brains at work to find out who she was, and did give him leave to use all means to find out who she was but pulling off her mask. He was mighty witty and she also, making sport of him very inoffensively, that a more pleasant rencontre I never heard. By that means lost the pleasure of the play wholly, to which now and then Sir Charles Sedley's exceptions against both words and pronouncing were very pretty.

151   Pepys comments on the changing composition of the audience
Pepys (Latham and Matthews eds.)

(A) 27 DECEMBER 1662 (vol. 3, pp. 295–6)

After dinner, with my wife to the Duke's Theatre and saw the second part of *Rhodes* done with the new Roxalana,[1] who does it rather better in all respects, for person, voice and judgement than the first Roxalana. Home with great content with my wife. Only not so well pleased with the company at the house today, which was full of citizens, there hardly being a gentleman or woman in the house but a couple of pretty ladies by us that made sport at it, being jostled and crowded by prentices.

[1] The first actress to play Roxalana was Hester Davenport who was enticed away from the theatre by the Earl of Oxford. The actress who replaced her and found such favour with Pepys was one Mrs Norton, about whom very little is known.

(B) 1 JANUARY 1668 (vol. 9, p. 2)

Thence I after dinner to the Duke of York's playhouse, and there saw *Sir Martin Marall*, which I have seen so often; and yet am mightily pleased with it and think it mighty witty and the fullest proper matter for mirth that ever was writ. And I do clearly see that they do improve in their acting of it. Here a mighty company of citizens, prentices and others; and it makes me observe that when I began first to be able to bestow a play on myself, I do not remember that I saw so many by half of the ordinary prentices and mean people in the pit at 2 s 6 d a piece, as now. I going for several years no higher than the 12 d and then the 18 d places, and though I strained hard to go in then when I did. So much the vanity and prodigality of the age is to be observed in this particular.

(C) 19 JANUARY 1661 (vol. 2, p. 18)

After dinner [. . .] went to the theatre where I saw *The Lost Lady* [Sir William Berkeley], which does not please me much. Here I was troubled to be seen by four of our office clerks who sat in the half-crown box and I in the 1 s 6 d.[1]

[1] The normal price of a box was 4 s. The reference here must be to a part of the middle gallery, closed off as a 2 s 6 d box.

152   Pepys comments on the prices of admission and the practice of gaining free entry for the last act of a play
Pepys (Latham and Matthews eds.)

(A) 16 DECEMBER 1661 (vol. 2, p. 234)

After dinner to the opera, where there was a new play [*Cutter of Coleman Street*] made in the year 1658, with reflections upon the late times. And it being the first time, the pay was doubled; and to save money, my wife and I went up into the gallery and there sat and saw very well; and a very good play it is – it seems of Cowley's making.

(B) 19 OCTOBER 1667 (vol. 8, p. 487)

At noon home to a short dinner, being full of my desire of seeing my Lord Orrery's new play this afternoon at the King's house, *The Black Prince*, the first time it is acted. Where, though we came by 2 o'clock, yet there was no room in the pit, but we were forced to go into one of the upper boxes at 4 s a piece, which is the first time I ever sat in a box in my life. And in the same box came by and by, behind me, my Lord Berkeley and his Lady; but I did not turn my face to them to be known so that I was excused from giving them my seat. And this pleasure I had, that from this place the scenes do appear very fine indeed and much better than in the pit.

(C) 25 NOVEMBER 1661 (vol. 2, p. 220)

Sir W. Penn and I to the theatre and there saw *The Country Captain* [Marquess of Newcastle], a dull play; and that being done, I left him with his tories [Irishmen] and went to the opera and saw the last act of *The Bondman* [Massinger].

(D) 11 FEBRUARY 1668 (vol. 9, pp. 62–3)

To the Duke of York's playhouse and there saw the last act for nothing; where I never saw such good acting of any creature as Smith's part of Zanger [in *Mustapha* by the Earl of Orrery].

153   The orange wenches and their patrons
Pepys (Latham and Matthews eds.)

(A) 11 MAY 1668 (vol. 9, p. 195)

But there happened one thing which vexed me, which is, that the orange-woman did come in the pit and challenge me for twelve oranges, which she delivered by my order at a late play at night to give to some ladies in a box, which was wholly untrue, but yet she swore it to be true. But, however, I did deny it and did not pay her; but for quiet did buy 4 *s* worth of oranges of her, at 6 *d* a-piece.

(B) 2 NOVEMBER 1667 (vol. 8, pp. 516–17)

And it was observable how a gentleman of good habit, sitting just before us, eating of some fruit in the midst of the play, did drop down as dead, being choked. But with much ado, Orange Moll did thrust her finger down his throat and brought him to life again.

(C) WILLIAM HOGARTH: *THE LAUGHING AUDIENCE*, 1733
Works of Hogarth, vol. 4, 1857–5–9–20. (Print Room, BM)

ATTEMPTS TO REGULATE AUDIENCE BEHAVIOUR AND SPORADIC REPORTS OF UNRULY CONDUCT

Audiences invariably establish their own unwritten rules and conventions. The Restoration was no exception. Much to the chagrin of the theatre managers, patrons of the Restoration playhouses asserted their importance by occasionally clambering onto the stage, wandering around backstage and importuning actresses in their dressing room. They also demanded free admission for the last act of a play. At frequent intervals, from the Restoration to the early eighteenth century, successive Lord Chamberlains issued edicts banning all or some of these practices. Presumably to little or no effect.

154   The Lord Chamberlain attempts to regulate audience behaviour in the playhouses

(A) ENTRANCE TO PLAYHOUSES, 7 DECEMBER 1663
PRO LC 7/1, p. 1

Whereas we are informed that diverse persons do rudely press and with evil language and blows force their way into the two theatres at the times of their public representations and acting without paying the prices established, to the great disturbance of our servants licensed by our authority and to the danger of the public peace: our will and pleasure therefore is, and we do hereby strictly charge and command, that no person of what quality soever presume rudely or by force to come into either of the two theatres till the plays are quite finished, without paying the prices established for the respective plays, as they will answer to the contrary at their peril, notwithstanding their pretended privilege by custom of forcing their entrance at the fourth or fifth acts without payment. And all our officers, civil and military, are required to be aiding and assisting therein. And whosoever shall presume to disobey our aforesaid orders, we do hereby command the officers and guards appointed to keep the peace of the said theatres that they immediately take the offenders into custody and bring them before the Lord Chamberlain of our Household to answer their misdemeanour.

(B) PRINTED BILL ON ENTRY TO PLAYHOUSES, 2 FEBRUARY 1673
PRO LC 7/3, f. 1

Whereas complaint has often been made to us that diverse persons do rudely press and with evil language and blows force their way into our theatres (called the Theatre Royal in Bridges Street and the Duke's Theatre in Dorset Garden) at the time of their public representations and acting, without paying the price established at both the said theatres, to the great disturbance of our servants, licensed by our authority, as well as others, and to the danger of the public peace: our will and pleasure therefore is, and we do hereby straightly charge and command, that no person of what quality soever do presume to come into either of the said theatres before and during the time of acting and until the plays are quite finished, without paying the price established for the respective places. And our further command is that the money which shall be so paid by any persons for their respective places shall not be returned again, after it is once paid, notwithstanding that such persons shall go out at any time before or during the play. And (to avoid future fraud) that none hereafter shall enter the pit, first or upper gallery, without delivering to the respective door-keeper the ticket or tickets which they received for their money paid at the first door.

And forasmuch as 'tis impossible to command those vast engines (which move the scenes and machines) and to order such a number of persons as must be employed in works of that nature, if any but such as belong thereunto be suffered to press in amongst them. Our will and command is that no person of what quality soever presume to stand or sit on the stage, or to come within any part of the scenes, before the play begins, while 'tis acting, or after 'tis ended. And we strictly hereby command our officers and guards of soldiers which attend theatres to see this order exactly observed. And if any person whatsoever shall disobey this our known pleasure and command, we shall proceed against them as contemners of our royal authority and disturbers of the public peace.

(c) PRINTED BILL. AUDIENCE FORBIDDEN TO COME ON STAGE, 2 MARCH 1708
PRO LC 7/3, f. 32

Whereas we are informed that frequent disorders have been occasioned of late in our theatres in the Haymarket and Drury Lane by persons coming behind the scenes and standing upon the stage during the performance of plays and operas, by which means they cannot be acted to the best advantage: our will and pleasure therefore is, and we do hereby strictly require and command the managers, sharers, etc. of both our theatres in the Haymarket and Drury Lane that they suffer no person whatever hereafter to come behind the scenes, or be upon the stage, either before or during the acting any play or opera, excepting the actors and servants necessary for the performance thereof, upon pain of our highest displeasure. And we further strictly command all our constables and others appointed to attend the theatres to be aiding and assisting to our managers therein. And if any person whatsoever shall disobey this our known will and pleasure and command, we shall proceed against them as contemners of our royal authority and disturbers of the public peace.

Disorderly conduct

From time to time, disorders in the audience got out of hand. When that happened, the offending theatre was normally closed for a brief period. On one such occasion in 1680, when some gentlemen in their cups interrupted the performance by speaking ill of the actors and, more importantly, of one of the King's mistresses, not only was the theatre closed, but the gentlemen concerned were reportedly prosecuted for riotous behaviour [see 155a and b]. On another occasion in 1682, two young hotheads quarrelled and fought a duel on stage, one of the combatants receiving a serious wound [see 155c and d]. In 1737, a London newspaper reported how disorderly conduct outside Covent Garden playhouse threatened to turn into a full-blown riot and to spill into the playhouse itself on an evening when the Prince and Princess of Wales were visiting the theatre [see 155e].

155   Reports of unruly behaviour in 1680 and 1682

(A) 5 FEBRUARY 1680 R.J. Smith: *A collection of material towards a history of the English stage*, vol. 20 (BL, 1825–40), f. 169

On Monday night last happened a great disorder in the Duke's playhouse. Some gentlemen in their cups entering the pit, flinging links at the actors and using several reproachful speeches against the Duchess of P[ortsmouth] and other persons of honour, which has occasioned a prohibition from further acting till His Majesty's further pleasure.

(B) NEWDIGATE NEWSLETTERS
Reproduced in J.H. Wilson: 'Theatre notes from the Newdigate newsletter' in *TN* 15 (1960–1), 80

9 FEBRUARY 1680

The late disorders at the playhouse have so much incensed His Majesty that 'tis said he has commanded the persons to be proceeded against as rioters.

12 FEBRUARY 1680

Those who lately made the disturbance in the Duke's playhouse are to be proceeded against as rioters.

(C) *IMPARTIAL PROTESTANT MERCURY*, 2 MAY 1682
Copy in Smith, vol. 20 (1825–40), f. 170

Mr Ch[arles] D[eering], son to Sir Edw. D. and Mr V[aughan] quarrelled in the Duke's playhouse and presently mounted the stage and fought, and Mr D. was very dangerously wounded and Mr V. secured lest it should prove mortal.

(D) NEWDIGATE NEWSLETTERS Reproduced in Wilson *TN* 15 (1960–1), 80

29 APRIL 1682

Mr Vaughan and Mr Charles Deering fought this week and the last dangerously hurt – on the playhouse stage.

(E) *THE LONDON DAILY POST*, 1 FEBRUARY 1737
Miscellaneous newspaper cuttings on the London theatres, June 1704 to March 1779, vol. 2 (BL)

There having been a great disturbance made on Saturday last at Covent Garden playhouse, the persons concerned in it were yesterday examined before Colonel De

Veil. And it appeared that one Francis Cooke, a gentleman's coachman, who had picked up a woman, did in a very impudent, saucy manner assault the sentry who had the care of His Royal Highness's chair in the playhouse passage and would force into the said chair the woman he had so picked up to make, as he had the impudence to call it, a bawdy house of the Prince's chair, which the sentry refusing to suffer, he struck him several blows over the head with his whip and in the same manner served three sentries more. This behaviour of his occasioned so great a disturbance and mob that the Captain of the Guard had much ado to quell the disturbance and prevent the mob from breaking into the playhouse where His Royal Highness, the Prince of Wales, and the Princess of Wales were. [. . .] The gentleman discharged his servant Francis Cook at Colonel De Veil's upon hearing the depositions taken against him.

References to contemporary events and to other colleagues

During the Restoration, any references by actors to contemporary events or important personalities were subtly or obliquely expressed. (Any actor departing from this practice, as Lacy discovered in 1667 [see 104], was immediately punished.) By the early eighteenth century, with a less sophisticated audience frequenting the theatre and a less autocratic monarch on the throne, actors at times encouraged a more obvious and immediate response to contemporary events or personalities. Uffenbach witnessed one such occasion, when the actors in a 1710 production of *The Recruiting Officer* mocked Marlborough, much to the delight of the audience, for his legendary meanness [see 156].

Some actors were rather less reticent about mocking the work of their colleagues, even if this eventually meant their dismissal from the company. The dancer and comic actor Joe Haines was notorious for his disorderly conduct in general and for his disrespect towards senior colleagues in particular. In 1677 Hart, who was managing Drury Lane at the time, dismissed him, following an episode where Haines had behaved outrageously on stage and had encouraged an audience to laugh at Hart's performance in Ben Jonson's *Catiline* [see 157]. In later life, following a number of adventures abroad, Haines returned to the London theatre and became famous for his ability to deliver satirical prologues and epilogues, the most famous of which he delivered sitting on an ass at Drury Lane in 1697, as shown in an early eighteenth-century frontispiece for the play, Scott's *The Unhappy Kindness* [see 158].

156   Uffenbach describes the actors and audience mocking Marlborough for his meanness in 1710

Uffenbach (1934), pp. 138–9. Original version in Uffenbach, vol. 2 (1753), pp. 598–9.

24 JULY 1710

In the afternoon we made purchases in various shops and in the evening went to the play, *The Recruiting Officer*. This is one of the most elegant and diverting pieces and is very frequently played. On this occasion the actors represented a prodigiously satirical interscenium, which was not to be found in the printed copy of the play. [. . .] In this interlude, a troop of soldiers came on, singing at the top of their voice an English song which had been made by the army in Flanders about the

Duke of Marlborough. In it Prince Eugene is praised for his open-handedness, while Marlborough on the other hand is blamed for his avarice, so that every verse ended:

> but Marlborough not a penny!

The people, who are very bitter against the whole family, even the Duke himself, laughed prodigiously and bandied about monstrous insults, although Marlborough's daughter, the Duchess of Montaigu, was herself at the play and was so greatly shamed that she was covered with blushes. I protest that I was myself greatly angered at their insolence in heaping public opprobrium on so brave a general, above all in the Queen's Theatre, though it cannot be denied that he has made for himself a most evil reputation through his excessive avarice. When the song was at an end, there was such a clapping and yelling that the actors were unable to proceed for nearly a quarter of an hour.

157   Joe Haines deliberately wrecks Hart's performance in *Catiline* in 1677

Tobias Thomas [Alias Thomas Brown]: *The life of the late famous comedian, Jo Haynes* (London: J. Nutt, 1701), pp. 23–4

There happened to be one night a play acted called *Catiline's Conspiracy*, wherein there was wanting a great number of senators. Now Mr Hart, being chief of the house, would oblige Joe to dress for one of these senators, although Joe's salary being then 50 s per week freed him from any such obligation.

But Mr Hart, as I said before, being sole governor of the playhouse and at a small variance with Joe, commands it and the other must obey. Joe, being vexed at the slight Mr Hart had put on him, he gets a Scaramouche dress; a large full ruff; makes himself whiskers from ear to ear; puts on his head a long Merry Andrews cap; a short pipe in his mouth; a little three-legged stool in his hand; and in this manner follows Mr Hart on stage, sets himself down behind him, and begins to smoke his pipe, to laugh and point at him.

Which comical figure put all the house in an uproar, some laughing, some clapping, and some hollowing. Now Mr Hart, as those that knew him can aver, was a man of that exactness and grandeur on the stage that, let what would happen, he'd never discompose himself or mind anything but what he then represented. And had a scene fallen behind him, he would not at that time look back to have seen what was the matter, which Joe, knowing, remained still smoking, the audience continued laughing, Mr Hart acting and wondering at this unusual occasion of their mirth, sometimes thinking it some disturbance in the house; again, that it might be something amiss in his dress. At last, turning himself towards the scenes, he discovered Joe in the aforesaid posture, whereupon he immediately goes off the stage, swearing he would never set foot on it again unless Joe was immediately turned out of doors; which was no sooner spoken but put in practice. So our grave senator was presently dismissed the Senate and turned out of the house [. . .].

158   Joe Haines delivers an epilogue sitting on an ass at Drury Lane in 1697

Thomas Brown: *Works, being a collection of poems, letters, essays, etc.*, vol. 5 (London: Sam Briscoe, 1721), facing p. 233

THE ACTRESSES AND THE MEN

The theatres of the Restoration were not large and anonymous institutions; on the contrary, they were small and compact, and built for close contact between actors and audience. Not surprisingly, members of the audience soon got to know actors and actresses on intimate terms. For the male patrons of the theatres, the friendship of an actress was highly valued, particularly as there was often an erotic component in the liaison. Pepys makes the point well, delighting in his close relationship with Mrs Knepp, until the understandable jealousy of his wife made him renounce this valued friendship.

159   Samuel Pepys's relationship with Elizabeth Knepp

Pepys (Latham and Matthews eds.)

2 FEBRUARY 1669 (vol. 9, pp. 435–6)

To the King's playhouse, where *The Heiress*, notwithstanding Kynaston's being beaten,[1] is acted; and they say the king is very angry with Sir Ch. Sedley for his being beaten; but he does deny it. [. . .] but that that pleased me most in the play is the first song that Knepp sings (she singing three or four); and indeed, it was very finely sung, so as to make the whole house clap her. To the office about my letters; and then home to supper and to bed, my wife being in mighty ill humour all night; and in the morning, I found it to be from her observing Knepp to wink and smile on me, and she says I smiled on her; and poor wretch, I did perceive that she did, and does on all such occasions, mind my eyes. I did with much difficulty pacify her and were friends, she desiring that hereafter at that house we might always sit either above in a box or, if there be room, close up to the lower boxes.

[1] Kynaston resembled Sir Charles Sedley and dressed like him in the production of *The Heiress*. To take his revenge, Sedley hired a villain to give Kynaston a beating in St James's Park, pretending that he mistook the actor for Sedley.

Becke Marshall

Other male members of the audience were less successful at establishing a happy rapport with the actresses of the period and insisted on forcing their unwanted attentions on a succession of unfortunate victims. One of Pepys's favourite actresses, Becke Marshall, was subjected to two violent assaults from well-born louts in the mid 1660s and complained of her treatment to the King.

160   Rebecca Marshall is attacked by two loutish admirers

(A) TO THE KING'S MOST EXCELLENT MAJESTY, THE HUMBLE PETITION OF REBECCA MARSHALL, 1665
PRO SP 29/142 pt. II, no. 160, p. 195

Humbly shows that your petitioner has been several times barbarously and insolently affronted by one Mark Trevor of the Temple Esq., as well upon the stage as off. Your petitioner has forborn to prosecute justice against him in hope he would henceforth forbear to injure her.

But so it is that this afternoon the said Trevor assaulted her violently in a coach and, after many horrid oaths and threats that he would be revenged of her for complaining to my Lord Chamberlain formerly of him, pursued her with his sword in his hand; and when by flight she had secured herself in a house, he continued his abusive language and broke the windows of the adjoining house. And by the manner of his carriage, your petitioner is in fear of her life.

Your petitioner therefore implores your Majesty's protection and prays the said Trevor may be restrained from doing her further injury according to your Majesty's great goodness and wisdom.

(B) THE DEPOSITION OF MRS REBECCA MARSHALL AGAINST SIR HUGH
MIDDLETON, 8 FEBRUARY 1666
PRO SP 29/191, no. 31, pp. 53–4. Copy in Smith, vol. 10 (1825–40), between ff. 153–4.
Reproduced in *BD*, vol. 7, pp. 426–7

On Saturday last, Sir Hugh entering into the tiring house or behind the scenes of
the playhouse, Mrs Marshall taxed him with some ill language he had cast out
against the women actors of that house and added that she wondered he would
come amongst them. Sir Hugh being disgusted at this, after a short discourse, grew
into a heat and told her she lied and concluded the injury with calling her a jade
and threatened he would kick her and that his footman should kick her.

Mrs Marshall on the Monday following, frightened with his menaces, complained of him to the King and desired His Majesty's protection from further
injuries.

Upon Tuesday in the evening, having acted in the play that day and returning
to her lodging, in the great entry going out of the playhouse into Drury Lane, she
saw Sir Hugh Middleton standing there, which gave her some apprehension that
he lay in wait to do her some mischief or affront, which she declared to Mr Quin
who led her home. Some few doors from the playhouse, a ruffian pressed hard
upon her, insomuch that she complained first of his rudeness and after turned
about and said, 'I think the fellow would rob me or pick my pocket.' Upon which,
he turned his face and seemed to slink away. And when she thought she was quite
rid of him, near the entrance of the court where she lodges (the street being there
free of coaches), the same ruffian ran close up to her and claps a turd upon her face
and hair and fled away in a trice.

That this was a formed design appears by the fellow's pursuit of her from the
playhouse to her lodging and that Sir Hugh suborned him appears:

    1. Because the said Mrs Marshall has no difference at present with any
other man or woman in England.

    2. Because it was the same day that the news broke out that she had been
at Court and received a gracious promise from His Majesty that she
should not be injured.

    3. Because Sir H. Middleton was seen by her in the entry of the playhouse
a good while after the play was done, a place where no people of quality do
stop at any time longer than to take coach or chair, which he could not
want, many coaches standing empty and all the audience wholly retired.

Mrs Marshall is ready to take her oath if this is required and does believe it may be
proved, if need be, that Sir Hugh did the same day discover a malicious design of
doing her a mischief. And the premises duly considered, she humbly implores His
Majesty's protection and justice as well for her vindication from these barbarous
injuries as for her security for the future.

THE REPERTOIRE AND CHANGES IN AUDIENCE COMPOSITION AND TASTE AT THE TURN
OF THE CENTURY

Theatre audiences are never static in composition. Audiences can vary from night to night,
and certainly do vary from year to year, in terms of their taste, social refinement, education

and class. Even in the early years of the Restoration, Pepys, as we have seen, complained of the increasing numbers of citizens and prentices attending the theatre around Christmas and the New Year.

By the turn of the century, the distinctive audience of the Restoration, boisterous and yet well educated, had largely disappeared. In 1702, John Dennis bemoaned the fact in one of his critical essays. With deft precision, he pinpoints the major changes that have taken place. A delight in the satirical treatment of individual patterns of behaviour has been replaced by a growing obsession with politics; a less sophisticated and well educated audience expects a correspondingly undemanding repertoire of light entertainment, including dance, music and farce; tired businessmen want soothing distraction, not food for thought [see 161]. The mixed repertoire of plays and lighter interludes of dance and music that resulted from such popular pressure is described by Uffenbach on one of his London theatre visits in 1710 [see 162].

The decline in the intellectual standard of the repertoire at the turn of the century was matched by an equal decline in the popularity of the theatre amongst the well-to-do. The monarchs of the 1690s and 1700s, William III and Anne, showed little enthusiasm for the theatre, in marked contrast to Charles and James. The amorous intrigues of the wealthy and beautiful were no longer to be observed in the public playhouses; instead, common prostitutes plied their trade in increasing numbers, much to the chagrin of those who wanted to see the theatre reformed and cleaned up [see 163]. The scene was set for the morality debates that were to radically affect the work of the London theatres after 1700.

161   John Dennis outlines the major changes in audience composition and taste since the Restoration, 1702

Edward Niles Hooker (ed.): *The critical works of John Dennis*, vol. 1 (Baltimore: The John Hopkins Press, 1939), pp. 289–94

'A large account of the taste in poetry and the causes of the degeneracy of it.' To the Honourable George Granville, Esq., 1702.

But Sir, whether the general taste of England ever was good or no, this I think cannot be controverted, that the taste of England for comedy [. . .] was certainly much better in the reign of King Charles the Second than it is at present. [. . .]

First then, in the reign of King Charles the Second, a considerable part of an audience had those parts which were requisite for the judging of comedy [. . .] principally a fine imagination and a sound judgement. [. . .]

Secondly then, in the reign of King Charles the Second, a considerable part of an audience had such an education as qualified them to judge of comedy. That reign was a reign of pleasure, even the entertainments of their closet were all delightful. Poetry and eloquence were then their studies and that human, gay and sprightly philosophy, which qualified them to relish the only reasonable pleasures which man can have in the world, and those are conversation and dramatic poetry. [. . .] All the sheer originals in town were known and in some measure copied. But now the case is vastly different. For all those great and numerous originals are reduced to one single coxcomb, and that is the foolish false politician. For from Westminster to Wapping, go where you will, the conversation turns upon politics. [. . .]

Besides, there are three sorts of people now in our audiences who have had no education at all and who were unheard of in the reign of King Charles the Second. A great many younger brothers, gentlemen born, who have been kept at home, by reason of the pressure of the taxes. Several people who made their fortunes in the late war and who, from a state of obscurity and perhaps of misery, have risen to a condition of distinction and plenty. I believe that no man will wonder if these people who, in their original obscurity, could never attain to any higher entertainment than tumbling and vaulting and ladder dancing and the delightful diversions of Jack Pudding, should still be in love with their old sports and encourage these noble pastimes still upon the stage. But a third sort of people who may be said to have had no education at all in relation to us and our plays is that considerable number of foreigners which, within these last twenty years, have been introduced among us. Some of whom, not being acquainted with our language and consequently with the sense of our plays, and others, disgusted with our extravagant, exorbitant rambles, have been instrumental in introducing sound and show, where the business of the theatre does not require it and particularly a sort of a soft and wanton music, which has used the people to a delight which is independent of reason, a delight that has gone a very great way towards the enervating and dissolving their minds.

But thirdly, in the reign of King Charles the Second, a considerable part of an audience had that due application, which is requisite for the judging of comedy. They had first of all leisure to attend to it. For that was an age of pleasure and not of business. They were serene enough to receive its impressions, for they were in ease and plenty. But in the present reign, a great part of the gentlemen have not leisure, because want throws them upon employments and there are ten times more gentlemen now in business than there were in King Charles's reign. Nor have they serenity [. . .] by reason that they are attentive to the events of affairs and too full of great and real events to receive due impressions from the imaginary ones of the theatre. They come to a playhouse full of some business which they have been soliciting, or of some harangue which they are to make the next day, so that they merely come to unbend and are utterly incapable of duly attending to the just and harmonious symmetry of a beautiful design. Besides, the faction which has been so long in their politics is got into their pleasures and they refuse to be delighted with what some people write, not because they really dislike it, but only because others are pleased with it, as if any one should be such a sot to refuse champagne because his enemy finds it delicious. [. . .]

162   Uffenbach describes the mixed repertoire of a typical London theatre in 1710

Uffenbach (1934), pp. 30–1. Original version in Uffenbach, vol. 2 (1753), pp. 456–7

13 JUNE 1710

In the evening we saw an extremely live comedy: *The Fair Quaker of Deal*, an uncommonly curious play, in which English quakers and quakeresses are represented most naturally. The female who played the chief part, that of a quaker, is a person well known throughout England, called Mrs Sandlow. She is universally admired for her beauty, matchless figure and the unusual elegance of her dancing and acting, and she is visited by those of the highest fashion in England. [. . .] The comedy was played in Drury Lane. The theatre here is neither so large nor near as elegant as that in the Haymarket. Between every act they introduced several dances for variety, which is never done there. The above-mentioned actress danced charmingly as Harlequin, which suits her excellently and much pleases the English. They make such a to-do about her that her portrait in this costume is painted on snuff-boxes and frequently sold. After her a man appeared as Scara-mouche, but he was far from being as elegant a dancer, though he excels in droll attitudes, leaping and contortions of the body, in which I never saw his equal. The most amazing of all was that he danced a chique [gigue] with great agility on the tips of his toes with his feet turned entirely inwards, so that one cannot conceive how he was able to bend his feet thus backwards, stand on tiptoes and spring about without straining his feet or breaking them at the ankle-joints. He jumped so high in the air and with such frequency, alighting each time on his toes, that, when he suddenly collapsed, his feet were not to be seen; then he immediately sprang up again without putting his hands to the ground to help himself. [. . .] Finally a person with a horse, who was dressed as a mountebank or gipsy, came on to the stage and sang very well a long song, which was much clapped by the English; but we could not understand it, as it was not printed with the play.

163   Wright describes the nuisance of prostitution in the London theatres at the turn of the century
Wright: *Historia Histrionica*. Cibber (Lowe ed.), p. xxvii

Do not wonder, but consider that though the town was then [in Elizabethan England] perhaps not much more than half so populous as now, yet then the prices were small (there being no scenes) and better order kept among the company that came, which made very good people think a play an innocent diversion for an idle hour or two, the plays themselves being then, for the most part, more instructive and moral. Whereas of late, the playhouses are so extremely pestered with vizard masks and their trade, (occasioning continual quarrels and abuses) that many of the more civilised part of the town are uneasy in the company and shun the theatre as they would a house of scandal.

THE MORALITY DEBATES AT THE TURN OF THE CENTURY

A dissenting High Church clergyman, called Jeremy Collier, summed up the feelings of a growing number of honest citizens in London, as well as members of polite society, when he wrote his vituperative critique of the stage in 1698: *A short view of the immorality and profaneness of the English stage*.[1] The explosive effect of this lengthy diatribe was both far-reaching and long-lasting. Initially, established playwrights such as Congreve and Vanbrugh felt impelled to write in their own defence.[2] In the long term, Collier's attack gave heart to men such as Steele and Addison who wanted to see a shift from the outspoken satiric approach of Restoration playwrights to the moralising sentimental approach to playwriting pioneered by Colley Cibber in his play *Love's Last Shift* of 1695.

As a direct result of Collier's attack, groups of puritan-minded guardians of morality initiated a spate of prosecutions against actors for uttering profane language on stage. They based their cases on a statute enacted in the days of James I [3 Jac I], forbidding profane utterance in public. Even Betterton found himself arraigned before the law.[3] The only prosecution that succeeded, however, was that brought against a relatively minor member of Betterton's troupe, George Bright, who complained bitterly to the Lord Chamberlain at being singled out in this fashion [see 164].

The outcome of his complaint is not known, although Queen Anne eventually entered a *nolle prosequi* in respect of the other cases.[4] In so doing she re-asserted the Crown's traditional control over the acting companies and their welfare, despite the fact that she herself was much in favour of the campaign to reform the stage.

Another effect of Collier's attack was to turn him into something of a public personality. His sermons and tracts were much in demand, and for a brief period in the early 1700s he kept his name in the public limelight with a series of astute variations on his anti-theatrical theme [see 165]. Such was the popularity of Collier's viewpoint that even would-be defenders of the theatre, such as James Wright, chose their words very carefully in expressing their opposition to Collier's stance [see 166].

[1] Much of the text is printed in J.E. Spingarn (ed.): *Critical essays of the seventeenth century*, vol. 3 (London: Oxford University Press, 1957), pp. 253–64.

[2] See William Congreve: *Amendments of Mr Collier's false and imperfect citations, etc. from The Old Bachelor, Double Dealer, Love for Love, Mourning Bride. By the author of those plays* (London, 1698). See also John Vanbrugh: *A short vindication of The Relapse and The Provoked Wife* (London, 1698).

[3] See Krutch (1924), pp. 170–4.

[4] *Ibid.*, p. 176.

164   George Bright complains of his prosecution to the Lord Chamberlain, 1701
PRO LC 7/3, f. 159. Reproduced in Krutch (1924), pp. 174–5.

The case of George Bright. Comedian at the Theatre in Lincoln's Inn Fields. That some time since, the said Bright was playing his part in the play called *Sir Fopling Flutter*, and in the conclusion of his part, these words are expressed: 'Please you, Sir, to commission a young couple to go to bed together, a' God's name.' Which being licensed and printed, the said Bright did humbly conceive that there was neither immorality or prophaneness therein; the said Bright as well as several others having often expressed the said words publicly on the stage, and no notice ever before taken thereof. But some maliciously busy person or persons informing against the said Bright have taken hold of the law, prosecuted him unknowingly and have surreptitiously obtained a verdict against him for £10, besides costs and charges, which amount to as much more. So that the said Bright is in continual danger of being taken up for the said £10 and costs and committed to gaol.

The said Bright therefore humbly begs your Honour to consider the hardness of this his case and hopes that, since the whole company are equally concerned in this matter, you will be pleased to order it so that the said company may be equal sharers in the payment of the said £10 with cost of suit, since by law it is ordered to be paid, or that you would be pleased to protect him, otherwise the said Bright and family must suffer.

(The case humbly presented to Sir John Stanley.)

165   Jeremy Collier continues his attack against the theatre, 1705

Jeremy Collier: *A letter to a lady concerning the new playhouse* (London: Joseph Downing, 1706), pp. 3–11

It was methought with some more than ordinary satisfaction that you seemed, when I was last to wait upon your Ladyship, to speak of the pleasant and convenient situation of your house, as being near the court, open to the park and but a little way from the new playhouse which is lately built in your neighbourhood. [. . .] I forgot then to ask your Ladyship at whose charge that topping playhouse was built, but I can't but think that the money contributed towards it would have been much better bestowed in building of churches, of which, at your end of the town, there is, I'm sure, much greater want than of playhouses. [. . .]

I can't but suspect, Madam, (though I hope I am mistaken in it) that your Ladyship has lent a helping hand to this work. But I'm sure your discourse gave me ground enough to believe that you intend, now it is finished, to partake of the benefit of it and to see plays more frequently than you could conveniently do, especially in the winter season, while the playhouses were at a greater distance. [. . .]

And, that I may not lay a stumbling block at the threshold, I do not now affirm that it is absolutely and altogether unlawful ever to go to see a play. But this I hope I may say with less offence: that to frequent the playhouse in the condition 'tis now in is not a matter of good report; that it is a thing which a good Christian may very well have some scruples about and consequently that it is much safer to be forborne, especially when no good reason can be given for going to see a play, but only for diversion sake. [. . .]

I never in my life saw a play and have not read very many; a few of them were sufficient to give me a surfeit and I never cared for them since. But so far as I can make a judgement from those which I have read, (and I'm sure I never chose to read the worst) their design is as wicked as their composure. For who and what is he that in our modern plays is commonly shown as a pattern to be imitated, the hero of the play, or the accomplished gentleman? What is he, I say, for the most part, but some accomplished debauchee that regards neither God nor man, who is above the discipline of priestcraft and can commit all manner of wickedness with a boon grace? Or, if he be not quite so bad as this, yet his greatest accomplishments usually are that he's well skilled in fashions and courtship and the humours of the town. This is the man that is usually shown to the spectators as one whose example 'tis fit all the young nobility and gentry should conform themselves to; and I'm sure they do it too much. And on the other side, what's he that from one end of the play to the other is represented as very silly and ridiculous beyond all the rest of mankind? Is it not commonly one that has more religion and more conscience than the rest? One that has not yet worn off all the impressions of a good and sober education? One that can't swear cleverly, nor damn roundly, nor sin impudently? [. . .] I have not, I confess, so much minded the women's characters. Your Ladyship, I suppose, may have done that better. But in those plays which I have happened to read, very few women have ever been brought upon the stage but under the notion of bawds, whores or jilts, or such as were easy to be wrought upon. Which respect commonly given by the playmakers to the fair sex should methinks work in the ladies some resentment. It should methinks somewhat abate of their forwardness to go to see themselves abused.

(Mr Collier's dissuasive from the playhouse in a letter to a person of quality, occasioned by the late calamity of the tempest. 29 September 1705.)

166   James Wright expresses cautious opposition to Collier's viewpoint
Wright: *Historia Histrionica*. Cibber (Lowe ed.), p. xxxiii

In my mind Mr Collier's reflections are pertinent and true in the main, the book ingeniously written and well intended. But he has overshot himself in some places, and his respondents perhaps in more. My affection inclines me not to engage on either side but rather mediate. If there are abuses relating to the stage, (which I think is too apparent), let the abuse be reformed and not the use, for that reason only, abolished.

THE DIVERGING INTERESTS OF THEATRE AUDIENCES DURING THE REIGN OF GEORGE I
Commercial exploitation of popular taste

After the turbulent start to the 1700s, when the issue of stage reform had greatly exercised the minds of contemporary theatre-goers and pamphleteers, the more stable theatrical climate that characterised the reign of George I saw quite disinct theatre audiences emerging, with widely differing tastes and interests. The less sophisticated theatre-goers showed an increasing fascination with pantomimes and masquerades, rather than with the plays themselves that still ostensibly made up the main part of an evening's theatre programme. Contemporary satirists, including Hogarth, took great delight in mocking the blatant commercialism of rival theatre managers pandering to popular taste.

167   Hogarth satirises commercial managers pandering to popular taste

William Hogarth: *The bad taste of the town*. The Burney Collection of Theatrical Portraits, vol. 4, no. 187, p. 101 (Print Room, BM)

Italian opera

The nobility and other wealthy theatre-goers turned their attention elsewhere, notably to the Italian operas mounted under the auspices of the Royal Academy of Music in the King's Theatre in the Haymarket. Foreign visitors to London noted the way contemporary audiences were obsessed by the personalities and rivalries of the virtuoso singing stars from Italy who now regularly graced the London operatic stage and commanded fabulous salaries in the process.

168   M. de Saussure describes the fascination of London theatre audiences with their operatic stars in 1728

Saussure (1902), pp. 271–3

There is an Italian opera in London, the contractors being certain noblemen at court. The symphony is composed of skilled musicians, both English and foreign, and the singers are all Italian. Two famous singers, the Faustina and the Cozzoni, and one of the brothers Senazini are at present singing here; they are said to be the finest singers in Europe, and are very well paid, the two former receiving each £1,500, and the latter £1,200 sterling, for singing three times a week for four months, besides a benefit night, which brings them in about £250 sterling each. The court and town, men and women, are divided into two parties, one admiring the Faustina and the other the Cozzoni, and both parties load their respective favourite with presents, compliments and flatteries. I must own that both these women are excellent and admirable singers and can do anything they wish with their throats; such excellent singers have never been heard before, and I cannot tell you which of the two I prefer.

There are no men or women dancers at the opera, neither is there any machinery, but the scenes and decorations are often changed, some of them being of rare beauty; and it is a delight to the eyes to see the King, the Queen, and the Royal Family, the peers and peeresses, always beautifully dressed. One cannot understand much about the intrigue of the piece; it is sung in Italian, and the words that suit the music are sung over and over again. The opera is expensive, for you must pay half a guinea for the best places.

Political theatre

Finally, the growing interest in politics, to which John Dennis had already drawn attention in 1702, led inevitably to the politicisation of the theatre. Beginning with Addison [see **169**], but culminating with Gay [see **170**] and Fielding, London theatre audiences were treated, during the reign of George I and well into the 1730s, to a series of politically biased productions in which factional interest and satiric comment introduced a completely novel kind of excitement and tension into the world of the theatre.[1]

---

[1] The only parallel that might be drawn here is with the theatre in England in the 1530s, when John Bale and others introduced Reformation propaganda into their morality plays and moral interludes and provoked the Crown into giving the Lord Chamberlain his initial powers of censorship.

169   George Berkeley describes the first night of Addison's *Cato* in 1713

Benjamin Rand (ed.): *Berkeley and Percival. The correspondence of George Berkeley and Sir John Percival* (Cambridge: Cambridge University Press, 1914), pp. 113–14
Berkeley to Percival. London, April 16th, 1713

On Tuesday last Mr Addison's play entitled *Cato* was acted the first time. I am informed the front boxes were all bespoke for nine days, a fortnight before the play was acted. I was present with Mr Addison, and two or three more friends in a side box, where we had a table and two or three flasks of burgundy and champagne, with which the author (who is a very sober man) thought it necessary to support his spirits in the concern he was then under; and indeed it was a pleasant refreshment to us all between the acts. He has performed a very difficult task with great success, having introduced the noblest ideas of virtue and religion upon the stage with the greatest applause, and in the fullest audience that ever was known. The actors were at the expense of new habits, which were very magnificent, and Mr Addison takes no part of the profit, which will be very great, to himself. Some parts of the prologue, which were written by Mr Pope, a Tory and even a Papist, were hissed, being thought to favour of whiggism, but the clap got much [the better of] the hiss. My Lord Harley, who sat in the next box to us, was observed to clap as loud as any in the house all the time of the play. Though some Tories imagine his play to have an ill design, yet I am persuaded you are not so violent as to be displeased at the good success of an author (whose aim is to reform the stage) because his hero was thought to be a Roman whig.

170   Macklin describes the political excitement when Walpole attended a performance of *The Beggar's Opera* in 1728
William Cooke: *Memoirs of Charles Macklin, comedian* (London, 1804), pp. 53-5

Gay, however, by frequently comparing highwaymen to courtiers and mixing other political allusions, drew the attention of the public to the character of Sir Robert Walpole, then Prime Minister, who, like most other Prime Ministers, had a strong party against him who constantly took care to make or find a comparison between the two characters. A particular anecdote of this nature is told of Sir Robert [. . .].

In the scene where Peachum and Lockit are described settling their accounts [II, x, Air XXX], Lockit sings the song,

When you censure the age, etc.

which had such an effect on the audience that, as if by instinct, the greater part of them threw their eyes on the stage box where the Minister was sitting and loudly *encored* it. Sir Robert saw this stroke instantly and saw it with good humour and discretion; for no sooner was the song finished then he *encored* it a second time himself, joined in the general applause, and by this means brought the audience into so much good humour with him that they gave him a general huzza from all parts of the house.

But, notwithstanding this escape, every night, and for many years afterwards that *The Beggar's Opera* was brought out, Macklin used to say, the Minister [Sir Robert Walpole] never could with any satisfaction be present at its representation on account of the many allusions which the audience thought referred to his character. The first song was thought to point to him. The name of Bob Booty, whenever mentioned, again raised the laugh against him: and the quarrelling scene between Peachum and Lockit was so well understood at that time to allude to a recent quarrel between the two ministers, Lord Townshend and Sir Robert, that the house was in convulsions of applause.

THEATRE CRITICISM
Steele in The Tatler and The Spectator

In the early decades of the eighteenth century, there was no theatre criticism in the modern sense of the word. London's first regular daily newspaper, *The Daily Courant* (founded in 1702), was modelled on the news-letters of the seventeenth century. It was a simple sheet newspaper that concentrated on politics, diplomacy and finance.[1] Theatre performances were advertised but not discussed.

The first moves towards theatre criticism followed as a direct consequence of the morality debates at the turn of the century. Where Collier and his supporters wrote with the aim of destroying the theatre as a public institution [see 165], a new generation of writers, headed by the journalist and playwright Richard Steele, wanted to see the theatre reformed. Some of Steele's papers written for *The Tatler* (published from April 1709 to December

1710), where he discusses plays and actors in a relaxed reformist tone, constitute the earliest examples of published theatre criticism in England [*see* 171]. His later essays published in *The Spectator* are more vigorously 'improving' in tone, as in the case of his outspoken attack on Etherege's *Man of Mode* [*see* 172]. In this essay, he makes extensive use of detailed quotation from the text to press home his objections to the play.

¹ See Gray (1931), p. 28.

171   Steele's thumbnail sketches of plays and actors in *The Tatler*, 1709

(A) *THE COUNTRY WIFE*. WILL'S COFFEE HOUSE, 14 APRIL 1709

This evening the comedy called *The Country Wife* was acted in Drury Lane for the benefit of Mrs Bignell. The part which gives name to the play was performed by herself. Through the whole action she made a very pretty figure and exactly entered into the nature of the part. Her husband in the drama is represented to be one of those debauchees who run through the vices of the town and believe, when they think fit, they can marry and settle at their ease. His own knowledge of the iniquity of the age makes him choose a wife wholly ignorant of it and place his security in her want of skill to abuse him.

The poet, on many occasions where the propriety of the character will admit of it, insinuates that there is no defence against vice but the contempt of it: and has, in the natural ideas of an untainted innocent, shown the gradual steps to ruin and destruction which persons of condition run into without the help of a good education to form their conduct. The torment of a jealous coxcomb, which arises from his own false maxims, and the aggravation of his pain by the very words in which he sees her innocence, makes a very pleasant and instructive satire. The character of Horner and the design of it is a good representation of the age in which that comedy was written; at which time love and wenching were the business of life, and the gallant manner of pursuing women was the best recommendation at court. To this only it is to be imputed that a gentleman of Mr Wycherley's character and sense condescends to represent the insults done to the honour of the marriage bed without just reproof; but to have drawn a man of probity with regard to such considerations had been a monster, and a poet had at that time discovered his want of knowing the manners of the court he lived in, by a virtuous character in his fine gentlemen, as he would show his ignorance by drawing a vicious one to please the present audience.

Mrs Bignell did her part very happily and had a certain grace in her rusticity, which gave us hopes of seeing her a very skilful player and in some parts supply our loss of Mrs Verbruggen.

I cannot be of the same opinion with my friends and fellow labourers, the reformers of manners, in their severity towards plays; but must allow that a good play acted before a well-bred audience must raise very proper incitements to good behaviour and be the most quick and most prevailing method of giving young people a turn of sense and breeding.

(B) *EPSON WELLS.* WILL'S COFFEE HOUSE, 25 APRIL 1709

This evening the comedy called *Epson Wells* [by Thomas Shadwell] was acted for the benefit of Mr Bullock who, though he is a person of much wit and ingenuity, has a peculiar talent of looking like a fool and therefore is excellently well qualified for the part of Bisket in this play. I cannot indeed sufficiently admire his way of bearing a beating, as he does in this drama, and that with such a natural air and propriety of folly that one cannot help wishing the whip in one's own hand; so richly does he seem to deserve his chastisement. Skilful actors think it a very peculiar happiness to play in a scene with such as top their parts. Therefore I cannot but say, when the judgement of any good author directs him to write a beating for Mr Bullock from Mr William Pinkethman, or for Mr William Pinkethman from Mr Bullock, those excellent players seem to be in their most shining circumstances and please me more, but with a different sort of delight, than that which I receive from those grave scenes of Brutus and Cassius, or Antony and Ventidius. The whole comedy is very just, and the low part of human life represented with much humour and wit.

(C) *THE EARL OF ESSEX.* WILL'S COFFEE HOUSE, 11 MAY 1709

Yesterday we were entertained with the tragedy of *The Earl of Essex* [by John Banks] in which there is not one good line, and yet a play which was never seen without drawing tears from some part of the audience. A remarkable instance that the soul is not to be moved by words but by things. For the incidents in this drama are laid together so happily that the spectator makes the play for himself by the force which the circumstance has upon his imagination. Thus, in spite of the most dry discourses and expressions almost ridiculous with respect to propriety, it is impossible for one unprejudiced to see it untouched by pity. I must confess, this effect is not wrought on such as examine why they are pleased; but it never fails to appear on those who are not too learned in nature to be moved by her first suggestions. It is certain the person and behaviour of Mr Wilks has no small share in conducing to the popularity of the play; and when a handsome fellow is going to a more coarse exit than beheading, his shape and countenance make every tender one reprieve him with all her heart, without waiting until she hears his dying words.

172 Steele attacks Etherege's comedy *The Man of Mode* in *The Spectator*
No. 65 (Tuesday, 15 May 1711)

[. . .] It cannot be denied but that the negligence of everything which engages the attention of the sober and valuable part of mankind appears very well drawn in this piece. But it is denied that it is necessary to the character of a fine gentleman that he should in that manner trample upon all order and decency. As for the character of Dorimant, it is more of a coxcomb than that of Fopling. He says of one of his companions that a good correspondence between them is their mutual interest. Speaking of that friend, he declares their being much together, 'makes the women think the better of his understanding and judge more favourably of my reputation. It makes him pass upon some for a man of very good sense and me upon others for a very civil person.'

This whole celebrated piece is a perfect contradiction to good manners, good sense and common honesty. And as there is nothing in it but what is built upon the ruin of virtue and innocence, according to the notion of merit in this comedy, I take the shoemaker to be in reality the fine gentleman of the play. For it seems, he is an atheist, if we may depend upon his character as given by the orange woman, who is herself far from being the lowest in the play. She says of a fine man, who is Dorimant's companion, 'There is not such another heathen in the town, except the shoemaker.' His pretension to be the hero of the drama appears still more in his own description of his way of living with his lady. 'There is', says he, 'never a man in town lives more like a gentleman with his wife than I do; I never mind her motions; she never enquires into mine. We speak to one another civilly, hate one another heartily, and because it is vulgar to lie and soak together, we have each of us our several settle bed.' That of 'soaking together' is as good as if Dorimant had spoken it himself. And, I think, since he puts human nature in as ugly a form as the circumstance will bear and is a staunch unbeliever, he is very much wronged in having no part of the good fortune bestowed in the last act.

To speak plainly of this whole work, I think nothing but being lost to a sense of innocence and virtue can make anyone see this comedy, without observing more frequent occasion to move sorrow and indignation than mirth and laughter. At the same time I allow it to be nature, but it is nature in its utmost corruption and degeneracy.

Steele's sentimental approach to comedy in *The Conscious Lovers*

In his introduction to his play *The Conscious Lovers* (1722), Steele defended his new sentimental style of playwriting, which aimed to present models of good behaviour to the 'goths and vandals' who frequented the theatre and to touch the hearts of men and women rather than appeal satirically to the mind [see 173]. The success of the play in production, with audiences tearfully applauding the scene where Mr Sealand discovers his long-lost daughter Indiana [see 174], coupled with Steele's impassioned defence of his work, opened up an aesthetic debate on sentimentality in the theatre that was to reverberate throughout the eighteenth century.

173   Steele defends his sentimental approach to comedy in *The Conscious Lovers*, 1722

Richard Steele: *The Conscious Lovers* (London: Tonson, 1735), preface

[. . .] The chief design of this was to be an innocent performance, and the audience have abundantly showed how ready they are to support what is visibly intended that way. Nor do I make any difficulty to acknowledge that the whole was written for the sake of the scene of the fourth act wherein Mr Bevil evades the quarrel with his friend; and hope it may have some effect upon the goths and vandals that frequent theatres, or a more polite audience may supply their absence.

But this incident, and the case of the father and daughter, are esteemed by some people no subjects of comedy, but I cannot be of their mind. For anything that has its foundation in happiness and success must be allowed to be the object of comedy. And sure it must be an improvement of it to introduce a joy too exquisite for laughter, that can have no spring but in delight, which is the case of this young lady. I must therefore contend that the tears which were shed on that occasion flowed from reason and good sense, and that men ought not to be laughed at for weeping, till we are come to a more clear notion of what is to be imputed to the hardness of the head and the softness of the heart. And I think it was very politely said of Mr Wilks to one who told him there was a General, weeping for Indiana, 'I'll warrant he'll fight ne'er the worse for that.' To be apt to give way to the impressions of humanity is the excellence of a right disposition and the natural working of a well-turned spirit.

174   The scene from *The Conscious Lovers* where Mr Sealand discovers his long-lost daughter Indiana
Richard Steele: *The Conscious Lovers* (London: Tonson, 1735), frontispiece. Bristol University Library

Theatre criticism in the 1720s

By the 1720s, an increasing number of newspapers and journals were published in London, but theatre performances were rarely discussed. Normally, critical commentary in the press was reserved for those occasions when plays provoked a heated aesthetic or political debate. (And in the 1720s, aesthetic and political views were inextricably inter-twined. The sentimental approach of Steele was clearly intended to be associated with Whig social philosophy, while the satirical approach of Gay and Fielding was equally clearly intended to be viewed as a product of Tory social and political thought.)[1] Accordingly, Steele's play *The Conscious Lovers* in 1722 and Gay's *Beggar's Opera* in 1728 were both greeted by a barrage of articles and squibs. Writing from deeply entrenched political standpoints, the journalists concerned responded to these two works in articles that were partisan and propagandist rather than descriptively accurate. In November 1722 *The Freeholder's Journal* comments ironically on the 'improving' tone of Steele's play. While in February 1728, *The Craftsman*, exhibiting a mock outrage at the satiric basis of *The Beggar's Opera*, provides a detailed key to the underlying political meaning of the play.

[1] See Loftis (1963), pp. 88–9 and 94–7.

175   Critical responses to *The Conscious Lovers* and *The Beggar's Opera*

(A) *THE CONSCIOUS LOVERS: THE FREEHOLDER'S JOURNAL*, 28 NOVEMBER 1722

What I report on this subject is only the sense of others, given historically, not my own criticism. This I insert to guard against a misunderstanding, as if I made my personal attack on the play, and to prevent the danger of a reply that might be levelled at me in particular.

It was remarked that Mr Bevil Junior is a much more gracious and hopeful young man of the kind than was ever observed. That nothing can be imagined to be like this draught of a person of gaiety, youth and fortune. That his nice and unlimited obedience to his good father (very towardly shown in Mr M), his very regular and cool passion, his pious homily against duelling [. . .] and his other parts are foreign to all reality and even probable observation in life.

It is true, the general sanctity of the play is the choice recommendation of it. And we rejoice to hear, the actors and audience so jointly approve it that old brethren in iniquity are now converts, go lovingly hand in hand as companions and allies in the cause of virtue, and like the two Kings of Brentford smell both to the same nosegay.

If all the effects of it that are rumoured be true, they are a proof that miracles are not ceased. It has produced on all sides a very amazing revolution: it has almost changed the old house in Drury Lane to a monastery. [. . .]

The audience are sent off with a sorrowful impression and tears in their eyes, not to be wiped off by the final event. In short, the whole is a very good lecture, held forth by the most able and experienced preacher of the age. The poet (like others) woud be thought to draw himself in his hero but has the fate of the actor of young Bevil and never was the person he represents.

(B) *THE BEGGAR'S OPERA: THE CRAFTSMAN*, 17 FEBRUARY 1728
Reproduced in *Contexts 1: The Beggar's Opera*, edited by J.V. Guerinot and R.D. Jilg (Hamden, Conn: Archon Books, 1976), pp. 85–92

But I shall go still deeper into this affair and undertake to prove beyond dispute that the *Beggar's Opera* is the most venomous allegorical libel against the G[overn-ment] that has appeared for many years past.

There are some persons who esteem Lockit the Keeper, or Prime Minister of Newgate, to be the hero of the piece. To justify which opinion, they take notice that he is set forth on the stage in the person of Mr Hall, as a very corpulent, bulky man; and that he hath a brother, named Peachum who, as represented by Mr Hippisley, appears to be a little awkward slovenly fellow.[1] They observe farther that these two brothers have a numerous gang of thieves and pickpockets under their direction, with whom they divide their plunder and whom they either screen or tuck up,[2] as their own interest and the present occasion requires. But I am obliged to reject this interpretation as erroneous, however plausible it may be, and to embrace another, which is more generally received. Viz. that Captain Macheath, who has also a goodly presence and has a tolerable bronze upon his face,[3] is designed for the principal character and drawn to asperse somebody in authority.[4] He is represented as the head of a gang of robbers who promise to stand by him against all the enquiries and coercive force of the law. He is often called a great man, particularly in the two following passages, viz., 'It grieves one's heart to take off a great man' – 'What a moving thing it is to see a great man in distress.' Which, by the bye, seems to be an innuendo that some great man will speedily fall into distress. [. . .]

His satirical strokes upon ministers, courtiers and great men in general abound in every part of this most insolent performance. [. . .] The second act begins with a scene of highwaymen drinking together who solemnly promise never to betray one another for interest or any other motive. Upon which one of them gets up and says: 'Show me a gang of courtiers who can say as much.' Innuendo, that courtiers have less honesty than highwaymen. [. . .]

In a scene between Peachum and his brother Lockit, Peachum takes upon him to say that he does not like these long arrears of the G[overnment] (innuendo that the G[overnment] is in arrears). Again, says he, can it be expected that we should hang our acquaintance for nothing when our betters will hardly save theirs without being paid for it. Innuendo that some persons have been well paid for saving or screening their former acquaintance. [. . .]

This is, I think, sufficient to demonstrate the malignant tendency of this piece and of my own good intentions. What reasons induce the G[overnment] to be thus passive under such repeated insults, I do not take upon me to determine. But though I am far from wishing, as I know it will be objected, to see the liberty of the stage entirely abolished, yet I think such licentious invectives on the most polite and fashionable vices require some immediate restraint. For if they continue to be allowed, the theatre will become the censor of the age and no man, even of the first quality or distinction, will be at liberty (which is certainly the birthright of every free Briton) without danger of becoming the may game of the whole town. I submit this to your sage judgement.

[1] A reference to Walpole and Townshend, his brother-in-law. The quarrel of Lockit and Peachum clearly parodies their own disagreement.
[2] Walpole had been accused of screening or protecting former directors of the South Sea Company.
[3] Walpole was both brazen and of a ruddy complexion.
[4] Namely Walpole.

Theatre criticism in the 1730s

It was not until 1734, when Aaron Hill and William Popple founded *The Prompter* that a London journal paid regular critical attention to the world of the theatre.[1] Hill was a dilettante critic (in much the same way that he was once a dilettante man of the theatre),[2] who was passionately committed to 'reforming' the theatre in the spirit of Steele's *Spectator* essays. His moralising zeal could lead him to make subjective and unbalanced judgements in terms of plays [see 176a], pantomimes and operas but his comments on reforms needed in acting and staging were often astute and to the point [see 176b and c].

[1] Richard Steele had founded a periodical called *The Theatre* in 1720, but his intention in doing so was not so much to provide a guide on current theatre matters as to plead his own case in his current dispute with the Lord Chamberlain. See p. 26 above.
[2] See [18].

176   Aaron Hill casts a reformer's eye on plays and theatre practice in the 1730s
The Prompter (Appleton and Burnim eds.)

(A) NO. 109, 25 NOVEMBER 1735, PP. 124–5 (The Prompter castigates Fleetwood's notion of reviving *The Maid's Tragedy*.)

The master of a theatre is a kind of general trustee for the nation. He holds in ward the morals of a rising race of people. Their manners, prejudices, gallantries, deportments, wit and breeding must take deep impression from his conduct. And, instead of leaving at election of unqualified judges what plays should be brought on, it ought to be his own most studied care, as being a determination from whose consequence the theatre becomes the great refiner or depraver of a hundred thousand families.

Shall then those prudent fathers who would guard with tenderness their daughters' modesty; those husbands whose whole happiness in life is centred in their wives' fidelity; the great, whose eminence is but a consequence of loyal principles; the beautiful, whose very power of charming must depend upon those soft and pure ideas which support the sex's honour – shall all these sit (insulted, under the shadow of receiving entertainment) and behold, without resentment and impatience, the most manifest and lewdest violations, even of common decency? – the cause of villainy, rebellion, impudence and cut-throat murder recommended from the stage, and that too perhaps amidst the horror-moving plaudits of an unreflecting auditory!

I will say no more of this play than that the amazement I am under at report of its being revived (in the present condition of the theatre) is so justly considerable that I apprehend but one thing which can possibly increase it, and that is, should our women, in disgrace of their modesty, condescend to appear at it, or our men, in neglect of their virtue, permit it a second time to be acted.

(B) NO. 62, 13 JUNE 1735, P. 78 (The Prompter makes some telling observations on actors who fail to listen to each other when on stage.)

An actor who assumes a character wherein he does not seem in earnest to be the person by whose name he calls himself, affronts instead of entertaining the audience. What excuse, then, can be given in defence of a custom that is almost as common among players as their vanity? They relax themselves as soon as any speech in their own part is over, into an absent unattentiveness to whatever is replied by another, looking round and examining the company of spectators with an ear only watchful of the cue, at which, like soldiers upon the word of command, they start suddenly back to their postures, tone over the unanimating sound of their lesson and then (like a caterpillar that has erected itself at the touch of a twig) shrink back again to their crawl and their quiet and enjoy their full ease till next rousing.

Now what judge of nature will not be shocked at this provoking neglect of a player's own duty and at so arrogant a contempt of that respect which he owes to this audience? Does it not imply a supposition that we are either too ignorant to observe his defects or too inconsiderable to deserve his attention? Have we not a right to the representation we have paid for? And is it possible to be deceived into a mistake of the player for the hero unless he *listens* as well as he *speaks*? Unless he *looks* the concern he *pretends* to? Unless his very silence is instructed to talk to the eye of the spectator by a thousand significant gestures, starts, changes and attitudes, whereby the soul, at work, inwardly throws out marks of its sensation?

(c) NO. 22, 24 JANUARY 1735, PP. 25–6 (The Prompter complains of improprieties of costume in the theatre.)

I have been greatly offended at the ridiculous dresses in which our inferior sons of the buskin generally make their appearance. I have frequently seen a Duke in a coat half a yard too long for him, and a Lord High Chamberlain that had shed most of his buttons. I have seen men of proud hearts submitting unnaturally to strut in tarnished lace, and there is a certain Knight of the Garter who condescends to tie back his wig with a packthread. When a King of England has honoured the stage, with his whole court in full splendour about him, I'd have undertaken to purchase the clothes of all his nobility for the value of five pounds. It exceeds (as my brother satirist has it) all power of face to be serious at the sight of so much shabbiness and majesty! [. . .]

The bounds of probability, in the mean time, may be as openly transgressed in the appearance of an actor as in the sentiments which he utters. And the dress therefore should always be *suited* to the person who takes it upon him. An old Roman could never with any propriety be made to look like a modern Frenchman, nor a Dutch burgomaster's wife like a Queen of Great Britain. When therefore persons of rank and figure are introduced upon the stage, they should be clothed so as to represent themselves and not the patchwork inconsistencies of their management.

7   Documents of control

INTRODUCTION

The document of fundamental importance to the shaping of the English theatre of the second half of the eighteenth century was the Licensing Act of 1737, even in those areas in which it was most ignored. Either negatively or positively, it influenced developments and changes for over a hundred years and left the legacy of a censorship system for over a century after that.

It influenced negatively because of its restrictive nature, particularly in confining legitimate theatrical performances initially to two patent playhouses in London. It influenced positively because this restriction, both in London and especially in the provinces, was either ignored or circumvented. This demonstrated the pressure, both social and artistic, for the theatre's survival and development and helped to ensure both. Eventually the pressure for expansion proved overwhelming. Foote's patent to run the Little Theatre at the Haymarket in 1766 was followed by a number of patents and licences for provincial playhouses in the final decades of the century as well as the Occasional Licensing Act of 1788.

THE BACKGROUND TO THE 1737 LICENSING ACT

Growing disorder in the patent acting companies, combined with the spread of small unlicensed playhouses in London and outside, form the essential prelude to the 1737 Act. In 1720 Thomas Potter had opened the Little Theatre in the Haymarket, close to Vanbrugh's Opera House. When Thomas Odell, in the autumn of 1729, proposed to erect and operate a theatre in the East End of London at Ayliffe Street in Goodman's Fields, there was strong opposition from the City, culminating in a formal petition by the Lord Mayor and Aldermen to the King in 1730, making use of the traditional argument over the stage's supposed immoral influence [see 177]. In April 1730, the Lord Chamberlain tried unsuccessfully to silence the theatre, a further element in his long-running battle with managements [see 178]. A contemporary source claims that the owner decided to ignore the order after taking legal advice.[1] Though there are no Goodman's Fields bills from 28 April to 11 May, they appear again regularly thereafter, and Odell still claimed to be playing 'By Authority'. He kept the theatre open throughout the 1730–1 season and then handed over the management to Henry Giffard.[2] The successful survival of Goodman's Fields raised the possibility of unlimited proliferation of small playhouses and companies, which naturally concerned the patent managers and their financial backers.

¹ See Nicholson (1906), chapter 2; P.J. Crean: 'The Stage Licensing Act of 1737' *Modern Philology* 35 (1937), 239–55; and S. Rosenfeld: 'Theatres in Goodman's Fields' *TN* 1 (1946), 49.
² See Crean, p. 240.

177   Petition of the Lord Mayor and Aldermen of the City of London, 1729–30
PRO LC 7/3, f. 28

To the King's Most Excellent Majesty
The humble petition of the court of the Lord Mayor and Aldermen of the City of London,
    Humbly sheweth,
That there having been lately erected a playhouse in a place called Goodman's Fields near adjoining to the said city (but not within their jurisdiction) and amidst great numbers of persons concerned in trade and particularly in the silk, woollen and other manufactures,
    And your petitioners having reason to be apprehensive of very many ill consequences from the continuance of the said playhouse and the representations performed in the same, more especially as affecting the morals, lessening the industry, and losing the time of those persons employed in the said manufactures which if not prevented may prove to be of very great prejudice to the trade of this city,
    And as the actors of the said playhouse pretend to act by authority, your petitioners most humbly apply to Your Majesty (with a full assurance of your most gracious disposition toward the trade, welfare and prosperity of this city) to give such orders for the suppressing an evil of so dangerous a consequence as to Your Majesty in your great wisdom shall seem meet. [. . .]

178   The Lord Chamberlain issues orders for silencing the playhouse in Goodman's Fields, 28 April 1730
PRO LC 5/160, p. 130

Whereas the Court of Lord Mayor and Aldermen of the City of London have by petition represented to His Majesty that many ill consequences have and may arise from plays being acted in the playhouse lately created in Goodman's Fields. In obedience to His Majesty's commands, I do, by virtue of my office of Chamberlain of His Majesty's Household, silence and strictly charge you, or any person, or persons listed in your service not to presume to act or represent any comedies, tragedies or other theatrical performances for the future, as you will answer the contrary at your peril. 28 April 1730.
    To the Master, Governor or Governors of the playhouse in Goodman's Fields.
    GRAFTON

THE 1737 LICENSING ACT AND ITS CONSEQUENCES

The major impetus to tighten control over theatrical activity came from the government and its supporters. They were stung into taking action by the outspoken and highly successful political satires of Gay and Fielding, written between 1728 and 1737. The final pretext came with the publication of *The Vision of the Golden Rump*, a scurrilous attack on Walpole and his colleagues, in March 1737.[1] This was dramatised and sent to Giffard at Goodman's Fields. He seems, for whatever motive, to have taken it to Walpole who paid him to hold it back from production, while he himself took the matter to the House of Commons. There on 20 May Walpole introduced a new bill to regain effective government control over the theatre, in the form of an amendment to a vagrancy Law passed in 1714 under Queen Anne. Though there was much controversy in the press, the only effective opponent in Parliament was Lord Chesterfield [*see* 180].[2] Without much opposition, the bill was rushed through Commons and Lords and received the Royal Assent on 21 June 1737.

One important consequence of the new act was the restriction of the King's power to grant letters patent for the erection of theatres, limited now to Westminster and elsewhere only during his residence. This led in turn to the closing in London of the Little Theatre in the Haymarket and the playhouses in Lincoln's Inn Fields and Goodman's Fields, leaving only Drury Lane, Covent Garden and the King's Theatre or Opera House. Thus a monopoly or cartel was given to Fleetwood at Drury Lane and Rich at Covent Garden, with no possibility in future of disaffected players being able to set up an independent company and ply their trade. (This was to be tested and proved in 1743–5.)[3] There was also reinforcement of the former stigma of 'vagrancy' on any players not protected by a patent and financial incentives to the laying of information against them. Finally, in future, the Lord Chamberlain was to be given statutory powers to examine all plays and to censor or prohibit at will any play or part of a play, backed by a £50 penalty and the threat of the loss of a licence.

[1] *Common Sense*, 19–26 March, 1737.
[2] *Journals of the House of Commons*, vol. 22, pp. 889–93 and vol. 22, pp. 134–7 and 148. See also Crean, pp. 252–4 and Nicholson (1906), chapter 3. Chesterfield also published an ironic article in *Common Sense* on 4 June 1737. See Fitzgerald, vol. 2 (1882), chapter 8.
[3] See Nicholson (1906), chapter 4.

179   The 1737 Licensing Act
10 Geo II, cap xxviii. Reprinted in J. Raithby (ed.): *Statutes at large*, vol. 5 (London: Eyre & Strahan, 1811), pp. 266–8

An act to explain and amend so much of an act made in the twelfth year of the reign of Queen Anne, entitled, *An act for reducing the laws relating to rogues, vagabonds, sturdy beggars and vagrants into one Act of Parliament; and for the more effectual punishing such rogues, vagabonds, sturdy beggars and vagrants, and sending them whither they ought to be sent*, as relates to common players of interludes.

[I.] Whereas by an Act of Parliament made in the twelfth year of the reign of Her late Majesty, Queen Anne, entitled, *An act for reducing the laws relating to rogues, vagabonds, sturdy beggars and vagrants into one Act of Parliament; and for the more effectual punishing such rogues, vagabonds, sturdy beggars and vagrants, and sending them whither they ought to be sent*,[(a)] it was enacted that all persons pretending themselves to be patent gatherers or collectors for prisons, gaols or hospitals, and wandering abroad for that purpose, all fencers, bearwards, common players of interludes and other persons therein named and expressed, shall be deemed rogues and vagabonds. And whereas some doubts have arisen concerning so much of the said Act as relates to common players of interludes; now for explaining and amending the same, be it declared and enacted by the King's most excellent Majesty, by and with the advice and consent of the Lords Spiritual and Temporal, and Commons, in this present Parliament assembled, and by the authority of the same, that from and after the twenty-fourth day of *June*, one thousand, seven hundred and thirty seven, every person who shall, for hire, gain or reward, act, represent or perform, or cause to be acted, represented or performed any interlude, tragedy, comedy, opera, play, farce or other entertainment of the stage, or any part or parts therein, in case such person shall not have any legal settlement in the place where the same shall be acted, represented or performed without authority by virtue of letters patent from His Majesty, his heirs, successors or predecessors, or without licence from the Lord Chamberlain of His Majesty's household for the time being, shall be deemed to be a rogue and a vagabond within the intent and meaning of the said recited Act, and shall be liable and subject to all such penalties and punishments, and by such methods of conviction as are inflicted on or appointed by the said Act for the punishment of rogues and vagabonds who shall be found wandering, begging and misordering themselves, within the intent and meaning of the said recited Act.

II. And be it further enacted by the authority aforesaid that if any person having or not having a legal settlement as aforesaid shall, without such authority or licence as aforesaid, act, represent or perform, or cause to be acted, represented or performed for hire, gain or reward any interlude, tragedy, comedy, opera, play, farce, or other entertainment of the stage, or any part or parts therein, every such person shall for every such offence forfeit the sum of fifty pounds; and in case the said sum of fifty pounds shall be paid, levied or recovered, such offender shall not for the same offence suffer any of the pains or penalties inflicted by the said recited act.

III. And be it further enacted by the authority aforesaid, that from and after the said twenty-fourth day of *June*, one thousand, seven hundred and thirty seven, no person shall for hire, gain or reward, act, perform, represent or cause to be acted, performed or represented any new interlude, tragedy, comedy, opera, play, farce, or other entertainment of the stage, or any part or parts therein; or any new act, scene or other part added to any old interlude, tragedy, comedy, opera, play, farce or other entertainment of the stage, or any new prologue or epilogue, unless a true copy thereof be sent to the Lord Chamberlain of the King's household for the time being, fourteen days at least before the acting, representing or performing thereof, together with an account of the playhouse or other place where the same shall be and the time when the same is intended to be first acted, represented or performed, signed by the master or manager, or one of the masters or managers of such playhouse or place, or company of actors therein.

IV. And be it enacted by the authority aforesaid that from and after the said twenty-fourth day of *June*, one thousand, seven hundred and thirty seven, it shall and may be lawful to and for the said Lord Chamberlain for the time being, from time to time, and when and as often as he shall think fit, to prohibit the acting, performing or representing any interlude, tragedy, comedy, opera, play, farce or other entertainment of the stage, or any act, scene or part thereof, or any prologue or epilogue. And in case any person or persons shall for hire, gain or reward act, perform or represent, or cause to be acted, performed or represented any new interlude, tragedy, comedy, opera, play, farce, or other entertainment of the stage, or any act, scene or part thereof, or any new prologue or epilogue before a copy thereof shall be sent as aforesaid, with such account as aforesaid, or shall for hire, gain or reward act, perform or represent, or cause to be acted, performed or represented, any interlude, tragedy, comedy, opera, play, farce or other entertainment of the stage, or any act, scene or part thereof, or any prologue or epilogue, contrary to such prohibition as aforesaid; every person so offending shall for every such offence forfeit the sum of fifty pounds and every grant, licence and authority (in case there be any such) by or under which the said master or masters or manager or managers set up, formed or continued such playhouse, or such company of actors, shall cease, determine and become absolutely void to all intents and purposes whatsoever.

V. Provided always that no person or persons shall be authorised by virtue of any letters patent from His Majesty, his heirs, successors or predecessors, or by the licence of the Lord Chamberlain of His Majesty's household for the time being, to act, represent or perform for hire, gain or reward, any interlude, tragedy, comedy, opera, play, farce or other entertainment of the stage, or any part or parts therein, in any part of Great Britain, except in the City of Westminster and within the liberties thereof, and in such places where His Majesty, his heirs or successors, shall in their royal persons reside, and during such residence only; anything in this Act contained to the contrary in any wise notwithstanding.[b]

VI. And be it further enacted by the authority aforesaid that all the pecuniary penalties inflicted by this Act for offences committed within that part of Great Britain called England, Wales and the town of Berwick upon Tweed, shall be recovered by bill, plaint or information in any of His Majesty's Courts of Record at Westminster, in which no essoin, protection or wager of law shall be allowed; and for the offences committed in that part of Great Britain called Scotland, by action or summary complaint before the Court of Session or Justiciary there; or for offences committed in any part of Great Britain, in a summary way before two Justices of the Peace for any county, stewartry, riding, division or liberty where any such offence shall be committed, by the oath or oaths of one or more credible witness or witnesses, or by the confession of the offender. The same to be levied by distress and sale of the offender's goods and chattels, rendering the overplus to such offender, if any there be above the penalty and charge of distress. And for want of sufficient distress, the offender shall be committed to any house of correction in any such county, stewartry, riding or liberty, for any time not exceeding six months, there to be kept to hard labour, or to the common gaol of any such county, stewartry, riding or liberty, for any time not exceeding six months, there to remain without bail or mainprize. And if any person or persons shall think him, her or themselves aggrieved by the order or orders of such Justices of the Peace, it shall and may be lawful for such person or persons to appeal therefrom to the next general Quarter-Sessions to be held for the said county, stewartry, riding or liberty, whose order therein shall be final and conclusive, and the said penalties for any offence against this Act shall belong, one moiety thereof to the informer or person suing or prosecuting for the same, the other moiety to the poor of the parish where such offence shall be committed.

VII. And be it further enacted by the authority aforesaid, that if any interlude, tragedy, comedy, opera, play, farce or other entertainment of the stage, or any act, scene or part thereof, shall be acted, represented or performed in any house or place where wine, ale, beer or other liquors shall be sold or retailed, the same shall be deemed to be acted, represented and performed for gain, hire and reward.

VIII. And be it further enacted by the authority aforesaid that no person shall be liable to be prosecuted for any offence against this Act, unless such prosecution shall be commenced within the space of six calendar months after the offence committed. And if any action or suit shall be commenced or brought against any Justice of the Peace or any other person for doing, or causing to be done, anything in pursuance of this Act, such action or suit shall be commenced within six calendar months next after the fact done; and the defendant or defendants in such action or suit shall and may plead the general issue and give the special matter in evidence. And if upon such action or suit, a verdict shall be given for the defendant or defendants, or the plaintiff or plaintiffs or prosecutor shall become nonsuit, or shall not prosecute his or their said action or suit, then the defendant or defendants shall have treble costs and shall have the like remedy for the same as any defendant or defendants have in other cases by law.[c]

[a] 12 Ann. Stat. 2.c.23. Repealed, 13. G.2.c.24.
[b] Repealed as to Edinburgh, 7.G.3.c.27, § 19; as to Bath 8.G.3.c.10; see as to Norwich, 8.G.3.c.28; repealed as to York and Kingston upon Hull, 9.G.3.Sess.2.c.17; as to Liverpool, 11.G.3.c.16; as to Manchester, 15.G.3.c.47; as to Chester, 17.G.3.c.14; as to Bristol, 18.G.3.c.8; as to Margate, 26.G.3.c.29; as to Newcastle upon Tyne, 27.G.3.c.50; as to Glasgow, 43.G.3.c.cxlii; as to Birmingham, 47.G.3.Sess.2.c.xliv.
[c] Justices at Quarter-Sessions may license plays, etc. as therein mentioned, 28.G.3.c.30.

CONTEMPORARY REACTIONS TO THE 1737 LICENSING ACT
Lord Chesterfield

Lord Chesterfield was the most vigorous opponent of the bill when it was debated in the House of Lords. Chesterfield's posthumous reputation has suffered much because of Dr Johnson's bitter comments on him (notably in his well-known letter on patronage and on the publication of Chesterfield's *Letter to his son* when Johnson commented that, 'they teach the morals of a whore and the manners of a dancing master'). Johnson's views have helped to attach to Chesterfield labels of arrogance, hypocrisy and duplicity. However, he clearly felt strongly about liberty and morality in public life as is demonstrated in the article he wrote for *Common Sense*, 4 June 1737 and the speech he delivered in the House of Lords opposing the new Licensing Act.

180   Lord Chesterfield's speech on the Licensing Bill, May 1737

Philip Dormer Stanhope, Earl of Chesterfield: *Miscellaneous works*, edited by M. Maty, Second edition, vol. 2 (London: E. & C. Dilly, 1779), pp. 319–39

MY LORDS

The bill now before you I apprehend to be of a very extraordinary, a very dangerous nature. It seems designed not only as a restraint on the licentiousness of the stage; but it will prove a most arbitrary restraint on the liberty of the stage. And I fear it looks yet further, I fear it tends towards a restraint on the liberty of the press, which will be a long stride towards the destruction of liberty itself. [. . .] When I considered how near it was to the end of the session, and how long this session had been protracted beyond the usual time of the year; when I considered that this bill passed through the other house with so much precipitancy [. . .], it set me upon enquiring, what could be the reason for introducing this bill at so unseasonable a time, and pressing it forward in a manner so very singular and uncommon. I have made all possible enquiry; and as yet, I must confess, I am at a loss to find out the great occasion. I have, it is true, learned from common report without doors, that a most seditious, a most heinous farce had been offered to one of the theatres, a farce for which the authors ought to be punished in the most exemplary manner, but what was the consequence? The master of that theatre behaved as he was in duty bound, and as common prudence directed; he not only refused to bring it upon the stage, but carried it to a certain honourable gentleman in the administration, as the surest method of having it absolutely suppressed. Could this be the occasion of introducing such an extraordinary bill, at such an extraordinary season, and pushing it in so extraordinary a manner? Surely no. The dutiful behaviour of the players, the prudent caution they showed upon that occasion, can never be a reason for subjecting them to such an arbitrary restraint: it is an argument in their favour and a material one, in my opinion, against the bill. Nay farther, if we consider all circumstances, it is to me a full proof that the laws now in being are sufficient for punishing those players who shall venture to bring any seditious libel upon the stage and consequently sufficient for deterring all players from acting anything that may have the least tendency towards giving a reasonable offence. [. . .]

But, my Lords, suppose it is true, that the laws now in being are not sufficient for putting a check to, or preventing, the licentiousness of the stage; suppose it absolutely necessary some new law should be made for that purpose. Yet it must be granted, that such a law ought to be maturely considered, and every clause, every sentence, nay every word of it, well weighed and examined, lest, under some of those methods presumed or pretending to be necessary for restraining licentiousness, a power should lie concealed, which might be afterwards made use of for giving a dangerous wound to liberty. Such a law ought not to be introduced at the close of a session. [. . .]

I am as much for restraining the licentiousness of the stage, and every sort of licentiousness, as any of your lordships can be. But, my Lords, I am, I shall always be, extremely cautious and fearful of making the least encroachment upon liberty [. . .]. The bill, my Lords, at first view, may seem to be designed only against the stage, but to me it plainly appears to point somewhere else. It is an arrow that does but glance upon the stage; the mortal wound seems designed against the liberty of the press. By this bill you prevent a play's being acted but you do not prevent its being printed; therefore, if a licence should be refused for its being acted, we may depend upon it the play will be printed. It will be printed and published, my Lords, with the refusal in capital letters upon the title page. People are always fond of what is forbidden. *Libri prohibiti* (prohibited books) are in all countries diligently and generally sought after. It will be much easier to procure a refusal, than it ever was to procure a good house or a good sale; therefore we may expect, that plays will be written on purpose to have a refusal; this will certainly procure a good house or a good sale. Thus will satires be spread and dispersed through the whole nation, and thus every man in the kingdom may, and probably will, read for sixpence what a few only could have seen acted and that not under the expense of half a crown. We shall then be told, What! will you allow an infamous libel to be printed and dispersed, which you would not allow to be acted? You have agreed to a law to prevent its being acted: can you refuse your assent to a law to prevent its being printed and published? I should really, my Lords, be glad to hear, what excuse, what reason one could give for being against the latter, after having agreed to the former; for I protest, I cannot suggest to myself the least shadow of an excuse. If we agree to the bill now before us, we must, perhaps next session, agree to a bill for preventing any plays being printed without a licence. Then satires will be written by way of novels, secret histories, dialogues, or under some such title. And thereupon we shall be told, What! will you allow an infamous libel to be printed and dispersed, only because it does not bear the title of a play? Thus, my Lords, from the precedent now before us, we shall be induced, nay, we can find no reason for refusing, to lay the press under a general licence and then we may bid adieu to the liberties of Great Britain. [. . .]

I shall admit, my Lords, that the stage ought not, upon any occasion, to meddle with politics. And for this very reason, among the rest, I am against the bill now before us. This bill will be so far from preventing the stage's meddling with politics that, I fear, it will be the occasion of its meddling with nothing else. But then it will be a political stage *ex parte*. It will be made subservient to the politics and the schemes of the court only. The licentiousness of the stage will be encouraged, instead of being restrained, but, like court-journalists it will be licentious only against the patrons of liberty, and the protectors of the people. Whatever man, whatever party, opposes the court in any of their most destructive schemes, will, upon the stage, be represented in the most ridiculous light the hirelings of a court can contrive. True patriotism, and love of public good, will be represented as madness, or as a cloak for envy, disappointment, and malice, whilst the most flagitious crimes, the most extravagant vices and follies, if they are fashionable at court, will be disguised and dressed up in the habit of the most amiable virtues. This has formerly been the case in King Charles the second's days: the playhouse was under a licence, what was the consequence? The playhouse retailed nothing but the politics, the vices and the follies of the court: not to expose them, no, but to recommend them, though it must be granted their politics were often as bad as their vices, and much more pernicious than their other follies [. . .].

My Lords, the proper business of the stage and that for which only it is useful, is to expose those vices and follies, which the laws cannot lay hold of; and to recommend those beauties and virtues, which ministers and courtiers seldom either imitate or reward. But by laying it under a licence, and under an arbitrary court licence too, you will, in my opinion, entirely pervert its use. For though I have the greatest esteem for that noble duke, in whose hands this power is at present designed to fall, though I have an entire confidence in his judgement and impartiality, yet I may suppose that a leaning towards the fashions of a court is sometimes hard to be avoided. It may be very difficult to make one, who is every day at court, believe that to be a vice or folly, which he sees daily practised by those he loves and esteems. By custom, even deformity itself becomes familiar, and at last agreeable. To such a person, let his natural impartiality be never so great, that may appear to be a libel against the court, which is only a most just and a most necessary satire upon the fashionable vices and follies of the court [. . .].

From hence, my Lords, I think it must appear, that the bill now before us cannot so properly be called a bill for restraining licentiousness, as it may be called a bill for restraining the liberty of the stage, and for restraining it too in that branch which, in all countries, has been the most useful. Therefore I must look upon this bill as a most dangerous encroachment upon liberty in general. Nay, farther, my Lords, it is not only an encroachment upon liberty, but it is likewise an encroachment upon property. Wit, my Lords, is a sort of property: it is the property of those who have it, and too often the only property they have to depend on. It is indeed but a precarious dependence. Thank God! we, my Lords have a dependence of another kind; we have a much less precarious support, and therefore cannot feel the inconveniences of the bill now before us. But it is our duty to encourage and protect wit, whosoever's property it may be. Those gentlemen who have any such property, are all, I hope, our friends. Do not let us subject them to any unnecessary or arbitrary restraint. I must own, I cannot easily agree to the laying of any tax upon wit. But by this bill it is to be heavily taxed, it is to be excised. For, if this bill passes, it cannot be retailed in a proper way without a permit, and the Lord Chamberlain is to have the honour of being chief-gauger, supervisor, commissioner, judge and jury. But what is still more hard, though the poor author, the proprietor I should say, cannot perhaps dine till he has found out and agreed with a purchaser, yet, before he can propose to seek for a purchaser, he must patiently submit to have his goods rummaged at this new excise office, where they may be detained for fourteen days, and even then he may find them returned as prohibited goods, by which his chief and best market will be forever shut against him. And that without any cause, without the least shadow of reason, either from the laws of his country, or the laws of the stage.

These hardships, this hazard, which every gentleman will be exposed to, who writes anything for the stage, must certainly prevent every man of a generous and free spirit from attempting anything in that way, and as the stage has always been the proper channel for wit and humour, therefore, my Lords, when I speak against this bill, I must think I plead the cause of wit, I plead the cause of humour, I plead the cause of the British stage, and of every gentleman of taste in the kingdom [. . .].

The last reason I shall trouble your lordships with, for my being against the bill, is that, in my opinion, it will in no way answer the end proposed; I mean the end openly proposed; and I am sure the only end which your lordships propose. To prevent the acting of a play which has any tendency to blasphemy, immorality, sedition, or private scandal, can signify nothing, unless you can prevent its being printed and published. On the contrary, if you prevent its being acted, and admit of its being printed, you will propagate the mischief. Your prohibition will prove a bellows, which will blow up the fire you intend to extinguish. This bill can therefore be of no use for preventing either the public or the private injury intended by such a play; and consequently can be of no manner of use, unless it be designed as a precedent, as a leading step towards another for subjecting the press likewise to a licenser. For such a wicked purpose it may indeed be of great use, and in that light it may most properly be called a step towards arbitrary power.

Let us consider, my Lords, that arbitrary power has seldom or never been introduced into any country at once. It must be introduced by slow degrees, and as it were step by step, lest the people should perceive its approach. The barriers and fences of the people's liberty must be plucked up one by one, and some plausible pretences must be found for removing or hood-winking, one after another, those sentries who are posted by the constitution of a great country, for warning the people of their danger. When these preparatory steps are once made, the people may then, indeed, with regret, see slavery and arbitrary power making long strides over their land, but it will be too late to think of preventing or avoiding the impending ruin. The stage, my Lords, and the press are two of our out-sentries; if we remove them, if we hood-wink them, if we throw them in fetters, the enemy may surprise us. Therefore I must look upon the bill now before us as a step, and a most necessary step too, for introducing arbitrary power into this kingdom. It is a step so necessary, that if ever any future ambitious king, or guilty minister, should form to himself so wicked a design, he will have reason to thank us, for having done so much of the work to his hand, but such thanks, or thanks from such a man, I am convinced, every one of your lordships would blush to receive and scorn to deserve.

CONTEMPORARY REACTIONS TO THE 1737 LICENSING ACT
Colley Cibber

Colley Cibber, in contrast to Chesterfield, supported the new bill. Having been for many years co-manager at Drury Lane with Wilks and Booth, in 1735 he had sold his share to John Highmore for 3000 guineas. At the age of sixty-five he had gone into semi-retirement. Although he continued to act occasionally, between 1737 and 1740 he was primarily engaged in writing his autobiography. It is in chapter 8 of this that he gives his rather rambling views on the subject of the Licensing Act. He takes up the main points made by Chesterfield in his speech, and attempts to refute them one by one. The concluding paragraph, however, makes it evident that his real support for the bill was on financial grounds, which clearly represents the established managerial attitude of the day.

181   Colley Cibber and the Licensing Act
Cibber, vol. 1, (Lowe ed.), pp. 289, 294, 297

When this law was in debate, a lively spirit and uncommon eloquence was employed against it. It was urged that one of the greatest goods we can enjoy is liberty. (This we may grant to be an incontestable truth, without its being the least objection to this law.) It was said too that to bring the stage under the restraint of a licenser was leading the way to an attack upon the liberty of the press. This amounts but to a jealousy at best, which I hope and believe all honest Englishmen have as much reason to think a groundless, as to fear it is a just jealousy. For the stage and the press, I shall endeavour to show, are very different weapons to wound with. If a great man could be no more injured by being personally ridiculed or made contemptible in a play than by the same matter only printed and read against him in a pamphlet, or the strongest verse, then indeed the stage and the press might pretend to be on an equal foot of liberty. But when the wide difference between these two liberties comes to be explained and considered, I dare say we shall find the injuries from one capable of being ten times more severe and formidable than from the other [. . .].

When direct arguments against this bill were found too weak, recourse was had to dissuasive ones. It was said that this restraint upon the stage would not remedy the evil complained of, that a play refused to be licensed would still be printed, with double advantage, when it should be insinuated that it was refused for some strokes of wit, etc. and would be more likely then to have its effect among the people. However natural this consequence may seem, I doubt it will be very difficult to give a printed satire or libel half the force or credit of an acted one. The most artful or notorious lie, or strained allusion that ever slandered a great man, may be read by some people with a smile of contempt, or at worst it can impose but on one person at once. But when the words of the same plausible stuff shall be repeated on a theatre, the wit of it among a crowd of hearers is liable to be over-valued and may unite and warm a whole body of the malicious or ignorant into a plaudit [. . .]. Against contempt and scandal, heightened and coloured by the skill of an actor ludicrously infusing it into a multitude, there is no immediate defence to be made or equal reparation to be had for it [. . .].

To conclude, let us now consider this law in a quite different light. Let us leave the political part of it quite out of the question. What advantage could either the spectators of plays or the masters of playhouses have gained by its never having been made? How could the same stock of plays supply four theatres which (without such additional entertainments as a nation of common sense ought to be ashamed of) could not well support two? Satiety must have been the natural consequence of the same plays being twice as often repeated as now they need be, and satiety puts an end to all tastes that the mind of man can delight in. Had therefore this law been made seven years ago, I should not have parted with my share in the patent, under a thousand pounds more than I received for it. So that, as far as I am able to judge, both the public as spectators, and the patentees as undertakers, are, or might be, in a way of being better entertained and more considerable gainers by it.

THE AFTERMATH OF THE ACT – THE CENSORSHIP

Under the new act, machinery was needed to carry out the examining functions given to the Lord Chamberlain. A Licenser of Stage Plays, William Chetwynd, was appointed at an annual salary of £400. His deputy or Examiner, at half the salary, was Thomas Odell, the founder of the Goodman's Fields Theatre. All new plays, adaptations or additions to old plays, prologues and epilogues had to be submitted by holders of the royal patent to the Lord Chamberlain for examination at least fourteen days before they were intended to be performed; if approved, a licence to perform would be given [see 182].[1]

Two manuscript plays quickly suffered. In the 1737–8 season, Henry Brooke's *Gustavus Vasa* and James Thomson's *Edward and Eleanora* were both proscribed. The former had actually been in rehearsal at Drury Lane when an order was sent from the Lord Chamberlain prohibiting its performance. This action provoked much controversy. Brooke immediately had the play printed, by subscription, with a preface recounting his side of the story. According to one contemporary source, he cleared £1000 as a result, confirming, if nothing else, Chesterfield's prediction.[2] Dr Johnson seized the opportunity for an ironical commentary on both Brooke and the new censorship [see 183].

The system was steadily developed and codified.[3] Though there was no legal warrant for this, it became the custom for the Examiner to retain the manuscript copies submitted to him. On his death in 1824, John Larpent, who had been Examiner since 1778, was in possession of more than 2,500 plays in manuscript form. The bulk of these are now preserved in the Huntington Library in California.[4]

---

[1] *Read's Weekly Journal*, 4 February 1733; Crean, p. 254; Nicholson (1906), pp. 70–1.

[2] See Victor, vol. 1 (1761), pp. 47–53; Nicholson (1906), p. 72.

[3] See D. Macmillan: 'The censorship in the case of Macklin's *The Man of the World*' *Huntington Library Bulletin* 10 (1936), 79–101. See also Connolly (1976).

[4] See Macmillan (1939), p. 53.

182   The wording of a licence to perform

Licence for the first performance of *The Hue and Cry*, translated and adapted from the French by Mrs Inchbald, at Drury Lane on 11 May 1791. Theatre Museum. Enthoven Collection

J.P. Kemble Esq.   April 1791
Theatre Royal
Drury Lane
It having been reported to me by the Examiner of all theatrical entertainments that a manuscript entitled *The Hue and Cry*, being a farce in two acts, does not contain in it anything immoral or otherwise improper for the stage, I, the Lord Chamberlain of His Majesty's household, in consideration of the same, do, by virtue of my office

and in pursuance of the Act of Parliament in that case provided, allow the said manuscript to be acted at your theatre, according to the copy thereof delivered to me and signed by yourself, without any variation whatsoever, unless such variation be likewise approved of by me in due form.
SALISBURY.

183   Dr Johnson on stage censorship

'A complete vindication of the Licensers of the stage from the malicious and scandalous aspersions of Mr Brooke, author of *Gustavus Vasa*, with a proposal for making the office of Licenser more extensive and effectual' [1739]. Samuel Johnson: *Works*, vol. 5 (Oxford: Pickering, Tallboys & Wheeler, 1825), pp. 329–44

[. . .] So far therefore is Mr Brooke from having received any hard or unwarrantable treatment that the Licenser has only acted in pursuance of that law to which he owes his power; a law which every admirer of the administration must own to be very necessary and to have produced very salutary effects.

I am indeed surprised that this great office is not drawn out into a longer series of deputations, since it might afford a gainful and reputable employment to a great number of friends of the government. And I should think, instead of having immediate recourse to the deputy-licenser himself, it might be sufficient honour for any poet, except the laureate, to stand bare-headed in the presence of the deputy of the deputy's deputy in the nineteenth subordination.

Such a number cannot but be thought necessary, if we take into consideration the great work of drawing up an index expurgatorius to all the old plays. Which is, I hope, already undertaken or, if it has been hitherto unhappily neglected, I take this opportunity to recommend.

The productions of our old poets are crowded with passages very unfit for the ears of an English audience and which cannot be pronounced without irritating the minds of the people.

This censure I do not confine to those lines in which liberty, natural equality, wicked ministers, deluded kings, mean arts of negotiation, venal senates, mercenary troops, oppressive officers, servile and exorbitant taxes, universal corruption, the luxuries of a court, the miseries of the people, the decline of trade or the happiness of independency are directly mentioned. These are such glaring passages, as cannot be suffered to pass without the most supine and criminal negligence. I hope the vigilance of the Licensers will extend to all such speeches and soliloquies as tend to recommend the pleasures of virtue, the tranquillity of an uncorrupted head and the satisfactions of conscious innocence. For though such strokes as these do not appear to a common eye to threaten any danger to the government, yet it is well known to more penetrating observers that they have such consequences as cannot be too diligently obviated or too cautiously avoided.

A man who becomes enamoured of the charms of virtue is apt to be very little concerned about the acquisition of wealth or titles and is therefore not easily induced to act in a manner contrary to his real sentiments or vote at the word of command; by contracting his desires and regulating his appetites, he wants much less than other men. And everyone versed in the arts of government can tell that men are more easily influenced in proportion as they are more necessitous. [. . .]

But alas! all those pernicious sentiments which we shall banish from the stage will be vented from the press and more studiously read because they are prohibited.

I cannot but earnestly implore the friends of the government to leave no art untried by which we may hope to succeed in our design of extending the power of the censor to the press and of making it criminal to publish anything without an IMPRIMATUR.

How much would this single law lighten the mighty burden of state affairs! With how much security might our ministers enjoy their honours, their places, their reputations and their admirers, could they once suppress those malicious invectives which are at present so industriously propagated and so eagerly read, could they hinder any arguments but their own from coming to the ears of the people and stop effectually the voice of cavil and enquiry [. . .].

EVASIONS AND THE LORD CHAMBERLAIN'S RESPONSE
Henry Giffard

The gaining of a licence for a play was only one aspect of the problem confronting playwrights and theatre managers. Obtaining permission to perform an approved play was quite another. Only those playhouses given a licence or patent by the Crown were allowed to perform plays for 'hire, gain or reward'. Soon various quasi-legal methods were tried to evade the monopoly in respect of legitimate theatre performances granted to London's two patent houses at Drury Lane and Covent Garden. When Henry Giffard re-opened the theatre at Goodman's Fields (on 15 October 1740), he proposed to avoid the 'hire, gain or reward' clause by claiming to charge only for the music and by giving the play free; this was a device that was soon followed elsewhere. Perhaps because of his co-operation over the *Golden Rump* affair, the authorities seem initially to have turned a blind eye to this.[1] However, when Garrick joined Giffard's company in 1741 and had a remarkable success, the patentees appear to have protested and threatened Giffard and Garrick with the Licensing Act. In the circumstances, both accepted engagements offered at Drury Lane, and once more Goodman's Fields was closed.[2]

[1] In his burlesque autobiography, Theophilus Cibber suggested that Giffard may even have written *The Golden Rump* at the instigation of Walpole, in return for which he was promised immunity from prosecution. See Loftis (1963), pp. 140–1.
[2] See Nicholson (1906), pp. 73–6.

184   Goodman's Fields reopens
LS, pt iii, p. 855. Nicholson (1906), p. 73

At the late theatre in Ayliffe Street [. . .], a concert of vocal and instrumental music. Divided into two parts. Tickets at four, three, two and one shilling. NB between the two divisions of the concert will be presented gratis a comedy called *The Stratagem*. By persons for their diversion [. . .].

Charles Macklin and Theophilus Cibber

Macklin used a similar device when, during the Drury Lane actors' revolt against their manager Fleetwood in 1743–4, he attempted to establish a young company at the Haymarket.[1] In September 1743 Theophilus Cibber took over the direction of this company and mounted a successful production of *Romeo and Juliet*. However, he neglected the formal evasion practised by his predecessors, and as a result the patentees complained to the Lord Chamberlain. A sharp reminder was duly sent from the Lord Chamberlain's office [*see* 185].

After a brief pause for thought, Cibber came up with the idea of a concert of music, followed by a free rehearsal on the part of his pupils.[2] This in turn produced a warning from a magistrate, Thomas de Veil, and finally, on 8 November 1743, a ban.[3] Cibber, however, remained attached to the idea of a public rehearsal. As late as 1756 at Richmond in Surrey he was using an even more imaginative version of the same device, claiming to be a snuff merchant who was organising snuff auctions [*see* 186].

[1] 6 February 1743. See *LS* pt iii, pp. 1085 and 1088; see also Nicholson (1906), p. 73.
[2] 11 September 1744. See *LS*, pt iii, pp. 1117–25.
[3] See *LS*, pt iii, pp. 1127–9 and Nicholson (1906), pp. 79–80. T. Cibber: *A serio-comic apology for part of his life* (London, 1748) recounts the whole affair from his point of view.

185 Order to the managers of the playhouse in the Haymarket, 1744
PRO LC 5/161, p. 192

Whereas you have presumed to entertain a company of comedians and act plays at the theatre in the Haymarket without any licence or authority from the Lord Chamberlain of His Majesty's household, as the law directs. These are strictly to charge and command you forthwith to dismiss the said company and forbear acting any more plays or other theatrical performances as you will answer the contrary at your peril. Given under my hand this 20th day of October 1744 in the 18th year of His Majesty's reign. W. FINCH

186 Snuff and a public rehearsal
R.J. Smith: *Material towards a history of the stage*, vol. 9, (BL, 1825–40), 1 July 1756

CIBBER AND COMPANY

SNUFF MERCHANTS

propose to open a snuff warehouse where will be sold a most excellent CEPHALIC SNUFF, whose virtues are of such efficacy as few words cannot easily express. Depending on its merits alone, they do not solicit a patent to puff or parade it.

As soon as a sufficient quantity is prepared, proper places will be appointed and opened for the sale of the said snuff, of which public notice will be given.

Mr Cibber will also open an ACADEMY for the instruction of young persons of genius in the art of ACTING, and purposes, for the better improvement of such pupils, etc., frequently to give PUBLIC REHEARSALS (without gain, hire or reward) for which no money will ever be taken, nor any persons admitted without pass tickets, which will be given by Mr Cibber and Company to their particular patrons and friends GRATIS.

The complex history of theatre patents during the eighteenth century may be briefly summed up as follows.[1] John Rich and his successors, first at Lincoln's Inn Fields and then at Covent Garden, operated under the Davenant patent and later (having bought the dormant Killigrew patent in 1742) under both the Restoration authorities. Drury Lane's authority was the Steele patent, renewed periodically as it expired. The first renewal, for twenty-one years, came in 1732, three years after Steele's death. When Garrick and Lacy took over the theatre in 1747, they arranged a renewal for the twenty-one years from 1753. Later renewals followed.[2] Apart from the omission of the long moral and religious preamble to the Steele patent in 1715, late eighteenth-century patents followed the same basic form.

In 1766, a new patent was granted to Samuel Foote, which gave him legal authority to operate at the Little Theatre in the Haymarket.[3] There were, however, two important restrictions specified in the patent. It was only valid for the summer season from 15 May to 15 September annually (when the other patent theatres were normally closed), and it was limited to the term of Foote's natural life. The patent appears to have been granted at the request of the Duke of York, who had witnessed an unfortunate riding accident involving Foote, which led to the amputation of one of his legs. The patent was clearly viewed as some form of recompense.[4] The restrictions in the patent were equally clearly introduced to safeguard the interests of the regular patent holders.

The Foote patent was the first major crack in the structure built around the 1737 Act. Indicative of a further easing of attitudes, is the fact that in 1777, before his death, Foote was able to sell his patent to the elder Colman (although this was expressly forbidden in the original wording of the patent) who then continued to operate on the basis of an annual licence.[5]

---

[1] For a comprehensive account of the history of theatre patents in the eighteenth century, see *Survey of London*, vol. 35, pp. 1–7.

[2] PRO c/66/3621.

[3] PRO c/66/3706.

[4] See Fitzgerald, vol. 2 (1882), chapter 4; Nicholson (1906), pp. 88–90; and Macqueen-Pope (1948), pp. 102–7.

[5] PRO lc 5/162, p. 230 (1778) and p. 259 (1781). See Nicholson (1906), p. 93. One of these licences survives in the Theatre Collection, University of Bristol. It is for 1781–2 and was granted under the terms of the 1752 Act for Regulating Places of Public Entertainment [*see* 190]. It was signed and sealed by six named Justices of the Peace and afterwards publicly read out in open court at the Michaelmas Quarter Sessions in Westminster on 11 October 1781. The cost to Colman was £3 13 s 6 d.

---

187   Foote's patent for the Little Theatre in the Haymarket, 1766

PRO c/66/3706 Patent Rolls

Samuel Foote Esq. Licence.

George the Third, by the grace of God, etc. [. . .] Know ye that we [. . .] have given and granted [. . .] to our trusty and well-beloved Samuel Foote of the parish of St Martin in the Fields, in the county of Middx, Esquire, from the twenty-fifth day of June in the year of our Lord 1766 and to continue for and during the term of the natural life of the said Samuel Foote, full power, licence and authority to gather together [. . .] and keep a company of comedians for our service, to exercise and act between the fifteenth day of May and the fifteenth day of September in every year (except on Sundays and at such times as the Chamberlain of our household shall judge it proper and expedient, either on account of mournings or otherwise to stop performances on the stage) such tragedies, plays, operas and other performances on the stage only as have already been or shall hereafter be licensed by the Chamberlain of our household, within the house commonly called or known by the name of the Little Theatre in the Haymarket or within any other house or theatre built or to be built, where the said Samuel Foote can best be fitted for that purpose within the City of Westminster, or within the liberties thereof: which said company shall subsist of such members as the said Samuel Foote shall from time to time think meet. And we do hereby [. . .] grant unto the said Samuel Foote full [. . .] authority to permit such persons to act plays and entertainments of the stage of all sorts, peaceably and quietly without the impeachment or impediment of any [. . .] persons whatsoever, for the honest recreation of such as shall desire to see the same. [. . .] and we do hereby [. . .] further grant to him [. . .] that it shall [. . .] be lawful [. . .] to take and receive of such persons as shall resort to see or hear such tragedies, plays, operas or other performances on the stage, [. . .] such sums of money as either have been customably given and taken in the like kind or as shall be thought reasonable by the said Samuel Foote in regard of the great expenses of scenes, music, dress and such new decorations as have not formerly been used. And further we do hereby [. . .] grant unto the said Samuel Foote full power to make such allowances out of the money which he shall so receive by the acting of plays and entertainments of the stage [. . .] to the actors and other persons employed in acting, representing or in any quality whatsoever about the said house or theatre as he [. . .] shall think fit. And that the said company shall be under the sole government of the said Samuel Foote, and all scandalous and mutinous persons shall from time to time by him be ejected and disabled from playing in the said theatre. And [. . .] we have thought fit hereby to declare that from henceforth no representation be admitted on the stage by virtue or under the colour of these our letters patent, whereby the Christian religion in general or the Church of England may in any manner suffer reproach, strictly prohibiting every degree of abuse or misrepresentation of sacred characters, tending to expose religion itself or to bring it into contempt, and that no such character be otherwise introduced or placed in any other light than such as may enhance the just esteem of those who truly answer the end of their sacred function. We further enjoin the strictest regard to such representations as any way concern civil policy or the constitution of our government that these may contribute to the support of our sacred authority and the preservation of order and good government. And it being our Royal will and pleasure that for the future our theatre may be instrumental to the promotion of virtue and instructive to human life, we do hereby command [. . .] that no new play or any old or revived play be acted under the authority hereby granted containing any passages or expressions offensive to piety and good manners, until the same be corrected and purged by the said governor from all such offensive and scandalous passages and expressions. Provided always [. . .]

that if the said Samuel Foote shall sell [. . .] or alienate in any manner to any [. . .] persons whatsoever these our letters patent granted to the said Samuel Foote that then these presents are and shall be to all intents and purposes [. . .] altogether void [. . .] In witness [. . .] ourself at Westminster, the fifth day July. By writ of Privy Seal, COCKS.

LEGISLATION FOR THE PROVINCES

A number of provincial cities had long theatrical traditions dating back to late mediaeval times, which were resumed in a much depleted form after the Restoration. Between 1660 and 1665, George Jolly with his company was visiting Norwich; other companies followed, among them those of Parker, Doggett and Power.[1] These performances usually took place at inns. The first purpose-built theatre in East Anglia was almost certainly that in Ipswich in 1736.[2] But over thirty years before that, in 1705, Power had built on the Borough Walls in Bath what was probably the earliest of all the provincial theatres.[3] In 1709 Penkethman set up a playhouse in Greenwich for a summer company of London players and in 1718 he opened the first of the theatres in Richmond, Surrey for a similar group. There was a theatre in Canterbury in 1726; in Bristol the Jacob's Wells theatre was opened in 1729; York had a theatre in the Minster Yard in 1734.[4] None of these seem to have been much affected by the 1714 Vagrancy Act; and at first the 1737 Licensing Act was not seen as a major threat.

Without benefit of royal patent, a company at Bath went so far as to build a new theatre in Orchard Street in 1750; however, in 1754, information was laid against the company, which led to a temporary closure and fines under the Act. Thereafter for some years all performances were advertised as 'Concerts of Music'.[5] Mrs Charke vividly describes a country arrest at Minchinhampton Gloucestershire at about the same time.[6] As late as 1769 the *Salisbury Journal* was using one of the standard protective devices to advertise a theatrical performance:

> We hear that Messrs Johnson and Collins have taken the new histrionic academy in Portsmouth in which they will deliver serious and comic lectures by subscription. This evening for the first time, *The Jealous Wife* and *Wit's Last Stake*. The academy is properly aired and cleaned. The lectures begin at precisely six o'clock.[7]

Provided no information was laid, performances seem normally to have gone ahead in comparative safety.

Despite the 1737 Licensing Act, theatrical activities in the provinces increased throughout the eighteenth century: there was steady pressure from audiences for more entertainment and there were a growing number of provincial companies. In Bristol, the surviving Account Book of the Jacob's Wells Theatre indicates steady summer activity from 1741 to 1748.[8] New playhouses were built in Norwich in 1758, Portsmouth in 1761 and in Bristol, in King's Street, in 1766.[9] James Dance opened a new playhouse in Richmond in Surrey on 15 June 1765, which had a summer company from the patent houses and Royal patronage.[10] When in 1766 Foote received his patent for the Little Theatre in the Haymarket, it was hardly surprising that demands should follow for similar protection for companies operating outside London.

The first, in 1767, was for Edinburgh [*see* 188], which, like Dublin, tended to regard itself, not so much as a provincial, but as a capital city. This repealed the provisions of earlier legislation in respect of the city, including the 1737 Licensing Act, and gave the company manager a twenty-one year patent to build a theatre, establish a company, discipline it (and its audiences), charge and disburse appropriate fees; the patent also set out the limits to be observed in respect of religion, morals and politics. All this was closely modelled on earlier London patents.[11]

Within months, the first provincial English city was petitioning for the same authority. Accordingly an Enabling Act was passed for the licensing of a playhouse in Bath, which was given the Royal Assent on 29 January 1768 [*see* **189**].[12]

Acts in similar form followed for Norwich (1768), York and Kingston upon Hull (1769), Liverpool (1771), Manchester (1775), Chester (1777), Bristol (1778), Margate (1786), Newcastle upon Tyne (1787), Glasgow (1803) and Birmingham (1807).[13]

1 See Rosenfeld (1939), chapters 2 and 3.
2 See Grice (1977), pp. 37–42. This was the playhouse in which Garrick made his first appearance on stage. See Nicoll (1980), p. 7.
3 See Rosenfeld (1939), chapter 8.
4 See Rosenfeld (1939), chapters 6, 10, 11, 13, 14.
5 See Hare (1977), pp. 6–10.
6 See Charke (1755, reprinted 1929), pp. 169–77.
7 *Salisbury Journal*, 1 May 1769. See Hare (1958), p. 80.
8 Bristol Reference Library. See Rosenfeld (1939), chapter 10.
9 See Grice (1977), chapter 4; Hare (1958), chapter 3; Barker (1974), chapter 1.
10 See Frederick Bingham: *A celebrated old playhouse: the history of Richmond Theatre from 1765 to 1884* (Richmond: Henry Vickers, 1886).
11 A similar document was issued on 10 October 1788 granting a twenty-one year patent from 29 September 1788 to the Duke of Hamilton and Henry Dundas.
12 See Raithby (1811) for appropriate years.
13 *Ibid.*

188   Royal Patent for establishing a playhouse in the City of Edinburgh, 1767
PRO LC 7/4, part I (box of unbound papers)

[The Act of 1737] is hereby repealed so far as the same respects to the City of Edinburgh, and it is hereby enacted that it shall and may be lawful to us, our heirs and successors to grant letters patent establishing a theatre or playhouse in the City of Edinburgh or suburbs thereof, which shall be entitled to all the privileges and subjected to all the regulations to which any theatre or playhouse in Great Britain is entitled and subjected. Know ye therefore that we [. . .] do give and grant to our trusty and well beloved Henry Davidson of Poland Street in the liberty of Westminster and County of Middlesex, solicitor, and his assigns, for and during the full end and terms of twenty-one years to commence from the twenty-ninth day of September in the year of our Lord one thousand, seven hundred and sixty seven, full power, licence and authority to erect, build and establish a theatre or playhouse in the City of Edinburgh or suburbs thereof, and to gather together [. . .], govern, privilege and keep a company of comedians for our service to exercise and to act such tragedies, plays and operas and other performances of the stage only as have already been or shall hereafter be licensed by the Chamberlain of our household, within the said theatre [. . .] (except at such times as the Chamberlain of our household shall judge it proper and expedient, either on account of mournings or otherwise, to stop performances of the stage): which said company of comedians shall consist of such numbers as the said Henry Davidson and his assigns shall from time to time think meet. And we do hereby grant [. . .] full power, licence and authority to permit such persons attached during the pleasure of the said Henry Davidson and his assigns from time to time to act plays and such entertainments of the stage of all sorts, peaceably and quietly without the impeachment or impediment of any person or persons whatsoever, for the honest recreation of such as shall desire to do the same [. . .]. And we do further grant [. . .] that it shall and may be lawful [. . .] to take and receive of such of our subjects as shall resort to the said theatre to see or hear such tragedies, plays, operas or other performances of the stage whatsoever such sum or sums of money as either have been customably given and taken in the like kind or as shall be thought reasonable by the said Henry Davidson and his assigns in regard to the great expense of building the said theatre and of scenes and music and such other decorations as are usual and necessary. And further, for us, our heirs and successors, we do hereby give and grant unto the said Henry Davidson and his assigns full power to make such allowances out of the money which shall be received by the acting such tragedies and plays, operas, or other performances of the stage as aforesaid to the actors and other persons employed in acting, representing or in any quality whatsoever about the said theatre or playhouse, as the said Henry Davidson and his assigns shall think fit. And that the said company shall be under the sole government and authority of the said Henry Davidson and his assigns, and all scandalous and mutinous persons shall from time to time by him or them be ejected and disabled from playing in the said theatre. And for the better attaining our royal purposes in this behalf, we have thought fit hereby to declare that henceforth no representations be admitted on the stage by virtue or under colour of these our letters patent whereby the Christian religion in general or the Church of England may in any manner suffer reproach, strictly inhibiting every degree of abuse or misrepresentation of sacred characters tending to expose religion itself and to bring it into contempt. And that no such character be otherwise introduced or placed in any other light than such as may enhance the best esteem of those who truly answer the end of their sacred function. We further enjoin the strictest regard to such representations as any way concern civil polity or the constitution of our government, that these may contribute to the support of our sacred authority and the preservation of order and good government. And it being our royal will and pleasure that for the future our theatre may be instrumental to the promotion of virtue and instructive to human life, we do hereby command and enjoin that no new play or any revived play be acted under the authority hereby granted containing any passage or expression offensive to piety and good manners until the same be corrected and purged by the said governor from all such offensive and scandalous passages and expressions [. . .].

By writ of Privy Seal. Cocks.

Entered at the Lord Chamberlain's Office, 2 September 1767.

189   An Act to enable His Majesty to license a playhouse in the City of Bath, 1768

J. Raithby (ed.): *Statutes at large*, vol. 7 (London: Eyre & Strahan, 1811), p. 3

Whereas a licensed playhouse is much wanted in the City of Bath, may it therefore please Your Majesty that it may be enacted. And be it enacted by the King's most excellent Majesty, by and with the advice and consent of the Lords Spiritual and Temporal, and Commons, in this present Parliament assembled, and by the authority of the same, that so much of an Act of Parliament which passed in the tenth year of His late Majesty's reign [. . .] as relates to common players of interludes (whereby all persons are discharged to represent any entertainment of the stage whatsoever, in virtue of letters patent from His Majesty or by licence of the Lord Chamberlain of His Majesty's household for the time being, except within the liberties of Westminster or where His Majesty is residing for the time being) be, and the same is hereby, repealed with respect to the said City of Bath. And that it shall and may be lawful for His Majesty, his heirs and successors, to grant letters patent for establishing a theatre or playhouse within the said city, which shall be entitled to all the privileges and subjected to all the regulations to which any theatre or playhouse in Great Britain is entitled and subjected.

THE MINOR THEATRES IN LONDON
Legislation in 1752

In London, one other piece of legislation had some relevance to the activity of minor theatrical establishments. This was an act designed to regulate places of popular entertainment and was first introduced in 1752. Such establishments might involve dancing, singing, juggling, rope-walking, pantomime and farce; there had been complaints that they encouraged thieving, drunkenness and fornication. In 1744, for instance, Sadler's Wells had been prosecuted as a disorderly and disreputable house and was closed down for a time. This was the background to the 'Act for regulating places of public entertainment' of 1752. After a trial period of three years, the act was renewed and made permanent in 1755.[1]

---

[1]   28 Geo II, cap xix (1755). See Raithby, vol. 6 (1811), p. 70.

190   An Act for the better preventing thefts and robberies and for regulating places of public entertainment and punishing persons keeping disorderly houses, 1752
J. Raithby (ed.): *Statutes at large*, vol. 6 (London, 1811), pp. 67–70, 25 Geo II cap xxxvi

[. . .] II. And whereas the multitude of places of entertainment for the lower sort of people is another great cause of thefts and robberies, as they are thereby tempted to spend their small substance in riotous pleasures and in consequence are put on unlawful methods of supplying their wants and renewing their pleasures. In order therefore to prevent the said temptation to thefts and robberies and to correct as far as may be the habit of idleness, which is become too general over the whole kingdom and is productive of much mischief and inconvenience, be it enacted by the authority aforesaid that from and after the first day of December, one thousand, seven hundred and fifty two, any house, room, garden or other place kept for public dancing, music, or other public entertainment of the like kind, in the cities of London and Westminster, or within twenty miles thereof, without a licence had for that purpose from the last preceding Michaelmas Quarter Sessions of the Peace, to be held for the county, city, riding, liberty or division in which such house, room, garden, or other place is situate (who are hereby authorised and empowered to grant such licences as they in their discretion shall think proper), signified under the hands and seals of four or more of the Justices there assembled, shall be deemed a disorderly house or place. [. . .] And it shall and may be lawful to and for any constable, or other person being thereunto authorised by warrant under the hand and seal of one or more of His Majesty's Justices of the Peace [. . .], to enter such house or place and to seize every person who shall be found therein, in order that they may be dealt with according to law. And every person keeping such house, room, garden or other place, without such licence as aforesaid, shall forfeit the sum of one hundred pounds to such person as will sue for the same and be otherwise punishable as the law directs in cases of disorderly houses.

III. Provided always [. . .] that in order to give public notice what places are licensed pursuant to this Act, there shall be affixed and kept up in some notorious place over the door or entrance to every such house, room, garden, or other place [. . .] an inscription in large capital letters in the words following: *videlicet*, LICENSED PURSUANT TO ACT OF PARLIAMENT OF THE TWENTY FIFTH OF KING GEORGE THE SECOND. And that no such house, room, garden, or other place, kept for any of the said purposes, although licensed as aforesaid, shall be open for any of the said purposes before the hour of five in the afternoon. And that the affixing and keeping up of such inscription as aforesaid, and the said limitation or restriction in point of time, shall be inserted in and made conditions of every such licence [. . .].

IV. Provided always that nothing in this Act contained shall extend, or be construed to extend, to the Theatres Royal in Drury Lane and Covent Garden or the theatre commonly called the King's Theatre in the Haymarket, or any of them. Nor to such performances and public entertainments as are or shall be lawfully exercised and carried on under or by virtue of letters patent or licence of the crown or the licence of the Lord Chamberlain of His Majesty's household, anything herein contained notwithstanding [. . .].

Sadler's Wells and the Royalty Theatre

Sadler's Wells was licensed under the provisions of the 1752 act, as were establishments like the China Hall Gardens at Rotherhithe, though this did not prevent them from being prosecuted for performing plays, if an information was laid against them.[1]

It was presumably on a generous interpretation of this act that John Palmer was relying in 1787 when he opened the newly-built Royalty Theatre in Wellclose Square and proposed to perform the standard repertory. Even though there was much controversy and a good deal of support for him, the patentees closed ranks and the scheme had to be abandoned [*see* **191**]. The theatre survived only as a house for burlettas, dances and pantomimes, like Sadler's Wells and Astley's.[2]

The Royalty affair, however, led Sadler's Wells to attempt to extend its privileges by a bill of 11 March 1788, which would enable it to be granted letters patent. When the bill came before the House, R.B. Sheridan, who was a patentee of Drury Lane as well as a Member of Parliament, was naturally called upon to speak [*see* **192**]. Sheridan argued against the creation of a new monopoly, while defending an existing monopoly and the financial advantages it brought the patentees; he also sought to divide the opposition by proposing a postponement rather than a vote against the bill. Ladbroke, who had brought in the bill, objected that if the second reading was put off as proposed, some of the most profitable part of the season would have elapsed before the bill could be decided upon; but the postponement was narrowly carried.

Opposition to the monopoly position of the patentees was growing, however, and an amended bill which would give greater freedom, not only to Sadler's Wells but also to the Royalty, Astley's and the Royal Circus, was approved by the Lords but rejected by the Commons on 25 June 1788.[3]

[1] See C.B. Hogan: 'The China Hall Theatre, Rotherhithe' *TN* 8 (1953–4), 76–8. See also Hare (1980), pp. 30–1.
[2] See Nicholson (1906), chapters 5 and 6.
[3] *Ibid.*, chapter 6.

191   John Palmer's address to the audience after the opening performance at the Royalty Theatre, 20 June 1787
Dodsley's London Chronicle, 21–3 June 1787

Ladies and Gentlemen.

I am sorry on the first night that I have the honour of seeing this theatre graced by so splendid an appearance, to be obliged to trouble you with the peculiar circumstances of my situation.

I had flattered myself that I should be able, during the summer months, to exert my best endeavours in your service.

This theatre was built under a letter of approbation from the Lord Lieutenant Governor of the Tower. And being situated in a palace and fortress, in a district immediately within his jurisdiction, his consent, added to a licence obtained from the Magistrates authorising a place of public entertainment, were deemed legal authority.

The first stone of the building was laid on 26 December 1785; at that time the Managers of the theatres at the West End of the town made no kind of objection.

In the course of the last summer, when I performed at the Little Theatre in the Haymarket, Mr Colman wrote a prologue, which I spoke on my benefit night; and, among others, were the following lines:

> For me, whose utmost aim is your delight,
> Accept the humble offering of this night;
> To please, wherever placed, be still my care,
> At Drury, Haymarket, or Wellclose Square.

As Mr Colman knew the plan I had then in view, it was fair to conclude that he did not meditate an opposition.

Mr Harris, the Manager of Covent Garden Theatre, gave his consent in writing, that Mr Quick should be engaged here.

After all this, to my great astonishment, when a large expense had been incurred and this house was completely ready for opening, the three Managers thought good to publish in the newspapers extracts from different Acts of Parliament, accompanied with their joint resolution to put the Act in force against this theatre.

They went a step further; they served me with a formal notice, signed Tho. Linley, Tho. Harris, Geo. Colman.

I have the satisfaction to find that those three gentlemen are the only enemies to this undertaking, and it will be for themselves to consider whether they are not, at the same time, opposing the voice of the public.

For myself, I have embarked my all in this theatre, persuaded that, under the sanction I obtained, it was perfectly legal: in the event of it, everything dear to my family is involved.

I was determined to strain every nerve to merit your favour, but when I consider the case of other performers, who have been also threatened with prosecutions, I own I shrink from the difficulty.

I had promised a benefit play for the use of the London Hospital, and all the performers agreed with me that one night at least should be employed for so useful a purpose.

We have not performed for hire, gain or reward, and we hope that the three Managers, with the Magistrates in their interest, will neither deem benevolence a misdemeanour nor send us, for an act of charity, to hard labour in the house of correction.

I beg pardon for trespassing thus long upon your patience; circumstanced as things are, and a combination being formed to oppress and ruin me, it is not at present in my power to give out another play.

Under the Act of Parliament which empowers the Magistrates to allow certain performances, I have obtained a licence, and to whatever purpose of innocent amusement this theatre may be converted, your future patronage will abundantly compensate for every difficulty I have to encounter.

Tumblers and dancing dogs might appear unmolested before you, but the other performers and myself standing forward to exhibit a moral play is deemed a crime.

The purpose, however, for which we have this night exerted ourselves, may serve to show that a theatre near Wellclose Square may be as useful as in Covent Garden, Drury Lane or the Haymarket.

All that remains at present is to return my most grateful thanks for the indulgence with which you have honoured me this night. I forbear to enlarge on that subject – my heart is too full – I have not words to express my feelings. I shall be ever devoted to your service.

Until it is announced that this house shall be again opened with a species of entertainment, not subjecting me to dangers, I humbly take my leave.

192   Sheridan opposes a bill to license performances at Sadler's Wells, 11 March 1788

Sheridan: *Speeches* (edited by a constitutional friend), vol. 2 (London: P. Martin. 1816). pp. 18–21

Mr Sheridan remarked that he had consented to the bill being read a first time because it was really his wish that the house should have an opportunity to consider the matter fairly and to understand what was demanded from them. [. . .]

He had ever been, and he trusted that he ever should be found, an enemy to anything like oppression in any matter, great or small; and on the present occasion, he confessed that the apprehensions of other people interested in the rights, supposed to be attacked by the bill in question, went beyond his own. But it was, however, to be remembered that those apprehensions related to a property upon which, taking the two winter theatres only, a sum little short of two hundred thousand pounds had been embarked. He felt it therefore his duty to endeavour to protect those rights according to their ideas of the injury they might sustain and not according to any more indulgent way of considering the subject which he might himself have entertained.

Mr Sheridan then proceeded to argue on the nature of the present application. The proprietors of Sadler's Wells had declared in their case that the cause of their application for a bill to enable His Majesty to grant them a licence to continue the entertainments of Sadler's Wells as heretofore was that, 'the proprietors of the winter theatres had lately instituted suits at law, not only against the last newly erected theatre [the Royalty] but intended to commence suits and prosecutions against all others indiscriminately'. To his own personal knowledge (Mr Sheridan said) that inference was wholly unfounded; and the proprietors of Sadler's Wells knew it to be groundless. There was no intention to proceed against them or to molest them in any way whatsoever. In another instance also the case of the proprietors of Sadler's Wells was fallaciously stated. They told the house that they came there only to ask that they might be legally empowered to continue their performances as usual. That was not the fact. Because what they asked for was a monopoly, as appeared clearly from a view and examination of the different parts of their case. There was some degree of unfairness also in their mode of reasoning against others who stood in a similar predicament. Speaking for themselves, they said, 'that doubts may arise whether, in strict construction of law, their performances might be strictly and minutely within the letter of their licence'. But when they spoke of the riding schools, the Circus and the new set of competitors, they stated them as performing in defiance of known laws upon the authority of musical licences only. Whereas their own licence contained not a letter of power more than the licences of their adversaries which they reprobated. The only difference being that the one was granted by the Surrey Justices and the other by those of Middlesex.

From this it appeared, nay indeed they avowed it, that their object was monopoly, not licence: and the house could grant them no relief, according to their own statement, unless they put down all similar places and shut their doors in future against all similar applications. Their claim to the preference might or might not be well founded. But he could not but think that places of similar amusement under the Surrey licences would afterwards come with a pretty strong case to Parliament for an equal indulgence: and that it would be an odd reason to give for refusing their requests that the proprietors of Sadler's Wells had the merit of transgressing the law first and had therefore received a protection from the legislature to which those who had only followed their example were not entitled. This, however, was a matter for Parliament to consider. If they chose to grant the preference and to establish the monopoly which the present bill aimed at, and as a matter of regulation and policy to stop there, the proprietors of the winter theatres would have little to complain of; for, he took it for granted, that certain alterations would be made in the bill and that no part of the new powers would be suffered to entrench in the least on the rights of the winter patents, either as to season or the species of performances.

Mr Sheridan concluded with observing that the winter theatres had a right to complain a little of those who had brought in the bill. The petition had been before the house nearly two months, and yet the bill had not been brought in till just at the last moment, close upon the commencement of the Sadler's Wells season, in order that its near approach might be used as an argument, and in order that it might come into discussion at a time when the winter proprietors could not so well be heard against it by their counsel, if they should judge that measure necessary. He should on that account, notwithstanding the surprise that had been attempted on the house, move, 'that the second reading of the bill be postponed to Friday, the fourth of April'.

THE ENABLING ACT OF 1788

If there was not yet agreement about the treatment of the minor theatres, there was by now a consensus that the 1737 act had become too restrictive and that some relaxation was necessary. In spite of general public support, respectable provincial companies could still be prosecuted, should an information be laid against them. There were, for example, successful prosecutions before the Bristol magistrates in 1773[1] and at the Salisbury Assizes on 21 July 1787, both of which aroused a great deal of public anger locally.[2] Since the principle of the granting of royal patents had already been tacitly accepted for certain provincial cities, the need for protection against unfair discrimination was now obvious. The possibility of limited licensing by Quarter Sessions had been canvassed during the discussions on some of the proposed legislation that had failed. In the autumn of 1788 it was put forward in a new bill that was passed by both Houses and became law [see **193a**]. The immediate effect of the bill was that even in those cases, as in Salisbury, where there had been a previous prosecution, there was now a proper mechanism for obtaining a theatrical licence [see **193b**].

This was an important move in the direction of freedom, but the legislation governing the work of theatres in London and the provinces was now complicated and cumbersome. In the City of Westminster, the Lord Chamberlain remained the chief authority in control of the patent theatres; within a twenty-mile radius of London and Westminster, magistrates might license certain kinds of theatrical entertainments; outside the twenty-mile radius, they could authorise 'legitimate' drama for a limited period each year; while individual Acts of Parliament gave to certain provincial theatres the same privileges as the metropolitan patent theatres.[3] There was an overlapping of jurisdiction here, as well as obvious anomalies, that were bound to cause trouble sooner or later. But it was another half century before the 'Theatre Regulation Bill' of 1843 brought some semblance of order into this chaos. The Lord Chamberlain's powers of censorship, first introduced by the Licensing Act of 1737, remained in force until the 'Theatres' Act' of 1968.

[1] Felix Farley's *Bristol Journal*, 23 Jan 1773 *et seq.*
[2] PRO *Western Circuit Minute Book* 1786–1800, Assizes 22–4. See also Hare (1958), pp. 17–28 and 116–18.
[3] See Nicholson (1906), pp. 138–9.

193 The Enabling Act of 1788
(a) An Act to enable Justices of the Peace to license theatrical representations occasionally, under the restrictions therein contained, 1788

J. Raithby (ed.): *Statutes at large*, vol. 9 (London, 1811), pp. 16–17. 28 Geo III, cap xxx.

Whereas by an Act passed in the tenth year of the reign of His late Majesty King George the Second, certain penalties and punishments were inflicted on every person who should, for hire, gain or reward, act, represent or perform or cause to be acted, represented or performed, any interlude, tragedy, comedy, opera, play, farce, or other entertainment of the stage, or any part or parts therein, except as in the said Act is excepted. And whereas diverse Acts of Parliament have since been solicited and obtained for diverse cities, towns and places for exempting them respectively from the provisions of the said law. And whereas it may be expedient to permit and suffer, in towns of considerable resort, theatrical representations for a limited time and under regulations; in which nevertheless it would be highly impolitic, inexpedient and unreasonable to permit the establishment of a constant and regular theatre. May it therefore please Your Majesty that it may be enacted [. . .] by and with the advice and consent of the Lords Spiritual and Temporal, and Commons, in this present Parliament assembled, and by the authority of the same, that it shall and may be lawful to and for the Justices of the Peace of any county, riding or liberty, in General or Quarter Sessions assembled, at their discretion, to grant a licence to any person or persons making application for the same by petition, for the performance of such tragedies, comedies, interludes, operas, plays or farces as now are or hereafter shall be acted, performed or represented at either of the patent or licensed theatres in the City of Westminster or as shall in the manner prescribed by law have been submitted to the inspection of the Lord Chamberlain of the King's household for the time being, at any place within their jurisdictions, or within any city, town or place situate within the limits of the same, for any number of days not exceeding sixty days, to commence within the then next six months and to be within the space of such four months as shall be specified in the said licence, so as there be only one licence in use at the same time within the jurisdiction so given, and so as such place be not within twenty miles of the cities of London, Westminster or Edinburgh, or eight miles of any patent or licensed theatre or ten miles of the residence of His Majesty, his heirs or successors, or of any place within the same jurisdiction at which within six months preceding a licence under this act shall have been had and executed, or within fourteen miles of either of the Universities of Oxford and Cambridge, or within two miles of the outward limits of any city, town or place having peculiar jurisdiction. And so also as no licence under this act shall have been had and exercised at the same place within eight months then next preceding; any law or statute for the punishment of persons employed in theatrical representations to the contrary in any wise notwithstanding.

II. Provided always that no such licence shall be granted by the Justices aforesaid to be exercised within any city, town or place having peculiar jurisdiction, unless proof shall be made that the majority of the Justices [. . .] have at a public meeting signed their consent and approbation to the said application [. . .]

III. Provided also that no such licence shall be granted by the Justices aforesaid within any city, town or place, unless notice shall have been given by the person or persons applying for such licence at least three weeks before such application to the mayor, bailiff, or other chief civil officer or officers of such city, town or place, of his or their intending to make such application.

(b) The Enabling Act in practice, Salisbury, October 1788

Wiltshire Quarter Sessions Minute Book 1782–95, p. 362 (Wiltshire County Records Office, Trowbridge)[1]

Players' Licence. By virtue of an Act of Parliament, made and passed in the twenty-eighth year of the reign of His present Majesty King George the Third over Great Britain and so forth, entitled 'An Act to enable Justices of the Peace to license theatrical representations occasionally under the restrictions therein contained', this court doth, on the application and petition of Thomas Collins and James Davis, license the said Thomas Collins and James Davis to perform such tragedies, comedies, interludes, operas, plays or farces as now or hereafter shall be acted, performed or represented at either of the patent theatres in the City of Westminster, or as shall in the manner prescribed by law have been submitted to the inspection of the Lord Chamberlain of the King's household, for the time being, at the City of New Sarum, being a city within the limits of the jurisdiction of this court, for fifty days between the twenty-fifth day of October instant and the fifth day of February now next ensuing, proof having been made to this court that the majority of the Justices acting for the City of New Sarum aforesaid have at a public meeting signed their consent and approbation to the said application.

[1] Subsequently Quarter Sessions records become a useful, though by no means exhaustive, source for company movements.

8 Contractual and company documents

INTRODUCTION

In the fifty years after 1737 there were five different types of theatrical company at work in the British Isles. First and foremost were the companies of the two London patent theatres, Drury Lane and Covent Garden, joined after 1766 by the Little Theatre in the Haymarket. In the early years there were *ad hoc* companies of London players making forays to certain provincial centres during the metropolitan summer closures. There were also winter companies outside London which, between 1767 and 1787, gained Royal patents, such as those in Edinburgh, Bath, Norwich, York, Bristol and Manchester. From these and alongside them developed the circuit companies in the last half of the century. And all the time there were the groups of poor strollers, moving wherever patronage seemed likely, playing in small towns or large villages, in inns, barns, or fairground booths; the lowest stratum of the profession, the bottom rung of the ladder from which many players ascended and learned their trade. Documents from all five are represented here, and they differ greatly in scale. The larger the organisation, the more complex its running became. But one common factor applied to all of them, from Garrick in London to Austin in Chester and the north – the steady search for reputation, reward and respectability. Not all achieved it. Of those who did, some made London the summit of their ambition; others, like Dimond, Wilkinson and Austin, settled for kingship in a smaller estate.

One other significant development should be recorded. Some players travelled further afield than the British Isles. English companies and players can be traced in the West Indies and North America during the second half of the century. The story of the Hallams, Hodgkinsons, John Henry and Joseph Jefferson, and theatres like those in Philadelphia, New York and Charleston will be told in a later volume in the context of the rise of the American theatre. But their seminal importance needs to be noted now.

MANAGEMENT IN LONDON

Provoked by the legal wrangles with Sir Richard Steele in the late 1720s, Colley Cibber set down in his *Apology* a useful working definition of the role of theatre manager [*see* **194**]. It was to be paid scant attention by the dilettante managers of Drury Lane during the 1730s and early 1740s. Highmore's incompetence as a manager provoked an actors' revolt in 1733 [*see* **23**]. Fleetwood's mismanagement provoked a similar revolt in April 1743, when the actors led by Garrick and Macklin left for Dublin. Although Garrick returned to Drury

Lane in December (which led to a bitter public quarrel with Macklin),[1] Fleetwood faced further public attacks for his mismanagement.[2]

[1] See *LS*, pt iii, pp. xciii–xcv and George W. Stone and George M. Kahrl *David Garrick a critical biography* (Carbondale & Edwardsville: Southern Illinois University Press, 1979), chapter 3.

[2] See *LS*, pt iii, p. xcv.

194   Colley Cibber's definition of the duties of a manager
Cibber (Lowe ed.), vol. 2, pp. 203–4

By our books it is apparent that the managers have under their care no less than a hundred and forty persons in constant daily pay; and among such numbers, it will be no wonder, if a great number of them are unskilful, idle and sometimes untractable, all which tempers are to be led or driven, watched and restrained by the continual skill, care and patience of the managers. Every manager is obliged in his turn to attend two or three hours every morning at the rehearsal of plays and other entertainments for the stage, or else every rehearsal would be but a rude meeting of mirth and jollity. The same attendance is as necessary at every play, during the time of its public action, in which one or more of us have constantly been punctual, whether we have any part in the play then acted or not. A manager ought to be at the reading of every new play when it is first offered to the stage, though there are seldom one of those plays in twenty, which, upon hearing, proves to be fit for it; and upon such occasions the attendance must be allowed to be as painfully tedious, as the getting rid of the authors of such plays must be disagreeable and difficult. Besides this, a manager is to order all new clothes, to assist in the fancy and propriety of them, to limit the expense and to withstand the unreasonable importunities of some who are apt to think themselves injured, if they are not finer than their fellows. A manager is to direct and oversee the painters, machinists, musicians, singers and dancers, to have an eye upon the doorkeepers, under-servants and officers who, without such care, are too often apt to defraud us or neglect their duty.

GARRICK AND LACY

Fleetwood was finally driven out after audience riots in November 1744, following his ill-judged attempt to increase prices. Fleetwood's patent was bought by the bankers Richard Green and Morton Amber for £3200.[1] They employed James Lacy as the new manager of Drury Lane; at the time he was under-manager for Rich at Covent Garden. Following the bankruptcy of his banker employers shortly afterwards, Lacy made the bold move of inviting Garrick to leave Rich's company and join him in full partnership at Drury Lane. Their collaboration was not without its difficulties, but it ushered in a new period of prosperity for Drury Lane. The Garrick–Lacy agreement [*see* 196] applies to an already large organisation which had a long history of disagreement, and the establishment of an 'honest broker' [*see* 197] was an attempt to find a simple machinery to obviate these for the future. The agreed division of labour [*see* 195] exploited the individual skills of the partners in an already recognised pattern of managerial responsibility.

[1] See *LS*, pt iii, p. xcvi.

195   Agreed division of labour between Garrick and Lacy

Thomas Davies: *Memoirs of the life of David Garrick Esq.*, vol. 1 [1780] (revised edition, London: Longman, 1808), pp. 144–9

Mr Garrick and Mr Lacy divided the business of the theatre in such a manner as not to encroach upon each other's province. Mr Lacy took upon himself the care of the wardrobe, the scenes and the economy of the household; while Mr Garrick regulated the more important business of treating with authors, hiring actors, distributing parts in plays, superintending rehearsals, etc. Besides the profits accruing from his half share, he was allowed an income of £500 for his acting, and some particular emoluments for altering plays, farces, etc.

Such was the confidence which the players had in Mr Garrick's abilities, that he had his choice of the most eminent amongst them, except Mr Quin who retired to Bath. Mrs Pritchard, Mrs Cibber and many others immediately entered into articles with the patentees of Drury Lane. Rich was almost deserted and, I believe, did not recover from his surprise and inactivity till very late in the season, when he brought out a favourite piece of mummery that drew vast crowds to it [. . .].

[. . .] Punctuality in attendance at rehearsals was exacted and complied with, and as much due attendance paid to the business of the scene as during the time of acting a play. Those players who had fallen into an unlucky habit of imperfection in their parts, and of being obliged to supply that defect by assuming a bold front and forging matter of their own, Mr Garrick steadily discouraged till, by being laid aside for some time, they had learned to pay a proper respect to the audience and the author. In distributing parts he consulted the genius of the actor; and though he was not without those prejudices which no man can be entirely divested of, yet, in general, the characters were very well suited to those who represented them [. . .].

196   1747 agreement between Garrick and Lacy regarding the management of Drury Lane

Forster Collection (Victoria and Albert Museum). Reproduced in Boaden (1831) vol. 1, pp. 50–3 and Little and Kahrl (1963), appendix B

Agreement made the 9th April, 1747, between James Lacy of Great Queen Street, near Lincoln's Inn Fields, in the County of Middlesex, gentleman, of the one part; and David Garrick, of James Street, Covent Garden, gentleman, of the other part [. . .][1]

[. . .] Now it is hereby agreed, that in case the said James Lacy shall and does within the time aforesaid procure such a new patent, on the terms aforesaid [. . .] they, the said James Lacy and David Garrick, their executors, administrators and assigns shall and will, from the end of this present acting season, become and be jointly and equally possessed of and interested in the said two several patents, and the said lease, wardrobe and scenes, subject to the respective encumbrances aforesaid, for the several terms that will remain and be in the said patents respectively, but without any benefit of survivorship; and shall and will enter into and execute proper articles of copartnership for the carrying on and managing the business of the said patents for their joint and equal benefit.

And that as soon as such new patent and right in the old patent, etc. shall be procured as aforesaid, the same shall be immediately conveyed to two persons, of which each of the said parties shall name and appoint one, upon trust, as a security from each of the said parties to the other for the performance of their respective agreements and covenants, both in these presents and in the said articles of copartnership to be contained.

That the said encumbrances on the said patents shall be paid off and discharged as soon as may be, by and out of the profits to arise in the said copartnership, or equally by and between the said parties.

Provided, that in case the said encumbrances (exclusive of the said annuities) shall exceed the said sum of £12,000, the difference or excess shall be made good, paid and discharged by the said James Lacy or his assigns; or out of his or their moiety of the said profits; and the said David Garrick and his assigns, and his or their moiety of the said patents, etc. are to be fully indemnified therefrom.

Provided also that each of the said parties shall or may, weekly or otherwise, take and retain for their private expenses, and under the title of managers, out of the money to be in the hands of the Treasurer or Cashier of the said copartnership, any sum not exceeding the rate of £500 per annum each. [. . .]

Provided also, and it is expressly agreed, that the said David Garrick shall have and be paid a clear salary of 500 gns per annum as an actor, with a clear benefit, or shall have such better terms as shall at any time during the said copartnership be given to any actor or actress; but the said David Garrick shall not, during the time of his being interested in the said patents, or either of them, act or perform, except for the joint benefit of the parties concerned in the said patents.

Provided also, that in settling the encumbrances aforesaid, the said James Lacy is to account for the receipts of this present season, it being the intent of the parties that the arrears due to the actors, performers and tradesmen, at the end of the last season, are to be the bases of their respective accounts, from or to which the profits or loss of this present season are to be respectively subtracted or added. [. . .]

Provided also that if either party shall be minded to sell or dispose of his share, the other party shall have the refusal thereof at such price, as two persons, one to be named by each party, shall value the same at.

Lastly, if any dispute or differences shall happen, the same are hereby agreed to be referred to two arbitrators, each of the parties to name one within twenty-four hours after notice from the other.

---

[1] The agreement lists Lacy's right to a patent at Drury Lane with six years' life remaining, and his ability to procure a new patent to follow it, together with all his debts and encumbrances.

197   Garrick and Lacy establish a system of mediation in case of disputes

Garrick Correspondence, vol. 36 (Forster Collection, Victoria and Albert Museum, undated). Reproduced in Little and Kahrl (1963), appendix B

Whereas at the time of signing the original agreements of copartnership between James Lacy and David Garrick Esquires on the 9th day of April 1747 it was verbally agreed that the business of the stage should be under the management of Mr Garrick, there being sufficient other matters of importance to employ Mr Lacy; and whereas there have of late some misunderstandings arisen between them touching the said management of the stage; and whereas it would be very inconvenient for the partners to meet to settle the said business by joint consent, and the plan of such business must frequently and sometimes be broken through and altered on account of various accidents *either of a foreign or domestic kind*, therefore to obviate such difficulties and prevent all misunderstandings for the future, it is hereby agreed between the said partners as follows: viz.

1st. That the settling or altering the business of the stage be left entirely to Mr Garrick who shall immediately communicate the same to the prompter for the information of Mr Lacy, with this proviso that whensoever Mr Lacy shall apprehend that Mr Garrick is pursuing measures injurious to his, Mr Lacy's, property, he shall state his objection to John Paterson Esq. (who undertakes to act as the common friend of both) and to him only; and Mr Garrick shall submit to his determination.

2nd. That all actors, actresses, singers, dancers and other servants shall be hired or discharged and their salaries or allowances settled or increased by joint consent and not otherwise.

3rd. That the accounts and all other business of the copartnership shall be jointly carried on at the office; Mr Garrick, by reason of his attendance upon the business of the stage being at liberty to employ his brother George Garrick to attend and act for him in the said office; but to give his personal attendance whensoever any matter of importance shall, in the judgement of Mr Lacy, appear to require it.

4th. That in the case of any future difference the partner who shall think himself injured shall (without venting any speeches in public to the disadvantage of the other) state his complaint to Mr Paterson, who shall decide thereon and finally settle the dispute between them.

5th. That in the case of any future misunderstanding between them being such as cannot be set right by Mr Paterson either party may give notice to the other of his desire to dissolve the copartnership, and both parties shall attend Mr Paterson at such time and place as he shall appoint in writing, when and where their joint property shall be put up to auction between them, their biddings being in writing and signed by them respectively; and when either party shall refuse or neglect to bid any more the best bidder shall be entitled to the whole joint property upon payment to the other of one half of the sum last bid by himself. And the other party shall upon such payment convey [. . .] his half part of the said property to the said best bidder free from all encumbrances [. . .].

6th. That in case of the death of either party there shall be the same auction and proceedings between the surviving partner, the executors and/or administrators of the partner deceased, as are hereinbefore directed [. . .].

7th. That this agreement is understood to be honorary and shall not be divulged upon any pretence whatsoever unless upon a breach of some part thereof, and in that case, only so far as relates to the article supposed to be broken.

CONDITIONS OF WORK FOR ACTORS AND ACTRESSES IN LONDON

From 1712 onwards, the triumvirate of managers at Drury Lane had avoided committing themselves to legally binding contracts with their actors and actresses. A number of actions for breach of contract had been brought by the actresses Letitia Cross and Jane Rogers against London managers, and the newly established triumvirate was determined to avoid similar difficulties.[1] The later eighteenth century saw a return to formal contracts of employment in London between managers and actors. This went hand-in-hand with a tightening up of company discipline and an improvement in salaries and conditions of work. These are reflected in the contractual agreement of 1785 made between Sheridan and his fellow patentees, on the one hand, and the actress Dorothea Jordan, on the other.

[1] See Judith Milhous and Robert D. Hume: 'Theatrical politics at Drury Lane: new light on Letitia Cross, Jane Rogers and Anne Oldfield' *Bulletin of research in the humanities* (1982), 412–29.

198   Conditions of employment at Drury Lane in 1785
Original document held in the Theatre Museum

Articles of agreement [. . .] agreed upon this sixteenth day of December in the year of our Lord 1785 between Richard Brinsley Sheridan, Thomas Linley and James Ford, patentees and proprietors of the Theatre Royal, of the one part, and Dorothea Jordan of Catherine Street in the parish of St Mary-le-Strand, spinster, of the other part.

The said Dorothea Jordan, for and in consideration of five shillings to her in hand paid by the said Richard Brinsley Sheridan, Thomas Linley and James Ford, the receipt whereof is hereby acknowledged, and also in consideration of the covenants and agreements hereinafter contained on the part of the said proprietors to be performed and kept, doth for herself, her executors and administrators, covenant and agree to and with the said proprietors and their successors in manner following. That is to say that the said Dorothea Jordan shall and will from the day of the date hereof for and during the residue and remainder of this present acting season and for and during the term of succeeding years for four acting seasons, diligently and duly attend the said Theatre Royal in her business or employment as a performer, and to the utmost of her power and capacity publicly act, sing or perform, on the stage of the said theatre, all and every such part or parts in all such tragedies and comedies, plays, operas, farces, pantomimes, entertainments, masques, interludes, dances and other theatrical performances as by or from the said proprietors or their successors or their manager or prompter for the time being shall be ordered, directed or required, or whereof notice shall be given by advertisement in the public newspapers and the fixing up the playbills in the usual and accustomed manner. As also that she, the said Dorothea Jordan, shall and will pay to the said proprietors and their successors or assigns, or allow to be deducted and retained by them for their own use and benefit out of the weekly payments hereinafter mentioned, all and every sum and sums of money which at any time or times within the time aforesaid she [. . .] may incur or become liable to forfeit or pay for her neglect, refusal or inability to attend, accept of study, practise, rehearse or publicly perform in the said theatre in such manner and in such proportions as in the Table of Forfeits bearing the date the twentieth day of March 1762 and now remaining affixed up in the Treasurer's Office belonging to the said theatre, for the inspection of all persons whom it may concern [. . .]; which said table hath been perused and approved of by the said Dorothea Jordan before the sealing and delivery of these presents. And further, that the said Dorothea Jordan shall not nor will at any time or times during the remainder of the present acting season and during the further term of four years to commence from the said first day of September next act, sing or perform any part or parts [. . .] in any other theatre or place whatsoever situate within the distance of ten miles from the said Theatre Royal without licence in writing for either of the said purposes from the said proprietors or the manager or managers for the time being first had and obtained.

In consideration of the covenants and agreements above mentioned, the said [. . .] proprietors [. . .] do hereby covenant and agree [. . .] that provided she, the said Dorothea Jordan shall well and truly keep and perform all [. . .] the covenants [. . .], she [. . .] shall have and be allowed the weekly playhouse payment of eight pounds, that is to say one pound, six shillings and eight pence for every night during the season on which any play or opera shall be performed at the said theatre (oratorios on Wednesdays and Fridays in Lent excepted) to be paid by the said proprietors or the Treasurer at the Treasury of the said theatre on every Saturday between the hours of eleven and one if demanded; they, the said proprietors or their successors, first deducting [. . .] all and every sum and sums of money that the said Dorothea Jordan shall become liable to forfeit or pay according to the Table of Forfeits herein aforementioned, or any other Table to be hereafter agreed upon by the said proprietors for the regulation and conduct of their undertaking at the said theatre.

And also that she [. . .], keeping and performing the covenants and agreements before entered into [. . .], shall be entitled to have one play for her benefit at the said Theatre Royal in this and every acting season during the said term of four years at such part of the season as comes within her order of salary, she first paying the sum of £105 and other small incidental charges into the Treasury for the use of the proprietors, or that not being required by them, they shall be empowered to stop that sum with such extras as are customary for the incidental charges of the performance from the receipt of her benefit night at the offices, and if there shall be any deficiency, to detain it from the salary until the whole charge shall be paid. Provided always, and it is hereby declared and agreed to be the true intent and meaning of these presents and of the parties hereto, that if at any time or times during the remainder of the present acting season and during the four succeeding acting seasons of the said term beforementioned, she [. . .] by sickness, lameness or other bodily indisposition or infirmity [. . .], accidental reason or cause whatsoever, shall be absent from or incapable of attending and performing at the said

Theatre Royal [. . .], then it shall and may be lawful for the said proprietors and their successors to stop and retain for their own use and benefit the said weekly sums for and during all the time or times of such absence or incapacity, and the said Dorothea Jordan shall not have any claim or demand on them or any of them for the same or any part thereof [. . .].

CONDITIONS OF WORK IN THE PROVINCES:
A TOURING CIRCUIT

Joseph Austin was manager of a company of players that toured in the north of England from about 1766 to his retirement at Chester in 1788. Austin's company was typical of the better provincial companies in the last third of the eighteenth century. He had built up his company to be a popular one with a wide-ranging circuit (James Winston estimated that they travelled 'about eleven hundred miles each year') which included Chester, Manchester, Lancaster, Preston, Whitehaven, Newcastle upon Tyne and Sheffield.

Austin was clearly concerned to maintain the discipline and social respectability of his company, as distinct from other more irregular and haphazard strolling companies. His set of rules and forfeits implies, sometimes amusingly, matters that had gone wrong in the past. These ARTICLES, from which a selection is printed below, seem to have been in use for about a decade from 1778, when Charles Whitlock became co-manager [see 199].

199   Contractual rules for a provincial touring company, c. 1778
Printed leaflet pasted in BL Playbills, vol. 307

Articles
To be observed by the members of Messrs AUSTIN and WHITLOCK'S Company of Comedians.
I

That forfeits shall be put in force, and rehearsals called as often as agreeable to the managers.

II

That the prompter shall put up in writing (or cause to be put up) every play night, between the hours of seven and nine in the Ladies' and Gentlemen's Dressing Rooms, the play or farce, or both, that is or are to be rehearsed next morning, with the hour that such play or farce is to begin, or to forfeit one shilling and sixpence neglecting it.

III

That the time of beginning rehearsals is to be regulated by the public clock nearest the theatre, and if the prompter is not at the house, to begin ten minutes after the time is expired, he shall forfeit one shilling for the first scene; and if absent the whole rehearsal of play or farce, he shall forfeit (sickness excepted) five shillings.

IV

That if any lady or gentleman neglects rehearsal on any account (sickness excepted) he or she shall forfeit sixpence for the first scene, and threepence for every scene afterwards, in either play, farce or pantomime: if absent the whole rehearsal, two shillings and sixpence; and if any member through irregularity of living or otherwise render himself or herself incapable of attending their business, at the proper hours, they shall be liable to the forfeits in this article and cannot have the privilege of pleading sickness as an excuse, if it is occasioned by their own intemperance. [. . .]

VII

That if any sharer shall advertise, or cause to be advertised in any newspaper, at full length, or by a (we hear) his or her benefit before the time allowed, such sharer so offending (on proof of it) shall forfeit his or her benefit; the profits of the house to be divided amongst the sharers.

VIII

That if any sharer sells, or agrees to let others sell their tickets under full price, they shall forfeit (on proof of it) his or her benefit; the profits arising from the house to be divided amongst the sharers. [. . .]

XI

That if any salary person shall neglect his or her business, they shall be liable to the same forfeits as the sharers are, as mentioned in the foregoing articles.[1]

XII

That if any sharer or salary person is drunk on a play night, and has any business to do on the stage, such sharer shall forfeit a crown; and such salary person, half a crown.

XIII

That any performer who, by *wilful neglect*, is not ready to begin the play at the time appointed in the bills of the day shall forfeit five shillings.

XIV

That if any performer or salary person shall put anyone into the theatre, either behind the scenes or in front of the house, by an order or any pretence, they must pay for them, unless it is their own hired servant.

XV

That if the musicians are not in the orchestra, to play the first music at the time appointed and mentioned to them, they shall forfeit sixpence for neglect of each music; and if absent the whole night they shall forfeit that night's salary.

XVI

That if any person's dog appears on the stage at rehearsal, the person to whom such dog belongs shall forfeit one shilling; and if any dog appears on the stage at night, the master or mistress of such dog shall forfeit two shillings and sixpence, unless the dog is wanted to attend his master or mistress in character.

XVII

That no person whatever shall be permitted to put in the bills of their benefit, any interlude, either speaking or pantomimical, as they only tend to disgrace the business in general; nor any *personal* or *written* application ever to be made at benefits.

XVIII

That any gentleman or lady not attending to perform, or neglecting to go on the stage (even if it is not to speak but as it may be thought necessary by the managers

to fill up the stage) when their name is inserted in the bills, to forfeit their night's
share or five shillings certain.

XIX

That if any sharer or salary person shall go home in any of the clothes, hats,
properties, etc. belonging to the stock, they shall forfeit half a crown.

XX

That no person shall be permitted to introduce a stranger to perform, sing, or
dance at their benefit, unless a person of known theatrical abilities and with the
consent of the managers.

XXI

That if any performer refuses any part or parts allotted to them by the managers,
which may be deemed necessary to carry on the business to the best advantage, to
forfeit ten shillings.

XXII

That if any performer does not agree to pay the forfeits incurred by these articles,
the managers will look on it that such performer dismisses himself or herself from
the company, and will set down such refusal as their warning, and certainly
provide someone to supply their cast of parts in two months or at the end of the
town.[2]

XXIII

As it is thought necessary by the managers, to add to their catalogue of plays and
farces, the managers are determined to get up a play or farce (which has not been
done in the company before) for each of their benefit nights in every town, which,
when they have settled, they will also assist in getting up two or three pieces for the
members' benefits in the company; but cannot think of doing any more, as the
parts they will be required to do in each piece are generally of that nature as to
render getting up more during benefits impossible. – Nor can this article be strange
to any performers who have seen the custom of other companies, where the
manager and some of the most *essential performers* always make it a rule to
introduce new plays or farces at their benefits, which tend to a *general* as well as a
private interest, as they are of great service to the business in every town.

XXIV

In drawing for benefits from night to night, there shall be no man and wife be
obliged to draw two nights together; but there shall be one play night between
their drawing, unless they choose to draw. This shall always be left to their own
determination to do as they please, whether they will run the chance of coming
after each other, or have a play night between drawing. If the benefits are all
drawn at one time, married and single must take the chance of such drawing.

XXV

That the plays and farces that are taken for benefits shall be performed as they
stand in the cast book for the stock night,[3] unless anyone choose to play any of the
managers' parts, which they may do (leaving them out of the bill for the night); but
one performer shall not play another performer's part at a benefit, as it only tends
to create disputes and very often is a detriment to the play or farce so altered.

XXVI

That no benefit bill shall be published without the managers first perusing it; nor any prologue, epilogue or any temporary or local piece that is not in print, spoken on the stage, without the managers' perusal, lest any offence should be offered therein to the public, which they must be answerable for; therefore think this caution necessary.

XXVII

That the ready money taken at the doors shall be given by the office keeper to the managers, and the remainder of the charges shall be paid into their hands before the Saturday morning in each week for them to pay the shares to the company, the salaries and other expenses.

XXVIII

That the managers here declare that they never will advance or lend any sum or sums of money to any performer on any account.

XXIX

That if any performer does not approve of his or her situation, they are expected to give two months warning in writing, on leaving the company; and the managers on their part bind themselves to give two months warning, unless anyone should behave in so bad a manner that the company in general find it necessary the dismission should be directly; as some such instances can be quoted but hope never to meet with them again.

XXX

That the managers and performers shall exchange an article, signed by both parties, that there be no misunderstanding between them in future.

XXXI

To prevent any altercation between the managers and performers, the former shall be by this empowered to stop all forfeits out of the shares or salaries of the latter. And these Articles shall always be considered in full force on the morning of the first rehearsal in every town.

---

[1] The early provincial companies were organised, much in the manner of the Restoration companies, with the various performers entitled to a single or part share in the company's profits. In London, this system withered away under the triumvirate at Drury Lane and Rich in Lincoln's Inn Fields. As the rival London managers increased their power and control over their respective companies, they employed their actors on a salaried basis. In the provinces, it was not until the late eighteenth century that this process began. By the 1770s, provincial managers began to employ certain actors on fixed salaries, often a guinea and a half per week (the village labourer's weekly wage was eight or nine shillings). See Hare (1958), p. 34; the Bristol Jacob's Wells Theatre Account Book in Bristol Public Library and Rosenfeld (1939).

[2] Touring companies would spend as long in any individual town as they could afford to hire the theatre, or gain legal permission to play, or expect to do good business. After the passing of the Enabling Act of 1788 this was normally limited to a maximum of sixty days. Before 'the end of the town', respectable managers would often advertise for outstanding accounts to be presented, so as not to depart leaving a trail of debts behind them.

[3] Members of well-established companies were engaged to play particular kinds of parts: leading lady, low comedian, Harlequin, walking gentleman, etc. The 'stock' was the standard range of plays that the company had in repertory, to be played whenever required and often at short notice. All these plays and the casting of them were recorded in the 'Stock Book' [see 202].

Dublin and Edinburgh regarded themselves as capital cities, but conditions of work there were in actuality more like those in the better provincial theatres. This emerges very clearly from the 'Articles and Conditions of Engagement' in force at the Theatre Royal Edinburgh in 1773.

200   Contractual rules at the Theatre Royal Edinburgh, 1773

York Minster Library. Reproduced in full in J. Curtis: 'A Theatrical Contract of 1773-4'. *TN* 30 (1976), 18-20.

The articles and conditions of engagement: to be observed and performed by every member of the Company of Comedians under the direction and management of West Digges Esq., Manager of the Theatre Royal of Edinburgh and also the Theatres of Glasgow and Aberdeen. [. . .]

IV

That every member of the company shall play, sing and dance in such plays and farces, and in such characters as the said West Digges shall think proper to allot them; and that every performer, whose salary does not exceed two guineas, shall go on to fill up the drama in such processions, pageants and scenes as they shall be required by the manager, or his prompter, by his order.

V

That the company shall only receive at the towns of Glasgow and Aberdeen, two-third parts of the salary which they respectively have at Edinburgh, excepting such persons as have only £1 10 s a week at Edinburgh, whose salaries are not to be reduced.

VI

That the company shall receive no salary for the time they are travelling from one place to another.

VII

As during the Sacrament Weeks the theatre is occasionally shut, the company shall be allowed salary only *wherever they are*, in proportion for such *number of nights playing* as the manager in that time chooses to perform on. [. . .]

X

That every member of the company shall observe and perform such laws and regulations concerning the proper management and good order of the theatres above mentioned, as shall from time to time be affixed upon the walls of the green rooms thereof, signed by the manager, and shall submit to the forfeitures there inserted.

XI

That every member of the company shall have a benefit at Edinburgh in rank of salary, upon paying the charges of the house, or giving security for the same; but no benefits can be allowed at Glasgow or Aberdeen.

XII

Whereas it often happens that objects of charity arise in the theatre by accidents, old age or otherwise; and that it is a duty incumbent on the manager and every individual of the company to contribute something to the support and relief of such objects: the manager binds and obliges himself to pay the sum of £4 sterling yearly for this purpose, and every person who shall become a member of this company shall be bound and obliged to allow a stoppage from their salary every week of the sum of three pence sterling for every 20s they have of salary. And that this sum shall be paid at Glasgow and Aberdeen as well as Edinburgh and shall be applied to the support of such persons as the manager shall think stand in need of such charity and shall merit the same. The money so to be raised and the application thereof to be marked in a book which shall lie in the office for the satisfaction and inspection of the company.

XIII

As it sometimes happens that persons are engaged in the theatre who, in the course of their business and otherwise, endeavour to foment disputes and divisions in the theatre, with a view to hurt the manager and the business of the stage, the manager hereby expressly provides and declares that, upon his having reason to believe or being convinced that any member or members of the company endeavour in this manner to foment divisions and disputes in the theatre, or endeavour to hurt his interest or the business of the stage, he shall be at liberty to go before a magistrate or other judge and make oath that he has such conviction and belief, and upon his making this oath, all engagements with such person or persons shall be void and null and he shall be at liberty to discharge them from the company without incurring any penalty or forfeiture of contract.

XIV

That every member of the company shall sign these articles in testimony of their agreement thereto, and of their undertaking to perform the same, under the penalty mentioned in their contract with the manager.

THE MOVE TO CORPORATE OWNERSHIP OF PROVINCIAL COMPANIES

As the circuit companies became more established, and their standards higher, their running became more costly and administratively burdensome; but the best of them were also clearly a good and, in general, reliable investment. Some therefore moved from being an individual enterprise, or a simple partnership, to corporate ownership, as the London theatres had already done by the beginning of the century. Norwich did this between 1758 and 1782. The surviving committee books of the Theatre Royal Norwich from 1768 to 1825 give a vivid insight into the workings of a provincial patent theatre and its circuit during a period of administrative change.

201   The evolution of a circuit company – private enterprise to corporate ownership at the Theatre Royal Norwich

Dorothy H. Eshleman (ed.): *The committee books of the Theatre Royal Norwich, 1768–1825* (London: STR, 1970), pp. 71–3

Mr Ivory[1] then engaged the former company of comedians to perform plays, etc. in this new theatre, and agreed with the former proprietor of this company and purchased of him all his scenes, wardrobe of clothes, and all other his right and title to all the leases, scenes, etc. throughout the different playhouses in the circuit in which the Norwich comedians performed plays etc. throughout the counties of Norfolk, Suffolk and Essex. The Norwich Theatre thus completed was opened for public exhibition in January 1758, at a considerable advantage to the then performers of the company, as they then received, exclusive of the advantage derived from their benefit plays, double the sum in the Norwich season to what they have received upon an average from the then preceeding ten years.

In 1764 Mr Ivory was induced by the company of comedians, etc., at the earnest request of the inhabitants of Colchester, to build a regular theatre there, as at that time the comedians had only a temporary building, erected in the Town Hall, whenever they went to Colchester, to perform plays in. This building was erected this year and elegantly fitted up with new scenery, painted by an eminent painter in London. There being now a regular theatre in Norwich for the winter season and a smaller one at Colchester for the summer expedition (and other playhouses on lease in the circuit), it gave an opportunity to increase the emoluments to the performers by making it, from a *sharing* to *a salary company*, which gave that degree of encouragement to performers of merit that the scheme commanded, and was supported by the best actors out of London.

In the year 1768, after having expended considerable sums of money in forming and completing the improvements in the entertainment of the stage, Mr Ivory procured an Act of Parliament to obtain the Grant of the Royal Protection to the theatre in Norwich. And thus, having with unwearied attention and great expense completed this scheme – which at the request of the public in 1757 – and devoting eleven years to the forming and improving it into a regular stage, he wished to return it back to the public and not to continue the sole proprietor of it longer than he had completed what he had been so earnestly requested in behalf of the public to attempt. And therefore offered his whole theatrical estate to public sale, to be divided into thirty shares, reserving two shares to himself, and proposed to dispose of twenty-eight shares only, which were immediately purchased by the following subscribers –

Thomas Ivory, original proprietor: 2 shares (no. 1, no. 2) and 28 shares, as follows:

3	Sir Wm Wiseman, Bart
4	Sir Edwd Ashley
5	Sir Harbd Harbord
6	Thos Sotherton Esq.
7	Miles Branthwayte Esq.
8	Mrs Sheen [. . .]

[1] Thomas Ivory was a Master Builder and timber importer and merchant, who was encouraged by the principal inhabitants of Norwich – 'to build this theatre, which was finished with every possible degree of elegance and convenience and furnished with scenes painted by one of the most eminent masters'.

STOCK BOOKS, PROGRAMME BUILDING AND PLANNING

The repertory policy of the eighteenth-century theatre involved frequent changes of programme: nightly in London and certain major provincial cities, three or four times a week elsewhere. This system required a seasonal stock of plays in repertory, with actors able to play specific types of character, often at short notice. The record of their capabilities was kept in the Stock Book, which was a vital tool for forward planning [*see* **202**]. No less important were the Registers or Diaries of performances kept by managers, such as Rich at Covent Garden and Cross and Hopkins at Drury Lane. These preserved a formal record of all performances given and sometimes the financial return involved [*see* **203**].

Less vital but extremely useful were two small volumes published in 1767 by Brownsmith, a former prompter at the Theatre Royal, Haymarket, listing the timings of the main plays in the repertory [*see* **204**] and the approximate length of various parts [*see* **205**]. (A 'length' – the unit of measurement used by actors of the time – was 42 lines.) In his preface to the volume on lengths, Brownsmith notes that the work is designed solely for 'theatrical persons' who can rely on its 'exactness; a majority of the parts having been written out (by the author) for the service of the houses'. He also stresses that managers using it will know how long each part will take to study and the performer will be able to 'judge whether it can be undertaken within the limited time'. Apart from the obvious relevance of the volumes as a programming tool, the preface to the volume on timing notes that the work will be of particular use to noblemen and gentlemen who may have carriages or appointments to attend to; it will prevent horses waiting long at playhouse doors in bad weather, and permit gentlemen to keep their servants at home till just before attendance is required, 'instead of assembling in public houses or houses of ill fame, to the destruction of their morals, properties and constitutions'. The preface also notes that the volume will be useful to those whom business prevents attending till after the third act, commonly called 'The Latter Account of it'. By allowing seven minutes between each act for the intervening music, one can be certain of when any act will be over. In pieces of three acts 'latter account' is taken from the end of the second act.

202   A company Stock Book[1]

Theatre Royal Bath (1770–77). Presented by General Palmer, Proprietor and Patentee, to B.W. Bellamy, Manager 1829. City Library, Bath

(Company)

1776

Mr Keasberry, ~~Henderson~~, Dimond, Blissett, Brookes, Didier, Edwin, ~~Brunsdon~~, Brett, Haughton, Payne, Rowbotham, Hitchcock, Summers, G. Summers, ~~Mast Sherriffe~~, Floor.

Mme ~~Mansell~~, ~~Sherriffe~~, Keasberry, Didier, Wheeler, ~~Hitchcock~~, Martin, Brett, Summers, E. Summers.

Band Markordt, Brookes Junr, Brookes Senr, S. Keasberry, Loader, Whitehead, Hopley, Low, Cantelo, S. Linley, Russell, Stevens.

	Hamlet
HAMLET	Mr Lee, Henderson, Dimond
HORATIO	Keasberry, ~~Siddons~~
KING	Gaudry, Furnival, Jackson, Egan, Rowbotham
GHOST	Brookes, Blissett, Egan
POLONIUS	Edwin, Blissett
LAERTES	Sherriffe, Robson, Guion, Dimond, Barnett
OSTRICK [*sic*]	Didier, Brunsdon

ROSENCRANS [sic]	Guion, Barret, Rowswell, Egan, ~~Barnett~~, Siddons
GUILDENSTERN	Harper, Haughton, Egan, Payne
MARCELLUS	Harper, Barret, Haughton
BERNARDO	Haughton, Summers
FRANCISCO	Moor, McGeorge, West, Brett, Griffin
PLAYER KING	Wood, Knight, Cooke, Sherriffe, Didier, Blissett, Haughton, Egan
LUCIANUS	Haughton, Floor, Summers
MESSENGER	Moor, Summers, Hitchcock, G. Summers
OFFICER	Floor, Payne, Summers
1st GRAVEDIGGER	Edwin, Haughton
2nd GRAVEDIGGER	Watts, Floor, Haughton
PRIEST '	Moor, Griffin, Hitchcock
ATTENDANTS	Watts, Moor, Wood, Summers, Payne
QUEEN	Mrs Sherriffe, Townshend, Mansell, Siddons
OPHELIA	Mahon, Keasberry, Arthur, Ward, Wheeler
PLAYER QUEEN	Kirby, Farran, Summers, Brett, Taylor
SAILOR	Watts

¹ Covering the years, 1770–77. The Bath Stock Book records the members of the company (and the changes) and the band. It also lists the parts the actors could be called upon to play in forty-one tragedies, seventy-four comedies and forty-eight afterpieces which were in the company's repertory during that period.

203   Rich's Register of Performances at Covent Garden[1]

Rich's Register, vol. 4, 1750–73. Chatsworth House (formerly in the possession of J.P. Kemble)[2]

	List of plays acted at the Theatre Royal, Covent Garden under the management of John Rich Esq., beginning on the 10th day of September 1750	List of plays acted at the Theatre Royal, Drury Lane, under the management of Mr Garrick and Mr Lacy
10th	No play	*The Merchant of Venice*
11th	No play	*The Beggar's Opera*
13th	No play	*Love's Last Shift*
15th	No play	*The Relapse*
18th	No play	*The London Merchant*
20th	No play	Ditto
21st	No play	*The Stratagem*
22nd	No play	*The Merry Wives of Windsor*
24th	*The Miser*, the part of the Miser acted by Mr Macklin	No play
25th	No play	*Hamlet*
26th	*The Busy Body*	No play
27th	No play	*The Conscious Lovers*

28th	*Romeo and Juliet*, the part of Romeo by Mr Barry and Juliet by Mrs Cibber, with a new scene of the funeral procession of Juliet the 1st night	*Romeo and Juliet*, the part of Juliet by Mrs Bellamy and Romeo acted by Mr Garrick
29th	*Romeo and Juliet*, the 2nd night	*Romeo and Juliet*
1st Oct	*Romeo and Juliet*, the 3rd night	*Romeo and Juliet*
2nd	*Romeo and Juliet*, the 4th night, by command of the Prince and Princess of Wales	*Romeo and Juliet*
3rd	*Romeo and Juliet*, the 5th night	*Romeo and Juliet*
4th	*Romeo and Juliet*, the 6th night	*Romeo and Juliet*
5th	*Romeo and Juliet*, the 7th night	*Romeo and Juliet*
6th	*Romeo and Juliet*, the 8th night	*Romeo and Juliet*
8th	*Romeo and Juliet*, the 9th night	*Romeo and Juliet*
9th	*Romeo and Juliet*, the 10th night	*Romeo and Juliet*
10th	*Romeo and Juliet*, the 11th night	*Romeo and Juliet*
11th	*Romeo and Juliet*, the 12th night	*Romeo and Juliet*, the 12th night
12th	*The Beggar's Opera*, because Mrs Cibber would not act in *Romeo* no longer	*Romeo and Juliet*, the 13th night
13th	*The Constant Couple*, the part of Sir Harry Wildair acted by Mrs Woffington	*The Masque of Comus*

[1] The various sections of Rich's Register are located in the following collections:
Vol. 1, 1714–23: Folger Shakespeare Library
Vol. 2, 1723–40: Garrick Club
Vol. 3, 1740–50: Harvard Theatre Collection
Vol. 4, 1750–73: Chatsworth House, Bakewell.
[2] This extract illustrates the famous battle between the two patent playhouses when Garrick at Drury Lane and Barry at Covent Garden played Romeo in rival productions that ran for thirteen consecutive performances.

204   Timing of plays

John Brownsmith: *The dramatic timepiece, or perpetual monitor*, being a calculation of the length of time every act takes in the performing in all the acting plays at the Theatre Royal of Drury Lane, Covent Garden and Haymarket, as minuted from repeated observations, during the course of many years practice, as also the time of night when the half-price will be taken and the certain period when any play will be over. (London: J. Almon, T. Davies, J. Hungeston, 1767)

EXAMPLES OF STANDARD FORM OF ENTRY FOR EACH PLAY[1]

Hamlet (p. 3)		Ho	Min		*Richard III* (p. 6)		Ho	Min
Act	I	0	40		Act	I	0	29
	II	0	22			II	0	27

III	O	40		III	Soft	O	29
IV	O	27		IV	music	O	36
V	O	30		V		O	32

Whole play   2   39   Whole play   2   33
Act III ends 56 min after 7   Act III ends 39 min after 7
Play over   3 min after 9   Play over   3 min after 9

EXAMPLES OF 'WHOLE PLAY' TIMINGS GIVEN FOR TRAGEDIES AND COMEDIES

Tragedies

Othello	2	23	*Lear*	2	34
Hamlet	2	39	*Richard III*	2	33
Tamerlane	2	28	*Cato*	2	10
Mourning Bride	1	47	*Macbeth*	2	20

Comedies

Love for Love	2	16	*Merry Wives*	1	26
Spanish Friar	2	5	*Drummer*	1	40
Stratagem	1	56	*Henry IV (1st)*	2	19
Bold Stroke	1	47	*Constant Couple*	1	56

[1] Sixty-six tragedies and eighty comedies are listed.

205   Length of parts

John Brownsmith: *The theatrical alphabet*. A catalogue of several hundred *parts* (both men's and women's) in different plays and farces; with the number of *lengths* noted that each part contains, carefully disposed in *alphabetical order* and accurately distinguished by initial letters denoting whether they are a *tragedy, comedy, opera, farce* etc. The number of lengths are justly calculated, as they are performed at the Theatres Royal, with a vacancy reserved to insert many more, as they may occur in new pieces or otherwise. (London: published by the author, 1767)[1]

EXTRACT FROM LETTER 'S'

(Key: t = tragedy; c = comedy; t.c = tragi-comedy; c.o = comic-opera; f.f.c = farce from comedy; b.f = ballad farce; f = farce; m = masque.)

Part	Play, etc.	Lengths	
Sir Harry	*High Life below Stairs*	f	4
Spirit, 2nd	*Comus*	m	2
Scroop	*Henry the Vth*	t	3
Simon	*Suspicious Husband*	c	1
Simple	*Merry Wives of Windsor*	c	2
Southampton	*Earl of Essex* (Jones)	t	5
Selim	*Mourning Bride*	t	2
Subtleman	*Twin Rivals*	c	5
etc.			

[1] Garrick's own copy survives in the British Library.

THE SELECTION OF NEW PLAYS

Traditionally, the selection of new plays was a managerial responsibility, and with social, commercial and dramatic pressures to contend with, an onerous one indeed. In the days of the triumvirate at Drury Lane, Colley Cibber was notoriously off-hand in his treatment of aspiring playwrights,[1] whereas Barton Booth appears to have been both assiduous and polite in exercising this particular duty [*see* **206**].

David Garrick was no less assiduous during his period of office as manager at Drury Lane. He was also extremely helpful in advising budding authors how to improve plays that caught his fancy [*see* **207**]. He was at times accused of prevarication, when faced by the delicate task of turning down a new play, but he could be very firm in his rejections [*see* **208**].

[1] See *BD*, vol. 3, pp. 213–40.

206   Booth arranges to hear a new play in 1732

Letter from Barton Booth, Sunday morning, 5 November 1732. Copy in R.J. Smith: *A collection of material towards an history of the English stage*, vol. 4 (BL, 1825–40)

Sir,

When I desired the favour of seeing you this evening, I had forgot that I had appointed a gentleman to hear his tragedy read at the same time. A message came to me this morning to put me in mind of the appointment. As the gentleman proposes to have his play acted (if it be approved of) before Xmas, I hope you will excuse my deferring the pleasure of hearing yours till tomorrow, or any other day and hour you please to appoint. I am downright ashamed of my forgetfulness, but if you knew what hurry our theatrical affairs have been in of late, you would more readily excuse

Your most obedient, humble servant, Barton Booth.

207   Garrick's response to the task of selecting new plays

Thomas Davies: *Memoirs of the life of David Garrick Esq.*, vol. 1 (1808), pp. 244–9

The most difficult and irksome task which a manager of a theatre can perhaps undergo arises from his connection with authors. To accept or refuse a play is a matter of more consequence than the world in general imagines. The writing a dramatic piece, without the assistance of a candid and intelligent manager and perhaps the farther support of a considerable party, will scarce answer the views of the author. The time bestowed in rehearsing the piece, and the expense of new scenes, dresses, music and other decorations, make it often very ineligible to a director of a theatre to accept a new play; especially when it is considered that the reviving of a good old play will answer his end of profit and reputation too perhaps, as well. [. . .]

But whatever other part of his conduct to authors might be deemed exceptionable, he never could be taxed with rudeness or incivility. He rather, in his treatment of writers, carried his politeness to excess, and in the first ardour of his friendship he was apt to promise more than he found it possible afterwards to perform. His inclination to temporize, I believe, was often productive of delays and excuses, which ended with a disappointment of the author, and a quarrel in consequence of it ensued, which a more decisive conduct might have prevented.

It is very certain that no manager we ever heard of was better qualified to serve an author in the correcting, pruning or enlarging of a dramatic piece than Mr Garrick. His acute judgement and great experience had rendered him a consummate judge of stage effect; and many authors now living, men of the greatest merit, will own their obligations to his taste and sagacity.

It was his misfortune sometimes to err egregiously, both in the choice and rejection of new plays. In the years 1756, 1758, 1759, he successively rejected the *Douglas* of Mr John Home, Dodsley's *Cleone*, and *The Orphan of China* by Mr Murphy. That great interest was made for *Douglas* cannot be questioned: the author's connections with some great persons at Leicester House, who encouraged his abilities and favoured his interest, we should have imagined would have superseded all objections and brought on the play without hesitation. But Mr Garrick's opinion of it could not be removed; he thought the plot was too simple and undramatic.

208   Garrick writes to the Earl of Bute, explaining his rejection of Home's *Douglas*

D.M. Little and G.M. Kahrl: *The letters of David Garrick*, vol. 1 (London: Oxford University Press, 1963), letter 166, pp. 244–7

It is with the greatest uneasiness that I trouble your lordship with my sentiments of Mr Hume's tragedy. The little knowledge I had of him gave me the warmest inclination to serve him, which I should have done most sincerely, had the means been put into my hands. But upon my word and credit, it is not in my power to introduce *Douglas* upon the stage with the least advantage to the author and the managers. The tragedy (if possible) is in its present situation as unfit for representation as it was before, and your lordship must be sensible that it wanted all the requisites of the drama to carry it even through the two first acts. Mr Hume is certainly a gentleman of learning and parts, but I am [as certain] that either his genius is not adapted to dramatic compositions or that he wants the proper exercise and experience to show it to advantage.

I am obliged my lord to be free in the delivery of my opinion upon this subject, as I think both Mr Hume's and my reputation concerned in it: I should have had the highest pleasure in forwarding any performance which your lordship should please to recommend; but nobody knows as well as you do that all the endeavour of a patron and the skill of a manager will avail nothing, if the dramatic requisites and tragic force are wanting. I am so strongly convinced that this is the case of the tragedy in question that I durst not upon any account venture it upon the stage of Drury Lane, and I would stake all my credit that the author would sorely repent it if ever it should be exhibited upon any theatre. As I ought to second these strong assertions with some few reasons, I will endeavour, for your lordship's and Mr Hume's satisfaction, to point out the (what I think) insurmountable objections to the tragedy.

The story is radically defective and most improbable in those circumstances which produce the dramatic action. For instance, Lady Barnet continuing seven years together in that melancholy miserable state, just as if it had happened the week before, without discovering the real cause; and on a sudden opening the whole affair to Anna without any stronger reason than what might have happened at any other time since the day of her misfortunes. This I think, which is the foundation of the whole, weak and unaccountable. The two first acts pass in tedious narratives, without anything of moment being planned or done. The introducing Douglas is the chief circumstance, and yet, as it is managed, it has no effect; it is romantic for want of those probable strokes of art, which the first poets make use of to reconcile strange events to the minds of an audience. Lady Barnet's speaking to Glenalvon immediately in behalf of Randolph, forgetting her own indelible sorrows, and Glenalvon's suspicions and jealousy upon it (without saying anything of *his* violent love for the lady, who cannot be of a love-inspiring age) are premature and unnatural. But these and many other defects, which I will not trouble your lordship with, might be palliated and altered perhaps; but the unaffecting conduct of the whole and which will always be the case, when the story is rather told than represented; when the characters do not talk or behave suitably to the passions imputed to them and the situation in which they are placed; when the events are such as cannot naturally be supposed to rise; and the language too often below the most familiar dialogue; these are the insurmountable objections, which in my opinion will ever make *Douglas* unfit for the stage. In short, there is no one character or passion which is strongly interesting and supported through the five acts. [. . .]

I have considered the performance by myself, I have read it to a friend or two with all the energy and spirit I was master of but without the wished for effect. The scenes are long without action, the characters want strength and pathos, and the catastrophe is brought about without the necessary and interesting preparations for so great an event. [. . .]

Had I thought that the tragedy could possibly have appeared, I would have submitted some alterations to the author; but upon my word and honour, I think the tragedy radically defective and in every act incapable of raising the passions or commanding attention. [. . .]

THE ROAD TO THE STAGE

Private drama teaching and elocution lessons were available; both Charles Macklin and Thomas Sheridan set up 'Academies' during some part of their careers, and there were others. But for the stage-struck youth, entry to a 'Spouting Club',[1] followed by a small (perhaps unpaid) engagement with a strolling company, and later working a passage through the circuits, was the usual route into the acting profession.

[1] An evening at a typical Spouting Club is described in an undated pamphlet (*c.* 1781) entitled *The new spouter's companion, or a selection of prologues and epilogues, [. . .] illustrated with the art of acting and the picture of a spouting club* (BL).

209   An actor's first engagement

A veteran stager: *An essay on the science of acting* [written *c.* 1773] (London: Cowie & Strange, 1828), pp. 108–10. Partially reproduced in Hare (1980), pp. 15–16

The allurements of a theatre are so strong that perhaps few, except those who have felt them, can conceive; [Cooke] felt them in their utmost force, and obeying their dictates accompanied by another stage-struck hero, a fellow apprentice who had just completed his time, named Colin Mitchell, took their departure from Berwick and arrived in London with a light heart and still lighter purse, their joint stock amounting to 17 s 6 d. Their first visit was to a noted theatrical tavern, in those days the Black Lion in Russell Street, kept at that time by a retired actor of the name of Waters. To mine host they told the motive of their visit to London, namely to procure a situation on the stage. The good-natured Waters felt for their condition, procured them beds for the night and on the morning painted to them in such doleful colours the misery of a strolling player, together with the impracticability of obtaining a situation on the London boards, as totally damped their youthful spirits. But what was to be done? [. . .]

In a very short time they were introduced to some of their own age and who, like themselves, were fond of the drama: a play was got up, *Richard the Third*; their theatre a hay loft; their only scene an old carpet, hung over a line, stretched across the building to support it; their lights, small candles stuck into lumps of clay, fashioned for the purpose; their seats, deal boards, supported by empty beer barrels; the orchestra had to boast of a Scotch bag-piper who, from that most harmonious instrument 'blew a blast so loud', and answered the purpose of drums and trumpets; and when Richard exclaimed 'a flourish, trumpets, strike alarm drums', was replied to by a blast from Sawney. Richard's dress was a borrowed vestment of a footman, consisting of a scarlet waistcoat with sleeves of the same colour; a red cloak, obtained of an ancient dame in the neighbourhood, fancifully decorated with strips of paper, embellished with Prince's metal, a star and garter made from the same materials.

Richmond was dressed much after the same fashion, with the addition of an enormous pair of trooper's boots; his head adorned with a grenadier's cap by way of helmet. The other heroes of Bosworth Field, as their characters were not of equal magnitude, did not perhaps adhere so pertinaciously to costume and propriety. The 'Dramatis Personae' ran thus, 'Richard: Mr Briarly' (since which a respectable manager and good actor in the northern district of Scotland); the 'Earl of Richmond: Mr Colin Mitchell', to which he added Tressel; 'King Henry by Mr Cooke'; 'Buckingham by Mr Joseph Munden'. The subsequent advancement and excellence of this great actor need not, we trust, be here set down, but to show what he then was, we have only to observe, in repeating the lines of Buckingham which ran thus, 'his fall unmourned and bloody as their own', Master Joe exclaimed 'his fall *un-a-mourned and bul-wudy* as their own'. However, all were extremely pleased with their own individual exertions. On the night in question there chanced to be present the eccentric Roger Wright who at that time was the best representative of the motley-coloured hero that had then appeared, who declared in the presence of

Jemmy Miller, the Northampton and Shrewsbury manager, that if he was not much deceived that long-nosed, raw Scotchman [Cooke] would one day prove to be a d—d good actor. Honest Jemmy, who was in town for the purpose of picking up recruits, repaired to the Black Lion, saw our hero and engaged him for his company at the enormous salary of 10 s per week.

THE APPOINTMENT OF ACTORS

The appointment of actors to a company could be a hit-or-miss process. Garrick had his talent scouts and would also use his influence to arrange an appointment with one of the better provincial companies for an actor whom he deemed unready yet for London – as he did at Bath for John Henderson – for these were the best training schools. Bath was for many years rated particularly highly in this respect (after her first failure at Drury Lane, Sarah Siddons joined the company there for three years before returning to London).

210   Garrick uses a talent scout, 1765
James Boaden (ed.): *The private correspondence of David Garrick with the most celebrated persons of his time*, vol. 1 (London: Colburn & Bentley, 1831–2), pp. 183–6

Dr Hoadly to Mr Garrick, St Cross, nr Winchester, 23 May 1765
I was prevented from making observations on *the Dodd* in *The Suspicious Husband* (which I much longed for) by an ugly cold, which confined me at home; but I employed a judicious friend to go and make me his report. Of what I saw in *The Wife's Resentment, Love in a Village, Double Gallant* and *Jealous Wife*, I will give you my own opinion.

My friend's report was that in Ranger he could not quite enough cast off the coxcombly character that sticks so close to him; and when he was to express joy and rapture, he only exalted his voice into a very disagreeable untuneful noise: but in the main, that the part was done with spirit and propriety enough. [. . .]

My own opinion of him in general is that his *person* is good enough, but his motion is too much under restraint and form; more the stalk and *menage* of a dancing-master than the ease of a gentleman. I speak of his legs; his action seems easy enough and unstudied. He has a white *calf-like* stupid face that disgusted me much till I heard him speak and throw some sensibility into it. His voice is good and well heard everywhere; and he seems sensible, alive and attentive to what is going on and properly so. I fear there must be a dash of the *coxcomb* in every part in which you would see him in perfection, and in that cast [*sic*] he will be an excellent successor to O'Brien; in the *easy gentleman* I much doubt, though there were some strokes in Atall that promised well. He sings agreeably and with more *feeling* than he acts with; though there is a formal kind of parade kept up by the singing gentry (not easily to be avoided in the strange unnatural circumstances and attitudes that the songs and their symphonies, etc. place them in, in the front of the stage), that hides and disguises nature, but which he reconciles better than I remember any body. In singing, his voice seemed to me remarkably low, but that might only be by comparing it with his *speaking* voice, which is very distinct. One excellence I observed in him that he is not in a hurry and his *pauses* are sensible and filled with proper action and looks.

My general idea of Mrs Dodd is that of a very genteel sensible woman, fit to fill any part of high life, especially if written with any sensibility and tenderness. Lady Townley and Mrs Conquest (of the last) pleased me much. Her raillery in Mrs C. rather wanted spirit. The affected drawl of Lady Dainty became her much; and in Mrs Oakley, I could not see a fault. She was not a moment out of the character, and amazingly proper and ready in the repartee, and taking up the half sentences before they fell to nothing, which abound in that natural comedy, as in all easy discourse. After all, I wish that these excellencies may not be almost totally lost, for want of that force of voice requisite to pierce all parts of a large and crowded theatre. In many places she put me in mind of Mrs Heron, who succeeded Mrs Oldfield.– *longo intervallo!* – but has a much genteeler person, though a face not unlike her; not handsome, but I think better for a stage. [. . .]

Dodd is reckoned *charming* in the gardener in *Love in a Village*; and indeed I think he makes the most of such precious stuff. They say his Macheath is excellent. I suppose his wife must sing tolerably at least, for she played Polly with him.

He played Atall well in the main, particularly as Col. Standfast; and his formality of motion became him in the grave Mr Freeman. In the character of Atall himself, he seemed not to know precisely what character to assume.

In Lord Trinket in *The Jealous Wife*, I thought him admirable. He was every inch the coxcomb and unfeeling man of quality. The whole play was acted well enough to be a rational entertainment to the best judges (except poor Charles by Mr Sheriffe whose contemptible figure and snuffling nose never became him so well as when he was drunk). [. . .]

I am now pretty well arrived at the end of my tether and hope my characters are pretty true, notwithstanding the deception of comparison, which I know to be very great.

FINANCIAL ARRANGEMENTS IN PROVINCIAL SHARING COMPANIES

For a large part of the eighteenth century, the financial basis on which provincial companies operated was that of profit sharing. Company managers offered their employees a specified share in the profits of the company (both money and goods) rather than a salary: if a given performance produced no profits, there was no money to be shared. Some of these sharing companies were very modest indeed, as were their profits. Charles Morison's notebook records the profits of a small company of strollers, some six actors who had left another strolling company at Cardigan on 8 May 1741. They were, it seems, making their way back to London. By 3 June, three members had left, but in July the remaining players performed at Malmesbury, Cricklade and Lechlade on the Wiltshire–Gloucestershire borders. The profit to be shared between the remaining three actors varied from 4 s 6 d in Cricklade on 8 July to 18 s 0 d at Lechlade on 13 July. The entry for Malmesbury on 2 July 1741 gives a very clear notion of how modest, indeed spartan their undertaking in fact was.

211   The accounts of a small strolling company in 1741
Charles Morison's Notebook. BL Add.MS 33,488, f. 28.

Thursday. Began at Malmesbury. July the 2nd 1741.

The Spanish Friar and *Parting Lovers*

By desire of Mr Collins.	£	s	d
Taken	0	16	0
Music	0	0	6
Candles	0	0	$10\frac{1}{2}$
Ale	0	0	$1\frac{1}{2}$
Paper	0	0	$4\frac{1}{2}$
Rent	0	2	0
Nails and packthread	0	0	$2\frac{1}{2}$
Lent at Newland	0	0	4
Charges	0	4	5
Remains	0	11	7
Shared at 3 shares 4 s	0	12	0
Lent	0	0	5

FINANCIAL ARRANGEMENTS AT THE JACOBS WELLS THEATRE IN BRISTOL

The company of actors performing during the summer season at the small Jacobs Wells Theatre in Bristol during the 1740s included actors and actresses of some stature. (Macklin played there in 1741 and Mrs Pritchard from 1741 to 1747.)[1] As one might expect, their finances were on a more secure basis. Even so poor weather or an unpopular play could drastically affect the takings [see 212a]. On an exceptional evening, the share per person might rise as high as £2.9.0. The average sum was, however, between 5 s and 12 s per person for each performance [see 212b].

[1] See Rosenfeld (1939), p. 205.

212   Accounts of a sharing company in Bristol, 1747–8
MS *account book of the Jacob's Wells Theatre Bristol, 1741–1748.* Bristol Library, Reference Department

(A) A GENERAL ACCOUNT FOR PLAYS PERFORMED IN JUNE AND JULY, 1747

1747 JUNE	Plays	Taken	Share	Rent	Clothes	In hand
10	*Provoked Husband*	14. 4.6.	—	4.4.0.	1. 1.0.	4. 1. 3.
12	*Committee*	12. 6.0.	—	4.4.0.	1. 1.0.	2.10. $8.\frac{1}{2}$
15	*Jane Shore*	19. 6.0.	0. 9.0.	4.4.0.	1. 1.0.	0.11. $7.\frac{1}{2}$
17	*Conscious Lovers*	27.11.0	0.15.0.	4.4.0.	1. 1.0.	—
19	*Merry Wives*	24. 7.6.	0.12.0.	4.4.0.	1. 1.0.	0. 7.10.

22	Constant Couple	14. 7.0.	0. 3.0.	4.4.0.	1. 1.0.	0. 9. 5.
24	Mr Hippisley's					
	benefit	38. 5.0.	0. 5.0.	—	—	—
26	Careless Husband	16. 9.0.	0. 4.6.	4.4.0.	1. 1.0.	0. 2. 7.½
29	Hamlet	16. 9.6.	0. 7.0.	4.4.0.	1. 1.0.	0. 0. 8.½

JULY

1	Merry Wives	13.18.6.	0. 4.6.	4.4.0.	1. 1.0.	0. 7. 9.
3	Suspicious Husband	30. 4.6.	0.17.0.	4.4.0.	1. 1.0.	0.14.10.
6	Suspicious Husband	24.16.0.	0.15.0.	4.4.0.	1. 1.0.	0.11. 4.
8	Suspicious Husband	16. 4.0.	0. 6.0.	4.4.0.	1. 1.0.	0.16. 4.
10	Busy Body	19. 2.6.	0. 9.0.	4.4.0.	1. 1.0.	0.14. 1.
13	Love for Love	48.19.0.	2. 8.0	—	1. 1.0.	0.19. 2.
15	Venice Preserved	7.18.0.	—	—	2.12.6.	0. 6. 6.
17	Conscious Lovers	12.11.6.	0. 4.0	—	1.11.6.	—
20	Recruiting Officer	18. 9.0.	0. 5.6.	—	2. 2.0	0. 7. 8.½
22	Mr Pritchard's					
	benefit	51. 7.0.	—	—	—	—
24	As you like it	22. 7.0.	0.11.0.	—	2. 2.0.	0. 7. 8.½
27	Hamlet	14.10.6.	0. 8.0.	—	2. 2.0.	0. 1. 2.
28	Provoked Husband	18.13.0.	0.11.0.	—	2. 2.0.	0. 4. 6.
	Recvd of Mr Plomer	4. 4.0.	—	4.4.0.	—	—
29	Jane Shore	18.10.6.	0.12.0.	—	—	0. 0. 6.
31	Mr Barrington	49. 7.0.	0. 5.0.	—	—	—

(B) A DETAILED ACCOUNT FOR THE PERFORMANCE OF *THE TEMPEST*,
6 AUGUST, 1742

Tempest	Taken	20	5	6
	Music	0	13	6
	Candles	0	9	0
	Bills	0	10	0
	Prompter	0	3	0
	Boy	0	2	0
	Miss Lee	0	4	0
	Mr Efran	0	2	6
	Men's dresser	0	3	0
	Stage keeper	0	3	0
	Women's ditto	0	2	6
	Door keeper	0	2	6
	Bill porter	0	2	0
	Bill sticker	0	2	0
	Molly Clark	0	1	0
	Sceneman Taylor	0	2	0
	Properties	0	5	0½

Carpenter's bill	I	18	11
Mr Garland's ditto	I	5	6
Music's dinner	O	12	O
For Mrs Clark's chair	O	5	O
Washing	O	2	6
For dresses [?]	O	1	6
Gallery keeper	O	1	10
Bill for foils	O	16	O
Paid boy for simples [?]	O	O	3
	8	11	2$\frac{1}{2}$
18 shares $\frac{1}{2}$ at 6 s 6 d each	6	O	3
Carriage bill back	6	O	O
	£20	11	5$\frac{1}{2}$

NB Paid Mrs Pritchard £50 and the stock debt[1] settled and remains in hand 11 pence. Witness W. Pritchard, O. Castrell (?), Henry Woodward.

[1] See [214] below.

STOCK DEBT AND DEAD SHARES

One of the most persistent causes of aggravation amongst actors who were paid a share in the profits of touring companies was the manipulation of the 'stock debt' and 'dead shares' by some unscrupulous theatre managers. As happened in the Restoration theatres in London, provincial theatre managers in the eighteenth century kept back for themselves a certain number of additional or dead shares (normally four) to defray expenses incurred in respect of scenery, costume and administration [see 213].[1]

In addition, they also retained a proportion of money to pay off or reduce what became known as the stock debt, i.e. exceptionally large managerial expenses that could not be met by the dead shares. Some of the more dishonest managers made sure that the stock debt was never cleared or even reduced to a reasonable level, and used it as an excuse to syphon off additional profits to themselves [see 214].

[1] See Rosenfeld (1939), p. 29.

213   An actor describes the function of dead shares

Thomas Weston: *Memoirs of that celebrated comedian and very singular genius, Thomas Weston* (London: S. Bladon, 1776), p. 18

In most country (or strolling) companies, the members form a kind of partnership or commonwealth, and all share alike; but the manager for his trouble, care and finding clothes and scenes, etc. is entitled for the same to four shares, which are called *dead ones*. He manages, fixes the plays, is treasurer and shares the money, after paying bills, servants, lights, carriage of goods from town to town, erecting buildings, and all manner of incidental charges, and is to keep a book, wherein they are to be set down for the inspection of the company.

214   The stock debt and dead shares manipulated by a ruthless manager

The secret history of the Green Room, vol. 1 (London: J. Owen, 1795), pp. 183–4

The manager, out of the money taken at doors, playbills, candles, etc. being first paid, divides the overplus equally among all the performers; excepting that the manager is allowed four shares for the scenery and dresses, one share for his trouble in superintending the stage, one for his services as an actor and another for his wife. And as he is an absolute monarch, as soon as his children can lisp out a few words, he sends them on the boards and takes a share for each of them. The expense of scenery and dresses, and the deficiencies of bad houses, he throws into a fund called the stock debt; and if he is an adept, he takes good care that the sum may always be very large, so that when the company is successful, he is sure to pay it off. By this business, in the course of a number of years, Mr Stanton[1] has amassed a tolerable fortune and has made several purchases in Staffordshire, particularly in the borough of that name [. . .].

[1] Stanton was for many years manager of a sharing company in Staffordshire. His daughter Charlotte was a member of the Bath Company 1783–8 (Orchard St Calendar); there she married a naval lieutenant from Bristol and become Mrs Goodall. She went to Drury Lane under that name in 1788. [See *The secret history of the Green Room,* vol. 1, pp. 183–6 and *LS,* pt v, p. 1090.]

FROM SHARE TO SALARY

Towards the latter half of the eighteenth century, the more successful provincial managers followed the lead of the London patent companies and moved over to a salary-based structure for their employees. The working capital for such companies was provided through private investment and shareholding. The one concession to profit-sharing was the retention of a benefit night for all actors. In some small provincial companies, however, the offer of a benefit was used as an excuse to keep salaries as low as possible, with the result that actors selling tickets for their own benefits often felt like beggars and vagabonds.

215   Terms of engagement in a small provincial touring company

'A manager's letter', *Salisbury Journal,* 7 February 1774

To Thomas Robson   Southton, 5 October 1773.

Sir, In reply to yours of the 2nd inst., the most advantageous terms it is in our power to offer you is one guinea *per week certain*; a single benefit at Salisbury and Winchester, paying only the incidental expenses of the night, as music, servants, etc. (which will not be above £4.4.0.). We shall open at Sarum about the 26th or 27th of this month, shall be there till the middle of January and the remainder of the winter at Winchester, three and twenty miles only distant. If these terms are acceptable, let me know, and I will send you a list of parts.

I remain, Sir, your very humble servant, Tho. Collins.

SALARIES AND SUBSCRIPTIONS

The surviving accounts of well-run provincial theatres or circuits from the 1760s onwards indicate at its best a stable profession with the possibility of long years of secure employment for established and popular actors [see 216]. Many provincial companies invited their audiences to subscribe for a season of plays and in this way provide a useful and known source of guaranteed income [see 217]. The detailed procedures for preventing fraud at the Box Office, and the importance of the Company Treasurer as guarantor of thrift (even down to the candle ends), are underlined in a set of rules for the administration of a provincial company (probably Manchester) in the 1770s [see 218].

In mid-eighteenth-century London, the rewards for outstanding actors were more generous. A leading London actor could earn as much per day as a provincial actor in a week. By the 1760s, the London patent companies had grown steadily in size and importance. Their accounts are discernibly more complex than they were at the beginning of the century, offering regular employment, as they now did, to a large number of performing artists, craftsmen, cleaners, dressers, barbers, doormen and bill stickers.[1]

---

[1] The Covent Garden MS Account Books [BL Eg 2267–72] reflect these changes from 1735 to 1767. An extract from Eg 2271 listing the overhead expenses for a full season (1760–1) is reproduced in *LS*, pt iv, pp. 814–17. The Drury Lane situation in 1748–9, from John Powel's unpublished MS *Tit for Tat*, and the salary lists of 1766–7 extracted from Winston's MS 9, can be compared from transcripts in *LS*, pt iv, pp. 121–8 and 1213–15.

216   Weekly salary list of an established circuit company, York, January 1784

Tate Wilkinson's Yorkshire Company. MS account book in York Public Library

	Men		Women	£	s	d
Mr	Wilkinson			1	11	6
	Cummins	Mrs	Cummins	2	11	6
	Smith		Smith	2	16	6
	Leng		Leng	1	11	0
	Dancer		Dancer	1	17	0
	Powell		Powell	2	4	0
	Kayne		Kayne	1	14	0
	Mills		Mills	2	16	6
			Jordan	1	11	6
			Ward	1	5	0
	Knight			1	5	0
	Butler			1	5	0
	Inchbald			1	1	0
	Barrett			0	18	0
	Creswell			0	18	0
	Colby			0	16	0
				26	1	6

Mr	Earby		0	15	0
	Swalwell		1	0	0
	Ned		0	15	0
	French		1	1	0
	Ward		0	16	0
	Lundie		0	16	0
		Betty	0	12	0
	Lloyd		0	12	0
	Large		0	10	0
	Thornton		0	8	0
	Callboy		0	2	0
			7	7	0

217   Invitation to subscribers

Drewry's *Derby Mercury*, 10 January 1782

Gosley's (late Whitley's) Derby and Nottingham Company. Season opening Friday, 25 January.

PROPOSALS FOR A SUBSCRIPTION

For FOURTEEN plays, to be performed in rotation, at the New Theatre on Monday, Wednesday and Friday evenings, to commence on Monday, 28 January 1782.

The company, during the course of the subscription, intend to perform all the most approved and fashionable pieces, as published by BELL, or shall be published this winter. They also engage, on a week's notice, to exhibit any tragedy or comedy that any ten or more subscribers shall appoint.

	£	s	d
Each subscriber for the boxes	1	1	0
Ditto for the pit	0	14	0

The subscription money to be paid on delivery of a silver ticket, which will be transferable.

218   Rules for the efficient financial administration of a company, *c.* 1777[1]

BL Add.MS 40,166, ff. 106–7

[. . .] Mr Barry[2] is to return the account of his numbering sealed up to Mr Younger or in his absence to Mr Powell every night before he takes the office keeper's accounts.

The money is to be put in one box and the checks in another, and if any person wants their money again before the curtain is drawn up, the check taker is to deliver them a card of which each check taker is to have twenty on a night and, on their giving this card to the office keeper, he is to return their money, and the card to tell as cash for him against the checks in the settling [of] his accounts.

Every office keeper to be furnished with silver to the value of . . . each night to give change with.[3]

If any check taker is found to let any person pass him without delivering his check, which he is to put directly into the box, or if he receives anything but checks or is found delaying the putting of them in the box, he will be discharged directly.

A written notice viz:

'No money is taken at this hatch or anything admitted but copper tickets' to be stuck up at the place of each check taker.

The money boxes and accounts to be sent every night to Mr Barry; the check boxes to Mr Younger when there; when he is absent to Mr Powell.

The office keeper to have his remaining checks counted every night; if any missing, to pay the value of admission for each.

The check taker to do the same by his cards, which he is to send with the check boxes to Mr Younger or, in his absence, to Mr Powell.

Mr Younger or Mr Powell and Mr Barry to settle the accounts of the house every morning after the rehearsal of the play. Door keeper's accounts to be sent for at different times of the night and fresh boxes given them, to look after them and note them and see they put the checks in the boxes.

The number of candles wanted for the stage and dressing rooms to be ascertained and delivered out every night by Mr Barry and in the morning as many pieces returned into the cellar in his presence. Once a month they are to be recounted and returned to the chandler and the value allowed against his account. No pieces are to be used on any account.

The oil is to be measured and delivered out in the presence of Mr Barry every morning. No person but himself is to have the key of the cellar [. . .]

[1] Probably for the company at Manchester in the season 1777–8. See J.L. Hodgkinson and R. Pogson *The early Manchester Theatre* (London: STR, 1960), pp. 80–176.
[2] William Barry, the company treasurer.
[3] The gaps in the MS are presumably to be filled in later or altered in the light of experience.

BENEVOLENT FUNDS FOR ACTORS

For most of the eighteenth century, actors' contracts with management made no provision for any security in cases of accident or illness [*see* **198**]. Occasional charity benefits might be given to alleviate hardship in specific instances.[1] However, in the mid 1760s the London patent theatres established benevolent funds for their companies, thus going some way to freeing managements from the moral dilemma of having to keep ageing, sick, or inadequate actors in their companies, to the detriment of artistic standards, or discharging them into a state of penury. These were later properly constituted as public trusts by Acts of Parliament [*see* **219**]. Members of the company at Covent Garden had to contribute 6 *d* per £1 from their salaries, plus one full day's pay annually. They were only entitled to claim benefits after seven years' contribution on a carefully laid-down scale. Even after leaving the company, however, they could elect to continue paying contributions from their salary into the fund and thus remain eligible for benefit.[2] Theatres in Dublin, Bath and Edinburgh soon followed the example of the London theatres and established benevolent funds of their own.

[1] See *LS*, pt iv, appendices B and C.
[2] See *Regulations for the theatrical fund at Covent Garden* (London, 1811).

219   A benevolent trust fund is formally established by Act of Parliament for the Theatre Royal, Drury Lane, 1776

An act for the better securing a fund belonging to certain persons of the Theatre Royal in Drury Lane, applicable to charitable uses; and for other purposes therein mentioned. 16 Geo III Cap XIII. J. Raithby (ed.); *Statutes at large*, vol. 7 (London. 1811), pp. 466–7

[I.] Whereas in or about the year 1766 a contribution was begun at the Theatre Royal in Drury Lane towards the charitable purpose of establishing a fund for the support of such performers belonging to the said theatre, as through age, infirmity or accident should be obliged to retire from the stage; the managers of which charity have since extended the same to the occasional relief of performers in case of sickness, and also the relief and support of the widows and children of deceased performers belonging to the said theatre; and whereas by the profits arising from several plays acted for the benefit of the said charity, and the voluntary contributions of the performers belonging to the said company, and other persons, a fund to the amount of £4000 or thereabouts is now in the hands of certain trustees applicable to the purposes aforesaid. To the end therefore that the money contributed as aforesaid, or which may hereafter be contributed towards increasing the said fund, may be applied to the purposes aforesaid, and to prevent, as far as may be, any misapplication or embezzlement thereof, may it please Your Majesty that it may be enacted [. . .] that from and after the passing of this act, all and every the subscribers to the said fund for the time being, during such time as he, she and they respectively shall pay to the same, shall be and are hereby declared to be one body corporate [. . .] and shall be called by the name of *The Society established for the relief of indigent persons belonging to His Majesty's Company of Comedians of the Theatre Royal in Drury Lane*. And by the same name they shall have perpetual succession, and a common seal; and they and their successors by the same name may sue and be sued, implead and be impleaded, answer and be answered unto, in all or any Court or Courts of Record and Places of Judicature within this Kingdom of Great Britain. And that they and their successors, by the name aforesaid, shall be able and capable in law to have, hold, receive, enjoy, possess and retain for the purposes aforesaid, all and every such sum and sums of money as have been paid, given, devised or bequeathed, or shall at any time or times hereafter be paid, given, devised or bequeathed to and for the ends and purposes herein before mentioned. And that they and their successors, by the name aforesaid, shall and may at any time hereafter [. . .] purchase, take or receive, hold and enjoy any lands, tenements or hereditaments not exceeding the yearly value of five hundred pounds.

    II. And be it further enacted, that from and after the passing of this act Thomas King, John Packer, John Moody, James Aickin, James William Dodd, Robert

Baddeley, Francis Waldron, Richard Hurst, William Brereton, James Wrighten, William Parsons, John Palmer and William Davies shall be and they are hereby appointed directors for managing the said fund until the 5th day of April [. . .] 1777. [. . .]

IV. And be it further enacted, that such subscribers to the said fund as may hereafter be entitled to receive any benefit therefrom, shall meet together at some convenient place in or near the said theatre, on the 25th day of March [. . .] 1777, or within ten days after, for electing directors for the year ensuing; and that previous to such election the names of all the directors for the time being shall be written on distinct pieces of paper, being all of an equal size, and rolled up in the same manner, as near as may be, and shall be put into a box, or some other convenient receptacle, and shall be shaken together, after which some person not interested in such election shall draw out the said names one by one, until the number remaining in the said box or receptacle shall be reduced to six, and the six persons whose names shall so remain shall be six of the directors for the ensuing year. After which the said subscribers present shall proceed to elect seven other persons from amongst themselves (either such as were or were not directors for the preceding year), and the seven persons so elected, together with the six persons whose names remained undrawn as aforesaid, shall be the directors for putting this act in execution for the year next ensuing [. . .]

V. Provided always, and be it further enacted, that notice of every such election shall be affixed in writing in some conspicuous part of the said theatre, for three days at the least, immediately preceding such election, and that all elections shall be decided by a majority of votes; and that every subscriber to the said fund shall have a right to vote in any such election.

VI. Provided also that at every annual election of directors for the purposes of this act, a majority of the directors for the ensuing year shall consist of persons belonging to or employed at the said theatre.

9   Playhouses

INTRODUCTION

For half a century after the Licensing Act no new playhouses were erected in London. In the patent theatres there were periodical interior redecorations and some rearrangements to improve and increase audience accommodation. It was not until 1787 that a totally new theatre was built: the Royalty in Wellclose Square. It was designed for the presentation of plays, but opposition from the patent holders confined the house for some time to general entertainments (see chapter 7). Sadler's Wells, rebuilt in 1765, had always been confined in that way.[1] In 1789 fire destroyed the King's Theatre, which was rebuilt and reopened in 1791.[2] However, it was the demolition of Wren's Drury Lane in 1791 and its rebuilding on a much larger scale by Holland (reopening in 1794) that truly marked the beginning of a new era. Both that theatre and Holland's enlargement of Covent Garden in 1792 were burned down in 1809 and 1808 respectively. Smirke's new Covent Garden in 1809 and Wyatt's Drury Lane in 1812 belong essentially to the Romantic theatre.[3]

For most of the eighteenth century, it is to the provinces that we must look for new playhouses. The earliest were small, often far too small to meet the needs of their audiences; like that in Bath (1750), which by 1775 had to be doubled in size.[4] In contrast, some theatre buildings survived into the nineteenth century, as was the case, for example, at Norwich (1758) and Portsmouth (1761).[5] An important prototype for many later playhouses was the Richmond Theatre in Surrey (1765). It was built by James Love as a summer theatre under royal authority and patronage, with a company drawn largely from the patent theatres. It was designed by Sanderson who was the stage carpenter at Drury Lane.[6] When at about the same time the Bristol proprietors wanted a new theatre, they obtained plans from both Covent Garden and Drury Lane and also consulted Sanderson.[7] The resulting theatre, built in King Street in 1766, was larger than the Richmond theatre but bore a distinct relationship to it. Two years later the new Edinburgh playhouse was to be designed, 'on the model of that lately built at Bristol which has been justly admired' [*see* **249**]. Others followed suit.

The basic characteristics of the Georgian playhouse were thus modelled on the shape of the London houses, although scaled down in capacity.[8] Boxes, pit and gallery were standard in provincial auditoria; a second gallery as in London was not added for the most part until the nineteenth century. Receipts for a full house in London might be two or three times that of a provincial theatre, in round figures £300 as against £80 to £120, though average houses in London and the provinces could be much less.[9]

The basic lay-out of the stage was the same in provincial houses as in London, though

266

often with less elaborate decoration and equipment. A forestage flanked on either side by a stage box and proscenium door gave onto a scenic stage with wings and shutters. A machine room below stage and a vista recess to make possible longer perspectives were added in certain theatres [*see* 248].[10] Dressing rooms and green room (however small), along with a scene store, were considered essential in all theatre buildings. Lighting was by candlelight (initially candelabra, sconces and footlights – see chapter 4); this basic lighting system survived in the provinces long after it was abandoned in London where the stage candelabra were replaced by more sophisticated methods involving a combination of wing lighting and footlights.[11] Oil lighting was also used in varying degrees [*see* 224, 285–9, 314].

In contrast to the purpose-built or permanently converted playhouses in many provincial cities, travelling or improvised theatres or fairground booths had little or no technical equipment and had to rely on primitive lighting effects [*see* 258, 260, 261].

There were in addition a number of private theatres built or converted at major town or country houses for the diversion of stage-struck amateurs: for instance at Wargrave, Richmond House, Wynnstay and Brandenburg House. From such interior engravings as have survived [*see* 256], it is clear that they too followed the same basic pattern established in the design of London's playhouses, though on a much smaller scale.[12]

[1] See Arundell (1965), chapters 1–3.
[2] Nalbach (1972), chapter 5. *Survey of London*, vol. 30, chapter 8.
[3] See *Survey of London*, vol. 35, chapters 4 and 6.
[4] Hare (1977), pp. 12–14.
[5] See Burley (1928), chapter 1; Grice (1977), chapter 4; Eshleman (1970); Hare (1958), chapter 8.
[6] See Bingham (1886), p. 11.
[7] See Barker (1974), chapter 1.
[8] See Nicoll (1980), chapters 2 and 3; Southern (1948); E.A. Langhans: 'The theatres' in R.D. Hume (ed.): *The London theatre world 1660–1800* (Southern Illinois University Press, 1980), pp. 35–65.
[9] Cf. annotated Bath playbills in Harvard Theatre Collection for 1787–8 and 1790–1 with Drury Lane and Covent Garden receipts in *LS*, pt iv, for same years.
[10] See chapter 4 and chapter 10.
[11] See Gösta M. Bergman: *Lighting in the theatre* (Stockholm: Almqvist & Wiksell, 1977), pp. 214–16; Nicoll (1980), chapter 5.
[12] See Rosenfeld (1978).

THE PLAYHOUSES IN GEORGIAN LONDON
Drury Lane[1]

There was an enlargement of the first gallery in 1747 and interior redecoration in 1753. However, the first significant development under Garrick's managership was the ending of the audience's right to occupy the stage on special occasions and to go behind the scenes. Ever since the Restoration, this had been a cause of irritation to theatre managers and actors (see chapters 4 and 5). In Dublin, Thomas Sheridan had been supported by the law as well as public opinion in banning the audience from the stage after the Kelly affair in 1747 when a drunken patron had tried to rape one of the actresses.[2] After several abortive attempts to introduce a similar ban in London, Garrick and Lacy felt there was sufficient support in 1762 to make this change; in the process, they were able to enlarge the seating capacity of the theatre. In 1771 there were further redecorations.

[1] See *Survey of London*, vol. 25, chapter 4.
[2] See Sheldon (1967), chapter 4.

220   Drury Lane: Garrick bans the audience from the stage and enlarges the auditorium, 1762

Thomas Davies: *Memoirs of the life of David Garrick Esq.* [1780] (London, 1808), pp. 375–8

To the disgrace of common apprehension we have often seen likewise in our theatres two audiences, one on the stage and another before the curtain; more especially at the actors' benefits, when a large amphitheatre has covered almost the whole stage, and the battle of Bosworth Field has been fought in a less space than that which is commonly allotted to a cock match.

Mr Garrick was fully sensible of all the incoherence arising from this glaring offence against what the painters call the costume but knew not how to bring about a reformation. He was reminded that Mr Sheridan, by his spirited behaviour, had conquered the refractory tempers of the Irish gentlemen by shutting his stage door against them; and, after suffering many vexations and much opposition, had supported his right with the sanction of legal authority [. . .].

[. . .] The comedians, by waiving the advantage of an amphitheatre on a benefit night, would be considerable losers; and to remedy that evil, Mr Garrick very judiciously observed that the plan of reformation must be preceded by a considerable enlargement of the playhouse; and if it could be so contrived that the space before the curtain might contain as many persons as had formerly filled the pit, boxes, galleries and the stage, nobody could have any pretence to murmur.

Mr Lacy was of the same opinion and he concurred with his partner in the prosecution of his scheme; and having a taste for architecture, he took upon himself the enlarging of the theatre, which was completely finished in the year 1762. From that time scarcely any but the performers were permitted to visit the scenes of the playhouse.

Drury Lane: the Adam reconstruction

Garrick's final and major legacy to the playhouse before his retirement was an extensive reconstruction commissioned from the Adam brothers in 1775 [*see* 221 and 222]. This in turn was altered in 1780. The exuberant nature of the Adam decoration was toned down and the stage doors were removed [*see* 223]. A further toning down was carried out by Thomas Greenwood and William Capon in 1783; the overall colour was now a faint pea-green, with the boxes lined in red [*see* 224]. More alterations were made, probably in 1785 [*see* 225], and a further repainting in white and gold occurred in 1787. At which of these redecorations the stage doors and a much reduced fretwork ornamentation were restored remains unclear.

221   Drury Lane: the Adam reconstruction of 1775

Public Advertiser, 30 September 1775. Reproduced in *Survey of London*, vol. 35, p. 46.

At first view I was a good deal surprised to find that by some means or other the ingenious artists had contrived to give the appearance of greater magnitude to the house. I knew it was *not* rebuilt but only repaired; and consequently that there could be no additional space between the old walls and roof. Upon reflection I perceived that one way by which this was effected was from having removed the old heavy square pillars on each side of the stage and by that means I suppose they have procured more width from one side box to the other.

I also observed that the sounding board was much raised on the part next the stage and that the height given to it increased greatly the appearance of magnitude in the house. This having brought the ceiling or sounding board nearly on a level has a wonderful good effect to the eye. And what astonished me greatly was to find that the sound of the music and actors' voices both improved by this additional height. All the people round me agreed with me in this fact and owned they thought it a very uncommon effort of art.

Small pilasters, the height of which is confined to the different tiers of boxes, support and adorn them. They are made more light and more gay by inserting in front of each a panel of plate glass which, in the lower order, is placed over a foil or varnish of spangled crimson, which looks both rich and brilliant. The capitals are gilt and are what our artists call the Grecian Ionic. The glass of the second order is placed over a green spangled foil or varnish and has an effect no less beautiful than the former. The capitals of this order are also gilt and are a sort of Corinthian, which I don't recollect to have seen before.

The upper tier of boxes is adorned with therms, of which the busts are gilt and the panels underneath are filled with painted ornaments. I admire the judgement of the artists for having laid aside pilasters in this last tier, it being too low for that species of decoration; and besides, the repetition would have become dull.

All the ornaments in the friezes and on the dados or fronts of the boxes are elegant and splendid. Nothing can, in my opinion, answer better than the festoon drapery upon the front of the first tier. The gilt ornaments on the faces of the two orders of pilasters (from whence the branches for the candles spring) ought not to be omitted in the catalogue of elegant ornaments. Neither must I omit the decoration of the ceiling or sounding board, which consists of octagon panels rising from an exterior circular frame to the opening, or ventilator, in the centre. The diminishing of these panels towards the centre, and the shade thrown next to the exterior frame, give the ceiling the appearance of a dome, which has a light and airy effect.

I can never give you a complete list of all the ornaments that struck me in this theatre. The stage doors, the spangled borders on each side of the stage, and many other new ornamental decorations, perfectly answered my ideas of elegance and splendour. Indeed I heard some critics allege that they thought the decorations of the house *too* elegant and too splendid and that it obscured the lustres of the scenery and dresses. My answer to these observations was that I thought the decorations of a theatre could *not* be too brilliant and that I did not doubt but, by the assistance of a Loutherbourg, the managers could and would soon remove these objections and bring the whole into perfect harmony.

Were I to hazard a criticism, where almost everything is so much to my satisfaction, it would be that the crimson drapery over the stage is too dark for the objects round it; and that the gold fringe has not the brilliant effect it ought to have in such a situation.

I had almost forgot to observe that the side boxes are much improved by the additional height given to each tier, which admits of the seats being raised considerably above each other and consequently gives a much better view of the stage. The boxes are now lined with crimson spotted paper and gilt border, which makes a fine background to all the decorations.

222   Auditorium of Drury Lane by R. Adam, 1775
Theatre Collection, University of Bristol. Reproduced in Leacroft (1973), p. 120

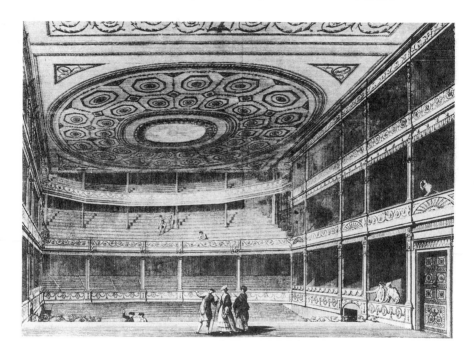

223   Drury Lane: renovations in 1780
Smith, vol. 19 (BL, 1825–40). [Unattributed newspaper cutting referring to the opening of the season, 16 September 1780.]

The house since the close of the last season has been much altered and in some degree improved. The boxes are new papered, an additional seat has been made to the pit, many of the scenes have been repainted, and the stage is better lighted than before. The box lobby also, and the avenues to the house, are rendered more agreeable by being less in the dark. But though the managers have gained two additional side boxes by taking away the stage doors, we fear they will feel the want of those necessary helps to the drama. And we could not but wonder they should sagaciously play a farce the very first night, in which one of the stage doors is a positive requisite in the representation.[1] The appearance of the stage is prodigiously mended in consequence of the removal of the tawdry fretwork border which joined to the stage boxes and has stood as the disgrace of the theatre for these four years past. The elegant fluted columns which the new side wings exhibit give it at once a grand, a neat and a theatrical appearance.

[1] This was *High Life Below Stairs*. See *LS*, pt v, p. 372.

224 The interior of Drury Lane as it appeared in 1783
Theatre Collection, University of Bristol. Reproduced in *Survey of London*, vol. 35, plate 116

225   Drury Lane: further alterations, *c.* 1785

Collection of memoranda relating to Drury Lane Theatre, arranged by James Winston, vol. 5.
Undated press cutting, probably 1785. Reprinted in *Survey of London,* vol. 35, pp. 48–9

The back of the front boxes, which two years ago, by being changed from the old
plan into enclosures, became a nest for prostitutes of both sexes, are now entirely
opened. The ceiling is raised in order to give room for the lustres to display their
lights and the seats are formed into recesses which communicate with the other
boxes and afford a full view of the stage. There is a circular regularity of arches
from the King's box round to the Prince's, which have a most pleasing effect. These
are formed at the back of the boxes from whence the former paper covering is
taken and a wainscot substituted. The wainscot is painted of a crimson colour in
festoons, which gives a richness to the view and deceives the eye into a perspective
that makes the boxes look much deeper than they really are. Great pains have
been bestowed on the galleries and upper boxes, the fronts of which are newly
decorated with festoons, which have a most beautiful appearance. On each wing
of the two shilling gallery are placed three pilasters, fluted and gilded, which
occupy the space formerly filled by false boxes. The pillars through the whole
house have changed their whole drapery and put on new livery. Nay even those of
iron in the back boxes are capped, cased, fluted and gilt. The colouring of the boxes
and gallery is a new fancy mixture. It is what may be called, in the artist's phrase, a
warm lilac; the appearance of which, contrasted with the glowing crimson at the
back of the boxes and the gilded pillars in front, give elegance, beauty, taste and
richness to a scene which does honour to the painter. The upper boxes, as to
convenience and intercourse, remain as formerly. They have been all new painted
and their pillars are richly gilded [. . .] (The stage was also illuminated) with patent
lamps. The effect of this light which is, in a manner, a new kind of artificial light,
was brilliant beyond all expectation.

THE PLAYHOUSES IN GEORGIAN LONDON
Covent Garden[1]

The basic shape of Covent Garden remained unchanged for some fifty years. Its intimate feel
is reflected in a drawing from the 1770s depicting the performance of a harlequinade [*see*
226]. Most of the alterations made during the early part of the century affected the backstage area in an attempt to improve conditions of work. However, a major renovation was
carried out in 1782 when Shepherd's fan-shaped auditorium was replaced by a new
parallel-sided auditorium, designed by J.I. Richards, the theatre's principal scene painter
[*see* **227, 228, 229**].[2] Richards was unable to extend the shell of the building but
nevertheless managed substantially to increase the seating capacity of the auditorium.

[1] See *Survey of London,* vol. 35, chapter 5.
[2] See also chapter 10 and later.

226   A harlequinade at Covent Garden, *c.* 1770

Theatre Collection, University of Bristol

227   Covent Garden: remodelling of the interior by J.I. Richards, 1782

Morning Chronicle. 24 September 1782

The two first and principal perfections to be considered are *seeing* and *hearing*. These have been particularly and very successfully attended to. The next are accommodating the audience with *room*, *air* and a *safe* and *easy* access. The advantages the present has over the late theatre we shall endeavour to explain to our readers by comparison.

The ground-plan of the late theatre was eight feet three inches wider at the back row of the pit than at the curtain, by which error the spectators in the side boxes were turned from the stage. In the present, it is nearly parallel. The sounding board and pit ceiling were in two parts, making an obtuse angle, inclining upwards from the front of the stage where the curtain drops. This is raised eight feet, making one level ceiling only.

The late pit was so low that the spectators on the three first rows were too much under the level of the stage to see with ease or satisfaction. The passages at the end of the benches on each side are now a step lower than the floor on which the benches are placed to prevent the standers from intercepting the view of the company in the front boxes. By altering the elevation of the seats in the pit, those in the front boxes are raised about five inches and the ceiling about two feet six inches.

Within the front boxes are eight enclosed or upper boxes, more elevated than the rest, which open immediately into the lobby, not interfering with the entrances to the general range of front boxes.

The side boxes are equally divided, having each the same number of benches, length and breadth; the ceilings are raised and the entrance is level with the lobby. In the old theatre there were at some boxes one, at others, two steps to get in. This improvement is made throughout the house. [. . .]

The front and side boxes form one colonnade round the house of the Ionic order. In the front, it terminates with a balustrade, which forms the first gallery. At the sides, it is continued up, with a second range of columns of the Corinthian order [. . .].

The upper gallery is supported by pilasters from the first gallery, with an entablature and balustrade.

The ornaments are few and simple, the colours a light pearl and a degree darker of a green tint for the panels, flutes of the columns, etc. The balustrades, capitals, fillets of the columns and other ornaments are gilt and the mouldings in parts. The tops of all the side and upper front boxes are ornamented with crimson festoon curtains. A small neat lustre hangs by a chain against every column below and against every other column above. The front boxes are lighted by four lustres and a large girandole at each end.

The doors on the stage are omitted, as the using them in any performance was certainly an impropriety, being the audience part of the house. The design of the frontispiece is entirely altered and distinct from either the audience or scenic parts of the house and is now in two pieces; the advantage of which is, it opens the stage considerably to the side boxes and gives an opportunity of introducing a door and balcony, which may be used with propriety and is placed on such an angle as to be seen by the spectators on the same side.

The sound board, which could not be made an ornamental ceiling from its extent without appearing too heavy for its support, is painted as a sky in imitation of the Roman theatres, which were open at the top, and from the lights below give the audience a lively idea of the morning dawn.

This magnificent structure was completed according to the design and immediately under the direction of that very ingenious artist Mr Richards. In our opinion, this gentleman not only deserves the warmest approbation of the public, but of his employers. The theatre is so considerably augmented that we take for granted the receipts on a full night cannot be less than £80 more than the house formerly contained. If the manager has secured a succession of good pieces during the winter (which we are informed is the case), the expense, great as it has been in completing the new theatre, will soon return into the treasury.

228   The Theatre Royal, Covent Garden, after remodelling by John Inigo Richards in 1782
Private Collection. Reproduced in *Survey of London*, vol. 35, pl. 43 [plan at pit level]

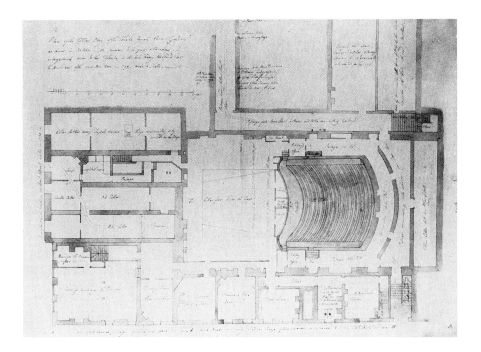

229   Covent Garden audience in 1786
Coloured aquatint by Thomas Rowlandson. George 7063. (Print Room, BM). Reproduced in *Survey of London*, vol. 35, plate 43

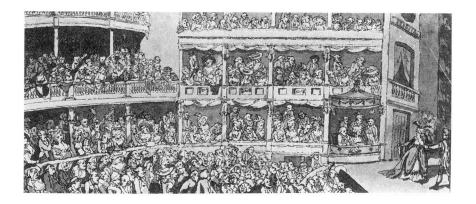

THE PLAYHOUSES IN GEORGIAN LONDON
Little Theatre in the Haymarket

Little is known about the interior of John Potter's original building of 1720.[1] A frontispiece illustration of Fielding's *Pasquin* from 1737 gives some idea of the intimate relationship between stage and auditorium [*see* **89**]. A print published in 1815 shows the theatre after Foote's remodelling and extension of 1766 (it reopened on 14 May 1767) [*see* **230**]. Apart from periodic redecoration, this house then remained largely unaltered until it was replaced on a slightly different site by the present Haymarket theatre in 1821.[2]

[1] See *Survey of London*, vol. 20, pp. 98–9.
[2] See Macqueen-Pope (1948).

230   Interior of the Little Theatre in the Haymarket, 1815
University of Bristol, Theatre Collection

THE PLAYHOUSES IN GEORGIAN LONDON
King's Theatre in the Haymarket[1]

When R.B. Sheridan of Drury Lane and T. Harris of Covent Garden gained a controlling interest in the Opera House in 1778, they altered and redecorated the auditorium.[2] William Taylor bought Sheridan's interest in 1781 and in 1782 employed a scene painter, Michael Novosielski, to make a much more radical reconstruction. The plan is reproduced in Saunders's *Treatise on theatres* [*see* **232**], following his own jaundiced account of the alterations [*see* 231]; by the time this volume was published in 1790, the theatre had been destroyed by fire. The 1782 interior is represented in William Capon's drawing [*see* 233]. Novosielski was engaged to redesign and rebuild the theatre after the fire. The plan in the Soane Museum [*see* 234], which has been attributed to the 1782 state,[3] may be more likely to represent his plans for the 1791 rebuilding. An engraving from *The Carlton House Magazine* (published some time between January 1792 and February 1796), held in the Theatre Museum, seems to confirm this suggestion [*see* 235]; though whether it incorporates Marinari's improvements of 1796 is not clear.[4]

[1] See *Survey of London*, vol. 30, chapter 8.
[2] *Ibid.*
[3] Most recently in *BD*, vol. 4, p. 564.
[4] See Nalbach (1972), pp. 81–3.

231   The King's Theatre in 1782

George Saunders: *A treatise on theatres* [London: published by the author, 1790] (reprinted by Benjamin Blom: New York, 1968), pp. 79–81

[. . .] This theatre underwent several alterations, the principal of which was in 1782, when it was enlarged under the direction of Mr Novosielski. The form was then made an oblong rounded off at the end of the stage. The length was, from the stage front to the opposite boxes, about 58 feet and 23 feet more to the scene; the breadth between the boxes 43 feet; and the height 44 feet from the centre of the pit to the ceiling. There were three ranges of boxes, 34 in each range, besides 18 in a line with the gallery; in all 116, allowing the space of two for entrances into the pit. Each box was from 5 to 6 feet wide, from 7 to 7 feet 6 inches high and 6 feet deep. Those in the first range, being on a level with the stage, had their fronts continued in one even line to the central box. But all the ranges above, as also the first gallery, projected in curved lines over the pit. A second gallery was managed in the cove of the ceiling, which was groined for that purpose. Five entrances led into the theatre: three from the Haymarket and two from Market Lane.

Being confined to the original walls, Mr Novosielski had not the opportunity of giving it a greater width. The form therefore remained extremely bad, and the stage and its appendages wretchedly confined and inconvenient. But I will desist from particularising these defects which were unavoidable and speak of such as in my opinion might have been avoided.

The only assistance sound can have to reach the end of a long confined space is plain and smooth surfaces to conduct it. Instead of which, the line of the box fronts in this theatre was continually broken by the projecting curves and these covered with paper ornaments, which were liberally distributed in every part of the theatre. The first gallery was low and inconvenient, and very little could be either discerned or heard there by those who were situated behind. The second gallery by being next to the ceiling was the best situation in the house for hearing but very prejudicial to every other part. And thus that which was of necessity bad was rendered still worse by adopting almost every means in the finishings that could oppose the progress of sound.

232   Plan of the King's Theatre in the Haymarket, 1782

George Saunders: *A treatise on theatres* [1790] (1968), plate 10

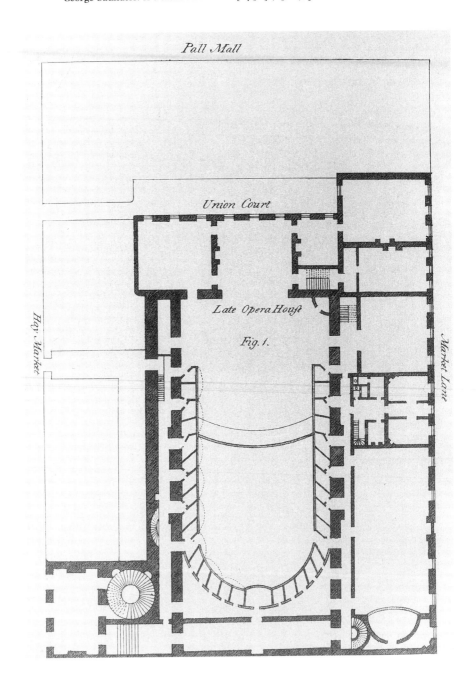

233   Pit and stage of the King's Theatre arranged for a masquerade, 1785
Drawing by William Capon. University of Bristol, Theatre Collection

234   Plan of the King's Theatre after the fire in 1789
Soane Museum. Reproduced in *BD*, vol. 4

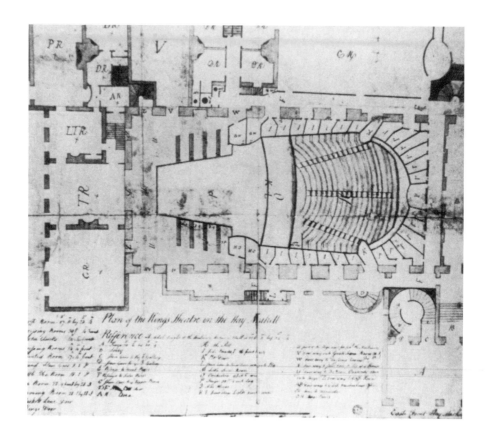

235   Interior of the King's Theatre in the early 1790s

The Carlton House Magazine. Theatre Museum

THE PLAYHOUSES IN GEORGIAN LONDON

The Royalty Theatre

Opened in 1787, the Royalty Theatre fits into the size and pattern of the better provincial theatres of the time. It was planned for normal playhouse use in the east of the city, but, because of the opposition of the patentees of Drury Lane and Covent Garden, for many years after the opening night had to be confined to burlettas, dances and pantomimes under the 1752 Act.[1]

[1] See chapter 7 above and Nicholson (1926), chapters 5 and 6. Various pamphlets were published as the controversy raged, including *A review of the present contest between the managers* (1787) and *A very plain state of the case, or The Royalty Theatre versus the Theatres Royal* (1787). See also W.F. Oulton: *History of the theatres of London 1771–95*, vol. 1 (London, 1796), pp. 167–96.

236   The opening of the Royalty Theatre, June 1787

(A) *LONDON CHRONICLE*, 19–21 JUNE 1787 p. 589

The theatre, within-side, is a very commodious and neat building, but the entrances are too contracted and thence rather inconvenient. The size of the audience part of the house is something between that of Covent Garden and that of the Haymarket, but on a different scale. The colouring is white, with a plain gold beading. The motto over the stage, *vincit qui patitur*. The ceiling of the boxes is more than usually lofty, which makes the area of the pit so extremely high that unfortunately the voice of the performers does not well carry itself to the audience but is lost in the expanse.

The dresses were new and proper and the scenery remarkably well painted but rather of too golden a cast. All the woods and landscapes savoured of autumn. The yellow leaf was somewhat too visible.

(B) UNATTRIBUTED NEWSPAPER CUTTING IN I. REED: *NOTITIA DRAMATICA* vol. 3, 1786–95. (BL Add.MS 25,392, f. 17).[1]

The scenes are well designed and beautifully painted. They are the production of a Mr Dixon who has proved himself equally skilled in architecture as in painting; for the whole superstructure has been designed and executed agreeably to his orders.

The house was illuminated with considerable splendour and indeed made a very beautiful appearance. It is very commodious, and every part before the curtain commands a full view of the stage. The boxes are not numerous but they are convenient. The pit is small and the galleries large: an excellent accommodation for that part of the town. The stage has a most pleasing effect: it is large and well lighted; and the orchestra holds a very good band of instrumental performers. [. . .] we shall content ourselves with observing that the experience of this night fully proved that it is constructed in such a manner as to be no less peculiarly commodious to the hearing than to the sight.

The motto which Mr Palmer has chosen for the front of the stage is: VINCIT QUI PATITUR (He conquers who endures).

---

[1] Both reports (and the *London Chronicle* for 21–3 June and 23–6 June) contain in addition an account of the opening performances (*As You Like It* and *A Miss in her Teens*); Palmer's farewell address; and subsequent correspondence from Quick, Ryder and Harris, opposing the theatre's licensing.

237   **Stage of the Royalty Theatre, Wellclose Square, 1787**
University of Bristol, Theatre Collection

238   **Auditorium of the Royalty Theatre in 1794**
University of Bristol, Theatre Collection

GEORGIAN PLAYHOUSES OUTSIDE LONDON

By the end of the eighteenth century, many towns in England, Scotland, Wales and Ireland had playhouses. The twenty-four illustrated and commented on in James Winston's *The theatric tourist* (1805) were in Andover, Bath, Birmingham, Brighton, Chichester, Edmonton, Exeter, Grantham, Lewes, Liverpool, Maidstone, Manchester, Margate, Newbury, Newcaste-upon-Tyne, Norwich, Plymouth, Portsmouth, Reading, Richmond (Surrey), Southampton, Tunbridge Wells, Winchester and Windsor;[1] there were many others, purpose built or converted. From the manuscript notes of Winston, William Douglas and Peter Davey,[2] over 300 can be listed, and on many of these much research remains to be done. The oldest surviving in working condition (modified or restored) are in Bristol (1766) and Richmond (Yorks), (1788).

The overall dimensions of the playhouses were based on those of Drury Lane (*c.* 110 ft by 60 ft) and Covent Garden (120 ft by 60 ft), sometimes slightly smaller or more irregular, depending on the site.

Bath

Bath in its original (1750) form was much smaller (*c.* 60 ft by 40 ft); its 1775 extension brought the length up to approximately 100 ft, though it must always have remained narrow [*see* 240, 241 and 242]. Hippisley's original proposals for Bath in 1747 [*see* 239] are interesting in the presumption made that since performances had been given regularly in the city during the ten years since the 1737 Licensing Act without objection, it was safe to erect a proper playhouse. However, in March 1754 information was laid against the new theatre and it had to be temporarily closed.[3]

[1] These have been reprinted in *BD*, vol. 5.
[2] MSS copies in New York Public Library (Winston), Johannesburg Public Library (Douglas) and the Theatre Museum (Davey).
[3] See Hare (1977), p. 6. The 1748 proposals for building by subscription are reproduced in Penley (1892), p. 25.

239   John Hippisley's proposals for a new theatre in Bath, 1747

John Wood: *A description of Bath*, second edition (London: W. Bathoe, 1765), pp. 443–6

Plays are acted some of the other evenings of the week in a cellar under part of the ballroom of Simpson's Assembly House. And the late Mr John Hippisley, finding that this had been constantly done without the least molestation for more than ten years after the suppression of playhouses by the Act of Parliament which took place on 24th June 1737, he, in November 1747, formed a scheme to raise the Bath theatre from its languishing condition and thereupon addressed the public in the following lines:

> 'TO THE NOBILITY, MAGISTRACY AND GENTRY AT BATH
> "Plays are like mirrors made, for men to see
> How BAD they are, how GOOD they ought to be."

In all ages and in all countries where liberty and learning flourished, the stage never failed of receiving sanction and protection from the great and noble.

Theatrical performances, when conducted with decency and regularity, have been always esteemed the most rational amusements by the polite and thinking part of mankind. Strangers therefore must be greatly surprised to find at Bath entertainments of this sort in no better perfection than they are, as it is a place, during its seasons, honoured with so great a number of persons eminent for politeness, judgement and taste, and where might reasonably be expected (next to London) the best theatre in England.

The present playhouse, or rather playroom, is so small and incommodious that 'tis almost impossible to have things better done in it than they are. The profits arising from the performance, as now conducted, will not support a larger or better company of actors. And nothing can be more disagreeable than for persons of the first quality, and those of the lowest rank, to be seated on the same bench together, which must be the case here if the former will honour and the latter have an inclination to see a play.

To remedy this, and for the better entertainment of the quality, it is humbly proposed to erect a regular, commodious theatre on the most convenient spot of ground that can be got, to be managed by Mr Hippisley (who for many years has been a performer in London) and others; and to add such a sufficient number of good performers to the present company as will (it is hoped) never fail of giving pleasure and satisfaction to the most judicious audience and greatly contribute towards rendering Bath the most agreeable place in the kingdom.'

[. . .] The house was proposed to have been sixty feet long and forty feet broad in the clear. It was to front westward to Orchard Street, and the front was to have consisted of a rustic basement, supporting the Doric order. The expense of building it was computed at about one thousand pounds; and this was three hundred pounds less than the theatre cost that was erected in the year 1705, though the new house would have been much larger than the old theatre was.

Theatrical performances making part of the amusements of Bath, (notwithstanding the severe law against the performers and such as shall cause them to be performed) while the custom continues, invalids will run much less hazard in going to a regular theatre than to an occasional playroom to become partakers of the amusements of the stage. And it was upon that very consideration that I granted Messrs Hippisley and Watts the piece of ground marked in the plan [. . .] with the letter E.

240   Interior of the Orchard Street Theatre Bath

From a watercolour by Nixon, reproduced in Mowbray Aston Green: *The eighteenth-century architecture of Bath* (Bath: George Gregory, 1902). The original is now untraceable

241   Enlargement of the Orchard Street Theatre Bath in 1775

Bath Journal, 25 September 1775

The alterations and improvements were, as I am informed, designed and conducted by Mr Palmer, architect and builder of this city, and are very striking. And will, I hope, be lasting monuments of his elegant taste, good judgement and expeditious and punctual performance. The house is in every respect highly improved both in convenience and beauty. The considerable enlargement of it backwards has enabled it to accommodate more company and at the same time rendered it more airy and agreeable. The heat formerly so much complained of will be for the future prevented increasing to any disagreeable degree by a new ventilator erected at the top of the building. This will supply a quantity of fresh air equally diffused over the whole house and prevent its rushing in streams or currents which are so apt to give cold. In cold weather it will I suppose be kept close shut and may at any time be open in such degree only as to admit such a quantity of air as is necessary.

The house is likewise now furnished with a large lobby or waiting room and proper retiring rooms. The pit is raised higher and the space between the seats enlarged and made more convenient. The dome that was so injurious in many parts of the theatre both to the sight and hearing, and its furniture of Apollo and the Muses so preposterously mixed with the gothic architecture, is removed. The Grecian orders are now introduced, so much more proper to a theatre than the Gothic. The stage itself appears much enlarged and the whole building improved in such a manner that not only the performers but the audience appear to much greater advantage. What is very extraordinary, I am informed that Mr Palmer the architect, when the theatre was last altered and enlarged (1767), gave in the plan it is now finished from (so striking for its simplicity, convenience and elegance) to the manager; and proved to him that it could be executed even at a less expense than the very strange one he persisted in adopting. The consequence has been that after a few years' trial, a great loss of entertainment to the public and profit to the proprietor, his advice is at last followed at an additional expense of at least a thousand pounds. He has really shown in the present work an elegance of taste and soundness of judgement that would not disgrace an architect in Europe. Add to this that he has executed it in a less space of time than can well be credited, considering the quantity of work and the accuracy and neatness of its execution.

242 The exterior of the Orchard Street Theatre Bath, 1750/1775

James Winston: *The theatric tourist* (London: T. Woodfall, 1805), plate 1

243   The Theatre Royal Bath in Orchard Street at the end of the eighteenth century
Winston (1805), pp. 5–7

The theatre is commodious and elegant, but we think the custom of using the lobby for a box-office would be more 'honoured in the breach than the observance'; for notwithstanding the doors of the boxes are secured, it certainly hazards a disturbance of rehearsal. This department is under the able regulation of the father of Mr Bartley of Drury Lane. The great space allowed for the stage doors gives the frontispiece a heavy appearance, being more than double the customary dimensions. The auditory is semi-circular: the whole designed and executed by Mr Palmer, architect; and it reflects on his professional abilities, take it for all in all, considerable credit [. . .].

[Exterior] The first door is the avenue leading to the stage; the second to the galleries; and the third the pit. The fourth was made about two or three years back for the convenience of entering the boxes, it being found that two chairs were sufficient to block up the regular entrance, which is pointed out by the wide adjoining door. The sixth entrance is a private door appointed for chairs only, close to which, on the other side of the projection, may be seen the upper part of a passage to the boxes intended for the convenience of carriages coming by way of St James's Street. From the paved court you descend a few steps into another court in which this door is situated.

GEORGIAN PLAYHOUSES OUTSIDE LONDON
Richmond (Surrey)

The Richmond plan [see **244a**] shows a pioneering attempt to fit a fan-shaped auditorium into an oblong space, with the clear aim of improving the sightlines for patrons in the side boxes. The stage plan also shows the relative position of wings and grooves and the vista arch at the rear.

A drawing of the theatre completed just before its demolition in 1884 gives a clear indication of the disposition of stage doors, stage boxes and the elegantly shaped proscenium opening [see **244b**]. (The same architectural idiom may be seen in Bristol's King Street theatre, which opened in the following year [see **247**].) Since it was expected to cater for a largely upper-class audience [see **245**], there was originally no upper gallery.

244a Ground-plan of the new theatre at Richmond, Surrey, 1765
Theatre Museum

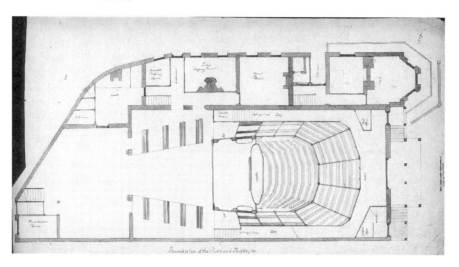

244b The stage of the new theatre at Richmond, Surrey, viewed from the auditorium
Frederick Bingham: *A celebrated old playhouse: the history of Richmond Theatre from 1765 to 1884* (Richmond: Henry Vickers, 1886), p. 15

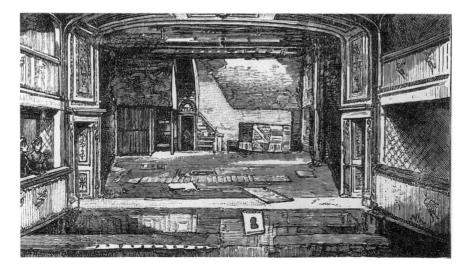

245   The new theatre on Richmond Green, Surrey: opened 15 June 1765

The Universal Museum and Complete Magazine, August 1765, pp. 391–2

A new theatre having been opened at Richmond during the course of this summer, of which the public have received very little, if any, satisfactory account, we thought it would not be an unentertaining circumstance to our readers to present them with a cursory history of this additional temple to the muses. [. . .]

The old theatre at the bottom of the hill was in a most tottering situation and was both too crazy and too inconvenient to be repaired with any prospect of success. The nobility and gentry had neglected it for a long time, on account of these circumstances. And the actors, though many of them people of some merit, gradually dwindled into insignificance and disesteem from the impossibility they lay under of representing those pieces in which they were most capital and in which the public had always found the greatest share of entertainment.

Mr Love,[1] seeing to what the utter disregard of the old house had been owing, immediately conceived a design of erecting a new one. With this in view he looked out for a convenient spot of ground and, meeting with a piece upon the Green, he purchased it and went to work. Mr Sanderson, the machinist of Drury Lane Theatre, drew the plan; and in a few months, what the builders call the shell was entirely completed. In the prosecution of this undertaking every imperfection in either of our royal houses was studiously avoided and every advantage most sedulously retained. In the embellishment, simplicity and elegance alone had the direction. And it may be said with the greatest justice that, for the size, it is by much the best constructed theatre in the British dominions. The boxes form a kind of crescent, which renders them remarkably commodious, because by this means they all have nearly a front view of the stage. They are lined with a crimson worsted damask. And the lobby is to the full as spacious for the entrance of the company as either of the lobbies at Covent Garden or Drury Lane. There is but one gallery. This, however, turns out not a little to the advantage of the audience, as it totally prevents the necessity of having pillars, which so frequently obstruct the view and hinder a spectator from enjoying many of the most interesting incidents of a play. The pit, if anything, is too small for the rest of the house; but perhaps it may have been made so on purpose, as the principal part of the spectators usually occupy the boxes and the gallery, there being but few of what may be called the middling station in the neighbourhood. The smallness of the pit has given Mr Love an opportunity for allowing a handsome space for an orchestra, which he has judiciously taken care to fill with a very good band of music. One particular improvement we cannot upon this occasion avoid to mention, which is that the gingerbread stuccoing, which we see round the boxes at the royal theatres, is totally omitted. All the panels being painted of a dark colour, which gives the stage an additional degree of light when the curtain is drawn up and makes everything on it appear with a double advantage. As to the scenes, they are the workmanship of the ingenious Mr French, the scene painter of Drury Lane house; and to the connoisseurs in that science a farther recommendation is utterly unnecessary.

[1] James Love, actor from Drury Lane, formerly manager in Edinburgh.

GEORGIAN PLAYHOUSES OUTSIDE LONDON
Bristol

The general disposition of stage and auditorium at Bristol bears some similarity to that of Richmond [*see* 246], as one might expect, since Sanderson was involved in the planning of both playhouses. In addition, a vista arch, similar to that of Richmond, survived until recently at Bristol [*see* 247]. At Bristol there was also a novel arrangement for naming boxes at the King Street theatre after famous playwrights [*see* 248a]: a notion that pleased both patrons and critics [*see* 248b]. (In Bath, before the enlargement of 1775, the boxes were named after early English kings.)[1]

[1] See Box Plan for 5 January 1775 in Bath Reference Library.

246   The stage and auditorium of the Theatre Royal, King Street, Bristol
Theatre Collection, University of Bristol

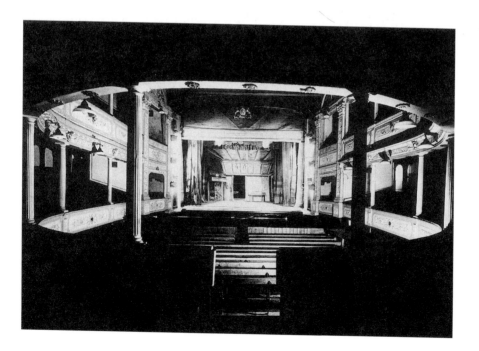

247   **The vista arch at the rear of the stage in Bristol's King Street Theatre: demolished in 1972**
Theatre Collection, University of Bristol

248a   Plan of the lower dress boxes and upper side boxes named after famous playwrights at Bristol's King Street Theatre
Theatre Collection, University of Bristol

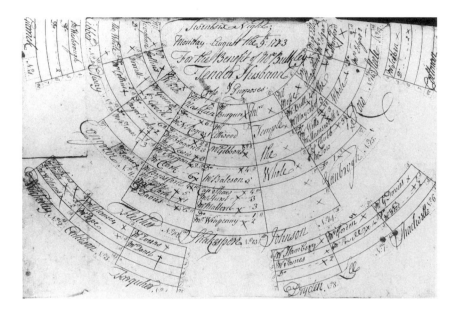

248b   The King Street Theatre Bristol, 1766
Richard Jenkins: *Memoirs of the Bristol stage* (Bristol: published by the author and W.H. Somerton, 1826), pp. 71–4

The architect of the theatre was Mr James Paty; the builder Mr Gilbert Davis, house carpenter; the mason, Mr Foote; and the smith, Mr Franklyn, father of Mr John Franklyn; all of this city. The house was painted by Mr Michael Edkins, father of the present artist of that name, who executed the same under Mr Simmons, city painter. The front panels of the boxes were painted in green and gold. The crimson curtains over the balconies and the flock paper with which the back part of the boxes was fitted up were furnished by Mr Marmaduke Cowles, upholder [*sic*], who kept his warehouse on St Augustin's parade. The first scenes displayed at this theatre were executed by Mr John French, a pupil of Loutherbourg, in a very masterly style.

I will now enter upon a description of the new theatre.

The internal part was formed semi-circular, and the whole decorated with carving, painting and gilding, executed with much taste.

In order to distinguish the several lower or dress boxes, which are nine in number, the names of the following dramatic poets were placed over the box doors in gilt letters, viz. that of SHAKESPEARE over the centre box; on the right-hand of the centre were the names of JONSON, VANBRUGH, ROWE and STEELE; and on the left those of FLETCHER, CONGREVE, OTWAY and CIBBER. Over the doors of the eight upper side boxes appeared the names of GARRICK, WYCHERLEY, ADDISON, FARQUHAR, DRYDEN, LEE, SHADWELL and COLMAN.

This mode of designating the boxes was so very convenient with respect to securing places that I wonder much it had not been continued.

There were not, when the theatre was first opened nor for many years afterwards, any upper front boxes. Those we have at this time then constituted the gallery. Neither was there a boudoir, or receiving room, for the company who preferred going to the play at half price. The ladies and gentlemen were therefore under the necessity of cooling their heels on the stone floor of a long passage leading to the house until the end of the third act. And it being impossible to know the precise time when such act would terminate, as it varied with the different plays which were performed, many persons impatient at being kept sometimes for an hour on their legs in the cold went home disappointed of their expected amusement rather than remain any longer waiting for admission.

This theatre contains as follows:–

The boxes	750	persons		£150	0	0
Pit	320	persons		40	0	0
Gallery	530	persons		39	15	0
Total	1600	persons	Amounting to	£229	15	0

The first cost of the theatre was, I am informed, upwards of £5000 [. . .]. [The] property is vested in five trustees for the proprietors, the whole number of shares being forty-eight. These shares entitle the holders to silver tickets of free admission to every kind of performance at the theatre.

GEORGIAN PLAYHOUSES OUTSIDE LONDON
Edinburgh

The proposals for building a new theatre in Edinburgh in 1768 offer an interesting example of how wealthy investors were encouraged to support the building of a new theatre away from London [see 249]. Shareholders might expect a combination of interest and free access to all performances; or they might choose to take a higher rate of interest without any free access to the theatre. Those who simply wished to donate a generous sum of money to the enterprise might have their names inscribed on a large plaque in the box-office lobby.[1]

It was claimed that the new Edinburgh playhouse would be built nearly on the model of that in Bristol, but the ground-plan seems more markedly rectangular than was the case in Bristol [see 250].

[1] Another method of financing the building of a playhouse was the 'Tontine' system, a gamble in which shares held descended on death to the surviving shareholders: the longest living could become sole owner. In 1780 the Worcester Theatre was erected by this method. See, for instance, William Douglas MS, vol. 1, p. 16.

249   Proposals for building a new Theatre Royal in Edinburgh 1768
Edinburgh Reference Library

Edinburgh, March 1st 1768

Proposals for building a new Theatre Royal in the New Streets of Edinburgh, the ground being feued by Mr Ross behind the orphan hospital to the east side of the New Bridge.

A Theatre Royal, to the honour of this city, is now established by legal authority, favoured by our most gracious sovereign's protection. A theatre properly conducted redounds to the honour and profit of every metropolis. The state of arts and literature in any kingdom, and the taste of the people, are best known by the amusements they follow: those of the theatre are the most rational in which the human mind can delight. [. . .]

A well regulated theatre will not only be an inducement to students to come to Edinburgh but of infinite utility to those in particular who are to speak in public and to the people in general as a standard of the English language.

It is needless to point out the absolute necessity of building a new theatre. Without such a building, the favour of the legislature and royal grant would be defeated, and the people deprived of an amusement they seem to taste and be willing to encourage.

Mr Ross therefore proposes to raise two thousand, five hundred pounds by twenty-five shares at one hundred pounds a share. For which subscribers shall receive three pounds per cent, paid every half year, and free access at all performances to any part of the house (except behind the scenes which will never be open for any access but to the performers). Those who choose five per cent, without the freedom, shall have it and the interest paid half yearly. The patentee to have it in his power, upon giving six months' notice, to pay off each subscriber; and each subscriber to have a right to demand his or her money upon giving nine months' notice.

The house is to be built one hundred feet long and fifty feet broad, nearly on the model of that lately built at Bristol, which has been justly admired by all those who have seen it.

It is computed that to furnish new scenes, and a new and proper wardrobe and other necessary decorations, will cost at least fifteen hundred pounds more than the two thousand, five hundred: which sum Mr Ross will lay out. And the whole building, etc. shall be mortgaged as a security to pay the interest half yearly.

A proper deed shall be drawn and approved by council as a solid heretable security, each share transferable as stock in London: the freedom of the house to go with the property, besides three pounds per cent, for his or her money while possessed of a share. If any of the nobility, gentry, or other lovers of the stage will favour the undertaking with a voluntary subscription by way of gift, from five guineas to any sum they please, such sum will be thankfully received by Mr Ross, the patentee, and inscribed on a large tablet to be placed in the box lobby, to perpetuate their names and bounty. The theatre will be insured for £4000 sterling.

The value of money being greatly decreased and labour and every article increased almost double, it will be impossible to procure good performers in each department, should the tickets remain at the low prices which are now paid, being just the same as they were sixty years ago when half a crown was of equal value as five shillings now. It is therefore proposed to make the boxes four shillings, the pit three shillings, the first gallery two shillings, and the upper gallery one shilling. These are the prices paid at the new theatre lately built at Cork, the second city in Ireland: and the same prices are paid at the village of Richmond, near London. And indeed, without these prices, it would be in vain to expect a decent stage, as men and women of merit expect salaries considerably larger than they were formerly.

For these prices this stage shall vie with those of London or Dublin. There shall be five capital men actors; one good man singer; one second ditto; three capital women actresses; two capital women singers; one capital man dancer; and one woman ditto; the rest as good as can be had. The orchestra shall be conducted with a good first fiddle as a leader; a harpsichord; and the rest of the band persons of merit.

All the singing pieces shall be performed in a manner hitherto not seen in Edinburgh. And the whole stage, scenes, dresses, machinery, etc., put and conducted on the most elegant footing the polite and sensible in the kingdom can expect.

Mr Ross proposes to go early in the spring to London to make engagements with the first performers to be had; and to induce them, no pains or expense will be spared.

Subscriptions will be taken in by Messrs Drummond and Co, Charing Cross, London; by Messrs Gibson and Balfour, bankers in Edinburgh; and by Mr Ross at his house in Cooper's Land, Canongate.

250   Ground-plan of the proposed Theatre Royal Edinburgh, 1768 (see facing page)
Edinburgh Reference Library

GEORGIAN PLAYHOUSES OUTSIDE LONDON
Norwich

Wilkins's survey of the Norwich playhouse in 1799 before taking it over is both an amusing account of design problems and a significant indication of the increasing expectations of audiences [see **251**]. These in turn may well reflect the changing social composition of late eighteenth-century audiences. The narrow entrance in the original building, to which he refers in his survey, is clearly visible in a drawing of the exterior [see **252**].

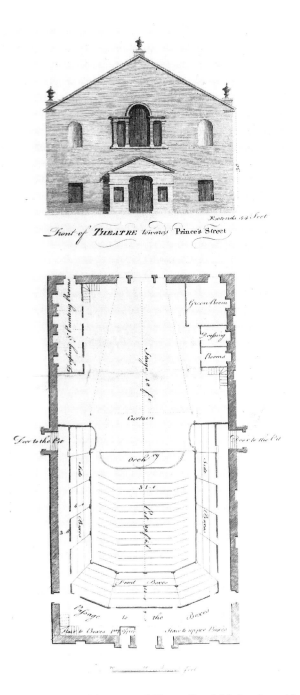

250 Ground-plan of the proposed Theatre Royal Edinburgh, 1768

251   The Theatre Royal Norwich at the end of the eighteenth century

William Wilkins's survey of 1799, reproduced in Dorothy H. Eshleman: *The committee books of the Theatre Royal Norwich, 1768–1825* (London: STR, 1970), appendix B, pp. 152–4

The public [. . .] have, even in the hardest times, evinced their fondness for theatrical exhibitions. Although it is pretty notorious that their comforts (in all the subsequent alterations that have been made in the house) have been the least consulted. In the audience part, the boxes that were separately enclosed have been opened and in no other respect has there been an alteration or improvement made but when it served to give greater room for filling and increasing the receipt. The entrances and avenues are so ill contrived that only one person can approach the lobby; a lady must be separated from the arm of her protector both on entering and leaving the lobby. The audience from the boxes, green boxes and pit are here huddled together and, on leaving the house, they must pass singly to the entrance where they are obliged to run the gauntlet through coachmen, footmen and porters; and if a carriage is not in readiness at the door, it is almost impossible to return 'till the house is nearly emptied. To avoid this bustle and extreme inconvenience, is it not common to see a great part of the boxes deserted before the end of the farce? It is really otherwise impossible that ladies can reach their carriages without danger of spoiling their dresses and being squeezed perhaps between doorkeepers, porters and prostitutes, who are forcing their way without regard to beauty or dress. With respect to the gallery, one of its approaches being stopped and the remaining outlet very narrow, makes it very long in emptying on full nights. And there is in consequence a dread which deters many people from entering the house. Should there be an alarm of fire, this outlet would be choked in a few minutes and the destruction of numbers would be the consequence.[1]

An alteration has been made in front of the stage, and the orchestra, which was before too cramped for the performers, is now become almost intolerable; there is so little room for the violincello players that they are obliged to be raised so high as to intercept the sight of numbers in the pit. The object obtained by this incautious alteration gives an additional seat or two in the pit but as they are of necessity on the same level with the seat behind, it is, with the additional standing room obtained at each end of the orchestra, the constant cause of disturbance on full nights [. . .].

The lobby is so managed that in it is a constant (crowd) of doorkeepers, cheque takers and prostitutes, a frequent interruption to the entertainments of the evening. A number of other inconveniences might also be mentioned, such as the small rise of the seats in the boxes and pit, the want of room for the knees in sitting, etc. The audience part of the theatre is become nearly a scene of darkness and more so in the last eight or nine years.

I am now become a candidate for a lease. Before I offer my terms, I shall premise my ideas of the improvements I think necessary and which, if I am successful, I not only premise but I am ready to engage for putting into immediate execution after the expiration of the present lease.

Viz.: I propose gutting the whole of the audience part; making a complete orchestra in length equal to the whole width of the pit; making the plan of the boxes a perfect semi-circle; giving the seats so much width and rising the floors so as to give the beholder ease and comfort; making the ingress and egress commodious; and to this, as the access to the pit. I propose by other passages that the entrances shall be quite as easy and perhaps even less interrupted than the approach to the Assembly Rooms. The approach to the pit I propose under the box lobby with a passage to run at the whole back of the pit so that persons, without running up and down and across the lobby as at present, shall not by any means interfere with the approach to the boxes. They shall also have the opportunity of quitting the house by two outlets. The staircase to the gallery shall be broad and more commodious and shall not interfere with either of the other approaches and the gallery shall be accessible to two inlets.

I presume it is unnecessary I should explain the effect on the audience part of the house by my improvements. It shall be so lighted that company in the back seats of the boxes shall appear equally splendid with those on the front seats; and the chandeliers shall be, as they were before the last lease was granted, of glass. The outside of the house shall yield up its barn-like appearance and shall assume that of a public building.

With respect to the stage part of the house, I am equally desirous of improving it. At present, I confess myself by no means prepared to suggest the whole of the improvements necessary to be done there although I am aware of many that must indispensably be made. The machinery to the dropping scenes, I am informed, is dangerous. The furnishing of new scenes and wings too are matters which should keep pace with the improvements in the front of the house and they shall be done in the best style. It will not I hope be presuming too much on your time to observe that, since the first erection of the house, the splendour of this part of the entertainments has been gradually decreasing until, it may be said, there is not a scene that is worth little more than the canvas. [. . .]

The roof and the stage are in bad plight, something serious must be done with them. It is incumbent of course on the landlord to deliver the premises wind and water-proof to his incoming tenant. And I flatter myself that the liberal proposals I make will not only entitle me to the preference of the proprietors but also to their patronage and protection. [. . .]

I estimate the improvements to be made at the sum of a thousand pounds, which I propose taking on myself. (Or, if the proprietors will expend that sum on the improvements and plans I will suggest, I will allow them £150 per ann.) I will give them a rental clear of six hundred pounds per ann. – equal to twenty pounds a year on each share. And as at a former meeting, the proprietors in consideration of all the necessities of Mrs Barrett, whose husband it must be admitted was the first who stamped any value whatever on the shares of the theatre (and in consideration also of her father's having been a very respectable and worthy magistrate of this city), were pleased to grant her an annuity of fifty pounds; in addition to the rental I have proposed, I will also continue the same annuity, making together a total rental of eight hundred pounds per annum. I propose taking the above on lease for seven or fourteen years as the proprietors may please to determine. William Wilkins.

[1] Fire in playhouses lit and heated by open flame was a constant hazard, and panic consequent on the raising of alarms of fire (not always justified) was another. Perhaps the most spectacular fire recorded in London during this period was that in 1789 which caused the rebuilding of the King's Theatre. But major fires followed at Covent Garden in 1808 and Drury Lane in 1809, fortunately with little loss of life since they occurred at night, but with almost total destruction of property and irreplaceable manuscripts and records. There were provincial examples too, as well as the rather more unexpected destruction of much of the scenery and properties of the Bath Company on Salisbury Plain, while they were on tour in 1757, due to the overheating of wagon wheels. The cost of damage on this occasion was estimated at over £2000, a considerable amount then [See Hare (1958), pp. 48–9].

252   The exterior of the Theatre Royal Norwich, built in 1758
J.A. Mitchley, Private Collection

GEORGIAN PLAYHOUSES OUTSIDE LONDON
Manchester

A foreign visitor to Manchester, C.G. Küttner, commented favourably on the way the theatre seemed designed to avoid the crushes and the mixing of the social classes that Wilkins deplored in Norwich [see 253]. A view of the exterior shows the separate entrances to which he refers [see 254].

253   The Theatre Royal Manchester (1775) as seen by a German visitor in 1783–4

C.G. Küttner: *Beiträge zur Kenntniss vorzüglich des Innern von England und seiner Einwohner* (Leipzig, 1791–6). Translated and quoted in J.L. Hodgkinson and R. Pogson: *The early Manchester theatre* (London: Anthony Blond for the Society for Theatre Research, 1960), pp. 107–8

The local theatre is small and hardly bigger than the former wooden one at Leipzig, but graceful, warm and comfortable; and the scenes, curtains and effect machines are very good indeed. The proscenium consists of six Corinthian pillars and above it is written: *spectas ut tu spectaberis*. In spite of its size, the house has three different entrances, none of which are in connection with the others. It is incomprehensible to me that when the Leipzig theatre was being planned no-one thought of the difficulties and the dangers which are a necessary consequence of one general entrance when all the spectators from different seats must pile up on each other. In all the larger theatres I know, each section has its own entrance and one can only get from one part to another by going out of the theatre and entering again from the street. [. . .]

254   The Theatre Royal Manchester

Winston (1805), plate 13

THEATRES IN PRIVATE HOUSES

The various theatres in private houses of course avoided this problem [*see* **255** and **256**]. They were built primarily for social purposes as examples of conspicuous consumption. Important instances were Wargrave, Richmond House, Blenheim, Brandenburgh House, Seaton Delaval, Wynnstay. The performers were usually a mixture of ladies and gentlemen of society and professional players engaged for the occasion, some of considerable eminence, e.g. Palmer, Bannister, Munden, Mrs Goodall *et al.* Macklin coached Sir Francis Delaval's players when they presented *Othello* at Drury Lane in 1751.[1]

[1] See Rosenfeld (1978) and Price (1948), chapter 11.

255   Lord Barrymore's private theatre at Wargrave

Anthony Pasquin (pseud. of John Williams): *The life of the late Earl of Barrymore, including a history of the Wargrave theatricals* (London: H.D. Symonds, 1793), pp. 14–16 and 23–6

The theatricals at Wargrave, though eventually so brilliant, commenced but humbly. The first performance there was Garrick's farce of *Miss in her Teens* in which Lord Barrymore enacted Flash [. . .]. This juvenile attempt was made when the eldest of the dramatis personae was under seventeen; the other characters were sustained by the most intelligent young men of the village. To this Thespian struggle, only the tradesmen and the farmers and their wives were invited, as the exhibition was in a barn and the commodiousness of the auditory not very remarkable. Eighteen months after this scenic endeavour, Lord Barrymore employed Mr Cox, late carpenter to Covent Garden Theatre, to erect the late noble and matchless structure, which was the admiration of all who viewed it. The mechanism of the traps for pantomime could not be exceeded by art. This superb building was pulled down in the summer of 1792 and the materials sold by auction. [. . .] Adjoining to the theatre was a lofty and spacious saloon, to which the company retired for refreshment between the acts and at the conclusion of the performances. From a recess in the centre of this building, six men-servants, dressed in scarlet and gold, delivered chocolate, coffee, tea, sweetmeats, orgeat, lemonade, etc. to all who required such a pleasant allay for a half-formed appetite. Over the niche of the recess, the family arms of the Barrys were emblazoned in full order. [. . .]

[Lord Barrymore] carried his passion for the drama to the very threshold of indiscretion and was literally a common protector to the stage in general. He frequently performed himself, and very ably, in such characters as Scrub, Hob, Bobadil and Gregory Gubbins. His playhouse at Wargrave, which he was persuaded to have pulled down last summer, had cost him upwards of sixty thousand pounds. It was universally allowed to be the most splendid private theatre in the kingdom! His dramatic establishment was proverbially superb and is supposed to have been the cause of several hundred thousand pounds having been expended in the vicinity of that temple of enchantment! [. . .]

256   Lord Barrymore's theatre at Wargrave

General Magazine and impartial review (April, 1793)

STROLLERS AND THEIR IMPROVISED PLAYHOUSES

Throughout the eighteenth century, temporary stages were hastily erected in town halls, inns, assembly rooms, barns or fairground booths by the poorer or less well established touring companies. Many of the established circuits, with their purpose-built playhouses, evolved from the earlier activities of such strolling players. It is interesting to note what they considered essential: a basic sense of illusion, created through improvised scenery, costume and lighting; and a forceful acting style to transport their audiences into an imaginary world. It is, however, worth bearing in mind, when reading any contemporary account of such work or viewing contemporary prints, that writers and artists alike were often more concerned to make the best of what they saw as a good story rather than give a descriptively accurate account.

257   'Jackson's Theatre' at the Black Bull, Farnham, c. 1772

John Bernard: *Retrospections of the stage* (London: Colburn and Bentley, 1830), pp. 9–14

[...] I was casually informed that a dramatic wanderer (well known in the west of England), Manager Jackson by name, had pitched his tent; and to the Red Cow or the Black Bull, or some other agricultural beast, I bent my steps. I soon discovered him in the village by perceiving a flag flying from the upper windows of an inn on which was inscribed the words 'Jackson's Theatre' and which, I afterwards learnt, performed the double office of an advertisement by day and the triumphal banner of a king or hero at night.

On the steps of the door I encountered the old man, a silver-haired Adam Winterton; and well I remember the awe and veneration with which I approached him. [. . .] I expressed my wishes in a very few words and he, as briefly, his willingness to gratify them. I wanted to play George Barnwell and promised I would fill his house by way of remuneration. He requested me to name the night and first rehearsal, then desired to show me over his theatre and introduce me to his company.

[. . .] He had engaged the largest room at the said Black Bull; suspended a collection of green tatters along its middle for a curtain; erected a pair of paper screens right-hand and left for wings; arranged four candles in front of said wings to divide the stage from the orchestra (the fiddlers' chairs being the legitimate division of the orchestra from the pit); and with all the spare benches of the inn to form boxes and a hoop suspended from the ceiling (perforated with a dozen nails to receive as many tallow candles) to suggest the idea of a chandelier; he had constructed and embellished what he denominated a theatre! The scenery consisted of two drops, simply and comprehensively divisible into the inside of a house and the outside of a house. The former (which was an original of about the same date as the manager) was a bona fide representation at bottom of a kitchen, with all the culinary implements arranged about it. But by the simple introduction of two chairs and a table, this was constituted a gentleman's parlour; and in the further presence of a crimson-cushioned, yellow-legged elbow chair, with a banner behind and a stool in front, was elevated into a royal hall of audience! This was clever stage managing. The other drop (which I have termed outside of a house) was somewhat younger than its companion and very ingeniously presented on its surface two houses peeping in at the sides, a hill, a wood, a stream, a bridge, and a distant plain. So that, from the general indistinctness of the whole, the eye of the spectator might single out a particular feature and agreeably to the locality of the scene that was passing, imagine himself in a street, a wood, by a stream, etc. alternately. This was also a very clever contrivance. The manager at least disencumbered himself of four scenes by it and, with the chair and table manoeuvring, did without two. I cannot remember now the condition of his wardrobe, but I have some general impression of its consistency with the above [. . .]

258   A theatric booth at Bartholomew Fair, Smithfield

C.A.G. Goede, translated by T. Horne: *Memorials of nature and art, collected on a journey in Great Britain during the years 1802 and 1803*, vol. 2 (London: J. Mawman, 1808), pp. 150–2

At length we have reached the theatre. How significantly are the various emotions of surprise, curiosity and admiration depicted upon the countenances of the spectators! This booth is the most spacious and magnificent of all. The fore-walls are hung with a tapestry of green cloth and bordered with gold fringe. Every side is illuminated with a row of lamps. At the upper extremity, an inscription in large gilt capitals announces that this is another Drury in miniature, just arrived from the North, in order to provide for the amusement of the respectable audience. A winding gallery encompasses the middle part of the building. Here the actors

appear, all bespangled with gold and silver and costly gems, and parade alternately in picturesque groups before the eyes of the multitude. Now a young damsel
steps forth, trailing a long shining robe of silver brocade. With dignified aspect, and
with measured steps, she advances along the gallery and darts a few side-long
glances of conscious dignity at the astonished populace. The whole assembly gazes
at her with wonder. Low whispers run through the busy crowds, 'That is the
princess!' The door of the gallery is again thrown open and a young man sallies
forth in a rich suit of embroidery and emblazoned with the order of the garter. A
negro and several spruce domestics are in attendance. With a look of divine
complacency the princess takes his hand. Thrice happy mortal! Doubtless he is the
prince, to whom this blooming bride is betrothed. The spectators are strangely
prepossessed with the idea that the actors are going to treat them with a spectacle
of high life; and the rabble make a furious assault upon the theatre, full of wistful
curiosity to learn the arcana of the court. 'Shall we enter and survey this
exhibition?' said my friend to me in a low whisper. We did so, but we were
presently obliged to relinquish our design. The atmosphere was so thoroughly
tainted by the noxious exhalations of these plebeian customers that it was
absolutely a mystery to me how such a crowd of bystanders could remain for
hours together under its pestilential influence.

259 A temporary theatre built into a barn, 1788
Aquatint by J. Wright after W.R. Pyne. George 7811 (Print Room, BM)

260   Richardson's booth at Greenwich Fair
Watercolour by Rowlandson (Print Room, BM)

261   A country fair booth
Engraved by Thomas Tagg after Rowlandson (Print Room, BM)

10 Stage presentation

INTRODUCTION

The changes in stage presentation during the eighteenth century are a study in evolution: the solution of one problem reveals another not previously thought of, which in turn requires the provision of appropriate new machinery. With the exception of opera and pantomime, the emphasis in the early eighteenth century was on the play, not the setting. Acting, especially in the comedies, was confined predominantly to the forestage, which meant that the scenic stage needed no more than comparatively dim lighting. In addition, stock scenery was generally thought adequate. However, after the removal of the audience from the stage area (along with a consequent reduction of the forestage in order to accommodate patrons who had been displaced from the stage), there was more need for actors to move into the scenic stage even in performances of comedies. The scenic stage now needed better lighting; this in turn showed up any obvious defects in the scenery (for instance, shadows thrown by directional light might clash with those painted on wings or shutters). With more flexible and controllable lighting, more transformations and special effects could be achieved; these, in turn, provoked the need for more machinery to control the movement of wings, shutters and borders.

Until the middle of the eighteenth century, scenery was still shifted manually using grooves or rollers. The scene shifting was synchronised (just as the music was cued) by the prompter's whistle and bell [see **147**]. By the late eighteenth century, new machinery for scene shifting made synchronisation much easier and facilitated more complex combinations. The demands of spectacle in opera and the variety of transformation scenes in pantomime meant that a growing body of knowledge was developed during the century as to what might be achieved with transparencies, free-standing, movable pieces, traps, flying machines and many other devices. Along with the ability to provide more complex settings went a shift of interest from the man-made to the natural, from architecture to nature (analogous to the change of interest from formal to landscape gardening).[1] Later, with the beginnings of Romanticism, a desire for the picturesque, the sublime, the exotic or the romantic past fed the end-of-century interest in antiquarian scenery and costume.

The need for new lighting techniques was felt all over Europe by the late eighteenth century.[2] Garrick visited Paris in 1763, bringing back with him new ideas that involved the abandoning of stage chandeliers, replacing them instead with concealed candles backed by reflectors in footlights and scene ladders (hidden from view behind the wings). The latter were easily controlled and manipulated, making much more effective transparencies

307

possible. Experiments were made with coloured reflective screens and oiled-silk, semi-transparent filters; in addition, synchronising machinery was installed. By 1791, for example, all the lighting posts in the King's Theatre could be turned by one mechanism.[3] With the new techniques came the appointment of artists like de Loutherbourg and J.I. Richards to design for them.

With respect to costume, most comedies were played in modern dress, provided haphazardly by the players themselves or out of stock. Tragic costumes were chosen, in the early years of the century, on much the same basis. There was little accurate knowledge of historical or exotic costume, which meant that, in some cases, individual choice, in others, long-standing stage tradition were the arbiters. There were traditional ways of dressing Greek or Roman, Spanish, Persian or Oriental figures; there were traditional costumes for some characters, like Falstaff or Hamlet; there were also traditional details of costuming involving certain figures, as, for instance, the business of the grave-diggers' waistcoats in *Hamlet*. Only for spectacular productions might efforts be made to provide costumes in uniform style, but this procedure became more widespread from the 1760s,[4] as did advertisements announcing the company, 'to be dressed in old English habits' or 'the olde English taste'.

Macklin's costumes for Shylock and Macbeth [*see* **304** and **281b**] shocked some spectators and were laughed at by others, but they duly caught on and the idea was copied. Gradually more attention was paid to overall production planning and the control and conduct of rehearsals,[5] making possible by the end of the century J.P. Kemble's antiquarianism and the forays into historical accuracy of William Capon. But these developments in turn were to be hampered by the inadequacy of antiquarian and historical knowledge and bedevilled by the Romantic passion for the exotic rather than the realistic.

[1] This was a social and intellectual movement in society, not purely an artistic fashion. See Rosenfeld (1981), chapter 4.
[2] See Bergman (1977), p. 180.
[3] See Rosenfeld (1981), p. 61.
[4] See Nicoll (1980), chapter 6.
[5] *Ibid.*, pp. 170–3.

STAGE CONDITIONS

In the 1740s, some of the inherited stage conditions and traditions undoubtedly hindered the use and development of elaborate scenic settings. The admittance of members of the audience onto the stage (especially on benefit nights) ruined any attempt at verisimilitude [*see* **262** and **263**],[1] and in such circumstances (when also the scenic area of the stage may not have been very adequately lit) there was little incentive to provide much more than stock scenery. With a domestic interior, a town exterior, a landscape, woodland or park, and a castle background, most plays could be covered. Where special efforts were made to provide new scenery for productions, there were usually attempts to ban the audience temporarily from the stage. After the popularity of the piece had waned, the new scenes would be added to the stock or put in store for repainting in due course [*see* **271** and **273**]. The development of the scenic stage had, of course, made life much more difficult for the smaller travelling companies. For them, one multiple backcloth or pair of shutters, along with a couple of pillared wings or screens, might have to do permanent duty.

There were other distracting practices. The spreading of a tragic carpet on the stage when a heroine was about to perform a dying fall might have preserved her costume from damage but it destroyed any possibility of empathy [*see* **264**]. Equally, the presence on the forestage of two soldiers standing guard to preserve order throughout the performance was hardly likely to foster a sense of dramatic illusion [*see* **265** and **314**].[2] Garrick's success in banishing the audience from the stage in 1762 and suppressing the amphitheatre [*see* **267**] began the process of reformation. The grenadiers were abandoned at some point in the sixties. In the same decade, the introduction of more sophisticated lighting techniques, helped to increase the possibility of scenic illusion [*see* **288** and **289**].

[1] See also Hogarth's painting of *The Beggar's Opera* [**98**].
[2] See Lawrence (1935), chapter 24 – 'stage sentinels'.

262   Audiences on the stage in 1741
Isaac Reed: *Notitia Dramatica*, vol. 2, 1734–85, f. 50 (BL Add.MSS 25,391)[1]

Pit and boxes laid together at 4 *s*, gallery 1 *s* 6 *d*. [. . .] Note. The stage will be commodiously built after the manner of an amphitheatre, and servants will be allowed to keep places in it who are desired to be there by three o'clock.

[1] An announcement for Garrick's benefit 'at the late theatre in Goodman's Fields, 2 December 1741'. He was due to play Lothario in *The Fair Penitent* for the first time.

263   Quin suffers from the inhibiting effect of the audience on stage at his last performance in 1753
Tate Wilkinson: *Memoirs of his own life* by *Tate Wilkinson, patentee of the Theatres Royal, York and Hull*, vol. 3 (Dublin edition, 1791), pp. 163–5

I can well remember, when I was thirteen years of age, viewing Mr Quin on Monday, March 19, 1753, for the benefit of Mr Ryan, play the character of Falstaff [*Henry IV* at Covent Garden]. He was thus announced in the play bill: 'The part of Falstaff will be performed by Mr Quin', which was his last night of performing. The stage was at 5 *s*; pit and boxes all joined together at 5 *s*. There was only one entrance on each side the stage, which was always particularly crowded. First, they sported their own figures to gratify self consequence and impede and interfere with the performers who had to come on and go off the stage. Affronting the audience was another darling delight; particularly, offending the galleries and thereby incurring the displeasure of the gods who showed their resentment by dispersing golden showers of oranges and half-eaten pippins; to the infinite terror of the ladies of fashion seated in the pit on such public nights, where they were so closely wedged as to preclude all possibility of securing a retreat or obtaining relief till the *finale*, when they all moved from their situation by general consent.

The stage spectators were not content with piling on raised seats till their heads reached the theatrical cloudings (which seats were closed in with dirty, worn-out scenery, to enclose the painted round from the first wing [*sic*], the main entrance being up steps from the middle of the back scene): but when that amphitheatre was filled, there would be a group of ill-dressed lads and persons sitting on the stage in front, three or four rows deep, otherwise those who sat behind could not have seen and a riot would have ensued. So in fact, a performer on a popular night could not step his foot with safety, lest he either should thereby hurt or offend or be thrown down amongst scores of idle, tipsy apprentices [. . .].

Mr Quin, aged sixty-five, with the heavy dress of Falstaff (notwithstanding the impatience of the audience to see their old acquaintance) was several minutes before he could pass through the numbers that wedged and hemmed him in, he was so cruelly encompassed around. What must the reader suppose at so barbarous and general a custom being not only yielded to but approved by the performers [. . .].

264   Goldsmith's advice on the tragic carpet and other scenic distractions

Oliver Goldsmith: 'Remarks on our theatres' in *The Bee*, no. 1 (October 1759). Reprinted in Masson (ed.): *Miscellaneous works* (London: Macmillan, 1907), pp. 355–7

The magnificence of our theatres is far superior to any others in Europe where plays only are acted. The great care our performers take in painting for a part, their exactness in all the minutiae of dress and other little scenical proprieties, have been taken notice of by Ricoboni, a gentleman of Italy who travelled Europe with no other design but to remark upon the stage. But there are several improprieties still continued or lately come into fashion. As, for instance, spreading a carpet punctually at the beginning of the death scene, in order to prevent our actors from spoiling their clothes. This immediately apprises us of the tragedy to follow; for laying the cloth is not a more sure indication of dinner than laying the carpet of bloody work at Drury Lane. Our little pages also with unmeaning faces that bear up the train of a weeping princess and our awkward lords in waiting take off much from her distress. Mutes of every kind divide our attention and lessen our sensibility, but here it is entirely ridiculous, as we see them seriously employed in doing nothing. If we must have dirty-shirted guards upon the theatres, they should be taught to keep their eyes fixed on the actors and not roll them round upon the audience as if they were ogling the boxes. [. . .]

265   The stage sentry still in post in 1763

Dougald Macmillan: *Drury Lane calendar, 1747–1776* (Oxford: Clarendon Press, 1938), p. 99[1]

October 28 1763

Twelfth Night. The Witches. In the fourth Act, Mr O'Brien ran up to the sentry, when Olivia draws her sword, and frightened the poor soldier that he fell down flat upon his back to the great mirth of the audience. [Hopkins's Diary no. 10.]

¹ See *LS*, pt iv, p. 1016.

In contrast to Continental practice, scene designers and painters in Georgian England did not attract the same public attention as actors and writers. It was not, for instance, until the 1770s and 1780s that their names were printed on playbills. However, in the final decades of the eighteenth century, the growing popularity and complexity of spectacular settings ensured an increased awareness of the contribution made by the scene designer. O'Keeffe's description of the work of the scene designer [*see* 266] is based upon the practice established at the two patent theatres in the 1770s and 1780s, where design sketches produced by the scene designer were executed under his supervision by individual scene painters.¹

¹ See also Angelo (1828), p. 12.

266   The role of the scene designer

John O'Keeffe: *Recollections of his life*, vol. 2 (London: Colburn, 1826), p. 39

The mode of the theatre is this: a copy of the drama is put into the hands of the artist who is to plan the scenes (Richards, an R.A. highly distinguished, had the office at this time); he considers upon it, makes models in card paper and gives his orders to the painters. The author is often brought into the scene room to give his opinion on the progress of their work. The wardrobe keepers, having also their copy of the play, produce the dresses of each character to the author. After this, the several performers when dressed, before the curtain goes up on the first night, make their appearance before the author to obtain his approbation.

The new scene designers

With the advent, in the 1770s and 1780s, of a new generation of gifted scene designers, such as Philip de Loutherbourg at Drury Lane and John Inigo Richards at Covent Garden, some fundamental changes in design practice began to take place. De Loutherbourg experimented with asymmetrically designed flats and free-standing pieces for interior and exterior scenes, as may be seen in two scenic models that may have been intended for productions of *Robinson Crusoe* and *Omai* at Covent Garden [*see* 267a and b]. By the end of the century, the traditional interior setting, using wings and shutters painted in perspective, began to give way to other design alternatives. A solution attempted in the 1790s involved the use of laterally placed flats to suggest an interior setting [*see* 268]. This particular design solution may be seen as the direct forerunner of the nineteenth-century box set, while de Loutherbourg's asymmetrical designs clearly foreshadow the practice of the Romantic theatre.

267   Scenic models by de Loutherbourg for Covent Garden
Victoria and Albert Museum

(A) SEA COAST SCENE, POSSIBLY FOR *ROBINSON CRUSOE*, 1781[1]

(B) INTERIOR SCENE POSSIBLY FOR O'KEEFFE'S *OMAI*, 1785[2]

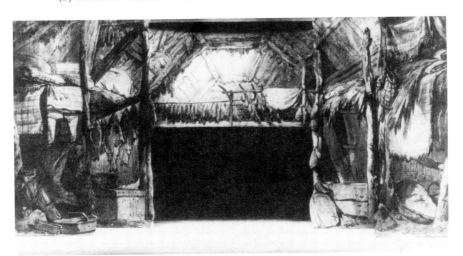

[1] Nicoll makes this ascription in *The Garrick Stage* (1980), pp. 138–9.
[2] Iain Mackintosh and Geoffrey Ashton make this ascription in the catalogue for the Arts Council exhibition *The Georgian playhouse* (1975), no. 287.

268   *The Three and the Deuce* at the Little Theatre in the Haymarket, 1795

Private Collection. Copy in Theatre Collection, University of Bristol. Reproduced in Rosenfeld (1973), p. 82

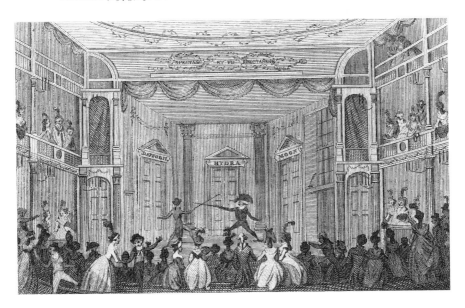

Scenic design in the provinces

Theatre in the provinces made valiant attempts to emulate the scenic achievements of the London theatres. An illustration of a perspective setting from the Sunderland Theatre in *c.* 1758 [*see* **269**] is reminiscent of Lediard's transparency work at the Little Theatre in the Haymarket in the 1730s [*see* **99**]. The illustration may well represent 'The Temple of Fame', the setting for *An Appeal to the Muses,* presented at the opening of the New Theatre in Sunderland on 16 November 1758, with Cawdell himself pleading the cause of culture in the north and receiving advice from the Muses of Tragedy [Mrs Hart] and Comedy [Mrs Hamilton].[1]

A number of advertisements and descriptions of plays and pantomimes make it clear that managements made a deliberate attempt to exploit scenic ideas that had found favour in London [*see* **270a**]. Obviously touring companies did not have at their disposal the same technical facilities as in the London theatres, but what they lacked in terms of technical equipment they made up for by ingeniously exploiting local colour [*see* **270b**].

[1] See J. Cawdell: *Miscellaneous poems* (Sunderland, 1785), pp. 137–50.

269   Trompe l'oeil perspective at the Sunderland Theatre, *c.* 1758

J. Cawdell: *The miscellaneous poems of J. Cawdell, comedian* (Sunderland: published for the author, 1785), frontispiece. Reproduced in Nicoll (1980), p. 73[1]

[1] Nicoll, in giving the date as 1785, is probably mistaking the date of publication for the date of production.

270   Spectacle in Derby in 1782

(A) *DRURY'S DERBY MERCURY*, 7 FEBRUARY 1782
[In the New Theatre, Bold Lane.[1] For a performance on 11 February of *Oriental Magic, or Harlequin Sorcerer*.]

The principal scenery consists of a new pavilion, the Bower of Fancy, with cupids waving a canopy of crimson and gold round the pavilion, under which Fancy is discovered asleep on a bed of roses, attended by an hermit and witch. A large cloud descends, then opens and discovers Harlequin dressed as a nabob, seated with an Eastern Magician in a flying chariot. When they get out of the cloud, it shuts up and ascends and discovers a new-cut wood, which separates and discovers a perspective north view of London from Highgate Hill. Also an entire new apothecary's shop made for that purpose, in which Harlequin will jump through a looking glass, which will instantly change to a skeleton; and finish[es] with a capital piece of machinery, representing a piece of water in motion, a waterfall and cascade of two sphinxes, spouting water out of their mouths into a basin, most beautifully reflecting in the stream. Besides other tricks and deceptions the same as in London. On account of the vast expense attending this entertainment, nothing under full price can possibly be taken.

[1] Built in 1773.

(B) *DRURY'S DERBY MERCURY*, 7 MARCH 1782
[For a performance on 7 March 1782 of *The Rape of Proserpine* or *Harlequin in the Peak of Derbyshire*.]

[. . .] Founded on a tradition that there existed a Genius of the Peak called Salmandore, who assisted the miners and endowed many of them with supernatural gifts as that of the hazel rod (by which mines were supposed to have been discovered) and the attendance of fairies, etc., [. . .] and including the birth of Harlequin in a shell which gradually breaks open, [. . .] the pantomime will finish with a most extensive prospect of one of the wonders of Derbyshire, being an exact representation of that most wonderful place called Castleton in the Peak, with a full view of that prodigious cave, called the Cavern of Castleton (one of the wonders). Likewise the huts that are built in it, inhabited by poor subterranean people who live by rope spinning and showing the inside of the cavern with lights, etc. A perspective view of the Shivering Mountain between Buxton and Castleton: the whole forming a most beautiful landscape of the adjacent country by daybreak, of the hills over the lead mines above Dovedale, Matlock and the High Tor. This vast rock's perpendicular height above the water is three hundred and fifty four feet. Painted by Mr Gamble of Derby. Concludes with a dance by miners and Derbyshire spinners. Nothing under full price.

Scene inventories

The volume of work accomplished in the Georgian theatre, with its swiftly changing repertoire of plays and afterpieces, meant that few productions had special scenery designed for them. With the exception of spectacular pantomimes and operas, most new productions made use of stock scenes that were refurbished from time to time. If new scenery was used, this was generally mentioned in advertisements and playbills and was often taken as sufficient reason to refuse admission at less than the full price [*see* **270**]. Subsequently, new scenery went into stock. There were often glaring discrepancies in stock scenes between wings, shutters and back flats. Nor did the costumes necessarily match the setting. In the well-known 'Fitzgiggo' engraving, for instance [*see* **285**], the singers in Dr Arne's opera *Artaxerxes* are shown wearing Persian or Eastern costumes within a general neo-classic setting. A further visual disparity may be seen within the set itself. While the wings are rounded classical columns, the shutter depicts an interior panelled wall.[1] An even more glaring discrepancy can be seen in an illustration showing the interior of the Orchard Street Theatre in Bath. The ghost scene from *Hamlet* is set against a rustic landscape shown on a back cloth, while the wings are formal neo-classic pillars [*see* **240**].

A close investigation of the few scene inventories that have survived from the Georgian theatre confirms that only exceptionally were wings designed to match shutters (or flats) and back cloths (or back flats and back drops). The Covent Garden inventory of 1744, for instance, indicates that the theatre kept in store some eighteen sets of wings as opposed to forty-three flats (or shutters) and back flats.[2] Few of the sets of wings are designed to match specific scenes depicted on the various flats [*see* **271**]. (Occasionally scenes depicted on the flats are named after the painter who last completed the work, e.g. 'Harvey's hall', or alternatively after the name of the play, e.g. 'Othello's hall'.) The inventory of the Crow Street Theatre in Dublin of 1776 shows the same discrepancy, listing some eighteen sets of wings and fifty-two flats or back drops [*see* **272**]. Only two sets of borders are listed, 'five palace borders' and 'five sky borders', which suggests that these two sets were used for all interior and exterior sets as appropriate in the theatre's productions.[3] Another point worth noting is the substantial proportion of scenes listed as very bad or damaged in one way or another. Clearly the extensive use given to stock scenery, particularly when it was moved from store to stage, was bound to harm the painted finish of canvas flats and wings.

The final inventory from Tate Wilkinson's touring company in 1784 indicates the type of stock scenes held by a good circuit company at the end of the eighteenth century [*see* **273**]. It also shows the movement of scenery between theatres on the circuit (with a record of their whereabouts), together with arrangements for periodic refurbishment (including the re-use of old canvases to save the cost of new materials). Generally speaking, the three theatres on the circuit at York, Leeds and Hull each had their own stock scenes, while new scenes were transported between all three theatres.[4]

---

[1] Richard Southern first drew attention to these discrepancies in *Changeable scenery* (1952), pp. 228–9.

[2] Richard Southern gives a very detailed analysis of the scenery listed in the Covent Garden inventory in *Changeable scenery* (1952), pp. 200–11. Sybil Rosenfeld corrects Southern's original figure of nineteen sets of wings in her analysis of the Covent Garden inventory in *Georgian scene painters and scene painting* (1981), p. 24.

[3] Sybil Rosenfeld has made a more detailed comparison in *Georgian scene painters and scene painting* (1981), pp. 25–6.

[4] For a more detailed analysis, see Rosenfeld (1981), pp. 26–7.

271   Inventory of scenes and properties at Covent Garden, 1744

BL Add.Ch 9319 and BL Add.MS 12,201, ff. 61–73. A full transcription by P.H. Highfill may be found in *Restoration and eighteenth-century theatre research* 5–6 (1966–7), 7–17, 17–26, 27–35[1]

[f. 61] A list of scenes.

Flats in the scene room: cottage and long village; Medusa's cave and 3 pieces grotto that changes to country house; inside of Merlin's cave; outside of ditto; dairy; hermitage; clock chamber; farm yard; country house; church; town; chimney chamber; fort; Rialto;[2] Harvey's hall; Othello's new hall; hell transparent[3] and 2 pieces inn yard; arch to waterfall; back of timber yard; short village; second hell; front of timber yard; garden; short wood.

Flat in the top flies: ship flat.[4]

Flats in the shop: a large palace arch; an old low flat of a tower and church; an open flat with cloudings on one side and palace on the other.

Back flats in scene room: Harvey's palace; bishop's garden; waterfall; long village; long wood; corn fields; the arch of Harvey's palace; back arch of Ariodante's palace;[5] a canal; a sea port.

Back flats in great room: the flat to the arch and groves; open country cloth.

Ditto [i.e. back flats] in the top flies: the sea back cloth; the King's Arms curtain.

Wings in the scene room: 4 Ariodante's palace: 12 Harvey's palace;[6] ditto rock; ditto wood; ditto Atalanta's garden; ten town; tent; Ceres's garden; 6 vault; ditto hell; ditto inn yard; ditto fine chamber; ditto plain chamber.

Wings in great room: eight moonlight.

Ditto [i.e. wings] in painter's room: 2 of Ariodante's palace but are rubbed out and not painted;[7]

Ditto [i.e. wings] in the shop: 2 tapestry; 2 old rock [f. 62].

Painted pieces[8] in scene room: 6 tent pieces; Shakespeare's monument; Macbeth's cave; Oedipus's tower; the moon in *Emperor of ditto*[9]; an arbour; 2 pieces transparent hell; a balcony; old garden wall; a balcony pedestal; front of gallery in *Ariodante*; a small palace border in ditto; a frontispiece in ditto; [. . .] 6 ground pieces to the trees in *Orpheus*; a figure in Harvey's palace; 2 stone figures in Medusa's cave.

Ditto [i.e. painted pieces] in great room: 7 open country pieces; 6 pieces corn fields; 4 open country pieces; 4 orange trees in pots; 6 garden pieces; hedge, stile & fence – 4 pieces; a ground piece in two parts; front of garden that changes to house – 4 pieces; 6 rock pieces with trees [. . .]; two pieces the back of machine in *Jupiter and Europa*; the moon in *Emperor of ditto*, a blind to the back machine; the back of the back machine; a ground piece of Atalanta's garden [. . .]; the King's and Prince's box complete; the front of great machine in *Jupiter and Europa*; the water piece to bridge; a pedestal in *Winter's Tale*; a piece ground landscape.

Ditto [i.e. painted pieces] in yard: 2 wings and 1 border to the back machine, 8 wings to great machine in *Rape [of Proserpine]*; 4 borders to ditto; the falling rock in

Alcina – 4 pieces; the compass border to Atalanta's garden; the bridge in *The Rehearsal*; 3 pieces the front of a small chariot; clouding; 6 Gothic chamber borders; for false stage, 2 large borders fixed to battens used in opera.

Painted pieces [f. 63] in first flies: a gibbet tree in *Apollo and Daphne*; a transparent in *Oedipus King of Thebes*[. . .]; a small rock flat; 8 pieces of old clouding; a marble pedestal; 3 figures on pedestals; 6 ditto with braces; corn fields in 6 pieces; a tomb in *Timon*; a garden wall in two pieces; the front of an altar.

Ditto [i.e. painted pieces] in the top flies: 6 waves & 2 shore pieces to ditto; a piece of falling rock in the operas; 3 old wings; the horses to front of back machine in *Apollo and Daphne*. Ditto [i.e. painted pieces] in painting room: a tomb with figure & lamp; 6 columns to Fame's temple; 2 water pieces out of use; 2 large branches for coronation.

Ditto [i.e. painted pieces] in shop: a piece of 2 columns and arches with hinges; arch and balustrade; part of an old pal[isade] – 2 pieces; an arbour; a large border of Ariodante's palace; a small transparent in *Atalanta*; the front of a ship; the front of Ceres's chariot; the figure of Massinello on a pedestal; an old rock; two oxen in *Justin*; an old small landscape; a clouding to a machine; a large frame for scaffold; a border to frontispiece in *Ariodante* [. . .].

Properties in scene room: the Spanish table; study of books [. . .]; a coffin; a tub; 5 stage ladders [. . .]; a gibbet in *Orpheus*; 6 doublers and 8 lighting sticks; the grave, skull and bones in *Hamlet*; 2 candlesticks and 3 twin lamp hangers.

Properties in great room: 4 long tables; 6 pedestals; common throne; steps, boards and 3 trestles; barrel, frame, iron braces & handles to new mount the cage; a haycock in two pieces; the mill in *Faustus*; supper table & 2 chairs; carpet; table and meal; [. . .] a red curtain fixed to batten lines and pullies; a throne board and 2 low trestles; four blocks com[prising] 9 tin candlesticks. [. . .]

[1] There is also a transcription by H. Saxe Wyndham of parts of the inventory published in his *Annals of Covent Garden Theatre*, vol. 2 (1906), pp. 309–14. Some of the detail is inaccurate.

[2] Presumably a scene from *The Merchant of Venice*.

[3] A transparent scene that would be of use in pantomimes.

[4] Richard Southern admits to being puzzled at this one item stored in the top fly gallery. See Southern (1952), pp. 207–8.

[5] *Ariodante* was an opera by Handel. It was clearly intended to be a spectacular production, which is why wings and shutters matched.

[6] The repeated number of twelve wings indicates that Covent Garden was able to accommodate a maximum of six pairs of wings on stage.

[7] Presumably these wings are in the paint room in order to be refurbished, having been 'rubbed out'.

[8] Pieces are 'any odd bits of scenery that do not fit into the principal categories'. Southern (1952), p. 201.

[9] A reference to *The Emperor in the Moon*, a popular Restoration farce by Aphra Behn.

272   An inventory of the scenes, properties, etc. belonging to the Theatre Royal in Crow Street Dublin, 1776

James Boaden: *Memoirs of the life of John Philip Kemble Esq.*, vol. 1 (London: Longman, Hurst et al., 1825), pp. 469–77

STAGE

[...] Stage table, one form broken. Three bells under the stage. Thunder bell, alarm bell, large bell and curtain bell. Two tin shades to shade light of the boxes. Two step ladders for the use of the stage. One long ladder for the use of the carpenter's gallery. One large wooden branch, hung but out of repair. Two stage chairs.

SCENES

[...] A drop wood. A drop palace. A town flat. Three chambers, *holes in one of them*; the doors of the door-chamber very bad. Prison. Canal garden. Blasted heath, *Macbeth*. Grand tent. Cut wood, *Hamlet*. Cave with catacombs painted on the back. Statue palace. Gothic palace. Garden. Long wood, a *hole* in it. Part of the hovel in the *Sorcerer*. Tiled chamber. Statue in *Merope*. Back of the bower. Patty's house, *very bad*. Doctor's brick house, in *Mercury Harlequin*. A small cut tree. Front of the orchestra, catacombs on the back. Map chamber out of repair. Part of the bridge in *King Arthur*. Rialto. The statue of Osiris. Aimworth's house, one stile *broken*. Palace arch. Toy house. Battlements, *torn*, Garden wall, very bad. Tomb in the *Grecian Daughter*. Library. An old Patagonian chamber in *Mother Shipton*.

Changeable flat in *Mercury Harlequin*. Waterfall in the *Dargle, very bad*. Cob's house, outside. Portico. Statue arch in *Mercury Harlequin*, very bad. Frost scene in *King Arthur*. Inside of Cob's house, *torn*. Long wood. Apothecary's shop in the *Dargle*, very bad. Outside of the miller's house (brick work) one part. Scene with sacks, one half. Waterfall. Scene of swords. Two pieces of plain paling. A small single tent. Altar piece in *Theodosius*. Palace arch of Corinthian order. Blue striped chamber. Iron yard painting, almost defaced. Garden arch. Two large wood wings, *greatly damaged*. One piece of clouding, very old and little worth.

Three pair of picture chamber wings. Six pair of wood wings, long used. Five pair of statue wings, one greatly damaged. Five pair of Gothic wings (five holes in the canvas). One pair of Gothic wings, very bad and torn. Five pair of town wings. One Sedan chair, no. 5, for the pantomime. Three pair of striped chamber wings. Two pair of marbled wings. Two pair of bower wings, all in bad order. Four pair of boat wings, the painting much damaged. Two pair of marble palace wings, long used. Two pair of back cloud wings. One pair of back town and wood wings. Two pair of rock wings. Five small tents, used in the fair, old. A small cabin. Temple in the *Maid of the Mill* (brick work). A Chinese temple, old. Juliet's balcony. Outside of a Chinese temple in the *Orphan of China*. Three small bower wings with hinges on them. Balcony in the *Suspicious Husband*, old. An old tree. Two pair of wood frames for flats, not covered. Padlock scene. The bridge in *King Arthur*. Two small trees. A green stage cloth. Juliet's bier. Jobson's bed. Five palace borders. Five sky borders. Mill house in the *Maid of the Mill*, torn very much. Rostrum in *Julius Caesar*.

PROPERTIES

Three pieces of black cloth. Four gentlemen's turbans. Six common ditto. Three white hats. Bow, quiver and bonnet for Douglas. Four gentlemen's helmets. Five soldiers' ditto. [. . .] Four small paper tarts. One green table cloth. An old pedlar's box. Four single chains. One ditto for the hall door. Two green covers for stage forms. One settee cover and two pillows. [. . .] Two grates in the men's wardrobe. Two pieces of scantling to hang clothes on. Four very small racks to hang clothes on. Twelve oak chairs, very good. Six washing basins, one broken; four black pitchers. Twenty-eight candlesticks for dressing. Eleven metal thunder bolts, sixty-seven wood ditto, five stone ditto. Three baskets for thunder balls. One canopy. The pedestal and horse in the *Sorcerer*, out of repair. Hob's well, two water wheels, boat in the *Dargle*. Two sets of fly grooves with barrels. Four long barrels with multiplying wheels. Two short barrels, not movable. Curtain barrel. Rack in *Venice Preserved*. Elephant in the *Enchanted Lady*, very bad. Alexander's car, some of it wanting. The star King Arthur cut across. Three pairs of cut drapery drops with figures and back, made for the *Enchanted Lady*. Midas's scaffold and barrel, with balance weight. One short barrel at the back of the stage. One frame with three barrels in the carpenter's gallery. [. . .] Two old scene barrels in carpenter's gallery. A small ship curtain. Two old trestles. A flag and mullet for painters. Five pair of arches and back in *Mother Shipton*. Three pair of wings in *Mother Shipton*, changeable. Four pair of small wheels. A back drop palace. Six small traps with cords, no balance weights. One grave trap with cords, no weights. Two barrels under the stage not in use, with one ring only. The scaffold in *Venice Preserved*. A small cabinet. Four buckets, iron bound. Total: twenty-four footlights. Total: seventy-six wing lights. Several old pantomime tricks and useless pieces of scenes. [. . .]

273   Scene stock of a circuit company, *c.* 1784

MS account book of Tate Wilkinson's Yorkshire company. York Public Library[1]

[One]

Cave scene. Jobson's house. Best chamber. Front chamber. Back scene, York Minster. Front chamber. Palace. Cave scene – left at Leeds. Garden. Dover Scene. Masons yard & street. Mount Vesuvius – left at Leeds. Cut grove – go to York. Prison. Picture scene – go to Hull. Moonlight scene – left at Leeds. Genii palace. Garden – left at Leeds. Mount Vesuvius – left at Leeds for a cut cave. Genii garden arched – go to Hull. Palace, Mr Colby's – left at Leeds to be refreshed.
Street. St Ustatia. Moonlight garden. Greenwich Hospital. Cyprus grove. [All] left at Leeds.

[Two]

Old hall chamber – go for use to Leeds. Cornfield to go for [. . .] & be repaired. Portsmouth scene forward. Camp scene, both sides good for camp scenes [. . .] shore. Genii's palace go to Leeds to be refreshed. Leeds painter's chamber to Leeds for *him* to repair. Garden scene to be refreshed. [. . .] picture scene stay at York. Other Leeds [. . .] Scene to Leeds, him to repair. Genii [. . .] garden – stay at York to be refreshed. Crusoe's [. . .] scene to Leeds for alterations. Old palace to Leeds to be refreshed. Cymon palace and wings go to Hull after the races. Sherwood forest to Leeds, Hull, etc. Old inn scene for a street scene: Leeds, Hull & be altered. Old inn scene wants immediate alteration. Prison scene wanted. Wings at Leeds. Masons yard, go as a street scene. Greenwich Hospital. Prison paper scene & black ground to padlock scene to serve as prison. Rock of Gibraltar go. Old chamber at Leeds. Camp scene at York. Fort Omon – York. Library at York.

[1] There are two hands, with the possibility of a third. Hand 2 adds comments on the page originally written by Hand 1.

COSTUME

In sharp contrast to the relative dearth of visual material showing stage settings in the Georgian theatre, there is almost an *embarras de richesses* when it comes to illustrations of well-known actors and actresses in costume during the eighteenth century. Not all the illustrations are reliable. Sometimes actors are depicted in roles they never played on stage. On other occasions, the same print is reproduced in several editions with completely different colours for the costume in the various versions.[1] Nevertheless, the many engravings, watercolours and oil paintings of Georgian actors in a wide variety of parts permit certain broad conclusions to be reached about the way plays were costumed during the eighteenth century.

In the early part of the century, as Tate Wilkinson recalls in his *Memoirs* (1791), there was no real attempt at cohesion in terms of costuming [*see* 274]. Actors made do with what could be found in the wardrobe of their theatre or provided their own attire. Traditional Baroque costumes were used for a wide range of tragic roles: the plumed helmets, perukes and tunics associated with Roman shapes (a 'shape' being the name given to any suit or dress in the wardrobe store of a theatre); and the flowing robes, turbans, scimitars associated with Persian shapes. An engraving of a scene from Whitehead's *The Roman Father* at Drury Lane in 1750 shows Henderson wearing a traditional Roman shape, while the actress is wearing a contemporary tragic gown [*see* 275]. A frontispiece from an edition of Rowe's *Tamerlane*, published in 1776, shows the actor Palmer playing the role of Bajazet in a Persian shape [*see* 276]. Again the actress Miss Hopkins, playing the role of Selima, is shown in contemporary tragic dress.

[1] See Nicoll (1980), pp. 147–54. The same is true of the china figurines of actors in well-known roles, as in the case of David Garrick as Richard III in his tent. The posture and costume are identical but the colours different.

274   Tate Wilkinson recalls costuming practice in the middle of the eighteenth century
Tate Wilkinson (Dublin, 1791), vol. 3 pp. 140–5

I have now worn occasionally [. . .] (for old characters of wealth) a suit of purple cloth, with gold vellum holes, that I frequently wore when a young man as a fashionable dress, and spoke the Prologue to the Author, gave tea, etc. on the London stage, and after that used it as my common dress to parade the streets at noon. But I must justly coincide with the point of truth and declare, the character-istic dressing of plays forty years ago was very inferior indeed to what is seen in these riper years, particularly the comedians. At that time, no more than two or three principal characters (at Covent Garden in particular) were well dressed, and those not with any variety as now. Mrs Woffington's wardrobe had only the increase of one tragedy suit in the course of the season, in addition to the clothes allotted to her, unless she indulged herself. And she had a new suit for Sir Harry Wildair, in which character Mrs Woffington looked the man of fashion. And Mrs Jordan sports now in Sir Harry one of the best legs in the kingdom. Sir Joshua Reynolds is a judge of legs and has, like Paris with his apple, given his decree on that said leg.

But the gentlemen and ladies in modern-dressed tragedies forty years ago at Covent Garden Theatre wore the old laced clothes which had done many years service at Lincoln's Inn Fields, besides having graced the original wearers, and the ladies were in large hoops; and the velvet petticoats, heavily embossed, proved extremely inconvenient and troublesome; and always a page behind to hear the lover's secrets and keep the train in graceful decorum. If two princesses met on the stage, with the frequent stage crossing then practised, it would now seem truly entertaining to behold a page dangling at the tail of each heroine (and I have seen a young lady, not of the most delicate form who sustained that office frequently – a Miss Mullart). They are now dismissed, as judged unnecessary and super-fluous. [. . .]

Strict propriety of habiliment not any manager has yet arrived at, even in London. And though it is so highly improved these last twenty years, yet the achievement not even money will ever be able to obtain, that is, while the stage is honoured with pretty women, as I sincerely hope it ever will be. For common sense, reason, persuasion, nor intreaty will ever persuade handsome women to appear in a farmer's daughter, or a witch, or a servant maid, but with the head dressed in full fashion and the feet decked in satin shoes. Yet I think they would be gainers by trying dear variety. For what will attract more than the simple Quaker or the truly neat chambermaid? And it is not every man that wishes for a duchess. Besides, what an advantage to be seen in a gaudy attire one night and another arrayed in pure simplicity and be viewed with propriety in a green stuff gown, etc.; and not as Madge in *Love in a Village*, or Betsy Blossom, with a French head, white silk stockings and white satin shoes. By such contradictions, nature is as distant from the stage now as she was an hundred years ago. And stuff shoes and clean cotton stockings would look not only as well but better by the preservation of character. [. . .]

275 Henderson as Horatio, wearing a Roman shape in William Whitehead's *The Roman Father* at Drury Lane, 1750 (see facing page)
Burney Collection of Theatrical Portraits, vol. 4, no. 206, p. 110 (Print Room, BM)

276 Palmer wearing a Persian shape in the character of Bajazet in Rowe's *Tamerlane*, 1776 (see facing page)
Frontispiece of the edition of N. Rowe's *Tamerlane* (London: Lowndes & Partners, 1776)

275   Henderson as Horatio, wearing a Roman
        shape

276   Palmer wearing a Persian shape in the
        character of Bajazet

Wardrobe inventories

Wardrobe inventories from respectively Covent Garden in 1744 and Norwich in 1784 confirm the tendency for the Georgian theatre to use standardised tragic costume; in the Covent Garden inventory one accordingly finds a large preponderance of Roman and Persian shapes [*see* 277], while the inventory of the ladies' wardrobe at Norwich lists a number of 'tragedy dresses' [*see* 278].

277   Inventory of the wardrobe at Covent Garden in 1744

BL Add.Ch 9319 and BL Add.MS 12,201, ff. 34–61. A complete transcript by P.H. Highfill may be found in *Restoration and eighteenth-century theatre research*, 5 (1966), 7–35

In the great wardrobe: No. A. – old shapes out of wear.

A blue satin Persian. A scarlet velvet. A scarlet silk roman. A blue satin Persian. A green silk ditto. A scarlet satin Turkish. Three black plush. A copper-coloured ditto. A scarlet plush Persian. A yellow tabby. A blue plush Turkish. A green ditto. A crimson ditto. A blue ditto. A blue satin Roman. A crimson plush. Twenty-six sleeves to the above shapes. Nine pair of breeches to ditto. A straw satin petticoat. 2 sets of lamberkins.

No. B. A blue satin Roman, a scarlet ditto, a crimson ditto [. . .]

No. C. – shapes in wear.

A black velvet Roman shape trimmed with beads. A blue plush. A scarlet ditto. A black ditto. A blue ditto. A brown ditto. 2 scarlet ditto. A crimson ditto. A scarlet ditto. A crimson ditto. A blue ditto Persian. 6 pair of bases to ditto. A red satin Roman shape. A black plush ditto. A blue satin. A yellow plush. Sixteen pair of breeches to the above shapes. A blue plush Persian shape. A red plush Roman.

No. D. Four purple changeable silk jackets and caps. 6 Scots jackets and caps. 2 stuff plaid sashes & 6 bonnets to ditto. 2 dark knit, 1 blue baize & 2 green silk bonnets. A Merry mantua. A buffoon's dress. White puffs and copper lace. 4 brown stuff peasants jackets trimmed with white, pinked silk. 4 red satin waistcoats to ditto [. . .].

No. K. A gold satin Roman shape. A yellow ditto. A blue ditto. A black plush. Pluto's shape. A black satin. Yellow spangled shape. A yellow tabby shape. The trimming taken off an ash-coloured satin shape for Momus. A yellow tabby shape. A green and copper tabby ditto. A cherry satin ditto. 8 pair of breeches to ditto. Volpone's black plush dress wrapped in a yellow tabby Turkish vest. Volpone's old blue plush jacket & breeches ditto. Mountebank's dress. Mosca's black baize dress. A blue linen friezeland gown & cap. The fool's dress. Falstaff's new dress. Justice Shallow's ditto. Falstaff's old dress. 2 old jackets of Falstaff's. Sir Hugh Evans's dress. Ditto disguise of white satin. Jack Rugby's coat. 2 buff coats. 2 white high crowned hats. 1 black ditto. Mr Slender's coat & waistcoat. Sir Hugh's old black bugle coat. Hearn the Hunter's dress.

No. L. – King Charles's chest.

Aesop's dress in the chimney corner. King Charles's dress. Duke of Gloucester's ditto. Duke of York's cloak. A black baize Spanish shape & breeches. A yellow satin spangled jacket. A black velvet Spanish jacket embroidered with black silk. [. . .]

278   Inventory of the Ladies' wardrobe at Norwich, 1784

Bolingbroke MSS. Reprinted in Dorothy H. Eshleman: *The committee books of the Theatre Royal Norwich, 1768–1825* (London, 1970), Appendix A, pp. 143–8[1]

1. Black cotton petticoat for *Cymon*: train & jacket.
2. Pink Persian jacket, train, etc., altered into gown for Mrs Holland. Worn out.
3. A white lawn coat & jacket.
4. 6 ladies' trains for the coronation; red trimmed with flannel.
5. A long purple train, 6 yards, for Anna Bullen. Trimmed with flannel for ermine.
6. 4 white and 2 yellow petticoats. 2 vests painted for *Comus*.
7. Green Persian dress. Vest, petticoat and train.
8. A blue plain silk tragedy dress.
9. A crimson satin tragedy dress – plain.
10. A silver tissue brocade. A tragedy dress – with furs.
11. A silver tissue Italian nightgown with pink and green flowers.
12. A garnet Italian nightgown – silver flowers.
13. A laylock silk nightgown.
14. A striped lutestring dancing dress, died a maroon.
15. Black puckered sack satin with a coat for the Duenna.
16. A tragedy vest, scarlet & silver.
17. 2 white silk brocaded petticoats, silk and purple flowers. [. . .]
71. A blue stuff gown with red & blue patches.
72. Worn out.
73. 2 shepherdesses' dresses for *Daphne & Nysa*. White stuff trimmed with black.
74. A brown stuff dress trimmed with white for Mysis.
75. A light brown Alpine jacket & coat. Puffs with X crossed out. [. . .]
230. White satin petticoat. Lost, it is said. Mrs Miller had it. [. . .]
244. A white satin tragedy dress. [. . .]

[1] There are 245 items in the inventory, plus valuations.

The growth of historical awareness in costume practice

John Hill's plea in the 1750s for greater naturalism and appropriateness of costume marks the beginning of a changing attitude [*see* **279**]. The debate began to focus on the suitability of modern dress for historical tragedy. Macklin had startled his contemporaries in 1741 with his historically based interpretation of Shylock [*see* **304** and **305**]: he was to repeat the process with his interpretation of Macbeth in 1773 as an ancient Scottish laird [*see* **281a** and **b**].[1] At the time, Othello, Macbeth, Lear and Hamlet were all played in contemporary dress: Garrick, for instance, played Macbeth dressed in scarlet and gold with a tail wig, like a contemporary military officer [*see* **280a**]. Even as late as the mid 1770s, Lichtenberg was still debating and ultimately defending the validity of Garrick's decision to play Hamlet in modern dress [*see* **282** and **283**]. By the end of the century, the historicist approach had won over many supporters [*see* **284**].

[1] See M. St. C. Byrne. 'The stage costuming of *Macbeth* in the 18th century' *Studies in English theatre history* (London: STR 1952), 52–64.

279   John Hill pleads for greater naturalism and appropriateness in costume

John Hill: *The actor* (London, 1750), pp. 222–9

The dresses of the actors is another particular that we are usually as careless about as the scenery in our plays. We should indeed be offended if we saw a person, who performed the part of a man of rank and quality, act in a plain suit. But we are very unconcerned to see an actress, whose part is that of a chambermaid, enter upon the stage in a habit that in real life might be worn by a duchess. We forget the necessary plainness that a person of the character and station represented to us ought to appear in, and only say upon the occasion that Mrs Clive has a great many very good clothes. The general taste which we have for extravagance in dress makes us forget the interest we have in the truth of the representation.

This is another folly which we have imported from France, where it is carried to so much a greater height than with us that it is as common for a stranger at first sight to mistake the waiting gentlewoman for the sister of the lady she belongs to, as it is for him to hear the gentlemen in the pit call out to those on the stage to entreat they will favour them so far as not to stand between them and the performers.

We are no more to expect that the generality of players will ever be brought of their own choice to prefer the dress under which they may best and most naturally affect the heart, to that by which they may charm the eyes and make the audience believe them to be genteel and clever people, than that the master of the house will of his own motion deny himself the crowns that offer at the stage door for the sake of representing the play the more naturally to us. Let us at least, however, desire that the manager will draw his magic circle in each of the openings of the scenes, beyond which the persons admitted behind them may not advance; that they may be kept, in as great a measure as may be, out of our sight. And let us entreat of the players that they would regulate, as well as they can, their vanity and love of finery by the nature of the part they are to perform; and not by their native pride make it impossible for us to know what character it is they are playing, unless we are informed of it beforehand.

One great source of these abuses in the parts of the waiting maids is that the authors of our farces in general have made persons of that rank the principal characters of the piece, while their mistresses have been little better than cyphers. But we are apt to believe that the authors of those pieces intended that the superiority of character in the servant should be discovered in the course of performance, not by the habit. And that the whole would have somewhat more the air of nature if, when they are both to appear often together upon the stage, the maid were at least not better dressed than the mistress. We are not without instances where the footman is made the hero of a farce and his master a mighty insignificant person in it. Yet we have never found the absurdity carried so high among the men as to see the Lying Valet better dressed than his master [. . .]. The men, though in general much less blamable than the women on this occasion, yet are not without their errors in it, and those such as greatly hurt the air of probability in the representation. We would entreat of them in general to remember that their parts concern them not only in what we see of them on the stage, but in everything which we hear passes without, in which they are concerned. We would not desire things to be carried so far indeed on this occasion as to expect a beau to enter in dirty boots because he is to mention his having come a journey. But then we would not have an Orestes return from the temple, where at the instigation of Hermione, he has been causing Pyrrhus to be assassinated, without one curl of his peruke out of order. Let the look of reality be kept up; and when the actor tells us of some dreadful bustle he has been in, we would have him show some marks of it by the disorder of his person.

The first time that Mr Garrick played Macbeth, he took occasion in one of his scenes of greatest confusion to enter upon the stage with his coat and waistcoat both unbuttoned and with some other discomposures in his dress that added greatly to the resemblance of nature in that part of his character. He did this, however, only the first night and lost, by omitting it afterwards, all the merit of having done it at all. We are apt to believe that some of his friends, who assume themselves the character of critics on stage performances, advised him to omit this striking particular in the following representations [. . .].

We are very sensible of the merit that some of our modern players claim to themselves from their judgement in dressing their characters [. . .]. But some late instances on one of the theatres make it necessary that we should remind the people who are so fond of their talents in this way that the habits of characters on the stage should be proper as well as pretty; and that the actors are not only to dress so as not to offend probability, but they are to be tied down as much as painters to the general customs of the world. Alexander the Great or Julius Caesar would appear as monstrous to us in bag wigs on the stage as in a picture [. . .].

We have in a former part of this treatise occasionally mentioned the general and vague resemblance which there ought always to be between the original and the copy of it on the stage. But we here enter on the subject of a much more particular and more determinate similarity.

We remember very lately an excellent actress, Mrs Pritchard, playing the part of Jane Shore. She spoke it, as she does everything else, at least as well as anybody could. But we were shocked in the first scenes at the face and figure of this actress, under the representation of all those charms that are so lavishly ascribed by the poet to that unfortunate heroine. And in the conclusion, nothing could be so unnatural as to see that plump and rosy figure endeavouring to present us with a view of the utmost want and starving [. . .].

If the player would have the representation carry with it an entire air of truth, he must be cautious not only to conduct his action and recitation with a strict regard to nature, but he must never select a character to appear in, which is remarkable for any particular striking singularity which is not in himself. He cannot too frequently remember that the representation of a play is a sort of painting which owes all its beauty to a close imitation of nature and that its touches are expected to be even vastly more expressive than those of the pencil. That the more advantages the stage has for the making the illusion perfect, the more perfection we expect to find in it there. And that it is not enough that the fictions it exposes to our view seem to bear a resemblance to the events which they are intended to figure to us, but that we expect that resemblance to be so perfect that we shall be able to persuade ourselves that what is in reality but a copy is an original, and that the very events themselves and the very persons concerned in them are really and truly present before our eyes.

280   Contemporary dress used in Shakespearian tragedy

(A) DAVID GARRICK AS MACBETH
Private collection. Bell's edition of Shakespeare's plays (London, 1775)

(B) THOMAS GRIST AS OTHELLO AT DRURY LANE, 1775
Burney Collection of Theatrical Portraits, vol. 4, no. 84, p. 45 (Print Room, BM)

281   Antiquarian naturalism – Macklin's 'Scottish' Macbeth, 1773

(A) JOHN TAYLOR
Quoted in E.A. Parry: *Charles Macklin* (London: Kegan Paul *et al.*, 1891), p. 161. Reprinted in Nagler (1952), p. 398

The character of Macbeth had been hitherto performed in the attire of an English general.[1] But Macklin was the first who performed it in the old Scottish garb. His appearance was previously announced by the Coldstream march. [. . .] When Macklin appeared on the bridge, he was received with shouts of applause, which were repeated throughout the performance. I was seated in the pit and so near the orchestra that I had a full opportunity of seeing him to advantage. Garrick's representation of the character was before my time. Macklin's was certainly not marked by studied grace of deportment but he seemed to be more in earnest in the character than any actor I have subsequently seen.

[1] See W. Cooke: *Memoirs of Charles Macklin, comedian* (London: J. Asperne, 1804), pp. 283–4

(B) CHARLES MACKLIN AS MACBETH
Private Collection. Theatre Museum. H.R. Beard Collection.

282   Lichtenberg debates the validity of Garrick acting Hamlet in modern dress

Lichtenberg's visits to England, as described in his letters and diaries, edited and translated by M.L. Mare and W.H. Quarrell (Oxford: Clarendon Press, 1938), pp. 21–3

I believe that I have already told you that [Garrick] plays Hamlet in a French suit. That seems, in truth, an odd choice. I have frequently heard him blamed for this, though never between the acts, nor on the way home, nor at supper after the play; but always after the impression made by him has had time to fade; and the intellect has revived sufficiently for cool discussion in which, as you know, learned is taken to be synonymous with good and striking with ingenious. I must confess that this criticism has never appealed to me. [. . .]

For my part, I am convinced that Garrick is an extremely ingenious man who, being able to gauge to a nicety the taste of his fellow countrymen, certainly attempts nothing on the stage without good reason and besides has a whole house full of ancient costumes. He is, moreover, a man who makes use of his experience of everyday life at fitting times and places, not for any monstrous heightening of his eloquence, but for the promotion of a harmonious growth of common sense. Is it likely that such a man could not comprehend what every London Macaroni would dare swear was as plain as a pikestaff? He, who thirty years ago had already become that which one would scarce concede to most of his critics at the present time. So instead of agreeing, I began to reflect as to what can have moved him to do such a thing. I pondered every aspect of the matter, so as to explain it, at least to my own satisfaction, until at last I found myself in agreement with what are presumably Garrick's sentiments, on the second occasion on which I saw *Hamlet* played, at the moment when he draws his sword on Horatio. As far as I am concerned, he is entirely justified, and would indeed, in my opinion, lose much of his effect if he appeared otherwise. [. . .] I cannot pass over in silence my reasons which, though not perhaps those of Garrick himself, may yet serve to guide a few thoughtful actors to better things.

It seems to me that if we are not vastly learned, ancient costumes on the stage are too reminiscent of a disguise worn at a masquerade, which is indeed pleasing, if it be pretty. But the trifling pleasure it gives can seldom contribute much to the sum total of all which heightens the impression of a play. [. . .] I have therefore come to the conclusion that we should by all means retain modern dress in a play, so long as it does not offend the susceptibilities of imperious pedants. [. . .] When Garrick, in the situation mentioned above, had partly turned his back on the audience, and I perceived that his exertions had produced that well-known diagonal crease from the shoulder to the opposite hip, it was in truth worth the play of facial expression twice over. In the inky cloak, of which Hamlet once speaks, I should assuredly not have remarked this. A well-formed actor (as all at any rate should be who have anything to do with tragedy) will certainly lose something by wearing a costume differing too greatly from such as might have been either earlier or later in life not the least object of any man's desires and the sweetest gratification of youthful vanity; in which, moreover, the eye can detect to a hair's breadth the least excess or deficiency. You must understand of course that I do not suggest that Caesar and England's Henries and Richards should appear on the stage in the uniform of the Guards, with scarf and gorget. Everyone has acquired at school and from engravings, medals and firebacks, enough knowledge and antiquarian pride to be sensible of, and resent, these and similar deviations from general custom. I think, however, that where the public is not yet awake to a certain point of antiquarian interest, the player should not be the first to disturb their slumbers. The trifling momentary pleasure, so to speak, given me by the worthless splendour of a masquerade costume, does not make amends for the harm done to the play in every other respect. All the spectators are aware that something is lacking, though all do not believe this to be the cause of it. The taste of an actor of tolerable discernment, who knows the strength and the foibles of the public before which he must appear, in this transcends all rules. In the case I have taken, London, as regards Hamlet the Dane, is in this situation, so is there any need for Garrick to be wise at the expense of both parties? Garrick can well dispense, on the one hand, with a modicum of praise for his learning if, on the other, the hearts of thousands are drawn to him.

283   Garrick as Hamlet, 1754

Burney Collection of Theatrical Portraits, Garrick Portfolio, no. E.e.3.106 (Print Room, BM)

284   Growing support for a historicist approach to costume at the turn of the century

Henry Siddons: *Practical illustrations of rhetorical gesture and action* (London: Sherwood *et al.*, 1822), pp. 366–8

To Mr Garrick the stage owes great obligation, and his memory will be dear to the lovers of drama as long as the works of Shakespeare continue to be the admiration of a British audience. Yet in tracing the progression of dress, we may surely be permitted to make a few passing observations, without detracting from the merit of that immortal man. There was nothing ridiculous in his wearing a wig in the character of Ranger, but such a dress would now excite the risible faculties of the audience. The characters of Macbeth and Romeo, which he represented so perfectly, would have been improved by the Scottish and Italian garb. King Richard is said to have been so exquisitely delineated by this great actor that none but those who had the happiness of seeing him can form any idea of the sublimity of his conception of that arduous part. The dress of Richard was as correct then as it is at present. But the other characters were attired in embroidered coats and waistcoats, cocked hats, powdered heads, bags and court swords. The general effect must have been considerably impaired by such a distinction, and with an actor of less ability, the illusion would have been weakened if not destroyed. But while Garrick acted, attention was employed on him and him alone; all exterior objects were put to flight by his transcendent genius.

It will be generally allowed that the actors of the present day maintain a decided superiority over their predecessors in the art of dressing their characters and in strict attention to costume. Trifling as this advantage may appear when opposed to the more noble portions of the drama, its importance will be readily admitted by the real connoisseur. When Macbeth appears on the wild heath with his plaid-covered chieftains, is not the fiction more aided by the substitution of the warlike Caledonian garb than when he marched down the stage with a powdered head and a gold-laced coat and waistcoat? When Alexander the Great was attired in silk stockings, was it not a total violation of history, truth and propriety?

LIGHTING

Few illustrations survive from the eighteenth century (and none at all from the Restoration) showing in any detail the lighting systems used in contemporary playhouses. Piecing together the evidence of verbal accounts from the Restoration and comparing these with the few visual illustrations that exist of lighting in Georgian playhouses, it seems that no significant changes were made to the basic format of stage lighting between the Restoration and the major alterations undertaken by Garrick in 1765.

One of the illustrations of the Fitzgiggo riots in 1763 [*see* 285] clearly shows the hooped chandeliers, the footlights and wall sconces that were all part of the original lighting system introduced into the Restoration playhouse by Davenant in the 1660s. The other illustration of the Fitzgiggo riots [*see* 286] shows an ornate chandelier painted onto the back shutter, which was obviously a scenic device used to suggest, through trompe l'oeil, an alternative lighting source to the one provided in reality by the simple iron hoops of the stage chandeliers. Zoffany's painting of Garrick and Mrs Pritchard in *Macbeth* [*see* **314**] captures the atmospheric effect achieved by chandeliers, footlights and wall sconces when the actors stand near the front of the brightly lit forestage while the upstage scenic area is significantly darker.[1]

[1] In his book *Lighting in the theatre* (1977), Gösta Bergman suggests that, following contemporary artistic practice, the artist has simply omitted the footlights from his portrait, [see p. 214]. However, it is clear from the swathe of light cast across the stage floor and up onto the characters' faces that the footlights are merely concealed behind a solid reflector.

285   A satire on the 'Fitzgiggo' riots of 1763 at Covent Garden

A broadsheet sold by E. Sumpter, print and bookseller at the *Bible and Crown*, three doors from Shoe Lane, Fleet Street, 26 February 1763. Theatre Collection, University of Bristol. Also in Burney Collection of Theatrical Portraits, vol. 9, p. 41 (Print Room, BM)

(A)

(B)

Lighting and the Covent Garden inventory

From the evidence of the Covent Garden inventory of 1744, it seems likely that the footlights might be raised and lowered to alter the lighting levels of particular scenes. It is also clear that scene ladders were available to provide wing lighting in productions making significant use of the scenic stage [*see* 286].

In addition to these various forms of stage lighting, sconces placed around the first and second rank of boxes (often with cutglass or crystal mounts to enhance the reflections), [*see* 286, 220, 225 and 227] and one or more chandeliers suspended above the pit, ensured that audiences could see each other almost as well as they might see the play.

286   Inventory of scenes and properties at Covent Garden, 1744
BL Add.Ch 9319 BL Add.MS 12,201, ff. 61–73[1]

Ditto, etc. contained in the cellar.
The lamps in front fixed with barrel cordage, weights, etc. The grave trap and 3 others with ditto. The scene barrel fixed with cog wheels, etc. 12 pair of scene ladders fixed with ropes. Banquo's trap with barrel & cordage. Throne ditto, weights & ditto. Pluto's ditto and chariot grooves, etc.[. . .] 41 sconce candlesticks. The cauldron in Macbeth. 5 tin blinds to stage lamps, 2 large iron pans. A tin basket & shovel & 2 watering pots, 3 stage hair brooms. 115 three-corner tin lamps. 2 long iron braces & screws in *Orpheus*. One large ditto in *Merlin*. 3 small ditto. A tub for water. 6 old iron rings and chains for branches brought from

Lincoln's Inn.² 2 short iron braces to Duke's box. 2 iron beams & 3 braces to the lustres at the King and Prince's box. The trap bell and sconce bell.

¹ For details of a complete transcript of the inventory, see [271].
² Obviously Rich had brought with him the old hooped stage chandeliers from Lincoln's Inn Fields which he now kept in store.

Garrick's lighting reforms

In 1765, following a visit to Paris two years earlier, Garrick decided to dispense with the hooped chandeliers at Drury Lane and to concentrate the lighting sources in the wings and footlights. Batteries of wax lights, mounted on moving poles and with reflectors recommended to Garrick in Paris [see 287],¹ enabled him to control the intensity and the direction of the lighting sources in the wings [see 288 and 317]. Some of Garrick's correspondence with Jean Monnet (formerly director of the Paris Opéra Comique), whose acquaintance he had made during his travels in Europe in the years 1763–5, has survived. Monnet's letters offer advice on candle and oil lanterns of new design, using reflectors [see 287].²

Further improvements were made in the 1785 alterations to Drury Lane with the introduction of patent lamps known as Argand lamps: these were much more efficient and enabled a brighter, more even light to be thrown onto the scenery (by using lamps in tin enclosures with only small apertures through which directional lighting could emerge) [see 224].³

Following Garrick's innovations in 1765, it was possible to exploit directional lighting even in contemporary interior settings, such as that for *The School for Scandal* in 1777 [see 289a and b]. (Interestingly James Roberts, in his oil painting of the scene indicates directional light coming from the side of the stage with a large painted window in it: the engraver, however, has reversed the image to show directional light coming from the opposite side to the painted window!) In addition, the use of coloured silks, gauzes and glass enabled designers to achieve dramatic and atmospheric lighting effects in particular scenes [see 290], though not everyone approved, as emerges from a letter sent by Gainsborough to Garrick in 1772 [see 291]. In the final decades of the century, illuminated transparencies were commonplace [see 292], as were scenes of conflagration and disaster.

¹ See Rosenfeld (1981), p. 61.
² See Little and Kahrl (1963), letter 347; Boaden, vol. 2 (1831–2), pp. 441, 446, 500, 507–8; D.C. Mullin: 'Lamps for Garrick's footlights' *TN* 26 (1971–2), 92–4.
³ See Bergman (1977), pp. 196–207.

287   Jean Monnet's correspondence with Garrick regarding new lighting appliances

James Boaden: *The private correspondence of David Garrick with the most celebrated persons of his time*, vol. 2 (London: Colburn & Bentley, 1831–2), pp. 441, 446, 500, 507–8

Paris, 15 June, 1765. [. . .] I have carried out your two commissions, and I shall send you, along with M. Bouquet's designs, a reflector and two different models of the lamp you want for the footlights in your theatre. There are two kinds of reflectors: those that are placed in a niche in the wall and which have one wick; and those which are hung up like a chandelier and have five wicks. The first, which are, I fancy, the more suitable for lighting your theatre cost 15 [French] pounds, and the others from 36 to 62 [French] pounds, according to their size and the ornaments applied to them. To start with, I shall send you one costing 15 pounds. If subsequently you want a large model, you must let me know and be sure to indicate its precise location and the size of the area for which you have chosen it.

As for the lamps for lighting your stage, there are two kinds: one of earthenware and in biscuit form, with six or eight wicks, and in which you use oil; the others of tin, in the shape of a candle, with a spring in which you place the candles. The first are less costly and give more light. But for them not to smell, you must use the best oil and keep the lamps very clean.

288   Lighting changes at Drury Lane and Covent Garden in 1765

The Universal Museum and Complete Magazine (August 1765), p. 451

One very considerable improvement introduced by Mr Garrick on the stage this season is the removal of the six rings that used to be suspended over the stage in order to illuminate the house. The French theatre is illuminated by another method, but the light that is cast on their stage is extremely faint and disagreeable. Our English improver has availed himself of the hint from the French and given to Drury Lane those perfections which the other wants. The public were agreeably surprised on the opening of Drury Lane Theatre to see the stage illuminated with a clear and strong light and the rings removed that used to supply it (though to the great annoyance of many of the audience and frequently the actors themselves).

The managers of Covent Garden have attempted the like improvement, but not with the same success. Instead of wax, they have given oil, and their lights may be said to smell too much of the lamp. That theatre, in consequence of this deviation, has more of the gloom of the *Comédie Française* than of the cheerfulness of Drury Lane. But as Messrs Beard and Co. have ever shown themselves attentive to please the public, there is no doubt but a laudable emulation will soon induce them to make the necessary alterations.

289   Directional lighting in the screen scene from *The School for Scandal*, Drury Lane, 1777

(A) OIL PAINTING BY JAMES ROBERTS, SHOWING THOMAS KING AS SIR PETER
TEAZLE, WM SMITH AS CHARLES SURFACE, JOHN PALMER AS JOSEPH AND
MRS ABINGTON AS LADY TEAZLE   Garrick Club

(B) ENGRAVING   Theatre Museum

290   Experiments with coloured lighting, *c.* 1759
Henry Angelo: *Reminiscences*, vol. 1 (London: Colburn, 1828), pp. 10–12

[Signior Amiconi, the scene painter]'s professional employment, however, was not confined to the Opera House. Rich, on his removal to the new theatre at Covent Garden (when he quitted Lincoln's Inn), engaged him conjointly with the celebrated George Lambert, the founder of the Beef Steak Club, in preparing the scenery for this new stage. It is not generally known that the ceiling of this theatre was magnificently painted and decorated with groups of heathen deities amusing themselves and banqueting in the clouds. Amiconi, moreover, designed the plafond to that magnificent staircase at Buckingham House, which has been removed in the recent alterations of that royal residence.

But to return to Garrick and the improvements of the scenic department of Drury Lane. It was in consequence of the little stage produced by the elder Angelo and Signior Servandoni that Garrick first seriously bent his thoughts to these pictorial reformations.

One evening, after dining with my father and sitting over the wine, Garrick, conversing upon a speaking pantomime which he had long projected, asked him to contrive a scene such as would be likely to attract by its novelty.

The projected piece was *Harlequin's Invasion* and Garrick, describing the various situations in which the character of the 'Tailor in armour' (Joseph Snip) was to be placed, it was suggested to lead him through an enchanted wood in the pursuit of Harlequin for whose head a reward was offered and this hero of the shears was a candidate for the prize.

French, an artist of no mean talent, at that time was principal designer of scenes for Drury Lane Theatre. He, however, like most of his contemporaries, was not very liberally rewarded for his studies, and that department was usually executed with little attention to stage effect.

Excited to exertion on this occasion, he produced a very fine composition, which was painted with masterly execution: the slips or screens in the usual opaque manner, but the back scene was a transparency behind which visionary figures were seen flitting across upon the plan of the *tableau mouvant*.

That which rendered this scene apparently the work of enchantment, however, was a contrivance which originated in the inventive faculties of my father.

He caused screens to be placed diagonally, which were covered with scarlet, crimson and bright blue moreen, which, having a powerful light before them, by turning them towards the scenes reflected these various colours alternately, with a success that astonished and delighted the audience. Indeed, the whole stage appeared on fire.

The success of this novel experiment gave rise to other scenes in which transparent paintings were adopted. And French drew crowded audiences to a scene in some popular melodrama in which was an admirable view of Ludgate Hill, describing a night scene on a general illumination for some recent victory. [. . .]

291   Gainsborough comments on Garrick's experiments in coloured lighting

Forster Collection, vol. 10 (1772), Victoria and Albert Museum

Bath, Sunday morning

My dear Sir,

When the streets are paved with brilliants and the skies made of rainbows, I suppose you'll be contented and satisfied with red, blue and yellow. It appears to me that fashion, let it consist of false or true taste, will have its run like a runaway horse. For when eyes and ears are thoroughly debauched by glare and noise, the returning to modest truth will seem very gloomy for a time. And I know you are cursedly puzzled how to make this retreat without putting out your lights and losing the advantage of all our new discoveries of transparent painting etc. How to satisfy your tawdry friends whilst you steal back into the mild evening gleam and quiet middle term.

Now I'll tell you, my sprightly genius, how this is to be done: maintain all your light, but spare the abused colours till the eye rests and recovers. Keep up your music by supplying the place of *noise* by more sound, more harmony and more tune, and split that cursed fife and drum.

Whatever so great a genius as Mr Garrick may say or do to support our false taste, he must feel the truth of what I am now saying, that neither our plays, paintings or music are any longer real works of invention, but the abuse of nature's lights and what has already been invented in former times.

Adieu my dear friend. Any commands to Bath.

292   A transparency scene at Sadler's Wells in 1779

Thomas Greenwood: *Prophecy of Queen Elizabeth at Tilbury*. Sadler's Wells, 1779. Engraved by Cook after Dodd. Reproduced in Rosenfeld (1981), pl. 26

11 Actors and acting

INTRODUCTION

In the second half of the eighteenth century, some leading actors began to think analytically about the nature of their art. The older tradition of there being one correct way to play a character, and that way being handed down from master to apprentice, was no longer accepted without question. There was also growing opposition to the formal, exaggerated method of playing tragedy that had been established in the early decades of the century. The special tones of voice (the degrees of artificiality are represented by references to them as 'rants', 'tones' or 'cadences') and the studied gestures, which had more affinity with formal rhetoric than with acting technique, came under increasing attack. The actor's task was now seen as one of understanding and revealing, rather than of presentation. To understand the character first (which meant close study of the text); to feel the emotions involved; to explore human behaviour under the spell of those emotions, either in oneself or in others; and to speak and behave in as easy and familiar a manner as was consistent with being seen and heard in a playhouse – these were at the heart of Macklin's and Garrick's attack on the inheritance of Booth and Wilks. Hence the shift from tradition to originality, which meant not only the acceptance of the actor's right to freedom of interpretation but, by the time of Cooke and Kemble, to a positive encouragement of it, almost to novelty for its own sake. Macklin's Shylock and Garrick's Richard III in 1741 made the impact they did because they combined emotional involvement and imaginative effort into new interpretations of great depth and subtlety. For many who saw them, they were an overwhelming theatrical experience.

These two interpretations marked the start of a conflict between the formal school of acting, as represented by Quin, and a new naturalist approach. The issue was debated for several decades. The new naturalism of Macklin and Garrick did not eclipse at a stroke the formalism of delivery and gesture to which theatre-goers and actors alike were accustomed. As may be seen in many contemporary prints, 'grace' was deemed an important attribute for the actor's art throughout the eighteenth century. Even at the end of the century, actors were urged to study painting (especially history painting) and sculpture to improve the quality of their stage presence. Yet by the end of the century, the actress Sarah Siddons, who had clearly mastered the art of acting with sculptured grace, felt that it was not enough to copy nature, what was important was to interpret it. Her approach, which was seen as a new kind of classicism, was one that sprang from inner depth of feeling and understanding rather than from a rhetorical tradition.

To refer to four schools of eighteenth-century acting and label them the schools of

Betterton, Cibber–Booth–Wilks, Macklin–Garrick and Siddons–Kemble[1] is no more than a convenient shorthand. It gives some idea of the shifts of emphasis that took place during the century, but it can be misleadingly rigid. Throughout the century, there was a lively debate about the nature of the actor's art and a considerable overlap of acting approaches and styles.

[1] See, for instance, Downer, *PMLA* 58 (Dec 1943), 1002–37 and Campbell, *PMLA* 32 (June 1917), 163–200.

ACTING THEORY

A number of acting handbooks were published during the latter part of the eighteenth century, but they need to be read and interpreted with care. In many instances, the authors concerned were exploiting personal hobby-horses in their attempts to reduce nature into method. Generally, however, the same issue continued to preoccupy the thoughts of late eighteenth-century theorists as was the case in the work of Charles Gildon and Aaron Hill in the early part of the century. Aaron Hill's very real insights have to be dug out from behind a screen of categories and definitions and seemingly mechanical analyses, but they were influential for a large part of the eighteenth century.[1] John Hill (a failed actor and Grub-Street journalist who was nevertheless a discriminating critic) borrowed the ideas of a contemporary French writer, Rémond de Sainte-Albine,[2] who had emphasised the need for emotional and imaginative involvement in the actor [*see* **293a**]. He went on to illustrate the Frenchman's ideas perceptively from current English theatre practice. He also stressed the actor's need to find ways of communicating emotional insight through gesture, facial expression, diction and pointing, without falling into mannerism or monotony [*see* **293b**].

[1] *The actor; or a guide to the stage* (1821) was largely based on Aaron Hill's essay. Furthermore, H. Siddons in *Practical illustrations of rhetorical gesture and action* [second edition] (London: Sherwood *et al.*, 1822) included an appendix of sixty-nine plates based substantially on Hill's analyses.
[2] Rémond de Sainte-Albine: *Le Comédien* (Paris: Desaint et Saillant, 1747). Hill's book, published anonymously, makes no acknowledgement that it is a translation of Sainte-Albine's work.

293   John Hill writes on the art of the actor
[John Hill]: *The actor: a treatise on the art of playing* (London: R. Griffiths, 1750)

(A) THE NEED FOR EMOTIONAL INVOLVEMENT IN ACTING [pp. 16 and 25]

The performer who does not himself feel the several emotions he is to express to the audience will give but a lifeless and insipid representation of them. All the art in the world can never supply the want of sensibility in the player; if he is defective in this essential quality, all the advantages of nature, all the accomplishments he may have acquired by study, are thrown away upon him. He will never make others feel what he does not feel himself and will always be as different from the thing he is to represent as a mask from a face. [. . .]

If in playing comedy it is necessary that the player be able to make the most different impressions succeed one another readily and easily in his heart, it is not less essential to the performer in tragedy that he feel, much more strongly than the other needs to do, every one of those which he is to express to the audience. Sensibility in the comic actor therefore must be a more universal agent and, in the tragedian, it must be a more powerful one. [. . .]

The first intent of all playing is to affect and move the audience and, in all theatrical performances, it is an invariable rule that the coldest representation is the most defective. The principal thing the actor has to observe, when the circumstances of his part make it necessary that he should be vehement, is that he does not strain his voice so as to render it incapable of carrying him through the rest of the piece. [. . .]

Our players conduct themselves very differently on this occasion and run into the two contrary faults: some of ranting themselves hoarse in the first scenes so as to be incapable of speaking the succeeding and finer parts of the character in such a manner as to be heard: and others of saving themselves for these most interesting passages at the expense of being cold, insipid and contemptible in all the rest. In the character of Orestes in *The Distressed Mother*, there is one capital scene in which the player is to exert his utmost power and which requires him to be in a condition far from tired when he enters on it. We cannot but think, however, that Mr Ryan, though excellent in this peculiar scene of that play, ought to be reminded that this is only a small part of the character of that hero and that we purchase his excellence in it at too dear a rate when he is so very tame as he has lately been in the preceding scenes of the play, in order to the saving himself for this. [. . .]

We remember the time when Mr Garrick, through a disdain of the meanness of this sort of artifice, ran into the other extreme in many parallel cases; when he always ran himself so out of voice in some of the first scenes in the character of Pierre in *Venice Preserved* that he could not even be heard when he came afterwards to that great scene in which he reproaches the senate. And when in *Richard* he cried out to Richmond, 'Richard is hoarse with calling thee to battle', the audience was so sensible of the truth of the expression that they could scarce distinguish the sounds that conveyed it to them. But to the honour of this inimitable player, he has now fallen into so happy a method of moderating his fire in the beginnings of these characters, in order to the preserving himself intelligible to their end, that he might be set up as an example to the performer we have just named, had not we an opportunity of recommending the yet more masterly address of the veteran of the other house in this very part of Pierre [Quin], who has formed the true rule by which to proportion the due strength of voice to every part of that noble character, so as not to let us perceive a want of force anywhere; and yet to keep a reserve to support himself in the most violent scenes with a power and energy that the rest of the great performers of the time must allow us to say, nobody ever did, or perhaps ever will, come up to. [. . .]

Another powerful obstacle to the truth of a player's recitation is monotony. Of this fault in delivery there are properly three kinds: first, a continual perseverance in the same modulation of voice; secondly, a too great resemblance in the closest of periods or speeches; and thirdly, a too frequent repetition of the same inflexions.

The first of these kinds of monotony is much more general in this age than it is commonly supposed to be and is equally the fault of our players in comedy and in tragedy. A great number of the present race of actors are from this fault eternally piping out the same tune, like those little wind instruments with which people teach birds to sing. The second kind is yet more common among our actors than the first, but is in a manner peculiar to tragedy. The very people who play in comedy with some sort of natural cadence, frequently when they have blank verse put into their mouths, take up a sort of cant tone and seem to think it a duty to close every sentence with an octave below. We are sorry to bear hard upon the other sex; but as everything that carries the face of censure here is not meant as raillery but as hints for improvement, we cannot but observe that the actresses in tragedy are more faulty in this kind of monotony than the performers of the other sex. And that some who are now but in a middling rank upon the stage would rise much higher in the judgements of all those who are worth pleasing, if they could break themselves of this absurd and unnatural custom. [. . .]

The players in comedy are very rarely to be reproached with the third species of monotony, the too frequent repetitions of the same inflexions of voice. But we find those who perform in tragedy have a great deal of trouble to guard against it. Where the numbers and measure are the same, it is very natural that the pronunciation should run into the same equality; and the necessity that the performers in the modern tragedy are under from time to time of delivering with a pompous accent a long chain of blank verses, exposes them too much to it. [. . .]

Macklin's naturalistic approach

Both as teacher and actor, Macklin advocated a robustly naturalistic approach: in some of his training methods may be seen, in embryo, the kind of improvisation work associated with the later naturalist theatre [see **294**]. He was firmly opposed to traditional rhetoric and formal gestures [see **295**].

294   Macklin's method of training the voice
John O'Keeffe: *Recollections of his life*, vol. 1 (London, 1826), pp. 285–6

In Macklin's garden there were three long parallel walks, and his method of exercising their voices was thus. His two young pupils with back boards (such as they use in boarding schools) walked firmly, slow and well, up and down the two side walks. Macklin himself paraded the centre walk. At the end of every twelve paces he made them stop. And, turning gracefully, the young actor called out across the walk, 'How do you do, Miss Ambrose?' She answered, 'Very well, I thank you, Mr Glenville'. They then took a few more paces and the next question was, 'Do you not think it a very fine day, Mr Glenville?' 'A very fine day indeed, Miss Ambrose,' was the answer. Their walk continued, and then, 'How do you do, Mr Glenville?' 'Pretty well, I thank you, Miss Ambrose'. And this exercise continued for an hour or so (Macklin still keeping in the centre walk), in the full hearing of their religious next-door neighbours. Such was Macklin's method of training the management of the voice. If too high, too low, a wrong accent, or a faulty inflection, he immediately noticed it and made them repeat the words twenty times till all was right.

295   Macklin's insistence on greater naturalism

[John Hill]: *The actor: a treatise on the art of playing* (second edition) (London: R. Griffiths, 1755), p. 239

There was a time when that extravagance, which has just been recommended for farce, had its place in tragedy, both in action and delivery. The gestures were forced and beyond all that ever was in nature, and the recitation was a kind of singing. We are at present getting more into nature in playing, and if the violence of gesture be not quite suppressed, we have none of the recitative of the old tragedy.

It is to the honour of Mr Macklin that he began this great improvement. There was a time he was excluded the theatres and supported himself by a company whom he taught to play and some of whom afterwards made no inconsiderable figure.[1] It was his manner to check all the cant and cadence of tragedy; he would bid his pupil first speak the passage as he would in common life, if he had occasion to pronounce the same words; and then giving them more force, but preserving the same accent, to deliver them on stage.

When the player was faulty in his stops or accents, he set him right. And with nothing more than this attention to what is natural, he produced out of the most ignorant persons, players that surprised everybody.

[1] In 1744 Macklin brought together a group of young student actors at the Little Theatre in the Haymarket including Samuel Foote and John Hill. He instructed them and managed the company. His first production with this group was *Othello*, which opened on 6 February 1744.

A rhetorical approach to acting training

In complete contrast to Macklin's approach, acting manuals published by Roger Pickering in 1755 [*see* **296**] and Dr Hiffernan in 1770 [*see* **297**] were firmly rooted in the rhetorical traditions first outlined by Charles Gildon in 1710, although there was general agreement on the need for emotional identifications on the part of the actor.

296   A rhetorical approach to action and gesture

Roger Pickering: *Reflections upon theatrical expression in tragedy* (London: W. Johnstone, 1755), p. 31

In astonishment and surprise, arising from terror, the left leg is drawn back to some distance from the other. Under the same affection of the mind, but resulting from an unhoped-for meeting with a beloved object, the right leg is advanced to some distance before the left.

[. . .] Anger and threatening may be strongly supplied with grand expressions from these limbs [. . .].

The frequent traverses and sudden turnings upon the stage make the management of the feet and legs no trivial concern of the actor. The bombast strut; the diminutive trip; the unwieldy and awkward movement of the feet in turnings; the toes turned in or placed in a straight line with the bone of the leg: will lessen all the dignity and gracefulness of the other parts of attitude.

297   Dr Hiffernan's formal advice on the use of head and eyes
Paul Hiffernan: *Dramatic genius* (London: published by the author, 1770), p. 79

The entire body is to bear firmly on the floor and not to shift its place or change its attitude every moment, which would incur the charge of an unballasted restlessness.

There must be a meaning of necessity or of grace for every diversified direction of the head. [. . .]

The countenance is always to be turned toward the speaker and, from the eyes through an escaping look, no consciousness is to be gathered of any spectators being present even in soliloquies, which are but thinking aloud, or in side speaking [i.e. speaking asides]. [. . .]

Wherefore it follows that the direction of the eyes must always illustrate the sense of the words. [. . .]

The duty of the eyebrows is to be neither too sluggishly quiescent nor too wantonly active, but to observe a free, easy and well-timed obsequiousness to the sentimental expression of the eyes, which may poetically be called the soul of the countenance.

Emotional involvement in acting

Two of the most distinguished practitioners of the period, David Garrick and Sarah Siddons, expressed the need for emotional identification in their work. Commenting on his acting of Macbeth, Garrick makes it clear that he can only express in the role what he feels; even theatrical techniques, such as the use of pauses or inflections of the voice, need to be informed by feeling [see **298**]. Writing about the acting of Sarah Siddons, Leigh Hunt stresses the emotional intensity and commitment that she brought to her playing, so that she herself felt the distress and agitation of her characters [see **299**]. She was so completely absorbed in the characters she played that it was impossible to know whether her constant playing of tragic characters affected her off-stage personality, as one spectator implied [see **300**] or whether, as Boaden suggested, her own personality and interests affected her acting style [see **301**]. Boaden also implies that the increasing formality of her acting style in her later career, was occasioned partly by her fascination with statuary and partly by the sheer size of the metropolitan theatres she worked in during later life, notably the large new theatres at Drury Lane and Covent Garden.

298   Garrick stresses how emotional involvement in the portrayal of a character informs acting technique
The letters of David Garrick (1963), vol. 1, letter 281 (24 January 1762)[1]

[. . .] *Shakes so my single* – if I stop at the last word, it is a glaring fault, for the sense is imperfect. But my idea of that passage is this: Macbeth is absorbed in thought and struck with the horror of the murder, though but in idea (*fantastical*), and it naturally gives him a slow, tremulous undertone of voice. And though it might appear that I stopped at every word in the line, more than usual, yet my intention was far from dividing the substantive from its adjective, but to paint the horror of Macbeth's mind and keep the voice suspended a little, which it will naturally be in such a situation. And here, sir, you must give me leave to explain a little what I mean by suspending the voice, which in many cases I reckon a beauty in the speaker, when a stop would be a great fault. I have been frequently abused by the gentlemen of the pen for false stops; and one in particular wrote against me for stopping injudiciously in this line in *Hamlet*, *I think it was to see – my mother's wedding*. I certainly never *stop* there (that is, close the sense), but I as certainly *suspend* my voice, by which your ear must know that the sense is suspended too. For Hamlet's grief causes the break, and with a sigh he finishes the sentence – *my mother's wedding*. I really could not from my feelings act it otherwise. And were I to have the pleasure of talking this matter over with you, I flatter myself that I could make you, by various examples, feel the truth of my position. [. . .]

My notions, as well as execution, of the lines in the second appearance of Banquo are, I fear, opposite to your opinion. Should Macbeth sink into pusillanimity, I imagine it would hurt the character and be contrary to the intentions of Shakespeare. The first appearance of the spirit overpowers him more than the second, but before it vanishes at first, Macbeth gains strength. *If thou can'st nod, Speak too* must be spoken with terror, but with a recovering mind. And in the next speech with him, he cannot pronounce *Avaunt and quite my sight!* without a stronger exertion of his powers under the circumstance of horror. The *Why so – being gone*, etc. means, in my opinion, 'I am returning to my senses, which were before mad and inflamed with what I have seen'. I make a great difference between a mind sunk by guilt into cowardice and one rising with horror to acts of madness and desperation, which last I take to be the case of Macbeth. I certainly (as you say) recollect a degree of resolution, but I never advance an *inch*, for notwithstanding my agitation, my feet are immovable. [. . .]

¹ The letter is a reply to one signed H.H., dated two days previously and containing comments on his performance as Macbeth. See Boaden (1831), vol. 1, pp. 132–5

299   Leigh Hunt stresses the importance of feeling in Sarah Siddons's acting

Leigh Hunt: *Dramatic essays*, ed. by W. Archer and R.W. Lowe (London: Walter Scott, 1894), pp. 11–14

To write a criticism on Mrs Siddons is to write a panegyric, and a panegyric of a very peculiar sort, for the praise will be true. Like her elder brother, she has a marked and noble countenance and a figure more dignified than graceful, and she is like him in all his good qualities but not any of his bad ones. If Mr Kemble studiously meditates a step or an attitude in the midst of passion, Mrs Siddons never thinks about either, and therefore is always natural because on occasions of great feeling it is the passions should influence the actions. Attitudes are not to be studied, as old Havard¹ used to study them, between six looking glasses: feel the passion, and the action will follow. I know it has been denied that actors sympathise with the feelings they represent, and among other critics Dr Johnson is supposed to have denied it. [. . .] It appears to me that the countenance cannot express a single passion perfectly unless the passion is first felt. It is easy to grin representations of joy and to pull down the muscles of the countenance as an imitation of sorrow, but a keen observer of human nature and its effects will easily detect the cheat. There are nerves and muscles requisite to expression that will not answer the will on common occasions. But to represent a passion with truth, every nerve and muscle should be in its proper action, or the representation becomes weak and confused: melancholy is mistaken for grief and pleasure for delight. It is from this feebleness of emotion so many dull actors endeavour to supply passion with vehemence of action and voice, as jugglers are talkative and bustling to beguile scrutiny. I have somewhere heard that Mrs Siddons has talked of the real agitation which the performance of some of her characters has made her feel.

To see the bewildered melancholy of Lady Macbeth walking in her sleep, or the widow's mute stare of perfected misery by the corpse of the gamester Beverly, two of the sublimest pieces of acting on the English stage, would argue this point better than a thousand critics. Mrs Siddons has the air of never being the actress; she seems unconscious that there is a motley crowd called a pit waiting to applaud her, or that there are a dozen fiddlers waiting for her exit. This is always one of the marks of a great actor. The player who amuses himself by looking at the audience for admiration may be assured he never gets any. [. . .]

[1] William Havard (1710–78) actor.

300   A spectator comments on the off-stage personality of Mrs Siddons

N. Mangin (ed.): *Piozziana, or recollections of the late Mrs Piozzi* (London: Edward Moxon, 1833), pp. 85–6

[Mrs Siddons] though somewhat large of bone, was thin and surprisingly graceful. Her countenance might, with strict justice, be called beautiful. It was composed of the finest proportions imaginable. Her mouth was wonderfully expressive of good sense, sweetness and scorn. Her eyes were brilliant and piercing and could be seen to sparkle or glare at an incredible distance on the stage, as all must recollect who saw her as Lady Macbeth, when she rose from her throne at the solemn supper and was descending to chide her terrified husband. Or when with swathed jaws and corpse-like aspect, she stalked in her sleep from the back of the scene [*see* 316]. The effect of her eyes was greatly assisted by a power she had of moving her eyebrows and the muscles of her forehead. By her countenance alone, she could signify anger, revenge, sarcasm, sorrow, pride and joy so perfectly that it was impossible to misunderstand her, though she had not spoken a word. She so constantly acted the character of personages in affliction that, on the whole, she had a mournful visage and an awful tone of voice, very detrimental to the success of her comic attempts, and indeed unfriendly to her effects in the less impassioned scenes of tragedy or when she played merely genteel women in middle life. At times, in private company, she gave one a notion of a wicked, unhappy queen rather than of a purely well-bred gentlewoman.

When I made such remarks as these to Mrs Piozzi, she said I was partly right, but that her friend Mrs Siddons could be infinitely comic when she pleased and was among her intimates, though anything but a comedian on the boards. [. . .]

301   Boaden comments on the later work of Mrs Siddons
James Boaden: *Memoirs of Mrs Siddons*, vol. 2 (London: Longman *et al.*, 1827), pp. 288–92

Conspiring with the larger stage to produce some change in her style was her delight in statuary, which directed her attention to the antique and made a remarkable impression upon her as to simplicity of attire and severity of attitude. The actress had formerly complied with fashion and deemed the prevalent becoming. She now saw that tragedy was debased by the flutter of light materials and that the head, and all its powerful action from the shoulder, should never be encumbered by the monstrous inventions of the hairdresser and the milliner. She was now therefore prepared to introduce a mode of stage decoration and of deportment parting from one common principle [. . .]. What Mrs Siddons had chosen remains in a great degree the standard female costume to the present hour; and any little successes by degrees dropped off and left our ladies the heirs of her taste and its inseparable modesty. I have said that her deportment now varied considerably [. . .]. In a small space the turns are quick and short. Where the area is considerable, the step is wider, the figure more erect and the whole progress more grand and powerful; the action is more from the shoulder, and we now first began to hear of the perfect form of Mrs Siddons's arm. Her walk has never been attempted by any other actress and, in deliberate dignity, was as much alone as the expression of her countenance. [. . .]

Conflicting acting styles and problems caused by traditional casting methods

Despite the efforts of leading critics and actors, there was no general commitment in the Georgian theatre to an acting style based on emotional involvement. Garrick at times complained of having to work with actors whose externalised rhetorical approach to acting was diametrically opposed to his search for emotional and intellectual truth [*see* 302]. Even more disturbing was the uneven quality of performance produced by the stock company tradition of allowing players rights to certain parts [*see* 303]. The complaints expressed at this practice are a timely reminder that the Georgian theatre, despite the achievements of its leading actors, was more often than not characterised by a motley pattern of conflicting styles and conventions.

302   Garrick complains of Jane Cibber's rhetorical style of acting
The letters of David Garrick (1963), vol. 1, p. 158, letter 97 to the Countess of Burlington (18 October 1750)

[. . .] We go on vastly well at Drury Lane, nothing is talked of now but the theatres, and I have the pleasure of assuring your ladyship that we don't lose ground in the contest. Tomorrow a grand-daughter of Mr Cibber plays the part of Alicia in *Jane Shore* [by Rowe]. She has been instructed by him for some time. The young lady may have genius for ought I know, but if she has, it is so eclipsed by the manner of speaking the laureate has taught her that I am afraid it will not do. We differ greatly in our notions of acting (in tragedy, I mean). And if he is right, I am and ever shall be in the wrong road. [. . .]

303   Problems caused by actors retaining their monopoly of parts within companies
The Universal Museum and Complete Magazine (August, 1765), 392–3

And here we cannot help expressing the strongest disapprobation of the injudicious custom which is kept up by the managers of Drury Lane and Covent Garden in continuing a number of characters to several of their performers, when they have people of superior abilities at the same time unemployed in their houses. We will make the best supposition in our power and even admit that the managers keep up this custom out of tenderness to the actors in possession of the parts who would, in all probability, be highly mortified at being stripped of the least, and might possibly suffer in their interest, was it to be placed in any other hand.

With the greatest deference, however, to the opinion of our managers, we must beg leave to ask whether the tenderness thus shown to an actor of little or no merit is not the greatest cruelty imaginable to a man who may possess a great deal. [. . .]

We have too long seen the sprightliest parts of comedy taken up by people who could scarcely hobble without crutches. And have beheld, till we are surfeited, a youthful lover without a tooth expiring for a blooming virgin of fourscore. Let propriety therefore be a little consulted for the future, and let us at least show a little regard to nature, if we are ever so dead to the nicer feelings of a polished understanding.

TRAGIC ACTING
Macklin as Shylock

Macklin's epoch-making interpretation of Shylock as a tragic figure was first performed at Drury Lane on 14 February 1741 [*see* **304** and **305**]. For a generation of theatre-goers, it successfully displaced the earlier interpretation of Shylock as a comic figure. Lichtenberg's account of it was written over thirty years later, about the time that Parkinson's portrait was drawn. But Lichtenberg's reactions were so sensitive and acute that his description remains the best contemporary account of the performance.

304   Macklin as Shylock

Bell's British Theatre, edition of Shakespeare (1775). Private collection. Also in University Library, Bristol

305   Lichtenberg describes Macklin in the role of Shylock

Lichtenberg (1938), pp. 40–1

I saw Macklin, who is well known for his extraordinary excellence [. . .] and his physiognomy, play Shylock in Shakespeare's *Merchant of Venice*. You know that Macklin as Shylock sounds as well on a playbill as Garrick as Hamlet. [. . .] When he came on the stage, he was thrice greeted with general applause, which on each occasion lasted for quite a quarter of a minute. It cannot be denied that the sight of this Jew is more than sufficient to arouse once again in the mature man all the prejudices of his childhood against this race. Shylock is not one of those mean, plausible cheats who could expatiate for an hour on the virtues of a gold watch-chain of pinchbeck. He is heavy and silent in his unfathomable cunning and, when the law is on his side, just to the point of malice. Imagine a rather stout man with a coarse yellow face and a nose generously fashioned in all three dimensions, a long double chin and a mouth so carved by nature that the knife appears to have slit him right up to the ears, on one side at least, I thought. He wears a long black gown, long wide trousers and a red tricorne, after the fashion of Italian Jews, I suppose. The first words he utters, when he comes onto the stage, are slowly and impressively spoken: 'Three thousand ducats'. The double 'th' and the two sibilants, especially the second after the 't', which Macklin lisps as lickerishly as if he were savouring the ducats and all that they would buy, make so deep an impression in the man's favour that nothing can destroy it. Three such words uttered thus at the outset give the keynote of his whole character. In the scene where he first misses his daughter, he comes on hatless, with disordered hair, some locks a finger long standing on end, as if raised by a breath of wind from the gallows, so distracted was his demeanour. Both his hands are clenched and his movements abrupt and convulsive. To see a deceiver, who is usually calm and resolute, in such a state of agitation is terrible. [. . .]

Contrasting performances of Hamlet

Many of the most vivid accounts of tragic acting from this period relate to performances in Shakespeare's plays. This was partly due to Shakespeare's quality as a dramatist and the current vogue for his work; partly due to the relative dearth of outstanding new playwriting following the introduction of strict theatrical censorship in 1737. But above all, Shakespeare's approach to character drawing gave much greater scope to the meticulously prepared interpretations of Macklin and Garrick and other gifted actors who followed them.

Garrick as Hamlet

Three contrasting interpretations of *Hamlet* are illustrated, all of them, except Garrick's, tried and tested in the provinces before being presented in London. Garrick's Hamlet in 1775, as described by Lichtenberg, manifests all the emotional and intellectual subtlety that had come to be associated with his acting style [*see* 306 and 283].

306   Garrick's Hamlet in 1775
Lichtenberg (1938), pp. 9–11

Hamlet appears in a black dress, the only one in the whole court, alas! still worn for his poor father who has been dead scarce a couple of months. Horatio and Marcellus, in uniform, are with him and they are awaiting the ghost. Hamlet has folded his arms under his cloak and pulled his hat down over his eyes; it is a cold night and just twelve o'clock. The theatre is darkened, and the whole audience of some thousands are as quiet, and their faces as motionless, as though they were painted on the walls of the theatre; even from the farthest end of the playhouse one could hear a pin drop. Suddenly, as Hamlet moves towards the back of the stage slightly to the left and turns his back on the audience, Horatio starts, and saying: 'Look, my lord, it comes', points to the right where the ghost has already appeared and stands motionless before any one is aware of him. At these words Garrick turns sharply and at the same moment staggers back two or three paces with his knees giving way under him. His hat falls to the ground and both his arms, especially the left, are stretched out nearly to their full length, with the hands as high as his head, the right arm more bent and the hand lower and the fingers apart. His mouth is open. Thus he stands rooted to the spot, with legs apart but no loss of dignity, supported by his friends who are better acquainted with the apparition and fear lest he should collapse. His whole demeanour is so expressive of terror that it made my flesh creep even before he began to speak. The almost terror-struck silence of the audience, which preceded this appearance and filled one with a sense of insecurity, probably did much to enhance this effect. At last he speaks, not at the beginning, but at the end of a breath, with a trembling voice: 'Angels and ministers of grace defend us!' words which supply anything this scene may lack and make it one of the greatest and most terrible which will ever be played on stage.

The ghost beckons to him; I wish you could see him, with eyes fixed on the ghost, though he is speaking to his companions, freeing himself from their restraining hands as they warn him not to follow and hold him back. But at length, when they have tried his patience too far, he turns his face towards them, tears himself with great violence from their grasp and draws his sword on them with a swiftness that makes one shudder, saying: 'By Heaven! I'll make a ghost of him that lets me'. That is enough for them. Then he stands with his sword upon guard against the spectre, saying: 'Go on, I'll follow thee', and the ghost goes off the stage. Hamlet still remains motionless, his sword held out so as to make him keep his distance, and at length, when the spectator can no longer see the ghost, he begins slowly to follow him, now standing still and then going on, with sword still upon guard, eyes fixed on the ghost, hair disordered, and out of breath, until he too is lost to sight. You can well imagine what loud applause accompanies this exit. It begins as soon as the ghost goes off the stage and lasts until Hamlet also disappears. What an amazing triumph it is. [. . .][1]

---

[1] Joshua Steele, in *Prosodia rationalis, or a treatise on the melody and measure of speech* [second edition] (London: T. Payne & Son, 1779), pp. 40–8, illustrated his attempt to work out a method for recording speech, using a technique based on symbols analogous to musical notation, by reproducing the pace and tone of an eighteenth-century actor speaking the soliloquy 'to be, or not to be' from *Hamlet*. Having subsequently heard Garrick, he added the variants which in his view Garrick made from this. It is a fascinating but tantalising glimpse into Garrick's art, but ultimately, given the purely private nature of the notation, impossible to interpret meaningfully.

Henderson as Hamlet

Henderson was seen by his contemporaries as a likely successor to Garrick, following the latter's retirement in 1776. Garrick himself had advised Henderson to serve a period of apprenticeship in Bath, where he first appeared, acting under a pseudonym, on 6 October 1772. When he began work in London, playing Hamlet in 1777 [see **307** and **308**], Henderson seemed poised to follow Garrick's example as an actor of emotional and intellectual depth. However, his premature death in 1785 cut short that early promise.

307   John Henderson as Hamlet, c. 1777

[F. Pilon]: *An essay on the character of Hamlet as performed by Mr Henderson at the Theatre Royal in the Haymarket* (London: W. Flexney, [?] 1777), pp. 5–8

Mr Henderson's person is far from striking; it is rather under the middle size and moulded with no extraordinary elegance or symmetry. His eye is good and all his other features bold and marking, but his countenance seemed incapable of assuming the pathetic engaging look which should peculiarly distinguish the character. His deportment was easy but not graceful, and was considerably injured by his appearing over-solicitous about the disposal of his hands; it is particular and ungraceful to confine them too much to the bosom. Mr Henderson's first impression therefore was not very favourable to him. But if he appeared inadequate to the character in aspect and deportment, he soon convinced his auditors that he was not deficient in judgement and feeling. When the Queen charges Hamlet, almost in direct terms, with hypocrisy, persevering in obstinate sorrow for a loss which could not be retrieved, Mr Henderson delivered his pathetic reply with great sensibility. His look, tone and gesture were as well conceived as executed and finely marked the resentment of a delicate and liberal spirit hurt by a reproach it was conscious of not meriting.

Excellence in speaking a soliloquy is one of the greatest difficulties in the art of acting. Nature is the only dictator in spirited and impassioned scenes, moreover in dialogue the eye of the speaker is fixed by the person addressed. But in those cool deliberations which the mind holds with itself, when reason drops a curtain before the eye of sense and every external object is excluded, it is then the genius of the actor is tried. For unless he has a strong imagination to render him thoroughly possessed of the character, united to a sound judgement and the happiest powers of execution, his attention will unavoidably be solicited by the audience and render his words ridiculous and unnatural. Though we cannot pronounce Mr Henderson excellent in this department of the histrionic art, yet he was far from reprehensible; he appeared to want practice more than judgement, and a young actor seldom possesses his powers at once in full flexibility.

When the mind is strongly agitated, the body is restless and unsettled. Therefore Mr Henderson's walking to and fro during the time he waited to see his father's spirit was extremely natural. However, we most earnestly entreat him never in future to prepare us for a start by pulling off his hat immediately before the appearance of the ghost. If he apprehends that appendage to dress may conceal the part of his face where terror and anxiety are most strongly expressed, let him contrive to get rid of it in his first confusion, which if he cannot do with ease, let him remember that in the fine arts nothing is a beauty which militates with nature and truth. In the solemn address to the ghost, Mr Henderson's voice was low, tremulous and interrupted, rising gradually to a more confirmed tone as his fears subsided. But his ejaculation to the protecting Angels of Grace was offered up before he saw the spirit. His succeeding pause was just and natural, for terror incites an instantaneous wish for safety, and it is always some time before the mind recovers itself enough to attend to any other object. There is a very capital blunder in the conduct of this scene, of which most Hamlets are guilty. When the spirit appears, Horatio and Marcellus, instead of consulting their own safeties, seize Hamlet's arms, as if from their prior acquaintance with the ghost, they were become familiar. This is not only absurd and unnatural, but robs the principal object of a picturesque and striking attitude. [. . .]

308   John Henderson as Hamlet, Haymarket, 1777
Burney Collection of Theatrical Portraits, vol. 4, no. 211, p. 111 (Print Room, BM)

Kemble as Hamlet

Kemble's Hamlet in 1783 was a deliberately new reading, dignified and solemn, intellectually probing and aimed at a well-informed audience [see 309 and 310]. He had studied the play long and deeply and worked on it in the provinces (especially in the north-west) when held back from performing it in London. His Hamlet was graceful and formal, with a fixed melancholy and lacking in sudden outbursts of passion. John Taylor, an experienced actor, reacted at first to it as 'stiff, conceited and unnatural'.[1] Richard Sharp, writing to John

Henderson, felt that 'very careful study appears in all he says and he does; but there is more singularity and ingenuity than simplicity and fire'.[2] However, when audiences had time to adjust to this new approach, it became the established Hamlet of the last decade of the century.

[1] John Taylor: *Records of my life*, vol. 1 (London: Edward Bull, 1832), p. 131.
[2] Quoted in Russell (1872), p. 249.

309   J.P. Kemble as Hamlet, 1783

James Boaden: *Memoirs of the life of John Philip Kemble Esq.*, vol. 1 (London: Longman *et al.*, 1825), pp. 88–105

It was on Tuesday, 30th September 1783 that Mr Kemble made his first appearance at Drury Lane Theatre in the character of Hamlet. [. . .]

On Mr Kemble's first appearance before the spectators, the general exclamation was, 'How very like his sister!' and there was a very striking resemblance. His person seemed to be finely formed and his manners princely, but on his brow hung the weight of 'some intolerable woe'. Apart from the expression called up by the situation of Hamlet, there struck me to be in him a peculiar and personal fitness for tragedy. What others assumed seemed to be inherent in Kemble. 'Native and to the manner born', he looked an abstraction, if I may so say, of the characteristics of tragedy.

The first great point of remark was that his Hamlet was decidedly original. He had seen no great actor whom he could have copied. His style was formed by his own taste or judgement, or rather grew out of the peculiar properties of his person and his intellectual habits. He was of a solemn and deliberate temperament. His walk was always slow and his expression of countenance contemplative; his utterance rather tardy for the most part but always finely articulate and in common parlance seemed to proceed rather from organisation than voice.

It was soon found that the critic by profession had to examine the performance of a most acute critic. To the general conception of the character I remember but one objection: that the deportment was too scrupulously graceful. But besides that Hamlet is represented by the poet as, 'the glass of fashion and the mould of form', I incline to think the critic's standard was too low rather than Kemble's too high. The manners were not too refined for such a person as Mr Kemble's.

There were points in the dialogue in almost every scene which called upon the critic, where the young actor indulged his own sense of the meaning. And these were to be referred to the text or context in Shakespeare and also to the previous manner of Garrick's delivery or the existing one of Henderson's. The enemies of Kemble, that is, the injudicious friends of other actors, called these points NEW READINGS, which became accordingly a term of reproach among the unthinking. The really judicious, without positively deciding, admitted the ingenuity and praised the diligence of the young artist. They freely confessed that there might be endless varieties in the representation of such a character, justifiable too by very plausible reasonings, and congratulated themselves and the public upon a new and original actor whose performances, at all events, would never disgust them by

common place but would at all times tend to make Shakespeare better known by
the necessity for his being more studied; that the reference must be perpetual from
the actor to the works, and in thus contributing to the fame of the poet, the
performer might eventually establish his own.

A pretty extensive list of such points is before me, noticed by myself and by
others, where Mr Kemble differed from Garrick or Henderson, or both. I am
therefore quite sure that I do not attribute to the beginning of his career what I
only noticed in the progress. [. . .][1]

[1] Boaden describes and comments on these new readings on pp. 94–104.

310   John Philip Kemble as Hamlet, Drury Lane, 1783

Bell's British Theatre (1785). Private collection. Also in Mander and Mitchenson Collection

Cooke as Hamlet in 1785 and an eighteenth-century prompt book

It is from this period that very detailed prompt books have begun to survive.[1] Though they
vary in scope and interest, from the best of them much detail of production and playing can
be deduced, as in that of Kemble's great rival Cooke [see 311].[2] If Kemble's Hamlet was
graceful and solemn, Cooke's appeared to some spectators in London in 1801 to be harsh

and lacking in appeal to the emotions. But it is clear that, like Kemble, Cooke had worked out his own unique approach to the character.[3]

The scene shown below is valuable for its indications of production technique, suggesting the level aimed at in the provinces as well as London. Lighting control (with the stage darkened), distant martial music and the sound of the great dog are all used to build up atmosphere in a sophisticated sequence of effects that would be well beyond the reach of a simple strolling company. It is also worth comparing this scene, as described in the prompt book, with the Bath Orchard Street water-colour sketch of the same scene [see **240**], which must refer to a performance at around the same time. In both, the ghost points off-stage with his truncheon. However, the apparent incongruity of the Bath setting, as drawn, would have been less obvious in the gloom of a darkened stage, which the artist has omitted to indicate.

[1] See Shattuck (1965).
[2] The prompt book is written in Cooke's own hand and represents the performance first given by him in Joseph Austin's company at Chester in 1785. No doubt it formed the basis of his London interpretation of 1801.
[3] See M. St. C. Byrne: 'The earliest *Hamlet* prompt book in an English library' *TN* 15 (1960), 21–31 and plates 5–8. See also Hare (1980), pp. 42–3 and 200–4.

311   G.F. Cooke's prompt book for *Hamlet*, 1785

Library of the Literary and Philosophical Society, Newcastle upon Tyne [pp. 18–19]

SCENE, *a Platform*

+ (*Enter Hamlet, Horatio and Marcellus*)   + The stage darkened –

HAM. The air bites shrewdly; it is very   Hamlet enters from the top.
cold.   Horatio on his R.H. Marcel-

HOR. It is a nipping and an eager air.   lus on L.H. They speak as

HAM. What hour now?   they come down.

HOR. I think it lacks of twelve.

MAR. No, it is struck.

HOR. Indeed! I heard it not. It then
draws near the season
Wherein the spirit held his wont
to walk. +   + Martial music heard at a

(Stage direction deleted)   distance. Afterwards the
What does this mean, my lord?   great dog appears and barks

HAM. The king doth wake tonight and   and barks at back scene of
takes his rouse,   the stage.
(line deleted)
And, as he drains his draughts of
Rhenish down,
The kettledrum and trumpet thus
(deletion) proclaim
The triumph of his pledge.

MAR. Is it a custom?

HAM. Ay, marry, is't:
But, to my mind – though I am

native here,

And to the manner born – it is a custom

More honoured in the breach than the observance

(**22 lines deleted**)

(*Enter Ghost*). W.L.H.

HOR. Look, my lord, it comes! +

HAM. Angels and ministers of grace defend us!

Be thou a spirit of health, or goblin damn'd,

Bring with thee airs from heavn'n, or blasts from hell,

Be thy intents wicked or charitable,

Thous com'st in such questionable shape

That I will speak to thee. I'll call thee Hamlet,

King, father, **royal Dane** (Loyal Dane): oh! answer me;

Let me not burst in ignorance! but tell

Why thy canoniz'd bones, hearsed in death,

Have burst their cearments? Why the sepulchre,

Wherein we saw thee quietly in-**ured** (terr'd)

Hath op'd **his** (its) ponderous and marble jaws,

To cast thee up again? What may this mean –

That thou, dead corse, again, in complete steel,

Revisit'st thus the glimpses of the moon,

Making night hideous; and **we** (us) fools of nature,

So horribly to shake our disposition

With thoughts beyond the reaches of our souls?

+ When the Ghost appears Hamlet starts, – a short pause – speaks the first line – a longer pause – at the word 'father': – pause – & during the whole scene, never takes his eye off the Ghost. Hor. & Mar. handle their swords, but do not draw. Their attention is likewise rivetted.

('**royal Dane**' deleted)

('**ured**' deleted)
('**his**' deleted)

('**we**' deleted)

	Say, why is this? Wherefore?	
	What should we do? +	+ Ghost waves his trun-
HOR.	It beckons you to go away with it,	cheon & points off L.H.
	As if it some impartment did desire	
	To you alone. +	+ With an action of earnest
		entreaty, waves again.

Contrasting performances of Macbeth and Lady Macbeth

Francis Gentleman's comparison of different actors playing the role of Macbeth [*see* 312] seems designed to underline Garrick's pre-eminence in the role. There were other distinguished actors who attempted the part, but there were none who excelled in it in quite the same way as Garrick [*see* 280a].

312   A comparison of different actors and actresses playing in *Macbeth*

Francis Gentleman: *The dramatic censor, or critical companion*, vol. 1 (London: J. Bell, 1770), pp. 106–13

[. . .] Through all the soliloquies of anxious reflections in the first act; amidst the pangs of guilty apprehensions and pungent remorse in the second; through all the distracted terror of the third; all the impetuous curiosity of the fourth and all the desperation of the fifth, Mr Garrick shows uniform, unabating excellence. Scarce a look, motion or tone but takes possession of our faculties and leads them to a just sensibility.

As Shakespeare rises above himself in many places so does this his greatest and best commentator, who not only presents his beauties to the imagination but brings them home feelingly to the heart. Among a thousand other instances of almost necromantic merit, let us turn our recollections only to a few in the character of Macbeth. Whoever saw the immortal actor start at and trace the imaginary dagger previous to Duncan's murder without embodying, by sympathy, unsubstantial air into the alarming shape of such a weapon? Whoever heard the low but piercing notes of his voice when the *deed is done*, repeating those inimitable passages which mention the sleeping grooms and murder of sleep, without feeling a vibration of the nerves? Whoever saw the guilty distraction of features he assumes on Banquo's appearance at the feast, without sacrificing reason to real apprehension from a mimic ghost? Who has heard his speech, after receiving his death wound, uttered with the utmost agony of body and mind, but trembles at the idea of future punishment, and almost pities the expiring wretch, though stained with crimes of the deepest die?

Theatrical performance to most spectators appears a mechanical disposition of limbs and a parrotted mode of speech: so indeed it really is too often. But intrinsic merit soars far beyond such narrow, barren limits; she traces nature through her various windings, dives into her deepest recesses and snatches ten thousand beauties which plodding method can never display. The dullest comprehension may be taught to enter on this side or that, to stand on a particular board, to raise the voice here and fall it there; but unless motion and utterance are regulated by a cultivated knowledge of life and self-born intelligent feelings, no greater degree of excellence can be attained than unaffecting propriety. Like a fair field whose native fertility of soil produced a beauteous luxuriant crop of spontaneous vegetation, which art can only regulate not enrich, Mr Garrick's matchless genius not only captivates our sportive senses but also furnishes high relished substantial food for our minds to strengthen by.

Mr Quin, whose sole merit in tragedy was declamation or brutal pride, was indescribably cumbersome in *Macbeth*. His face, which had no possible variation from its natural grace except sternness and festivity, could not be expected to exhibit the acute sensations of this character. His figure was void of the essential spirit and his voice far too monotonous for the transitions which so frequently occur. Yet, wonderful to be told, he played it several years with considerable applause.

Mr Sheridan showed more variety of acting in this part than any other and made an astonishing good use of his limited powers. Without any exaggeration of compliment to that gentleman, we must place him in a very reputable degree of competition with Mr Garrick in the dagger scene, and at the same time confess a doubt whether any performer ever spoke the words, 'this is a sorry sight', better. As to the third, fourth and fifth acts, his meaning well was all we could ever perceive to recommend him.

Mr Barry, as a capital actor, indeed a very capital one in his proper cast, made, in our comprehension, but a luke-warm affair of Macbeth. His amorous harmony of features and voice could but faintly, if at all, describe passions incident to a tyrant in such circumstances as he is placed. His commanding figure and other requisites preserved him from being insipid, though far beneath himself. [. . .]

Lady Macbeth, as to the detestable composition of her character, has been sufficiently animadverted on, therefore little more is necessary than to observe that, though there does not appear much call for capital merit, yet several first-rate actresses have made but a languid figure in representing her.

Notwithstanding Mrs Woffington was extremely well received and really did the part as well as her deplorable tragedy voice would admit, we must place Mrs Pritchard foremost, who made a very just distinction in the scene where Banquo's ghost appears between reproving Macbeth's behaviour with passion or the anxiety of apprehension, lest he should betray his guilt. This latter method she happily pursued and here, as well as in the sleeping scene, gained manifest superiority. Mrs Yates at present comes nearest the point of praise, but certainly displays no very conspicuous merit in the character. And to mention Mrs Barry would be to injure her, as it certainly does not at all coincide with her capabilities. [. . .]

Garrick and Mrs Pritchard in Macbeth

Thomas Davies seems to imply that Garrick's success in the part owed something to the acting of Mrs Pritchard who was his constant companion as Lady Macbeth: they seemed to complement each other perfectly [*see* **313**]. The dagger scene was one of the major highlights of their performance, depicted in graphic detail by Zoffany [*see* **314**].[1]

[1] The Fuseli version of this scene concentrates on dramatic effect. See Nicoll (1980), p. 108.

313 Hannah Pritchard as Lady Macbeth
Davies, vol. 2 (1808), pp. 182–9

Her few defects in tragedy proceeded from a too loud and profuse expression of grief and want of grace in her manner. Her natural ease of deportment and grandeur of person generally hid the defect of this last requisite from the common spectator. [. . .]

Lady Macbeth is the chief agent of the poet to carry on his plot. A woman of unbounded ambition, divested of all human feelings, to gain a crown urges her reluctant husband to the murder of the king. Mrs Pritchard's action, before and after the commission of the horrid deed, was strongly characteristical. It presented an image of a mind insensible to compunction and inflexibly bent to gain its purpose. When she snatched the daggers from the remorseful and irresolute Macbeth, despising agitations of a mind unaccustomed to guilt and alarmed at the terrors of conscience, she presented to the audience a picture of the most consummate intrepidity in mischief. When she seized the instruments of death and said, 'Give me the daggers!', her look and action cannot be described and will not soon be forgotten by the surviving spectators. At the banquet scene in the third act of the play, she still discovered more characteristical skill, if possible, than in the preceding act. The guilty king, whose mind is full of horrors resulting from the murder of Banquo, by his alarming terrors betrays himself to his guests. Pritchard's art in endeavouring to engage the attention of the company and draw them from the observation of Macbeth's feelings equalled anything that was ever seen in the art of acting.

In exhibiting the last scene of Lady Macbeth, in which the terrors of a guilty conscience keep the mind broad awake while the body sleeps, Mrs Pritchard's acting resembled those sudden flashes of lightning which more accurately discover the horrors of surrounding darkness.

314   The dagger scene from *Macbeth*: Garrick as Macbeth, Mrs Pritchard as Lady Macbeth, 1768

Painting by Zoffany. Original in Baroda Museum.

Sarah Siddons as Lady Macbeth

Sarah Siddons's notes on her experiences in the part of Lady Macbeth [*see* 315] indicate vividly the emotional power she found in the role even as a young and inexperienced actress. Her lively description is even more revealing than the portrait that has survived showing her in the role of Lady Macbeth [*see* 316].

315   Sarah Siddons's notes on preparing and playing Lady Macbeth

'Remarks on the character of Lady Macbeth' in T. Campbell: *The life of Mrs Siddons*, vol. 2 (London: Effingham Wilson, 1834), pp. 35–9

It was my custom to study my characters at night when all the domestic cares and business of the day were over. On the night preceding that in which I was to appear in this part for the first time, I shut myself up as usual, when all the family were retired, and commenced my study of Lady Macbeth. As the character is very short, I thought I should soon accomplish it. Being then only twenty years of age, I believed, as many others do believe, that little more was necessary than to get the words into my head; for the necessity of discrimination and the development of character at that time of my life had scarcely entered into my imagination. But, to proceed. I went on with tolerable composure in the silence of the night (a night I never can forget), till I came to the assassination scene, when the horrors of the scene rose to a degree that made it impossible for me to get farther. I snatched up my candle and hurried out of the room in a paroxysm of terror. My dress was of silk, and the rustling of it, as I ascended the stairs to go to bed, seemed to my panic-struck fancy like the movement of a spectre pursuing me. At last I reached my chamber, where I found my husband fast asleep. I clapt my candlestick down upon the table, without the power of putting the candle out, and I threw myself on my bed, without daring to stay even to take off my clothes. At peep of day, I rose to resume my task, but so little did I know of my part when I appeared in it at night that my shame and confusion cured me of procrastinating my business for the remainder of my life.

About six years afterwards I was called upon to act the same character in London. By this time I had perceived the difficulty of assuming a personage with whom no one feeling of common general nature was congenial or assistant. One's own heart could prompt one to express, with some degree of truth, the sentiments of a mother, a daughter, a wife, a lover, a sister, etc., but to adopt this character must be an effort of the judgement alone.

Therefore it was with the utmost diffidence, nay terror, that I undertook it, and with the additional fear of Mrs Pritchard's reputation in it before my eyes. The dreaded first night at length arrived when, just as I had finished my toilette and was pondering with fearfulness my first appearance in the grand fiendish part, comes Mr Sheridan knocking at my door and insisting, in spite of all my entreaties not to be interrupted at this to me tremendous moment, to be admitted. He would not be denied admittance, for he protested he must speak to me on a circumstance which so deeply concerned my own interest that it was of the most serious nature. Well, after much squabbling, I was compelled to admit him that I might dismiss him the sooner and compose myself before the play began. But what was my distress and astonishment when I found that he wanted me, even at this moment of anxiety and terror, to adopt another mode of acting the sleeping scene. He told me he had heard with the greatest surprise and concern that I meant to act it without holding the candle in my hand. And when I urged the impracticability of washing out that 'damned spot' with the vehemence that was certainly implied by both her own words and by those of her gentlewoman, he insisted that if I did put the candle out of my hand, it would be thought a presumptious innovation, as Mrs Pritchard had always retained it in hers. My mind, however, was made up and it was then too late to make me alter it, for I was too agitated to adopt another method. My deference for Mr Sheridan's taste and judgement was, however, so great that, had he proposed the alteration whilst it was possible for me to change my own plan, I should have yielded to his suggestion. Though even then, it would have been against my own opinion and my observation of the accuracy with which somnambulists perform all the acts of waking persons. The scene of course was acted as I had myself conceived it, and the innovation, as Mr Sheridan called it, was received with approbation. Mr Sheridan himself came to me after the play and most ingenuously congratulated me on my obstinacy. When he was gone out of the room, I began to undress and, while standing up before my glass and taking off my mantle, a diverting circumstance occurred to chase away the feelings of this anxious night. For, while I was repeating and endeavouring to call to mind the appropriate tone and action to the following words, 'Here's the smell of blood still!', my dresser innocently exclaimed, 'Dear me, ma'am, how very hysterical you are tonight. I protest and vow, ma'am, it was not blood but rose-pink water, for I saw the property man mix it up with my own eyes.'

316   Sarah Siddons as Lady Macbeth
Theatre Collection, University of Bristol. Painted by Harlowe, engraved by Robert Casper. Published 1822

Contrasting performances in *Romeo and Juliet* and *Venice Preserved*

In 1750 both Covent Garden and Drury Lane mounted productions of *Romeo and Juliet* for a competitive run that lasted for thirteen consecutive nights.[1] At Covent Garden, Spranger Barry played Romeo, while Susannah Cibber played Juliet: at Drury Lane Garrick played Romeo while George Anne Bellamy played Juliet [*see* **317**]. A fascinating comparison of the two interpretations of Romeo by Francis Gentleman suggests that while Garrick, in terms of his vivacity and ability to convey a shifting series of emotions, may have been the better actor, Barry was by far the best at bringing tears to the eyes of his audience [*see* **318** and **319**].

[1] See the extract from Rich's Register in chapter 8 giving details of this run [**203**].

317   The tomb scene from Garrick's version of *Romeo and Juliet*, 1750

Engraving by Ravenet (1765) after Benjamin Wilson (*c.* 1753). Burney Collection of Theatrical Portraits, Garrick Portfolio, no. E.e.3.182 (Print Room, BM). Reproduced in Rosenfeld (1981), plate 11

318   Spranger Barry as Romeo and Isabel Nossiter as Juliet in the 1754 production of *Romeo and Juliet* at Covent Garden
Mander and Mitchenson Theatre Collection

319   Barry and Garrick compared as Romeo
Gentleman, vol. 1 (1770), pp. 189–90

[. . .] a character upon the stage was never supported with more luxuriant merit than this [Romeo] by Messrs Garrick and Barry, or Barry and Garrick. For when those inimitable performers contested it sixteen or seventeen years since, it was extremely difficult to say who should stand first [. . .].

As to figure, though there is no necessity for a lover being tall, yet we apprehend Mr Barry had a peculiar advantage in this point. His amorous harmony of features, melting eyes and unequalled plaintiveness of voice seemed to promise everything we could wish. And yet the superior grace of Mr Garrick's attitudes, the vivacity of his countenance and the fire of his expression showed there were many essential beauties in which his great competitor might be excelled. Those scenes in which they most evidently rose above each other are as follow: Mr Barry, the garden scene of the second act; Mr Garrick, the friar scene in the third; Mr Barry, the garden scene in the fourth; Mr Garrick, in the first scene, description of the apothecary, etc.; fifth act, Mr Barry, first part of the tomb scene; and Mr Garrick, from where the poison operates to the end.

Having seen this play three times at each house during the contention, and having held the critical scale in as just an equilibrium as possible, by not only my own feelings but those of the audience in general, I perceived that Mr Garrick commanded most applause, Mr Barry most tears [. . .].

Spranger Barry

Generally, Barry excelled in emotive parts. He was known as the outstanding stage lover of his day. His good looks (he was tall, charming and had 'melting eyes'), and his naturally gentle temper, made him perfectly suited to parts requiring a display of the 'softer passions', as Thomas Davies points out in his assessment of Barry's acting.

320   Thomas Davies assesses the quality of Spranger Barry's acting
Davies, vol. 2 (1808), pp. 259–62

Of all the tragic actors who have trod the English stage for these last fifty years, Mr Barry was unquestionably the most pleasing. Since Booth and Wilks, no actor had shown the public a just idea of the hero or the lover; Barry gave dignity to the one and passion to the other. In his person he was tall, without awkwardness; in his countenance handsome without effeminacy; in his uttering of passion, the language of nature alone was communicated to the feelings of an audience.

If any player deserved the character of an unique, he certainly had a just claim to it. [. . .] It has been said that Colley Cibber preferred his Othello to the performances of Betterton and Booth in that part, and I should not wonder at it. For they, I believe, though most excellent actors, owed a great deal of their applause to art. Every word which Barry spoke in this the greatest character of the greatest poet seemed to come from the heart. [. . .] But indeed the same heart-rending feelings which charmed the audience in Othello diffused themselves through all Barry's acting when the softer passions predominated: in Jaffier, Castalio, Romeo, Varanes, Phocyas, Orestes. Richard the Third and Macbeth he never should have attempted, for he was deficient in representing the violent emotions of the soul; nor could a countenance so placid as his ever wear the strong impressions of despair and horror. His Lear, though not equal to Garrick's perfect exhibition of that part, from the dignity of his figure and his tenderness of expression, perfectly adapted to some scenes of the part, was very respectable. Booth, from a too classical taste, had no relish for the rants of Alexander and could never be prevailed upon to act that part, which Montfort and Betterton had so highly graced. But Barry gave new vigour to the wild flights of the mad hero; he charmed the ladies repeatedly by the soft melody of his love complaints and the noble ardour of his courtship.

Mrs Cibber, Mrs Barry and Mrs Siddons

Susannah Cibber, who had played Juliet to Barry's Romeo in 1750, was also best suited to emotive roles. An assessment of her in *Biographia Dramatica* points to her plaintive and musical voice and her ability (similar to Barry's) to affect the hearts of an audience [*see* 321]. In 1762, she played Belvidera in Otway's *Venice Preserved*, while Garrick played Jaffier. Zoffany's portrait of the famous dagger scene, where Jaffier threatens to stab his wife, shows a resolute Garrick dominating Belvidera who languishes on the ground at his feet [*see* 322]. Roberts's 1776 engraving of Mr and Mrs Barry (later Mrs Crawford) in precisely the same scene is revealing for its similarities and differences. In both, the gestures and the poses are studied and graceful, as befits the self-conscious rhetoric of Otway's Restoration tragedy. However, by comparison with Garrick, Barry seems altogether softer and more irresolute in the role of Jaffier (and arguably closer to the character Otway created); his wife stands upright, side by side with him, his equal both emotionally and professionally [*see* 323]. Something of the forcefulness of her personality and acting style emerges from Boaden's comparison of her approach with that of the more thoughtful, graceful and melancholic approach of Sarah Siddons [*see* 324].

321   A portrait of Susannah Cibber

David Erskine Baker (ed.): *Biographia Dramatica, or a companion to the playhouse*, vol. 1 (London: Longman *et al.*, 1812), pp. 123–4

Her person was perfectly elegant, for although she somewhat declined beyond the bloom of youth and even wanted that *embonpoint* which sometimes is assistant in concealing the impression made by the hand of time, yet there was so complete a symmetry and proportion in the different parts which constituted this lady's form that it was impossible to view her figure and not think her young or look in her face and not consider her handsome. Her voice was beyond conception plaintive and musical, yet far from deficient in powers for the expression of resentment and disdain. And so much equal command of feature did she possess for the representation of pity or rage, of complacence or disdain, that it would be difficult to say whether she affected the hearts of an audience most when playing the gentle, the delicate Celia, or the haughty, the resenting Hermione, in the innocent love-sick Juliet, or in the forsaken, the enraged Alicia. In a word, through every cast of tragedy she was admirable; and could we forget the excellence of a Pritchard, we should be apt to say inimitable. [. . .]

322   David Garrick as Jaffier and Susannah Cibber as Belvidera in *Venice Preserved*, Drury Lane, 1762

Engraving by Wilson after Zoffany. Burney Collection of Theatrical Portraits, Garrick Portfolio, no.E.e.3.207 (Print Room, BM). Portraits in The Garrick Club and the National Theatre

323   Mr and Mrs Barry in the characters of Jaffier and Belvidera in *Venice Preserved*

Bell's British Theatre (1776). University Library, Bristol

324   Mrs Barry and Mrs Siddons compared, 1783

James Boaden: *Memoirs of the life of John Philip Kemble Esq.*, vol. 1 (London: Longman *et al.*,
1825), pp. 129–30

[Mrs Barry] looked still a fine woman, though time, while it had taken something
from the elegance of her figure, had also begun to leave its impression upon her
features. It soon appeared the great actresses were of very different schools. That
what was unimpassioned in the dialogue was somewhat rapidly given by Mrs
Crawford [Mrs Barry][1] who evidently reserved herself for striking effects, while
Mrs Siddons seemed to consider that everything in the part she played required the
utmost care, and that where declamation was not to be lifted by passion, it was to
charm by a kind of tender and melancholy music, disposing the soul to the
superior effects when they arose. Although no comparison could be made except
as to the general style of the two artists, it was yet not very difficult to anticipate in
what points they would be found to differ in the performance of the character in
question.

The voice of Mrs Crawford was somewhat harsh and what might be termed
broken. In level speaking it resembled the tone of passion in other speakers. It was
at no time agreeable to the ear. But when thrown out by the vehemence of her
feeling, it had a transpiercing effect that seemed absolutely to wither up the hearer.
It was a flaming arrow; it was the lightning of passion. Such was the effect of her
almost shriek to Old Norval, 'Was he alive?' It would be ungenerous to ask
whether even a mother, hanging with breathless terror over every word of the old
shepherd's narrative, could summon force enough for such an explosion. The fact
was that reason here had nothing to do. It was an electric shock that drove the
blood back from the surface suddenly to the heart and made you cold and
shuddering with terror in the midst of a crowded theatre.

[1] Mrs Barry, before her marriage, was known as Mrs Dancer. After Spranger Barry's death in 1777,
she became Mrs Crawford.

Contrasting performances of Richard III
Garrick as Richard III

In the same year as Macklin presented his naturalistic reading of Shylock (14 February
1741), Garrick offered a fiery re-interpretation of Richard III at Goodman's Fields on 19
October. It was clearly intended as a challenge to the rhetorical bias of Quin's approach to
acting. Though some members of the audience were inclined to query the propriety of
Garrick's natural style of delivery, Thomas Davies points out that most were won over by
the energy and subtlety of his reading [*see* **325a**]. Francis Gentleman, in his account of
Garrick's acting in the role, stressed the carefully balanced nature of his interpretation [*see*
325b]. As he saw it, Garrick avoided the opposing temptations to play Richard as buffoon or
brute. The well-known portrait of Garrick as Richard III by Hogarth conveys directly and
vividly the emotional fire and intensity that Garrick brought to his acting of the part [*see*
326].

325   Garrick as Richard III

(A) DAVIES Davies, vol. 1 (1808), pp. 39–41

An actor who, in the first display of his talents, undertakes a principal character, has generally amongst other difficulties, the prejudices of the audience to struggle with, in favour of an established performer. Here indeed, they were not insurmountable. Cibber, who had been much admired in Richard, had left the stage. Quin was the popular player, but his manner of heaving up his words and his laboured action prevented his being a favourite Richard.

Mr Garrick's easy and familiar, yet forcible, style in speaking and acting at first threw the critics into some hesitation concerning the novelty as well as propriety of his manner. They had been long accustomed to an elevation of the voice, with a sudden mechanical depression of its tones calculated to excite admiration and to entrap applause. To the just modulation of the words, and concurring expression of the features from the genuine workings of nature, they had been strangers, at least for some time. But after he had gone through a variety of scenes, in which he gave evident proofs of consummate art and perfect knowledge of character, their doubts were turned into surprise and astonishment, from which they relieved themselves by loud and reiterated applause. They were more especially charmed when the actor, after having thrown aside the hypocrite and politician, assumed the warrior and hero. When news was brought to Richard that the Duke of Buckingham was taken, Garrick's look and action, when he pronounced the words, 'Off with his head! So much for Buckingham!' were so significant and important, from his visible enjoyment of the incident that several loud shouts of approbation proclaimed the triumph of the actor and satisfaction of the audience. The death of Richard was accompanied with the loudest gratulations of applause.

(B) FRANCIS GENTLEMAN Gentleman, vol. 1 (1770), pp. 11–12

The public have set up Mr Garrick as a standard of perfection in this laborious, difficult part, and if we consider the essentials, his claim to such distinction will immediately appear indisputable. A very deformed person never rises above, and seldom up to, the middle stature; it is generally attended with an acuteness of features and sprightliness of eyes. In these three natural points our Roscius stands unexceptionable: variations of voice and climax of expression, in both which he stands without an equal; graceful attitudes, nervous action, with a well-regulated spirit to animate within natural bounds every passage, even from the coldest up to the most inflamed.

Mr Garrick also preserves a happy medium and dwindles neither into the buffoon or the brute: one, or both of which, this character is made by most other performers. 'Tis true, there are many passages which have a ludicrous turn, yet we may rest assured that he who occasions least laughter is most right. [. . .]

Having placed Mr Garrick far before all other competitors in this character, as supporting every scene throughout the whole with very capital merit, it would be ungenerous not to acknowledge that Mr Mossop displays great powers, Mr Sheridan much judgement and Mr Smith considerable spirit. But had the first more delicacy with less labour; the second more harmony and less stiffness; the third more variation with less levity, their merit would rise several degrees beyond what it is.

326 Portrait of Garrick as Richard III by Hogarth

Engraving by Hogarth and Grignon in Burney Collection of Theatrical Portraits, Garrick Portfolio, no E.e. 3.119 (Print Room, BM). Original portrait in Walker Art Gallery, Liverpool.

Cooke as Richard III

Equally startling in his impact on London audiences some 60 years later was G.F. Cooke in his playing of Richard III. At the heart of his interpretation was the attempt to achieve a consistently studied approach to the character, embodied in a series of emotional and visual leitmotifs. Cooke viewed Richard III as a subtle, sarcastic villain, detestable and yet understandable, seeing himself cut off from others because of his deformity. He explored various ways of communicating his understanding of the part both visually and emotionally to his audiences. A thorough analysis of his approach may be found in the *Monthly Mirror* [*see* 327].[1] A portrait of him in the same role is less revealing, in terms of overall interpretation, but it does underline the carefully sustained nature of his approach to Richard III as a calculating villain [*see* 328].

[1] Important also is a pamphlet: *Remarks on the character of Richard III as played by Cooke and Kemble* [second edition, revised and corrected] (London, 1801).

327   George Frederick Cooke as Richard III

'Retrospect of new performers' in *Monthly Mirror*, 10 (November 1800), 318–21

This gentleman has excited the public attention more than any actor that has appeared on the London boards for many years. He has already played Richard and Shylock four times and Sir Archy MacSarcasm in *Love à la Mode* twice to crowded houses and with the most unbounded approbation. [. . .]

Richard has always been considered one of the most difficult of Shakespeare's characters from the varieties of situation in which he is placed. [. . .] the performer who undertakes the task must bring to it a mature judgement and extensive powers: the most skilful discrimination, an exhaustless spirit and a voice that will sustain itself through a rapid series of the most difficult transitions. Blunt, yet hypocritical; barbarous and unrelenting, but occasionally checked by the small still voice of conscience; an ardent lover, but a tyrannical husband; frightened by a dream and yet disdaining to be subdued by it; suspicious, yet daring; politic in council and courageous in the field of battle. [. . .]

Arduous as a character thus versatile must be, it is yet one of the most favourable parts which an actor can possibly select for his appearance. Such a man is Cooke, who seems to possess an active and capacious intellect with a profound knowledge of the science of acting. He has read and thought for himself. He appears to have borrowed neither from contemporary nor deceased excellence. He sometimes passes over what have been usually conceived to be great points in the character, and he exalts other passages into importance which former Richards have not thought significant enough for particular notice. His object seems to have been to form a grand, characteristic and consistent whole, and that whole is the result of deep thinking and well-directed study, judiciously adapted to his individual powers of action. For Mr Cooke not only thinks originally, but he looks, speaks and walks unlike any other man we ever saw. 'He is himself alone.' He is therefore in some degree a mannerist, but his settled habits are not injurious to the characters he has hitherto played, or is likely to play, in Covent Garden. And his talents are so uncommonly brilliant that, though we cannot be altogether blind to his defects, they are forgotten almost as soon as noticed. [. . .]

In all the subtle, ludicrous, sarcastic turns of the character, he conveyed the poet's intention with uncommon force; this indeed seems to be the governing excellence of his performance. We have seen Richard rendered more awful and terrific, but never more thoroughly detestable; and this is the proper feeling that he should excite during nearly the whole of the first four acts. In the last he becomes an object of deeper interest. As his fate approaches, commiseration of his sufferings and admiration of his valour are blended with our disgust at his crimes. Perhaps Mr Cooke is somewhat deficient in the kingly and heroic part of the character; and his expression of terror after the dream is not so vivid and impressive as it should be. But there must always be imperfection somewhere, and Mr Cooke's merits can afford to suffer some abatement. [. . .]

His delivery of the passage [. . .], 'Why I can smile and murder while I smile',

[. . .] conveyed the idea of a man, sensible of his personal deformities and the barriers which separated him from the rest of his brethren, hugging himself up and enjoying a horrible satisfaction in the possession of a faculty by which he hoped to overreach the rest of mankind and secure the grand object he had in his eye. This was the great preparatory feature of his performance.

The soliloquies were all finely given; not addressed, as too commonly is the case, to the audience, like a chorus to explain the plot; but they actually appeared to be the secret deliberations of the soul, forming themselves into words as they arose in the mind. Nothing was ever more natural than his management of the short soliloquy in which he meditates upon the place where the young king is to hold his court. 'The tower – ay, the tower' – there was no side glance at the pit; no grin of malignant delight at the arrangement he had planned. He seemed to settle the point as a man of Richard's policy, studious of his own immediate interest, would settle it and who was satisfied that he had settled it rightly.

Richard had a common habit of gnawing his lip when he was offended. 'The king is angry; see, he gnaws his lip.' And this peculiarity, Mr Cooke exhibited with great effect in several parts of the play. Indeed his perturbation under all the circumstances is extremely natural and forcibly expressed.

During the murder of the princes, where Richard reflects for the first time upon the enormity of his conduct and its probable consequences, Mr Cooke was highly interesting. And his hesitation and walking to and fro just before the tent scene, with some admirable byplay (which to be properly estimated must be seen), finely denoted the misgivings of his mind as to the event of the approaching battle, and suitably prepared the audience for the awful visitation that was at hand, when the ghosts of those he had murdered were to sit heavy on his soul. [. . .]

It will be impossible, in an article like this, to notice all the particulars in which Mr Cooke varies from, or improves on, the manner of other representatives of Richard. But it would be unpardonable to forget the mingled irony and displeasure in his reply to Stanley, father-in-law to Richmond and of course an object of mistrust to his enemy. [. . .] It is easy to discover new points, but the skill consists in making them, as is done here, conformable to season, place and character. [. . .]

328   Portrait of George Frederick Cooke as Richard III
[Artist and date unknown] National Theatre

COMIC ACTING
Garrick as a comic actor

Most leading players in the Georgian theatre prided themselves on their ability to play both tragic and comic parts. However, audiences frequently valued them more highly in one type of role than the other. With Garrick, there was general agreement that he excelled in both kinds of role. An article in *The Theatrical Review* (1763) underlines this very point.

329   Garrick's skill as both a tragic and a comic actor
The theatrical review or annals of the drama (London: S. Williams *et al.*, 1763). Reprinted in Agate: *The English dramatic critics – an anthology* (n.d.), pp. 47–50

In many parts of tragedy, by his judgement in conceiving and his talents in executing, he never fails exciting similar feelings in the breasts of his audience. In that picturesque display in *Hamlet* of the poor parade of vestimental mourning, compared to the genuine grief of an affected heart, who can hear him without sympathy repeat, 'But I have that within which passeth show'?

In the scene with Lady Ann in *Richard*, with what masterly judgement and surprising powers, with what a well dissembled passion, does he work the lady to a firm belief of his sincerity! – When the ghost of Banquo rises, how repeatedly astonishing his transition from the placidly merry to the tremendously horrific!

Though Mr Garrick's merit in tragedy is very apparent, we are nevertheless inclined to think that comedy is his more peculiar forte. The manner of his playing his Bayes he entirely struck out himself; and in our opinion it is a test of much judgement, infinite vivacity, ready invention and every other quality which composes the genuine *vis comica*. In Benedick he has given us the highest specimen of the sprightly and the humorous; in Kitely, of the jealous; in Chalk-stone, of the persevering debauchee. And in a variety of other parts, almost every character within the compass of the comic muse.

But it is not to be understood that we think Mr Garrick utterly exempt from faults; no, there are some few which we propose to enumerate. It gives us pain to see him sometimes exert a sort of theatrical parade in tragedy to catch the eyes and applause of the multitude. He too frequently uses a sort of hesitating stammering when there is no natural obstacle to occasion it, merely to strike a seeming show of something out of nothing. A great objection has been raised by the critics to the propriety of Mr Garrick's pauses. [. . .]

We must admit that we have seen him make use of them where judgement could not warrant the adoption; sometimes as a trap for applause where he could reasonably expect none; sometimes indeed they have been occasioned by the too great length of a period, where he would have rendered himself absolutely inarticulate, had he endeavoured implicitly to conform to exact propriety. [. . .]

If Mr Garrick has any particular defect as a comedian, 'tis barely this (and from which few actors are exempt): namely, an occasional compliance with the vitiated taste of too many of the audience in introducing the *outré* for the sake of a laugh, where the author never intended it. The first is that of boxing in Abel Drugger. This character, as drawn by Jonson, is that of a most credulous, timid, pusillanimous wretch. The Broughtonian attitudes into which Mr Garrick throws himself are utterly inconsistent with the part. And consequently the weakness of those who are pleased with, and applaud it, is obviously manifest.

The next instance is Scrub. We can see no cause for Mr Garrick's affecting almost throughout this character a voice scarcely audible and a deportment as if in expectation of the chastisement of his master whenever he is called to only the performance of his duty. Nor can we assign any other reason for this peculiar method of exhibiting Scrub but that, as the expectation of the people was raised by so great a performer's undertaking the part, there appeared to him a necessity of deviating from the manner of others, however characteristic, lest the public should deem him a copy.

Upon a review of the whole, we will venture to affirm that impartial justice must pronounce Mr Garrick as the first of his profession: and that the amazing blaze of his excellencies greatly obscures, if not totally eclipses his defects.

Garrick as Archer in The Beaux' Stratagem

Commenting on Garrick's acting of Archer in Farquhar's play *The Beaux' Stratagem*, Lichtenberg points to his ability to play off against a colleague (in this case Weston who was a splendid if more limited comic actor), in such a way as to strike continuous sparks of hilarity by apparently the simplest means [*see* 330]. His description of the scene between Archer and Scrub is particularly interesting for the way it compares the scene as performed on stage with an engraved record of the scene drawn by Smith and Sayer in 1771 [*see* 331]. Despite the element of caricature in the engraving, to which Lichtenberg draws attention, the visual record, placed side by side with his description, brings the scene alive in all its comic subtlety.

330   Garrick as Archer and Weston as Scrub in a performance of *The Beaux' Stratagem*, 1775

Lichtenberg (1938), pp. 24–7

I mentioned, I believe, in my first letter a scene in Farquhar's *Stratagem* in which I saw Garrick and Weston together. I will describe it to you to the best of my ability, although I very much doubt whether my outline will be even tolerable. [. . .]

Garrick plays Archer, a gentleman of quality disguised as a servant for reasons which may easily be guessed; and poor Weston takes the part of Scrub, a tapster in a wretched inn at which the former is lodging[1] [. . .]. Garrick wears a sky-blue livery, richly trimmed with sparkling silver, a dazzling beribboned hat with a red feather, displays a pair of calves gleaming with white silk and a pair of quite incomparable buckles, and is indeed a charming fellow. And Weston, poor devil, oppressed by the burden of greasy tasks, which call him in ten different directions at once, forms an absolute contrast in a miserable wig spoilt by the rain, a grey jacket which had been cut perhaps thirty years ago to fit a better-filled paunch, red woollen stockings and a green apron. He is all pious astonishment when this gentleman's gentleman [. . .] appears. Garrick, sprightly, roguish and handsome as an angel, his pretty little hat perched at a rakish angle over his bright face, walks on with firm and vigorous step, gaily and agreeably conscious of his fine calves and new suit, feeling himself head and shoulders taller beside the miserable Scrub. And Scrub, at the best of times a poor creature, seems to lose even such powers as he had and quakes in his shoes, being deeply sensible of the marked contrast between the tapster and the valet. With dropped jaw and eyes fixed in a kind of adoration, he follows all of Garrick's movements. Archer, who wishes to make use of Scrub for his own purposes, soon becomes gracious and they sit down together. An engraving has been made of this part of the scene, and Sayer has included a copy of it among his well-known little pictures. But it is not particularly like either Weston or Garrick, and of the latter, in especial, it is an abominable caricature, although there are in the same collection of pictures such excellent likenesses of him as Abel Drugger and Sir John Brute that they can scarce be surpassed. This scene should be witnessed by anyone who wishes to observe the irresistible power of contrast on the stage, when it is brought about by a perfect collaboration on the part of author and player so that the whole fabric, whose beauty depends entirely on correct balance, be not upset, as usually happens. Garrick throws himself into a chair with his usual ease of demeanour, places his right arm on the back of Weston's chair and leans towards him for a confidential talk; his magnificent livery is thrown back and coat and man form one line of perfect beauty. Weston sits, as is fitting, in the middle of his chair, though rather far forward and with a hand on either knee, as motionless as a statue, with his roguish eyes fixed on Garrick. If his face expresses anything, it is an assumption of dignity, at odds with a paralysing sense of the terrible contrast. And here I observed something about Weston which had an excellent effect. While Garrick sits there at his ease with an agreeable careless- ness of demeanour, Weston attempts, with back stiff as a poker, to draw himself up to the other's height, partly for the sake of decorum and partly in order to steal a glance now and then, when Garrick is looking the other way, so as to improve on his imitation of the latter's manner. When Archer at last with an easy gesture crosses his legs, Scrub tries to do the same, in which he eventually succeeds, though not without some help from his hands and with eyes all the time either gaping or making furtive comparisons. And when Archer begins to stroke his magnificent silken calves, Weston tries to do the same with his miserable red woollen ones, but, thinking better of it, slowly pulls his green apron over them with an abjectness of demeanour, arousing pity in every breast. In this scene, Weston almost excels Garrick by means of the foolish expression natural to him and the simple demeanour that is apparent in all he says and does and which gains not a little from the habitual thickness of his tones. And this is indeed saying a great deal.

[1] Lichtenberg's memory has obviously let him down here. Scrub is not a tapster, but manservant to Squire Sullen.

331   Garrick as Archer and Weston as Scrub, 1771
Engraving by J. Smith and R. Sayer. Burney Collection of Theatrical Portraits, Garrick Portfolio, no.E.E.3–191 (Print Room, BM)

Garrick as Sir John Brute

One of Garrick's most famous comic roles was that of Sir John Brute in Vanbrugh's play *The Provoked Wife*. In its original version, Vanbrugh had shown Sir John Brute, during a night of drink and violence, stealing a parcel of clothes from a tailor and dressing up as clergyman, only to engage in a fight with the watch. The scene gave such offence to puritan minds that is was amended to show Sir John dressing up as a woman. This was how it was played throughout the eighteenth century, providing delightful scope for comic actors to show their paces in drag. Garrick excelled in the part, offering a satiric view of Sir John's behaviour and dress that became more polished but also more extravagant as the years went by [*see* 332 and 334]. Lichtenberg's description of him in this role showed the grudging admiration, tinged with mild disapprovement, that the part still provoked in the puritan-minded even in its revised state [*see* 333 and 369].

332   Portrait of Garrick playing Sir John Brute, 1765

Mezzotint by Finlayson, after Zoffany. Burney Collection of Theatrical Portraits, Garrick Portfolio, 1872/1.13/875 (Print Room, BM). Original painting by Zoffany in Wolverhampton Art Gallery

333   Garrick as Sir John Brute, *c.* 1775

(A) LICHTENBERG Lichtenberg (1938), pp. 17–19

Sir John Brute is not merely a dissolute fellow, but Garrick makes him an old fop also, this being apparent from his costume. On top of a wig, which is more or less suitable for one of his years, he has perched a small, beribboned modish hat so jauntily that it covers no more of his forehead than was already hidden by his wig. In his hand he holds one of those hooked oaken sticks, with which every young poltroon makes himself look like a devil of a fellow in the Park in the morning (as they call here the hours between 10 and 3). It is in fact a cudgel, showing only faint traces of art and culture, as is generally the case also with the lout who carries it. Sir John makes use of this stick to emphasise his words with bluster, especially when only females are present, or in his passion to rain blows where no-one is standing who might take them amiss.

In all playhouses there is generally one or another of the actors who can represent a drunken man very tolerably. The reason for this is not far to seek. There is no lack of opportunity for observation and, whatever may be the main motive of the play, such a part must, in the nature of things, have no narrow or sharply defined limits. In spite of this, Mr Garrick plays the drunken Sir John in such a way that I should certainly have known him to be a most remarkable man, even if I had never heard anything of him and had seen him in one scene only in this play. At the beginning, his wig is quite straight, so that his face is full and round. Then he comes home excessively drunk and looks like the moon a few days before its last quarter, almost half his face being covered by his wig. The part that is still visible is indeed somewhat bloody and shining with perspiration, but has so extremely amiable an air as to compensate for the loss of the other part. His waistcoat is open from top to bottom, his stockings full of wrinkles, with the garters hanging down and, moreover, which is vastly strange, two kinds of garters. One would hardly be surprised indeed if he had picked up odd shoes. In this lamentable condition he enters the room where his wife is and, in answer to her anxious enquiries as to what is the matter with him (and she has good reason for enquiring), he, collecting his wits, answers, 'Wife, as well as a fish in the water.' He does not, however, move away from the doorpost, against which he leans as closely as if he wanted to rub his back. Then he again breaks into coarse talk and suddenly becomes so wise and merry in his cups that the whole audience bursts into a tumult of applause.

I was filled with amazement at the scene where he falls asleep. The way in which, with shut eyes, swimming head and pallid cheeks, he quarrels with his wife and, uttering a sound where 'r' and 'l' are blended, now appears to abuse her and then to enunciate in thick tones moral precepts to which he himself forms the most horrible contradiction; his manner also of moving his lips so that one cannot tell whether he is chewing, tasting or speaking. All this, in truth, as far exceeded my expectations as anything I have seen of this man. If you could but hear him articulate the word 'prerogative'; he never reaches the third syllable without two or three attempts. Vanbrugh has made an excellent use of this. It is the perfect watchword, the signal for blows of ale-house politicians in England; they do not trouble themselves about its meaning, but it can set them all by the ears when the protagonists have reached the point of being unable to pronounce it. But however excellently they represent this play, for Lady Brute was played by Miss Young and Lady Fanciful by the famous Mrs Abington, I am yet convinced that it would be better never to produce it. They have indeed altered the shameful scene where Sir John Brute disguises himself as a parson and wrestles with the watch, so that he performs these mighty deeds clad only in a hooped petticoat, saloppe and head-dress, to which there can be no objection. But in spite of this, there are here and there abominable things offending ear and eye.

(B) UNATTRIBUTED NEWSPAPER CUTTING DATED IN PENCIL 7 FEB 1776[1]
Smith, vol. 11 (BL, 1825–40)

The female head-dress has now reached the highest degree of ridicule. It was time for the stage to lay hold of such extreme folly and to expose it to the derision of the public. Mr Garrick, in the part of Sir John Brute, exhibited a most extraordinary lady's cap, ornamented with such a plume of feathers, ribbons of various colours, oranges and lemons, flowers, etc. and so formidable a toupee that the audience gave repeated bursts of applause with such peals of laughter that the roof of the theatre seemed to be in danger. The ladies in the boxes drew back their heads, as if ashamed of the picture; and it is to be hoped that for the future they will take a reef in, as the sailors say, and lower their topsails.

[1] There is no record of a performance of the play on that date, but there were other performances that season. See *LS*, pt iv, p. 1950.

334   Garrick as Sir John Brute, 1775
Engraving by J. Roberts. *Bell's British Theatre*, vol. 2 (1796). Engraving first published 1 June 1776. University Library, Bristol

Comic actresses

Eighteenth-century actresses, like their male colleagues, were expected to be versatile, to be equally at home in comedy and tragedy, and many of them were. Inevitably, however, there were those whose style and talents better fitted the comic stage: among the most famous were Margaret Woffington, Dorothy Jordan, Catherine Clive and Frances Abington.

Margaret Woffington

The colourful details of Mrs Woffington's private life, including her early affair with Garrick and her later Green-Room battle with George Ann Bellamy, often obscured the fact that this Dublin-born bricklayer's daughter became a brilliant comedienne with a strong professional commitment, who served the theatrical public faithfully. Apart from her lively portrayals of society women, she was adept at 'breeches parts', a vogue, which Mrs Clive, Mrs Barry and Mrs Jordan, among others, successfully pursued.

335   Mrs Woffington's acting style
Davies, vol. 1 (1808), pp. 340–3

Mrs Margaret Woffington was born at Dublin in 1718. For her education, in the very early part of life, she was indebted to Madame Violante, a French woman of good reputation and famous for feats of agility [. . .]. From her instructions, little Woffington learned that easy action and graceful deportment, which she afterwards endeavoured, with unremitting application, to improve. When *The Beggar's Opera* was first acted at Dublin, it was so much applauded and admired that all ranks of people flocked to see it. A company of children, under the title of Lilliputians, were encouraged to represent this favourite piece at the Theatre Royal, and Miss Woffington, then in the tenth year of her age, made a very distinguished figure among these pigmy comedians.

She appeared for the first time in London at the theatre in Covent Garden in 1738. Her choice of character excited the curiosity of the public: Sir Harry Wildair,[1] acted by a woman, was a novelty. This gay, dissipated, good-humoured rake, she represented with so much ease, elegance and propriety of deportment that no male actor has since equalled her in that part. She acquitted herself so much to the general satisfaction that it became fashionable to see Mrs Woffington personate Sir Harry Wildair. The managers soon found it to be their interest to announce her frequently for that favourite character; it proved a constant charm to fill their houses.

In Dublin she tried her powers of acting a tragedy rake, for Lothario[2] is certainly of that cast. But whether she was as greatly accomplished in the manly tread of the buskined libertine, as she was in the genteel walk of the gay gentleman in comedy, I know not. But it is certain that she did not meet with the same approbation in the part of Lothario as in that of Wildair.

Her chief merit in acting, I think, consisted in the representation of females in high rank and of dignified elegance, whose graces in deportment, as well as foibles, she understood and displayed in a very lively and pleasing manner. The fashionable irregularities and sprightly coquetry of a Millamant, a Lady Townly, Lady Betty Modish,[3] and Maria in *The Non-juror*, were exhibited by Woffington with that happy ease and gaiety, and with such powerful attraction, that the excesses of these characters appeared, not only pardonable, but agreeable.

But this actress did not confine herself to parts of superior elegance. She loved to wanton with ignorance, when combined with absurdity, and to play with petulance and folly, with peevishness and vulgarity. Those who remember her Lady Pliant in Congreve's *Double Dealer* will recollect with pleasure her whimsical discovery of passion and her awkwardly assumed prudery. In Mrs Day, in *The Committee*, she made no scruple to disguise her beautiful countenance by drawing on it the lines of deformity and the wrinkles of old age, and to put on the tawdry habiliments and vulgar manners of an old hypocritical city vixen.

[1] In Farquhar's *The Constant Couple*.
[2] Rowe's *The Fair Penitent*.
[3] *The Careless Husband*.

336   Mrs Woffington speaking an epilogue as a volunteer, 1746
Contemporary engraving. Mander and Mitchenson Theatre Collection

Dorothy Jordan

Dorothy Jordan's acting début in London in 1785 came after a turbulent apprenticeship in Dublin (where an affair with the company manager led to an unwanted pregnancy) and some difficult years with Tate Wilkinson's troupe on the York circuit. In London, she became famous for her skill in breeches parts, adding Sir Harry Wildair to her repertoire in 1787 [*see* **337**]. Tate Wilkinson speaks wistfully of her in this role in his memoirs [*see* **274**], remarking that the painter Sir Joshua Reynolds was much taken with Mrs Jordan's legs. Even John Genest agreed that she sported, 'the best leg ever seen on the stage' [*see* **338**]. But the finest tribute to her, written from memory, but *con amore*, came from Charles Lamb [*see* **339**]. It remains a verbal portrait in some ways more vivid and revealing than Hoppner's brush [*see* **340**] – certainly a worthy complement to it.

337   Mrs Jordan as Sir Harry Wildair
Burney Collection of Theatrical Portraits, vol. 5, no. 91, p. 42 (Print Room, BM)

London. Pub. by Wm Holland. at Garrick's Richard N.50 Oxford Street. November 10. 1788

338   Mrs Jordan in breeches parts

John Genest: *Some account of the English stage from the Restoration in 1660 to 1800* (Bath: Carrington, 1832)

[vol. 6, p. 375]

Mrs Jordan was not a beauty, nor was she elegant in her person or manners, but she fascinated the town at the time and continued to do so – she was peculiarly comic, but perfectly natural.

[vol. 8, pp. 430–1]

As an actress she never had a superior in her proper line. Mrs Clive no doubt played Nell as well as Mrs Jordan: it was hardly possible for her to have played the part better. Mrs Jordan's Country Girl, Romp, Miss Hoyden and all characters of that description were exquisite. In breeches parts, no actress can be put in competition with her but Mrs Woffington. And to Mrs Woffington she was as superior in point of voice, as Mrs Woffington was superior to her in beauty. [. . .] she was never handsome, but she was peculiarly pleasing, and as Wilkinson says, she sported the best leg ever seen on the stage. She latterly grew too fat for the breeches characters: this was her misfortune, not her fault.

339a   Charles Lamb recalls Mrs Jordan, as she was *c.* 1788

Charles Lamb: 'On some of the old Actors'. *Dramatic essays* (edited by Brander Matthews) (London: Chatto & Windus, 1891), pp. 44–5

[. . .] Those who have only seen Mrs Jordan within the last ten or fifteen years, can have no adequate notion of her performance of such parts as Ophelia; Helena, in *All's Well that Ends Well*; and Viola in this play [*Twelfth Night*]. Her voice had latterly acquired a coarseness, which suited well enough with her Nells and Hoydens, but in those days it sank, with her steady melting eye, into the heart. Her joyous parts – in which her memory now chiefly lives – in her youth were outdone by her plaintive ones. There is no giving an account how she delivered the disguised story of her love for Orsino. It was no set speech that she had foreseen so as to weave it into an harmonious period, line necessarily following line, to make up the music – yet I have heard it so spoken, or rather *read*, not without its grace and beauty – but, when she had declared her sister's history to be a 'blank,' and that she 'never told her love,' there was a pause, as if the story had ended – and then the image of the 'worm in the bud' came up as a new suggestion – and the heightened image of 'Patience' still followed after that, as by some growing (and not mechanical) process, thought springing up after thought, I would almost say, as they were watered by her tears. So in those fine lines –

> Write loyal cantos of contemned love –
> Hollow your name to the reverberate hills –

there was no preparation made in the foregoing image for that which was to follow. She used no rhetoric in her passion; or it was nature's own rhetoric, most legitimate then, when it seemed altogether without rule or law.

339b Mrs Jordan as Viola
Painting by John Hoppner, The Iveagh Bequest, Kenwood

Frances Abington

Frances Abington was another of those rare women who worked her way up from very humble beginnings (she was a cobbler's daughter who had sold flowers in the streets of Covent Garden at the age of fourteen) to become a celebrated comic actress and an equally celebrated beauty and socialite. Unlike Mrs Jordan, she never felt the need to appear in a breeches part. Instead, she set an example of exquisite dressing on the stage that was intended to make her the envy of the town. She largely succeeded in this aim, charming the men, as one might expect, and becoming an arbiter of fashion to ladies of quality. Garrick, however, heartily disliked her.

340   Mrs Abington's appeal as a comic actress

(A) JAMES BOADEN Boaden: *The Life of Mrs Jordan*, vol. 1 (London: Edward Bull, 1831), pp. 16–18. Quoted in W.C. Russell: *Representative actors* (London: Warne, 1872), pp. 160–1

She, I think, took more entire possession of the stage than any actress I have seen. There was, however, no assumption in her dignity. She was a lawful and grateful sovereign who exerted her full power and enjoyed her established prerogatives. The ladies of her day wore the hoop and its concomitant train. The *Spectator's* exercise of the fan was really no play of fancy. Shall I say that I have never seen it in a hand so dexterous as that of Mrs Abington? She was a woman of great application: to speak as she did required more thought than usually attends female study. Far the greater part of her sex rely upon an intuition which seldom misleads them: such discernment as it gives becomes habitual, and is commonly sufficient or sufficient for common purposes. But commonplace was not the station of Abington. She was always beyond the surface; untwisted all the chains which bind ideas together and seized upon the exact cadence and emphasis by which the point of dialogue is enforced. Her voice was of a high pitch and not very powerful. Her management of it alone made it an organ. Yet this was so perfect that we sometimes converted the mere effect into a cause and supposed it was the sharpness of the tone that gave the sting. [. . .] Her deportment is not so easily described: more womanly than Farren; fuller, yet not heavy, like Younge;[1] and far beyond even the conception of modern fine ladies, Mrs Abington remains in memory as a thing for chance to restore to us rather than design, and revive our polite comedy at the same time.

[1] For pen-portraits of Miss Farren, later Countess of Derby, and Miss Younge, later Mrs Pope, see *The secret history of the Green Room*, vol. 1 (1795), pp. 19–27 and 105–17.

(B) CHARLES DIBDIN Dibdin: *Complete history of the English stage*, vol. 5 (London: published by the author, 1797–1800), pp. 357–9. Quoted in W.C. Russell: *Representative actors* (London: Warne, 1872), pp. 160–1

With Mrs Abington came a species of excellence which the stage seems never before to have boasted in the same perfection. The higher parts in comedy had been performed chastely and truly; perhaps in these particulars more so than by this actress. There was peculiar goodness gleamed across the levity of Mrs Pritchard and by what we can learn of Mrs Bracegirdle (who seems to have possessed the same captivating sort of manner which distinguished Mrs Abington), she was in these characters natural and winning. But it remained for her successor to add a degree of grace, fashion and accomplishment to sprightliness, which was no sooner seen than it was imitated in the politest circles. [. . .] In addition to the grace, the ease, and the elegance with which Mrs Abington personated characters in high life and aped politeness in chambermaids, her taste for dress was novel and interesting. She was consulted by ladies of the first distinction, not from caprice, as we have frequently seen in other instances, but from a decided conviction of her judgement in blending what was beautiful with what was becoming. Indeed, dress took a sort of *ton* from her fancy, and ladies both on the stage and off piqued themselves with decorating their persons with decency and decorum.

341   Mrs Abington in the character of Aurelia in *The Twin Rivals*, 1777

Bell's British Theatre, vol. 8 (1777). University Library, Bristol

Contrasting interpretations of Falstaff

A good many comic actors exploited their natural attributes in choosing which roles to play on stage. This was certainly the case with Weston when he played Scrub [*see* 330]. But it was no less true of the heavyweight Quin who, by temperament and shape, seemed almost destined to play Falstaff: a role in which he was justly famous [*see* 342]. The opposite was true of Henderson. His youth, shape and temperament were all against him in the part of Falstaff. But it is a mark of his versatility (and an indication of the potential lost by his early death) that he played the part so well [*see* 343].

342   Quin as Falstaff

Mezzotint by J. McArdell. Burney Collection of Theatrical Portraits, vol. 7, no. 154, p. 66
(Print Room, BM)

343   Quin and Henderson compared in the role of Falstaff

Thomas Davies: *A genuine narrative of the life and theatrical transactions of Mr John Henderson,
commonly called the Bath Roscius* (London: T. Evans, 1777), pp. 53–6

I am of opinion that Falstaff is the masterpiece of Henderson. He had no original
before his eyes to draw from, so that the acting of this part was entirely of his own
creation. I know that some of the old jovial bottle companions of Quin look upon
this attempt of our young comedian as high treason against the memory of their
friend; no man must dare to act Falstaff after Quin.

Let us fairly examine the pretensions of this great comedian to such superiority.
I have often conversed with those who knew him well. A man of quick conception
and ready wit he certainly was, but his general turn of mind was prone to the
sarcastical, and his poignant wit was calculated to excite laughter often at the
expense of others. His mirth was not generally of the joyous, liberal and jovial
kind. He had little of the milk of human kindness about him; he took too much
pleasure in wounding and degrading those whom he saw were inferior to himself.

But it must be owned that he had his happy intervals of festivity and good humour. He was particularly lively and gay when his venison was well flavoured and his claret of the genuine sort; then indeed was he a most excellent companion and the very soul of mirth. Though little acquainted with books, Quin knew mankind perfectly. He discerned with a quick eye characteristic folly and absurdity and took delight in exposing them by strong and pungent ridicule.

Such a man, with the advantage too of a large figure, an expressive countenance, with a full and well-toned voice, was not ill qualified to act Falstaff. When we make allowance for the applause he really deserved and the partiality of friends and admirers, we cannot help saying that upon the whole, though he pointed out many essential beauties of Falstaff's character, he fell short in some of the frolicsome, licentious and joyous scenes of the humorous knight. The actor was easily to be unmasked; he was still the surly James Quin, with that sternness of brow and severe gravity of speech, of which he could never divest himself entirely.

I will grant that in some of the high domineering scenes of Falstaff, Quin must have excelled all that went before him or may possibly succeed him. But in the loose, easy, merry, ludicrous, gay, and elbow-chair situations and attitudes of the character, Henderson is greatly his superior, by the confession of many judicious persons who have seen both actors. For a young man to forget himself so far as to adopt all the infirmities and encumbrances of an old fat fellow of sixty is certainly a difficult task; nay, to give the proper tones of voice peculiar to such a part is no easy matter. But that he should enter strongly into the high impudent roguery of Falstaff is scarce to be believed. And yet Henderson's bragging of his unmatched valour and his arch recovery from his being detected by the Prince and Poins in the second act; his high-finished satirical description of Bardolph's fall in the third; and his inimitable soliloquy where he enjoys the cheating the King of his press money in the fourth act are such irrefragable proofs of comic powers as must place him, in my opinion, amongst the first-rate actors of the age.

REHEARSALS AND MANAGEMENT

The system evolved during the first half of the century did not change fundamentally, but it did become more complex as the patent theatres grew larger. If the leading actor was part proprietor, as Garrick, Foote and Kemble were, then the ultimate authority in all matters lay with him. If not, artistic planning and control might be given to a deputy or acting manager, financial affairs to a treasurer. The preparation of scripts and control of stage action, both at rehearsal and performance, remained in the hands of the prompter. Artistic direction in the case of new productions was often in the hands of the leading actor, in collaboration or association with the playwright. Once a new production became established, the responsibility for supervising its revivals lay with the prompter. Gibbon's Journal provides a fleeting glimpse of the furious pace at which rehearsals could take place in order to meet the demands of a swiftly changing repertoire [see 344].

The diaries of Cross and Hopkins, successively prompters at Drury Lane, survive in the Folger Library and are a mine of information. The Hopkins Memorandum Book quoted here [see 345] seems to have been kept to provide a formal record of problems experienced by the prompter in respect of particular actors. His difficulties with Mr and Mrs Barry are a striking example of the hindrances that could be experienced in trying to persuade leading actors to adhere to an agreed rehearsal schedule. Barry was a genuinely sick man at the time, but he was also very difficult to handle.

344   Mrs Pritchard rehearses two plays simultaneously

D.M. Low (ed.): *Gibbon's Journal to 28 Jan 1763* (London: Chatto & Windus, 1929), pp. 186–6.

26 Nov 1762

I went with Mallet to breakfast with Garrick; and from thence to Drury Lane house, where I assisted at a very private rehearsal in the green room of a new tragedy of Mallet's called *Elvira*. As I have since seen it acted, I shall defer my opinion of it till then.[1] But I can't help mentioning here the surprising versatility of Mrs Pritchard's talents, who rehearsed almost at the same time the part of a furious queen in the green room and that of a coquette on the stage,[2] and passed several times from one to the other with the utmost ease and happiness.

I dined with Darrel, saw *The Way of the World* afterwards, and finished the evening at the Cocoa Tree.

[1] The first night of *Elvira* was 19 Jan 1763. Gibbon's comments may be read in his *Journal*, pp. 202–4.
[2] She was playing Millamant in the evening.

345   The trials of a prompter

Smith, vol. 8 (BL, 1825–40)[1]

Sept 1769

Thursday 21st. Wrote to Mr Barry to know when they could play. Received a letter from him on Monday, desiring they might be excused playing till Saturday sennight [week] as they were both ill; and wrote to him the same day desiring they would send me word what play they would choose to appear in and when they would rehearse. Received a letter on Thursday 28th that the soonest they could appear would be the latter end of the next week. May play King Lear on Sat 7th of October.

The Fair Penitent was advertised for Wednesday 11th [October]. A rehearsal was called on Tuesday 10th. About nine o'clock in the morning, Mr Barry sent for me and told me he was so ill that it would be impossible for him to play for some time and that he would give up his salary till he was able to play.

Thursday 12th [October]. Waited on Mr and Mrs Barry to know if it would be agreeable to them to go in the Pageant[2] on Saturday. They both agreed they would and Mr Barry said he could be able to walk in the Pageant if he could not play. Thursday 12th. A rehearsal of *As You Like It* was called by Mrs Barry's desire. At ten she sent word to have the rehearsal put off for half an hour. The performers stayed for her till past eleven, but, she not coming, they went away.

Monday 14th. Waited on Mrs Barry to know if it would be agreeable to her to play Lady Townly with Mr Reddish. She said she had no clothes fit for it. I asked if she had any objection to Mrs Abington's playing the part. She answered no.

[. . .] Saturday 21st. Mrs Barry sent word she was so ill she could not come out for the Pageant. If she did, she could not play *The Mourning Bride* on Monday. I waited on her by the managers' order and told her they would excuse her playing on Monday if she would come out and do her part in the Pageant. And as it was a thing of great consequence to them, they desired and expected, as she had begun it, that she would continue it as long as she was able. Her answer was that, as they seemed to think it of such consequence, she would come out and do it tonight and Monday night, but after that desired to be excused from doing it. On Tuesday morn, Mr Barry sent a note that Mrs Barry was ill in her bed and could not come out till she was better. *Tancred and Sigismunda* was called, and I did not receive the note till the rehearsal was begun. I also on Saturday delivered a message to Mrs Barry from Mr Garrick that he would never ask her to play in anything in which he was particularly interested. Her answer was, that was in his rage, but if his mind should alter, she was ready and willing to do anything he would desire her to do.

Thursday 26th. I called upon Mr Barry: he was not at home. In the afternoon, I sent him a note desiring they would send notice when they were able to perform. He sent me an angry note in answer on Friday. I, by the managers' [instruction], answered it on Friday morning, both which letters Mr Garrick has.

On Saturday 28th received a message that Mrs Barry was better and should be able to rehearse on Monday and that Mr Barry would be able to play Lord Townly on Thursday next. [. . .]

---

[1] Vol. 8 contains a thin notebook in marbled covers with a note in Smith's handwriting: 'A memorandum book formerly belonging to Mr Hopkins, the father of Mrs Brereton, afterwards Mrs John Kemble.' Mr Hopkins was prompter of Drury Lane Theatre for 20 years and died on 22 December 1780. Letters relating to this episode are reprinted in J. Boaden (ed.): *The private correspondence of David Garrick*, vol. 1 (London: Colburn & Bentley, 1831), pp. 369–71.

[2] The Pageant referred to was Garrick's Shakespeare Jubilee.

12 Audiences, taste, theatre criticism

THE COMPOSITION OF THE AUDIENCE

Audiences in mid- and late-eighteenth-century England were not drawn exclusively from the middle and upper classes, as has sometimes been suggested, but from all sections of society. There was, however, clear social stratification, which was marked in the prices charged for admission to different parts of the theatre. Places in the boxes normally cost 5 *s*, admission to the pit cost 3 *s*, to the first or middle gallery 2 *s*, and to the second or upper gallery 1 *s* [*see* **347**]. (In the provinces, the corresponding prices were 3 *s* for the boxes, 2 *s* for the pit, 1 *s* 6 *d* for the middle gallery and 1 *s* for the upper gallery, though many provincial theatres had only one gallery at 1 *s*.) As may be seen by comparing these prices with those charged in Pepys's day [*see* **152**], there had been remarkably little increase in the cost of theatre going for more than a century.

The great, the rich, and the middle sort (to use three of Defoe's seven social categories) could well afford such prices. Equally the cost of a gallery ticket was well within the economic reach of working-class patrons: journeymen, apprentices, servants, soldiers and sailors. With a jar of ale costing 3 *d*, an evening in the tavern was likely to prove more expensive than a visit to the theatre.[1] Especially when one bears in mind the half-price tradition, applicable after the third act of the main piece, so that effectively the afterpiece entertainments, including acrobatics, line dancing, farces and pantomimes were available for 6 *d*.

The social stratification in the audience remained much as it was at the beginning of the century, with the wealthy and the privileged occupying the boxes; the 'bucks', 'critics' and other men about town in the pit; citizens and their wives from the middle classes in the middle gallery (when Fielding's Tom Jones took Partridge, Mrs Miller and her daughter to Drury Lane, they sat in the first row of the middle gallery); the lower classes, often noisy and uninhibited, in the upper gallery [*see* **346**]. Whores traditionally plied their trade in the upper or 'green' boxes [*see* **348**; *see also* **153c**]. There was movement between pit and boxes, pit and middle gallery, middle and upper gallery; there was also a discernible influx into the upper gallery after half price and a corresponding vacating of box places on those nights when the behaviour of the gallery audiences was particularly troublesome. Following Garrick's reforms in the early 1760s, audiences were finally banished from the stage.

[1] See Pedicord (1954).

346   The composition of the audience in Dublin

The trick of the town laid open, or a companion for country gentlemen (Dublin, n.d.), p. 37.
Reprinted in L.T. Stockwell: *Dublin theatres and theatre customs, 1637–1820* [1938],
(London and New York: Blom, 1968), p. 193

In our playhouse at Dublin, besides an upper gallery for Abigails, servingmen,
journeymen and apprentices, we have three other different and distinct classes.
The first is called the boxes, where there is one peculiar to the Lord Lieutenant, and
the rest for the persons of quality, and for the ladies and gentlemen of the highest
rank, unless some fools that have more wit than money, or perhaps more
impudence than both, crowd in among them. The second is called the pit, where
sit the judges, wits and censurers without either wit or judgement. These are the
bully judges that damn and sink the play at a venture; 'tis a play, and they are the
judges, and so it must be damned, cursed and censured in course; in common with
these sit the squires, sharpers, beaus and bullies and here and there an extravagant male citizen. The third is distinguished by the title of the middle gallery where
the citizens' wives and daughters take their place.

347   The Little Theatre in the Haymarket in 1782

Carl Philip Moritz: *Journeys of a German in England in 1782*, translated and edited by R. Nettel
(London: Cape, 1965), pp. 60–4

Last week [June 1782], I went twice to an English theatre. On the first occasion,
The Nabob by the late Samuel Foote was played, and the afterpiece was a comic
opera called *The Agreeable Surprise*, which certainly lived up to its name. On my
next visit I saw *The English Merchant*, which is well known in its German
translation under the title, *Die Schottländerin, oder das Kaffeehaus*.

I have not visited Covent Garden or Drury Lane theatres because they are
closed in summer. The best actors are travelling in the country from May to
October and act only in the winter. With few exceptions the players whom I saw
were nothing extraordinary.

It costs five shillings for a seat in a box, three shillings in the pit, two shillings in
the circle and one shilling in the gallery; and the gallery certainly makes the most
noise for its shilling. I sat in the pit, which slopes upwards from the orchestra to the
far end and is filled from top to bottom with benches. Every moment a rotten
orange came whizzing past me or past my neighbour; one hit my hat, but I dared
not turn round for fear one hit me in the face.

Oranges are eaten practically everywhere in London, for they can be bought as
cheaply as one or even two for a halfpenny. In the theatre I was charged sixpence
for a single orange!

In addition to pelting from the gallery there is no end to their shrieking and
banging with sticks until the curtain goes up. I have seen a tall baker's boy
reaching over the rails and beating with his stick on the outside of the gallery with
all his might, visible to everyone but quite unabashed. I sometimes also heard
people in the circle quarrelling with those in the gallery.

Behind me in the pit sat a young fop who continually put his foot on my bench in order to show off the flashy stone buckles on his shoes; if I didn't make way for his precious buckles, he put his foot on my coat-tails.

In the boxes sat servants of the gentry, who dared not look out or let themselves be seen for fear of being pelted with orange peel [. . .]. The theatre seemed to me to be somewhat bigger than that in Hamburg and on both occasions was very full.

348   The 'green boxes', or the 'flesh market'
The Connoisseur, 21 November 1754. Reprinted in Pedicord (1954), p. 50

I must take notice of that division of the upper boxes properly distinguished by the name of the flesh market. There is frequently as much art used to make the flesh exhibited here look wholesome and, as Tim says in the farce, 'all over red and white, like the inside of a shoulder of mutton', as there is by the butchers to make their veal look white; and it is as often rank carrion and flyblown. If these ladies would appear in any other quarter of the house, I would only beg of them, and those who come to market, to drive their bargains with as little noise as possible. But I have lately observed with some concern that these women deign to appear in the lower boxes, to the destruction of all order and great confusion of all modest ladies. It is to be hoped that some of their friends will advise them not to pretend to appear there, anymore than at court; for it is as absurd to endeavour the removal of their market into the front and side boxes, as it would be in the butchers of St James's market to attempt fixing the shambles in St James's Square.

THE POWER OF THE AUDIENCE

In the Restoration, actors, as sworn servants of the monarch, enjoyed some limited royal protection. In the commercial cut-and-thrust of Georgian England, this was no longer the case. Actors were considered fair game by most audiences; and apart from those actors working in the two patent companies, they could be seen, in strictly legal terms, as rogues and vagabonds. The treatment meted out to actors by Georgian playgoers could be savage in the extreme. Plays and individual performances were sometimes greeted by vocal and physical abuse; playgoers refused to accept changes of casting or programming they did not like [*see* 349]; any attempt to increase ticket prices was howled down or taken as the excuse for a riot; other changes in established practice led to the demand for abject public apologies by the manager or actor concerned and even dismissal for the offenders. In the provinces, actors had to beg and plead in public for support on benefit nights [*see* 350 and 351].

Members of the patent companies in London, as well as leading provincial companies, found this demeaning. Garrick and other managers at the time regarded themselves as gentlefolk and were ill disposed to tolerate such abuse. As the century proceeded, there was a gradual improvement in the status of actors and some success in the struggle for social acceptance and respectability.

349   The rights and power of the audience

(A) *PUBLIC ADVERTISER*, 23 FEBRUARY 1767

COUNTRY NEWS. Bath, 19 February

Last Monday night, a most remarkable contest happened at our theatre between the audience and the manager, the former of whom unanimously insisted on Mr Reddish's performing the character of Richard, in the room of Mr Sherriffe whose name was in the bills. As soon as the curtain drew up, the manager was called for, who, refusing to comply with their demand, was obliged to make a hasty retreat. And after repeated efforts made not to consent (which kept the house an hour in suspense), the point was carried in favour of the town and the play received by a numerous audience with universal applause.

(B) WILLIAM HOPKINS [PROMPTER AT DRURY LANE] Ms diary notes, transcribed by J.P. Kemble in Huntington playbills. Reprinted in Macmillan (1938), pp. 134–5 and in LS, pt iv, pp. 1356–7

5 October 1768. This morning a printed paper was handed about requesting the lovers of theatrical performances to meet this evening at the theatre to insist upon the doors not being opened till five o'clock. As soon as the curtain was up, they called for Mr Garrick and would not suffer the play to begin. Mr King went on and told the audience, 'that he was desired by the managers to tell them the doors for the future should not be opened till five,' – a great clap – he added, 'that [the] managers were always willing to oblige the public in everything that was in their power; but they thought that on very full nights it would be attended with some inconveniences,' – They would not hear of any alteration – he then told them, 'the doors should always for the future be opened at five, unless the public applied to have it altered.' – All then was quiet and the play began. Mr Weston, whose name was in the bills for Jerry, was taken suddenly ill, and Mr W. Palmer went on for it without an apology. – [sic] called out, 'Mr Holland, what is the reason we have not Mr Weston according to your publication in the bills?' They then were told he was taken suddenly ill – 'then, pray make an apology for him', they said. – Another gentleman called out, 'Don't answer him, Mr Holland, you do him too much honour by deigning to answer him.' – Then all was quiet and the play went on.

(C) SYLAS NEVILLE B. Cozens-Hardy (ed.): The Diary of Sylas Neville (London: Oxford University Press, 1950), pp. 120–1

Wednesday, 25 September 1771. About 7 o'clock we went into the pit at C.G. Theatre to see Hamlet. The entertainment was to have been Midas, but Shuter having sprained his ankle, the managers changed it to Thomas and Sally and distributed hand-bills assigning the reason, which satisfied the pit, but the gods would not receive anything but Midas. There was a great noise – different actors were sent to make an apology, but they would not hear any of them. After waiting half an hour, Wiggin and I left the house, being obliged to stand and being almost stewed. So how the dispute ended, I do not know.[1]

[1] Almost certainly the performance was abandoned. Rich's Register, vol. 4, at Chatsworth House records the performance of Hamlet but there is no mention of an afterpiece.

350   Traditional customs to attract audience support in the provinces, c. 1763

Tate Wilkinson vol. 2 (Dublin 1791), pp. 248–52

It was at that time not only the custom there [Norwich] (and a horrid custom it certainly was), but also at York, Hull, etc. for the performer, whether man or woman, to attend the playbill man round the town, knock humbly at every door honoured with or without a rapper, and supinely and obediently stop at every shop and stall to leave a playbill and request the favour of Mr and Mrs Griskin's company at the benefit. The heroine (if unmarried) was equally responsible for steering her steps, no matter whether the Juliet, the Cleopatra, the Lady Townly, or the Queen Elizabeth. No dignity of any kind allowed for such an omission, without being construed a violation of duty. That severe law of custom then in force must be complied with or looked on as an infringement of rules and respect and would incur censure, with the appellation of pride, impudence, insolence and want of reverence. No matter how severe the weather, if frost, snow, rain, or hail, Jane Shore and the proud Lady Macbeth were expected equally to pay the same homage. If the Lady Turtle Dove was blessed with a loving mate, her attendance was dispensed with, but not otherwise on any pretext whatever; in that case the honour devolved on the husband. These laws (thank God) I had not been accustomed to: and having a plentiful well-supplied pocket had no need to comply or trouble myself to use such a practice. Which I dare say superior minds to my own have, from the dictates of prudence and necessity, against their will too often complied with.

Another custom was, after the play the performer was to return thanks and, if married, both husband and wife to appear. Mr Frodsham, once at York, spoke a comic epilogue on his benefit night and actually carried his wife (now living) on and off the stage on his back, to comply with the expected homage. On particular occasions, four or five children to make up weight, courtesying and bowing in frocks, had a wonderful effect, as the audience in general and the ladies in particular prided themselves upon bestowing their bounty on such a painstaking man, or such a painstaking couple as they proved themselves to be [. . .].

Another strange custom they had at Norwich and, if abolished, it has not been many years, which was for a drummer and a trumpeter (not the King's) in every street to proclaim in an audible voice, having been assisted by his shrill notes to summons each garreteer, without which ceremony the gods would not submit to descend from their heights into the streets to enquire what play was to be acted, nor ascend into the gallery.

A custom of this kind prevailed so far with a Mr Herbert's Lincolnshire company in the time of our revered, well-remembered and beloved Marquis of Granby, that when at Grantham the players determined to omit the usual ceremony of the drum, wishing to grow more polite; and by obstinate perseverance, Lady Jane Grey, Mary Queen of Scots, King Henry the Eighth, the King of France, nay even Cardinal Wolsey had no command, attraction or power over the populace when they lost their accustomed and so much loved sound of the drum and trumpet. The ladies were obstinate, though they could not by all their arts or by all their charms obtain a livelihood; and their heroism was so great that they preferred death, honourable death, rather than submit to slavish terms. The Marquis of Granby sent for the manager of the troupe and said to him, 'Mr Manager, I like a play, I like a player, and shall be glad to serve you. But, my good friend, why are you all so suddenly offended at and averse to the noble sound of a drum? I like it', said the Marquis, 'and all the inhabitants like it. Put my name on your playbill, provided you drum, but not otherwise. Try the effect on tomorrow night. If then you are as thinly attended as you have lately been, shut up your playhouse at once, but if it succeeds, drum away.' The manager communicated this edict to the princes, princesses, peers and peeresses. And not only they, but even the ambitious step-mother gave up all self-consideration for the public weal, and it was after some debate voted *nem. con.* in favour of the drum. They deigned to try Lord Granby's suggestion, and to their pleasing astonishment their little theatre was brim-full on the sound of the drum and Lord Granby's name. After which night, they row-didi-dowed away, had a very successful season, and drank flowing bowls to the health of the noble Marquis. They left Grantham in great credit, without being drummed out of town, though accompanied by their friend the drummer; and I am told the custom is continued at Grantham to this day.

351　Delivering playbills in the country

Anon. Harvard Theatre Collection. Reproduced in Nicoll (1980), p. 62

THE BEHAVIOUR OF THE AUDIENCE
The Fitzgiggo riots

Audience behaviour in the playhouses was a good deal less decorous than we are accustomed to in the twentieth century. In London, as in other major cities, rowdyism occasionally spilt over into full-blown riots. These might be provoked by a variety of issues. Sometimes they were the result of misplaced patriotism.[1] More frequently they were occasioned by management attempts to increase the prices of admission.

Perhaps the most notorious of the eighteenth-century theatre riots was sparked off by animosity between a young buck called Thaddeus Fitzpatrick and David Garrick. Fitzpatrick had attacked Garrick in a series of published letters in 1760; Garrick replied in 1761 with a satire called *The Fribbleriad*, in which the principal character was a comically effeminate caricature of Fitzpatrick. He, in turn, led a riot in January 1763 at Drury Lane, ostensibly in protest against the management's refusal to allow half-price concessions on certain occasions. After two nights of violence, Garrick was forced to give an undertaking that this would not recur and was also coerced into dismissing Moody, one of his company [*see* 352]. The rioters then turned their attention to John Beard at Covent Garden who defended himself vigorously, but was also in the end forced to capitulate. The episodes produced partisan letters and statements in the press; a number of pamphlets, of which one is quoted here [*see* 352]; and the satirical burlesque which contained one of the best known engravings of the Covent Garden stage at this time [*see* 285a and b].

[1] There were demonstrations against French players at the Haymarket in 1738 (see Victor, vol. I (1761), pp. 54–60 and *LS*, pt iii, pp. 734–5) and further demonstrations during Garrick's *Chinese Festival* at Drury Lane in November 1755 (see Davies, vol. I (1808), p. 187 ff. and *LS*, pt iv. pp. 507–10).

352   **The Fitzgiggo riot at Drury Lane, 25 January 1763**
Anon: *An historical and succinct account of the late riots at the Theatres of Drury Lane and Covent Garden* (London: W. Morgan, 1763), pp. 5–19

On the day of performance of *The Two Gentlemen of Verona*, the following hand-bill was delivered at all the public places and coffee-houses in London.

'To the frequenters of the theatres, GENTLEMEN,

You have long complained as individuals of the unjustifiable innovation, introduced by the managers of the playhouses, in advertising, "that nothing under the full price would be taken during the performance". But hitherto this imposition has been carried on successfully, as no-one thought proper to take the lead in rectifying so flagrant an abuse. The public for a long time past, though dissatisfied, submitted to an additional tax, upon producing entertainments, evidently attended with extraordinary expense – but will you acquiesce, gentlemen, in this *insolent* extortion, without any other pretence than new dressing the characters of an old play in linsey woolsey; or reviving a spurious comedy under the respectable name of Shakespeare? Perhaps you have been told by the partisans of our theatrical directors that it has been always customary to insist on the full price during the run of a new performance of every species. This I deny and insist on my own knowledge that, until a very moderate period, this privilege was confined to a new pantomime. I likewise add on the same certainty that the managers did not venture on so *impudent* an attempt on the public at the representation of *Barbarossa Boadicea* [*sic*] – *The Apprentice* – *Agis* – *The Upholsterer*

– The Englishman returned from Paris – The Orphan of China – or *The Siege of Aquileia –* I do not apprehend that anyone will be daring enough to allege that an improvement of the diversions of the theatre authorises this increase of the prices. But should such an outrage on your understanding be attempted, permit me to rouse your indignation by reminding you that we formerly could see for four shillings a play performed by Booth, Wilks, Cibber, Dogget, Norris, Pinkethman, Johnson, Griffin, Porter, Oldfield – and are now obliged to pay five shillings for half a play performed by Garrick, Holland, O'Brien, Blakes, King, Yates, Palmer, Bransby, Packer, Ackman, Cibber and Yates. It is impossible to draw the line and determine where the imposition will end; nor can any reasonable man take upon him to ensure that our Lords and Masters will not require opera prices of the public when they have fully established the present insult on their forbearance. One way only is left us to obtain redress, which is to assemble at the playhouses and demand with decency and temper an explanation on this grievance, which I am certain, cannot be supported and owes its establishment to an opinion that every imposition, not openly opposed, acquires the sanction of prescription.

I am, Gentlemen, Your humble servant, *An Enemy to Imposition.* The reason of addressing the town in this manner is that all communications with the public by the channel of the newpapers is cut off through the influence of one of the theatrical managers, who has found means to lay that restraint upon the liberty of the press which no minister of state has hitherto been able to effect in this country. [. . .]'

At night, the pit and boxes were filled with men who soon began to cry for Garrick, Garrick! An actor appeared to tell them a messenger was gone for him and Mr Garrick himself soon appeared before them. Silence was at last with difficulty obtained by the signals of a person in the centre of the pit who seemed by his actions as if he proposed to speak, and when the noise was subsided began to pour forth his oratory in the following vehement manner, addressing himself to Mr Garrick. 'I call on you in the name of the public to answer for your rascally impositions.' The word RASCAL was immediately echoed through the house, the orator all this while continuing his violent action, cried, 'Answer it, Sir, answer me, Sir.' Mr Garrick made some answer, but noise hindered our hearing it. But the orator hastily replied, 'Speak to the audience, Sir, speak to the house.' To which the manager attempted, but for a long time in vain. At last he asked, 'for time to answer so sudden a charge; that he had a partner to consult who was then at a great distance'. He was then called on to read their paper. He said 'he would do more than read it, he would answer it, if they would give him time'. This was denied him, and peremptorily YES or NO was demanded by the orator who called on him as follows, 'Will you, or will you not, admit the public at half prices to all entertainments, except the first winter of a new pantomime?' To this the manager answered as before, that he desired time to consult his partner – and to answer a question of that importance – but he would lay his answer before the public in a few days, which very greatly enraged them. And the manager, after standing their hissings for some time, bowed and retired.

After some time spent in noise and uproar, the great majority of unprejudiced persons in the house were desirous the play should be no longer interrupted and called loudly for it. The actors appeared several times, but were obliged to retire from the clamour and outrage of the rioters. And thus it continued till eight of the clock, when the ladies were called on by them to retire that the house might be burnt and destroyed, as was the voice of several of those enraged heroes. The glass lustres were broke and the lighted candles fell to the ground. When the mischief was done to the boxes and pit, a magistrate appeared with a guard, upon which the rioters thought proper to decamp, and so the affair ended for that night.

We cannot help remarking what a contradiction of behaviour this was to what they promised in their hand-bill, where they say, 'One way only is left us to obtain redress, which is to assemble at the playhouses and demand with decency and temper an explanation of this grievance.' No prologue till Mr Garrick comes on – off – off – off. Mr Garrick appears, bows submissively, but is not allowed to speak. Did you not call for him to be heard? Remonstrances are vain; mischief must be done to testify the resentment of the town. The benches are torn up, the sconces broke, the actors pelted, the chandeliers destroyed, and all is anarchy and confusion. This is the equitable manner in which the town makes theatrical regulations![1] [. . .]

The next day, January 26th, [. . .] the bills of *Elvira* also were posted up for the sixth night for the benefit of the author, with nothing under the full price.

The rioters were again assembled at the theatre and the manager when called for came upon the stage with a full resolution to comply with their commands. Yet they would not hear him speak. He stood sweating upon the stage near twenty minutes before he was permitted to say YES.

In the performance of the tragedy, a scene drew and discovered Mr Ackman* among the train, attending on the King. The rioting gentry immediately called him forth. He came forward and said, 'he was extremely sorry he had done anything to give offence to the gentlemen, that it was far from his intention and humbly asked them pardon', upon which he was pardoned and walked back to his place. They then called for Mr Moody and were told he had nothing to do at the house that night and was not there. The rioters immediately cried, 'send for him, we will have him, send for him'. Nor would they suffer the play to go on until one of the actors told them, he should be sent for. At the end of the act, Moody was again loudly called for and in a little time appeared. And after the noise which the sight of him occasioned was quelled, he said, 'Gentlemen, if my saving the house last night from being burned was an offence, I ask your pardon', and went off. At which the whole house roared out to bring him back. And he appeared again, every one cried out, 'Knees, knees! Down on your knees!' Moody finding that nothing but going on his knees would satisfy them, he clapt his hand on his breast and walked off, in seeming contempt of their demand. The manager was then called for to order his discharge, which he did, and was applauded for it. And so ended the disturbance of that night.

* (On the first night, when the rioters were determined upon mischief, two of the actors, namely Ackman and Moody, ran round the boxes to see what was doing, and the sight of

them made the rioters suspect they were sent as spies. But Moody did more. He saw a gentleman strike the glass lustre, and down fell the candle alight, which another slyly shoved with his foot against the wainscot. This candle Mr Moody put out and kept his eye upon the person. When the magistrate with the guard appeared, he pointed him out to be apprehended, but his brethren either bribed or shouldered the soldiers that the person escaped.)

[1] The following day, 26 January, an advertisement was issued in *The Public Advertiser* confirming Garrick's assertion that the management was not conscious of any breaking with precedent and reiterating his promise of publishing a full answer to the charges made in the printed paper.

The Blackamoor washed White

Other quarrels were provoked by the choice of particular plays or afterpieces, sometimes deliberately fomented by enemies of the author. In 1776, for instance, at the very end of Garrick's period of management, a new farce by Henry Bate called *The Blackamoor washed White* was the target for such a demonstration. The ensuing brawl lasted for over half an hour. A contemporary print shows members of the audience fighting on stage as well as the sticks and fruit thrown at the hapless performers [*see* 353]. At its subsequent performance Garrick was obliged to appear on stage and beg for calm, which was only restored when the audience was informed that the author had taken the prompt copy of the play away from the theatre and that it would not be performed again [*see* 354].

353 The theatrical dispute, Drury Lane, 1776

Anonymous engraving. Theatre Collection, University of Bristol. Reproduced in Nicoll (1980), p. 89

354   The affair of *The Blackamoor washed White*, Drury Lane, 1776

William Hopkins's Diary, no. 3. Folger Shakespeare Library. Transcribed in Macmillan (1938), pp. 193–4

Feb 1   *Matilda. The Blackamoor washed White* (never acted before)
The Blackamoor washed White – a new comic opera of two acts writted by (The Revd) Mr Bate (Bate Dudley) – much hissed and crying out 'No more, no more'. Mr Reddish was desired to give out the next day's play at the end of *Matilda* [. . .] and could not get the play given out till after the farce was over. When the *Blackamoor* was given out for the next night, they cried out, 'No more – give out another farce' and kept a great noise, but at last went away.

Feb 2   *The School for Lovers*. Ditto
Great applause to the play. The first act of the farce went off pretty well, but the beginning of the second act, began to hiss and cry, 'Off'. A great tumult and noise ensued and with great difficulty got through the farce.

Feb 3   *Zara*. Ditto
The farce was much hissed from the second act. Captain Roper and another gentleman came in drunk and kept such a noise in the boxes that the pit and gallery resented it. A great hubbub ensued. Mr King went to know their pleasure if the farce should go on; great clapping and much hissing. Numbers of the pit and boxes got upon the stage and blows passed between some of them, and I thought the house would have been pulled to pieces. At length, they were again pacified and we finished the farce.

Feb 5   *The Provoked Wife*. Ditto
Soon after the farce began, 'Off, off – no more' and much hissing. Mr King went on to know their pleasure – a great noise and would not hear him speak. At length, Mr Garrick went on – a great noise continued, and they would not hear him for a long while, though he attempted several times to speak. At length they cried, 'Hear him, hear him.' Mr Garrick told them he, 'would wait their commands till morning with pleasure, if they required it'. At last they consented to hear him. He desired, 'to know their pleasure – if they would please to have any other farce, or if they would choose the *Blackamoor* to go on'. A great noise ensued and nothing determined. At last Mr Garrick told them, 'his theatrical life would be very short and he should be glad to end it in peace'. A man in the pit cried out, 'If you have a mind to die in peace, don't let the *Blackamoor* be played again.' Mr Garrick was on and off the stage several times and Mr King also. Nothing would pacify them. At length Mr King went and told them 'In order to make everything quiet that the author had taken the copy from the prompter and that it should not be done again.' Even this would not do, and Mr Garrick went on again; they would not hear, till a gentleman in the boxes cried, 'For shame! hear Mr Garrick speak.' And then they condescended to hear him. He confirmed what Mr King said and told the author's friends that, 'it was now out of his power to oblige them by performing the *Blackamoor* and desired to know what farce they would please to have, etc.'

In the provinces, audience behaviour could be just as noisy as in London. Dublin was known to be particularly rowdy[1], but there were also problems associated with garrison towns on the mainland. The high spirits of serving men in the audience led on occasions to scenes of drunken excess and violence.

Because theatre riots were usually well written up, they perhaps loom larger than they should and they therefore need to be kept in perspective. It is worth recalling that during Garrick's managership at Drury Lane, which lasted some thirty years, there were no more than seven theatre riots.[2]

[1] See Stockwell (1938), chapter 3.
[2] See Pedicord (1954), p. 52.

355   The problems of playing in a garrison town: Portsmouth

(A) E.C. EVERARD A.C. Everard: *Memoirs of an unfortunate son of Thespis*, (Edinburgh: Ballantyne, 1818), pp. 104–5 and 136

The house was nearly full almost every night, but a very turbulent noisy audience, when the fleet or much shipping was in, and frequently a whole evening's performance would be gone through and not ten lines distinctly heard from beginning to end. That might suit an indifferent or imperfect actor very well, but was enough to spoil a good one. Our situation on the stage, from being often rendered unpleasant, was sometimes dangerous. Apples and oranges we got pretty well used to from their frequency of appearing. But when our unthinking spectators would sometimes salute us with a potato, or even a pint or quart bottle, it was above a joke. Half that came did not know what it was to be – it was a play, and that was enough. We could not, however, but observe that in general our tragedies such as *Macbeth*, *Richard* and *Hamlet* brought us much better houses than our comedies, and still more remarkable, they were not so clamorous. One night, we were playing Sheridan's elegant comedy of *The School for Scandal*, of which not three words were heard, till, in the third act Charles was discovered with his companions, drinking. Upon which, many of the sailors from the gallery got round to the slips over the boxes and dropped themselves down upon the stage till it was filled, coming up to Charles, exclaiming, 'My eyes, you're a hearty fellow! Come, my tight one, hand us a glass!' We were obliged to drop the curtain and use all the fair means we could think of, for we knew foul or forcible efforts would not do. At length, with a deal of persuasion, after permitting them to send for half a dozen bottles and helping to empty them, they were prevailed on to resume their seats. But they were as noisy during the remainder of the play as at first. Yet upon all occasion where there was dancing or a pantomime, they were silent among themselves and attentive to us, as we wished them to be at other times. [. . .]

[. . .] At Portsmouth, a midshipman, without any provocation, suddenly killed our carpenter. He was tried at Winchester, but having powerful friends, he got acquitted by paying only [a] one shilling fine! The Judge was applauded for his opinion, but shame on the Jury. In consequence of this calamity, the Old Theatre, as then called in Portsmouth, was shut up and as a theatre, I believe has never been allowed to be opened since, only as a warehouse. In consequence of this poor man being quite killed, I was half-murdered. We lay idle for three months or more till we were allowed to open the New Theatre and then, when our benefits came on, there was no fleet or scarcely a theatrical person in town.

(B) *HAMPSHIRE CHRONICLE*, 16 FEBRUARY 1795

A few nights since, some young officers, belonging to a regiment now quartered in Portsmouth, paraded the streets with drawn swords and they rushed into the theatre with a hideous yell, where they wounded several persons and terminated the performance, which was *Everyone has his Fault*. Since this insolent and brutal conduct, the theatre has been shut up, to the manifest injury of the managers and performers and to the disappointment and annoyance of the town. We have witnessed so many instances of unqualified violence on the part of subaltern officers towards poor country actors that it is worth some enquiry to ask from where such little tyranny originates.

(C) CHARLES DIBDIN Charles Dibdin: *Observations on a tour through almost the whole of England and a considerable part of Scotland*, vol. 2 (London: G. Goulding, 1801–2), pp. 373–4

I must not take leave of Portsmouth without doing justice on a subject which I had mistaken, as well as others. I own I always dreaded to occupy the theatre there, for I had conceived that, in a sea port, where it cannot but be that vice and infamy must be found, a playhouse would of course exhibit every sort of riot and quarrelling. I never was so much mistaken in my life. An assembly room, regulated by a master of ceremonies, could not be better conducted. It is true, prostitutes were seen there in plenty, but there was a space set apart for them where they were obliged to conform to rules and order or be turned out. They did not dare to bar up the lobbies and insult modest women. Better discipline never was observed. They were permitted to be happy as long as their conduct was inoffensive. And so good an effect had this wholesome established regulation on their conduct that, if I may judge by what I myself witnessed, there is more barefaced profligate indecency practised at Drury Lane or Covent Garden Theatres in an evening than at Portsmouth Theatre in a season.

ATTITUDES AND TASTE OF AUDIENCES

With audiences so heterogeneous, it is not surprising that tastes and demands differed, sometimes radically, not only between London and the provinces [*see* 356 and 357], but within a given performance between the various social sections of the audience or between the naive and the sophisticated.

O'Keeffe's fashionable gentleman in Dublin [*see* 359] is arguably no more than the genteel equivalent of Everard's roistering Portsmouth sailors [*see* **355a**]; they at least did sometimes listen when Shakespearean tragedies were performed. From an actor's point of view, such disparate audiences must have been extremely difficult to please or even control.

356 Differences in taste between town and country
Tate Wilkinson vol. 2 (Dublin 1791), p. 241

The differences of audiences [. . .] is amazing. A farce, if it possesses true humour, in London will be greatly relished and applauded. In the country, very possibly the same (even decently acted) shall be termed vile, low, vulgar and indelicate. The *Love for Love* of Congreve, the *Trip to Scarborough, The Way of the World, The Confederacy* and others are in London attended to as plays of wit and merit (witness their constant repetition), but in the country not permitted, or if permitted to appear, not upon any account fashionable, which is just as bad.

357 Rowlandson contrasts London and country audiences
Rowlandson: *Comedy in the Country* and *Tragedy in London*, George 7606 (Print Room. BM)

358   Differences between sections of the audience
Garrick's Epilogue to Arthur Murphy's *All in the Wrong* (1761)

[. . .] What shall we do your different tastes to hit?
  You relish satire (*to the pit*), you ragouts of wit (*to the boxes*),
  Your taste is humour and high-seasoned joke (*first gallery*).
  You call for hornpipe and for hearts of oak (*second gallery*).

359   An exhibitionist spectator
John O'Keeffe: *Recollections of his life*, vol. 1 (London: Colburn, 1826), pp. 153–5

One of the finest gentlemen in Dublin about this time [1760s], indeed the most remarkable for his dress and manner, was a young merchant in Cow Lane who troubled himself no more about business than my Bouquet, the hop merchant in St Mary Axe. This grand gentleman was one night at Crow Street (the play, Murphy's *Orphan of China*). He sat in the left-hand stage box and, though he had the front seat all to himself, this did not content him. Turning his back upon the stage, (upon Barry's Zamti and Mrs Fitzhenry's Mandane) he placed himself upon the edge of the box, his legs stretched out at full length, crossing each other, his arms also folded and his shoulder resting against the side of the box. Under him was the door opening to the pit and the flooring was rather deep. Thus he remained, enjoying his prime wish of an ample display of his person and dress to the whole house. His clothes were silk and richly embroidered; his hair, tastefully dressed with ringlets that played round his ears; his sword, with a large and magnificent silver sword-knot, stretched itself all along by the side of his legs to complete the view. The eyes of the audience were upon him full front, the eyes of the performers upon the back of his head and shoulder. In the very height of this proud and careless display of his six-feet-long person, whilst lolling with a smile of complacent nonchalance, he at an instant overbalanced himself and tumbled into the pit. A clamour of mirth burst through the whole house and, as no bones were broke, nobody was sorry for his downfall. This, though not the first, was most likely his last attempt to captivate the notice of the audience and turn it from the stage, the true point of attraction, to his own fine self-admired self.

360   A naive spectator
Tate Wilkinson vol. 3 (Dublin 1791), p. 165

The first time Holland acted Hamlet it was for his own benefit [. . .]. On seeing the Ghost, he was much frightened and felt the sensation and terror usual on that thrilling occasion, and his hat flew *à-la-mode* off his head. An inoffensive woman in a red cloak (a friend of Holland's), hearing Hamlet complain the air bit shrewdly and was very cold, with infinite composure crossed the stage,[1] took up the hat and with the greatest care placed it fast on Hamlet's head, who on the occasion was as much alarmed in reality as he had just then been feigning. But the audience burst out into such incessant peals of laughter that the Ghost moved off without any ceremony and Hamlet, scorning to be outdone in courtesy, immediately followed with roars of applause. The poor woman stood astonished, which increased the roar, etc. It was some time before the laughter subsided and they could not resist a repetition (that merry tragedy night) on the re-appearance of the Ghost and Hamlet.

¹ An amphitheatre had been constructed on the stage for the benefit performance [*see* **263**].

CRITICAL THEORY AND THEATRE CRITICISM

The state of critical theory in the mid-eighteenth-century theatre was somewhat confused. From the Renaissance and the seventeenth century it had inherited respect for the three classical unities, of action, time, and place; the separation of kinds, which meant that tragi-comedy was viewed as an illegitimate form; decorum, which was concerned with the kind of characters appropriate to tragedy and comedy and how they should behave, so that a king should speak or act in a manner appropriate to a king, a peasant to a peasant, etc. Tragedy was to show terrible actions in an elevated style; comedy the familiar and domestic. The trouble was that a playwright like Shakespeare broke all of these 'rules' at times, yet it was not possible to deny his greatness or popularity (hence, they believed, the need for some re-writing of his worst transgressions). It was also undeniable that the witty upper-class comedy inherited from the seventeenth century was unashamedly elitist in character and tone, whereas comedy was expected to deal satirically with the vices and follies of those of low or at best middle rank.

   The relics of the morality debates and Steele's reformism, together with the influence of the contemporary French stage, led to the desire for retribution and repentance, not reconciliation, in comedy. Ridicule was not enough, what was required was the inculcation of moral sentiments and the dictatorship of 'good taste'. Yet at the same time it had to be admitted that this new elevated style often bore little relation, if any, to reality, while good taste and moral sentiment were often boring in the extreme. As a result of such confusion, opinions were often sharply divided.

The battle over sentimentality

There was not a clear and decisive victory for sentimentality in the Georgian theatre, as has sometimes been supposed. For one thing, most of the sentimental comedies were dull and unpopular, whereas much of the successful comedy writing and playing was carried on in farces and other afterpieces. The greatest popular acclaim in mainpiece comedy went to those writers (including Garrick, Hoadly, Colman, Murphy, Goldsmith, Sheridan) who subordinated, or ignored, the demands of sentimentality and wrote for social and theatrical effect. The point is well illustrated in Samuel Foote's defence of Hoadly's play *The Suspicious Husband*.

361   Samuel Foote approves of Hoadly's comedy *The Suspicious Husband*

Samuel Foote: *The Roman and English comedy considered and compared* (London: T. Waller, 1747), pp. 26–34

It will (I doubt not) be often mentioned by future generations, that in the year 1746, Dr Hoadly produced a comedy called *The Suspicious Husband*, in which he has found means to give the highest delight, without having recourse to the low usual arts of bawdy and buffoonery.

But that we may not appear tainted with the common partiality that generally attends novelty, let us venture at the discovery of those qualities in this piece which have recommended it to the general favour of the public, and have obtained for it our particular approbation.

In the first place, then, most of the characters are real, the incidents are interesting, the catastrophe affecting, and the language pure, spirited and natural.

The character of Mr Strickland (who names the play) is as well drawn and supported as any I have met with. And amongst the scenes which the author has designed to ridicule the folly and absurdity of suspicion, none seems so well calculated for the purposes as that where Strickland is desirous, and yet afraid, of engaging one of his domestics in the service of his passion. The perplexity at who he shall trust, or whether he shall trust either, with the doubts, resolutions, hesitations on that occasion, make up so natural and comic a description of that disease of the mind, that the play, on this account only, deserves the highest encomiums.

Mrs Strickland is described as such a woman ought to be, in order to render the husband's extravagant humour without excuse. Her innocence, joined to her other amiable qualities, interest the audience strongly in her favour, and place the passion of jealousy in a more hated and ridiculous light.

The two Fine Gentlemen of this comedy are not (as I can perceive) different from the fine gentlemen of other writers: they laugh, sing, say good things, and are in love.

The Rake is a lively portrait of that character in life. His errors arise from the want of reflection; a lively imagination, with a great flow of spirits, hurries him into all the fashionable follies of the town; but throw the least shadow of wickedness or dishonour on an action, and he avoids it with the same care that he would a precipice.

The natural good qualities of this youth obtain for him on the stage the same indulgence that attends him in the world; we are blind to his foibles, entertained with his adventures, and wish to see (in which, I suppose, by the conduct of the author, we are wrong) the wild rogue reclaimed.

I sat (the first night this comedy was exhibited) by a plain, honest, well-meaning citizen, whose imagination was strongly possessed by the incidents of the play. At dropping of the curtain, I could not help complaining to my neighbour that I was displeased at seeing Ranger go off as he came on. Could not, said I, the author throw this youth, in the course of his nocturnal rambles, into some ridiculous scene of distress which might, with propriety, have reclaimed him. But as he now stands, who knows but the rogue, after all the pleasure he has given us, may spend the night in a round-house. By G—d! says the cit, if it happen in my ward, I'll release him; for I'm sure he is too honest a fellow to run away from his bail.

The amiable light in which this character appears will, I am afraid, draw many a templar into troublesome scrapes. I have now no less than ten friends, since the appearance of Ranger, who are under prosecution for ravishing kisses from girls in the street and beating the Watch. It is therefore necessary to let these sprightly boys know that these are not the particulars of Ranger's character that procure our regard; we are only tempted to overlook these blemishes in his conduct, on the score of some amiable beauties.

But that we may not appear partial to the productions of this author, let me take a view of such of his characters as appear liable to exception.

That the critics, then, might not be deprived of their daily food, the poet has thrown them a couple of characters to nibble at; the Coquette and the Coxcomb.

The last is of a species pretty common amongst us, but hitherto neglected. The importation of fopperies from France we have laughed at till we are tired: our author was willing to see whether Italy could not furnish us with a fool as ridiculous and diverting as her neighbour. And had the character in question been supported with the same spirit that it is begun, I doubt not but we should have been fully satisfied. But no sooner has this merry gentleman raised our attention but he slips through our fingers like an eel, and we hear no more of him. Mr Meggot does, in truth, survive the loss of his Monkey, but he never forgets his affection so far as to be tolerable company after.

I did indeed flatter myself with the hopes of seeing that gentleman interested in the conduct of the play, and every minute expected to find my friend Ranger very jocose upon his foible.

But whether the author did not choose to expose so good-natured a fellow, or was above being obliged to any nation but his own for the entertainment he was to give us, Jackie Meggot is of very little more consequence in *The Suspicious Husband*, than is Lieutenant Story in *The Committee*.

The next character for the snarlers to mumble is Clarinda. This lady, at the opening of the play, would put herself upon us for a finished coquette; but she does it so awkwardly, that few of us are imposed upon. She is, indeed, at first a little waggish with Jacintha, about giving ease, etc. but this was only a copy of her countenance, for I do not find but she is as ready to satisfy the desires of her lover (in an honourable way) as the other.

But all this while, are we not imposing on ourselves? How are we sure that Dr Hoadly intended Clarinda for a coquette? Indeed she sometimes talks like one, but her actions are directly opposite; and as I, for my own part, choose to rely more on the latter than the former, I shall not scruple to pronounce that this lady is no more a coquette than Jacintha . . .

[. . .] But were we to answer all the trifling remarks of these eternal cavillers there would be no end to the subject; therefore I shall dismiss them with one general answer, that I defy them to produce a comedy, since the year twenty-six, that has a tithe of the merit of *The Suspicious Husband*. And though we may be deficient as to the *vis comica*, and our characters may not be altogether so highly drawn as might be wished, yet, upon the whole, we are at least equal to the best of the Roman comic poets, Terence; and that is reputation enough to satisfy our ambition.

362   Garrick and Mrs Pritchard in Hoadly's *The Suspicious Husband*, 1747

From a painting by Francis Hayman, The London Museum. Reproduced in *The Revels history of drama in English*, vol. 5 (1976), plate 33; Mander and Mitchenson (1957), pl. 69

Richard Cumberland

In the late sixties and early seventies, fashion gave some renewed impetus to the vein of sentimentality, so that a play like Cumberland's *The West Indian* had an initial run of twenty-eight nights following its first performance on 17 January 1771. In his *Memoirs*, Cumberland records what he was trying to achieve with the play.

363   Richard Cumberland sets out his aims as a dramatist

Richard Cumberland: *Memoirs* [1806], edited by H. Flanders [Philadelphia, 1856] (New York: Blom, 1969) pp. 141–2

As the writer for the stage is a writer to the passions, I hold it matter of conscience and duty in the dramatic poet to reserve his brightest colouring for the best characters, to give no false attractions to vice and immorality, but to endeavour, as far as is consistent with that contrast, which is the very essence of his art, to turn the fairer side of human nature to the public, and, as much as in him lies, to contrive so as to put men into good humour with one another. Let him therefore in the first place strive to make worthy characters amiable, but take great care not to make them insipid. If he does not put life and spirit into his man or woman of virtue and render them entertaining as well as good, their morality is not a whit more attractive than the morality of a Greek chorus. He had better have let them alone altogether.

Congreve, Farquhar, and some others have made vice and villainy so playful and amusing that either they could not find in their hearts to punish them, or not caring how wicked they were, so long as they were witty, paid no attention to what became of them. Shadwell's comedy is little better than a brothel. Poetical justice, which has armed the tragic poet with the weapons of death, and commissioned him to wash out the offence in the blood of the offender, has not left the comic writer without his instruments of vengeance. For surely, if he knows how to employ the authority that is in him, the scourge of ridicule alone is sharp enough for the chastisement of any crimes which can fall within his province to exhibit. A true poet knows that, unless he can produce works whose fame will outlive him, he will outlive both his works and his fame; therefore, every comic author who takes the mere clack of the day for his subject and abandons all his claims upon posterity, is no true poet; if he dabbles in personalities, he does considerably worse.

When I began therefore, as at this time, to write for the stage, my ambition was to aim at writing something that might be lasting and outlive me. When temporary subjects were suggested to me, I declined them: I formed to myself in idea what I conceived to be the character of a legitimate comedy, and that alone was my object, and though I did not quite aspire to attain, I was not altogether in despair of approaching it. I perceived that I had fallen upon a time when great eccentricity of character was pretty nearly gone by, but still I fancied there was an opening for some originality, and an opportunity for showing at least my good-will to mankind, if I introduced the characters of persons who had been usually exhibited on the stage as the butts for ridicule and abuse, and endeavoured to present them in such lights as might tend to reconcile the world to them and them to the world. I thereupon looked into society for the purpose of discovering such as were the victims of its national, professional, or religious prejudices; in short for those suffering characters which stood in need of an advocate, and out of these I meditated to select and form heroes for my future dramas, of which I would study to make such favourable and reconciliatory delineations, as might incline the spectators to look upon them with pity and receive them into their good opinion and esteem.

Opponents of sentimentality

Cumberland's work provoked a powerful counter-attack. Goldsmith's was the classic exposition of the anti-sentimental position, though in his polemic approach he probably exaggerated the popularity and strength of the *comédie larmoyante* [*see* 364]. 'Bossu', while firing his own broadside, reminds us of Foote's satirical contribution to the argument in

1772 and 1773 in the theatre itself [*see* **365**]. But Cooke [*see* **366**], looking back after the battle makes it clear that the result was finally inconclusive, or at best a pyrrhic victory for those opposed to sentimental comedy. For a time at least, traditional satirical comedy gave way to a debased form of comedy we associate with the romantic theatre and the early nineteenth century.

364   Oliver Goldsmith on sentimental comedy

O. Goldsmith: 'An essay on the theatre: or, a comparison between laughing and sentimental comedy' [1772] in O. Goldsmith: *Miscellaneous works* (Globe edition, edited by David Masson, London: Macmillan, 1868, and later reprints), pp. 346–7

The theatre, like all other amusements, has its fashions and its prejudices; and when satiated with its excellence, mankind begins to mistake change for improvement. For some years tragedy was the reigning entertainment; but of late [*c.* 1770] it has entirely given way to comedy, and our best efforts are now exerted in these lighter kinds of composition. The pompous train, the swelling phrase, and the unnatural rant are displaced for that natural portrait of human folly and frailty, of which all are judges, because all have sat for the picture.

But as in describing nature it is presented with a double face, either of mirth or sadness, our modern writers find themselves at a loss which chiefly to copy from. And it is now debated, whether the exhibition of human distress is likely to afford the mind more entertainment than that of human absurdity.

Comedy is defined by Aristotle to be a picture of the frailties of the lower part of mankind, to distinguish it from tragedy, which is an exhibition of the misfortunes of the great. When comedy therefore ascends to produce the characters of princes or generals upon the stage, it is out of its walk, since low life and middle life are entirely its object. The principal question therefore is whether, in describing low or middle life, an exhibition of its follies be not preferable to a detail of its calamities. Or, in other words, which deserves the preference – the weeping sentimental comedy so much in fashion at present, or the laughing and even low comedy which seems to have been last exhibited by Vanbrugh and Cibber?

If we apply to authorities, all the great masters in the dramatic art have but one opinion. Their rule is that as tragedy displays the calamities of the great, so comedy should excite our laughter by ridiculously exhibiting the follies of the lower part of mankind. Boileau, one of the best modern critics, asserts that comedy will not admit of tragic distress:

> Le comique, ennemi des soupirs et des pleurs,
> N'admet point dans ses vers de tragiques douleurs.[1]

Nor is this rule without the strongest foundation in nature, as the distresses of the mean by no means affect us so strongly as the calamities of the great. When tragedy exhibits to us some great man fallen from his height, and struggling with want and adversity, we feel his situation in the same manner as we suppose he himself must feel, and our pity is increased in proportion to the height from which he fell. On the contrary, we do not so strongly sympathise with one born in humbler circumstances, and encountering accidental distress; so that while we melt for Belisarius, we scarce give halfpence to the beggar who accosts us in the street. The one has our pity; the other our contempt. Distress therefore is the proper object of tragedy, since the great excite our pity by their fall; but not equally so of comedy, since the actors employed in it are originally so mean, that they sink but little by their fall.

Since the first origin of the stage, tragedy and comedy have run in distinct channels and never till of late encroached upon the provinces of each other. Terence, who seems to have made the nearest approaches, always judiciously stops short before he comes to the downright pathetic. And yet he is even reproached by Caesar for wanting the *vis comica*. All the other comic writers of antiquity aim only at rendering folly or vice ridiculous, but never exalt their characters into buskined pomp or make what Voltaire humorously calls 'a tradesman's tragedy'.

Yet notwithstanding this weight of authority, and the universal practice of former ages, a new species of dramatic composition has been introduced under the name of sentimental comedy, in which the virtues of private life are exhibited rather than the vices exposed, and the distresses rather than the faults of mankind make our interest in the piece. These comedies have had of late great success, perhaps from their novelty, and also from their flattering every man in his favourite foible. In these plays, almost all the characters are good and exceedingly generous. They are lavish enough of their tin money on the stage and, though they want humour, have abundance of sentiment and feeling. If they happen to have faults or foibles, the spectator is taught, not only to pardon, but to applaud them, in consideration of the goodness of their hearts; so that folly, instead of being ridiculed, is commended, and the comedy aims at touching our passions without the power of being truly pathetic. In this manner, we are likely to lose one great source of entertainment on the stage. For while the comic poet is invading the province of the tragic muse, he leaves her lovely sister quite neglected. Of this, however, he is no way solicitous, as he measures his fame by his profits.

But it will be said that the theatre is formed to amuse mankind, and that it matters little, if this end be answered, by what means it is obtained. If mankind find delight in weeping at comedy, it would be cruel to abridge them in that or any other innocent pleasure. If those pieces are denied the name of comedies, yet call them by any other name and, if they are delightful, they are good. Their success, it will be said, is a mark of their merit, and it is only abridging our happiness to deny us an inlet to amusement.

These objections, however, are rather specious than solid. It is true that amusement is a great object of the theatre, and it will be allowed that these sentimental pieces do often amuse us. But the question is whether the true comedy would not amuse us more. The question is whether a character supported throughout a piece with its ridicule still attending would not give us more delight than this species of bastard tragedy, which only is applauded because it is new.

A friend of mine who was sitting unmoved at one of these sentimental pieces was asked how he could be so indifferent. 'Why truly', says he, 'as the hero is but a tradesman, it is indifferent to me whether he be turned out of his counting house on Fish Street Hill, since he will still have enough left to open shop in St Giles's.'

The other objection is as ill-grounded. For though we should give these pieces another name, it will not mend their efficacy. It will continue a kind of mulish production, with all the defects of its opposite parents, and marked with sterility. If we are permitted to make comedy weep, we have an equal right to make tragedy laugh and set down in blank verse the jests and repartees of all the attendants in a funeral procession.

But there is one argument in favour of sentimental comedy which will keep it on the stage, in spite of all that can be said against it. It is, of all others, the most easily written. Those abilities that can hammer out a novel are fully sufficient for the production of a sentimental comedy. It is only sufficient to raise the characters a little, to deck out the hero with a ribbon or give the heroine a title, then to put an insipid dialogue without character or humour into their mouths, give them mighty good hearts, very fine clothes, furnish a new set of scenes, make a pathetic scene or two, with a sprinkling of tender melancholy conversation through the whole, and there is no doubt but all the ladies will cry and all the gentlemen applaud.

Humour at present seems to be departing from the stage, and it will soon happen that our comic players will have nothing left for it but a fine coat and a song. It depends upon the audience whether they will actually drive those poor merry creatures from the stage or sit at a play as gloomy as at the tabernacle. It is not easy to recover an art when once lost. And it will be but a just punishment that when, by our being too fastidious, we have banished humour from the stage, we should ourselves be deprived of the art of laughing.

[1] Boileau: *L'art poétique* (1674), canto III, lines 401–2. Sir William Soame and John Dryden, in their translation and adaptation published in 1683, rendered the lines as follows:

> The comic wit, born with a smiling air,
> Must tragic grief and pompous verse forbear:

A more literal translation would run as follows:

> Comic art, foe to sighs and tears,
> Banishes from its verses all tragic grief.

365 Another attack on sentimentality
St James's Chronicle, 9 March 1773

Sir,
Urged by those feelings which naturally lead me to espouse the interests of literature and taste, I publicly censured a new tragedy which did not appear to me to do honour to the former or to correspond with the latter. I was willing to awaken the attention of a heedless audience, some of whom are too incapable and others too idle to judge for themselves. In this I was opposing my single powers to the torrent of degeneracy which threatens to overwhelm our theatre and our fair

literary fame, and though the effort may be vain, I know it to be generous. The goddess of dullness walks abroad, her murky wings grow every day more extensive, and we must endeavour to clip them.

Guided by these sentiments, I confess to have received uncommon pleasure from the new representations of Mr Foote at the Haymarket.[1] This classical humorist has trod closely upon the heels of the modern drama; he has exposed its follies and marked its weaknesses with that accumulated ridicule which they merit and which on that account ought to be patronised by the public.

The sharpest arrows of Mr Foote's satire seem to be levelled at that sentimental writing which, like a cloud, wraps our drama universally in its foggy folds, that string of feeble, formal, useless declamation which fills the plays of Cumberland, Bickerstaffe, Griffiths, etc. and all the pieces written by Mr Colman since he quitted Mr Garrick. These are the men who banished invention, wit and nature from the stage, and who introduced in their room French plays without plots, scenes without business and declamation without meaning. These men, like all the founders of new fashions, have pushed their progress to an unpardonable extreme, and one of them (Mr Cumberland) like the good son of a good bishop, seems to have made free even with his father's sermons and has transplanted into his comedy expression enough to be ridiculed even in the canting Methodists of Bunhill Fields.

A want of taste is always preceded by a want of judgement. Let these writers know [...] that the admission of many sentiments into a comedy is the latest error of the judgement. When a multiplicity of these appear in a dialogue, it is not possible they *all* can be made to appear with propriety. Some of them, in spite of all the author's art, will seem to be forced into their places without connection or judgement, and the scene will be in a dilemma similar to that of the city lady who lately sallied to the west end of the town loaded with such a profusion of jewels injudiciously huddled each upon the other that she was received by the courtiers with an universal titter. Had this honest bourgeoise selected about one half of her jewels and disposed them with taste, instead of disgracing they would have adorned her – an observation which I recommend to the writers of the modern drama.

But these sentiments (say they), the more numerous they are, the more instruction they impart to us. Indeed! I was pleased with an arch incident in Foote's sentimental mock comedy to this purpose. After the squire has poured out a great profusion of generous sentiments to dissuade the housekeeper from treating the housemaid with severity, he immediately, in the next breath, generously endeavours to debauch the same housemaid. In this a poignant sarcasm is couched and exhibits to us the strong tendency of sentiment to reform the age. And a melancholy observation it is that after these honest gentlemen, the pious comic writers, have supplied our stage so liberally with expressions not obscene and with chaste sentiments, this wicked age will not reform and cease to be the wickedest age that ever existed. And yet sentiment! sentiment! is the fashionable echo. The pit have it in high *gusto* and the galleries wear it upon their tongue tips.

The scoundrel pick-pocket, having first crammed well his pockets with plunder among the crowd, sits in the lofty gallery and roars out Bravo! at every fine sentiment in the play. The crop-eared boy invites his trull to see the *West Indian* because why, it is very pretty and very sentimental! And the gayer youth who yawns in the pit or lounges in the boxes, after repeating fifty times 'Ah fine!' and 'Oh noble!' and 'D—n'd excellent!' retires instantly from this feast of sentiment to bagnios and stews to revel in debauch, to riot in lust and to put sentiments in practice. So unimportant are the labours of those idle men who sacrifice nature to affectation and who strive to tickle the ear rather than to touch the heart.
BOSSU

¹ This refers to Foote's Primitive Puppet Show and 'anti-sentimental' farce contained in it, *The Handsome Housemaid, or Piety in Pattens* (15 February 1773, revised version 6 March 1773). See *TS* 14 (autumn 1973).

366   William Cooke on sentimental comedy
William Cooke: *Memoirs of Samuel Foote*, vol. 1 (London: Richard Phillips, 1805), pp. 182–6

Having thus rode his *Nabob* over the course with success and credit, [Foote] next year [1773] brought out two new pieces: one called *Piety in Pattens*, in which he introduced what he called a primitive puppet-show, the other a comedy of three acts entitled *The Bankrupt*.¹ The first of these was intended to ridicule a species of writing known under the name of sentimental comedy, which was then very much gaining ground upon the stage. This was a sort of moral essay thrown into dialogue which, as it demanded little or no knowledge of the human character in all the various and contrasted shapes of comic situation, was readily caught at by every smatterer in dramatic knowledge who thus gained money and reputation without deserving either.

The mass of the public saw the innovation with a kind of indolent pleasure not entirely devoid of self-gratification. It was so much like the light fantastic kind of novel writing which their wives and daughters read in the parlour that they were thus far critics when they came to the theatre. Having a previous knowledge how a modern love match should be commenced, entangled, disentangled and con-cluded, they became umpires of the drama instead of mere spectators. And as those pieces were generally well sprinkled with commonplace axioms of morality, instead of waiting for the hand of criticism to lead them as heretofore, they would now decide at once for themselves; and in their newly acquired censorial charac-ter announced, 'that the theatre was at last become what it ought to be, a public school of virtue and morality'.

Dr Goldsmith was the first to attack this illegitimate species of writing by his successive productions of *The Good Natured Man* and *She Stoops to Conquer*. Our hero followed with his *Piety in Pattens*, in which he introduces in the true ballad style, 'how a maiden of low degree, by the mere effects of morality and virtue, raised herself to riches and honours'. These two being supported by other writers soon laid the ghost of sentimental comedy, and John Bull was once more restored to his usual laugh and good humour.

But it sometimes unfortunately happens in mental as well as in corporeal diseases that in curing one species of complaint, unskilful physicians induce another equally dangerous. This was the case in the cure of sentimental comedy. Those writers who succeeded Goldsmith and Foote in their design, but could not follow them in their talents, perceiving the success of the ridicule against gravity, thought that by making comedy still more laughable it would accommodate more the taste of the public. They therefore, to banish the style of *The Whole Duty of Man* and *The Economy of Human Life*, took their model from Joe Miller. Whence it resulted that by a profusion of stale jests clumsily fitted to modern circumstances and pantomimic tricks which were called dramatic situations, the stage in general is even at present so contaminated that not only our best poets on the stock list are out of fashion but many men of real dramatic knowledge feel the shame as well as the risk of writing under such a degrading and discouraging patronage.

[1] *The Nabob*, 29 July 1772. *The Bankrupt*, 21 July 1773.

THEATRE CRITICISM

The great contribution of the later eighteenth century was its recognition of the art of 'theatrical' rather than 'dramatic' criticism. Nurtured, no doubt, by the passion for theatre of fashionable young men with time on their hands and little enough to do, and the welcome given to them by the printers of many of the new newspapers, its achievement was to find ways to write about the theatrical experience, not the play as literature.

During the second half of the eighteenth century, writing of all kinds about the theatre proliferates. The increasing number of newspapers carry more information, sometimes simply as announcements of performances, or playbills, or managerial puffs; but there is also independent comment, which develops into the first true dramatic and theatrical criticism. It is sporadic and uneven. In London, newspapers like Dodsley's *London Chronicle* in the fifties and sixties, as well as the *St James's Chronicle*, the *General Evening Post*, the *Public Advertiser*; later the *Morning Chronicle* and *Post* and *Bell's Weekly Messenger*, are all important sources, as are periodicals like the *Gentleman's Magazine*, the *Westminster Magazine*, the *Universal Museum and Complete Magazine*. The best period overall for theatre criticism seems to be between 1760 and 1780.[1]

There are occasional flares in the provinces too, like 'Frank Freeman' and others in the *Bath Chronicle* of 1767–8 [*see* **367a** and **b**]. After 1795, the *Monthly Mirror* carries regular reports and critical comments from provincial correspondents as well as its London criticism.[2]

[1] See Gray (1931).
[2] Francis Gentleman's *Dramatic Censor* (1770) and Baker, Reed and Jones's *Biographia Dramatica* (1764/1782/1812) are primarily concerned with plays and playwrights but do contain occasional theatrical criticism. John Hill's *The Actor* (1750/1755) has critical comments on both plays and actors. One reprinted collection of contributions to the *Public Ledger* – *The theatrical review or new companion to the playhouse* (2 vols., 1772) gives a complete survey of the 1771–2 London season, and its extended title summarises its aim and emphasises its independence:

> 'A critical and historical account of every tragedy, comedy, opera, farce, etc. exhibited at the theatre during the last season, with remarks on the actors who performed the principal characters. The whole interspersed with occasional reflections on dramatic poetry in general; the characters of the best English dramatic authors; and observations on the conduct of the managers. Calculated for the entertainment and instruction of every lover of theatrical amusements. By a society of gentlemen, independent of managerial influence.'

367   Reviews of productions in Bath in the 1770s

(A) AN ANONYMOUS REVIEW OF *HAMLET Bath Chronicle*, 4 November 1773

[. . .] Mr Henderson's performance of Hamlet displayed to us striking abilities, masterly execution, and great sensibility. The unaffected concern, unabated assiduity and nobleness of friendship of good Horatio for his prince, was so strongly apparent in Mr Keasberry that it excited our regard and esteem. Mr Jackson rendered the King very respectable. The obsequious, busy, garrulous courtier, old Polonius, seems to have taken leave of our stage with the exit of Mr Arthur. To hit off this character with strict propriety is a task so difficult that few can attain it. Some, we have observed, ambitious for the laughter of the gallery, have delivered his cautious precepts, arguments and insinuations with a degree of buffoonery that, to the judicious, has rendered him at once contemptible and ridiculous, whilst others, to avoid this, have entered into the other extreme, and by throwing too much gravity and affected consequence into his character, have sunk him into insipidity. Mr Blisset in his caution to Ophelia deserved our approbation, but in those insinuative scenes where Polonius would be thought to possess more knowledge than the whole court together, the character rose above him. Mr Didier was truly characteristic in the Fop and Mr Brookes merits much of our applause in the Ghost. There sometimes appeared a few faint sketches of the Queen in Mrs Sherriffe. Ophelia! Patience, criticism! Should the lady who played it attempt it again, we shall certainly conclude she must be in reality deprived of her most ingenious sense.

(B) FRANK FREEMAN REVIEWS *KING LEAR The Bath Chronicle*, 10 December 1767

Mr Sherriffe in Lear fell vastly short of perfection. There is a quick sensibility of love, anger, resentment, etc., required in the character, which this actor is by no means capable of expressing. But we must do him the justice to own that we believe no performer on this stage can play the part so well. He is a just speaker, but has not power to support the capital parts in some of our best tragedies: the second parts he will always be able to represent with decency and often with applause.

Mr Collins in Edgar exceeded our expectation in the feigned madness so peculiar to that character, but the tender scenes with Cordelia he overacted to a fault. However, he has much improved his tragic genius since he was last here and may be looked upon as a valuable acquisition by the present manager. His talents in comedy are well known, and we hope to see him introduced (for the sake of our theatrical amusements) into those characters wherein he is known to excel. We are afraid he thinks himself all perfection and, if so, any hints to him would be useless. However, we can't help advising him to avoid throwing his hands so much above his head and to leave off the disagreeable manner of seeming to pull the words out of his mouth with his fingers. There are many things unpleasing to an audience that an actor cannot himself find out. Therefore, 'tis of great service to him to be told of it; and if he takes the hint, he shows himself a man of sense. If not, he deserves to be laughed at for his folly and to be ranked with those who are below criticism.

Mr Keasberry was very great in the last scene of the bastard, but he was too careless in some of the best speeches of the part, particularly the first, in which he spoke nonsense. We would not be understood to say that we think he knew not the meaning of his part, but impute it to inattention.

Mr Furnival, in Gloster, became the part well but his memory seems to fail him. However, there are great allowances to be made to declining age; he has been, and still is, a very good actor.

Mr Wood, in Albany, very indifferent. He frequently laid the emphasis on the most insignificant words, which quite altered the sense of what he spoke. But as it was a part of no great consequence, we readily excused it; though we hope he will take this as a hint to study meaning (for the future) as well as words.

Mr Brookes, in Kent, and Mr Didier, in the Gentleman Usher, passable.

As to the women, not one of the characters was bearable, except Cordelia. Such a Goneril and such a Regan were surely never matched so well before! Miss Read, in Cordelia, made us amends for her two sisters. She performed the part very natural and displayed great sensibility.

Tragedies are conducted here in a very odd manner. When Cordelia tells us she hears the drum afar off, not to have it sounded then is an unpardonable omission in the person who is entrusted with the care of the representation. The same may be said of the storm, to represent which properly there should be a noise like falling rain, etc., as well as thunder and lightning, but our present manager seems to care but little about tragedies, as his own cast of parts does not lie that way. [. . .]

Arthur Murphy's criticism

Perhaps the best exponent of theatre criticism in the late eighteenth century was Arthur Murphy, playwright, failed actor, journalist, lawyer and, it must be admitted, prickly and quarrelsome Irishman. Murphy's contributions to 'The Theatre' in Dodsley's *London Chronicle* in 1757–8 are mostly unattributed, but there can be little doubt that the bulk of the fifty-six articles are by him.[1] Though his career as a critic lasted only two years, Murphy may well be regarded as one of the founding fathers of English theatrical criticism.

His love–hate relationship with the theatre did not affect his sensitivity to its art. He wrote genuine theatre criticism, noting down his responses to particular performances immediately after he had seen them. His lengthy comparison of Garrick and Woodward as Marplot in Mrs Centlivre's play *The Busy Body* [see **368**], though perhaps a little coloured by his latest quarrel with Garrick, is a shrewd technical study. His analysis of David Garrick as Sir John Brute struggling with sleep [see **369**] is equally revealing. It says something about contemporary attitudes and taste, more about the writer's sensitivity. It also says a great deal about the art of the actor and the effect on an eighteenth-century audience of a brilliant theatrical experience.

[1] See Dunbar (1946), appendix A, pp. 305–10.

368   Garrick and Woodward compared in Mrs Centlivre's *The Busy Body*

London Chronicle, 19–21 December 1758

[...] THE COUNTENANCE. In this Mr Woodward was perfectly happy for the character in question. He appeared innocent of an idea, till some present object excited it and even then it seemed but a kind of half conception, which however served him as a will-o'-the-wisp to lead him on blundering, as it were, into sense, but ever mistaking his path and running into absurdity. In this, however, he seemed to have no harm but, on the contrary, strong appearances of the characteristic goodness of Marplot. He does mischief so innocently that we all forgive him from our hearts. And whenever he goes wrong, they who suffer by it see plainly that his meddling disposition carries its atonement along with it. His looks are busy but foolishly so; and he is like the Absent Man in this point that, while a crowd of circumstances are about him claiming his attention, he is attached to a single point, namely his eagerness to know every thing that he may be of service to his friends and, on that account, he very naturally is regardless of all other consequences.

Mr Garrick's face is strongly marked with great sensibility; it ever has the pale cast of thought; the traces of care are rather too legible. Every look of his seems to carry with it a degree of cunning and of sharp discernment. He has sometimes the curiosity of the Double Dealer rather than that of Marplot and, when he would appear undesigning, is it not something of a counterfeit thoughtfulness which seems to gleam but faintly over features generally fixed in habitual intenseness of thought? In short, Mr Garrick cannot look undesigning; nor can his curiosity be thought to have its source in a total inattention to his own affairs and the good-natured principle of helping others. It looked to me as if he had a sly intention to mar the projects of his friends and, when the mischief is done, he assures them that, 'He has a great regard for them and meant them well, – But – a, – things have so fallen out that a – but to be sure he never loved anybody so well in his life.' [...]

369   Vanbrugh – comedy and morality; Garrick as Sir John Brute

The Theatre, no. 19. *London Chronicle*, 3 March 1757, p. 223[1]

Sir John Vanbrugh's comedy called *The Provoked Wife* was acted this evening. It is judiciously remarked by Mr Pope concerning this writer that 'Van wants grace that never wanted wit.' The truth is Sir John's comedies are generally too licentious and vice is rather exhibited in an attractive garb than in that odious and forbidden mien which it should be the business of writers for the stage to represent, in order to serve the purpose of virtue and good manners. Had Lady Brute been provoked to a noble indignation at the conduct of her husband, after endeavouring to reclaim him by becoming patience and correct behaviour on her side, had she then given vent to the emotions of spirit natural to a slighted woman and, with the intercession of her relations, demanded a separation, what a beautiful contrast would the poet have given us between the brutality of a hardened debauchee and the amiable deportment of a virtuous wife. But when at present we see the provoked wife only excited to an emulation of vice, when we perceive her endeavouring to outstrip her husband in a dereliction of morals, and see them both pursuing their separate paths of wickedness, we revolt from the witty and humorous writer and cannot help condemning him for the looseness of his principles.

If his admirable genius were exerted to set our passions on the side of truth, to provoke our merriment by the ridiculous appearance of folly and to make us recoil from the turpitude of corrupt manners, this author would perhaps have deserved the precedence among all our English writers. His dialogue is always natural and enlivened, abounding in wit, humour and quick and unexpected turns; his images are generally familiar and entertaining from their agreeable association. His fable is well conducted, full of what the players call 'business', tending to produce entertaining situations and frequent opportunities for lively traits of character.

These different talents are all assembled in the play before us. Sir John's soliloquy inimitably opens the play and the whimsical foibles of his own character. He does not come forth tamely to tell a dull story, but he is instantly thrown into action, and everything has manners. Lady Brute, it cannot be denied, is well drawn, though not well imagined, for the reasons already given. Lady Fanciful has the air of a caricature, but, if strictly examined, she exhibits a just imitation of a person who has bid adieu to the native ornaments of her sex and is fantastically ridiculous. The character is admirably acted by Mrs Clive who, besides that spirited éclat which instantly seizes her audience, never fails to give us many little touches of imitation perceptible only to the nice observer.

Mr Garrick is not generally allowed[2] to play Sir John Brute as well as many other parts: we cannot help thinking the critics who have determined this matter somewhat mistaken. A large uncouth figure, with a deep toned voice, is by no means necessary. On the contrary, perhaps the appearance of one worn out with excessive debauchery is the more natural of the two, and it is probable, if the ladies of quality were called upon as evidence, we should find that men of flimsy texture have, to all intents and purposes, as much brutality as more robust constitutions. Mr Garrick is not morosely sullen but peevishly fractious with his wife. In his manner there is an appearance of acrimony rather than downright insensibility and rudeness. And this is certainly a just conception of the character. For it appears that the knight is naturally of a lively turn, with an unmannerly vein of wit. He sees things in a pleasant light, that is to say a light that diverts others, though he does not seem to be entertained himself with his own ideas. This appears to be the intention of the poet, and this is the intention of this fine comedian.

How full of frolic festivity is he in the tavern scene, when free from women and elevated by wine and my Lord Rake! Even temperance and sobriety wish to be of the party and to enjoy the knight's company. When examining the tailor, how finely does he, like all drunken men, lose sight of his intended idea and gape and stare and change those meaning eyes into the most unideal that ever were seen! When personating Lady Brute, you would swear he had often attended the toilet and there gleaned up the many various airs of the fair sex: he is perfectly versed in the exercise of the fan, the hips, the adjustment of the tucker and even the minutest conduct of the finger. When he returns home, nature, at his first appearance, seems to be harassed out, and through the rest of the scene he is extremely laughable. His voice, his looks, his attitude are comic to the highest degree when he makes his solemn reflection, 'He comes to my house', etc'. Whoever has seen him sit down in his chair must acknowledge that sleep comes upon him by the most natural gradations: not the minutest circumstance about a man in that situation escapes him. The struggle between sleep and his unwillingness to give way to it is perfectly just: the lid depressed, yet faintly raised, the change of his voice from distinct articulation to a confused murmuring, the sudden oppression of his senses and the recovery from it. His then beginning again his broken chain of thought, and the malicious smile that unexpectedly gleams from him, till he is at length totally overpowered, are all such acknowledged strokes of art that they keep the whole house agitated at once with laughter and admiration of the comedian who can thus exhibit both the mental and external workings of nature, without exaggeration.

[1] The play was performed at Drury Lane on 3 March 1757.
[2] Namely, 'considered'.

THE CLOSE OF THE CENTURY

If Murphy was the best of the early theatre critics, he was by no means alone, as many of the pen-portraits and assessments of players in chapter 11 bear witness. Lichtenberg, Gentleman and Davies, in their portrayals of Garrick, Macklin, Henderson and others, were all concerned with analysing the distinctive ways in which the outstanding actors of the period approached and illuminated the different roles they presented to contemporary audiences. By the turn of the century, an analytic and descriptively detailed approach to theatre criticism could be taken for granted, as we have seen in examples of the work of, for instance, Leigh Hunt, Lamb and Boaden. This was one of the many important legacies of the Georgian theatre to the newly developing Romantic theatre.

The last decade of the eighteenth century marked something of a watershed in the British theatre. Playhouses and their equipment, actors and their techniques, audience assumptions and taste were all changing discernibly, as were the playwrights who wrote to satisfy them. These various changes involved a series of cumulative shifts in terms of theatre practice and theatre architecture: it was a process of evolution rather than revolution (even if revolution, in the world of politics, was in the air at the time). However, the net result was a decisive move away from the intimacy of the Georgian theatre towards the larger scale and broader sweep of the Romantic theatre – the subject matter of a later volume in the series.

Bibliography 1660–1788

(1) WORKS OF REFERENCE

Armstrong, Norma. *The Edinburgh stage 1715–1820*, 3 vols. [typescript] (Edinburgh Public Library, 1968)

Arnott, J.F. and Robinson, J.W. *English theatrical literature, 1559–1900. A bibliography.* (London: STR, 1970)

Avery, E.L., Scouten, A.H., Stone, G.W. and Hogan, C.B. (eds.). *The London stage.* Part I: 1660–1700; Part II: 1700–1729, 2 vols.; Part III: 1729–1747, 2 vols.; Part IV: 1747–1776, 3 vols.; Part V: 1776–1800, 3 vols. (Carbondale and Edwardsville: Southern Illinois University Press, 1960–5)

Bentley, Gerald Eades. *The Jacobean and Caroline Stage.* 7 vols. (Oxford: Clarendon Press, 1941–68)

BUCOP. *British Union catalogue of periodicals (seventeenth century to the present).* 4 vols. and later supplements. (London: Butterworth Scientific Publications, 1955–8)

Chambers, E.K. *The Elizabethan stage.* 4 vols. (Oxford: Clarendon Press, 1923)

Conolly, L.W. *A directory of British theatre research resources in North America.* (London: British Theatre Institute, 1978)

Fitzsimmonds, L. and McDonald, A. *The Yorkshire stage 1766–1803.* 2 vols. (to be published in 1989, Metuchen, New Jersey: Scarecrow Press)

Hall, Lilian A. *Catalogue of dramatic portraits in the Theatre Collection of the Harvard College Library.* 4 vols. (Cambridge Mass.: Harvard University Press, 1930–4)

Hare, Arnold (ed.). *Theatre Royal Bath – The Orchard Street Calendar 1750–1805.* (Bath: Kingsmead Press, 1977)

Highfill, Philip Jr, Burnim, Kalman A. and Langhans, Edward (eds.). *A biographical dictionary of actors, actresses, musicians, dancers, managers and other stage personnel in London. 1660–1800.* 8 vols. [A–R] to 1987. (Carbondale and Edwardsville: Southern Illinois University Press, 1973–)

Howard, Diana. *Directory of theatre research information resources in the UK* (2nd edition). (London: STR and Library Association, 1986)

Kerslake, J.F. (ed.). *Catalogue of theatrical portraits in London public collections.* (London: STR, 1961)

Loewenberg, Alfred. *The theatre of the British Isles (excluding London). A bibliography.* (London: STR, 1950)

Mackintosh, Iain and Ashton, Geoffrey. *The Georgian playhouse – actors, artists, audiences and architecture* (Catalogue of an exhibition at the Hayward Gallery, London) (London: Arts Council of Great Britain, 1975)

Macmillan, Dougald. *Catalogue of the Larpent plays in the Huntington Library.* (San Marino: Huntington Library Lists, 1939)

Drury Lane calendar 1747–1776. (Oxford: Clarendon Press, in association with Huntington Library, 1938). [265, 349b, 354]

Nagler, A.M. *A source book in theatrical history.* [New York: Theatre Annual, 1952] (New York: Dover, 1959)

Nicoll, Allardyce. *A history of English drama, 1660–1900* (vols. 1–3 and 6). [Cambridge: Cambridge University Press, 1923, 1925 and 1927] (Cambridge: Cambridge University Press, 1959)

425

Shattuck, Charles H. *The Shakespeare prompt books – a descriptive catalogue*. (Urbana and London: University of Illinois Press, 1965)

Sheppard, F.H.W. (ed.). *Survey of London*, vols. 20, 29, 30 and 35. (London: Athlone Press, 1960 and 1970)

The Revels history of drama in English (general editors: Clifford Leech and T.W. Craik), vols. 5 and 6. (London: Methuen, 1975–6)

(2) MANUSCRIPT SOURCES

Bath Reference Library

B792 (strong room)

Orchard Street Theatre Royal, Bath: company stock book 1770–7. Presented to B.P. Bellamy, Manager of the Bath Theatre, by General Palmer, Proprietor and Patentee (1829). [202]

Bristol Reference Library

MS account book of the Jacob's Wells Theatre Bristol, 1741–8. [212]

British Library

11826.r.s

R.J. Smith: *A collection of material towards an history of the English stage* (consisting of memoirs, plates, playbills, cuttings from books, newspapers and magazines, copious MS notes by the author, collected during the years 1825–40). 25 vols. [Vol. 1: a historical account of the English stage. Vol. 2: notes on *Roscius anglicanus*. Vols. 3 and 4: notes on *An apology for the life of Colley Cibber*. Vols. 5–8: notes on Davies's *Life of Garrick*. Vols. 9–11: letters, adverts, engravings. Vols. 12–13: notes on Cooke's *Memoirs of Macklin*. Vols. 14–19: notes on Boaden's *Life of Kemble*. Vols. 20–4: Dramatic chronology. Vol. 25: Index.] [155a, 155c, 186, 206, 223, 333b, 345]

Add.Ch 17,753

Licence to erect a theatre 1664

Add.Ch 26,514

Assignment of a share in Lisle's Tennis Court Theatre, 1661

Add.Ch 9295–9321 (Additional charters relating to the London theatres, 1660–1760)

Add.Ch 9295

Articles of agreement between Sir William Davenant and a company of players relative to Salisbury Court and the New Theatre. Dated 5 Nov 1660. [25]

Add.Ch 9303

Indenture by which Christopher Rich [...] and Rupert Clarke [...] declare the trusts under which they hold a lease of the theatre in Little Lincoln's Inn Fields for thirty nine and a half years to be in favour of the Rt. Hon Lionell (Sackville), Earl of Dorset and others, 3 Sept 1714. [68]

Add. Ch 9308

Articles of agreement indented between Sir Richard Steele, Robert Wilks, Colley Cibber and Barton Booth, managers of the Theatre Royal Drury Lane and John Rich and Christopher Mosyer Rich, managers of Lincoln's Inn playhouse, respecting the engagement of actors, 12 April 1722. The schedules of the actors' names are attached. [41]

Add.Ch 9319

Indenture tripartite between John Rich [...], Martha Launder [...], and Hutchinson Mure [...], assigning in trust to the said Hutchinson, the lease of the messuage and ground on the north side of the Piazza, Covent Garden, with the theatre built thereon and all the wardrobes and furniture of the same, 30 Jan 1744/5. With a schedule of wardrobes, etc. [271, 277, 286]

Add.MS 12,201

Papers relating to Drury Lane, 1674–1722 (including material copied from Add.MS 20,726). Schedule of the properties belonging to Covent Garden theatre 1744. [26, 41, 52, 271, 277, 286]

Add.MS 18,584–5

Alphabetical list of English dramatic pieces from the sixteenth century to the year 1836; with notices of authors, where and when first acted and when published. By B.P. Bellamy of the Bath Theatre

Add.MS 18,586
Alphabetical catalogue of performers in the London theatres from the earliest period to the present time (1833). At the end are notices of the different theatres of London. By B.P. Bellamy of the Bath theatre

Add.MS 18,590
A collection of printed play bills from 1762 to 1836 formed by B.P. Bellamy

Add.MS 19,256
Papers, partly original and partly copies, relating to the Office of the Master of the Revels (1660-3). [1, 3, 5, 6, 7, 25]

Add.MS 20,726
Papers relating to Drury Lane, 1674–1711. [15, 17, 26, 29, 52]

Add.MS 21,508
John Rich's agreement with David Garrick 1746

Add.MS 25,390–2
Notitia Dramatica; being notes of performances on the English stage [. . .] from 1702 to 1795 by Isaac Reed. 3 vols

Add.MS 25,915
Letters and receipts relating to Drury Lane, 1787–1809

Add.MS 29,709–11
Accounts of Drury Lane, 1772–1826

Add.MS 31,972–6
J.P. Kemble's Memorandum Books 1788–1815

Add.MS 32,249–52
Handwritten transcriptions of play bills, 1702–46

Add.MS 32,428
Original list of shareholders at Covent Garden Theatre 1731

Add.MS 32,685
(ff. 13–51) Newcastle papers. Letters and papers relating to the drama, 1714–24; in particular letters from Steele and Congreve to the Duke of Newcastle. [21]

Add.MS 33,488
Charles Morison's notebook, containing accounts, cast lists, etc. of a company touring in Wales. Miscellaneous notes on London theatres, 1733–82. [211]

Add.MS 35,118
Papers relating to R.B. Sheridan and Drury Lane Theatre, 1770–1826

Add.MS 35,177
(ff. 79–80) François Brunet: *Voyage en Angleterre*, 1676. [59]

Add.MS 36,129
(f. 184) Licence to Colley Cibber, etc. for the Drury Lane company in 1731

Add.MS 38,620–1
Collections for a history of the English stage up to 1817, by R.J. Smith

Add.MS 38,622
Songs for Harlequin Omai by J. O'Keeffe, 1785

Add.MS 40,166 (o), section 5, ff. 106–10
Financial regulations at the Theatres Royal of Manchester and Liverpool, *c.* 1777

Add.MS 40,379
(ff. 304–9) Abstract of documents (1618–1710) in the State Paper Office, relative to the early English stage, and the licensing of theatres from the reign of King James I to that of George I, prepared for Mr Peel's information, 22 Dec 1824

Add.MS 44,919 (i), ff. 38–46
Documents relating to Drury Lane, 1774–5. Legal opinions and accounts relating to the purchase from David Garrick of his share in Drury Lane by Sheridan, Linley and partners. [218]

c.120.h.1
A collection of material relating to Drury Lane theatre

Eg 1,957
Papers and letters relating to Sheridan's management of Drury Lane, 1780–1812

Eg 2,265–6
Accounts of Lincoln's Inn Fields theatre, containing the items of receipt and expenditure, the titles of the pieces performed on each night, the names and salaries of the actors. Sept 1724–June 1727

Eg 2,267–72
Covent Garden account books: vol. 1, 1735–6; vol. 2, 1746–7; vol. 3, 1749–50; vol. 4, 1757–8; vol. 5, 1760–1; vol. 6, 1766–70; vol. 7, 1771–4

Eg 2,273–2,319
Ledger of Covent Garden Theatre 1767–1822. 47 vols.

Eg 2,320
Diary, apparently by Benjamin Griffen, actor and dramatist, of plays acted at Lincoln's Inn Fields, Sept 1715–June 1721; Drury Lane, Sept 1721–May 1733 and March 1734–Nov 1736; and at the Haymarket, Sept 1733–March 1734

Eg 2,321–2
Register of pieces performed nightly at Drury Lane, the Opera House, Lincoln's Inn Fields from Oct 1710 to July 1729

Eg 2,334
Proposals of Charles Macklin to the managers of Drury Lane

Eg.Ch 362
Sir Richard Steele's covenant with Robert Wilks and others for the share in the profits of Drury Lane, 1721

Playbills, vol. 307
Inserted into this volume are printed contractual rules for a provincial touring company, 1778. Also inserted is an MS list, naming and commenting on fifty-three players. [199]

Chatsworth House

Rich's Register, vol. 4, 1750–73 [203]

Folger Library

Rich's Register, vol. 1, 1714–23

Garrick Club

Rich's Register, vol. 2, 1723–40

Harvard Theatre Collection

James Winston: MS notes for *The theatric tourist* (1805)
Rich's Register, vol. 3, 1740–50
George Frederick Cooke: MS diary and recollections 1794–1807

Johannesburg Public Library

William Douglas: MS notes on provincial theatres in the United Kingdom, vol. 1

New York Public Library

William Douglas: MS notes on provincial theatres in the United Kingdom, vol. 2

Newcastle upon Tyne Library of the Literary and Philosophic Society

George Frederick Cooke: Prompt book for *Hamlet* in 1785. [311]

Norfolk and Norwich Records Office

Committee books of the Theatre Royal Norwich, 1768–1825. 2 vols.

Public Records Office

c/66/3013
Copy of Killigrew's patent [8]

c/66/3501
Steele's patent [19]
c/66/3621
The Garrick–Lacy patent
c/66/3706
Samuel Foote's patent for the Little Theatre in the Haymarket 1766 [187]
c11/2662/1
Rich's bill of complaint against Shepherd, 1732 [70]
c7/298/35
Copy of Killigrew's contract with builders [24]
cp40/2751, m 317
The Red Bull players submit to Herbert's authority, 1660 [2]

Lord Chamberlain: warrants original
LC 5/118 (1660–71) to LC 5/130 (Geo III)

LC 5/119
1660–71 [51]

Lord Chamberlain: warrant books general
LC 5/137 (1660–3) to LC 5/163 (1793–1810)

LC 5/141
1674–76 [27]
LC 5/142
1677 [11]
LC 5/154
1704–9 [13, 14, 15, 16]
LC 5/155
1710–14 [18]
LC 5/157
1717–21 [20, 22, 36]
LC 5/160
1727–37 [178]
LC 5/161
1738–53 [185]

Lord Chamberlain: petitions
LC 5/184 (1660–2) to LC 5/192 (1689–97)

LC 5/191
1677–85 [30, 31]

Lord Chamberlain: theatres

LC 7/1
1661–1700 Warrants and orders [10, 39, 154a]
LC 7/2
1706–14 Contracts
LC 7/3
1673–1797 Papers bound [12, 32, 33, 34, 35, 37, 38, 40, 42, 154b, 154c, 164, 177]
LC 7/4
1767–1852 Papers unbound [188]

Minutes, depositions and letters

Western Circuit Civil Minute Book 1786–1800, Assizes 22–4
sp29/10, no. 108
Sir Geoffrey Palmer's note to Charles II [4]

SP29/142 (ii) no. 160
Rebecca Marshall's petition to Charles II, 1660 [160a]
SP29/191 no. 31
Rebecca Marshall's deposition against Sir Hugh Middleton, 1666 [160b]
SP29/195, no. 109
Charles II orders George Jolly to surrender his licence [9]

Theatre Museum

Enthoven Collection
Licence from the Lord Chamberlain to J.P. Kemble in respect of *The Hue and Cry*, May 1791 [182]
Articles of agreement between R.B. Sheridan and Dorothea Jordan, 16 Dec 1785 [198]
Original of Killigrew's patent [8]
Davey, Peter. *Old country theatres, eighteenth and nineteenth century.* 36 vols. (a collection of MS notes,
    excerpts from books, cuttings and letters)
George Frederick Cooke. Two MS notebooks

University of Bristol Theatre Collection

Licence renewal for New Theatre, Haymarket 1781–2, Manager George Colman

Victoria and Albert Museum

John Forster Collection of Garrick's private papers. 40 vols. [196, 197, 291]

Wiltshire Records Office, Trowbridge

Wiltshire Quarter Sessions Minute Book, 1782–5 [193b]

York Minster Library

Collection of Tate Wilkinson's playbills

York Public Library

MS account book of Tate Wilkinson's Yorkshire Company [216, 273]

(3) PUBLISHED SOURCES

A collection of cuttings relating to London theatres, 1704–1779. (British Library: Th.Cts. 1–6). [155e]
A veteran stager. *An essay on the science of acting.* (London: Cowie & Strange, 1828). [209]
Adams, J.Q. (ed.). *The dramatic records of Sir Henry Herbert.* (New Haven and London: Yale University
    Press, 1917)
Addison, Joseph and Steele, Sir Richard. *The Spectator* (edited by Donald F. Bond). 5 vols. (Oxford:
    Clarendon Press, 1965). [172]
Agate, James. *The English dramatic critics – an anthology.* (New York: Hill & Wang, n.d.). [329]
Angelo, Henry. *Reminiscences.* (London: Colburn, 1828). [290]
Anon. *Letters from a Moor at London.* (London: F. Noble, [?] 1739). [97]
Anon. *A review of the present contest between the Managers of the winter theatres, the Little Theatre in the
    Haymarket, and the Royalty Theatre in Wellclose Square.* (London: Stalker, 1787)
Anon. *Considerations upon how far the present winter and summer theatres can be affected by the application
    to Parliament for an act to enable His Majesty to license, as a playhouse for the summer season, the
    Royalty Theatre in Well Street, in the liberty of the Tower Hamlets.* (London: [s.n.], 1794)
Anon. (? George Colman). *A very plain state of the case, or the Royalty Theatre versus the Theatres Royal.*
    (London: published by the author, 1787)
Anon. *Remarks on the character of Richard III, as played by Cooke and Kemble* (2nd edition). (London:
    Parsons, 1801)
Anon. *The life of James Quin, comedian.* (London: S. Bladon, 1766)

Anon. *The new spouter's companion, or a selection of prologues and epilogues . . . illustrated with the art of acting and the picture of a spouting club* (6'd pamphlet). (London: R. Rusted, undated, but possibly c. 1781)

Anon. *The secret history of the Green Room, containing authentic and entertaining memoirs of the actors and actresses in the three Theatres Royal.* (A new edition, with improvements, to which is prefixed a sketch of the history of the English stage). 2 vols. (London: J. Owen, 1795)

Anon. *An essay upon the present state of the theatre in France, England and Italy.* (London: Pottinger, 1760)

Anon. *An historical and succinct account of the late riots at the Theatres of Drury Lane and Covent Garden.* (London: W. Morgan, 1763). [352]

Anon. *Fitz-Giggo* (Broadsheet with 1 print). (London: E. Sumpter, 26 Feb 1763). [285]

Anon. *The second and last act of Fitzgiggo* (Broadsheet with 1 print). (London: E. Sumpter, 3 March 1763)

Anon. *The theatrical review, or Annals of the drama.* (London: Williams, Wilson & Fell, 1763)

Anon. *Thoughts on the late disturbance at the Theatre Royal Newcastle.* (Newcaste upon Tyne: M. Brown, 1789)

Anon. (by a society of gentlemen): *The theatrical review, or New companion to the playhouse.* 2 vols. (London: Crowdes, Wilkkie & Walter, 1772)

Articles and conditions of engagement at the Theatre Royal Edinburgh. (York Minster Library) [200]

Aston, Anthony. *A brief supplement to Colley Cibber Esq. his lives of the famous actors and actresses.* [London: published for the author, 1747] (reprinted in Cibber [Lowe edition], vol. 2, 1889). [114, 126]

Aubrey, John. *Brief lives* (edited by Andrew Clark). 2 vols. (Oxford: Clarendon Press, 1898)

Baker, David Erskine, Reed, Isaac and Jones, Stephen. *Biographia Dramatica; or, a companion to the playhouse.* 3 vols. (London: Longman, Hurst et al., 1812). [321]

Bellamy, George Anne. *Apology for her life.* 5 vols. (4th edition) (London: published for the author, 1786)

Bernard, John. *Retrospections of the stage.* 2 vols. (London: Colburn & Bentley, 1830). [257]

[Betterton, Thomas]. *The history of the English stage from the Restoration to the present time.* (London: E. Curll, 1741). [117]

Boaden, James. *Memoirs of the life of John Philip Kemble Esq., including a history of the stage from the time of Garrick to the present period.* 2 vols. (London: Longman, Hurst et al., 1825). [272, 309, 324]

Memoirs of Mrs Siddons. 2 vols. (London: Longman et al., 1827). [301]

Memoirs of Mrs Inchbald. 2 vols. (London: Bentley, 1833).

The life of Mrs Jordan. 2 vols. (London: Edward Bull, 1831). [340a]

Boaden, James (ed.). *The private correspondence of David Garrick with the most celebrated persons of his time.* 2 vols. (London: Colburn & Bentley, 1831). [210, 287]

Brown, Thomas. *Works, being a collection of poems, letters, essays, etc.* 5 vols. (London: Sam Briscoe, 1721). [158]

Brownsmith, John. *The contrast, or, new mode of management.* (Salisbury: J. Hodson, 1776)

The dramatic timepiece, or perpetual monitor. (London: J. Almon, T. Davies & J. Hungeston, 1767). [204]

The theatrical alphabet. (London: published by the author, 1776–1767). [205]

Burney, Charles. *A general history of music.* [London: printed for the author, 1776–1789] [with critical and historical notes by Frank Mercer, London: G.T. Foulis & Co, 1935] (reprinted, New York: Dover, 1957)

Campbell, T. *The life of Mrs Siddons.* 2 vols. (London: Effingham Wilson, 1834). [315]

Cawdell, J: *The miscellaneous poems of J. Cawdell, comedian.* (Sunderland: published for the author, 1785) [269]

Charke, Charlotte. *A narrative of the life of Mrs Charlotte Charke.* [London: W. Reeve, 1755] (Reprinted, London: Constable, 1929)

Chetwood, William Rufus. *A general history of the stage.* (London: W. Owen, 1749). [135]

The British theatre. Containing the lives of the English dramatic poets, with an account of all their plays. Together with the lives of most of the principal actors. To which is prefixed a short view of the rise and progress of the English stage. (Dublin: Peter Wilson, 1750)

Clark, Barrett H. *European theories of the drama* (revised edition). (New York: Crown, 1947)

Cibber, Colley. *An apology for the life of Mr Colley Cibber, written by himself.* 2 vols. [London: Watts, 1740] [edited by R.W. Lowe, London, 1889] (reprinted, New York: AMS Press, 1966). [61, 65, 92, 106, 107c, 110a, 118, 119, 121, 122, 124, 130, 139, 181, 194]

The Provoked Husband (preface). (London: J. Watts, 1728). [134]

Cibber, Theophilus. *A serio-comic apology for part of his life*. (London: C. Corbett, 1748)
    The lives and characters of the most eminent actors and actresses of Great Britain & Ireland, from Shakespeare to the present time. Interspersed with a general history of the stage. (London: R. Griffiths, 1753)
Clayton, Thomas. *Arsinoe, Queen of Cyprus. An opera after the Italian manner. As it is performed at the Theatre Royal in Drury Lane by Her Majesty's Servants* (preface). (London: Jacob Tonson, 1705). [**85**]
Collier, Jeremy. *A letter to a lady concerning the new playhouse.* (London: Joseph Downing, 1706). [**165**]
    A short view of the immorality and profaneness of the English stage. (London: S. Keble, 1698)
Congreve, William. *Amendments of Mr Collier's false and imperfect citations, etc. from The Old Bachelor, Double Dealer, Love for Love, Mourning Bride, by the author of those plays.* (London: J. Tonson, 1698)
Cooke, William. *The elements of dramatic criticism.* (London: Kearsley & Robinson, 1775)
    Memoirs of Charles Macklin, comedian. (London: J. Asperne, 1804). [**170, 366**]
    Memoirs of Samuel Foote. 3 vols. (London: Richard Phillips, 1805)
Cumberland, Richard. *Memoirs.* [London: Lackington, Allen & Co., 1806] [Philadelphia, 1856] (New York: Blom, 1969). [**137, 363**]
Curll, E. [pseud. William Egerton]. *Faithful memoirs of the life, amours and performances of the justly celebrated and most eminent actress of her time, Mrs Anne Oldfield.* (London: [s.n.], 1731). [**132**]
Davenant, Sir William. *The Siege of Rhodes. Made a representation by the art of prospective in scenes and the story sung in recitative music* (address to the reader and stage directions). (London: Henry Herringman, 1656). [**74, 75**]
Davies, Thomas. *Memoirs of the life of David Garrick Esq.* 2 vols. [1780] (London: Longman, Hurst et al., revised edition 1808). [**195, 207, 313, 320, 325a, 335**]
    Dramatic miscellanies. 3 vols. (London: Thomas Davies, 1784). [**127, 136a, 144**]
    A genuine narrative of the life and theatrical transactions of Mr John Henderson, commonly called the Bath Roscius. (London: T. Evans, 1777). [**343**]
Deutsch, Otto E. *Handel: a documentary biography.* [London: A. & C. Black, 1955] (New York: Da Capo Press, 1974)
Dibdin, Charles. *Observations on a tour through Scotland and England.* 2 vols. (London: G. Goulding et al., 1801–2)
    A complete history of the English stage. 5 vols. (London: published by the author, 1797–1800). [**340b**]
Dibdin, Thomas. *Reminiscences.* 2 vols. (London: Colburn, 1827)
Downes, John. *Roscius Anglicanus or an historical review of the stage.* [edited by Montague Summers, London: The Fortune Press (n.d.)] (edited by J. Milhous and R.D. Hume, London: STR, 1987). [**81, 102a, 107a, 109, 111b, 113, 123**]
Dryden, John. *Albion and Albanius* (preface and stage directions). (London: Jacob Tonson, 1685). [**83**]
Dumont, G.P.M. *Parallèle des plans des plus belles salles de spectacles d'Italie et de France.* (Paris: [s.n.], 1774). [**67, 71**]
Dunlap, W. *The life of George Frederick Cooke.* (2nd edition, revised, London: Colburn, 1815)
Eshleman, Dorothy H. *The committee books of the Theatre Royal Norwich, 1768–1825.* (London: STR, 1970). [**201, 251, 278**]
Evelyn, John. *The diary of John Evelyn* (edited by E.S. de Beer). 6 vols. (Oxford: Clarendon Press, 1955). [**76, 77, 102d, 111c**]
Everard, Edward Cape. *Memoirs of an unfortunate son of Thespis.* (Edinburgh: Ballantyne & Everard, 1818). [**355**]
Flecknoe, Richard. *A short discourse of the English stage.* (London: R. Wood, 1664). [**79**]
Foote, Samuel. *The Roman and English comedy considered and compared.* (London: T. Waller, 1747). [**361**]
Freeman, Arthur (ed.). *The English stage. Attack and defense, 1570–1730.* 50 vols. (facsimile reproductions of original works). (New York and London: Garland, 1973)
Genest, John. *Some account of the English stage from the Restoration in 1660 to 1830.* 10 vols. (Bath: Carrington, 1832). [**338**]
Gentleman, Francis. *The dramatic censor, or critical companion.* 2 vols. [London: J. Bell, 1770] (reprinted, Farnborough: Gregg, 1969). [**312, 319, 325b**]
Gibbon, Edward. *Gibbon's journal to 28 Jan 1763* (edited by D.M. Low). (London: Chatto & Windus, 1929). [**344**]

Gildon, Charles. *The life of Mr Thomas Betterton the late eminent tragedian.* (London: Robert Gosling, 1710). [**120, 145, 148**]

Goede, C.A.G. *Memorials of nature and art, collected on a journey in Great Britain during the years 1802 and 1803* (translated by T. Horne). 3 vols. (London: J. Mawman, 1808)
The stranger in England. 3 vols. (London: Matthews & Leigh, 1807). [**259**]

Goldsmith, Oliver. *An enquiry into the present state of polite learning.* (London: R. & J. Dodsley, 1759)
Miscellaneous works. [London, 1775] (Globe edition, edited by David Masson, London: Macmillan, 1868, and later reprints). [**264, 364**]

Guerinot, J.V. and Jilg, R.D. (eds.). *Contexts 1: 'The Beggar's Opera'* (Hamden, Conn: Archon Books, 1976). [**175b**]

Hamilton, Count Anthony. *Memoirs of the life of the Count of Gramont* (translated from the French by Mr Boyer). (London: J. Round, 1714)

[Harding, Silvester and Edward]. *The biographical mirrour, comprising a series of ancient and modern English portraits of eminent and distinguished persons, from original pictures and drawings.* 3 vols. (London: Silvester and Edward Harding, 1795–1802). [**125**]

Hazlitt, William. *Dramatic essays* (edited by W. Archer and R.W. Lowe) (London: Walter Scott, 1895)

Hiffernan, Paul. *Dramatic genius.* (London: published by the author, 1770). [**297**]

Highfill, P.H. 'Rich's 1744 inventory of Covent Garden properties'. *Restoration and eighteenth-century Theatre Research,* 5, no. 1 (1966), 7–17; 5, no. 2 (1966), 17–26; 6, no. 1 (1967), 27–35

Hill, Aaron. 'Essay on the art of acting'. *Works,* vol. 4. (London: published by subscription for the benefit of the family, 1753)

Hill, Aaron and Popple, William. *The prompter* (selections edited by William Appleton and Kalman A. Burnim). (New York: Blom, 1966). [**128, 140, 147, 149, 176**]

[Hill, John]. *The actor: a treatise on the art of playing.* [London: R. Griffiths, 1750] (2nd edition, London: R. Griffiths, 1755). [**136b, 279, 293, 295**]

Hogarth, William. *The analysis of beauty.* [London: published by the author, 1753] (facsimile reprint, Ilkley: Scolar Press, 1969)

Hooker, Edward Niles (ed.). *The critical works of John Dennis.* 2 vols. (Baltimore: The John Hopkins Press, 1939). [**160**]

Hunt, Leigh. *Dramatic essays* (edited by W. Archer and R.W. Lowe). (London: Walter Scott, 1894). [**299**]

Jackson, John. *The history of the Scottish stage.* (Edinburgh: Hill, 1793)

Jenkins, Richard. *Memoirs of the Bristol stage.* (Bristol: published by the author and W.H. Somerton, 1826). [**248b**]

Johnson, Samuel. *Works.* 9 vols. (Oxford: Pickering, Tallboys & Wheeler, 1825). [**183**]

Kelly, Michael. *Reminiscences* (compiled by Theodore Hook). (2nd edition, London, 1826) [reprinted by Blom, 1969] (edited by R. Fiske, London: Oxford University Press, 1975)

Kirkman, James Thomas. *Memoirs of the life of Charles Macklin Esq.* 2 vols. (London: Lackington, Allen & Co, 1799)

Küttner, C.G.. *Beiträge zur Kenntniss vorzüglich des Innern von England und seiner Einwohner.* (Leipzig: im Verlag der Dykischen Buchhandlung, 1791–6). [**253**]

La Motte, Marie Catherine. *Memoirs of the court of England.* 2 vols. (London: B. Bragg, 1707)

Lamb, Charles. *Essays of Elia.* (London: Taylor and Hessey, 1823). [**339a**]
Dramatic essays (edited by Brander Matthews). (London: Chatto & Windus, 1891)

Langbaine, Gerard. *An account of the English dramatic poets.* (Oxford: George West & Henry Clements, 1691). [**105b**]

Lediard, Thomas. *Britannia. An English opera. As it is performed at the New Theatre in the Haymarket. With the representation and description of a transparent theatre, illuminated and adorned with a great number of emblems, mottoes, devices and descriptions, and embellished with machines in a manner entirely new* (frontispiece and description of the transparent theatre). (London: J. Watts, 1732). [**99**]

Lichtenberg, Georg Christoph. *Lichtenberg's visits to England, as described in his letters and diaries* (translated and annotated by Margaret Mare and W.H. Quarrell). (Oxford: Clarendon Press, 1938). [**282, 305, 306, 330, 333a**]

Little, D.M. and Kahrl, G.M. (eds.). *The letters of David Garrick.* 3 vols. (London: Oxford University Press, 1963). [**208, 298, 302**]

Loftis, John (ed.). *Essays on the theatre from eighteenth-century periodicals.* (London: Augustan reprint society publication no. 85–6, 1960)

Magalotti, Lorenzo. *Travels of Cosmo the Third, Grand Duke of Tuscany, through England.* (London: J. Mawman, 1821). [55]

Malone, Edward (ed.). Introductory account of the history of the British theatre, in *The plays and poems of William Shakespeare.* Vol. 1, part 2 (London: H. Baldwin, 1790)

Mander, Raymond and Mitchenson, Joe. *A picture history of the British theatre.* (London: Hulton Press, 1957)

Misson, Henri. *Memoirs and observations in his travels over England* (translated by John Ozell). (London: D. Browne, 1719). [62]

Monconys, Balthasar de. *Journal des voyages de Monsier de Monconys.* 2 vols. (Lyons: Horace Boissat, 1666). [53]

Moore, Thomas. *Memoirs of Richard Brinsley Sheridan.* 2 vols. (London: Longman et al., 1825)

Moritz, Carl Philip. *Journeys of a German in England in 1782.* (London: Cape, 1965). [347]

Munden, J.S. *Memoirs of Joseph Shepherd Munden, comedian* (2nd edition). (London: Bentley, 1846)

Muralt, Béat Louis de. *Letters describing the character and customs of the English and French nations* (2nd edition). (London: T. Edlin, 1726). [90b]

   Lettres sur les anglais et les français et sur les voyages. (Cologne: [SN], 1726). [90b]

Murphy, Arthur. *The life of David Garrick Esq.* 2 vols. (London: J. Wright, 1801)

Neville, Sylas. *The diary of Sylas Neville* (edited by B. Cozens-Hardy). (London: Oxford University Press, 1950)

O'Keeffe, John. *Recollections of his life.* 2 vols. (London: Colburn, 1826). [266, 294, 359]

Oulton, Walley C. *The history of the theatres of London 1771–95.* 2 vols. (London: Martin & Bain, 1796)

Palmer, John. 'Address on the opening of the Royalty Theatre, 20 June 1787'. *Dodsley's London Chronicle* no. 4779, June 21–3 1787, p. 596. [191]

Pasquin, Anthony [pseud. of John Williams]. *The Life of the late Earl of Barrymore, including a history of the Wargrave Theatricals* (London: H.D. Symonds, 1793). [255]

Pepys, Samuel. *The diary of Samuel Pepys* (edited by Robert Latham and William Matthews). 11 vols. (London: G. Bell & Sons, 1970–83). [44, 48, 49, 57, 78, 102c, 104, 107b, 110b, 111a, 112a, 138, 141, 150–3, 159]

Pickering, Roger. *Reflections upon theatrical expression in tragedy.* (London: W. Johnston, 1755). [296]

[Pilon, F.]. *An essay on the character of Hamlet as performed by Mr Henderson at the Theatre Royal in the Haymarket.* (London: W. Flexney, [?] 1777). [307]

[Piozzi, Hester]. *Piozziana, or recollections of the late Mrs Piozzi* (edited by N. Mangin). (London: Edward Moxon, 1833). [300]

Price, Cecil (ed.). *The letters of Richard Brinsley Sheridan.* 3 vols. (Oxford: Clarendon Press, 1966)

Raithby, J. (ed.). *Statutes at large.* 10 vols. (London: Eyre & Strahan, 1811). [179, 189, 190, 193, 219]

Rand, Benjamin (ed.). *Berkeley and Percival. The correspondence of George Berkeley and Sir John Percival.* (Cambridge: Cambridge University Press, 1914). [169]

Reynolds, Sir Joshua. *A discourse delivered to the students of the Royal Academy, on the distribution of the prizes, 10 December 1778, by the President.* (London: T. Cadell, 1778)

   Discourses on art (edited by R.R. Wark). (New Haven: Yale University Press, 1975)

Russell, W. Clark. *Representative actors.* (London: Frederick Warne, 1872)

Rymer, Thomas. *Foedera, conventiones, literae et cujuscunque generis acta publica inter reges angliae, etc.,* vol. 20. (London: Tonson, 1735)

   The tragedies of the last age considered and examined by the practice of the ancients and by the common sense of all ages. (London: Tonson, 1678). [102b]

Sainte-Albine, Rémond de. *Le Comédien.* (Paris: Desaint et Saillant, 1747)

Saunders, George. *A treatise on theatres.* [London: published by the author 1790] (New York: Blom, 1968). [231, 232]

Saussure, César de. *A foreign view of England in the reigns of George I and George II* (translated and edited by Mme van Muyden). (London: John Murray, 1902). [95, 168]

Settle, Elkanah. *The Virgin Prophetess: or the fate of Troy. An opera performed at the Theatre Royal by His Majesty's Servants* (stage directions). (London: A. Roper, 1701). [84]

Shadwell, Thomas. *Psyche. A tragedy. Acted at the Duke's Theatre* (preface). (London: Henry Herringman, 1675)

Shattuck, Charles H. (ed.). *The Kemble prompt books.* 11 vols. (Charlottesville: University of Virginia Press, 1974)

Sherbo, Arthur (ed.). *New essays by Arthur Murphy.* (East Lansing: Michigan State University Press, 1963)

Sheridan, Richard Brinsley. *Speeches* (edited by a constitutional friend). 2 vols. (London: P. Martin, 1816). [192]

Siddons, Henry. *Practical illustrations of rhetorical gesture and action* (2nd edition). (London: Sherwood *et al.*, 1822). [284]

Sorbière, Samuel. *A voyage to England, containing many things relating to the stage of learning, religion and other curiosities of that kingdom.* (London: J. Woodward, 1709). [54]

   Relation d'un voyage en Angleterre. (Paris: Thomas Jolly, 1664). [54]

Spingarn, J.E. (ed.). *Critical essays of the seventeenth century.* 3 vols. [Oxford: Clarendon Press, 1908] (Reprinted, London: Oxford University Press, 1957 and Bloomington: Indiana University Press, 1968)

Stanhope, Philip Dormer, Earl of Chesterfield. *Miscellaneous works* (edited by M. Maty) (2nd edition), vol. 2. (London: E. & C. Dilly, 1779). [180]

Steele, Joshua. *Prosodia rationalis, or a treatise on the melody and measure of speech* (2nd edition). [London: J. Nichols, 1779] (Menston: Scolar Press, 1969)

Steele, Sir Richard. *The theatre* (edited by J. Loftis). (London: Oxford University Press, 1962)

   The Conscious Lovers (preface and frontispiece). (London: Tonson, 1735). [173, 174]

Swift, Jonathan. *Journal to Stella* (edited by Harold Williams). 2 vols. (Oxford: Clarendon Press, 1948). [143]

Taylor, John. *Records of my life.* 2 vols. (London: Edward Bull, 1832)

Theatrical fund regulations. *Theatrical fund instituted at the Theatre Royal, Covent Garden, 22 December 1765 and confirmed by Act of Parliament 1776.* (London: E. Macleish, 1811)

Thomas, Tobias [alias Thomas Brown]. *The life of the late famous comedian, Jo Haynes.* (London: J. Nutt, 1701). [157]

Uffenbach, Zacharius Conrad von. *London in 1710. From the travels of Z.C. von Uffenbach* (translated and edited by W.H. Quarrell and M. Mare). (London: Faber & Faber, 1934). [90a, 156, 162]

   Merkwürdige Reisen durch Niedersachsen, Holland und Engelland. 3 vols. (Ulm and Memmingen: Johann Friedrich Gaum, 1753). [90a, 156, 162]

Vanbrugh, Sir John. *The works of Sir John Vanbrugh* (edited by Geoffrey Webb). 4 vols. (London: The Nonesuch Press, 1927). [63, 66]

   A short vindication of The Relapse and The Provoked Wife. (London: H. Walwyn, 1698)

Victor, Benjamin. *The history of the theatres of London and Dublin from the year 1730 to the present time.* 3 vols. (London: Thomas Davies, 1761 (vols. 1 and 2), London: T. Becket 1771 (vol. 3)). [131, 146]

Villiers, George, Duke of Buckingham. *The Rehearsal.* (London: Thomas Dring, 1672). [142]

Weston, Thomas. *Memoirs of that celebrated comedian and very singular genius, Thomas Weston.* (London: S. Bladon, 1776). [213]

Wilkinson, Tate. *Memoirs of his own life by Tate Wilkinson, patentee of the Theatres Royal, York and Hull.* [4 vols., York: published for the author, 1790] (3 vols. Dublin: Byrne, Wogan *et al.*, 1791). [263, 274, 350, 356, 360]

   The wandering patentee or, a history of the Yorkshire theatres from 1770 to the present time. [4 vols., York: published for the author, 1795] (facsimile reprint, London and Ilkley: Scolar Press, 1973). Index by C.B. Hogan (London: STR, 1973)

Winston, James. *The theatric tourist.* (London: T. Woodfall, 1805). [242, 243, 254]

Wood, John. *A description of Bath* (2nd edition). 2 vols. (London: W. Bathoe, 1765). [239]

Wright, James. *Historia Histrionica. An historical account of the English stage, showing the ancient use, improvement and perfection of dramatic representations in this nation, in a dialogue of plays and players.* [London: William Haws, 1699] (reprinted in Cibber [Lowe ed.], vol. 1). [43, 100, 105a, 163, 166]

(4) STUDIES

Adams, J.Q. *Shakespearean playhouses. A history of English theatres from the beginnings to the Restoration.* (London: Constable, n.d.)

Aitken, George A. *The life of Richard Steele.* 2 vols. (London: William Isbister Ltd, 1889)

Appleton, William W. *Charles Macklin: an actor's life.* (Cambridge Mass.: Harvard University Press, 1960)

Arundell, Dennis. *The story of Sadler's Wells, 1683–1964.* (London: Hamish Hamilton, 1965)

Barker, Kathleen. *The Theatre Royal Bristol 1766–1966.* (London: STR, 1974)

Barlow, Graham. 'From tennis court to opera house'. Ph.D thesis, University of Glasgow, 1983

Baur-Heinhold, Margarete. Baroque theatre. (London: Thames & Hudson, 1967)

Baynham, Walter. The Glasgow stage. (Glasgow: Forrester, 1892)

Beljame, Alexandre. Men of letters and the English public in the eighteenth century, 1660–1744: Dryden, Addison, Pope. (London: Kegan Paul et al., 1948)

Bergman, Gösta M. Lighting in the theatre. (Stockholm: Almqvist & Wiksell, 1977)

Bevis, Richard W. The laughing tradition; stage comedy in Garrick's day. (Athens and London: University of Georgia Press, 1980)

Bingham, Frederick. A celebrated old playhouse: the history of Richmond Theatre [Surrey] from 1765 to 1884. (Richmond: Henry Vickers, 1886). [244b]

Boswell, Eleanore. The Restoration court stage, 1660–1702. [Cambridge Mass.: Harvard University Press, 1932] (New York: Benjamin Blom, 1965)

Broadbent, R.J. Annals of the Liverpool stage. (Liverpool: Howell, 1908)

Burley, T.L.G. Playhouses and players of East Anglia. (Norwich: Jarrold, 1928)

Burnim, Kalman A. David Garrick, director. (University of Pittsburgh Press, 1961)

Campbell, Lily B. Scenes and machines on the English stage during the Renaissance. (Cambridge: Cambridge University Press, 1923)

Campbell, Thomas. The life of Mrs Siddons. 2 vols. (London: Effingham Wilson, 1834)

Clark, William S. The Irish stage in the county towns 1720–1800. (Oxford: Clarendon Press, 1965)

Cole, Toby and Chinoy, Helen Krich (eds). Actors on acting. (New York: Crown Publishers, 1949)

Conolly, L.W. The censorship of English drama 1737–1824. (San Marino: The Huntington Library, 1976)

Cook, T.A. and Nickalls, G. Thomas Doggett deceased. (London: Archibald Constable & Co, 1908)

Cotton, William. The story of the drama in Exeter 1787–1823. (London: Hamilton Adams, 1887)

Croft-Murray, Edward. John Devoto, a Baroque scene painter. (London: STR, 1953)

Cunningham, J.E. Theatre Royal (Birmingham). (Oxford: George Ronald, 1950)

Dibdin, James C. The annals of the Edinburgh stage. (Edinburgh: Cameron, 1888)

Duerr, Edwin. The length and depth of acting. (New York: Holt, Rinehart & Winston, 1962)

Dunbar, Howard H. The dramatic career of Arthur Murphy. (London: Oxford University Press, 1946)

Dunbar, Janet. Peg Woffington and her world. (London: Heinemann, 1968)

Fiske, Roger. English theatre music in the eighteenth century. (London: Oxford University Press, 1973)

Fitzgerald, Percy. A new history of the English stage. From the Restoration to the liberty of the theatres, in connection with the patent houses, from original papers in the Lord Chamberlain's Office, the State Paper Office and other sources. 2 vols. (London: Tinsley Brothers, 1882)

  The life of David Garrick (new and revised edition). (London: Simpkin Marshall et al., 1899)

Fraser, Antonia. The weaker vessel. Woman's lot in seventeenth-century England. (London: Weidenfeld & Nicolson, 1984)

Galt, John. The lives of the players. 2 vols. (London: Henry Colburn & Richard Bentley, 1831)

Gray, Charles H. Theatrical criticism in London to 1795. (New York: Columbia University Press, 1931)

Green, Mowbray Aston. The eighteenth-century architecture of Bath. (Bath: George Gregory, 1902). [240]

Grice, E. Rogues and vagabonds, or the actors' road to respectability. (Lavenham Suffolk: Terence Dalton, 1977)

Hannam-Clark, T. Drama in Gloucestershire. (Gloucester: Minchin & Gibbs, 1928)

Hare, Arnold. The Georgian theatre in Wessex. (London: Phoenix House, 1958)

  George Frederick Cooke: the actor and the man. (London: STR, 1980)

  Richard Brinsley Sheridan (Windsor: Profile Books, 1981)

Hilson, J.C., Jones, M.M.B. and Watson, J.R. (eds.). Augustan worlds. (Leicester: University Press, 1978)

Hodgkinson, J.L. and Pogson, R. The early Manchester theatre. (London: STR, 1960)

Holland, Peter. The ornament of action. Text and performance in Restoration comedy. (Cambridge: Cambridge University Press, 1979)

Hotson, Leslie. The Commonwealth and Restoration stage. (Cambridge Mass.: Harvard University Press, 1928)

Hughes, Leo. The drama's patrons; a study of the eighteenth-century London audience. (Austin and London: University of Texas Press, 1971)

Hume, Robert D. (ed.). The London theatre world 1660–1800 (Carbondale and Edwardsville: Southern Illinois University Press, 1980)

Joseph, Bertram. The tragic actor. (London: Routledge & Kegan Paul, 1959)

Kelly, Linda. *The Kemble era. John Philip Kemble, Sarah Siddons and the London stage.* (London: The Bodley Head, 1980)

Langhans, Edward A. *Restoration promptbooks.* (Carbondale and Edwardsville: Southern Illinois University Press, 1981)

Lanier, Henry Wysham. *The first English actresses. From the initial appearance of women on the stage in 1660 till 1700.* (New York: The Players, 1930)

Laver, James. *Drama, its costume and decor.* (London: Studio Publications, 1951)

Lawrence, W.J. *Speeding up Shakespeare.* (London: Argonaut Press, 1937)
Old theatre days and ways. (London: G.G. Harrap, 1935)

Leacroft, Richard. *The development of the English playhouse.* (London: Eyre Methuen, 1973)

Liesenfeld, V.J. *The Licensing Act of 1737.* (Madison: University of Wisconsin Press, 1984)

Loftis, John. *Steele at Drury Lane.* (Berkeley and Los Angeles: University of California Press, 1952)
Comedy and society from Congreve to Fielding. (Stanford: University Press, 1959)
The politics of drama in Augustan England. (London: Oxford University Press, 1963)
Sheridan and the drama of Georgian England. (Oxford: Blackwell, 1976)

Loftis, John (ed.). *Restoration drama: modern essays in criticism.* (New York and London: Oxford University Press, 1966)

Lynch, James J. *Box, pit and gallery. Stage and society in Johnson's London.* (Berkeley and Los Angeles: University of California Press, 1953)

Macqueen-Pope, W. *Haymarket: theatre of perfection.* (London: W.H. Allen, 1948)

Mantzius, Karl. *A history of theatrical art in ancient and modern times,* vol 5. (London: Duckworth & Co., 1909)

Manvell, Roger. *Sarah Siddons, portrait of an actress.* (London: Heinemann, 1970)

Merchant, W.M. *Shakespeare and the artist.* (London: Oxford University Press, 1959)

Milhous, Judith. *Thomas Betterton and the management of Lincoln's Inn Fields, 1695–1708.* (Carbondale and Edwardsville: Southern Illinois University Press, 1979)

Milhous, Judith and Hume, Robert D. (eds.). *Vice Chamberlain Coke's theatrical papers, 1706–1715.* (Carbondale and Edwardsville: Southern Illinois University Press, 1982)

Moore, R. E. *Hogarth's literary relationships.* (Minneapolis: University of Minnesota Press, 1948)
Henry Purcell and the Restoration theatre. (Cambridge Mass.: Harvard University Press, 1961)

Mullin, Donald C. *The development of the playhouse.* (Berkeley: University of California Press, 1970)

Nalbach, Daniel. *The King's Theatre, 1704–1867: London's first Italian opera house.* (London: STR, 1972)

Nash, Mary. *The provoked wife: the life and times of Susannah Cibber.* (London: Hutchinson, 1977)

Nethercot, Arthur H. *Sir William D'Avenant. Poet Laureate and playwright–manager.* [University of Chicago Press, 1938] (New York: Russell & Russell, 1967)

Nicholson, Watson. *The struggle for a free stage in London.* (London: Constable, 1906)

Nicoll, Allardyce. *The development of the theatre.* [London: G.G. Harrap & Co., 1927] (London: Harrap, 1937)
Stuart masques and the Renaissance stage. [London: G.G. Harrap & Co., 1938] (New York: Blom, 1963)
The Garrick stage. (Manchester: University Press, 1980)

Oman, Carola. *David Garrick.* (London: Hodder & Stoughton, 1958)

Orrell, John. *The theatres of Inigo Jones and John Webb.* (Cambridge: Cambridge University Press, 1985)

Osborn, James M. *John Dryden: some biographical facts and problems.* [New York: Columbia University Press, 1940] (revised edition, Gainsville: University of Florida Press, 1965). [28]

Oswald, Harold. *The Theatres Royal in Newcastle upon Tyne.* (Newcastle upon Tyne: Northumberland Press, 1936)

Parry, E. A. *Charles Macklin.* (London: Kegan Paul *et al.,* 1891). [281]

Paulson, Ronald. *Hogarth: his life, art and times.* 2 vols. (New Haven and London: Yale University Press, 1971)

Pedicord, H.W. *The theatrical public in the time of Garrick.* (Carbondale and Edwardsville: Southern Illinois University Press, 1954). [348]

Penley, Belville S. *The Bath stage.* (London: Lewis & Son, 1892)

Powell, G. Rennie. *The Bristol stage.* (Bristol: Bristol Printing & Publishing Co., 1919)

Powell, Jocelyn. *Restoration theatre production.* (London: Routledge & Kegan Paul, 1984)

Price, Cecil. *The English theatre in Wales in the eighteenth and early nineteenth centuries.* (Cardiff: University of Wales Press, 1948)
Theatre in the age of Garrick. (Oxford: Basil Blackwell, 1973)

Price, Curtis A. *Music in the Restoration theatre. With a catalogue of instrumental music in the plays, 1665–1713.* (UMI Research Press, 1979)

Henry Purcell and the London stage. (Cambridge: Cambridge University Press, 1984)

Richards, Kenneth and Thomson, Peter (eds.). *The eighteenth-century English stage.* (London: Methuen, 1972)

Rogers, Pat. *Literature and popular culture in eighteenth-century England.* (Sussex: Harvester Press, 1985)

Rosenfeld, Sybil. *Strolling players and drama in the provinces 1660–1765.* (Cambridge: Cambridge University Press, 1939)

'*The York theatre*' (typescript, York Public Library, 1948)

Foreign theatrical companies in Great Britain in the 17th and 18th centuries. (London: STR, 1955)

The theatre of the London fairs in the eighteenth century. (Cambridge: Cambridge University Press, 1960)

A short history of scene design in Great Britain. (Oxford: Basil Blackwell, 1973)

Temples of Thespis. Some private theatres and theatricals in England and Wales 1700–1820. (London: STR, 1978)

Georgian scene painters and scene painting. (Cambridge: Cambridge University Press, 1981)

The Georgian theatre of Richmond, Yorkshire, and its circuit: Beverley, Harrogate, Kendal, Northallerton, Ulverston and Whitby. (London: STR, 1984)

Sawyer, Paul. *The new theatre in Lincoln's Inn Fields.* (London: STR, 1979)

Sheldon, E.K. *Thomas Sheridan of Smock Alley 1719–1788.* (New Jersey: Princeton University Press, 1967)

Smith, Dane Farnsworth. *The critic in the audience of the London theatres from Buckingham to Sheridan. A study of neoclassicism in the playhouse, 1671–1779.* (Albuquerque: University of New Mexico Press, 1953)

Southern, Richard. *The Georgian playhouse.* (London: Pleiades Books, 1948)

Changeable scenery. (London: Faber & Faber, 1952)

The seven ages of the theatre. (London: Faber & Faber, 1962)

Stein, E.P. *David Garrick dramatist.* [PMLA 1938] (New York: Blom, 1967)

Stockwell, L.T. *Dublin theatres and theatre customs, 1637–1820.* [Kingsport, Tenn: Kingsport Press, 1938] (London and New York: Blom, 1968). **[346]**

Stone, G. W. and Kahrl, G.M. *David Garrick, a critical biography.* (Carbondale and Edwardsville: Southern Illinois University Press, 1979)

Studies in English theatre history, in memory of Gabrielle Enthoven OBE. (London: STR, 1952)

Summers, Montague. *The Restoration theatre.* (London: Kegan Paul, 1934)

The playhouse of Pepys. [London: Kegan Paul, 1935] (New York: Humanities Press, 1964)

Thaler, Alwin. *Shakespeare to Sheridan. A book about the theatre of yesterday and today.* (Cambridge Mass.: Harvard University Press, 1922)

Troubridge, St Vincent. *The benefit system in the British theatre.* (London: STR, 1967)

Vaughan, Anthony. *Born to please: Hannah Pritchard, actress, 1711–1768.* (London: STR, 1979)

Wickham, Glynne. *Early English stages,* vol. 2, pt 2. (London: Routledge & Kegan Paul, 1972)

Wilmeth, D.B. *George Frederick Cooke, Machiavel of the stage.* (Westport, Conn: Greenwood Press, 1980)

Wilson, John Harold. *All the King's ladies. Actresses of the Restoration.* (Chicago: University of Chicago Press, 1958)

Mr Goodman the player. (Pittsburgh: University of Pittsburgh Press, 1964)

Wyndham, H. Saxe. *Annals of Covent Garden Theatre from 1732 to 1897.* 2 vols. (London: Chatto & Windus, 1906)

(5) ARTICLES

Allen, R.G. 'The wonders of Derbyshire; a spectacular eighteenth-century travelogue'. *TS* 2 (1961), 54–66

Avery, Emmet L. 'The defense and criticism of the pantomime entertainments in the early eighteenth century'. *Journal of English Literary History* 5 (June 1938), 127–45

'The Restoration audience'. *Philological Quarterly* 45 (1966), 54–61

Barker, K.M.D. 'Michael Edkins, painter'. *TN* 16 (1961–2), 39–55

'The theatre proprietors' story (Theatre Royal Bristol)'. *TN* 18 (1964–5), 79–91

Bell, Hamilton. 'Contributions to the history of the English playhouse'. *Architectural Record* 33 (1913), 359–68

Bogorad, S.M. and Noyes, R.G. 'Samuel Foote's Primitive Puppet Show and *Piety in Pattens* – a critical edition'. *TS* 14 (1973), complete issue

Burgess, C.F. 'Some unpublished items of John Rich and something of a puzzle'. *Restoration and eighteenth-century theatre research* 7, no. 2 (Nov 1966), 37–46

Burling, William J. and Hume, Robert D. 'Theatrical companies at the Little Haymarket, 1720–1737'. *Essays in Theatre* 4, no. 2 (1986), 98–118

Burnim, K.A. 'Eighteenth-century theatrical illustrations in the light of contemporary documents'. *TN* 14 (1959–60), 45–55

'Some notes on Aaron Hill and stage scenery'. *TN* 12 (1957–8), 29–33

Byrne, M.St.C. 'The earliest Hamlet prompt book in an English library'. *TN* 15 (1960), 21–31

'The stage costuming of *Macbeth* in the 18th century'. *Studies in English theatre history.* (London: STR, 1952), 52–66

Campbell, Lily B. 'The rise of a theory of stage presentation in England during the eighteenth century'. *PMLA* 32 (June 1917), 163–200

'A history of costuming on the English stage between 1660 and 1823'. *University of Wisconsin Studies* 2 (1918), 187–223

Chancellor, E.B. 'A MS account book of Drury Lane Theatre for 1746–8'. *The Connoisseur* (August 1926), 217–21; (October 1926), 90–4

Clark, W.S. 'The Siddons' in Dublin'. *TN* 9 (1954–5), 103–11

Coleman, W.S.E. 'Post Restoration Shylocks prior to Macklin'. *TS* 8 (1967), 17–36

Cooper, Charles W. 'The triple portrait of John Lacy'. *PMLA* 47 (1932), 759–65

Crean, P.J. 'The Stage Licensing Act of 1737'. *Modern Philology* 35 (1937–8), 239–55

Curtis, J. 'A theatrical contract of 1773–4'. *TN* 30 (1976), 18–20

'Tate Wilkinson's costume notebook'. *TN* 32 (1978), 11–24

Donohue, J.W. 'Kemble's production of Macbeth (1794)'. *TN* 21 (1966–7), 63–74

'Kemble and Mrs Siddons in Macbeth: the Romantic approach to tragic character'. *TN* 22 (1967–8), 65–86

Downer, A.S. 'Nature to advantage dress'd: eighteenth-century acting'. *PMLA* 58 (Dec 1943), 1002–37

Eddison, Robert. 'Capon and Goodman's Fields'. *TN* 14 (1959–60), 127–32. [72]

Fahrner, R. 'David Garrick presents *The Padlock*'. *TS* 13 (1972), 52–69

Fawcett, T. 'Scene painting at the Norwich Theatre 1758–99'. *TN* 26 (1971–2), 15–19

Freehafer, John. 'The formation of the London Patent companies in 1660'. *TN* 20 (1965–6), 6–30

'Brome, Suckling and Davenant's theatre project of 1639'. *Texas Studies in Literature and Language* 10 (1968), 367–88

'Perspective scenery and the Caroline playhouse'. *TN* 27 (1971–2), 98–113

Frushell, R.C. 'Contemporary commentary on the players' revolt of 1743 and the Licensing Act of 1737'. *TS* 14 (1973), 91–5

Green, Elvena M. 'John Rich's art of pantomime as seen in his *The Necromancer, or Harlequin Doctor Faustus:* a comparison of the two Faustus pantomimes at Lincoln's Inn Fields and Drury Lane'. *Restoration and eighteenth-century theatre research* 4, no. 1 (May 1965), 47–60

Grice, F. 'Roger Kemble's company at Worcester'. *TN* 9 (1954–5), 73–5

Gruber, C.P. 'Falstaff on an eighteenth-century battlefield'. *TN* 21 (1966–7), 120–1

Harbin, B.J. 'John Hodgkinson in the English provinces 1765–92'. *TN* 28 (1974), 106–16

Hare, Arnold. 'George Frederick Cooke's early years in the theatre'. *TN* 31 (1977), 12–21

Hauger, G. 'Ten years of a provincial theatre (Wakefield 1786–95)'. *Theatre – general and particular.* (London: Michael Joseph, 1966), 100–81

Hines, P. 'Theatre items from the Newdigate Newsletters'. *TN* 39 (1985), 76–83

Hogan, C.B. 'The MS of Winston's *theatric tourist*'. *TN* 1 (1946–7), 86–90

'The New Wells, Goodman's Fields 1739–52'. *TN* 3 (1948–9), 67–72

'The China Hall Theatre, Rotherhithe'. *TN* 8 (1953–4), 76–80

'An eighteenth-century prompter's notes'. *TN* 10 (1955–6), 37–44

Hook, Lucyle. 'Anne Bracegirdle's first appearance'. *TN* 13 (1958–9), 133–6

'Portraits of Elizabeth Barry and Anne Bracegirdle'. *TN* 15 (1960–1), 129–37

Hughes, L. 'Folger *Jul.Caes.8*: a Covent Garden prompt book (1766)'. *TN* 34 (1980), 86–91

Hume, Robert D. 'The Dorset Garden Theatre: a review of facts and problems'. *TN* 33 (1979), 4–17

Jackson, Allan S. 'Restoration scenery, 1656–1680'. *Restoration and eighteenth-century theatre research* 3, no. 2 (Nov 1964), 25–38

'The frontispiece to Eccles's Theatre Musick 1699'. *TN* 19 (1964–5), 47–9

'Little known theatrical prints of the eighteenth century'. *TN* 22 (1967–8), 113–16

Jordan, R. 'Some Restoration playgoers'. *TN* 35 (1981), 51–7

Keith, W.G. 'Designs for the first movable scenery on the English public stage'. *Burlington Magazine* 25 (April 1914), 29, 85

'John Webb and the Court theatre of Charles II'. *The Architectural Review* 57, no. 2 (1925), 49–55

Kennedy-Skipton, L. 'Notes on a copy of William Capon's plan of Goodman's Fields Theatre 1786 and 1802 . . . in the Folger Shakespeare Library'. *TN* 17 (1963–4), 86–9

Kern, Ronald C. 'Documents relating to company management, 1705–11'. *TN* 14 (1959–60), 60–5

Knapp, M.E. 'Additional entries to Arnold Hare: *The Georgian Theatre in Wessex* (1958)'. *TN* 35 (1981), 100–3

Koenig, B. 'Where was Garrick's prompter?'. *TN* 37 (1983), 9–14

Langhans, Edward A. 'New Restoration theatre accounts, 1682–92'. *TN* 17 (1962–3), 118–34

'Wren's Restoration playhouse'. *TN* 18 (1963–4), 91–100

'The Dorset Garden Theatre in pictures'. *TS* 6, no. 2 (1965), 134–46

'Pictorial material on the Bridges Street and Drury Lane Theatre'. *TS* 7, no. 7 (1966), 80–100

'The Vere Street and Lincoln's Inn Fields Theatres in pictures'. *Educational Theatre Journal* 20, no. 2 (1968), 171–85

'Players and playhouses, 1695–1710, and their effect on English comedy'. *Theatre Annual* 29 (1973), 28–39

Leacroft, Richard. 'The remains of the theatre at Ashby-de-la-Zouch and Loughborough'. *TN* 4 (1949–50), 12–21

'The remains of the Fisher Theatres at Beccles, Bungay, Lowestoft and North Walsham'. *TN* 5 (1950–1), 82–7

'The remains of the old theatre, Wisbech (1793)'. *TN* 32 (1978), 68–75

Linton, M. 'Prompt books in the Bute collection of English plays'. *TN* 11 (1956–7), 20–3

Love, Harold. 'The myth of the Restoration audience'. *Komos* 1 (1967), 49–56

Macdonald, A.W. 'The season of 1782 on the Yorkshire circuit'. *TN* 37 (1983), 104–9

'The social life of the performer on the Yorkshire circuit 1766–85'. *TS* 25 (1984), 167–76

Mackintosh, Iain. 'Inigo Jones – theatre architect'. *Tabs* 31 (Sept 1973), 99–105

Macmillan, Dougald. 'The censorship in the case of Macklin's *The Man of the World*'. *Huntington Library Bulletin* 10 (1936), 79–101

Marly, Diana de. 'The architect of Dorset Garden Theatre'. *TN* 29 (1975), 119–24

Martin, L.J. 'From forestage to proscenium: a study of Restoration staging techniques'. *TS* 4 (1963), 3–28

Milhous, Judith. 'An annotated census of Thomas Betterton's roles, 1659–1701'. *TN* 29 (1975), 33–43, 85–94

'The date and import of the financial plan for a united theatre company in PRO LC 7/3'. *Maske und Kothurn* 21 (1975), 81–8

'New light on Vanbrugh's Haymarket theatre project'. *TS* 17 (1976), 143–61

'The Duke's Company's profits, 1675–77'. *TN* 32 (1978), 76–88

Milhous, Judith and Hume, Robert D. 'The silencing of Drury Lane in 1709'. *Theatre Journal* 32 (1980), 439–40

'An annotated guide to the theatrical documents in PRO LC 7/1, 7/2 and 7/3'. *TN* 35 (1981), 25–31; 77–87; 122–9

'The London theatre cartel of the 1720s: British Library additional charters 9306 and 9308'. *TS* 26 (May 1985), 21–37

'A 1660s promptbook of Shirley's *Loves Crueltie*'. *Theatre Research International* 11, no. 1 (1986), 1–13

'Charles Killigrew's "Abstract of Title to the Playhouse" British Library Add.MS 20,726, fols. 1–4'. *Theatre History Studies* 6 (1986), 57–71

Mitchell, Louis D. 'Command performances during the reign of Queen Anne'. *TN* 24 (1969–70), 111–17

Mullin, Donald C. 'The Queen's Theatre Haymarket: Vanbrugh's Opera House'. *TS* 8 (1967), 84–105

'The Theatre Royal, Bridges Street. An architectural puzzle'. *TN* 25 (1970–1), 14–19

'Lamps for Garrick's footlights'. *TN* 26 (1971–2), 92–4

'Lighting on the eighteenth-century London stage: a reconsideration'. *TN* 34 (1980), 73–85

Mullin, Donald C. and Koenig, Bruce. 'Christopher Wren's Theatre Royal'. *TN* 21 (1966–7), 180–7

Olleson, P. 'Vanbrugh and opera at the Queen's Theatre Haymarket'. *TN* 26 (1971–2), 94–101

Orrell, John. 'Filippo Corsini and the Restoration theatre'. *TN* 34 (1980), 4–9

Pedicord, H.W. 'The second chronicler: a tentative identification of the unknown hand in the MS diaries of the Drury Lane Theatre'. *TS* 5 (1964), 79–86
  'Masonic theatre pieces in London 1730–80'. *TS* 25 (1984), 153–66
Pentzell, R.J. 'Garrick's costuming'. *TS* 10 (1969), 18–42
  'Kemble's Hamlet costume'. *TS* 13 (1972), 81–5
Price, Cecil. 'John Ward, stroller'. *TN* 1 (1945–7), 10–12
  'Some movements of the Bath Company 1729–34'. *TN* 1 (1945–7), 55–6
  'An eighteenth-century theatrical agreement'. *TN* 2 (1947–8), 31–4
  'Joseph Austin and his associates 1766–89'. *TN* 5 (1949–50), 89–94
Ranger, P. 'The Thornton Circuit 1784–1817'. *TN* 32 (1978), 130–6
Richards, J. 'Thomas Shaftoe Robertson and *The Theatric Tourist*'. *TN* 29 (1975), 4–9
Richards, Kenneth. 'Changeable scenery for plays on the Caroline stage'. *TN* 23 (1968–9), 6–20
  'The French actors in London, 1661–2'. *Restoration and eighteenth-century theatre research* 14, no. 2 (Nov 1975), 48–52
Rosenfeld, Sybil. 'Dramatic advertisements in the Burney newspapers 1660–1700'. *PMLA* 51 (1936), 123–52
  'The career of Thomas Lediard'. *TN* 2 (1947–8), 46–54
  'St George's Hall, King's Lynn'. *TN* 3 (1948–9), 24–7
  'Two provincial theatre MSS (James Douglas)'. *TN* 4 (1949–50), 32–5
  'The wardrobes of Lincoln's Inn Fields and Covent Garden'. *TN* 5 (Winter 1950), 15–19
  'Unpublished stage documents'. *TN* 11 (1956–7), 92–6
  'An Ipswich theatre book'. *TN* 13 (1958–9), 129–33
  'A Sadler's Wells scene book'. *TN* 15 (1960–1), 57–62
Rosenfeld, Sybil and Croft-Murray, Edward. 'Checklist of scene painters working in Great Britain and Ireland in the eighteenth century'. *TN* 19 (1964–5), 6–20; 49–64; 102–13; 133–45. 20 (1965–6), 36–44; 69–72; 113–18
Rostron, D. 'J. P. Kemble's *Coriolanus* and *Julius Caesar*. An examination of the prompt copies'. *TN* 23 (1968–9), 26–34
Scanlan, Elizabeth. 'Reconstruction of the Duke's Playhouse in Lincoln's Inn Fields, 1661–1671'. *TN* 10 (1955–6), 48–50
Scouten, A.H. 'On the origin of Foote's matinees'. *TN* 7 (1953), 28–31
  'The increase in popularity of Shakespeare's plays in the eighteenth century'. *Shakespeare Quarterly* 7 (Spring 1956), 189–202
Shattuck, C.H. 'The Shakespeare prompt books: first supplement'. *TN* 24 (1969–70), 5–17
Smith, John Harrington. 'Shadwell, the ladies, and the change in comedy'. *Modern Philology* 46 (1948), 22–33
Sorelius, Gunnar. 'The rights of the Restoration theatrical companies in the older drama'. *Studia Neophilologica* 27 (1965), 174–89
  'The early history of the Restoration theatre: some problems reconsidered'. *TN* 33 (1979), 52–61
Southern, Richard. 'Observations on Lansdowne MS no 1171'. *TN* 2 (1947–8), 6–19
  'Lediard and early eighteenth-century scene design'. *TN* 2 (Summer 1948), 49–54
  'The theatre remains at Wisbech'. *TN* 4 (1949–50), 21–3
Sprague, A.C. 'Did Betterton chant?' *TN* 1 (Oct 1945–July 1947), 54–5
Spring, John R. 'Platforms and picture stages: a conjectural reconstruction of the Duke of York's Theatre, Dorset Garden'. *TN* 31, no. 3 (1977), 6–19
  'Dorset Garden Theatre: playhouse or opera house?' *TN* 34 (1980), 60–9
Steer, F.W. 'Sources of information on eighteenth and early nineteenth-century theatres in Sussex'. *TN* 12 (1957–8), 58–64
Stone, G.W. 'Garrick's long-lost alteration of Hamlet'. *PMLA* 49 (Sept 1934), 890–921
Stow, Leonie. 'Inigo Jones and the use of scenery at the Cockpit-in-Court'. *TS* 19, no. 1 (May 1978), 35–48
Thaler, A. 'Strolling players and drama after Shakespeare'. *PMLA* 37 (1922), 243–80
Thieme, J.A. 'Spouting, spouting clubs and spouting companions'. *TN* 29 (1975), 9–16
Thomas, Russell. 'Stage decorations of London theatres, 1700–1800'. *Modern Philology* 42, no. 2 (1944), 65–78
Van Dijk, M. 'J.P. Kemble as King John: two scenes'. *TN* 29 (1975), 22–32
  'J.P. Kemble and the critics'. *TN* 36 (1982), 110–18
Van Lennep, William. 'Plays on the English stage, 1669–1672'. *TN* 16 (1961–2), 12–20
  'The death of the Red Bull'. *TN* 16 (1961–2), 126–34

Vincent, H.P. 'John Rich and the first Covent Garden Theatre'. *Journal of English Literary History* 17 (Dec 1950), 296–306

Visser, Colin. 'The anatomy of the early Restoration stage: *The Adventures of Five Hours* and John Dryden's Spanish comedies'. *TN* 29 (1975), 56–69; 114–19

'The Killigrew Folio: private playhouses and the Restoration stage'. *TS* 19, no. 2 (1978), 19–38

'Garrick's Palace of Armida: a neglected document'. *TN* 34 (1980), 104–12

Wasserman, E.R. 'The sympathetic imagination in eighteenth-century theories of acting'. *Journal of English-German Philology* 46 (July 1947), 264–72

White, E.W. 'Early theatrical performances of Purcell's operas 1690–1710'. *TN* 13 (1958–9), 43–65

'The rehearsal of an opera'. *TN* 14 (1959–60), 79–90

Whitty, J.C. 'The half-price riots of 1763'. *TN* 24 (1969–70), 25–32

Wickham, Glynne. 'The Cockpit reconstructed'. *New Theatre Magazine* 7, no. 2 (1967), 26–35

Wilson, J.H. 'Rant, cant and tone on the Restoration stage'. *Studies in Philology* 52 (Oct 1955), 592–8

'Theatre notes from the Newdigate Newsletters'. *TN* 15 (1960–1), 79–84. *TN* 16 (1961–2), 59

'Players' lists in the Lord Chamberlain's registers'. *TN* 18 (1963–4), 25–30

Winton, Calhoun. 'The London stage embattled: 1695–1700'. *Tennessee Studies in Literature* 19 (1974), 9–19

Wood, F.T. 'Goodman's Fields Theatres'. *Modern Language Review* 25 (Oct 1930), 443–56

Index

Abington, Frances, 381; Boaden and Dibdin describe her appeal as a comic actress, 388–9; depicted in the character of Aurelia, 389

Ackman (actor): provokes the wrath of the audience during the Fitzgiggo Riots, 402–3

Act for regulating places of public entertainment, 1752, 225–6

Act to enable Justices of the Peace to license theatrical representations occasionally, 1788, 231

Actors' riot, Drury Lane, 25, 27–8

Adam, Robert (architect): reconstruction of Drury Lane in 1775, 268–70

Addison, Joseph, 174, 189
Cato: Booth acts in, 154; Swift describes a rehearsal of, 163–4; George Berkeley describes the first night, 194

Albion and Albanius. See Dryden, John

Alexander the Great. See Lee, Nathaniel

All's Lost by Lust. See Rowley, William

Amber, Morton (banker): buys Fleetwood's patent, 234

Anne, Queen, 190, 207; grants a licence to Congreve and Vanbrugh, 22–3

Appius and Virgina. See Webster, John

Ariadne; or, the Marriage of Bacchus. See Perrin, Pierre; Grabu, Louis

Arne, Thomas (composer), 123; illustrations of 'Fitzgiggo' riots during a performance of Artaxerxes, 316, 330–4

Arsinoe. Queen of Cyprus. See Clayton, Thomas; Thornhill, Sir James; Motteux, Peter

Artaxerxes. See Arne, Thomas

Articles of Union between Charles Killigrew and Charles Davenant, 39–40

Aston, Anthony: describes the acting of Betterton and Barry, 144–5; describes the acting of Anne Bracegirdle, 151–2

Attorney General, 9, 11, 20. See also Palmer, Sir Geoffrey

Austin, Joseph (actor and manager of a touring company), 233; contractual rules for a provincial touring company, 240–4

Banister, John (composer): writes music for Circe, 101

The Bankrupt. See Foote, Samuel

Banks, John, The Earl of Essex: Steele writes a critical review for The Tatler, 197

Barry, Elizabeth (actress), 46, 127; signs the petition of the players, 21; given the first benefit, 41; complains of Rich's refusal to honour her benefit, 42–3; establishes a distinctive style of acting with Betterton, 143; Kneller's portrait of, 143, 146; trained by Rochester, 146; acting described by Cibber, 149; rivalry with Anne Oldfield, 157

Barry, Mrs (actress): depicted as Belvidera in Venice Preserved, 370; Boaden compares her with Mrs Siddons, 371; pleads illness for not attending rehearsals, 392–3

Barry, Spranger (actor): plays Romeo at Covent Garden in 1750, 366; depicted as Romeo, 367; Davies assesses the quality of his acting, 368–9; depicted as Jaffier in Venice Preserved, 370; pleads illness for not attending

443